50
BEST
AMERICAN
SHORT STORIES

1915–1939

50
BEST
AMERICAN
SHORT STORIES

1915 – 1939

Edited by

EDWARD J. O'BRIEN

THE LITERARY GUILD OF AMERICA, INC.
New York

The Riverside Press
CAMBRIDGE · MASSACHUSETTS
PRINTED IN THE U.S.A.

CONTENTS

INTRODUCTION

Twenty-five years have made a difference in the American short story comparable to the difference between the tone and feeling of Pope and the tone and feeling of Shelley. During this one short generation American writing has evolved from the point at which it could only be described as extremely provincial English writing to the point where it has achieved dignity and substance as a rich literature in its own right.

For the past twenty-five years my chief interest and preoccupation has been to watch this development and to mark the steps of it as far as possible by publishing annually what seem to me to be the best short stories which appeared in American periodicals. I must have published since 1914 well over five hundred American short stories in which I had faith. I have now sought to choose the fifty stories published during the past twenty-five years which are most representative in their distinction and thus to present to you a panoramic picture of the period. As the panorama unfolds, you will be able to watch the progress of the American short story from the point at which it was content to be simply narrative harking back to English models to the present day in which it aims at rather more.

These fifty stories will also give you a tolerably satisfactory portrait of the changes in mood and manners of the American people during the past twenty-five years. You will see the American temper changing from a mood of complacent self-satisfaction which felt that Americans were living the best of lives in the best of all possible worlds to an awakening realization, little by little, that we have not yet discovered, or perhaps not even asked ourselves, what were the foundations of our lives or even who and what we were.

The period under review in this book practically coincides at the start with the beginning of the World War. A careful reader of this volume will be able to detect the impact of the war on an America as yet unawakened to anything but the most material reality. You will be able to see curiosity about themselves awakening, for example, in the minds of such representative Americans of a hitherto inarticulate generation as Sherwood Anderson and Ernest Hemingway. These two men were the first Americans in our time to make the essentially simple but vitally important discovery that the little man next door was as important a subject for stories as any writer could possibly find.

Before Anderson and Hemingway came along, the American short-story writer almost always felt that his task required him to leave home. The neighbors were not thought interesting or important. One must go far afield to find a story. A few American writers who did not feel this way also instinctively set aside the material nearest to their hands of which one might suppose that they had the most intimate knowledge. It seemed colorless to them. If they stayed home and wrote about their village, they sought for what seemed to them to be quaint and unusual in their surroundings. If they lived in Provincetown, for example, they were not concerned with their own blood knowledge, but wrote romantically and artificially about the Portuguese fishermen whose emotions seemed to them foreign and strange.

Sherwood Anderson and Ernest Hemingway changed all this. They were content to write about America, and they wrote about America from the inside rather than from the outside. In other words, they wrote about themselves. Others came after them. The foundation of *Story* a few years ago was the second landmark of the change. Awakened to a new sense of discovery, partly by Anderson and Hemingway, and partly by the great depression which had swept away a familiar prosperous world, it became a necessity for the young American writer to examine himself and his environment much more closely than he had ever done before. America had begun to want to know. The young writer found that he had questions to ask, discoveries to make, perhaps even judgments to set down. In other words, the American short story had come of age.

The progress the American short story has made during the past twenty-five years in finding a satisfactory American subject matter rooted deeply in American earth and in American life has been closely paralleled by a remarkable evolutionary change in the form of the American short story. Twenty-five years ago the American short story was written with elaborate artificial hauteur. Rules for its correct structure abounded and the form was as artificial and cramping as the eighteenth-century rhymed couplet. Inside this rigid framework nothing was left to chance, or perhaps I should say rather that nothing was left to life. It seemed as if all American writers were afraid of life. Then little by little life began to creep in and take charge. The rigid inorganic structure collapsed. The critics complained that the American short story had become formless.

Actually it had not. On the contrary, it had begun to grow for the first time in an organic way. Human life is organic and shapes its own pattern as it grows. Naturally, it has growing pains. It is always difficult to recognize the form of new life while it is growing, and it is impossible to arrest that growth if it is a healthy growth. The American short story has been growing healthily, and growing, as a child and a man grows, without accepting any rules imposed from outside. It has its own physiology and morphology which the student has to learn, but anything the student learns in this respect he must learn from life.

Well, here are the living stories of the past twenty-five years. Suppose you watch them grow. If you are a story-writer, that will be one of your best lessons. Perhaps the simplest lesson that these stories will teach you is that America has made one discovery. It has learned to surprise the mood on the face of the man next door and to transfer it innocently to paper so that it tells us something we need to know about ourselves. That is what writing is for, and in no other country is it being done quite so well at present. Bear this in mind as you read these stories, and also bear in mind the fact that good American writers know now that the short story, like life, can seldom be shocked into a sudden surprise ending.

EDWARD J. O'BRIEN

50

BEST

AMERICAN

SHORT STORIES

1915–1939

THE YELLOW CAT[1]

WILBUR DANIEL STEELE

AT LEAST once in my life I have had the good fortune to board a deserted vessel at sea. I say 'good fortune' because it has left me the memory of a singular impression. I have felt a ghost of the same thing two or three times since then, when peeping through the doorway of an abandoned house.

Now that vessel was not dead. She was a good vessel, a sound vessel, even a handsome vessel, in her blunt-bowed, coastwise way. She sailed under four lowers across as blue and glittering a sea as I have ever known, and there was not a point in her sailing that one could lay a finger upon as wrong. And yet, passing that schooner at two miles, one knew, somehow, that no hand was at her wheel. Sometimes I can imagine a vessel, stricken like that, moving over the empty spaces of the sea, carrying it off quite well were it not for that indefinable suggestion of a stagger; and I can think of all those ocean gods, in whom no landsman will ever believe, looking at one another and tapping their foreheads with just the shadow of a smile.

I wonder if they all scream — these ships that have lost their

[1] From *Harper's Magazine*. Copyright, 1915, by Harper and Brothers. Copyright, 1916, by Wilbur Daniel Steele.

souls? Mine screamed. We heard her voice, like nothing I have ever heard before, when we rowed under her counter to read her name — the *Marionnette* it was, of Halifax. I remember how it made me shiver, there in the full blaze of the sun, to hear her going on so, railing and screaming in that stark fashion. And I remember, too, how our footsteps, pattering through the vacant internals in search of that haggard utterance, made me think of footsteps of hurrying warders roused in the night.

And we found a parrot in a cage; that was all. It wanted water. We gave it water and went away to look things over, keeping pretty close together, all of us. In the quarters the table was set for four. Two men had begun to eat, by the evidence of the plates. Nowhere in the vessel was there any sign of disorder, except one sea-chest broken out, evidently in haste. Her papers were gone and the stern davits were empty. That is how the case stood that day, and that is how it has stood to this. I saw this same *Marionnette* a week later, tied up to a Hoboken dock, where she awaited news from her owners; but even there, in the midst of all the waterfront bustle, I could not get rid of the feeling that she was still very far away — in a sort of shippish other-world.

The thing happens now and then. Sometimes half a dozen years will go by without a solitary wanderer of this sort crossing the ocean paths, and then in a single season perhaps several of them will turn up: vacant waifs, impassive and mysterious — a quarter-column of tidings tucked away on the second page of the evening paper.

That is where I read the story about the *Abbie Rose*. I recollect how painfully awkward and out of place it looked there, cramped between ruled black edges and smelling of landsman's ink — this thing that had to do essentially with air and vast colored spaces. I forget the exact words of the heading — something like 'Abandoned Craft Picked Up at Sea' — but I still have the clipping itself, couched in the formal patter of the marine-news writer:

'The first hint of another mystery of the sea came in today when the schooner *Abbie Rose* dropped anchor in the upper river, manned only by a crew of one. It appears that the outbound freighter *Mercury* sighted the *Abbie Rose* off Block Island on Thursday last, acting in a suspicious manner. A boat party sent aboard found the schooner in perfect order and condition, sailing under four lower sails, the topsails being pursed up to the mastheads but not stowed. With the exception of a yellow cat, the vessel was found to be utterly deserted, though her small boat still hung in the davits. No evidences of disorder were visible in any part of the craft. The dishes were washed up, the stove in the galley was still slightly warm to the touch, everything in its proper place with the exception of the vessel's papers, which were not to be found.

'All indications being for fair weather, Captain Rohmer of the *Mercury* detailed two of his company to bring the find back to this port, a distance of one hundred and fifteen miles. The only man available with a knowledge of the fore-and-aft rig was Stewart McCord, the second engineer. A seaman by the name of Björnsen was sent with him. McCord arrived this noon, after a very heavy voyage of five days, reporting that Björnsen had fallen overboard while shaking out the foretopsail. McCord himself showed evidences of the hardships he has passed through, being almost a nervous wreck.'

Stewart McCord! Yes, Stewart McCord would have a knowledge of the fore-and-aft rig, or of almost anything else connected with the affairs of the sea. It happened that I used to know this fellow. I had even been quite chummy with him in the old days — that is, to the extent of drinking too many beers with him in certain hot-country ports. I remembered him as a stolid and deliberate sort of a person, with an amazing hodgepodge of learning, a stamp collection, and a theory about the effects of tropical sunshine on the Caucasian race, to which I have listened half of more than one night, stretched out naked on a freighter's deck. He had not impressed me as a fellow who would be bothered by his nerves.

And there was another thing about the story which struck me as rather queer. Perhaps it is a relic of my seafaring days, but I have always been a conscientious reader of the weather reports; and I could remember no weather in the past week sufficient to shake a man out of a top, especially a man by the name of Björnsen — a thoroughgoing seafaring name.

I was destined to hear more of this in the evening from the ancient boatman who rowed me out on the upper river. He had been to sea in his day. He knew enough to wonder about this thing, even to indulge in a little superstitious awe about it.

'No sir-ee. Something *happened* to them four chaps. And another thing ——'

I fancied I heard a sea-bird whining in the darkness overhead. A shape moved out of the gloom ahead, passed to the left, lofty and silent, and merged once more with the gloom behind — a barge at anchor, with the sea-grass clinging around her waterline.

'Funny about that other chap,' the old fellow speculated. 'Björnsen — I b'lieve he called 'im. Now that story sounds to me kind of ——' He feathered his oars with a suspicious jerk and peered at me. 'This McCord a friend of yourn?' he inquired.

'In a way,' I said.

'Hm-m — well ——' He turned on his thwart to squint ahead. 'There she is,' he announced, with something of relief, I thought.

It was hard at that time of night to make anything but a black blotch out of the *Abbie Rose*. Of course I could see that she was pot-bellied, like the rest of the coastwise sisterhood. And that McCord had not stowed his topsails. I could make them out, pursed at the mastheads and hanging down as far as the crosstrees, like huge, over-ripe pears. Then I recollected that he had found them so — probably had not touched them since; a queer

way to leave tops, it seemed to me. I could see also the glowing
tip of a cigar floating restlessly along the farther rail. I called:
'McCord! Oh, McCord!'

The spark came swimming across the deck. 'Hello! Hello,
there — ah ——' There was a note of querulous uneasiness
there that somehow jarred with my remembrance of this man.

'Ridgeway,' I explained.

He echoed the name uncertainly, still with that suggestion of
peevishness, hanging over the rail and peering down at us. 'Oh!
By gracious!' he exclaimed abruptly. 'I'm glad to see you,
Ridgeway. I had a boatman coming out before this, but I guess
— well, I guess he'll be along. By gracious! I'm glad ——'

'I'll not keep you,' I told the gnome, putting the money in his
palm and reaching for the rail. McCord lent me a hand on my
wrist. Then when I stood squarely on the deck beside him he
appeared to forget my presence, leaned forward heavily on the
rail, and squinted after my waning boatman.

'Ahoy — boat!' he called out, sharply, shielding his lips with
his hands. His violence seemed to bring him out of the blank,
for he fell immediately to puffing strongly at his cigar and explaining in rather a shame-voiced way that he was beginning to
think his own boatman had 'passed him up.'

'Come in and have a nip,' he urged with an abrupt heartiness,
clapping me on the shoulder.

'So you've ——' I did not say what I had intended. I was
thinking that in the old days McCord had made rather a fetish of
touching nothing stronger than beer. Neither had he been of the
shoulder-clapping sort. 'So you've got something aboard?' I
shifted.

'Dead men's liquor,' he chuckled. It gave me a queer feeling
in the pit of my stomach to hear him. I began to wish I had not
come, but there was nothing for it now but to follow him into the
afterhouse. The cabin itself might have been nine feet square,

with three bunks occupying the port side. To the right opened the master's stateroom, and a door in the forward bulkhead led to the galley.

I took in these features at a casual glance. Then, hardly knowing why I did it, I began to examine them with greater care.

'Have you a match?' I asked. My voice sounded very small, as though something unheard of had happened to all the air.

'Smoke?' he asked. 'I'll get you a cigar.'

'No.' I took the proffered match, scratched it on the side of the galley door, and passed out. There seemed to be a thousand pans there, throwing my match back at me from every wall of the box-like compartment. Even McCord's eyes, in the doorway, were large and round and shining. He probably thought me crazy. Perhaps I was, a little. I ran the match along close to the ceiling and came upon a rusty hook a little aport of the center.

'There,' I said. 'Was there anything hanging from this — er — say a parrot — or something, McCord?' The match burned my fingers and went out.

'What do you mean?' McCord demanded from the doorway. I got myself back into the comfortable yellow glow of the cabin before I answered, and then it was a question.

'Do you happen to know anything about this craft's personal history?'

'No. What are you talking about! Why?'

'Well, I do,' I offered. 'For one thing, she's changed her name. And it happens this isn't the first time she's — well, damn it all, fourteen years ago I helped pick up this whatever-she-is off the Virginia Capes — in the same sort of condition. There you are!' I was yapping like a nerve-strung puppy.

McCord leaned forward with his hands on the table, bringing his face beneath the fan of the hanging-lamp. For the first time I could mark how shockingly it had changed. It was almost colorless. The jaw had somehow lost its old-time security and the eyes

seemed to be loose in their sockets. I had expected him to start at
my announcement; he only blinked at the light.

'I am not surprised,' he remarked at length. 'After what I've
seen and heard ——' He lifted his fist and brought it down with
a sudden crash on the table. 'Man — let's have a nip!'

He was off before I could say a word, fumbling out of sight in
the narrow stateroom. Presently he reappeared, holding a glass
in either hand and a dark bottle hugged between his elbows.
Putting the glasses down, he held up the bottle between his eyes
and the lamp, and its shadow, falling across his face, green and
luminous at the core, gave him a ghastly look — like a mutilation
or an unspeakable birthmark. He shook the bottle gently and
chuckled his 'Dead men's liquor' again. Then he poured two
half-glasses of the clear gin, swallowed his portion, and sat
down.

'A parrot,' he mused, a little of the liquor's color creeping into
his cheeks. 'No, this time it was a cat, Ridgeway. A yellow cat.
She was ——'

'Was?' I caught him up. 'What's happened — what's become
of her?'

'Vanished. Evaporated. I haven't seen her since night before
last, when I caught her trying to lower the boat ——'

'Stop it!' It was I who banged the table now, without any of
the reserve of decency. 'McCord, you're drunk — drunk, I tell
you. A cat. Let a cat throw you off your head like this! She's
probably hiding out below this minute, on affairs of her own.'

'Hiding?' He regarded me for a moment with the queer
superiority of the damned. 'I guess you don't realize how many
times I've been over this hulk, from decks to keelson, with a mal-
let and a foot-rule.'

'Or fallen overboard,' I shifted, with less assurance. 'Like this
fellow Björnsen. By the way, McCord ——' I stopped there on
account of the look in his eyes.

He reached out, poured himself a shot, swallowed it, and got up to shuffle about the confined quarters. I watched their restless circuit — my friend and his jumping shadow. He stopped and bent forward to examine a Sunday-supplement chromo tacked on the wall, and the two heads drew together, as though there were something to whisper. Of a sudden I seemed to hear the old gnome croaking, 'Now that story sounds to me kind of ——'

McCord straightened up and turned to face me.

'What do you know about Björnsen?' he demanded.

'Well — only what they had you saying in the papers,' I told him.

'Pshaw!' He snapped his fingers, tossing the affair aside. 'I found her log,' he announced in quite another voice.

'You did, eh? I judged from what I read in the paper that there wasn't a sign.'

'No, no; I happened on this the other night, under the mattress in there.' He jerked his head toward the stateroom. 'Wait!' I heard him knocking things over in the dark and mumbling at them. After a moment he came out and threw on the table a long, cloth-covered ledger, of the common commercial sort. It lay open at about the middle, showing close script running indiscriminately across the column ruling.

'When I said "log,"' he went on, 'I guess I was going it a little strong. At least, I wouldn't want that sort of log found around *my* vessel. Let's call it a personal record. Here's his picture, somewhere ——' He shook the book by its back and a common kodak blue-print fluttered to the table. It was the likeness of a solid man with a paunch, a huge square beard, small squinting eyes, and a bald head. 'What do you make of him — a writing chap?'

'From the nose down, yes,' I estimated. 'From the nose up, he will tend to his own business if you will tend to yours, strictly.'

McCord slapped his thigh. 'By gracious! that's the fellow!

He hates the Chinaman. He knows as well as anything he ought not to put down in black and white how intolerably he hates the Chinaman, and yet he must sneak off to his cubby-hole and suck his pencil, and — and how is it Stevenson has it? — the "agony of composition," you remember. Can you imagine the fellow, Ridgeway, bundling down here with the fever on him ——'

'About the Chinaman,' I broke in. 'I think you said something about a Chinaman?'

'Yes. The cook, he must have been. I gather he wasn't the master's pick, by the reading-matter here. Probably clapped on to him by the owners — shifted from one of their others at the last moment; a queer trick. Listen.' He picked up the book and, running over the pages with a selective thumb, read:

'"*August second.* First part, moderate southwesterly breeze —" and so forth — er — but here he comes to it:

'"Anything can happen to a man at sea, even a funeral. In special to a Chinyman, who is of no account to social welfare, being a barbarian as I look at it."

'Something of a philosopher, you see. And did you get the reserve in that "even a funeral"? An artist, I tell you. But wait; let me catch him a bit wilder. Here:

'"I'll get that mustard-colored —— (This is back a couple of days.) Never can hear the —— coming, in them carpet slippers. Turned round and found him standing right at my back this morning. Could have stuck a knife into me easy. 'Look here!' says I, and fetched him a tap on the ear that will make him walk louder next time, I warrant. He could have stuck a knife into me easy."

'A clear case of moral funk, I should say. Can you imagine the fellow, Ridgeway ——'

'Yes; oh, yes.' I was ready with a phrase of my own. 'A man handicapped with an imagination. You see he can't quite understand this "barbarian," who has him beaten by about thirty

centuries of civilization — and his imagination has to have something to chew on, something to hit — a "tap on the ear," you
know.'

'By gracious! That's the ticket!' McCord pounded his knee.
'And now we've got another chap going to pieces — Peters, he
calls him. Refuses to eat dinner on August the third, claiming he
caught the Chink making passes over the chowder-pot with his
thumb. Can you believe it, Ridgeway — in this very cabin here?'
Then he went on with a suggestion of haste, as though he had
somehow made a slip. 'Well, at any rate, the disease seems to be
catching. Next day it's Bach, the second seaman, who begins to
feel the gaff. Listen:

'"Back he comes to me tonight, complaining he's being
watched. He claims the —— has got the evil eye. Says he can
see you through a two-inch bulkhead, and the like. The Chink's
laying in his bunk, turned the other way. 'Why don't you go
aboard of him?' says I. The Dutcher says nothing, but goes over
to his own bunk and feels under the straw. When he comes back
he's looking queer. 'By God!' says he, 'the devil has swiped my
gun!'. . . . Now if that's true there is going to be hell to pay in
this vessel very quick. I figure I'm still master of this vessel."'

'The evil eye,' I grunted. 'Consciences gone wrong there somewhere.'

'Not altogether, Ridgeway. I can see that yellow man peeking.
Now just figure yourself, say, eight thousand miles from home,
out on the water alone with a crowd of heathen fanatics crazy
from fright, looking around for guns and so on. Don't you
believe you'd keep an eye around the corners, kind of — eh?
I'll bet a hat he was taking it all in, lying there in his bunk,
"turned the other way." Eh? I pity the poor cuss —— Well,
there's only one more entry after that. He's good and mad.
Here:

'"Now, by God! this is the end. My gun's gone, too; right

out from under lock and key, by God! I been talking with Bach this morning. Not to let on, I had him in to clean my lamp. There's more ways than one, he says, and so do I."'

McCord closed the book and dropped it on the table. 'Finis,' he said. 'The rest is blank paper.'

'Well!' I will confess I felt much better than I had for some time past. 'There's *one* "mystery of the sea" gone to pot, at any rate. And now, if you don't mind, I think I'll have another of your nips, McCord.'

He pushed my glass across the table and got up, and behind his back his shoulders rose to scour the corners of the room, like an incorruptible sentinel. I forgot to take up my gin, watching him. After an uneasy minute or so he came back to the table and pressed the tip of a forefinger on the book.

'Ridgeway,' he said, 'you don't seem to understand. This particular "mystery of the sea" hasn't been scratched yet — not even *scratched*, Ridgeway.' He sat down and leaned forward, fixing me with a didactic finger. 'What happened?'

'Well, I have an idea the "barbarian" got them, when it came to the pinch.'

'And let the —— remains over the side?'

'I should say.'

'And then they came back and got the "barbarian" and let *him* over the side, eh? There were none left, you remember.'

'Oh, good Lord, I don't know!' I flared with a childish resentment at this catechising of his. But his finger remained there, challenging.

'I do,' he announced. 'The Chinaman put them over the side, as we have said. And then, after that, he died — of wounds about the head.'

'So?' I had still sarcasm.

'You will remember,' he went on, 'that the skipper did not happen to mention a cat, a *yellow* cat, in his confessions.'

'McCord,' I begged him, 'please drop it. Why in thunder *should* he mention a cat?'

'True. Why *should* he mention a cat? I think one of the reasons why he should *not* mention a cat is because there did not happen to be a cat aboard at that time.'

'Oh, all right!' I reached out and pulled the bottle to my side of the table. Then I took out my watch. 'If you don't mind,' I suggested, 'I think we'd better be going ashore. I've got to get to my office rather early in the morning. What do you say?'

He said nothing for the moment, but his finger had dropped. He leaned back and stared straight into the core of the light above, his eyes squinting.

'He would have been from the south of China, probably.' He seemed to be talking to himself. 'There's a considerable sprinkling of the belief down there, I've heard. It's an uncanny business — this transmigration of souls ——'

Personally, I had had enough of it. McCord's fingers came groping across the table for the bottle. I picked it up hastily and let it go through the open companionway, where it died with a faint gurgle, out somewhere on the river.

'Now,' I said to him, shaking the vagrant wrist, 'either you come ashore with me or you go in there and get under the blankets. You're drunk, McCord — *drunk*. Do you hear me?'

'Ridgeway,' he pronounced, bringing his eyes down to me and speaking very slowly, 'you're a fool, if you can't see better than that. I'm not drunk. I'm sick. I haven't slept for three nights — and now I can't. And you say — you ——' He went to pieces very suddenly, jumped up, pounded the legs of his chair on the decking, and shouted at me: 'And you say that, you — you landlubber, you office coddler! You're so comfortably sure that everything in the world is cut and dried. Come back to the water again and learn how to wonder — and stop talking like a damn fool. Do you know where —— Is there anything in your

municipal budget to tell me where Björnsen went? Listen!' He
sat down, waving me to do the same, and went on with a sort of
desperate repression.

'It happened on the first night after we took this hellion. I'd
stood the wheel most of the afternoon — off and on, that is, because she sails herself uncommonly well. Just put her on a reach,
you know, and she carries it off pretty well ——'

'I know,' I nodded.

'Well, we mugged up about seven o'clock. There was a good
deal of canned stuff in the galley, and Björnsen wasn't a bad hand
with a kettle — a thoroughgoing Squarehead he was — tall and
lean and yellow-haired, with little fat, round cheeks and a white
mustache. Not a bad chap at all. He took the wheel to stand
till midnight, and I turned in, but I didn't drop off for quite a
spell. I could hear his boots wandering around over my head,
padding off forward, coming back again. I heard him whistling
now and then — an outlandish air. Occasionally I could see the
shadow of his head waving in a block of moonlight that lay on
the decking right down there in front of the stateroom door. It
came from the companion; the cabin was dark because we were
going easy on oil. They hadn't left a great deal, for some reason or
other.'

McCord leaned back and described with his finger where the
illumination had cut the decking.

'There! I could see it from my bunk, as I lay, you understand.
I must have almost dropped off once when I heard him fiddling
around out here in the cabin, and then he said something in a
whisper, just to find out if I was still awake, I suppose. I asked
him what the matter was. He came and poked his head in the
door.'

'"The breeze is going out," says he. "I was wondering if we
couldn't get a little more sail on her." Only I can't give you his
fierce Squarehead tang. "How about the tops?" he suggested.

'I was so sleepy I didn't care, and I told him so. "All right," he says, "but I thought I might shake out one of them tops." Then I heard him blow at something outside. "Scat, you ——!" Then: "This cat's going to set me crazy, Mr. McCord," he says, "following me around everywhere." He gave it a kick, and I saw something yellow floating across the moonlight. It never made a sound — just floated. You wouldn't have known it ever lit anywhere, just like ——'

McCord stopped and drummed a few beats on the table with his fist, as though to bring himself back to the straight narrative.

'I went to sleep,' he began again. 'I dreamed about a lot of things. I woke up sweating. You know how glad you are to wake up after a dream like that and find none of it is so? Well I turned over and settled to go off again, and then I got a little more awake and thought to myself it must be pretty near time for me to go on deck. I scratched a match and looked at my watch. "That fellow must be either a good chap or asleep," I said to myself. And I rolled out quick and went above-decks. He wasn't at the wheel. I called him: "Björnsen! Björnsen!" No answer.'

McCord was really telling a story now. He paused for a long moment, one hand shielding an ear and his eyeballs turned far up.

'That was the first time I really went over the hulk,' he ran on. 'I got out a lantern and started at the forward end of the hold, and I worked aft, and there was nothing there. Not a sign, or a stain, or a scrap of clothing, or anything. You may believe that I began to feel funny inside. I went over the decks and the rails and the house itself — inch by inch. Not a trace. I went out aft again. The cat sat on the wheel-box, washing her face. I hadn't noticed the scar on her head before, running down between her ears — rather a new scar — three or four days old, I should say. It looked ghastly and blue-white in the flat moonlight. I ran over and grabbed her up to heave her over the side — you understand how upset I was. Now, you know a cat will squirm around and grab something when you hold it like that, generally speaking. This one didn't. She just drooped and began to purr and looked up at me out of her moonlit eyes under that scar. I dropped her on the deck and backed off. You remember Björnsen had *kicked* her — and I didn't want anything like that happening to ——'

The narrator turned upon me with a sudden heat, leaned over, and shook his finger before my face.

'There you go!' he cried. 'You, with your stout stone buildings and your policemen and your neighborhood church — you're so damn sure. But I'd just like to see you out there, alone, with the moon setting, and all the lights gone tall and queer, and a shipmate ——' He lifted his hand overhead, the finger-tips pressed together and then suddenly separated as though he had released an impalpable something into the air.

'Go on,' I told him.

'I felt more like you do, when it got light again, and warm and sunshiny. I said "Bah!" to the whole business. I even fed the cat, and I slept awhile on the roof of the house — I was so sure. We lay dead most of the day, without a streak of air. But that night —! Well, that night I hadn't got over being sure yet. It takes quite a jolt, you know, to shake loose several dozen generations. A fair, steady breeze had come along, the glass was high, she was staying herself like a doll, and so I figured I could get a little rest lying below in the bunk, even if I didn't sleep.

'I tried not to sleep, in case something should come up — a squall or the like. But I think I must have dropped off once or twice. I remember I heard something fiddling around in the galley and I hollered "Scat!" and everything was quiet again. I rolled over and lay on my left side, staring at that square of moonlight, outside my door for a long time. You'll think it was a dream — what I saw there.'

'Go on,' I said.

'Call this table-top the spot of light, roughly,' he said. He placed a finger-tip at about the middle of the forward edge and drew it slowly toward the center. 'Here, what would correspond with the upper side of the companionway, there came down very gradually the shadow of a tail. I watched it streaking out there across the deck, wiggling the slightest bit now and then. When it had come down about halfway across the light, the solid part of the animal — its shadow, you understand — began to appear, quite big and round. But how could she hang there, done up in a ball, from the hatch?'

He shifted his finger back to the edge of the table and puddled it around to signify the shadowed body.

'I fished my gun out from behind my back. You see, I was feeling funny again. Then I started to slide one foot over the edge of the bunk, always with my eyes on that shadow. Now, I swear I didn't make the sound of a pin dropping, but I had no more than moved a muscle when that shadowed thing twisted itself around in a flash — and there on the floor before me was the profile of a man's head, upside down, listening — a man's head with a tail of hair.'

McCord got up hastily and stepped in front of the stateroom door, where he bent down and scratched a match.

'See,' he said, holding the tiny flame above a splintered scar on the boards. 'You wouldn't think a man would be fool enough to shoot at a shadow?'

He came back and sat down.

'It seemed to me all hell had shaken loose. You've no idea, Ridgeway, the rumpus a gun raises in a box like this. I found out afterward the slug ricocheted into the galley, bringing down a couple of pans — and that helped. Oh, yes, I got out of here quick enough. I stood there, half out of the companion, with my hands on the hatch and the gun between them, and my shadow running off across the top of the house shivering before my eyes like a dry leaf. There wasn't a whisper of sound in the world —

just the pale water floating past and the sails towering up like a
pair of twittering ghosts. And everything that crazy color ——

'Well, in a minute I saw it, just abreast of the mainmast,
crouched down in the shadow of the weather rail, sneaking off
forward very slowly. This time I took a good long sight before I
let go. Did you ever happen to see black-powder smoke in the
moonlight? It puffed out perfectly round, like a big, pale balloon,
this did, and for a second something was bounding through it —
without a sound, you understand — something a shade solider
than the smoke and big as a cow, it looked to me. It passed from
the weather side to the lee and ducked behind the sweep of the
mainsail like *that* ——' McCord snapped his thumb and forefinger under the light.

'Go on,' I said. 'What did you do then?'

McCord regarded me for an instant from beneath his lids,
uncertain. His fist hung above the table. 'You're ——' He hesitated, his lips working vacantly. A forefinger came out of the fist
and gesticulated before my face. 'If you're laughing, why, damn
me, I'll ——'

'Go on,' I repeated. 'What did you do then?'

'I followed the thing.' He was still watching me sullenly. 'I
got up and went forward along the roof of the house, so as to have
an eye on either rail. You understand, this business had to be
done with. I kept straight along. Every shadow I wasn't absolutely sure of I *made* sure of — point-blank. And I rounded the
thing up at the very stem — sitting on the butt of the bowsprit,
Ridgeway, washing her yellow face under the moon. I didn't
make any bones about it this time. I put the bad end of that gun
against the scar on her head and squeezed the trigger. It snicked
on an empty shell. I tell you a fact; I was almost deafened by
the report that didn't come.

'She followed me aft. I couldn't get away from her. I went and
sat on the wheel-box and she came and sat on the edge of the

house, facing me. And there we stayed for upwards of an hour, without moving. Finally she went over and stuck her paw in the water-pan I'd set out for her; then she raised her head and looked at me and yawled. At sundown there'd been two quarts of water in that pan. You wouldn't think a cat would get away with two quarts of water in ——'

He broke off again and considered me with a sort of weary defiance.

'What's the use?' He spread out his hands in a gesture of hopelessness. 'I knew you wouldn't believe it when I started. You *couldn't*. It would be a kind of blasphemy against the sacred institution of pavements. You're too damn smug, Ridgeway. I can't shake you. You haven't sat two days and two nights, keeping your eyes open by sheer teeth-gritting, until they got used to it and wouldn't shut any more. When I tell you I found that yellow thing snooping around the davits, and three bights of the boat-fall loosened out, plain on deck — you grin behind your collar. When I tell you she padded off forward and evaporated — flickered back to hell and hasn't been seen since, then — why, you explain to yourself that I'm drunk. I tell you ——'

He jerked his head back abruptly and turned to face the companionway, his lips still apart. He listened so for a moment, then he shook himself out of it and went on:

'I tell you, Ridgeway, I've been over this hulk with a foot-rule. There's not a cubic inch I haven't accounted for, not a plank I ——'

This time he got up and moved a step toward the companion, where he stood with his head bent forward and slightly to the side. After what might have been twenty seconds of this he whispered, 'Do you hear?'

Far and far away down the reach a ferryboat lifted its infinitesimal wail, and then the silence of the night river came down once more, profound and inscrutable. A corner of the wick above my head sputtered a little — that was all.

'Hear what?' I whispered back. He lifted a cautious finger toward the opening.

'Somebody. Listen.'

The man's faculties must have been keyed up to the pitch of his nerves, for to me the night remained as voiceless as a subterranean cavern. I became intensely irritated with him; within my mind I cried out against this infatuated pantomime of his. And then, of a sudden, there *was* a sound — the dying rumor of a ripple, somewhere in the outside darkness, as though an object had been let into the water with extreme care.

'You heard?'

I nodded. The ticking of the watch in my vest pocket came to my ears, shucking off the leisurely seconds, while McCord's fingernails gnawed at the palms of his hands. The man was really sick. He wheeled on me and cried out, 'My God! Ridgeway — why don't we go out?'

I, for one, refused to be a fool. I passed him and climbed out of the opening; he followed far enough to lean his elbows on the hatch, his feet and legs still within the secure glow of the cabin.

'You see, there's nothing.' My wave of assurance was possibly a little overdone.

'Over there,' he muttered, jerking his head toward the shore lights. 'Something swimming.'

I moved to the corner of the house and listened.

'River thieves,' I argued. 'The place is full of ——'

'*Ridgeway. Look behind you!*'

Perhaps it *is* the pavements — but no matter; I am not ordinarily a jumping sort. And yet there was something in the quality of that voice beyond my shoulder that brought the sweat stinging through the pores of my scalp even while I was in the act of turning.

A cat sat there on the hatch, expressionless and immobile in the gloom.

I did not say anything. I turned and went below. McCord was there already, standing on the farther side of the table. After a moment or so the cat followed and sat on her haunches at the foot of the ladder and stared at us without winking.

'I think she wants something to eat,' I said to McCord.

He lit a lantern and went into the galley. Returning with a chunk of salt beef, he threw it into the farther corner. The cat went over and began to tear at it, her muscles playing with convulsive shadow-lines under the sagging yellow hide.

And now it was she who listened, to something beyond the reach of even McCord's faculties, her neck stiff and her ears flattened. I looked at McCord and found him brooding at the animal with a sort of listless malevolence. 'Quick! She has kittens somewhere about.' I shook his elbow sharply. 'When she starts, now ——'

'You don't seem to understand,' he mumbled. 'It wouldn't be any use.'

She had turned now and was making for the ladder with the soundless agility of her race. I grasped McCord's wrist and dragged him after me, the lantern banging against his knees. When we came up the cat was already amidships, a scarcely discernible shadow at the margin of our lantern's ring. She stopped and looked back at us with her luminous eyes, appeared to hesitate, uneasy at our pursuit of her, shifted here and there with quick, soft bounds, and stopped to fawn with her back arched at the foot of the mast. Then she was off with an amazing suddenness into the shadows forward.

'Lively now!' I yelled at McCord. He came pounding along behind me, still protesting that it was of no use. Abreast of the foremast I took the lantern from him to hold above my head.

'You see,' he complained, peering here and there over the illuminated deck. 'I tell you, Ridgeway, this thing ——' But my eyes were in another quarter and I slapped him on the shoulder.

'An engineer — an engineer to the core!' I cried at him. 'Look aloft, man.'

Our quarry was almost to the cross-trees, clambering up the shrouds with a smartness no sailor has ever come to, her yellow body, cut by the moving shadows of the ratlines, a queer sight against the mat of the night. McCord closed his mouth and opened it again for two words: 'By gracious!' The following instant he had the lantern and was after her. I watched him go up above my head — a ponderous, swaying climber into the sky — come to the cross-trees, and squat there with his knees clamped around the mast. The clear star of the lantern shot this way and that for a moment, then it disappeared, and in its place there sprang out a bag of yellow light, like a fire-balloon at anchor in the heavens. I could see the shadows of his head and hands moving monstrously over the inner surface of the sail, and muffled exclamations without meaning came down to me. After a moment he drew out his head and called: 'All right — they're here. Heads! there below!'

I ducked at his warning, and something spanked on the planking a yard from my feet. I stepped over to the vague blur on the deck and picked up a slipper — a slipper covered with some woven straw stuff and soled with a matted felt, perhaps a half-inch thick. Another struck somewhere abaft the mast, and then McCord reappeared above and began to stagger down the shrouds. Under his left arm he hugged a curious assortment of litter, a sheaf of papers, a brace of revolvers, a gray kimono, and a soiled apron.

'Well,' he said when he had come to deck, 'I feel like a man who has gone to hell and come back again. You know I'd come to the place where I really believed that about the cat. When you think of it —— By gracious! we haven't come so far from the jungle, after all.'

We went aft and below and sat down at the table as we had been. McCord broke a prolonged silence.

'I'm sort of glad he got away — poor cuss! He's probably climbing up a wharf this minute, shivering and scared to death. Over toward the gas tanks, by the way he was swimming. By gracious! Now that the world's turned over straight again, I feel I could sleep a solid week. Poor cuss! can you imagine him, Ridgeway ——'

'Yes,' I broke in. 'I think I can. He must have lost his nerve when he made out your smoke and shinnied up there to stow away, taking the ship's papers with him. He would have attached some profound importance to them — remember, the "barbarian," eight thousand miles from home. Probably couldn't read a word. I suppose the cat followed him — the traditional source of food. He must have wanted water badly.'

'I should say! He wouldn't have taken the chances he did.'

'Well,' I announced, 'at any rate, I can say it now — there's another "mystery of the sea" gone to pot.'

McCord lifted his heavy lids.

'No,' he mumbled. 'The mystery is that a man who has been to sea all his life could sail around for three days with a man bundled up in his top and not know it. When I think of him peeking down at me — and playing off that damn cat — probably without realizing it — scared to death — by gracious! Ridgeway, there was a pair of funks aboard this craft, eh? Wow — yow — I could sleep ——'

'I should think you could.'

McCord did not answer.

'By the way,' I speculated. 'I guess you were right about Björnsen, McCord — that is, his fooling with the foretop. He must have been caught all of a bunch, eh?'

Again McCord failed to answer. I looked up, mildly surprised, and found his head hanging back over his chair and his mouth opened wide. He was asleep.

THE LOST PHOEBE[1]

THEODORE DREISER

T HEY lived together in a part of the country which was not so prosperous as it had once been, about three miles from one of those small towns that, instead of increasing in population, is steadily decreasing. The territory was not very thickly settled; perhaps a house every other mile or so, with large areas of corn- and wheat-land and fallow fields that at odd seasons had been sown to timothy and clover. Their particular house was part log and part frame, the log portion being the old original home of Henry's grandfather. The new portion, of now rain-beaten, time-worn slabs, through which the wind squeaked in the chinks at times, and which several overshadowing elms and a butternut-tree made picturesque and reminiscently pathetic, but a little damp, was erected by Henry when he was twenty-one and just married.

That was forty-eight years before. The furniture inside, like the house outside, was old and mildewy and reminiscent of an earlier day. You have seen the whatnot of cherry wood, perhaps, with spiral legs and fluted top. It was there. The old-fashioned four-poster bed, with its ball-like protuberances and deep curving incisions, was there also, a sadly alienated descendant of an early Jacobean ancestor. The bureau of cherry was also high and wide and solidly built, but faded-looking, and with a musty odour. The rag carpet that underlay all these sturdy examples of enduring furniture was a weak, faded, lead-and-pink-coloured affair woven by Phoebe Ann's own hands, when she was fifteen years younger than she was when she died. The creaky wooden loom on which it had been done now stood like a dusty, bony skeleton, along with a broken rocking-chair, a worm-eaten clothes-press — Heaven knows how old — a lime-stained bench that had once been used to keep flowers on outside the door, and other decrepit factors of household utility, in an east room that was a lean-to against this so-called main portion. All sorts of other broken-down furniture were about this place; an antiquated clothes-horse, cracked in two of its ribs; a broken mirror in an old cherry frame, which had fallen from a nail and cracked itself three days before their youngest son, Jerry, died; an extension hat-rack, which once had had porcelain knobs on the ends of its pegs; and a sewing-machine, long since outdone in its clumsy mechanism by rivals of a newer generation.

The orchard to the east of the house was full of gnarled old apple trees, worm-eaten as to trunks and branches, and fully ornamented with green and white lichens, so that it had a sad, greenish-white, silvery effect in moonlight. The low outhouses which had once housed chickens, a horse or two, a cow, and several pigs, were covered with patches of moss as to their roof, and the sides had been free of paint for so long that they were blackish grey as to colour, and a little spongy. The picket-fence in front, with its gate squeaky and askew, and the side fences of the stake-and-rider type were in an equally run-down condition. As a matter of fact, they had aged synchronously with the persons who lived here, old Henry Reifsneider and his wife Phoebe Ann.

They had lived here, these two, ever since their marriage,
forty-eight years before, and Henry had lived here before that
from his childhood up. His father and mother, well along in
years when he was a boy, had invited him to bring his wife here
when he had first fallen in love and decided to marry; and he had
done so. His father and mother were the companions of himself
and his wife for ten years after they were married, when both
died; and then Henry and Phoebe were left with their five children
growing lustily apace. But all sorts of things had happened since
then. Of the seven children, all told, that had been born to them,
three had died; one girl had gone to Kansas; one boy had gone to
Sioux Falls, never even to be heard of after; another boy had gone
to Washington; and the last girl lived five counties away in the
same State, but was so burdened with cares of her own that she
rarely gave them a thought. Time and a commonplace home-life
that had never been attractive had weaned them thoroughly, so
that, wherever they were, they gave little thought as to how it
might be with their father and mother.

Old Henry Reifsneider and his wife Phoebe were a loving
couple. You perhaps know how it is with simple natures that
fasten themselves like lichens on the stones of circumstance and
weather their days to a crumbling conclusion. The great world
sounds widely, but it has no call for them. They have no soaring
intellect. The orchard, the meadow, the cornfield, the pig-pen,
and the chicken-lot measure the range of their human activities.
When the wheat is headed it is reaped and threshed; when the
corn is browned and frosted it is cut and shocked; when the
timothy is in full head it is cut, and the haycock erected. After
that comes winter, with the hauling of grain to market, the saw-
ing and splitting of wood, the simple chores of fire-building, meal-
getting, occasional repairing, and visiting. Beyond these and the
changes of weather — the snows, the rains, and the fair days —
there are no immediate, significant things. All the rest of life is a

far-off, clamorous phantasmagoria, flickering like Northern lights in the night, and sounding as faintly as cowbells tinkling in the distance.

Old Henry and his wife Phoebe were as fond of each other as it is possible for two old people to be who have nothing else in this life to be fond of. He was a thin old man, seventy when she died, a queer, crotchety person with coarse grey-black hair and beard, quite straggly and unkempt. He looked at you out of dull, fishy, watery eyes that had deep-brown crow's feet at the sides. His clothes, like the clothes of many farmers, were aged and angular and baggy, standing out at the pockets, not fitting about the neck, protuberant and worn at elbow and knee. Phoebe Ann was thin and shapeless, a very umbrella of a woman, clad in shabby black, and with a black bonnet for her best wear. As time had passed, and they had only themselves to look after, their movements had become slower and slower, their activities fewer and fewer. The annual keep of pigs had been reduced from five to one grunting porker, and the single horse which Henry now retained was a sleepy animal, not over-nourished and not very clean. The chickens, of which formerly there was a large flock, had almost disappeared, owing to ferrets, foxes, and the lack of proper care, which produces disease. The former healthy garden was now a straggling memory of itself, and the vines and flower-beds that formerly ornamented the windows and dooryard had now become choking thickets. A will had been made which divided the small tax-eaten property equally among the remaining four, so that it was really of no interest to any of them. Yet these two lived together in peace and sympathy only that now and then old Henry would become unduly cranky, complaining almost invariably that something had been neglected or mislaid which was of no importance at all.

'Phoebe, where's my corn-knife? You ain't never minded to let my things alone no more.'

'Now you hush, Henry,' his wife would caution him in a cracked and squeaky voice. 'If you don't, I'll leave yuh. I'll git up and walk out of here some day, and then where would y' be? Y' ain't got anybody but me to look after yuh, so yuh just behave yourself. Your corn-knife's on the mantel where it's allus been unless you've gone an' put it sommers else.'

Old Henry, who knew his wife would never leave him in any circumstances, used to speculate at times as to what he would do if she were to die. That was the one leaving that he really feared. As he climbed on the chair at night to wind the old, long-pendulumed, double-weighted clock, or went finally to the front and the back door to see that they were safely shut in, it was a comfort to know that Phoebe was there, properly ensconced on her side of the bed, and that if he stirred restlessly in the night, she would be there to ask what he wanted.

'Now, Henry, do lie still! You're as restless as a chicken.'

'Well, I can't sleep, Phoebe.'

'Well, yuh needn't roll so, anyhow. Yuh kin let me sleep.'

This usually reduced him to a state of somnolent ease. If she wanted a pail of water, it was a grumbling pleasure for him to get it; and if she did rise first to build the fires, he saw that the wood was cut and placed within easy reach. They divided this simple world nicely between them.

As the years had gone on, however, fewer and fewer people had called. They were well known for a distance of as much as ten square miles as old Mr. and Mrs. Reifsneider, honest, moderately Christian, but too old to be really interesting any longer. The writing of letters had become an almost impossible burden, too difficult to continue or even negotiate via others, although an occasional letter still did arrive from the daughter in Pemberton County. Now and then some old friend stopped with a pie or cake or a roasted chicken or duck, or merely to see that they were well; but even these kindly-minded visits were no longer frequent.

One day in the early spring of her sixty-fourth year Mrs. Reifsneider took sick, and from a low fever passed into some indefinable ailment which, because of her age, was no longer curable. Old Henry drove to Swinnerton, the neighbouring town, and procured a doctor. Some friends called, and the immediate care of her was taken off his hands. Then one chill spring night she died, and old Henry, in a fog of sorrow and uncertainty, followed her body to the nearest graveyard, an unattractive space with a few pines growing in it. Although he might have gone to the daughter in Pemberton or sent for her, it was really too much trouble and he was too weary and fixed. It was suggested to him at once by one friend and another that he could come to stay with them awhile, but he did not see fit. He was so old and so fixed in his notions and so accustomed to the exact surroundings he had known all his days, that he could not think of leaving. He wanted to remain near where they had put his Phoebe; and the fact that he would have to live alone did not trouble him in the least. The living children were notified, and the care of him offered if he would leave, but he would not.

'I kin make a shift for myself,' he continually announced to old Dr. Morrow, who had attended his wife in this case. 'I kin cook a little, and, besides, it don't take much more'n coffee an' bread in the mornin's to satisfy me. I'll get along now well enough. Yuh just let me be.' And after many pleadings and proffers of advice, with supplies of coffee and bacon and baked bread duly offered and accepted, he was left to himself. For a while he sat idly outside his door brooding in the spring sun. He tried to revive his interest in farming, and to keep himself busy and free from thought by looking after the fields, which of late had been much neglected. It was a gloomy thing to come in of an evening, however, or in the afternoon and find no shadow of Phoebe where everything suggested her. By degrees he put a few of her things away. At night he sat beside his lamp and read in the papers that were left him occasionally or in a Bible that he had neglected for years, but he could get little solace from these things. Mostly he held his hand over his mouth and looked at the floor as he sat and thought of what had become of her, and how soon he himself would die. He made a great business of making his coffee in the morning and frying himself a little bacon at night; but his appetite was gone. The shell in which he had been housed so long seemed vacant, and its shadows were suggestive of immedicable griefs. So he lived quite dolefully for five long months, and then a change began.

It was one night, after he had looked after the front and the back door, wound the clock, blown out the light, and gone through all the selfsame motions that he had indulged in for years, that he went to bed not so much to sleep as to think. It was a moonlight night. The green-lichen-covered orchard just outside and to be seen from his bed where he now lay was a silvery affair, sweetly spectral. The moon shone through the east windows, throwing the pattern of the panes on the wooden floor, and making the old furniture, to which he was accustomed, stand out dimly in the room. As usual he had been thinking of Phoebe and the years when they had been young together, and of the children who had gone, and the poor shift he was making of his present days. The house was coming to be in a very bad state indeed. The bed-clothes were in disorder and not clean, for he made a wretched shift of washing. It was a terror to him. The roof leaked, causing things (some of them) to remain damp for weeks at a time, but he was getting into that brooding state where he would accept anything rather than exert himself. He preferred to pace slowly to and fro or to sit and think.

By twelve o'clock on this particular night he was asleep, however, and by two had waked again. The moon by this time had shifted to a position on the western side of the house, and it now shone in through the windows of the living-room and those of the kitchen beyond. A certain combination of furniture — a chair near a table, with his coat on it, the half-open kitchen door casting a shadow, and the position of a lamp near a paper — gave him an exact representation of Phoebe leaning over the table as he had often seen her do in life. It gave him a great start. Could it be she — or her ghost? He had scarcely ever believed in spirits; and still.... He looked at her fixedly in the feeble half-light, his old hair tingling oddly at the roots, and then sat up. The figure did not move. He put his thin legs out of the bed and sat looking at her, wondering if this could really be Phoebe. They had talked of ghosts often in their lifetime, of apparitions and omens; but they had never agreed that such things could be. It had never been a part of his wife's creed that she could have a spirit that could return to walk the earth. Her after-world was quite a different affair, a vague heaven, no less, from which the righteous did not trouble to return. Yet here she was now, bending over the table in her black skirt and gray shawl, her pale profile outlined against the moonlight.

'Phoebe,' he called, thrilling from head to toe and putting out one bony hand, 'have yuh come back?'

The figure did not stir, and he arose and walked uncertainly to the door, looking at it fixedly the while. As he drew near, however, the apparition resolved itself into its primal content — his old coat over the high-backed chair, the lamp by the paper, the half-open door.

'Well,' he said to himself, his mouth open, 'I thought shore I saw her.' And he ran his hand strangely and vaguely through his hair, the while his nervous tension relaxed. Vanished as it had, it gave him the idea that she might return.

Another night, because of this first illusion, and because his mind was now constantly on her and he was old, he looked out of the window that was nearest his bed and commanded a hen-coop and pig-pen and a part of the wagon-shed, and there, a faint mist exuding from the damp of the ground, he thought he saw her again. It was one of those little wisps of mist, one of those faint exhalations of the earth that rise in a cool night after a warm day, and flicker like small white cypresses of fog before they disappear. In life it had been a custom of hers to cross this lot from her kitchen door to the pig-pen to throw in any scrap that was left from her cooking, and here she was again. He sat up and watched it strangely, doubtfully, because of his previous experience, but inclined, because of the nervous titillation that passed over his body, to believe that spirits really were, and that Phoebe, who would be concerned because of his lonely state, must be thinking about him, and hence returning. What other way would she have? How otherwise could she express herself? It would be within the province of her charity so to do, and like her loving interest in him. He quivered and watched it eagerly; but, a faint breath of air stirring, it wound away toward the fence and disappeared.

A third night, as he was actually dreaming, some ten days later, she came to his bedside and put her hand on his head.

'Poor Henry!' she said. 'It's too bad.'

He roused out of his sleep, actually to see her, he thought, moving from his bedroom into the one living-room, her figure a shadowy mass of black. The weak straining of his eyes caused little points of light to flicker about the outlines of her form. He arose, greatly astonished, walked the floor in the cool room, convinced that Phoebe was coming back to him. If he only thought sufficiently, if he made it perfectly clear by his feeling that he needed her greatly, she would come back, this kindly wife, and tell him what to do. She would perhaps be with him much of the time, in the night, anyhow; and that would make him less lonely, his state more endurable.

In age and with the feeble it is not such a far cry from the subtleties of illusion to actual hallucination, and in due time this transition was made for Henry. Night after night he waited, expecting her return. Once in his weird mood he thought he saw a pale light moving about the room, and another time he thought he saw her walking in the orchard after dark. It was one morning when the details of his lonely state were virtually unendurable that he woke with the thought that she was not dead. How he had arrived at this conclusion it is hard to say. His mind had gone. In its place was a fixed illusion. He and Phoebe had had a senseless quarrel. He had reproached her for not leaving his pipe where he was accustomed to find it, and she had left. It was an aberrated fulfilment of her old jesting threat that if he did not behave himself she would leave him.

'I guess I could find yuh ag'in,' he had always said. But her crackling threat had always been:

'Yuh'll not find me if I ever leave yuh. I guess I kin git some place where yuh can't find me.'

This morning when he arose he did not think to build the fire in the customary way or to grind his coffee and cut his bread, as was his wont, but solely to meditate as to where he should search for her and how he should induce her to come back. Recently the one horse had been dispensed with because he found it cumbersome and beyond his needs. He took down his soft crush hat after he had dressed himself, a new glint of interest and determination in his eye, and taking his black crook cane from behind the door, where he had always placed it, started out briskly to look for her among the nearest neighbours. His old shoes clumped soundly in the dust as he walked, and his grey-black locks, now grown rather long, straggled out in a dramatic fringe or halo from under his hat. His short coat stirred busily as he walked, and his hands and face were peaked and pale.

'Why, hello, Henry! Where're yuh goin' this mornin'?' inquired Farmer Dodge, who, hauling a load of wheat to market, encountered him on the public road. He had not seen the aged farmer in months, not since his wife's death, and he wondered now, seeing him looking so spry.

'Yuh ain't seen Phoebe, have yuh?' inquired the old man, looking up quizzically.

'Phoebe who?' inquired Farmer Dodge, not for the moment connecting the name with Henry's dead wife.

'Why, my wife Phoebe, o' course. Who do yuh s'pose I mean?' He stared up with a pathetic sharpness of glance from under his shaggy, grey eyebrows.

'Wall, I'll swan, Henry, yuh ain't jokin', are yuh?' said the solid Dodge, a pursy man, with a smooth, hard, red face. 'It can't be your wife yuh're talkin' about. She's dead.'

'Dead! Shucks!' retorted the demented Reifsneider. 'She left me early this mornin', while I was sleepin'. She allus got up to build the fire, but she's gone now. We had a little spat last night, an' I guess that's the reason. But I guess I kin find her. She's gone over to Matilda Race's; that's where she's gone.'

He started briskly up the road, leaving the amazed Dodge to stare in wonder after him.

'Well, I'll be switched!' he said aloud to himself. 'He's clean out'n his head. That poor old feller's been livin' down there till he's gone outen his mind. I'll have to notify the authorities.' And he flicked his whip with great enthusiasm. 'Geddap!' he said, and was off.

Reifsneider met no one else in this poorly populated region until he reached the whitewashed fence of Matilda Race and her husband three miles away. He had passed several other houses *en route*, but these not being within the range of his illusion were not considered. His wife, who had known Matilda well, must be here. He opened the picket-gate which guarded the walk, and stamped briskly up to the door.

'Why, Mr. Reifsneider,' exclaimed old Matilda herself, a stout woman, looking out of the door in an answer to his knock, 'what brings yuh here this mornin'?'

'Is Phoebe here?' he demanded eagerly.

'Phoebe who? What Phoebe?' replied Mrs. Race, curious as to this sudden development of energy on his part.

'Why, my Phoebe, o' course.' My wife Phoebe. Who do yuh s'pose? Ain't she here now?'

'Lawsy me!' exclaimed Mrs. Race, opening her mouth. 'Yuh pore man! So you're clean out'n your mind now. Yuh come right in and sit down. I'll git you a cup o' coffee. O' course your wife ain't here; but yuh come in an' sit down. I'll find her fer yuh after a while. I know where she is.'

The old farmer's eyes softened, and he entered. He was so thin and pale a specimen, pantalooned and patriarchal, that he aroused Mrs. Race's extremest sympathy as he took off his hat and laid it on his knees quite softly and mildly.

'We had a quarrel last night, an' she left me,' he volunteered.

'Laws! laws!' sighed Mrs. Race, there being no one present with whom to share her astonishment as she went to her kitchen. 'The pore man! Now somebody's just got to look after him. He can't be allowed to run around the country this way lookin' for his dead wife. It's turrible.'

She boiled him a pot of coffee and brought in some of her new-baked bread and fresh butter. She set out some of her best jam and put a couple of eggs to boil, lying whole-heartedly the while.

'Now yuh stay right there, Uncle Henry, till Jake comes in, an' I'll send him to look for Phoebe. I think it's more'n likely she's over to Swinnerton with some o' her friends. Anyhow, we'll find out. Now yuh just drink this coffee an' eat this bread. Yuh must be tired. Yuh've had a long walk this mornin'.' Her idea was to take counsel with Jake, 'her man,' and perhaps have him notify the authorities.

She bustled about, meditating on the uncertainties of life, while old Reifsneider thrummed on the rim of his hat with his

pale fingers and later ate abstractedly of what she offered. His
mind was on his wife, however, and since she was not here, or
did not appear, it wandered vaguely away to a family by the
name of Murray, miles away in another direction. He decided
after a time that he would not wait for Jake Race to hunt his
wife but would seek her for himself. He must be on, and urge
her to come back.

'Well, I'll be goin',' he said, getting up and looking strangely
about him. 'I guess she didn't come here after all. She went
over to the Murrays, I guess. I'll not wait any longer, Mis' Race.
There's a lot to do over to the house to-day.' And out he marched
in the face of her protests, taking to the dusty road again in the
warm spring sun, his cane striking the earth as he went.

It was two hours later that this pale figure of a man appeared
in the Murrays' doorway, dusty, perspiring, eager. He had
tramped all of five miles, and it was noon. An amazed husband
and wife of sixty heard his strange query, and realized also that
he was mad. They begged him to stay to dinner, intending to
notify the authorities later and see what could be done; but
though he stayed to partake of a little something, he did not stay
long, and was off again to another distant farmhouse, his idea
of many things to do and his need of Phoebe impelling him. So
it went for that day and the next and the next, the circle of his
inquiry ever widening.

The process by which a character assumes the significance of
being peculiar, his antics weird, yet harmless, in such a community
is often involute and pathetic. This day, as has been said, saw
Reifsneider at other doors, eagerly asking his unnatural question
and leaving a trail of amazement, sympathy, and pity in his wake.
Although the authorities were informed — the county sheriff,
no less — it was not deemed advisable to take him into custody;
for when those who knew old Henry, and had for so long, reflected on the condition of the county insane asylum, a place

which, because of the poverty of the district, was of staggering aberration and sickening environment, it was decided to let him remain at large; for, strange to relate, it was found on investigation that at night he returned peaceably enough to his lonesome domicile there to discover whether his wife had returned, and to brood in loneliness until the morning. Who would lock up a thin, eager, seeking old man with iron-grey hair and an attitude of kindly, innocent inquiry, particularly when he was well known for a past of only kindly servitude and reliability? Those who had known him best rather agreed that he should be allowed to roam at large. He could do no harm. There were many who were willing to help him as to food, old clothes, the odds and ends of his daily life — at least at first. His figure after a time became not so much a commonplace as an accepted curiosity, and the replies, 'Why, no, Henry; I ain't see her,' or 'No, Henry; she ain't been here to-day,' more customary.

For several years thereafter then he was an odd figure in the sun and rain, on dusty roads and muddy ones, encountered occasionally in strange and unexpected places, pursuing his endless search. Under-nourishment, after a time — although the neighbours and those who knew his history gladly contributed from their store — affected his body: for he walked much and ate little. The longer he roamed the public highway in this manner, the deeper became his strange hallucination; and finding it harder and harder to return from his more and more distant pilgrimages, he finally began taking a few utensils with him from his home, making a small package of them, in order that he might not be compelled to return. In an old tin coffee-pot of large size he placed a small tin cup, a knife, fork, and spoon, some salt and pepper, and to the outside of it, by a string forced through a pierced hole, he fastened a plate, which could be released, and which was his woodland table. It was no trouble for him to secure the little food that he needed, and with a strange, almost religious dignity, he had no hesitation in asking for that much. By degrees his hair became longer and longer, his once black hair became an earthen brown, and his clothes threadbare and dusty.

For all of three years he walked, and none knew how wide were his perambulations, nor how he survived the storms and cold. They could not see him, with homely rural understanding and forethought, sheltering himself in haycocks, or by the sides of cattle, whose warm bodies protected him from the cold, and whose dull understandings were not opposed to his harmless presence. Overhanging rocks and trees kept him at times from the rain, and a friendly hayloft or corn-crib was not above his humble consideration.

The involute progression of hallucination is strange. From asking at doors and being constantly rebuffed or denied, he finally came to the conclusion that although his Phoebe might not be in any of the houses at the doors of which he inquired, she might nevertheless be within the sound of his voice. And so, from patient inquiry, he began to call sad, occasional cries, that ever and anon waked the quiet landscapes and ragged hill regions, and set to echoing his thin 'O-o-o Phoebe! O-o-o Phoebe!' It had a pathetic, albeit insane, ring, and many a farmer or ploughboy came to know it even from afar and say, 'There goes old Reifsneider.'

Another thing that puzzled him greatly after a time and after many hundreds of inquiries was when he no longer had any particular dooryard in view and no special inquiry to make, which way to go. These cross-roads, which occasionally led in four or even six directions, came after a time to puzzle him. But to solve this knotty problem, which became more and more of a puzzle, there came to his aid another hallucination: Phoebe's spirit or some power of the air or wind or nature would tell him. If he stood at the centre of the parting of the ways, closed his eyes, turned thrice about, and called 'O-o-o Phoebe!' twice, and

then threw his cane straight before him, that would surely indi-
cate which way to go for Phoebe, or one of these mystic powers
would surely govern its direction and fall! In whichever direction
it went, even though, as was not infrequently the case, it took
him back along the path he had already come, or across fields,
he was not so far gone in his mind but that he gave himself
ample time to search before he called again. Also the hallucination seemed to persist that at some time he would surely find
her. There were hours when his feet were sore, and his limbs
weary, when he would stop in the heat to wipe his seamed brow,
or in the cold to beat his arms. Sometimes, after throwing away
his cane, and finding it indicating the direction from which he
had just come, he would shake his head wearily and philosophi-
cally, as if contemplating the unbelievable or an untoward fate,
and then start briskly off. His strange figure came finally to be
known in the farthest reaches of three or four counties. Old
Reifsneider was a pathetic character. His fame was wide.

Near a little town called Watersville, in Green County, perhaps four miles from that minor centre of human activity, there
was a place or precipice locally known as the Red Cliff, a sheer
wall of red sandstone, perhaps a hundred feet high which raised
its sharp face for half a mile or more above the fruitful corn-fields
and orchards that lay beneath, and which was surmounted by a
thick grove of trees. The slope that slowly led up to it from the
opposite side was covered by a rank growth of beech, hickory,
and ash, through which threaded a number of wagon-tracks crossing at various angles. In fair weather it had become old Reifsneider's habit, so inured was he by now to the open, to make his
bed in some such patch of trees as this, to fry his bacon or boil
his eggs at the foot of some tree before laying himself down for
the night. Occasionally, so light and inconsequential was his sleep,
he would walk at night. More often, the moonlight or some sudden wind stirring in the trees or a reconnoitring animal arousing

him, he would sit up and think, or pursue his quest in the moon-light or the dark, a strange, unnatural, half wild, half savage-looking but utterly harmless creature, calling at lonely road-crossings, staring at dark and shuttered houses, and wondering where, where Phoebe could really be.

That particular lull that comes in the systole-diastole of this earthly ball at two o'clock in the morning invariably aroused him, and though he might not go any farther he would sit up and contemplate the darkness or the stars, wondering. Sometimes in the strange processes of his mind he would fancy that he saw moving among the trees the figure of his lost wife, and then he would get up to follow, taking his utensils, always on a string, and his cane. If she seemed to evade him too easily he would run, or plead, or, suddenly losing track of the fancied figure, stand awed or disappointed, grieving for the moment over the almost insurmountable difficulties of his search.

It was in the seventh year of these hopeless peregrinations, in the dawn of a similar springtime to that in which his wife had died, that he came at last one night to the vicinity of this self-same patch that crowned the rise to the Red Cliff. His far-flung cane, used as a divining-rod at the last cross-roads, had brought him hither. He had walked many, many miles. It was after ten o'clock at night, and he was very weary. Long wandering and little eating had left him but a shadow of his former self. It was a question now not so much of physical strength but of spiritual endurance which kept him up. He had scarcely eaten this day, and now exhausted he set himself down in the dark to rest and possibly to sleep.

Curiously on this occasion a strange suggestion of the presence of his wife surrounded him. It would not be long now, he coun-selled with himself, although the long months had brought him nothing, until he should see her — talk to her. He fell asleep after a time, his head on his knees. At midnight the moon began to rise, and at two in the morning, his wakeful hour, was a large silver disc shining through the trees to the east. He opened his eyes when the radiance became strong, making a silver pattern at his feet and lighting the woods with strange lustres and silvery, shadowy forms. As usual, his old notion that his wife must be near occurred to him on this occasion, and he looked about him with a speculative, anticipatory eye. What was it that moved in the distant shadows along the path by which he had entered — a pale, flickering will-o'-the-wisp that bobbed gracefully among the trees and riveted his expectant gaze? Moonlight and shadows combined to give it a strange form and a stranger reality, this fluttering of bogfire or dancing of wandering fireflies. Was it truly his lost Phoebe? By a circuitous route it passed about him, and in his fevered state he fancied that he could see the very eyes of her, not as she was when he last saw her in the black dress and shawl but now a strangely younger Phoebe, gayer, sweeter, the one whom he had known years before as a girl. Old Reifsneider got up. He had been expecting and dreaming of this hour all these years, and now as he saw the feeble light dancing lightly before him he peered at it questioningly, one thin hand in his grey hair.

Of a sudden there came to him now for the first time in many years the full charm of her girlish figure as he had known it in boyhood, the pleasing, sympathetic smile, the brown hair, the blue sash she had once worn about her waist at a picnic, her gay, graceful movements. He walked around the base of the tree, straining with his eyes, forgetting for once his cane and utensils, and following eagerly after. On she moved before him, a will-o'-the-wisp of the spring, a little flame above her head, and it seemed as though among the small saplings of ash and beech and the thick trunks of hickory and elm that she signalled with a young, a lightsome hand.

'O Phoebe! Phoebe!' he called. 'Have yuh really come?

Have yuh really answered me?' And hurrying faster, he fell once, scrambling lamely to his feet, only to see the light in the distance dancing illusively on. On and on he hurried until he was fairly running, brushing his ragged arms against the trees, striking his hands and face against impeding twigs. His hat was gone, his lungs were breathless, his reason quite astray, when coming to the edge of the cliff he saw her below among a silvery bed of apple trees now blooming in the spring.

'O Phoebe!' he called. 'O Phoebe! Oh, no, don't leave me!' And feeling the lure of a world where love was young and Phoebe as this vision presented her, a delightful epitome of their quondam youth, he gave a gay cry of 'Oh, wait, Phoebe!' and leaped.

Some farmer-boys reconnoitring this region of bounty and prospect some few days afterward, found first the tin utensils tied together under the tree where he had left them, and then later at the foot of the cliff, pale, broken, but elate, a moulded smile of peace and delight upon his lips, his body. His old hat was discovered lying under some low-growing saplings the twigs of which had held it back. No one of all the simple population knew how eagerly and joyously he had found his lost mate.

THE MENORAH[1]

BENJAMIN ROSENBLATT

IT WAS a secluded little town in Russia, a town within the Pale — unpretentious, undignified. Very narrow and crooked were the streets; dingy and dilapidated, the low-thatched shanties; bare and bleak, the surrounding country. And the inhabitants partook of the pervading grime. They stooped in their walk, and stuttered in their speech — unerring tokens of the Jewish dwellers in the dominions of the White Tsar.

Yet the town did not lack its few aristocrats, its scanty patricians, before whom all the rest bent the crooked knee. But woe to the erstwhile Croesus who lost his all, and joined the tatterdemalions. The victim and his progeny forever after stooped in their walk, faltered in their speech, and no wisdom or virtue could raise them from the dust.

The town had its prying eye on the ever-growing list of the once mighty who had slipped on the downhill road, soon to be cast into the trough of oblivion.

Among those who still received the homage of the populace, but whose star was on the wane, was Lea Reb Kalman's. Her

---

[1] From *The Bellman*. Copyright, 1916, by the Bellman Company. Copyright, 1917, by Benjamin Rosenblatt.

spouse, Reb Shloime, like Enoch, walked with God. His days were spent in the synagogue, enmeshed in a continuous maze of cabalistic hair-splitting. It was Lea who, living up to the lofty opinion of the Psalmist, toiled and spun for her household. The cares of the home, including the raising of funds, devolved on her shoulders. The town, therefore, brushed aside the master of the home, bearded Reb Shloime, who swallowed science and snuff to excess, and the family was universally known by the patronymic of Lea — the house of Lea Reb Kalman's.

Long after the demise of the first Reb Kalman, the grandfather of Lea, the town shook with the rumors of his vast wealth, the numbers of holy scrolls he donated, the silver and gold utensils that lined the shelves of his home. But grandpa Reb Kalman could not forestall the pending ruin of the saintly Lea. The family pedigree was rated at a premium, but the wolf at Lea's door grew more and more daring. Then, too, there was a marriageable daughter, but no dowry; a house filled with the furniture used by two generations, and no prospect of change. Lea's patience and self-control and dissimulation were never found wanting. The true situation had to be hidden from public gaze.

The very closest neighbors were kept in the dark. Lea blinded them by the only link that still bound her impoverished family to its ancestral glory, a seven-branched antique candelabrum of massive gold and of excellent workmanship which Lea placed on a pedestal in the center of the best room, to spread its halo of aristocracy over the largest possible area. This Menorah enjoyed a local fame, and from near-by towns people would often come to view the treasure of Reb Kalman. They entered the house with reverence and awe, and were sure to overlook all that was dingy.

Poor Lea played the financier, and felt the ground under her giving way. The store of dry goods and miscellanies, which was left in the family in her charge, dwindled away by degrees. What the town really knew to be her journeys for the sake of business were frequently no more than visits to some well-to-do branch of the family in a remote town. There she would give vent to her pent-up tears and beg a loan to uphold the family dignity, so that Reb Shloime would not be forced to leave his spiritual heights and join the wicked ways of the pursuers of wealth.

'My enemies shall never live to see me go to work like Esau!' he would often exclaim amidst a spasm of coughing. He looked upon Lea as the guilty party, and she could not but agree with him. Never would she have had the glory of being led to the canopy by such a saint, if it had not been for the rating of her family. She could not now drag him into the mire. On her rested the burden of keeping untarnished the crest of Reb Kalman.

Slowly the plaster on the once stately mansion detached itself from the moldy wall, and hung as if in mockery; more than one of the massive oak chairs and tables became wabbly and was about to give way. Lea's eyes followed the ruin to its minutest detail; but she clung desperately to the many-branched Menorah that cast its soft glamour over the sordid house.

The eyes of old Lea gradually took on a hungry, startled look. Her body was undersized. The face that looked out of the white kerchief was pinched and furrowed criss-cross. Still she felt a latent power that might turn her into a giant at the approach of danger to her only treasure.

For interwoven into her very fiber was the consciousness that the golden thread which bound her to her famed forefather was so feeble that she, and what was hers, might be instantly swallowed up by the crooked streets, initiated into their ragged fraternity, engulfed in their mud, wiped out — forgotten, forgotten. A cry of anguish would escape her breast, and she would gaze at the golden relic as at a living thing, so endeared to her heart. None would dare to impeach her standing with that talisman before her. Her husband must respect her. The town must not forget her.

Often, when the strain of making both ends meet became unbearable, Lea prayed only for a husband for her daughter. After that, let the Most High send what He willed. The town called her the wide-awake mother. All knew how she ran about, her kerchief halfway off her head, in search of a bridegroom for her only daughter. And she contrived to make appointments with the match-maker for no other day but the Sabbath. Then the candelabrum appeared more prominent on the silvery tablecloth, and radiated such awe that the Shadchan could not have the audacity to propose aught but the very flower of Israel. He could not for a moment forget that he faced Lea Reb Kalman's.

There had been times when it was not so difficult for Lea to keep the secret of her growing poverty from the world. Long after her marriage the house looked bright, and enjoyed many relics from the departed grandfather. There was a silver cup of rare design, the luster of which kept the neighbors for a long time from detecting that the home library of holy books was dwindling away. A string of pretty pearls hung from Lea's neck, distracting attention from the threadbare dress of *moiré* antique. A younger daughter was then alive, a slender, airy creature who added aristocratic grace to the bliss of the Sabbath, when the candles in the Menorah burned brightly, each little flame representing the soul of a departed kinsman. Old Shloime did not cough then, and he paced the room in his Sabbath caftan, his earlocks dangling, while he snapped his fingers and sang aloud his greetings to the angels that bring peace to the home.

Through the arts of Lea, the final disappearance of the pearls and books had little effect on the neighbors. She had let them go so gradually, with such finely shaded diminuendo, that her reputation had suffered but little.

When the town was in want of someone to go the rounds and

collect for the poor, it turned to Lea Reb Kalman's. She walked from house to house, her ears tingling, her eyes aflame; and she collected groschens for the needy.

To the silver cup she clung tenaciously for a long time; and used it, together with the candelabrum, as a stalking horse. The value of the cup was slight, but she dreaded its loss; and she feared Reb Shloime, who kept the mug for his 'wine of blessing.'

Once, however, when the younger child grew ill, Shloime noticed that Lea took the cup with her on one of her journeys. He fastened his eyes on her trembling hands, as she cast wild glances at the Menorah. For a moment he saw ruin before him, the devastation of everything. But she took only the cup, and with the little money tried to save the child, relying on the Almighty for the rest. When the girl died, and the mother threw her arms wildly in the air, and uttered her protest against the Lord, pious old Shloime shouted: 'Silence! You have not sacrificed enough; you ——' He was interrupted, for Lea was carried swooning into the open air.

Later, when the little corpse of their child lay on the ground, near its head two burning candles stuck into the lustrous candelabrum, and the assembled mourners, glancing at the celebrated relic, spoke in respectful whispers of the great Reb Kalman who died in the Lord, Reb Shloime felt a guilty shame, despite his habitual exaltation, toward his poor wife.

Lea would stay for hours near her golden gift, caressing it with her wrinkled hands, watching lest a speck of dust should dim its gloss. Every Friday, at sundown, as she stood with her face covered by her hands, murmuring her prayers over the lighted candles, she also prayed for the soul of the departed child. Then her husband's harsh words would suddenly startle her, 'You have not sacrificed enough,' and she would turn from the candelabrum, her face livid, her breast heaving.

One day, Lea returned from one of her journeys with a fire in her dimmed eyes that Shloime had never noticed before. In tones that sounded to him at first like an apology, and then like an atonement, she spoke of good news.

'A young man of birth, a family of means,' she related with scanty breath — 'an excellent match for our daughter. They wanted such high dowry. But thank God, as soon as you acquiesce we shall have her betrothed.'

Reb Shloime marveled at her abrupt speech. Even he noticed that Lea's lips were parched, her eyes aflame, and that she spoke as if she had swallowed her sobs. But he ascribed it all to the excitement of leading a daughter to the canopy.

For the first time since her marriage, Lea had a secret which she kept from her husband. She was aware that she could not ward off the inevitable. Soon, not only her husband, the entire town, would learn of her fall. Her little body was shaken by a chill that ran from the roots of her hair to the tips of her fingers. Her teeth chattered in her mouth with the effort to keep from shouting the terrible secret at the top of her voice. But her trembling old lips moved in a whisper, in a continuous mumble: 'O Lord of my fathers, O dear God, you know a mother's heart — I had to sell Grandpa's Menorah, my magic Menorah.'

Shloime could not make out her incoherent cry at night, 'I did not have enough for the dowry.'

It was one of her relatives on the paternal side who had bought Reb Kalman's legacy, the candelabrum, yielding to the condition that Lea should keep the treasure till after her daughter's betrothal.

In a frenzy, Lea had run to the tailor's long before it was time. While her husband was away at the synagogue, celebrating with his cronies, she was afraid to stay alone at the house with the treasure that was no longer hers. She managed to spend the days before the ceremony amid the rustle of linens, the clicking of scissors, the flying of needles.

The night of the wedding, she frisked about and danced so wildly that the guests eyed one another in astonishment. Even at 'the covering of the bride,' when the young girl sheds tears under her veil, while the bard, accompanied by the sighing violins and the wails of the women, speaks of happiness and misery, of life and death — even then Lea stood with eyes dry and staring.

Only for a moment her face contracted spasmodically, as she imagined that she was the cause of the wailing; even as the Talmud says: 'Yea, the poor are likened unto the dead.' Better had she been now a corpse — she, the daughter of Israel who reduced her learned spouse to penury; she, who was no more the aristocratic Lea Reb Kalman's. With an effort she straightened up, for fear that her husband might suspect something. She recalled a song she knew in her childhood, and, placing herself before the bride, she sang in a falsetto:

> And when you depart hence,
> And when you depart —
> Oh, think how lonely you leave me.

And Reb Shloime, with eyes somewhat the worse for wine, looked shyly at her and laughed hoarsely, and nudged his neighbors, with the incessant remark: 'Isn't she as blooming as a bride? As I am a Jew, she looks as young as a bride!'

ONNIE[1]

THOMAS BEER

MRS. RAWLING ordered Sanford to take a bath, and with the clear vision of seven years Sanford noted that no distinct place for this process had been recommended. So he retired to a sun-warmed tub of rain-water behind the stables, and sat comfortably arm-pit deep therein, whirring a rattle lately worn by a snake, and presented to him by one of the Varian tribe, sons of his father's foreman. Soaking happily, Sanford admired his mother's garden, spread up along the slope toward the thick cedar forest, and thought of the mountain strawberries ripening in this hot Pennsylvania June. His infant brother Peter yelled viciously in the big gray-stone house, and the great sawmill snarled half a mile away, while he waited patiently for the soapless water to remove all plantain stains from his brown legs, the cause of this immersion.

A shadow came between him and the sun, and Sanford abandoned the rattles to behold a monstrous female, unknown, white-skinned, moving on majestic feet to his seclusion. He sat deeper in the tub, but she seemed unabashed, and stood with a red hand on each hip, a grin rippling the length of her mouth.

[1] From *The Century Magazine.* Copyright, 1917, by The Century Company. Copyright, 1918, by Thomas Beer.

'Herself says you'll be comin' to herself now, if it's you that's Master San,' she said.

Sanford speculated. He knew that all things have an office in this world, and tried to locate this preposterous, lofty creature while she beamed upon him.

'I'm San. Are you the new cook?' he asked.

'I am the same,' she admitted.

'Are you a *good* cook?' he continued. 'Aggie wasn't. She drank.'

'God be above us all! And whatever did herself do with a cook that drank in this place?'

'I don't know. Aggie got married. Cooks *do*,' said Sanford, much entertained by this person. Her deep voice was soft, emerging from the largest, reddest mouth he had ever seen. The size of her feet made him dubious as to her humanity. 'Anyhow,' he went on, 'tell Mother I'm not clean yet. What's your name?'

'Onnie,' said the new cook. 'An' would this be the garden?'

'Silly, what did you think?'

'I'm a stranger in this place, Master San, an' I know not which is why nor forever after.'

Sanford's brain refused this statement entirely, and he blinked.

'I guess you're Irish,' he meditated.

'I am. Do you be gettin' out of your tub now, an' Onnie'll dry you,' she offered.

'I can't,' he said firmly, 'you're a lady.'

'A lady? Blessed Mary save us from sin! A lady? Myself? I'm no such thing in this world at all; I'm just Onnie Killelia.'

She appeared quite horrified, and Sanford was astonished. She seemed to be a woman, for all her height and the extent of her hands.

'Are you sure?' he asked.

'As I am a Christian woman,' said Onnie. 'I never was a lady, nor could I ever be such a thing.'

'Well,' said Sanford, 'I don't know, but I suppose you can dry me.'

He climbed out of his tub, and this novel being paid kind attention to his directions. He began to like her, especially as her hair was of a singular silky blackness, suggesting dark mulberries, delightful to the touch. He allowed her to kiss him and to carry him, clothed, back to the house on her shoulders, which were as hard as a cedar trunk, but covered with green cloth sprinkled with purple dots.

'And herself's in the libr'y drinkin' tea,' said his vehicle, depositing him on the veranda. 'An' what might that be you'd be holdin'?'

'Just a rattle off a snake.'

She examined the six-tiered, smoky rattle with a positive light in her dull black eyes and crossed herself.

'A queer country, where they do be bellin' the snakes! I heard the like in the gover'ment school before I did come over the west water, but I misbelieved the same. God's ways is strange, as the priests will be sayin'.'

'You can have it,' said Sanford, and ran off to inquire of his mother the difference between women and ladies.

Rawling, riding slowly, came up the driveway from the single lane of his village, and found the gigantic girl sitting on the steps so absorbed in this sinister toy that she jumped with a little yelp when he dismounted.

'What have you there?' he asked, using his most engaging smile.

''Tis a snake's bell, your Honor, which Master San did be givin' me. 'Tis welcome indeed, as I lost off my holy medal, bein' sick, forever on the steamship crossin' the west water.'

'But — can you use a rattle for a holy medal?' said Rawling.

'The gifts of children are the blessin's of Mary's self,' Onnie maintained. She squatted on the gravel and hunted for one of the big hairpins her jump had loosened, then used it to pierce the topmost shell. Rawling leaned against his saddle, watching the huge hands, and Pat Sheehan, the old coachman, chuckled, coming up for the tired horse.

'You'll be from the West,' he said, 'where they string sea-shells.'

'I am, an' you'll be from Dublin, by the sound of your speakin'. So was my father, who is now drowned forever, and with his wooden leg,' she added mournfully, finding a cord in some recess of her pocket, entangled there with a rosary and a cluster of small fish-hooks. She patted the odd scapular into the cleft of her bosom and smiled at Rawling. 'Them in the kitchen are tellin' me you'll be ownin' this whole country an' sixty miles of it, all the trees an' hills. You'll be no less than a President's son, then, your Honor.'

Pat led the horse off hastily, and Rawling explained that his lineage was not so interesting. The girl had arrived the night before, sent on by an Oil City agency, and Mrs. Rawling had accepted the Amazon as manna fall. The lumber valley was ten miles above a tiny railroad station, and servants had to be tempted with triple wages, were transient, or married an employee before a month could pass. The valley women regarded Rawling as their patron, heir of his father, and as temporary aid gave feudal service on demand; but for the six months of his family's residence each year house servants must be kept at any price. He talked of his domain, and the Irish girl nodded, the rattles whirring when she breathed, muffled in her breast, as if a snake were crawling somewhere near.

'When my father came here,' he said, 'there wasn't any rail-road, and there were still Indians in the woods.'

'Red Indians? Would they all be dead now? My brother

Hyacinth is fair departed his mind readin' of red Indians. Him is my twin.'

'How many of you are there?'

'Twelve, your Honor,' said Onnie, 'an' me the first to go off, bein' that I'm not so pretty a man would be marryin' me that day or this. An' if herself is content, I am pleased entirely.'

'You're a good cook,' said Rawling, honestly. 'How old are you?'

He had been puzzling about this; she was so wonderfully ugly that age was difficult to conjecture. But she startled him.

'I'll be sixteen next Easter-time, your Honor.'

'That's very young to leave home,' he sympathized.

'Who'd be doin' the like of me any hurt? I'd trample the face off his head,' she laughed.

'I think you could. And now what do you think of my big son?'

The amazing Onnie gurgled like a child, clasping her hands.

'Sure, Mary herself bore the like among the Jew men, an' no one since that day, or will forever. An' I must go to my cookin', or Master San will have no dinner fit for him.'

Rawling looked after her pink flannel petticoat, greatly touched and pleased by this eulogy. Mrs. Rawling strolled out of the hall and laughed at the narrative.

'She's appalling to look at, and she frightens the other girls, but she's clean and teachable. If she likes San, she may not marry one of the men — for a while.'

'He'd be a bold man. She's as big as Jim Varian. If we run short of hands, I'll send her up to a cutting. Where's San?'

'In the kitchen. He likes her. Heavens! if she'll only stay, Bob!'

Onnie stayed, and Mrs. Rawling was gratified by humble obedience and excellent cookery. Sanford was gratified by her address, strange to him. He was the property of his father's lumbermen, and their wives called him everything from 'heart's

love' to 'little cabbage,' as their origin might dictate; but no one
had ever called him 'Master San.' He was San to the whole
valley, the first-born of the owner who gave their children schools
and stereopticon lectures in the union chapel, as his father had
before him. He went where he pleased, safe except from blind
nature and the unfriendly edges of whirling saws. Men fished
him out of the dammed river, where logs floated, waiting conversion into merchantable planking, and the Varian boys, big, tawny
youngsters, were his bodyguard. These perplexed Onnie Killelia
in her first days at Rawling's Hope.

'The agent's lads are whistlin' for Master San,' she reported to
Mrs. Rawling. 'Shall I be findin' him?'

'The agent's lads? Do you mean the Varian boys?'

'Them's them. Wouldn't Jim Varian be his honor's agent?
Don't he be payin' the tenantry an' sayin' where is the trees to
be felled? I forbid them to come in, as Miss Margot — which is a
queer name! — is asleep sound, an' Master Pete.'

'Jim Varian came here with his honor's father, and taught his
honor to shoot and swim, also his honor's brother Peter, in New
York, where we live in winter. Yes, I suppose you'd call Jim
Varian his honor's agent. The boys take care of Master San
almost as well as you do.'

Onnie sniffed, balancing from heel to heel.

'Fine care! An' Bill Varian lettin' him go romping by the
poison ivy, which God lets grow in this place like weeds in a
widow's garden. An' his honor, they do be sayin', sends Bill to a
fine school, and will the others after him, and to a college like
Dublin has after. An' they callin' himself San like he was their
brother!'

As a volunteer nursemaid Onnie was quite miraculous to her
mistress. Apparently she could follow Sanford by scent, for his
bare soles left no traces in the wild grass, and he moved rapidly,
appearing at home exactly when his stomach suggested. He was

forbidden only the slate ledges beyond the log basin, where rattle-snakes took the sun, and the trackless farther reaches of the val-ley, bewildering to a small boy, with intricate brooks and fallen cedar or the profitable yellow pine. Onnie, crying out on her saints, retrieved him from the turntable pit of the narrow-gauge logging-road, and pursued his fair head up the blue-stone crags behind the house, her vast feet causing avalanches among the garden beds. She withdrew him with railings from the enchanting society of louse-infested Polish children, and danced hysterically on the shore of the valley-wide, log-stippled pool when the Varians took him to swim. She bore him off to bed, glowering at the actual nurse. She filled his bath, she cut his toenails. She sang him to sleep with 'Drolien' and the heart-shattering lament for Gerald. She prayed all night outside his door when he had a brief fever. When trouble was coming, she said the 'snake's bells' told her, talking loudly; and petty incidents confirmed her so far that, after she found the child's room ablaze from one of Rawling's cigarettes, they did not argue, and grew to share half-way her superstition.

Women were scarce in the valley, and the well-fed, well-paid men needed wives; and, as time went on, Honora Killelia was sought in marriage by tall Scots and Swedes, who sat dumbly passionate on the back veranda, where she mended Sanford's clothes. Even hawk-nosed Jim Varian, nearing sixty, made cautious proposals, using Bill as messenger, when Sanford was nine.

'God spare us from Purgatory!' she shouted. 'Me to sew for the eight of you? Even in the fine house his honor did be givin' the agent I could not stand the noise of it. An' who'd be mendin' Master San's clothes? Be out of this kitchen, Bill Varian!'

Rawling, suffocated with laughter, reeled out of the pantry and fled to his pretty wife.

'She thinks San's her own kid!' he gasped.

'She's perfectly priceless. I wish she'd be as careful of Margot and Pete. I wish we could lure her to New York. She's worth twenty city servants.'

'Her theory is that if she stays here there's someone to see that Pat Sheehan doesn't neglect — what does she call San's pony?' Rawling asked.

'The little horse. Yes, she told me she'd trample the face off Pat if Shelty came to harm. She keeps the house like silver, too; and it's heavenly to find the curtains put up when we get here. Heavens! Listen!'

They were in Rawling's bedroom, and Onnie came up the curved stairs. Even in list house-slippers she moved like an elephant, and Sanford had called her, so the speed of her approach shook the square upper hall, and the door jarred a little way open with the impact of her feet.

'Onnie, I'm not sleepy. Sing Gerald,' he commanded.

'I will do that same if you'll be lyin' down still, Master San. Now, this is what Conia sang when she found her son all dead forever in the sands of the west water.'

By the sound Onnie sat near the bed crooning steadily, her soft contralto filling both stories of the happy house. Rawling went across the hall to see, and stood in the boy's door. He loved Sanford as imaginative men can who are still young, and the ugly girl's idolatry seemed natural. Yet this was very charming, the simple room, the drowsy, slender child, curled in his sheets, surrounded with song.

'Thank you, Onnie,' said Sanford. 'I suppose she loved him a lot. It's a nice song. Goo'night.'

As Onnie passed her master, he saw the stupid eyes full of tears.

'Now, why'll he be thankin' me,' she muttered — 'me that 'u'd die an' stay in hell forever for him? Now I must go mend up the fish-bag your Honor's brother's wife was for sendin' him an' which no decent fish would be dyin' in.'

'Aren't you going to take Jim Varian?' asked Rawling.

'I wouldn't be marryin' with Roosyvelt himself, that's President, an' has his house built all of gold! Who'd be seein' he gets his meals, an' no servants in the sufferin' land worth the curse of a heretic? Not the agent, nor fifty of him,' Onnie proclaimed, and marched away.

Sanford never came to scorn his slave or treat her as a servant. He was proud of Onnie. She did not embarrass him by her all-embracing attentions, although he weaned her of some of them as he grew into a wood-ranging, silent boy, studious, and somewhat shy outside the feudal valley. The Varian boys were sent, as each reached thirteen, to Lawrenceville, and testified their gratitude to the patron by diligent careers. They were Sanford's summer companions, with occasional visits from his cousin Dennis, whose mother disapproved of the valley and Onnie.

'I really don't see how Sanford can let the poor creature fondle him,' she said. 'Denny tells me she simply wails outside San's door if he comes home wet or has a bruise. It's rather ludicrous, now that San's fourteen. She writes to him at St. Andrew's.'

'I told her St. Andrew's wasn't far from Boston, and she offered to get her cousin Dermot — he's a bell-hop at the Touraine — to valet him. Imagine San with a valet at St. Andrew's!' Rawling laughed.

'But San isn't spoiled,' Peter observed, 'and he's the idol of the valley, Bob, even more than you are. Varian, McComas, Jansen — the whole gang and their cubs. They'd slaughter anyone who touched San.'

'I don't see how you stand the place,' said Mrs. Peter. 'Even if the men are respectful, they're so familiar. And anything could happen there. Denny tells me you have Poles and Russians — all sorts of dreadful people.'

Her horror tinkled prettily in the Chinese drawing-room, but Rawling sighed.

'We can't get the old sort — Scotch, Swedes, the good Irish. We get any old thing. Varian swears like a trooper, but he has to fire them right and left all summer through. We've a couple of hundred who are there to stay, some of them born there; but God help San when he takes it over!'

Sanford learned to row at St. Andrew's, and came home in June with new, flat bands of muscle in his chest, and Onnie worshiped with loud Celtic exclamations, and bade small Pete grow up like Master San. And Sanford grew two inches before he came home for the next summer, reverting to bare feet, corduroys, and woolen shirts as usual. Onnie eyed him dazedly when he strode into her kitchen for sandwiches against an afternoon's fishing.

'Oh, Master San, you're all grown up sudden'!'

'Just five foot eight, Onnie. Ling Varian's five foot nine; so's Cousin Den.'

'But don't you be goin' round the cuttin' camps up valley, neither. You're too young to be hearin' the awful way these new hands do talk. It's a sin to hear how they curse an' swear.'

'The wumman's right,' said Cameron, the smith, who was courting her while he mended the kitchen range. 'They're foul as an Edinburgh fishwife — the new men. Go no place wi'out a Varian, two Varians, or one of my lads.'

'Good Lord! I'm not a kid, Ian!'

'Ye're no' a mon, neither. An' ye're the owner's first,' said Cameron grimly.

Rawling nodded when Sanford told him this.

'Jim carries an automatic in his belt, and we've had stabbings. Keep your temper if they get fresh. We're in hot water constantly, San. Look about the trails for whiskey-caches. These rotten stevedores who come floating in bother the girls and bully the kids. You're fifteen, and I count on you to help keep the property decent. The boys will tell you the things they hear. Use the Varians; Ling and Reuben are clever. I pay high enough wages for this riffraff. I'll pay anything for good hands; and we get dirt!'

Sanford enjoyed being a detective, and kept the Varians busy. Bill, acting as assistant doctor of the five hundred, gave him advice on the subject of cocaine symptoms and alcoholic eyes. Onnie raved when he trotted in one night with Ling and Reuben at heel, their clothes rank with the evil whiskey they had poured from kegs hidden in a cavern near the valley-mouth.

'You'll be killed forever with some Polak beast! Oh, Master San, it's not you that's the polis. 'Tis not fit for him, your Honor. Some Irish pig will be shootin' him, or a sufferin' Bohemyun.'

'But it's the property, Onnie,' the boy faltered. 'Here's his honor worked to death, and Uncle Jim. I've got to do something. They sell good whiskey at the store, and just smell me.'

But Onnie wept, and Rawling, for sheer pity, sent her out of the dining-room.

'She — she scares me!' Sanford said. 'It's not natural, Dad, d' you think?'

He was sitting on his bed, newly bathed and pensive, reviewing the day.

'Why not? She's alone here, and you're the only thing she's fond of. Stop telling her about things or she'll get sick with worry.'

'She's fond of Margot and Pete, but she's just idiotic about me. She did scare me!'

Rawling looked at his son and wondered if the boy knew how attractive were his dark, blue eyes and his plain, grave face. The younger children were beautiful; but Sanford, reared more in the forest, had the forest depth in his gaze and an animal litheness in his hard young body.

'She's like a dog,' Sanford reflected. 'Only she's a woman. It's sort of ——'

'Pathetic?'

'I suppose that's the word. But I *do* love the poor old thing. Her letters are rich. She tells me about all the new babies and who's courting who and how the horses are. It *is* pathetic.'

He thought of Onnie often the next winter, and especially when she wrote a lyric of thanksgiving after the family had come to Rawling's Hope in April, saying that all would be well and trouble would cease. But his father wrote differently:

'You know there is a strike in the West Virginia mines, and it has sent a mass of ruffians out looking for work. We need all the people we can get, but they are a pestiferous outfit. I am opening up a camp in Bear Run, and our orders are enormous already, but I hate littering the valley with these swine. They are as insolent and dirty as Turks. Pete says the village smells, and has taken to the woods. Onnie says the new Irish are black scum of Limerick, and Jim Varian's language isn't printable. The old men are complaining, and altogether I feel like Louis XVI in 1789. About every day I have to send for the sheriff and have some thug arrested. A blackguard from Oil City has opened a dive just outside the property, on the road to the station, and Cameron tells me all sorts of dope is for sale in the boarding-houses. We have cocaine-inhalers, opium-smokers, and all the other vices.'

After this outburst Sanford was not surprised when he heard from Onnie that his father now wore a revolver, and that the overseers of the sawmill did the same.

On the first of June Rawling posted signs at the edge of his valley and at the railroad stations nearest, saying that he needed no more labor. The tide of applicants ceased, but Mrs. Rawling was nervous. Pete declared his intention of running away, and riding home in the late afternoon, Margot was stopped by a drunken, babbling man, who seized her pony's bridle, with unknown words. She galloped free, but next day Rawling sent his wife and children to the seaside and sat waiting Sanford's coming to cheer his desolate house, the new revolver cold on his groin.

Sanford came home a day earlier than he had planned, and drove in a borrowed cart from the station, furious when an old cottage blazed in the rainy night, just below the white posts marking his heritage, and shrill women screamed invitation at the horse's hoof-beats. He felt the valley smirched, and his father's worn face angered him when they met.

'I almost wish you'd not come, Sonny. We're in rotten shape for a hard summer. Go to bed, dear, and get warm.'

'Got a six-shooter for me?'

'You? Who'd touch you? Someone would kill him. I let Bill have a gun, and some other steady heads. You must keep your temper. You always have. Ling Varian got into a splendid row with some hog who called Uncle Jim — the usual name. Ling did him up. Ah, here's Onnie. Onnie, here's ——'

The cook rushed down the stairs, a fearful and notable bedgown covering her night-dress, and the rattles chattering loudly.

'God's kind to us. See the chest of him! Master San! Master San!'

'Good Lord, Onnie. I wasn't dead, you know! Don't *kill* a fellow!'

For the first time her embrace was an embarrassment; her mouth on his cheek made him flush. She loved him so desperately, this poor stupid woman, and he could only be fond of her, give her a sort of tolerant affection. Honesty reddened his face.

'Come on and find me a hard-boiled egg, there's a ——'

'A hard-boiled egg? Listen to that, your Honor! An' it's near the middle of the night! No, I'll not be findin' hard-boiled eggs for you — oh, he's laughin' at me! Now you come into the dinin'-room, an' I'll be hottin' some milk for you, for you're wet as any drowned little cat. An' the mare's fine, an' I've the fishin'-sticks all dusted, an' your new bathin'-tub's to your bathroom, though ill fate follow that English pig Percival that put it in, for he dug holes with his heels! An' would you be wantin' a roast-beef sand-widge?'

'She's nearly wild,' said Rawling as the pantry door slammed. 'You must be careful, San, and not get into any rows. She'd have a fit. What is it?'

'What do you do when you can't — care about a person as much as they care about you?'

'Put up with it patiently.' Rawling shrugged. 'What else *can* you do?'

'I'm sixteen. She keeps on as if I were six. S-suppose she fell in love with me? She's not old — very old.'

'It's another sort of thing, Sonny. Don't worry,' said Rawling gravely, and broke off the subject lest the boy should fret.

Late next afternoon Sanford rode down a trail from deep forest, lounging in the saddle, and flicking brush aside with a long dog-whip. There was a rainstorm gathering, and the hot air swayed no leaf. A rabbit, sluggish and impertinent, hopped across his path and wandered up the side trail toward Varian's cottage. Sanford halted the mare and whistled. His father needed cheer-ing, and Ling Varian, if obtainable, would make a third at dinner. His intimate hurtled down the tunnel of mountain ash directly and assented.

'Wait till I go back and tell Reuben, though. I'm cooking this week. Wish Onnie'd marry Dad. Make her, can't you? Hi, Reu! I'm eating at the house. The beef's on, and Dad wants fried onions. Why won't she have Dad? *You're* grown up.'

He trotted beside the mare noiselessly, chewing a birch spray, a hand on his friend's knee.

'She says she won't get married. I expect she'll stay here as long as she lives.'

'I suppose so, but I wish she'd marry Dad,' said Ling. 'All this trouble's wearing him out, and he won't have a hired girl if we could catch one. There's a pile of trouble, San. He has rows every day. Had a hell of a row with Percival yesterday.'

'Who's this Percival? Onnie was cursing him out last night,' Sanford recollected.

'He's an awful big hog who's pulling logs at the runway. Used to be a plumber in Australia. Swears like a sailor. He's a — what d' you call 'em? You know, a London mucker?'

'Cockney?'

'Yes, that's it. He put in your new bathtub, and Onnie jumped him for going round the house looking at things. Dad's getting ready to fire him. He's the worst hand in the place. I'll point him out to you.'

The sawmill whistle blew as the trail joined open road, and they passed men, their shirts sweat-stained, nodding or waving to the boys as they spread off to their houses and the swimming-place at the river bridge.

A group gathered daily behind the engine-yard to play horse-shoe quoits, and Sanford pulled the mare to a walk on the fringes of this half-circle as old friends hailed him and shy lads with hair already sun-bleached wriggled out of the crowd to shake hands — Camerons, Jansens, Nattiers, Keenans, sons of the faithful. Bill Varian strolled up, his medical case under an arm.

'I'm eating with you. The boss asked me. He feels better already. Come in and speak to Dad. He's hurt because *he's* not seen you, and you stopped to see Ian at the forge. Hi, Dad!' he called over the felt hats of the ring, 'here's San.'

'Fetch him in, then!' cried the foreman.

Bill and Ling led the nervous mare through the group of pipe-smoking, friendly lumbermen, and Varian hugged his fosterling's son.

'Stop an' watch,' he whispered. 'They'll like seein' you, San. Onnie's been tellin' the women you've growed a yard.'

Sanford settled to the monotony of the endless sport, saluting known brown faces and answering yelps of pleasure from the small boys who squatted against the high fence behind the stake.

'That's Percival,' said Ling, as a man swaggered out to the pitching-mark.

'Six foot three,' Bill said, 'and strong as an ox. Drinks all the time. Think he dopes, too.'

Sanford looked at the fellow with a swift dislike for his vacant, heavy face and his greasy, saffron hair. His bare arms were tattooed boldly and in many colors, distorted with ropes of muscle. He seemed a little drunk, and the green clouds cast a copper shade into his lashless eyes.

'Can't pitch for beans,' said Ling as the first shoe went wide. When the second fell beside it, the crowd laughed.

'Now,' said Ian Cameron, 'he'll be mad wi' vain-glory. He's a camstearlie ring' it an' a claverin' fu'.'

'Ho! Larf ahead!' snapped the giant. ''Ow's a man to 'eave a bloody thing at a bloody stike?'

The experts chuckled, and he ruffled about the ring, truculent, sneering, pausing before Varian, with a glance at Sanford.

'Give me something with some balance. Hi can show yer. Look!'

'I'm looking,' said the foreman; 'an' I ain't deaf, neither.'

''Ere's wot you blighters carn't 'eave. Learned it in Auckland, where there's *real* men.' He fumbled in his shirt, and the mare snorted as the eight-inch blade flashed out of its handle under her nose. 'See? That's the lidy! Now watch! There's a knot-'ole up the palings there.'

The crowd fixed a stare on the green, solid barrier, and the knife soared a full twenty yards, but missed the knothole and rattled down. There was flat derision in the following laughter, and Percival dug his heel in the sod.

'Larf ahead! Hanyone else try 'er?'

'Oh, shut up!' said someone across the ring. 'We're pitchin' shoes.'

Percival slouched off after his knife, and the frieze of small boys scattered except a lint-haired Cameron who was nursing a stray cat busily, cross-legged against the green boarding.

'Yon's Robert Sanford Cameron,' said the smith. 'He can say half his catechism.'

'Good kid,' said Sanford. 'I never could get any ——'

Percival had wandered back and stood a yard off, glaring at Bill as the largest object near.

'Think I can't, wot?'

'I'm not interested, and you're spoiling the game,' said Bill, who feared nothing alive except germs, and could afford to disregard most of these. Sanford's fingers tightened on his whip.

'Ho!' coughed the cockney. 'See! You — there!'

Robert Cameron looked up at the shout. The blade shot between the child's head and the kitten and hummed gently, quivering in the wood.

'Hi could 'a' cut 'is throat,' said Percival, so complacently that Sanford boiled.

'You scared him stiff,' he choked. 'You hog! Don't ——'

''Ello, 'oo's the young dook?'

'Look out,' said a voice. 'That's San, the ——'

'Ho! 'Im with the Hirish gal to 'elp 'im tike 'is bloody barth nights? 'Oo's *he*? She's a ——'

A second later Sanford knew that he had struck the man over the face with his whip, cutting the phrase. The mare plunged and the whole crowd congested about the bellowing cockney as Bill held Cameron back, and huge Jansen planted a hand on Rawling's chest.

'No worry,' he said genially. 'Yim an' us, Boss, our job.'

Varian had wedged his hawk face close to the cockney's, now purple blotched with wrath, and Rawling waited.

'Come to the office an' get your pay. You hear? Then clear out. If you ain't off the property in an hour you'll be dead. You hear?'

'He ought to,' muttered Ling, leading the mare away. 'Dad hasn't yelled that loud since that Dutchman dropped the kid in the — hello, it's raining!'

'Come on home, Sonny,' said Rawling, 'and tell us all about it. I didn't see the start.'

But Sanford was still boiling, and the owner had recourse to his godson. Ling told the story, unabridged, as they mounted toward the house.

'Onnie'll hear of it,' sighed Rawling. 'Look, there she is by the kitchen, and that's Jennie Cameron loping 'cross lots. Never mind, San. You did the best you could; don't bother. Swine are swine.'

The rain was cooling Sanford's head, and he laughed awkwardly.

'Sorry I lost my temper.'

'I'm not. Jennie's telling Onnie. Hear?'

The smith's long-legged daughter was gesticulating at the kitchen trellis, and Onnie's feet began a sort of war-dance in the wet grass as Rawling approached.

'Where is this sufferin' pig, could your Honor be tellin' me? God be above us all! With my name in his black, ugly mouth! I *knew* there'd be trouble; the snake's bells did be sayin' so since the storm was comin'. An' him three times the bigness of Master San! Where'd he be now?'

'Jim gave him an hour to be off the property, Onnie.'

'God's mercy he had no knife in his hand, then, even with the men by an' Master San on his horse. Blessed Mary! I will go wait an' have speech with this Englishman on the road.'

'You'll go get dinner, Onnie Killelia,' said Rawling. 'Master San is tired, Bill and Ling are coming — and look there!'

The faithful were marching Percival down the road to the

valley-mouth in the green dusk. He walked between Jansen and Bill, a dozen men behind and a flying scud of boys before.

'An' Robbie's not hurt,' said Miss Cameron, 'an' San ain't, neither; so don't you worry, Onnie. It's all right.'

Onnie laughed.

'I'd like well to have seen the whip fly, your Honor. The arm of him! Will he be wantin' waffles to his dinner? Heyah! More trouble yet!' The rattles had whirred, and she shook her head. 'A forest fire likely now? Or a child bein' born dead?'

'Father says she's fey,' Jennie observed as the big woman lumbered off.

'You mean she has second sight? Perhaps. Here's a dollar for Robbie, and tell Ian he's lucky.'

Bill raced up as the rain began to fall heavily in the windless gray of six o'clock. He reported the cockney gone and the men loud in admiration of Sanford; so dinner was cheerful enough, although Sanford felt limp after his first attack of killing rage. Onnie's name on this animal's tongue had maddened him, the reaction made him drowsy; but Ling's winter at Lawrenceville and Bill's in New York needed hearing. Rawling left the three at the hall fireplace while he read a new novel in the library. The rain increased, and the fall became a continuous throbbing so steady that he hardly heard the telephone ring close to his chair: but old Varian's voice came clear along the wire.

'Is that you, Bob? Now, listen. One of them girls at that place down the station road was just talkin' to me. She's scared. She rung me up an' Cameron. That dam' Englishman's gone out o' there bile drunk, swearin' he'll cut San's heart out, the pup! He's gone off wavin' his knife. Now, he knows the house, an' he ain't afraid of nothin' — when he's drunk. He might get that far an' try breakin' in. You lock up ——'

'Lock up? What with?' asked Rawling. 'There's not a lock in the place. Father never had them put in, and I haven't.'

'Well, don't worry none. Ian's got out a dozen men or so with lights an' guns, an' Bill's got his. You keep Bill an' Ling to sleep downstairs. Ian's got the men round the house by this. The hog'll make noise enough to wake the dead.'

'Nice, isn't it, Uncle Jim, having this whelp out gunning for San! I'll keep the boys. Good night,' he said hastily as a shadow on the rug engulfed his feet. The rattles spoke behind him.

'There's a big trouble sittin' on my soul,' said Onnie. 'Your Honor knows there's nothing makes mortal flesh so wild mad as a whipping, an' this dog does know the way of the house. Do you keep the agent's lads tonight in this place with guns to hand. The snake's bells keep ringin'.'

'My God! Onnie, you're making me believe in your rattles! Listen. Percival's gone out of that den down the road, swearing he'll kill San. He's drunk, and Cameron's got men out.'

'That 'u'd be the why of the lanterns I was seein' down by the forge. But it's black as the bowels of Purgatory, your Honor, an' him a strong, wicked devil, cruel an' angry. God destroy him! If he'd tread on a poison snake! No night could be so black as his heart.'

'Steady, Onnie!'

'I'm speakin' soft. Himself's not able to hear,' she said, her eyes half shut. She rocked slowly on the amazing feet. 'Give me a pistol, your Honor. I'll be for sleepin' outside his door this night.'

'You'll go to bed and keep your door open. If you hear a sound, yell like perdition. Send Bill in here. Say I want him. That's all. There's no danger, Onnie; but I'm taking no chances.'

'We'll take no chances, your Honor.'

She turned away quietly, and Rawling shivered at this cool fury. The rattles made his spine itch, and suddenly his valley seemed like a place of demons. The lanterns circling on the lawn seemed like frail glow-worms, incredibly useless, and he leaned on the window-pane listening with fever to the rain.

'All right,' said Bill when he had heard. 'Phone the sheriff. The man's dangerous, sir. I doctored a cut he had the other day, and he tells me he can see at night. That's a lie, of course, but he's light on his feet, and he's a devil. I've seen some rotten curs in the hospitals, but he's worse.'

'Really, Billy, you sound as fierce as Onnie. She wanted a gun.'

The handsome young man bit a lip, and his great body shook.

'This is San,' he said, 'and the men would kill anyone who touched you, and they'd burn anyone who touched San. Sorry if I'm rude.'

'We mustn't lose our heads.' Rawling talked against his fear. 'The man's drunk. He'll never get near here, and he's got four miles to come in a cold rain. But ——'

'May I sleep in San's room?'

'Then he'll know. I don't want him to, or Ling, either; they're imaginative kids. This is a vile mess, Billy.'

'Hush! Then I'll sleep outside his door. I *will*, sir!'

'All right, old man. Thanks. Ling can sleep in Pete's room. Now I'll phone Mackintosh.'

But the sheriff did not answer, and his deputy was ill. Rawling shrugged, but when Varian telephoned that there were thirty men searching, he felt more comfortable.

'You're using the wires a lot, Dad,' said Sanford, roaming in. 'Anything wrong? Where's Ling to sleep?'

'In Pete's room. Good night, Godson. No, nothing wrong.'

But Sanford was back presently, his eyes wide.

'I say, Onnie's asleep front of my door and I can't get over her. What's got into the girl?'

'She's worried. Her snake's bells are going, and she thinks the house'll burn down. Let her be. Sleep with me, and keep my feet warm, Sonny.'

'Sure,' yawned Sanford. ''Night, Billy.'

'Well,' said Bill, 'that settles that, sir. She'd hear anything, or I will, and you're a light sleeper. Suppose we lock up as much as we can and play some checkers?'

They locked the doors, and toward midnight Cameron rapped at the library window, his rubber coat glistening.

'Not a print of the wastrel loon, sir; but the lads will bide out the night. They've whusky an' biscuits an' keep moving.'

'I'll come out myself,' Rawling began, but the smith grunted.

'Ye're no stirrin' oot yer hoos, Robert Rawling! Ye're daft! Gin you met this ganglin' assassinator, wha'd be for maister? San's no to lack a father. Gae to yer bit bed!'

'Gosh!' said Bill, shutting the window, '*he's* in earnest. He forgot to try to talk English even. I feel better. The hog's fallen into a hole and gone to sleep. Let's go up.'

'I suppose if I tell Onnie San's with me, she'll just change to my door,' Rawling considered; 'but I'll try. Poor girl, she's faithful as a dog!'

They mounted softly and beheld her, huddled in a blanket, mountainous, curled outside Sanford's closed door, just opposite the head of the stairs. Rawling stooped over the heap and spoke to the tangle of blue-shadowed hair.

'Onnie Killelia, go to bed.'

'Leave me be, your Honor. I'm —— '

Sleep cut the protest. The rattles sounded feebly, and Rawling stood up.

'Just like a dog,' whispered Bill, stealing off to a guest-room. 'I'll leave my door open.' He patted the revolver in his jacket and grinned affectionately. 'Good night, Boss.'

Rawling touched the switch inside his own door, and the big globe set in the hall ceiling blinked out. They had decided that, supposing the cockney got so far, a lightless house would perplex his feet, and he would be the noisier. Rawling could reach this button from his bed, and silently undressed in the blackness, laying the automatic on the bedside table, reassured by all these circling folk, Onnie, stalwart Bill, and the loyal men out in the rain. Here slept Sanford, breathing happily, so lost that he only sighed when his father crept in beside him, and did not rouse when Rawling thrust an arm under his warm weight to bring him closer, safe in the perilous night.

The guest-room bed creaked beneath Bill's two hundred pounds of muscle, and Ling snored in Peter's room. Rawling's nerves eased on the mattress, and hypnotic rain began to deaden him, against his will. He saw Percival sodden in some ditch, his knife forgotten in brandy's slumbers. No shout came from the hillside. His mind edged toward vacancy, bore back when the boy murmured once, then he gained a mid-state where sensation was not, a mist.

He sat up, tearing the blankets back, because someone moved in the house, and the rain could be heard more loudly, as if a new window were open. He swung his legs free. Someone breathed heavily in the hall. Rawling clutched his revolver, and the cold of it stung. This might be Onnie, anyone; but he put his finger on the switch.

'Straight hover — hover the way it was,' said a thick, puzzled voice. 'There, that one! 'Is bloody barth!'

The rattles whirred as if their first owner lived. Rawling pressed the switch.

'Your Honor!' Onnie screamed. 'Your Honor! Master San! Be lockin' the door inside, Master San! Out of this, you! You!'

Rawling's foot caught in the doorway of the bright hall, and he stumbled, the light dazzling on the cockney's wet bulk hurling itself toward the great woman where she stood, her arms flung cruciform, guarding the empty room. The bodies met with a fearful jar as Rawling staggered up, and there came a crisp explosion before he could raise his hand. Bill's naked shoulder cannoned into him, charging, and Bill's revolver clinked against his own. Rawling reeled to the stairhead, aiming as Bill caught at the man's shirt; but the cockney fell backward, crumpling down, his face purple, his teeth displayed.

'In the head!' said Bill, and bent to look, pushing the plastered curls from a temple. The beast whimpered and died; the knife rattled on the planks.

'Dad,' cried Sanford, 'what on ——'

'Stay where you are!' Rawling gasped, sick of this ugliness, dizzy with the stench of powder and brandy. Death had never seemed so vile. He looked away to the guardian where she knelt at her post, her hands clasped on the breast of her coarse white robe as if she prayed, the hair hiding her face.

'I'll get a blanket,' Bill said, rising. 'There come the men! That you, Ian?'

The smith and a crowd of pale faces crashed up the stairs.

'God forgie us! We let him by — the garden, sir. Alec thought he ——'

'Gosh, Onnie!' said Bill, 'excuse *me!* I'll get some clothes on. Here, Ian ——'

'Onnie,' said Sanford, in the doorway — 'Onnie, what's the matter?'

As if to show him this, her hands, unclasping, fell from the dead bosom, and a streak of heart's blood widened from the knife-wound like the ribbon of some very noble order.

BOYS WILL BE BOYS[1]

IRVIN S. COBB

W HEN Judge Priest, on this particular morning, came puffing into his chambers at the courthouse, looking, with his broad beam and in his costume of flappy, loose white ducks, a good deal like an old-fashioned full-rigger with all sails set, his black shadow, Jeff Poindexter, had already finished the job of putting the quarters to rights for the day. The cedar water bucket had been properly replenished; the jagged flange of a fifteen-cent chunk of ice protruded above the rim of the bucket; and alongside, on the appointed nail, hung the gourd dipper that the master always used. The floor had been swept, except, of course, in the corners and underneath things; there were evidences, in streaky scrolls of fine grit particles upon various flat surfaces, that a dusting brush had been more or less sparingly employed. A spray of trumpet flowers, plucked from the vine that grew outside the window, had been draped over the framed steel engraving of President Davis and his cabinet upon the wall; and on top of the big square desk in the middle of the room, where a small section of cleared green-blotter space formed an oasis in a dry and arid

---

[1] From *The Saturday Evening Post.* Copyright, 1917, by The Curtis Publishing Company. Copyright, 1918, by Irvin S. Cobb.

desert of cluttered law journals and dusty documents, the morning's mail rested in a little heap.

Having placed his old cotton umbrella in a corner, having removed his coat and hung it upon a peg behind the hall door, and
having seen to it that a palm-leaf fan was in arm's reach should
he require it, the Judge, in his billowy white shirt, sat down at his
desk and gave his attention to his letters. There was an invitation
from the Hylan B. Gracy Camp of Confederate Veterans of Eddy-
burg, asking him to deliver the chief oration at the annual reunion,
to be held at Mineral Springs on the twelfth day of the following
month; an official notice from the clerk of the Court of Appeals
concerning the affirmation of a judgment that had been handed
down by Judge Priest at the preceding term of his own court;
a bill for five pounds of a special brand of smoking tobacco;
a notice of a lodge meeting — altogether quite a sizable batch of
mail.

At the bottom of the pile he came upon a long envelope addressed to him by his title, instead of by his name, and bearing
on its upper right-hand corner several foreign-looking stamps;
they were British stamps, he saw, on closer examination.

To the best of his recollection it had been a good long time since
Judge Priest had had a communication by post from overseas.
He adjusted his steel-bowed spectacles, ripped the wrapper with
care, and shook out the contents. There appeared to be several
inclosures; in fact, there were several — a sheaf of printed forms,
a document with seals attached, and a letter that covered two
sheets of paper with typewritten lines. To the letter the recipient
gave consideration first. Before he reached the end of the opening paragraph he uttered a profound grunt of surprise; his reading of the rest was frequently punctuated by small exclamations, his face meantime puckering up in interested lines. At
the conclusion, when he came to the signature, he indulged himself in a soft, low whistle. He read the letter all through again,

and after that he examined the forms and the document which had accompanied it.

Chuckling under his breath, he wriggled himself free from the snug embrace of his chair arms and waddled out of his own office and down the long, bare, empty hall to the office of Sheriff Giles Birdsong. Within, that competent functionary, Deputy Sheriff Breck Quarles, sat at ease in his shirt-sleeves, engaged, with the smaller blade of his pocketknife, in performing upon his finger-nails an operation that combined the fine deftness of the manicure with the less delicate art of the farrier. At the sight of the Judge in the open doorway he hastily withdrew from a tabletop, where they rested, a pair of long, thin legs, and rose.

'Mornin', Breck,' said Judge Priest to the other's salutation. 'No, thank you, son. I won't come in; but I've got a little job for you. I wisht, ef you ain't too busy, that you'd step down the street and see ef you can't find Peep O'Day fur me and fetch him back here with you. It won't take you long, will it?'

'No, suh — not very.' Mr. Quarles reached for his hat and snuggled his shoulder holster back inside his unbuttoned waist-coat. 'He'll most likely be down round Gafford's stable. Whut's Old Peep been doin', Judge — gettin' himself in contempt of court or somethin'?' He grinned, asking the question with the air of one making a little joke.

'No,' vouchsafed the Judge; 'he ain't done nothin'. But he's about to have somethin' of a highly onusual nature done to him. You jest tell him I'm wishful to see him right away — that'll be sufficient, I reckin.'

Without making further explanation, Judge Priest returned to his chambers and for the third time read the letter from foreign parts. Court was not in session, and the hour was early and the weather was hot; nobody interrupted him. Perhaps fifteen min-utes passed. Mr. Quarles poked his head in at the door.

'I found him, suh,' the deputy stated. 'He's outside here in the hall.'

'Much obliged to you, son,' said Judge Priest. 'Send him on in, will you, please?'

The head was withdrawn; its owner lingered out of sight of His Honor, but within earshot. It was hard to figure the presiding judge of the First Judicial District of the State of Kentucky as having business with Peep O'Day; and, though Mr. Quarles was no eavesdropper, still he felt a pardonable curiosity in whatsoever might transpire. As he feigned an absorbed interest in a tax notice, which was pasted on a blackboard just outside the office door, there entered the presence of the Judge a man who seemingly was but a few years younger than the Judge himself — a man who looked to be somewhere between sixty-five and seventy. There is a look that you may have seen in the eyes of ownerless but well-intentioned dogs — dogs that, expecting kicks as their daily portion, are humbly grateful for kind words and stray bones; dogs that are fairly yearning to be adopted by somebody — by anybody — being prepared to give to such a benefactor a most faithful doglike devotion in return.

This look, which is fairly common among masterless and homeless dogs, is rare among humans; still, once in a while you do find it there too. The man who now timidly shuffled himself across the threshold of Judge Priest's office had such a look out of his eyes. He had a long, simple face, partly inclosed in gray whiskers. Four dollars would have been a sufficient price to pay for the garments he stood in, including the wrecked hat he held in his hands and the broken, misshaped shoes on his feet. A purchaser who gave more than four dollars for the whole in its present state of decrepitude would have been but a poor hand at bargaining.

The man who wore this outfit coughed in an embarrassed fashion and halted, fumbling his ruinous hat in his hands.

'Howdy do?' said Judge Priest heartily. 'Come in!'

The other diffidently advanced himself a yard or two.

'Excuse me, suh,' he said apologetically, 'but this-here Breck

Quarles he come after me and he said ez how you wanted to see me. 'Twas him ez brung me here, suh.'

Faintly underlying the drawl of the speaker was just a suspicion — a mere trace, as you might say — of a labial softness that belongs solely and exclusively to the children, and in a diminishing degree to the grandchildren, of native-born sons and daughters of a certain small green isle in the sea. It was not so much a suggestion of a brogue as it was the suggestion of the ghost of a brogue; a brogue almost extinguished, almost obliterated, and yet persisting through the generations — south of Ireland struggling beneath south of Mason and Dixon's Line.

'Yes,' said the Judge; 'that's right. I do want to see you.' The tone was one that he might employ in addressing a bashful child. 'Set down there and make yourself at home.'

The newcomer obeyed to the extent of perching himself on the extreme forward edge of a chair. His feet shuffled uneasily where they were drawn up against the cross rung of the chair.

The Judge reared well back, studying his visitor over the tops of his glasses with rather a quizzical look. In one hand he balanced the large envelope which had come to him that morning.

'Seems to me I heared somewheres, years back, that your regular Christian name was Paul — is that right?'

'Shorely is, suh,' assented the ragged man, surprised and plainly grateful that one holding a supremely high position in the community should vouchsafe to remember a fact relating to so inconsequent an atom as himself. 'But I ain't heared it fur so long I come mighty nigh furgittin' it sometimes, myself. You see, Judge Priest, when I wasn't nothin' but jest a shaver folks started in to callin' me Peep — on account of my last name bein' O'Day, I reckin. They been callin' me so ever since. Fust off, 'twas Little Peep, and then jest plain Peep; and now it's got to be Old Peep. But my real entitled name is Paul, jest like you said, Judge — Paul Felix O'Day.'

'Uh-huh! And wasn't your father's name Philip and your mother's name Katherine Dwyer O'Day?'

'To the best of my recollection that's partly so, too, suh. They both of 'em up and died when I was a baby, long before I could remember anything a-tall. But they always told me my paw's name was Phil, or Philip. Only my maw's name wasn't Kath — Kath — wasn't whut you jest now called it, Judge. It was plain Kate.'

'Kate or Katherine — it makes no great difference,' explained Judge Priest. 'I reckin the record is straight this fur. And now think hard and see ef you kin ever remember hearin' of an uncle named Daniel O'Day — your father's brother.'

The answer was a shake of the tousled head.

'I don't know nothin' about my people. I only jest know they come over frum some place with a funny name in the Old Country before I was born. The onliest kin I ever had over here was that there no-'count triflin' nephew of mine — Perce Dwyer — him that uster hang round this town. I reckin you call him to mind, Judge?'

The old Judge nodded before continuing:

'All the same, I reckin there ain't no manner of doubt but whut you had an uncle of the name of Daniel. All the evidences would seem to p'int that way. Accordin' to the proofs, this-here Uncle Daniel of yours lived in a little town called Kilmare, in Ireland.' He glanced at one of the papers that lay on his desktop, then added in a casual tone: 'Tell me, Peep, whut are you doin' now fur a livin'?'

The object of this examination grinned a faint grin of extenuation.

'Well, suh, I'm knockin' about, doin' the best I kin — which ain't much. I help out round Gafford's liver' stable, and Pete Gafford he lets me sleep in a little room behind the feed room, and his wife she gives me my vittles. Oncet in a while I git a chancet to do odd jobs fur folks round town — cuttin' weeds and splittin' stove wood and packin' in coal, and sech ez that.'

'Not much money in it, is there?'

'No, suh; not much. Folks is more prone to offer me old clothes than they are to pay me in cash. Still, I manage to git along. I don't live very fancy; but, then, I don't starve, and that's more'n some kin say.'

'Peep, whut was the most money you ever had in your life — at one time?'

Peep scratched with a freckled hand at his thatch of faded whitish hair to stimulate recollection.

'I reckin not more'n six bits at any one time, suh. Seems like I've sorter got the knack of livin' without money.'

'Well, Peep, sech bein' the case, whut would you say ef I was to tell you that you're a rich man?'

The answer came slowly:

'I reckin, suh, ef it didn't sound disrespectful, I'd say you was prankin' with me — makin' fun of me, suh.'

Judge Priest bent forward in his chair.

'I'm not prankin' with you. It's my pleasant duty to inform you that at this moment you are the rightful owner of eight thousand pounds.'

'Pounds of whut, Judge?' The tone expressed a heavy incredulity.

'Why, pounds in money.'

Outside, in the hall, with one ear held conveniently near the crack in the door, Deputy Sheriff Quarles gave a violent start; and then, at once, was torn between a desire to stay and hear more and an urge to hurry forth and spread the unbelievable tidings. After the briefest of struggles the latter inclination won; this news was too marvelously good to keep; surely a harbinger and a herald were needed to spread it broadcast.

Mr. Quarles tiptoed rapidly down the hall. When he reached

the sidewalk the volunteer bearer of a miraculous tale fairly ran. As for the man who sat facing the Judge, he merely stared in a dull bewilderment.

'Judge,' he said at length, 'eight thousand pounds of money oughter make a powerful big pile, oughten it?'

'It wouldn't weigh quite that much ef you put it on the scales,' explained His Honor painstakingly. 'I mean pounds sterlin' — English money. Near ez I kin figger offhand, it comes in our money to somewheres between thirty-five and forty thousand dollars — nearer forty than thirty-five. And it's yours, Peep — every red cent of it.'

'Excuse me, suh, and not meanin' to contradict you, or nothin' like that; but I reckin there must be some mistake. Why, Judge, I don't scursely know anybody that's ez wealthy ez all that, let alone anybody that'd give me sech a lot of money.'

'Listen, Peep: This-here letter I'm holdin' in my hand came to me by today's mail — jest a little spell ago. It's frum Ireland — frum the town of Kilmare, where your people come frum. It was sent to me by a firm of barristers in that town — lawyers, we'd call 'em. In this letter they ask me to find you and to tell you what's happened. It seems, from whut they write, that your uncle, by name Daniel O'Day, died not very long ago without issue — that is to say, without leavin' any children of his own, and without makin' any will.

'It appears he had eight thousand pounds saved up. Ever since he died those lawyers and some other folks over there in Ireland have been tryin' to find out who that money should go to. They learnt in some way that your father and your mother settled in this town a mighty long time ago, and that they died here and left one son, which is you. All the rest of the family over there in Ireland have already died out, it seems; that natchelly makes you the next of kin and the heir at law, which means that all your uncle's money comes direct to you.

'So, Peep, you're a wealthy man in your own name. That's the news I had to tell you. Allow me to congratulate you on your good fortune.'

The beneficiary rose to his feet, seeming not to see the hand the old Judge had extended across the desktop toward him. On his face, of a sudden, was a queer, eager look. It was as though he foresaw the coming true of long-cherished and heretofore unattainable visions.

'Have you got it here, suh?'

He glanced about him as though expecting to see a bulky bundle. Judge Priest smiled.

'Oh, no; they didn't send it along with the letter — that wouldn't be regular. There's quite a lot of things to be done fust. There'll be some proofs to be got up and sworn to before a man called a British consul; and likely there'll be a lot of papers that you'll have to sign; and then all the papers and the proofs and things will be sent across the ocean. And, after some fees are paid out over there — why, then you'll git your inheritance.'

The rapt look faded from the strained face, leaving it downcast. 'I'm afeared, then, I won't be able to claim that-there money,' he said forlornly.

'Why not?'

'Because I don't know how to sign my own name. Raised the way I was, I never got no book learnin'. I can't neither read nor write.'

Compassion shadowed the Judge's chubby face; and compassion was in his voice as he made answer:

'You don't need to worry about that part of it. You can make your mark — just a cross mark on the paper, with witnesses present — like this.'

He took up a pen, dipped it in the inkwell, and illustrated his meaning.

'Yes, suh; I'm glad it kin be done thataway. I always wisht I knowed how to read big print and spell my own name out. I ast a feller oncet to write my name out fur me in plain letters on a piece of paper. I was aimin' to learn to copy it off; but I showed it to one of the hands at the liver' stable and he busted out laughin'. And then I come to find out this-here feller had tricked me fur to make game of me. He hadn't wrote my name out a-tall — he'd wrote some dirty words instid. So after that I give up tryin' to educate myself. That was several years back and I ain't tried sence. Now I reckin I'm too old to learn. . . . I wonder, suh — I wonder ef it'll be very long before that there money gits here and I begin to have the spendin' of it?'

'Makin' plans already?'

'Yes, suh,' O'Day answered truthfully; 'I am.' He was silent for a moment, his eyes on the floor; then timidly he advanced the thought that had come to him. 'I reckin, suh, it wouldn't be no more'n fair and proper ef I divided my money with you to pay you back fur all this trouble you're fixin' to take on my account. Would — would half of it be enough? The other half oughter last me fur what uses I'll make of it.'

'I know you mean well and I'm much obliged to you fur your offer,' stated Judge Priest, smiling a little; 'but it wouldn't be fittin' or proper fur me to tech a cent of your money. There'll be some court dues and some lawyers' fees, and sech, to pay over there in Ireland; but after that's settled up everything comes direct to you. It's goin' to be a pleasure to me to help you arrange these-here details that you don't understand — a pleasure and not a burden.'

He considered the figure before him.

'Now, here's another thing, Peep; I judge it's hardly fittin' fur a man of substance to go on livin' the way you've had to live durin' your life. Ef you don't mind my offerin' you a little advice I would suggest that you go right down to Felsburg Brothers when you leave here and git yourself fitted out with some suitable clothin'. And you'd better go to Max Biederman's, too, and order a better pair of shoes fur yourself than them you've got on. Tell 'em I sent you and that I guarantee the payment of your bills. Though I reckin that'll hardly be necessary — when the news of your good luck gits noised round I misdoubt whether there's any firm in our entire city that wouldn't be glad to have you on their books fur a stiddy customer.

'And, also, ef I was you I'd arrange to git me regular board and lodgin's somewheres round town. You see, Peep, comin' into a property entails consider'ble many responsibilities right frum the start.'

'Yes, suh,' assented the legatee obediently. 'I'll do jest ez you say, Judge Priest, about the clothes and the shoes, and all that; but — but, ef you don't mind, I'd like to go on livin' at Gafford's. Pete Gafford's been mighty good to me — him and his wife both; and I wouldn't like fur 'em to think I was gittin' stuck up jest because I've had this-here streak of luck come to me. Mebbe, seein' ez how things has changed with me, they'd be willin' to take me in fur a table boarder at their house; but I shorely would hate to give up livin' in that there little room behind the feed room at the liver' stable. I don't know ez I could ever find any place that would seem ez homelike to me ez whut it is.'

'Suit yourself about that,' said Judge Priest heartily. 'I don't know but whut you've got the proper notion about it after all.'

'Yes, suh. Them Gaffords have been purty nigh the only real true friends I ever had that I could count on.' He hesitated a moment. 'I reckin — I reckin, suh, it'll be a right smart while, won't it, before that money gits here frum all the way acrost the ocean?'

'Why, yes; I imagine it will. Was you figurin' on investin' a little of it now?'

'Yes, suh; I was.'

'About how much did you think of spendin' fur a beginnin'?'

O'Day squinted his eyes, his lips moving in silent calculation.

'Well, suh,' he said at length, 'I could use ez much ez a silver dollar. But, of course, sence ——'

'That sounds kind of moderate to me,' broke in Judge Priest. He shoved a pudgy hand into a pocket of his white trousers. 'I reckin this detail kin be arranged. Here, Peep' — he extended his hand — 'here's your dollar.' Then, as the other drew back, stammering a refusal, he hastily added: 'No, no, no; go ahead and take it — it's yours. I'm jest advancin' it to you out of whut'll be comin' to you shortly.

'I'll tell you whut: Until sech time ez you are in position to draw on your own funds you jest drap in here to see me when you're in need of cash, and I'll try to let you have whut you require — in reason. I'll keep a proper reckinin' of whut you git and you kin pay me back ez soon ez your inheritance is put into your hands.

'One thing more,' he added as the heir, having thanked him, was making his grateful adieu at the threshold: 'Now that you're wealthy, or about to be so, I kind of imagine quite a passel of fellers will suddenly discover themselves strangely and affection-ately drawed toward you. You're liable to find out you've always had more true and devoted friends in this community than whut you ever imagined to be the case before.

'Now, friendship is a mighty fine thing, takin' it by and large; but it kin be overdone. It's barely possible that some of this-here new crop of your well-wishers and admirers will be makin' little business propositions to you — desirin' to have you go partners with 'em in business, or to sell you desirable pieces of real estate; or even to let you loan 'em various sums of money. I wouldn't be surprised but whut a number of sech chances will be comin' your way durin' the next few days, and frum then on. Ef sech should be the case I would suggest to you that, before committin' yourself to anybody or anything, you tell 'em that I'm sort of actin' as your unofficial adviser in money matters, and that they should come to me and outline their little schemes in person. Do you git my general drift?'

'Yes, suh,' said Peep. 'I won't furgit; and thank you ag'in, Judge, specially fur lettin' me have this dollar ahead of time.'

He shambled out with the coin in his hand; and on his face was again the look of one who sees before him the immediate fulfillment of a delectable dream.

With lines of sympathy and amusement cross-hatched at the outer corners of his eyelids, Judge Priest, rising and stepping to his door, watched the retreating figure of the town's newest and strangest capitalist disappear down the wide front steps of the courthouse.

Presently he went back to his chair and sat down, tugging at his short chin beard.

'I wonder now,' said he, meditatively addressing the emptiness of the room, 'I wonder whut a man sixty-odd-year-old is goin' to do with the furst whole dollar he ever had in his life!'

It was characteristic of our circuit judge that he should have voiced his curiosity aloud. Talking to himself when he was alone was one of his habits. Also, it was characteristic of him that he had refrained from betraying his inquisitiveness to his late caller. Similar motives of delicacy had kept him from following the other man to watch the sequence.

However, at second hand, the details very shortly reached him. They were brought by no less a person than Deputy Sheriff Quarles, who, some twenty minutes or possibly half an hour later, obtruded himself upon Judge Priest's presence.

'Judge,' began Mr. Quarles, 'you'd never in the world guess whut Old Peep O'Day done with the first piece of money he got his hands on out of that-there forty thousand pounds of silver dollars he's come into from his uncle's estate.'

The old man slanted a keen glance in Mr. Quarles' direction.

'Tell me, son,' he asked softly, 'how did you come to hear the glad tidin's so promptly?'

'Me?' said Mr. Quarles innocently. 'Why, Judge Priest, the word is all over this part of town by this time. Why, I reckin twenty-five or fifty people must 'a' been watchin' Old Peep to see how he was goin' to act when he come out of this courthouse.'

'Well, well, well!' murmured the Judge blandly. 'Good news travels almost ez fast sometimes ez whut bad news does — don't it, now? Well, son, I give up the riddle. Tell me jest whut our elderly friend did do with the first installment of his inheritance.'

'Well, suh, he turned south here at the gate and went down the street, a-lookin' neither to the right nor the left. He looked to me like a man in a trance, almost. He keeps right on through Legal Row till he comes to Franklin Street, and then he goes up Franklin to B. Weil & Son's confectionery store; and there he turns in. I happened to be followin' 'long behind him, with a few others — with several others, in fact — and we-all sort of slowed up in passin' and looked in at the door; and that's how I come to be in a position to see what happened.

'Old Peep, he marches in jest like I'm tellin' it to you, suh; and Mr. B. Weil comes to wait on him, and he starts in buyin'. He buys hisself a five-cent bag of gumdrops; and a five-cent bag of jelly beans; and a ten-cent bag of mixed candies — kisses and candy mottoes, and sech ez them, you know; and a sack of fresh-roasted peanuts — a big sack, it was, fifteen-cent size; and two prize boxes; and some gingersnaps — ten cents' worth; and a coconut; and half a dozen red bananas; and a half a dozen more of the plain yaller ones. Altogether I figger he spent a even dollar; in fact, I seen him hand Mr. Weil a dollar, and I didn't see him gittin' no change back out of it.

'Then he comes out of the store, with all these things stuck in his pockets and stacked up in his arms till he looks sort of like some new kind of a summertime Santy Klaws; and he sets down on a goods box at the edge of the pavement, with his feet in the gutter, and starts in eatin' all them things.

'First, he takes a bite off a yaller banana and then off a red banana, and then a mouthful of peanuts; and then maybe some mixed candies — not sayin' a word to nobody, but jest natchelly eatin' his fool head off. A young chap that's clerkin' in Bagby's grocery, next door, steps up to him and speaks to him, meanin', I suppose, to ast him is it true he's wealthy. And Old Peep, he says to him, "Please don't come botherin' me now, sonny — I'm busy ketchin' up," he says; and keeps right on a-munchin' and a-chewin' like all possessed.

'That ain't all of it, neither, Judge — not by a long shot it ain't! Purty soon Old Peep looks round him at the little crowd that's gathered. He didn't seem to pay no heed to the grown-up people standin' there; but he sees a couple of boys about ten years old in the crowd, and he beckons to them to come to him, and he makes room fur them alongside him on the box and divides up his knickknacks with them.

'When I left there to come on back here he had no less'n six kids squattered round him, includin' one little nigger boy; and between 'em all they'd jest finished up the last of the bananas and peanuts and the candy and the gingersnaps, and was fixin' to take turns drinkin' the milk out of the coconut. I s'pose they've got it all cracked out of the shell and et up by now — the coconut, I mean. Judge, you oughter stepped down into Franklin Street and taken a look at the picture whilst there was still time. You never seen sech a funny sight in all your days, I'll bet!'

'I reckin 'twould be too late to be startin' now,' said Judge Priest. 'I'm right sorry I missed it. . . . Busy ketchin' up, huh? Yes; I reckin he is. . . . Tell me, son, whut did you make out of the way Peep O'Day acted?'

'Why, suh,' stated Mr. Quarles, 'to my mind, Judge, there ain't no manner of doubt but whut prosperity has went to his head

and turned it. He acted to me like a plum' distracted idiot. A
grown man with forty thousand pounds of solid money settin'
on the side of a gutter eatin' jimcracks with a passel of dirty little
boys! Kin you figure it out any other way, Judge — except that
his mind is gone?'

'I don't set myself up to be a specialist in mental disorders,
son,' said Judge Priest softly; 'but, sence you ask me the question, I should say, speakin' offhand, that it looks to me more ez ef
the heart was the organ that was mainly affected. And possibly'
— he added this last with a dry little smile — 'and possibly, by
now, the stomach also.'

Whether or not Mr. Quarles was correct in his psychopathic
diagnosis, he certainly had been right when he told Judge Priest
that the word was already all over the business district. It had
spread fast and was still spreading; it spread to beat the wireless,
traveling as it did by that mouth-to-ear method of communication which is so amazingly swift and generally so tremendously
incorrect. Persons who could not credit the tale at all nevertheless lost no time in giving to it a yet wider circulation; so that, as
though borne on the wind, it moved in every direction, like ripples
on a pond; and with each time of retelling the size of the legacy
grew.

The *Daily Evening News*, appearing on the streets at 5 P.M.,
confirmed the tale; though by its account the fortune was reduced
to a sum far below the gorgeously exaggerated estimates of most
of the earlier narrators. Between breakfast and supper-time Peep
O'Day's position in the common estimation of his fellow citizens
underwent a radical and revolutionary change. He ceased —
automatically, as it were — to be a town character; he became,
by universal consent, a town notable, whose every act and every
word would thereafter be subjected to close scrutiny and closer
analysis.

The next morning the nation at large had opportunity to know
of the great good fortune that had befallen Paul Felix O'Day, for
the story had been wired to the city papers by the local corre-
spondents of the same; and the press associations had picked up
a stickful of the story and sped it broadcast over leased wires.
Many who until that day had never heard of the fortunate man,
or, indeed, of the place where he lived, at once manifested a concern in his well-being.

Certain firms of investment brokers in New York and Chicago
promptly added a new name to what vulgarly they called their
'sucker' lists. Dealers in mining stocks, in oil stocks, in all kinds
of attractive stocks, showed interest; in circular form samples of
the most optimistic and alluring literature the world has ever
known were consigned to the post, addressed to Mr. P. F.
O'Day, such-and-such a town, such-and-such a state, care of
general delivery.

Various lonesome ladies in various lonesome places lost no time
in sitting themselves down and inditing congratulatory letters;
object matrimony. Some of these were single ladies; others had
been widowed, either by death or request. Various other persons
of both sexes, residing here, there, and elsewhere in our country,
suddenly remembered that they, too, were descended from the
O'Days of Ireland, and wrote on forthwith to claim proud and
fond relationship with the particular O'Day who had come into
money.

It was a remarkable circumstance, which speedily developed,
that one man should have so many distant cousins scattered over
the Union, and a thing equally noteworthy that practically all
these kinspeople, through no fault of their own, should at the
present moment be in such straitened circumstances and in such
dire need of temporary assistance of a financial nature. Ticker
and printer's ink, operating in conjunction, certainly did their
work mighty well; even so, several days were to elapse before the

news reached one who, of all those who read it, had most cause to feel a profound personal sensation in the intelligence.

This delay, however, was nowise to be blamed upon the tardiness of the newspapers; it was occasioned by the fact that the person referred to was for the moment well out of contact with the active currents of world affairs, he being confined in a workhouse at Evansville, Indiana.

As soon as he had rallied from the shock this individual set about making plans to put himself in direct touch with the inheritor. He had ample time in which to frame and shape his campaign, inasmuch as there remained for him yet to serve nearly eight long and painfully tedious weeks of a three-months vagrancy sentence. Unlike most of those now manifesting their interest, he did not write a letter; but he dreamed dreams that made him forget the annoyances of a ball and chain fast on his ankle and piles of stubborn stones to be cracked up into fine bits with a heavy hammer.

We are getting ahead of our narrative, though — days ahead of it. The chronological sequence of events properly dates from the morning following the morning when Peep O'Day, having been abruptly translated from the masses of the penniless to the classes of the wealthy, had forthwith embarked upon the gastronomic orgy so graphically detailed by Deputy Sheriff Quarles.

On that next day more eyes probably than had been trained in Peep O'Day's direction in all the unremarked and unremarkable days of his life put together were focused upon him. Persons who theretofore had regarded his existence — if indeed they gave it a thought — as one of the utterly trivial and inconsequential incidents of the cosmic scheme were moved to speak to him, to clasp his hand, and, in numerous instances, to express a hearty satisfaction over his altered circumstances. To all these, whether they were moved by mere neighborly good will, or perchance were inspired by impulses of selfishness, the old man exhibited a mien of aloofness and embarrassment.

This diffidence or this suspicion — or this whatever it was — protected him from those who might entertain covetous and ulterior designs upon his inheritance even better than though he had been brusque and rude; while those who sought to question him regarding his plans for the future drew from him only mumbled and evasive replies, which left them as deeply in the dark as they had been before. Altogether, in his intercourse with adults he appeared shy and very ill at ease.

It was noted, though, that early in the forenoon he attached to him perhaps half a dozen urchins, of whom the oldest could scarcely have been more than twelve or thirteen years of age; and that these youngsters remained his cómpanions throughout the day. Likewise the events of that day were such as to confirm a majority of the observers in practically the same belief that had been voiced by Mr. Quarles — namely, that whatever scanty brains Peep O'Day might have ever had were now completely addled by the stroke of luck that had befallen him.

In fairness to all — to O'Day and to the town critics who sat in judgment upon his behavior — it should be stated that his conduct at the very outset was not entirely devoid of evidences of sanity. With his troupe of ragged juveniles trailing behind him, he first visited Felsburg Brothers' Emporium to exchange his old and disreputable costume for a wardrobe that, in accordance with Judge Priest's recommendation, he had ordered on the afternoon previous, and which had since been undergoing certain necessary alterations.

With his meager frame incased in new black woolens, and wearing, as an incongruous added touch, the most brilliant of neckties, a necktie of the shade of a pomegranate blossom, he presently issued from Felsburg Brothers' and entered M. Biederman's shoe store, two doors below. Here Mr. Biederman fitted

him with shoes, and in addition noted down a further order, which
the purchaser did not give until after he had conferred earnestly
with the members of his youthful entourage.

Those watching this scene from a distance saw — and perhaps
marveled at the sight — that already, between these small boys,
on the one part, and this old man, on the other, a perfect understanding appeared to have been established.

After leaving Biederman's, and tagged by his small escorts,
O'Day went straight to the courthouse and, upon knocking at the
door, was admitted to Judge Priest's private chambers, the boys
meantime waiting outside in the hall. When he came forth he
showed them something he held in his hand and told them something; whereupon all of them burst into excited and joyous
whoops.

It was at that point that O'Day, by the common verdict of
most grown-up onlookers, began to betray the vagaries of a disordered intellect. Not that his reason had not been under suspicion already, as a result of his freakish excess in the matter of
B. Weil & Son's wares on the preceding day; but the relapse that
now followed, as nearly everybody agreed, was even more pronounced, even more symptomatic than the earlier attack of
aberration.

In brief, this was what happened: To begin with, Mr. Virgil
Overall, who dealt in lands and houses and sold insurance of all
the commoner varieties on the side, had stalked O'Day to this
point and was lying in wait for him as he came out of the courthouse into the Public Square, being anxious to describe to him
some especially desirable bargains, in both improved and unim-
proved realty; also, Mr. Overall was prepared to book him for
life, accident, and health policies on the spot.

So pleased was Mr. Overall at having distanced his professional
rivals in the hunt that he dribbled at the mouth. But the warmth
of his disappointment and indignation dried up the salivary

founts instantly when the prospective patron declined to listen
to him at all and, breaking free from Mr. Overall's detaining
clasp, hurried on into Legal Row, with his small convoys trotting
along ahead and alongside him.

At the door of the Blue Goose Saloon and Short Order Restaurant its proprietor, by name Link Iserman, was lurking, as it
were, in ambush. He hailed the approaching O'Day most cor-
dially; he inquired in a warm voice regarding O'Day's health;
and then, with a rare burst of generosity, he invited, nay urged,
O'Day to step inside and have something on the house — wines,
ales, liquors, or cigars; it was all one to Mr. Iserman. The other
merely shook his head and, without a word of thanks for the offer,
passed on as though bent upon an important mission.

Mark how the proofs were accumulating: The man had dis-
dained the company of men of approximately his own age or
thereabout; he had refused an opportunity to partake of refreshment suitable to his years; and now he stepped into the Bon Ton
toy store and bought for cash — most inconceivable of acquisi-
tions! — a little wagon that was painted bright red and bore on
its sides, in curlicued letters, the name Comet.

His next stop was made at Bishop & Bryan's grocery, where,
with the aid of his youthful compatriots, he first discriminatingly
selected, and then purchased on credit, and finally loaded into the
wagon, such purchases as a dozen bottles of soda pop, assorted
flavors; cheese, crackers — soda and animal; sponge cakes with
weatherproof pink icing on them; fruits of the season; cove
oysters; a bottle of pepper sauce; and a quantity of the extra
large-sized bright green cucumber pickles known to the trade as
the Fancy Jumbo Brand, Prime Selected.

Presently the astounding spectacle was presented of two small
boys, with string bridles on their arms, drawing the wagon
through our town and out of it into the country, with Peep O'Day
in the rôle of teamster walking alongside the laden wagon. He

was holding the lines in his hands and shouting orders at his team, who showed a colty inclination to shy at objects, to kick up their heels without provocation, and at intervals to try to run away. Eight or ten small boys — for by now the troupe had grown in number and in volume of noise — trailed along, keeping step with their elderly patron and advising him shrilly regarding the management of his refractory span.

As it turned out, the destination of this preposterous procession was Bradshaw's Grove, where the entire party spent the day picnicking in the woods and, as reported by several reliable witnesses, playing games. It was not so strange that holidaying boys should play games; the amazing feature of the performance was that Peep O'Day, a man old enough to be grandfather to any of them, played with them, being by turns an Indian chief, a robber baron, and the driver of a stagecoach attacked by Wild Western desperadoes.

When he returned to town at dusk, drawing his little red wagon behind him, his new suit was rumpled into many wrinkles and marked by dust and grass stains; his flame-colored tie was twisted under one ear; his new straw hat was mashed quite out of shape; and in his eyes was a light that sundry citizens, on meeting him, could only interpret for a spark struck from inner fires of madness.

Days that came after this, on through the midsummer, were, with variations, but repetitions of the day I have just described. Each morning Peep O'Day would go to either the courthouse or Judge Priest's home to turn over to the Judge the unopened mail which had been delivered to him at Gafford's stables; then he would secure from the Judge a loan of money against his inheritance. Generally the amount of his daily borrowing was a dollar; rarely was it so much as two dollars; and only once was it more than two dollars.

By nightfall the sum would have been expended upon perfectly useless and absolutely childish devices. It might be that he would buy toy pistols and paper caps for himself and his following of urchins; or that his whim would lead him to expend all the money in tin flutes. In one case the group he so incongruously headed would be for that one day a gang of make-believe banditti; in another, they would constitute themselves a fife-and-drum corps — with barrel tops for the drums — and would march through the streets, where scandalized adults stood in their tracks to watch them go by, they all the while making weird sounds, which with them passed for music.

Or again, the available cash resources would be invested in provender; and then there would be an outing in the woods. Under Peep O'Day's captaincy his chosen band of youngsters picked dewberries; they went swimming together in Guthrie's Gravel Pit, out by the old Fair Grounds, where his spare naked shanks contrasted strongly with their plump, freckled legs as all of them splashed through the shallows, making for deep water. Under his leadership they stole watermelons from Mr. Dick Bell's patch, afterward eating their spoils in thickets of grapevines along the banks of Perkins' Creek.

It was felt that mental befuddlement and mortal folly could reach no greater heights — or no lower depths — than on a certain hour of a certain day, along toward the end of August, when O'Day came forth from his quarters in Gafford's stables, wearing a pair of boots that M. Biederman's establishment had turned out to his order and his measure — not such boots as a sensible man might be expected to wear, but boots that were exaggerated and monstrous counterfeits of the red-topped, scroll-fronted, brass-toed, stub-heeled, squeaky-soled bootees that small boys of an earlier generation possessed.

Very proudly and seemingly unconscious of, or at least oblivious to, the derisive remarks that the appearance of these new belongings drew from many persons, the owner went clumping about in them, with the rumply legs of his trousers tucked down in them, and ballooning up and out over the tops in folds which overlapped from his knee joints halfway down his attenuated calves.

As Deputy Sheriff Quarles said, the combination was a sight fit to make a horse laugh. It may be that small boys have a lesser sense of humor than horses have, for certainly the boys who were the old man's invariable shadows did not laugh at him, or at his boots either. Between the whiskered senior and his small comrades there existed a freemasonry that made them all sense a thing beyond the ken of most of their elders. Perhaps this was because the elders, being blind in their superior wisdom, saw neither this thing nor the communion that flourished. They saw only the farcical joke. But His Honor, Judge Priest, to cite a conspicuous exception, seemed not to see the lamentable comedy of it.

Indeed, it seemed to some almost as if Judge Priest were aiding and abetting the befogged O'Day in his demented enterprises, his peculiar excursions, and his weird purchases. If he did not actually encourage him in these constant exhibitions of witlessness, certainly there were no evidences available to show that he sought to dissuade O'Day from his strange course.

At the end of a fortnight one citizen, in whom patience had ceased to be a virtue and to whose nature long-continued silence on any public topic was intolerable, felt it his duty to speak to the Judge upon the subject. This gentleman — his name was S. P. Escott — held with many that, for the good name of the community, steps should be taken to abate the infantile, futile activities of the besotted legatee.

Afterward Mr. Escott, giving a partial account of the conversation with Judge Priest to certain of his friends, showed unfeigned annoyance at the outcome.

'I claim that old man's not fittin' to be runnin' a court any longer,' he stated bitterly. 'He's too old and peevish — that's what ails him! For one, I'm certainly not never goin' to vote fur him again. Why, it's gettin' to be ez much ez a man's life is worth to stop that-there spiteful old crank in the street and put a civil question to him — that's whut's the matter!'

'What happened, S. P.?' inquired someone.

'Why, here's what happened!' exclaimed the aggrieved Mr. Escott. 'I hadn't any more than started in to tell him the whole town was talkin' about the way that daffy Old Peep O'Day was carryin' on, and that somethin' had oughter be done about it, and didn't he think it was beholdin' on him ez circuit judge to do somethin' right away, sech ez havin' O'Day tuck up and tried fur a lunatic, and that I fur one was ready and willin' to testify to the crazy things I'd seen done with my own eyes — when he cut in on me and jest ez good ez told me to my own face that ef I'd quit tendin' to other people's business I'd mebbe have more business of my own to tend to.

'Think of that, gentlemen! A circuit judge bemeanin' a citizen and a taxpayer' — he checked himself slightly — 'anyhow, a citizen, thataway! It shows he can't be rational his ownself. Personally I claim Old Priest is failin' mentally — he must be! And ef anybody kin be found to run against him at the next election you gentlemen jest watch and see who gits my vote!'

Having uttered this threat with deep and significant emphasis Mr. Escott, still muttering, turned and entered the front gate of his boarding house. It was not exactly his boarding house; his wife ran it. But Mr. Escott lived there and voted from there.

But the apogee of Peep O'Day's carnival of weird vagaries of deportment came at the end of two months — two months in which each day the man furnished cumulative and piled-up material for derisive and jocular comment on the part of a very considerable proportion of his fellow townsmen.

Three occurrences of a widely dissimilar nature, yet all closely interrelated to the main issue, marked the climax of the man's new rôle in his new career. The first of these was the arrival of his legacy; the second was a one-ring circus; and the third and last was a nephew.

In the form of sundry bills of exchange the estate left by the late Daniel O'Day, of the town of Kilmare, in the island of Ireland, was on a certain afternoon delivered over into Judge Priest's hands, and by him, in turn, handed to the rightful owner, after which sundry indebtednesses, representing the total of the old Judge's day-to-day cash advances to O'Day, were liquidated.

The ceremony of deducting this sum took place at the Planters' Bank, whither the two had journeyed in company from the court-house. Having, with the aid of the paying teller, instructed O'Day in the technical details requisite to the drawing of personal checks, Judge Priest went home and had his bag packed, and left for Reelfoot Lake to spend a week fishing. As a consequence he missed the remaining two events, following immediately thereafter.

The circus was no great shakes of a circus; no grand, glittering, gorgeous, glorious pageant of education and entertainment, traveling on its own special trains; no vast tented city of world's wonders and world's champions, heralded for weeks and weeks in advance of its coming by dead walls emblazoned with the finest examples of the lithographer's art, and by half-page advertisements in the *Daily Evening News*. On the contrary, it was a shabby little wagon show, which, coming overland on short notice, rolled into town under horse-power, and set up its ragged and dusty canvases on the vacant lot across from Yeiser's drugstore.

Compared with the street parade of any of its great and famous rivals, the street parade of this circus was a meager and disappointing thing. Why, there was only one elephant, a dwarfish and debilitated-looking creature, worn mangy and slick on its various angles, like the cover of an old-fashioned haircloth trunk; and obviously most of the closed cages were weather-beaten stake wagons in disguise. Nevertheless, there was a sizable turnout of people for the afternoon performance. After all, a circus was a circus.

Moreover, this particular circus was marked at the afternoon performance by happenings of a nature most decidedly unusual. At one o'clock the doors were opened; at one-ten the eyes of the proprietor were made glad and his heart was uplifted within him by the sight of a strange procession, drawing nearer and nearer across the scuffed turf of the Common, and heading in the direction of the red ticket wagon.

At the head of the procession marched Peep O'Day — only, of course, the proprietor didn't know it was Peep O'Day — a queer figure in his rumpled black clothes and his red-topped, brass-toed boots, and with one hand holding fast to the string of a captive toy balloon. Behind him, in an uneven jostling formation, followed many small boys and some small girls. A census of the ranks would have developed that here were included practically all the juvenile white population who otherwise, through a lack of funds, would have been denied the opportunity to patronize this circus or, in fact, any circus.

Each member of the joyous company was likewise the bearer of a toy balloon — red, yellow, blue, green, or purple, as the case might be. Over the line of heads the taut rubbery globes rode on their tethers, nodding and twisting like so many big iridescent bubbles; and half a block away, at the edge of the lot, a balloon vender, whose entire stock had been disposed of in one splendid transaction, now stood, empty-handed but full-pocketed, marveling at the stroke of luck that enabled him to take an afternoon off and rest his voice.

Out of a seemingly bottomless exchequer Peep O'Day bought tickets of admission for all. But this was only the beginning. Once inside the tent he procured accommodations in the reserved-seat section for himself and those who accompanied him. From such superior points of vantage the whole crew of them witnessed the performance, from the thrilling grand entry, with spangled ladies and gentlemen riding two by two on broad-backed steeds, to the tumbling-bout introducing the full strength of the company, which came at the end.

They munched fresh-roasted peanuts and balls of sugar-coated popcorn, slightly rancid, until they munched no longer with zest but merely mechanically. They drank pink lemonade to an extent that threatened absolute depletion of the fluid contents of both barrels in the refreshment stand out in the menagerie tent. They whooped their unbridled approval when the wild Indian chief, after shooting down a stuffed coon with a bow and arrow from somewhere up near the top of the center pole while balancing himself jauntily erect from the haunches of a coursing white charger, suddenly flung off his feathered headdress, his wig, and his fringed leather garments, and revealed himself in pink fleshings as the principal bareback rider.

They screamed in a chorus of delight when the funny old clown, who had been forcibly deprived of three tin flutes in rapid succession, now produced yet a fourth from the seemingly inexhaustible depths of his baggy white pants — a flute with a string and a bent pin attached to it — and, secretly affixing the pin in the tail of the cross ringmaster's coat, was thereafter enabled to toot sharp shrill blasts at frequent intervals, much to the chagrin of the ringmaster, who seemed utterly unable to discover the whereabouts of the instrument dangling behind him.

But no one among them whooped louder or laughed longer than their elderly and bewhiskered friend, who sat among them, paying the bills. As his guests they stayed for the concert; and, following this, they patronized the side show in a body. They had been almost the first upon the scene; assuredly they were the last of the audience to quit it.

Indeed, before they trailed their confrère away from the spot, the sun was nearly down; and at scores of supper tables all over town the tale of poor old Peep O'Day's latest exhibition of freak-ishness was being retailed, with elaborations, to interested auditors. Estimates of the sum probably expended by him in this crowning extravagance ranged well up into the hundreds of dollars.

As for the object of these speculations, he was destined not to eat any supper at all that night. Something happened that so upset him as to make him forget the meal altogether. It began to happen when he reached the modest home of P. Gafford, adjoining the Gafford stables, on Locust Street, and found sitting on the lowermost step of the porch a young man of untidy and unshaved aspect, who hailed him affectionately as Uncle Paul, and who showed deep annoyance and acute distress upon being rebuffed with chill words.

It is possible that the strain of serving a three-months sentence, on the technical charge of vagrancy, in a workhouse somewhere in Indiana had affected the young man's nerves. His ankle bones still ached where the ball and chain had been hitched; on his palms the blisters induced by the uncongenial use of a sledge-hammer on a rock pile had hardly as yet turned to calluses. So it is only fair to presume that his nervous system felt the stress of his recent confining experiences also.

Almost tearfully he pleaded with Peep O'Day to remember the ties of blood that bound them; repeatedly he pointed out that he was the only known kinsman of the other in all the world, and therefore had more reason than any other living being to expect kindness and generosity at his uncle's hands. He spoke socialistically of the advisability of an equal division; failing to make any impression here he mentioned the subject of a loan — at first hopefully, but finally despairingly.

When he was done Peep O'Day, in a perfectly colorless and unsympathetic voice, bade him good-bye — not good night but good-bye! And, going inside the house, he closed the door behind him, leaving his newly returned relative outside and quite alone.

At this the young man uttered violent language; but, since

there was nobody present to hear him, it is likely he found small satisfaction in his profanity, rich though it may have been in metaphor and variety. So presently he betook himself off, going straight to the office in Legal Row of H. B. Sublette, Attorney-at-Law.

From the circumstance that he found Mr. Sublette in, though it was long past that gentleman's office hours, and, moreover, found Mr. Sublette waiting in an expectant and attentive attitude, it might have been adduced by one skilled in the trick of putting two and two together that the pair of them had reached a prior understanding sometime during the day; and that the visit of the young man to the Gafford home and his speeches there had all been parts of a scheme planned out at a prior conference.

Be this as it may, so soon as Mr. Sublette had heard his caller's version of the meeting upon the porch he lost no time in taking certain legal steps. That very night, on behalf of his client, denominated in the documents as Percival Dwyer, Esquire, he prepared a petition addressed to the circuit judge of the district, setting forth that, inasmuch as Paul Felix O'Day had by divers acts shown himself to be of unsound mind, now, therefore, came his nephew and next of kin praying that a committee or curator be appointed to take over the estate of the said Paul Felix O'Day, and administer the same in accordance with the orders of the court until such time as the said Paul Felix O'Day should recover his reason, or should pass from this life, and so forth and so on; not to mention whereases in great number and aforesaids abounding throughout the text in the utmost profusion.

On the following morning the papers were filed with Circuit Clerk Milam. That vigilant barrister, Mr. Sublette, brought them in person to the courthouse before nine o'clock, he having the interests of his client at heart and perhaps also visions of a large contingent fee in his mind. No retainer had been paid. The state of Mr. Dwyer's finances — or, rather, the absence of any finances — had precluded the performance of that customary detail; but to Mr. Sublette's experienced mind the prospects of future increment seemed large.

Accordingly he was all for prompt action. Formally he said he wished to go on record as demanding for his principal a speedy hearing of the issue, with a view to preventing the defendant named in the pleadings from dissipating any more of the estate lately bequeathed to him and now fully in his possession — or words to that effect.

Mr. Milam felt justified in getting into communication with Judge Priest over the long-distance phone; and the Judge, cutting short his vacation and leaving uncaught vast numbers of bass and perch in Reelfoot Lake, came home, arriving late that night.

Next morning, having issued divers orders in connection with the impending litigation, he sent a messenger to find Peep O'Day and to direct O'Day to come to the courthouse for a personal interview.

Shortly thereafter a scene that had occurred some two months earlier, with His Honor's private chamber for a setting, was substantially duplicated: there was the same cast of two, the same stage properties, the same atmosphere of untidy tidiness. And, as before, the dialogue was in Judge Priest's hands. He led and his fellow character followed his leads.

'Peep,' he was saying, 'you understand, don't you, that this-here fragrant nephew of yours that's turned up from nowheres in particular is fixin' to git ready to try to prove that you are feeble-minded? And, on top of that, that he's goin' to ask that a committee be app'inted fur you — in other words, that somebody or other shall be named by the court, meanin' me, to take charge of your property and control the spendin' of it frum now on?'

'Yes, suh,' stated O'Day. 'Pete Gafford he set down with me

and made hit all clear to me, yestiddy evenin', after they'd done served the papers on me.'

'All right, then. Now I'm goin' to fix the hearin' fur tomorrow mornin' at ten. The other side is askin' fur a quick decision; and I rather figger they're entitled to it. Is that agreeable to you?'

'Whutever you say, Judge.'

'Well, have you retained a lawyer to represent your interests in court? That's the main question that I sent fur you to ast you.'

'Do I need a lawyer, Judge?'

'Well, there have been times when I regarded lawyers ez bein' superfluous,' stated Judge Priest dryly. 'Still, in most cases litigants do have 'em round when the case is bein' heard.'

'I don't know ez I need any lawyer to he'p me say whut I've got to say,' said O'Day. 'Judge, you ain't never ast me no questions about the way I've been carryin' on sence I come into this-here money; but I reckin mebbe this is ez good a time ez any to tell you jest why I've been actin' the way I've done. You see, suh ——'

'Hold on!' broke in Judge Priest. 'Up to now, ez my friend, it would 'a' been perfectly proper fur you to give me your confidences ef you were minded so to do; but now I reckin you'd better not. You see, I'm the judge that's got to decide whether you are a responsible person — whether you're mentally capable of handlin' your own financial affairs, or whether you ain't. So you'd better wait and make your statement in your own behalf to me whilst I'm settin' on the bench. I'll see that you git an opportunity to do so and I'll listen to it; and I'll give it all the consideration it's deservin' of.

'And, on second thought, p'raps it would only be a waste of time and money fur you to go hirin' a lawyer specially to represent you. Under the law it's my duty, in sech a case ez this here one is, to app'int a member of the bar to serve durin' the proceedin's ez your guardian ad litem.

'You don't need to be startled,' he added, as O'Day flinched at the sound in his ears of these strange and fearsome words. 'A guardian ad litem is simply a lawyer that tends to your affairs till the case is settled one way or the other. Ef you had a dozen lawyers I'd have to app'int him jest the same. So you don't need to worry about that part of it.

'That's all. You kin go now ef you want to. Only, ef I was you, I wouldn't draw out any more money frum the bank 'twixt now and the time when I make my decision.'

All things considered, it was an unusual assemblage that Judge Priest regarded over the top rims of his glasses as he sat facing it in his broad armchair, with the flat top of the bench intervening between him and the gathering. Not often, even in the case of exciting murder trials, had the old courtroom held a larger crowd; certainly never had it held so many boys. Boys, and boys exclusively, filled the back rows of benches downstairs. More boys packed the narrow, shelf-like balcony that spanned the chamber across its far end — mainly small boys, barefooted, sunburned, freckle-faced, shock-headed boys. And, for boys, they were strangely silent and strangely attentive.

The petitioner sat with his counsel, Mr. Sublette. The petitioner had been newly shaved, and from some mysterious source had been equipped with a neat wardrobe. Plainly he was endeavoring to wear a look of virtue, which was a difficult undertaking, as you would understand had you known the petitioner.

The defending party to the action was seated across the room, touching elbows with old Colonel Farrell, dean of the local bar and its most florid orator.

'The court will designate Colonel Horatio Farrell as guardian ad litem for the defendant during these proceedings,' Judge Priest had stated a few minutes earlier, using the formal and grammatical language he reserved exclusively for his courtroom.

At once old Colonel Farrell had hitched his chair up alongside O'Day; had asked him several questions in a tone inaudible to those about them, had listened to the whispered answers of O'Day, and then had nodded his huge, curly white dome of a head, as though amply satisfied with the responses.

Let us skip the preliminaries. True, they seemed to interest the audience; here, though, they would be tedious reading. Likewise, in touching upon the opening and outlining address of Attorney-at-Law Sublette let us, for the sake of time and space, be very much briefer than Mr. Sublette was. For our present purposes, I deem it sufficient to say that in all his professional career Mr. Sublette was never more eloquent, never more forceful, never more vehement in his allegations, and never more convinced — as he himself stated, not once but repeatedly — of his ability to prove the facts he alleged by competent and unbiased testimony. These facts, he pointed out, were common knowledge to the community, nevertheless, he stood prepared to buttress them with the evidence of reputable witnesses, given under oath.

Mr. Sublette, having unwound at length, now wound up. He sat down, perspiring freely and through the perspiration radiating confidence in his contentions, confidence in the result, and, most of all, unbounded confidence in Mr. Sublette.

Now Colonel Farrell was standing up to address the court. Under the cloak of a theatrical presence and a large, orotund manner, and behind a Ciceronian command of sonorous language, the Colonel carried concealed a shrewd old brain. It was as though a skilled marksman lurked in ambush amid a tangle of luxuriant foliage. In this particular instance, moreover, it is barely possible that the Colonel was acting on a cue, privily conveyed to him before the court opened.

'May it please Your Honor,' he began, 'I have just conferred with the defendant here; and, acting in the capacity of his guardian ad litem, I have advised him to waive an opening address by counsel. Indeed, the defendant has no counsel. Furthermore, the defendant, also acting upon my advice, will present no witnesses in his own behalf. But, with Your Honor's permission, the defendant will now make a personal statement; and thereafter he will rest content, leaving the final arbitrament of the issue to Your Honor's discretion.'

'I object!' exclaimed Mr. Sublette briskly.

'On what ground does the learned counsel object?' inquired Judge Priest.

'On the grounds that, since the mental competence of this man is concerned — since it is our contention that he is patently and plainly a victim of senility, an individual prematurely in his dotage — any utterances by him will be of no value whatsoever in aiding the conscience and intelligence of the court to arrive at a fair and just conclusion regarding the defendant's mental condition.'

Mr. Sublette excelled in the use of big words; there was no doubt about that.

'The objection is overruled,' said Judge Priest. He nodded in the direction of O'Day and Colonel Farrell. 'The court will hear the defendant. He is not to be interrupted while making his statement. The defendant may proceed.'

Without further urging, O'Day stood up, a tall, slabsided rack of a man, with his long arms dangling at his sides, half facing Judge Priest and half facing his nephew and his nephew's lawyer. Without hesitation he began to speak. And this was what he said:

'There's mebbe some here ez knows about how I was raised and fetched up. My paw and my maw died when I was jest only a baby; so I was brung up out here at the old county porehouse ez a pauper. I can't remember the time when I didn't have to work my board and keep, and work hard. While other boys was goin' to school and playin' hooky, and goin' in washin' in the

creek, and playin' games, and all sech ez that, I had to work.
I never done no playin' round in my whole life — not till here jest
recently, anyway.

'But I always craved to play round some. I didn't never say
nothin' about it to nobody after I growed up, 'cause I figgered it
out they wouldn't understand and mebbe'd laugh at me; but all
these years, ever sence I left that-there porehouse, I've had a
hankerin' here inside of me' — he lifted one hand and touched
his breast — 'I've had a hankerin' to be a boy and to do all the
things a boy does; to do the things I was chiseled out of doin'
whilst I was of a suitable age to be doin' 'em. I call to mind that
I uster dream in my sleep about doin' 'em; but the dream never
come true — not till jest here lately. It didn't have no chancet to
come true — not till then.

'So, when this money come to me so sudden and unbeknownst-
like I said to myself that I was goin' to make that-there dream
come true; and I started out fur to do it. And I done it! And
I reckin that's the cause of my bein' here today, accused of bein'
feeble-minded. But, even so, I don't regret it none. Ef it was all
to do over ag'in, I'd do it jest the very same way.

'Why, I never knowed whut it was, till here two months or so
ago, to have my fill of bananas and candy and gingersnaps, and
all sech knickknacks ez them. All my life I've been cravin'
secretly to own a pair of red-topped boots with brass toes on 'em,
like I used to see other boys wearin' in the wintertime when I was
out younder at that porehouse wearin' an old pair of somebody
else's cast-off shoes — mebbe a man's shoes, with rags wropped
round my feet to keep the snow frum comin' through the cracks
in 'em, and to keep 'em from slippin' right spang off my feet.
I got three toes frostbit oncet durin' a cold spell, wearin' them
kind of shoes. But here the other week I found myself able to
buy me some red-top boots with brass toes on 'em. So I had 'em
made to order and I'm wearin' 'em now. I wear 'em reg'lar even

ef it is summertime. I take a heap of pleasure out of 'em. And
also, all my life long I've been wantin' to go to a circus. But not
till three days ago I didn't never git no chancet to go to one.

'That gentleman yonder — Mister Sublette — he 'lowed jest
now that I was leadin' a lot of little boys in this-here town into bad
habits. He said that I was learnin' 'em nobody knowed whut
devilment. And he spoke of my havin' egged 'em on to steal
watermelons frum Mister Bell's watermelon patch out here three
miles frum town, on the Marshallville gravel road. You-all
heared whut he jest now said about that.

'I don't mean no offense and I beg his pardon fur contradictin'
him right out before everybody here in the big courthouse; but,
mister, you're wrong. I don't lead these-here boys astray that
I've been runnin' round with. They're mighty nice clean boys,
all of 'em. Some of 'em are mighty near ez pore ez whut I uster be;
but there ain't no real harm in any of 'em. We git along together
fine — me and them. And, without no preachin', nor nothin' like
that, I've done my best these weeks we've been frolickin' and
projectin' round together to keep 'em frum growin' up to do mean
things. I use chawin' tobacco myself; but I've told 'em, I don't
know how many times, that ef they chaw it'll stunt 'em in their
growth. And I've got several of 'em that was smokin' cigarettes
on the sly to promise me they'd quit. So I don't figger ez I've
done them boys any real harm by goin' round with 'em. And I
believe ef you was to ast 'em they'd all tell you the same, suh.

'Now about them watermelons: Sence this gentleman has brung
them watermelons up, I'm goin' to tell you-all the truth about
that too.'

He cast a quick, furtive look, almost a guilty look, over his
shoulder toward the rear of the courtroom before he went on:

'Them watermelons wasn't really stole at all. I seen Mister
Dick Bell beforehand and arranged with him to pay him in full fur
whutever damage mout be done. But, you see, I knowed water-

melons tasted sweeter to a boy ef he thought he'd hooked 'em out
of a patch; so I never let on to my little pardners yonder that
I'd the same ez paid Mister Bell in advance fur the melons we
snuck out of his patch and et in the woods. They've all been
thinkin' up till now that we really hooked them watermelons.
But ef that was wrong I'm sorry fur it.

'Mister Sublette, you jest now said that I was fritterin' away
my property on vain foolishment. Them was the words you used
— "fritterin'" and "vain foolishment." Mebbe you're right, suh,
about the fritterin' part; but ef spendin' money in a certain way
gives a man ez much pleasure ez it's give me these last two
months, and ef the money is his'n by rights, I figger it can't be so
very foolish; though it may 'pear so to some.

'Excusin' these-here clothes I've got on and these-here boots,
which ain't paid fur yet, but is charged up to me on Felsburg
Brothers' books and Mister M. Biederman's books, I didn't spend
only a dollar a day, or mebbe two dollars, and once three dollars
in a single day out of whut was comin' to me. The Judge here, he
let me have that out of his own pocket; and I paid him back.
And that was all I did spend till here three days ago when that-
there circus come to town. I reckin I did spend a right smart then.

'My money had come frum the old country only the day before; so I went to the bank and they writ out one of them pieces of
paper which is called a check, and I signed it — with my mark;
and they give me the money I wanted — an even two hundred
dollars. And part of that-there money I used to pay fur circus
tickets fur all the little boys and little girls I could find in this
town that couldn't 'a' got to the circus no other way. Some of 'em
are settin' back there behind you-all now — some of the boys,
I mean; I don't see none of the little girls.

'There was several of 'em told me at the time they hadn't never
seen a circus — not in their whole lives. Fur that matter, I
hadn't, neither; but I didn't want no pore child in this town to

grow up to be ez old ez I am without havin' been to at least one
circus. So I taken 'em all in and paid all the bills; and when night
come there wasn't but 'bout nine dollars left out of the whole two
hundred that I'd started out with in the mornin'. But I don't
begredge spendin' it. It looked to me like it was money well
invested. They all seemed to enjoy it; and I know I done so.

'There may be bigger circuses'n whut that one was; but I don't
see how a circus could 'a' been any better than this-here one I'm
tellin' about, ef it was ten times ez big. I don't regret the investment and I don't aim to lie about it now. Mister Sublette, I'd do
the same thing over ag'in ef the chance should come, lawsuit or no
lawsuit. Ef you should win this-here case mebbe I wouldn't have
no second chance.

'Ef some gentleman is app'inted ez a commitee to handle my
money it's likely he wouldn't look at the thing the same way I do;
and it's likely he wouldn't let me have so much money all in one
lump to spend takin' a passel of little shavers that ain't no kin to
me to the circus and to the side show, besides lettin' 'em stay fur
the grand concert or after show, and all. But I done it once; and
I've got it to remember and think about in my own mind ez long
ez I live.

'I'm 'bout finished now. There's jest one thing more I'd like to
say, and that is this: Mister Sublette he said a minute ago that
I was in my second childhood. Meanin' no offense, suh, but you
was wrong there too. The way I look at it, a man can't be in his
second childhood without he's had his first childhood; and I was
cheated plum' out of mine. I'm more'n sixty years old, ez near
ez I kin figger; but I'm tryin' to be a boy before it's too late.'

He paused a moment and looked round him.

'The way I look at it, Judge Priest, suh, and you-all, every man
that grows up, no matter how old he may git to be, is entitled to
'a' been a boy oncet in his lifetime. I — I reckin that's all.'

He sat down and dropped his eyes upon the floor, as though

ashamed that his temerity should have carried him so far. There was a strange little hush filling the courtroom. It was Judge Priest who broke it.

'The court,' he said, 'has by the words just spoken by this man been sufficiently advised as to the sanity of the man himself. The court cares to hear nothing more from either side on this subject. The petition is dismissed.'

Very probably these last words may have been as so much Greek to the juvenile members of the audience; possibly, though, they were made aware of the meaning of them by the look upon the face of Nephew Percival Dwyer and the look upon the face of Nephew Percival Dwyer's attorney. At any rate, His Honor hardly had uttered the last syllable of his decision before, from the rear of the courtroom and from the gallery above, there arose a shrill, vehement, sincere sound of yelling — exultant, triumphant, and deafening. It continued for upward of a minute before the small disturbers remembered where they were and reduced themselves to a state of comparative quiet.

For reasons best known to himself, Judge Priest, who ordinarily stickled for order and decorum in his courtroom, made no effort to quell the outburst or to have it quelled — not even when a considerable number of the adults present joined in it, having first cleared their throats of a slight huskiness that had come upon them, severally and generally.

Presently the Judge rapped for quiet — and got it. It was apparent that he had more to say; and all there hearkened to hear what it might be.

'I have just this to add,' quoth His Honor. 'It is the official judgment of this court that the late defendant, being entirely sane, is competent to manage his own affairs after his preferences.

'And it is the private opinion of this court that not only is the late defendant sane but that he is the sanest man in this entire jurisdiction. Mister Clerk, this court stands adjourned.'

Coming down the three short steps from the raised platform of the bench, Judge Priest beckoned to Sheriff Giles Birdsong, who, at the tail of the departing crowd, was shepherding its last exuberant members through the doorway.

'Giles,' said Judge Priest in an undertone, when the worthy sheriff had drawn near, 'the circuit clerk tells me there's an indictment for malicious mischief ag'in this-here Perce Dwyer knockin' round amongst the records somewheres — an indictment the grand jury returned several sessions back, but which was never pressed, owin' to the sudden departure frum our midst of the person in question.

'I wonder if it would be too much trouble fur you to sort of drap a hint in the ear of the young man or his lawyer that the said indictment is apt to be revived, and that the said Dwyer is liable to be tuck into custody by you and lodged in the county jail sometime during the ensuin' forty-eight hours — without he should see his way clear durin' the meantime to get clean out of this city, county, and state! Would it?'

'Trouble? No, suh! It won't be no trouble to me,' said Mr. Birdsong promptly. 'Why, it'll be more of a pleasure, Judge.'

And so it was.

Except for one small added and purely incidental circumstance, our narrative is ended. That same afternoon Judge Priest sat on the front porch of his old white house out on Clay Street, waiting for Jeff Poindexter to summon him to supper. Peep O'Day opened the front gate and came up the graveled walk between the twin rows of silver-leaf poplars. The Judge, rising to greet his visitor, met him at the top step.

'Come in,' bade the Judge heartily, 'and set down a spell and rest your face and hands.'

'No, suh; much obliged, but I ain't got only a minute to stay,' said O'Day. 'I jest come out here, suh, to thank you fur whut you done today on my account in the big courthouse, and — and to make you a little kind of a present.'

'It's all right to thank me,' said Judge Priest, 'but I couldn't accept any reward fur renderin' a decision in accordance with the plain facts.'

''Tain't no gift of money, or nothin' like that,' O'Day hastened to explain. 'Really, suh, it don't amount to nothin' at all, scursely. But a little while ago I happened to be in Mr. B. Weil & Son's store, doin' a little tradin', and I run acrost a new kind of knickknack, which it seemed like to me it was about the best thing I ever tasted in my whole life. So, on the chancet, suh, that you might have a sweet tooth, too, I taken the liberty of bringin' you a sack of 'em and — and — and here they are, suh; three flavors — strawberry, lemon, and vanilly.'

Suddenly overcome with confusion, he dislodged a large-sized paper bag from his side coat pocket and thrust it into Judge Priest's hands; then, backing away, he turned and clumped down the graveled path in great and embarrassed haste.

Judge Priest opened the bag and peered down into it.

It contained a sticky, sugary dozen of flattened confections, each molded round a short length of wooden splinter. These sirupy articles, which have since come into quite general use, are known, I believe, as all-day suckers.

When Judge Priest looked up again, Peep O'Day was outside the gate, clumping down the uneven sidewalk of Clay Street with long strides of his booted legs. Half a dozen small boys, who, it was evident, had remained hidden during the ceremony of presentation, now mysteriously appeared and were accompanying the departing donor, half trotting to keep up with him.

THE MEEKER RITUAL[1]

JOSEPH HERGESHEIMER

I. THE ROCK OF AGES

THE entire pretension is so ridiculous that it is difficult to credit the extent of its acceptance. I don't mean McGeorge's story, but the whole sweep of spiritism. It ought to be unnecessary to point out the puerility of the evidence — the absurd babble advanced as the speech of wise men submerged in the silent consummation of death, the penny tricks with bells and banjos, the circus-like tables and anthropomorphic Edens. Yet, so far as the phrase goes, there is something in it; but whatever that is, lies in demonstrable science, the investigations of the subconscious by Freud and Jung.

McGeorge himself, a reporter with a sufficient education in the actual, tried to repeat impartially, with the vain illusion of an open mind, what he had been told; but it was clear that his power of reasoning had been disarranged. We were sitting in the Italian restaurant near his paper to which he had conducted me, and he was inordinately troubled by flies. A small, dark man, he was never without a cigarette; he had always been nervous, but I had no memory of such uneasiness as he now exhibited.

---

[1] From *The Century Magazine.* Copyright, 1919, by The Century Company. Copyright, 1920, by Joseph Hergesheimer.

'It's rather dreadful,' he said, gazing at me for an instant, and then shifting his glance about the white plaster walls and small flock of tables, deserted at that hour. 'I mean this thing of not really dying — hanging about in the wind, in space. I used to have a natural dread of death; but now I'm afraid of — of keeping on. When you think of it, a grave's quite a pleasant place. It's restful. This other ——' He broke off, but not to eat.

'My editor,' he began anew, apparently at a tangent, 'wouldn't consider it. I was glad. I'd like to forget it, go back. There might be a story for you.'

Whatever he had heard in connection with the Meeker circle, I assured him, would offer me nothing; I didn't write that sort of thing.

'You'd appreciate Lizzie Tuoey,' he asserted.

McGeorge had been sent to the Meeker house to unearth what he could about the death of Mrs. Kraemer. He described vividly the location, which provided the sole interest to an end admitted normal in its main features. It was, he said, one of those vitrified wildernesses of brick that have given the city the name of a place of homes; dreadful. Amazing in extent, it was without a single feature to vary the monotony of two-storied dwellings cut into exact parallelograms by paved streets; there was a perspective of continuous façades and unbroken tin roofs in every direction, with a grocery or drugstore and an occasional saloon at the corners, and beyond, the sullen red steeple of a church.

Dusk was gathering when McGeorge reached the Meekers'. It was August, and the sun had blazed throughout the day, with the parching heat; the smell of brick dust and scorched tin was hideous. His word. There was, too, a faint metallic clangor in the air. He knew that it came from the surface cars, yet he could not rid himself of the thought of iron furnace doors.

He had, of course, heard of the Meekers before. So had I, for that matter. A crack-brained professor had written a laborious, fantastic book about their mediumship and power of communication with the other world. They sat together as a family: the elder Meekers; the wife's sister; a boy, Albert, of fourteen; Ena, close to twenty; and Jannie, a girl seventeen years old and the medium proper. Jannie's familiar spirit was called Stepan. He had, it seemed, lived and died in the reign of Peter the Great; yet he was still actual, but unmaterialized, and extremely anxious to reassure everyone through Jannie of the supernal happiness of the beyond. What messages I read, glancing over hysterical pages, gave me singularly little comfort, with the possible exception of the statement that there were cigars; good cigars, Stepan, or Jannie, explained, such as on earth cost three for a quarter.

However, most of what McGeorge told me directly concerned Lizzie Tuoey. The Meekers he couldn't see at all. They remained in an undiscovered part of the house — there was a strong reek of frying onions from the kitchen — and delegated the servant as their link with the curious or respectful or impertinent world.

Lizzie admitted him to the parlor, where, she informed him, the sittings took place. There wasn't much furniture beyond a plain, heavy table, an array of stiff chairs thrust back against the walls, and on a mantel a highly painted miniature Rock of Ages, with a white-clad figure clinging to it, washed with a poisonous green wave, all inclosed in a glass bell. At the rear was a heavy curtain that, he found, covered the entrance to a smaller room.

Lizzie was a stout, cheerful person, with the ready sympathies and superstitions of the primitive mind of the south of Ireland. She was in a maze of excitement, and his difficulty was not to get her to talk, but to arrest her incoherent flood of invocations, saints' names, and credulity.

Her duties at the Meekers' had been various; one of them was the playing of mechanical music in the back room at certain opportune moments. She said that Stepan particularly requested it; the low strains made it easier for him to speak to the dear folks on this side. It couldn't compare, though, Stepan had added, with the music beyond; and why should it, Lizzie had commented, and all the blessed saints bursting their throats with tunes! She swore, however, that she had had no part in the ringing of the bells or the knocks and jumps the table took.

She had no explanation for the latter other than the conviction that the dear God had little, if any, part in it. Rather her choice of an agent inclined to the devil. Things happened, she affirmed, that tightened her head like a kettle. The cries and groaning from the parlor during a sitting would blast the soul of you. It was nothing at all for a stranger to faint away cold. The light would then be turned up, and water dashed on the unconscious face.

She insisted, McGeorge particularized, that the Meekers took no money for their sittings. At times some grateful person would press a sum on them; a woman had given two hundred and seventy dollars after a conversation with her nephew, dead, as the world called it, twelve years. All the Meekers worked but Jannie; she was spared every annoyance possible, and lay in bed till noon. At the suggestion of Stepan, she made the most un-expected demands. Stepan liked pink silk stockings. He begged her to eat a candy called Turkish paste. He recommended a 'teeny' glass of Bénédictine, a bottle of which was kept ready. He told her to pinch her flesh black to show — Lizzie Tuoey forgot what.

Jannie was always dragged out with a face the color of wet laundry soap. She had crying fits; at times her voice would change, and she'd speak a gibberish that Mr. Meeker declared was Russian; and after a trance she would eat for six. There was nothing about the senior Meeker Lizzie could describe, but she disliked Mrs. Meeker intensely. She made the preposterous state-ment that the woman could see through the blank walls of the house. Ena was pale, but pretty, despite dark smudges under her eyes; she sat up very late with boys or else sulked by herself.

Albert had a big grinning head on him, and ate flies. Lizzie had often seen him at it. He spent hours against the panes of glass and outside the kitchen door.

It wasn't what you could name gay at the Meekers, and, indeed, it hadn't been necessary for the priest to insist on the girl finding another place; she had decided that independently after she had been there less than a month. Then Mrs. Kraemer had died during a sitting. She would be off, she told McGeorge, the first of the week.

The latter, whose interest at the beginning had been commendably penetrating, asked about Mrs. Meeker's sister; but he discovered nothing more than that — Lizzie Tuoey allowed for a heretic — she was religious. They were all serious about the spiritism, and believed absolutely in Jannie and Stepan, in the messages, the voices and shades that they evoked.

However, questioned directly about Mrs. Kraemer's presence at a sitting, the servant's ready flow of comment and explanation abruptly dwindled to the meager invocation of holy names. It was evidently a business with which she wanted little dealing, even with Mrs. Kraemer safely absent, and with no suspicion of criminal irregularity.

The reporting of that occurrence gave a sufficiently clear impression of the dead woman. She was the relict of August, a naturalized American citizen born in Salzburg, and whose estate, a comfortable aggregate of more than two millions, came partly from hop-fields in his native locality. There was one child, a son past twenty, not the usual inept offspring of late-acquired wealth, but a vigorously administrative youth who spent half the year in charge of the family investment in Germany. At the beginning of the Great War the inevitable overtook the Salzburg industry; its financial resources were acquired by the Imperial Government, and young Kraemer, then abroad, was urged into the German Army.

McGeorge, with a great deal of trouble, extracted some additional angles of insight on Mrs. Kraemer from the reluctant Lizzie.

She was an impressive figure of a lady in fine lavender muslin ruffles, a small hat, blazing diamonds, and a hook in her nose, but Roman and not Jew. A bullying voice and a respectful chauffeur in a glittering car completed the picture. She had nothing favorable to say for the location of the Meeker house; indeed, she complained pretty generally, in her loud, assertive tones, about the inefficiency of city administration in America, but she held out hopes of improvement in the near future. She grew impatiently mysterious — hints were not her habit — in regard to the good shortly to enfold the entire earth. Lizzie gathered somehow that this was bound up with her son, now an officer in a smart Uhlan regiment.

A man of Mrs. Kraemer's type, and the analogy is far closer than common, would never have come to the Meekers' for a message from a son warring in the north of France. It is by such lapses that women with the greatest show of logic prove the persistent domination of the earliest emotional instincts. After all, Lizzie Tuoey and Mrs. Kraemer were far more alike than any two such apparently dissimilar men.

At this point McGeorge was lost in the irrelevancy of Lizzie's mind. She made a random statement about Mrs. Meeker's sister and a neighbor, and returned to the uncertain quality of Jannie's temper and the limitations of a medium. It seemed that Jannie was unable to direct successful sittings without a day between for the recuperation of her power. It used her up something fierce. Stepan as well, too often recalled from the joys of the beyond, the cigars of the aroma of three for a quarter, grew fretful; either he refused to answer or played tricks, such as an unexpected sharp thrust in Albert's ribs, or a knocked message of satirical import, 'My! Wouldn't you just like to know!'

McGeorge had given up the effort to direct the conversation; rather than go away with virtually nothing gained, he decided to let the remarks take what way they would. In this he was wise, for the girl's sense of importance, her normal pressing necessity for speech, gradually submerged her fearful determination to avoid any contact with an affair so plainly smelling of brimstone. She returned to Miss Brasher, the sister, and her neighbor.

The latter was Mrs. Doothnack, and, like Mrs. Kraemer, she had a son fighting in the north of France. There, however, the obvious similitude ended; Edwin Doothnack served a machine-gun of the American Expeditionary Forces, while his mother was as poor and retiring as the other woman was dogmatic and rich. Miss Brasher brought her early in the evening to the Meekers', a little person with the blurred eyes of recent heavy crying, excessively polite to Lizzie Tuoey. Naturally, this did nothing to increase the servant's good opinion of her.

The sister soon explained the purpose of their visit: Edwin, whose regiment had occupied a sacrifice position, was missing. There his mother timidly took up the recital. The Meekers were at supper, and Lizzie, in and out of the kitchen, heard most of the developments. When the report about Edwin had arrived, Mrs. Doothnack's friends were reassuring; he would turn up again at his regiment, or else he had been taken prisoner; in which case German camps, although admittedly bad, were as safe as the trenches. She had been intensely grateful for their good will, and obediently set herself to the acceptance of their optimism, when — it was eleven nights now to the day — she had been suddenly wakened by Edwin's voice.

'O God!' Edwin had cried, thin, but distinct, in a tone of exhausted suffering — 'O God!' and 'Mummer!' his special term for Mrs. Doothnack. At that, she declared, with straining hands, she knew that Edwin was dead.

Miss Brasher then begged darling Jannie to summon Stepan

and discover the truth at the back of Mrs. Doothnack's 'message'
and conviction. If, indeed, Edwin had passed over, it was their
Christian duty to reassure his mother about his present happiness,
and the endless future together that awaited all loved and loving
ones. Jannie said positively that she wouldn't consider it. A
sitting had been arranged for Mrs. Kraemer tomorrow, so that
she, without other means, might get some tidings of the younger
August.

Mrs. Doothnack rose at once with a murmured apology for disturbing them, but Miss Brasher was more persistent. She had
the determination of her virginal fanaticism, and of course she
was better acquainted with Jannie. Lizzie wasn't certain, but
she thought that Miss Brasher had money, though nothing
approaching Mrs. Kraemer; probably a small, safe income.

Anyhow, Jannie got into a temper, and said that they all had
no love for her, nobody cared what happened so long as they had
their precious messages. Stepan would be cross, too. At this
Albert hastily declared that he would be out that evening; he had
been promised moving pictures. That old Stepan would be sure
to bust his bones in. Jannie then dissolved into tears, and cried
that they were insulting her dear Stepan, who lived in heaven.
Albert added his wails to the commotion, Mrs. Doothnack sobbed
from pure nervousness and embarrassment, and only Miss
Brasher remained unmoved and insistent.

The result of this disturbance was that they agreed to try a
tentative sitting. Stepping out into the kitchen, Mrs. Meeker
told Lizzie that she needn't bother to play the music that evening.

Here the latter, with a sudden confidence in McGeorge's
charitable knowledge of life, admitted that Jannie's bottle of
Bénédictine was kept in a closet in the room behind the one
where the sittings were held. The Meekers had disposed themselves about the table, the circle locked by their hands placed on
adjoining knees, with Jannie at the head and Mrs. Doothnack

beyond. The servant, in the inner room for a purpose which she had made crystal-clear, could just distinguish them in a dim, red-shaded light through the opening of the curtain.

By this time familiarity with the proceeding had bred its indifference, and Lizzie lingered at the closet. The knocks that announced Stepan's presence were a long time in coming; then there came an angry banging and a choked cry from Albert. The table plainly rocked and rose from the floor, and Jannie asked in the flat voice of the tranced:

'Is Edwin there? Here's his mother wanting to speak to him.'

The reply, knocked out apparently on the wood mantel, and repeated for the benefit of the visitor, said that those who had won to the higher life couldn't be treated as a mere telephone exchange. Besides which, a party was then in progress, and Stepan was keeping waiting Isabella, consort of King Ferdinand, a lady who would not be put off. This business about Edwin must keep. Miss Brasher said in a firm voice:

'His mother is much distressed and prays for him to speak.'

The answer rattled off was not interpreted, but Lizzie gathered that it was extremely personal and addressed to Miss Brasher. There was a silence after that, and then the table rose to a perceptible height and crashed back to the floor. In the startling pause which followed a voice, entirely different from any that had spoken, cried clear and low:

'O God!'

This frightened Lizzie to such an extent that she fled to the familiar propriety of the kitchen; but before she was out of hearing, Mrs. Doothnack screamed, 'Edwin!'

Nothing else happened. The firm Miss Brasher and her neighbor departed immediately. Jannie, however, looked a wreck, and cold towels and Bénédictine were liberally applied. She sobbed hysterically, and wished that she were just a plain girl without a call. Further, she declared that nothing could in-

duce her to proceed with the sitting for Mrs. Kraemer tomorrow.
Stepan, before returning to Isabella of Castile, had advised her
against it. With such droves of soldiers coming over, it was more
and more difficult to control individual spirits. Things in the
beyond were in a frightful mess. They might see something that
would scare them out of their wits.

Mrs. Meeker, with a share of her sister's aplomb, said that
she guessed they could put up with a little scaring in the interest
of Mrs. August Kraemer. She was sick of doing favors for people
like Agnes's friend, and made it clear that she desired genteel
associates both in the here and the hereafter. Jannie's face began
to twitch in a manner common to it, and her eyes grew glassy.
At times, Lizzie explained, she would fall right down as stiff as a
board, and they would have to put her on the lounge till she
recovered. Her sentimental reading of Jannie's present seizure
was that she was jealous of Ferdinand's wife.

Not yet, even, McGeorge confessed, did he see any connection
between the humble little Mrs. Doothnack and Mrs. Kraemer,
in her fine lavender and diamonds. He continued putting the
queries almost at random to Lizzie Tuoey, noting carelessly, as if
they held nothing of the body of his business, her replies. While
the amazing fact was that, quite aside from his subsequent
credulity or any reasonable skepticism, the two presented the
most complete possible unity of causation and climax. As a
story, beyond which I have no interest, together they are ad-
mirable. They were enveloped, too, in the consistency of mood
loosely called atmosphere; that is, all the details of their surrounding combined to color the attentive mind with morbid
shadows.

It was purely on Lizzie Tuoey's evidence that McGeorge's
conversion to such ridiculous claims rested. She was not capable
of invention, he pointed out, and continued that no one could
make up details such as that, finally, of the Rock of Ages. The

irony was too biting and inevitable. Her manner alone put what she related beyond dispute.

On the contrary, I insisted, it was just such minds as Lizzie's that could credit in a flash of light — probably a calcium flare — unnatural soldiers, spooks of any kind. Here simple pictorial belief readily accepted the entire possibility of visions and wonders.

I could agree or not, he proceeded wearily; it was of small moment. The fate waited for all men. 'The fate of living,' he declared, 'the curse of eternity. You can't stop. Eternity,' he repeated, with an uncontrollable shiver.

'Stepan seemed to find compensations,' I reminded him.

'If you are so damned certain about the Tuoey woman,' he cried, 'what have you got to say about Mrs. Kraemer's death? You can't dismiss her as a hysterical idiot. People like her don't just die.'

'A blood clot.' His febrile excitement had grown into anger, and I suppressed further doubts.

He lighted a cigarette. The preparations for Mrs. Kraemer's reception and the sitting, he resumed, were elaborate. Mr. Meeker lubricated the talking-machine till its disk turned without a trace of the mechanism. A new record — it had cost a dollar and a half and was by a celebrated violinist — was fixed, and a halftone semi-permanent needle selected. Lizzie was to start this after the first storm of knocking, or any preliminary jocularity of Stepan's, had subsided.

Jannie had on new pink silk stockings and white kid slippers. Her head had been marcelled special, and she was so nervous that she tore three hair-nets. At this she wept, and stamped her foot, breaking a bottle of expensive scent.

When Mrs. Kraemer's motor stopped at the door, Lizzie went forward, and Mrs. Meeker floated down the stairs.

Stopping him sharply, I demanded a repetition of the latter

phrase. It was Lizzie's. McGeorge, too, had expressed surprise, and the girl repeated it. Mrs. Meeker, she declared, often 'floated.' One evening she had seen Mrs. Meeker leave the top story by a window and stay suspended over the bricks twenty feet below.

Mrs. Kraemer entered the small hall like a keen rush of wind; her manner was determined, an impatience half checked by interest in what might follow. She listened with a short nod to Mr. Meeker's dissertation on the necessity of concord in all the assembled wills. The spirit world must be approached reverently, with trust and thankfulness for whatever might be vouchsafed.

The light in the front room, a single gas-burner, was lowered, and covered by the inevitable red-paper hood, and the circle formed. Lizzie was washing dishes, but the kitchen door was open, so that she could hear the knocks that were the signal for the music. They were even longer coming than on the night before, and she made up her mind that Stepan had declared a holiday from the responsibilities of a control. At last there was a faint vibration, and she went cautiously into the dark space behind the circle. The curtains had always hung improperly, and she could see a dim red streak of light.

The knocks at best were not loud; several times when she was about to start the record they began again inconclusively. Stepan finally communicated that he was exhausted. Someone was being cruel to him. Could it be Jannie? There was a sobbing gasp from the latter. Mrs. Kraemer's voice was like ice-water; she wanted some word from August, her son. She followed the name with the designation of his rank and regiment. And proud of it, too, Lizzie added; you might have taken from her manner that she was one of us. Her version of Mrs. Kraemer's description sounded as though August were a ewe-lamb. McGeorge, besotted in superstition, missed this.

Independently determining that the moment for music had

come, Lizzie pressed forward the lever and carefully lowered the
lid. The soft strains of the violin, heard through the drawn curtains, must have sounded illusively soothing and impressive.

'Stepan,' Jannie implored, 'tell August's mamma about him,
so far away amid shot and shell.'

'Who is my mother?' Stepan replied, with a mystical and
borrowed magnificence.

'August, are you there?' Mrs. Kraemer demanded. 'Can you
hear me? Are you well?'

'I'm deaf from the uproar,' Stepan said faintly. 'Men in a
green gas. He is trying to reach me; something is keeping him
back.'

'August's alive!' Mrs. Kraemer's exclamation was in German,
but Lizzie understood that she was thanking God.

'Hundreds are passing over,' Stepan continued. 'I can't hear
this voice, but there are medals. He's gone again in smoke. The
other ——' The communication halted abruptly, and in the
silence which followed Lizzie stopped the talking-machine, the
record at an end.

It was then that the blaze of light occurred which made her
think the paper shade had caught fire and that the house would
burn down. She dragged back the curtain.

McGeorge refused to meet my interrogation, but sat with his
gaze fastened on his plate of unconsumed gray macaroni. After
a little I asked impatiently what the girl thought she had seen.

After an inattentive silence McGeorge asked me, idiotically I
thought, if I had ever noticed the game, the hares and drawn
fish, sometimes frozen into a clear block of ice and used as an
attraction by provision stores. I had, I admitted, although I
could see no connection between that and the present inquiry.

It was, however, his description of the column of light Lizzie
Tuoey saw over against the mantel, a shining white shroud
through which the crudely painted Rock of Ages was visible,

insulated in the glass bell. Oh, yes, there was a soldier, but in the uniform that might be seen passing the Meekers' any hour of the day, and unnaturally hanging in a traditional and very highly sanctified manner. The room was filled with a coldness that made Lizzie's flesh crawl. It was as bright as noon; the circle about the table was rigid, as if it had been frozen into immobility, while Jannie's breathing was audible and hoarse.

Mrs. Kraemer stood wrung with horror, a shaking hand sparkling with diamonds raised to her face. It was a lie, she cried in shrill, penetrating tones. August couldn't do such a thing. Kill him quickly!

The other voice was faint, McGeorge said, hardly more than a sigh; but Lizzie Tuoey had heard it before. She asserted that there was no chance for a mistake.

'O God!' it breathed. 'Mummer!'

This much is indisputable, that Mrs. Kraemer died convulsively in the Meeker hall. Beyond that I am congenitally incapable of belief. I asked McGeorge directly if it was his contention that, through Stepan's blunder, the unfortunate imperialistic lady, favored with a vignette of modern organized barbarity, had seen Mrs. Doothnack's son in place of her own.

He didn't, evidently, think this worth a reply. McGeorge was again lost in his consuming dread of perpetual being.

II. THE GREEN EMOTION

Virtually buried in a raft of ethical tracts of the Middle Kingdom, all more or less repetitions of Lao-tsze's insistence on Heaven's quiet way, I ignored the sounding of the telephone; but its continuous burr — I had had the bell removed — triumphed over my absorption, and I had answered curtly. It was McGeorge. His name, in addition to the fact that it constituted an annoying interruption, recalled principally that, caught in the stagnant marsh of spiritism, he had related an absurd fabrication in connection with the Meeker circle and the death of Mrs. August Kraemer.

Our acquaintance had been long, but slight. He had never attempted to see me at my rooms, and for this reason only — that his unusual visit might have a corresponding pressing cause — I directed Miss Maynall, at the telephone exchange, to send him up. Five minutes later, however, I regretted that I had not instinctively refused to see him. It was then evident that there was no special reason for his call. It was inconceivable that anyone with the least knowledge of my prejudices and opinions would attempt to be merely social, and McGeorge was not without both the rudiments of breeding and good sense.

At least such had been my impression of him in the past, before he had come in contact with the Meekers. Gazing at him, I saw that a different McGeorge was evident, different even from when I had seen him at the Italian restaurant where he had been so oppressed by the fear not of death, but of life. In the first place, he was fatter and less nervous, he was wearing one of those unforgivable soft black ties with flowing ends, and he had changed from Virginia cigarettes to Turkish.

A silence had lengthened into embarrassment, in which I was combating a native irritability with the placid philosophical acceptance of the unstirred Tao, when he asked suddenly:

'Did you know I was married?' I admitted that this information had eluded me, when he added in the fatuous manner of such victims of a purely automatic process, 'To Miss Ena Meeker that was.'

I asked if he had joined the family circle in the special sense, but he said not yet; he wasn't worthy. Then I realized that there was a valid reason for his presence, but, unfortunately, it operated slowly with him; he had to have a satisfactory audience for the astounding good fortune he had managed. He wanted to talk, and McGeorge, I recalled, had been a man without intimates or family in the city. Almost uncannily, as if in answer to my thought, he proceeded:

'I'm here because you have a considerable brain and, to a certain extent, a courageous attitude. You are all that and yet you won't recognize the truth about the beyond, the precious world of spirits.'

'Material.'

However, I indicated in another sense that I wasn't material for any propaganda of hysterical and subnormal séances. His being grew inflated with the condescending pity of dogmatic superstition for logic.

'Many professors and men of science are with us, and I am anxious, in your own interest, for you to see the light. I've already admitted that you would be valuable. You can't accuse me of being mercenary. I couldn't. I must tell you!' he actually cried out, in sudden surrender to the tyrannical necessity of self-revelation. 'My marriage to Ena was marvelous, marvelous, a true wedding of souls. Mr. Meeker,' he added in a different, explanatory manner, 'like all careful fathers, is not unconscious of the need, here on earth, of a portion of worldly goods. For a while, and quite naturally, he was opposed to our union.

'There was a Wallace Esselmann.' A perceptible caution overtook him, but which, with a gesture, he evidently discarded. 'But I ought to explain how I met the Meekers. I called.' I expressed a surprise, which he solemnly misread. 'It became necessary for me to tell them of my admiration and belief,' he proceeded.

'I saw Mrs. Meeker and Ena in the front room where the sittings are held. Mrs. Meeker sat straight up, with her hands folded; but Ena was enchanting.' He paused, lost in the visualization of the enchantment. 'All sweet curves and round ankles and little feet.' Then he unexpectedly made a very profound remark: 'I think pale girls are more disturbing than red cheeks. They've always been for me, anyway. Ena was the most disturbing thing in the world.'

Here, where I might have been expected to lose my patience disastrously, a flicker of interest appeared in McGeorge and his connection with the Meekers. A normal, sentimental recital would, of course, be insupportable; but McGeorge, I realized, lacked the co-ordination of instincts and faculties which constitutes the healthy state he had called, by implication, stupid. The abnormal often permits extraordinary glimpses of the human machine, ordinarily a sealed and impenetrable mystery. Hysteria has illuminated many of the deep emotions and incentives, and McGeorge, sitting lost in a quivering inner delight, had the significant symptoms of that disturbance.

He may, I thought, exhibit some of the primitive 'complex sensitiveness' of old taboos, and furnish an illustration, for a commentary on the sacred Kings, of the physical base of religious fervor.

'An ordinary prospective mother-in-law,' said McGeorge, 'is hard enough, but Mrs. Meeker ——' He made a motion descriptive of his state of mind in the Meeker parlor. 'Eyes like ice,' he continued; 'and I could see that I hadn't knocked her over with admiration. Ena got mad soon, and made faces at her mother when she wasn't looking, just as if she were a common girl. It touched me tremendously. Then — I had looked down at the carpet for a moment — Mrs. Meeker had gone, without a sound, in a flash. It was a good eight feet to the door and around a table. Space and time are nothing to her.'

Silence again enveloped him; he might have been thinking of the spiritistic triumphs of Mrs. Meeker or of Ena with her sweet curves. Whatever might be said of the latter, it was clear that she was no prude. McGeorge drew a deep breath; it was the only expression of his immediate preoccupation.

'It was quite a strain,' he admitted presently. 'I called as

often as possible and a little oftener. The reception, except for
dear Ena, was not prodigal. Once they were having a sitting,
and I went back to the kitchen. Of course Lizzie Tuoey, their
former servant, was no more, and they had an ashy-black African
woman. Someone was sobbing in the front room — the terrible
sobs of a suffocating grief. There was a voice, too, a man's, but
muffled, so that I couldn't make out any words. That died away,
and the thin, bright tones of a child followed; then a storm of
knocking, and blowing on a tin trumpet.

'A very successful sitting. I saw Jannie directly afterward, and
the heroic young medium was positively livid from exhaustion.
She had a shot of Bénédictine and then another, and Mr. Meeker
half carried her up to bed. I stayed in the kitchen till the confusion was over and Albert came out and was pointedly rude.
If you want to know what's thought of you in a house, watch
the young.

'Ena was flighty, too; it irritated her to have me close by —
highly strung. She cried for no reason at all and bit her finger-
nails to shreds. There was a fine platinum chain about her neck,
with a diamond pendant, I had never seen before, and for a long
while she wouldn't tell me where it had come from. The name,
Wallace Esselmann, finally emerged from her hints and evasions.
He was young and rich, he had a waxed mustache, and the favor
of the Meekers generally.

'Have you ever been jealous?' McGeorge asked abruptly.
Not in the degree he indicated, I replied; however, I compre-
hended something of its possibilities of tyrannical obsession.
'It was like a shovelful of burning coals inside me,' he asserted.
'I was ready to kill this Esselmann or Ena and then myself. I
raved like a maniac; but it evidently delighted her, for she took
off the chain and relented.

'At first,' McGeorge said, 'if you remember, I was terrified
at the thought of living forever; but I had got used to that truth,

and the blessings of spiritualism dawned upon me. No one could ever separate Ena and me. The oldest India religions support that ——'

'With the exception,' I was obliged to put in, 'that all progression is toward nothingness, suspension, endless calm.'

'We have improved on that,' he replied. 'The joys that await us are genuine twenty-two carat — the eternal companionship of loving ones, soft music, summer ——'

'Indestructible lips under a perpetual moon.'

He solemnly raised a hand.

'They are all about you,' he said; 'they hear you; take care. What happened to me will be a warning.'

'Materialize the faintest spirit,' I told him, 'produce the lightest knock on that Fyfe table, and I'll give you a thousand dollars for the cause.' He expressed a contemptuous superiority to such bribery. 'By your own account,' I reminded him, 'the Meekers gave this Esselmann every advantage. Why?'

McGeorge's face grew somber.

'I saw him the next time I called, a fat boy with his spiked mustache on glazed cheeks, and a pocketful of rattling gold junk, a racing car on the curb. He had had Ena out for a little spin, and they were discussing how fast they had gone. Not better than sixty-eight, he protested modestly.

'Albert hung on his every word; he was as servile to Esselmann as he was arrogant to me. He said things I had either to overlook completely or else slay him for. I tried to get his liking.' McGeorge confessed to me that, remembering what the Meekers' old servant had told him about Albert's peculiar habit, he had even thought of making him a present of a box of flies, precisely in the manner you would bring candy for a pretty girl.

'It began to look hopeless,' he confessed of his passion. 'Ena admitted that she liked me better than Wallace, but the family wouldn't hear of it. Once, when Mr. Meeker came to the door, he shut it in my face. The sittings kept going right along, and the manifestations were wonderful; the connection between Jannie and Stepan, her spirit control, grew closer and closer. There was a scientific investigation — some professors put Jannie on a weighing-machine during a séance and found that, in a levitation, she had an increase in weight virtually equal to the lifted table. They got phonograph records of the rapping ——'

'Did you hear them?' I interrupted.

'They are still in the laboratory,' he asserted defiantly. 'But I have a photograph that was taken of an apparition.' He fumbled in an inner pocket and produced the latter. The print was dark and obscured, but among the shadows a lighter shape was traceable: it might have been a woman in loose, white drapery, a curtain, light-struck; anything, in fact. I returned it to him impatiently.

'That,' he informed me, 'was a Christian martyr of ancient times.'

'Burned to a cinder,' I asked, 'or dismembered by lions?'

'Can't you even for a minute throw off the illusion of the flesh?'

'Can you?'

He half rose in a flare of anger; for my question, in view of his admissions, had been sharply pressed.

'All love is a sanctification,' McGeorge said, recovering his temper admirably. 'The union of my beloved wife and me is a holy pact of spirits, transcending corruption.'

'You married her against considerable opposition,' I reminded him.

'I had the hell of a time,' he said in the healthy manner of the former McGeorge. 'Everything imaginable was done to finish me; the powers of earth and of the spirit world were set against me. For a while my human frame wasn't worth a lead nickel.'

'The beyond, then, isn't entirely the abode of righteousness?'

'There are spirits of hell as well as of heaven.'

'The Chinese,' I told him, 'call them Yin and Yang, spirits of dark and light. Will you explain — it may be useful, if things are as you say — how you fought the powers from beyond?'

'Do you remember what Lizzie Tuoey thought about Jannie and Stepan?' he asked, apparently irrelevantly. 'That time Stepan had an engagement with Isabella of Spain.' I didn't. 'Well, she said that Jannie was jealous of the queen.'

McGeorge had, by his own account, really a dreadful time with what was no better than common or, rather, uncommon murder. Two things were evident on the plane of my own recognition — that he had succeeded in holding the illusive affections of Ena, no small accomplishment in view of her neurotic emotional instability, and that the elder Meekers had an interest in the most worldly of all commodities, not exceeded by their devotion to the immaculate dream of love beyond death.

The girl met McGeorge outside the house; he called defiantly in the face of an unrelenting, outspoken opposition. It was in the Meeker front room that he first realized his mundane existence was in danger. He could give no description of what happened beyond the fact that suddenly he was bathed in a cold, revolting air. It hung about him with the undefinable feel and smell of death. A rotten air, he described it, and could think of nothing better; remaining, he thought, for half a minute, filling him with instinctive abject terror, and then lifting.

Ena, too, was affected; she was as rigid as if she were taking part in a séance; and when she recovered, she hurried from the room. Immediately after McGeorge heard her above quarrelling with Jannie. She returned in tears, and said that they would have to give each other up. Here McGeorge damned the worlds seen and unseen, and declared that he'd never leave her. This, with his complete credulity, approached a notable courage or frenzy of desire. He had no doubt but they would kill him. Their facilities, you see, were unsurpassed.

Worse followed almost immediately. The next morning, to be accurate, McGeorge was putting an edge on his razor — he had never given up the old type — when an extraordinary seizure overtook him; the hand that held the blade stopped being a part of him. It moved entirely outside his will; indeed, when certain possibilities came into his shocked mind, it moved in opposition to his most desperate determination.

A struggle began between McGeorge in a sweating effort to open his fingers and drop the razor to the floor, and the will imposing a deep, hard gesture across his throat. He was twisted, he said, into the most grotesque positions; the hand would move up, and he would force it back perhaps an inch at a time. During this the familiar, mucid feel closed about him.

I asked how the force was applied to his arm, but he admitted that his fright was so intense that he had no clear impression of the details. McGeorge, however, did try to convince me that his wrist was darkly bruised afterward. He was, he was certain, lost, his resistance virtually at an end when, as if from a great distance, he heard the faint ring of the steel on the bathroom linoleum.

That, he told himself, had cured him; the Meekers, and Ena in particular, could have their precious Wallace Esselmann. This happened on Friday, and Sunday evening he was back at the Meeker door. The frenzy of desire! Love is the usual, more exalted term. Perhaps. It depends on the point of view, the position adopted in the attack on the dark enigma of existence. Mine is unpresumptuous.

They were obviously surprised to see him — or, rather, all were but Ena — and his reception was less crabbed than usual. McGeorge, with what almost approached a flash of humor, said that it was evident they had expected him to come from the realm of spirits. In view of their professed belief in the endless time for junketing at their command, they clung with amazing energy to the importance of the present faulty scheme.

Ena was wonderfully tender, and promised to marry him whenever he had a corner ready for her. McGeorge, a reporter, lived with the utmost informality with regard to hours and rooms. He stayed that night almost as long as he wished, planning, at intervals, the future. Sometime during the evening it developed that Jannie was in disfavor; the sittings had suddenly become unsatisfactory. One the night before had been specially disastrous.

Stepan, in place of satisfying the very private curiosity of a well-known and munificent politician, had described another party that had made a wide ripple of comment and envious criticism among the shades. It had been planned by a swell of old Rome, faithful in every detail to the best traditions of orgies; and Stepan's companion, a French girl of the Maison Dorée, had opened the eyes of the historic fancy to the latent possibilities of the dance.

Jannie, at this, had spoiled everything, but mostly the temper of the munificent politician, by a piercing scream. She had gone on, Ena admitted, something terrible. When Mr. Meeker had tried to bundle her to bed, she had kicked and scratched like never before. And since then she declared that she'd never make another effort to materialize shameless spirits.

Argument, even the temporary absence of Bénédictine, had been unavailing. Very well, Mrs. Meeker had told her grimly, she would have to go back to cotton stockings; and no more grilled sweetbreads for supper, either; she'd be lucky if she got scrapple. She didn't care; everything was black for her. Black it must have been, I pointed out to McGeorge; it was bad enough with worry limited to the span of one existence, but to look forward to a perpetuity of misery ——

McGeorge returned the latter part of the week with the plans for their marriage, an elopement, considerably advanced; but only Jannie was at home. She saw him listlessly in the usual formal room, where — he almost never encountered her — he sat in a slight perplexity. Jannie might be thought prettier than Ena, he acknowledged, or at least in the face. She had quantities of bright brown hair, which she affected to wear, in the manner of much younger girls, confined with a ribbon, and flowing down her back. Her eyes, too, were brown and remarkable in that the entire iris was exposed. Her full under lip was vividly rouged, while her chin was unobtrusive.

That evening she was dressed very elaborately. The pink silk stockings and preposterous kid slippers were in evidence; her dress was black velvet, short, and cut like a sheath; and there was a profusion of lacy ruffles and bangles at her wrists. To save his soul, McGeorge couldn't think of anything appropriate to talk about. Jannie was a being apart, a precious object of special reverence. This, together with her very human pettishness, complicated the social problem. He wanted excessively to leave, — there was no chance of seeing Ena — but neither could he think of any satisfactory avenue of immediate escape.

Jannie's hands, he noticed, were never still; her fingers were always plaiting the velvet on her knees. She would sigh gustily, bite her lips, and accomplish what in an ordinary person would be a sniffle. Then suddenly she drew nearer to McGeorge and talked in a torrent about true love. She doubted if it existed anywhere. Spirits were no more faithful than humans.

This, for McGeorge, was more difficult than the silence; all the while, he told me, his thoughts were going back to the scene in the bathroom. He had no security that it wouldn't be repeated and with a far different conclusion. He had a passing impulse to ask Jannie to call off her subliminal thugs; the phrasing is my own. There was no doubt in his disordered mind that it was she who, at the instigation of the elder Meekers, was trying to remove him in the effort to secure Wallace Esselmann.

She dissolved presently into tears, and cried that she was the

most miserable girl in existence. She dropped an absurd con-
fection of a handkerchief on the floor, and he leaned over, returning
it to her. Jannie's head dropped against his shoulder, and, to
keep her from sliding to the floor, he was obliged to sit beside
her and support her with an arm. It had been a temporary
measure, but Jannie showed no signs of shifting her weight; and,
from wishing every moment for Ena's appearance, he now prayed
desperately for her to stay away.

McGeorge said that he heard the girl murmur something that
sounded like, 'Why shouldn't I?' Her face was turned up to
him in a way that had but one significance for maiden or medium.
She was, he reminded me, Ena's sister, about to become his
own; there was a clinging seductive scent about her, too, and a
subtle aroma of Bénédictine; and, well, he did what was expected.

However, no sooner had he kissed her than her manner grew
inexplicable. She freed herself from him, and sat upright in an
expectant, listening attitude. Her manner was so convincing
that he straightened up and gazed about the parlor. There was
absolutely no unusual sight or sound; the plain, heavy table in
the center of the room was resting as solidly as if it had never
playfully cavorted at the will of the spirits, the chairs were back
against the walls, the minature Rock of Ages, on the mantel,
offered its testimony to faith.

One insignificant detail struck his eye — a weighty cane of Mr.
Meeker's stood in an angle of the half-opened door to the hall,
across the floor from where Jannie and he were sitting.

III

After a little, with nothing apparently following, the girl's
expectancy faded; her expression grew petulant once more, and
she drew sharply away from McGeorge, exactly as if he had
forced a kiss on her and she was insulted by the indignity. Lord!

he thought, with an inward sinking, what she'll do to me now will be enough!

He rose uneasily and walked to the mantel, where he stood with his back to Jannie, looking down absently at the fringed gray asbestos of a gas hearth. An overwhelming oppression crept over him when there was a sudden cold sensation at the base of his neck, and a terrific blow fell across his shoulders.

McGeorge wheeled instinctively, with an arm up, when he was smothered in a rain of stinging, vindictive battering. The blows came from all about him, a furious attack against which he was powerless to do anything but endeavor to protect his head. No visible person, he said solemnly, was near him. Jannie was at the other side of the room.

'Did you see her clearly while this was going on?' I asked.

Oh, yes, he assured me sarcastically; he had as well glanced at his diary to make sure of the date. He then had the effrontery to inform me that he had been beaten by Mr. Meeker's cane without human agency. He had seen it whirling about him in the air. McGeorge made up his mind that the hour of his death had arrived. A fog of pain settled on him, and he gave up all effort of resistance, sinking to his knees, aware of the salt taste of blood. But just at the edge of unconsciousness the assault stopped.

After a few moments he rose giddily, with his ears humming and his ribs a solid ache. The cane lay in the middle of the room, and Jannie stood, still across the parlor, with her hands pressed to scarlet cheeks, her eyes shining, and her breast heaving in gasps.

'Why not after such a violent exercise?'

McGeorge ignored my practical comment.

'She was delighted,' he said; 'she ran over to me and, throwing her arms about my neck, kissed me hard. She exclaimed that I had helped Jannie when everything else had failed, and she wouldn't forget it. Then she rushed away, and I heard her falling upstairs in her high-heeled slippers.

Naturally he had half collapsed into a chair, and fought to supply his laboring lungs with enough oxygen. It's an unpleasant experience to be thoroughly beaten with a heavy cane under any condition, and this, he was convinced, was special.

I asked if he was familiar with Havelock Ellis on hysterical impulses, and he replied impatiently that he wasn't.

'There are two explanations,' I admitted impartially, 'although we each think there is but one. I will agree that yours is more entertaining. Jannie was jealous again. The Roman orgies, the young person from the *grands boulevards*, were more than she could accept; and she tried, in the vocabulary lately so prevalent, a reprisal. But I must acknowledge that I am surprised at the persistent masculine flexibility of Stepan.'

'It was at the next sitting,' McGeorge concluded, 'that Stepan announced the wedding of Ena and me. The spirits awaited it. There was a row in the Meeker circle; but he dissolved, and refused to materialize in any form until it was accomplished.'

'To the music of the spheres,' I added, with some attempt at ordinary decency.

TURKEY RED[1]

FRANCES GILCHRIST WOOD

THE old mail-sled running between Haney and Le Beau, in the days when Dakota was still a Territory, was nearing the end of its hundred-mile route.

It was a desolate country in those days: geographers still described it as The Great American Desert, and in looks it certainly deserved the title. Never was there anything as lonesome as that endless stretch of snow reaching across the world until it cut into a cold gray sky, excepting the same desert burned to a brown tinder by the hot wind of summer.

Nothing but sky and plain and its voice, the wind, unless you might count a lonely sod shack blocked against the horizon, miles away from a neighbor, miles from anywhere, its red-curtained square of window glowing through the early twilight.

There were three men in the sled: Dan, the mail-carrier, crusty, belligerently Western, the self-elected guardian of everyone on his route; Hillas, a younger man, hardly more than a boy, living on his pre-emption claim near the upper reaches of the stage line; the third a stranger from that part of the country vaguely defined as 'the East.' He was traveling, had given his name as

---

[1] From *The Pictorial Review*. Copyright, 1919, by The Pictorial Review Company. Copyright, 1921, by Frances Gilchrist Wood.

Smith, and was as inquisitive about the country as he was reticent about his business there. Dan plainly disapproved of him.

They had driven the last cold miles in silence when the stage-driver turned to his neighbor. 'Letter didn't say anything about coming out in the spring to look over the country, did it?'

Hillas shook his head. 'It was like all the rest, Dan. Don't want to build a railroad at all until the country's settled.'

'God! Can't they see the other side of it? What it means to the folks already here to wait for it?'

The stranger thrust a suddenly interested profile above the handsome collar of his fur coat. He looked out over the waste of snow.

'You say there's no timber here?'

Dan maintained unfriendly silence and Hillas answered. 'Nothing but scrub on the banks of the creeks. Years of prairie fires have burned out the trees, we think.'

'Any ores — mines?'

The boy shook his head as he slid farther down in his worn buffalo coat of the plains.

'We're too busy rustling for something to eat first. And you can't develop mines without tools.'

'Tools?'

'Yes, a railroad first of all.'

Dan shifted the lines from one fur-mittened hand to the other, swinging the freed numbed arm in rhythmic beating against his body as he looked along the horizon a bit anxiously. The stranger shivered visibly.

'It's a God-forsaken country. Why don't you get out?'

Hillas, following Dan's glance around the blurred sky-line, answered absently, 'Usual answer is, "Leave? It's all I can do to stay here!"'

Smith regarded him irritably. 'Why should any sane man ever have chosen this frozen wilderness?'

Hillas closed his eyes wearily. 'We came in the spring.'

'I see!' The edged voice snapped, 'Visionaries!'

Hillas's eyes opened again, wide, and then the boy was looking beyond the man with the far-seeing eyes of the plainsman. He spoke under his breath as if he were alone.

'Visionary, pioneer, American. That was the evolution in the beginning. Perhaps that is what we are.' Suddenly the endurance in his voice went down before a wave of bitterness. 'The first pioneers had to wait, too. How could they stand it so long!'

The young shoulders drooped as he thrust stiff fingers deep within the shapeless coat pockets. He slowly withdrew his right hand holding a parcel wrapped in brown paper. He tore a three-cornered flap in the cover, looked at the brightly colored contents, replaced the flap, and returned the parcel, his chin a little higher.

Dan watched the northern sky-line restlessly. 'It won't be snow. Look like a blizzard to you, Hillas?'

The traveler sat up. 'Blizzard?'

'Yes,' Dan drawled in willing contribution to his uneasiness, 'the real Dakota article where blizzards are made. None of your Eastern imitations, but a ninety-mile wind that whets slivers of ice off the frozen drifts all the way down from the North Pole. Only one good thing about a blizzard — it's over in a hurry. You get to shelter or you freeze to death.'

A gust of wind flung a powder of snow stingingly against their faces. The traveler withdrew his head turtlewise within the handsome collar in final condemnation. 'No man in his senses would ever have deliberately come here to live.'

Dan turned. 'Wouldn't, eh?'

'No.'

'You're American?'

'Yes.'

'Why?'

'I was born here. It's my country.'

'Ever read about your Pilgrim Fathers?'

'Why, of course.'

'Frontiersmen, same as us. You're living on what they did. We're getting this frontier ready for those who come after. Want our children to have a better chance than we had. Our reason's same as theirs. Hillas told you the truth. Country's all right if we had a railroad.'

'Humph!' With a contemptuous look across the desert. 'Where's your freight, your grain, cattle ——'

'*West*-bound freight, coal, feed, seed-grain, work, and more neighbors.'

'One-sided bargain. Road that hauls empties one way doesn't pay. No Company would risk a line through here.'

The angles of Dan's jaw showed white. 'Maybe. Ever get a chance to pay your debt to those Pilgrim pioneers? Ever take it? Think the stock was worth saving?'

He lifted his whip-handle toward a pin-point of light across the stretch of snow. 'Donovan lives over there and Mis' Donovan. We call them "old folk" now; their hair has turned white as these drifts in two years. All they've got is here. He's a real farmer and a lot of help to the country, but they won't last long like this.'

Dan swung his arm toward a glimmer nor' by nor'east. 'Mis' Clark lives there, a mile back from the stage road. Clark's down in Yankton earning money to keep them going. She's alone with her baby holding down the claim.' Dan's arm sagged. 'We've had women go crazy out here.'

The whip-stock followed the empty horizon half round the compass to a lighted red square not more than two miles away.

'Mis' Carson died in the spring. Carson stayed until he was too poor to get away. There's three children — oldest's Katy, just eleven.' Dan's words failed, but his eyes told. 'Somebody will brag of them as ancestors some day. They'll deserve it if they live through this.'

Dan's jaw squared as he leveled his whip-handle straight at the traveler. 'I've answered your questions, now you answer mine! We know your opinion of the country — you're not traveling for pleasure or for your health. What are you here for?'

'Business. My own!'

'There's two kinds of business out here this time of year. 'Tain't healthy for either of them.' Dan's words were measured and clipped. 'You've damned the West and all that's in it good and plenty. Now I say, damn the people anywhere in the whole country that won't pay their debts from pioneer to pioneer; that lets us fight the wilderness barehanded and die fighting; that won't risk ——'

A gray film dropped down over the world, a leaden shroud that was not the coming of twilight. Dan jerked about, his whip cracked out over the heads of the leaders, and they broke into a quick trot. The shriek of the runners along the frozen snow cut through the ominous darkness.

'Hillas,' Dan's voice came sharply, 'stand up and look for the light on Clark's guide-pole about a mile to the right. God help us if it ain't burning.'

Hillas struggled up, one clumsy mitten thatching his eyes from the blinding needles. 'I don't see it, Dan. We can't be more than a mile away. Hadn't you better break toward it?'

'Got to keep the track 'til we — see — light!'

The wind tore the words from his mouth as it struck them in lashing fury. The leaders had disappeared in a wall of snow, but Dan's lash whistled forward in reminding authority. There was a moment's lull.

'See it, Hillas?'

'No, Dan.'

Tiger-like the storm leaped again, bandying them about in its paws like captive mice. The horses swerved before the punishing blows, bunched, backed, tangled. Dan stood up, shouting his orders of menacing appeal above the storm.

Again a breathing space before the next deadly impact. As it came Hillas shouted: 'I see it — there, Dan! It's a red light. She's in trouble.'

Through the whirling smother and chaos of Dan's cries and the struggling horses the sled lunged out of the road into unbroken drifts. Again the leaders swung sidewise before the lashing of a thousand lariats of ice and bunched against the wheel-horses. Dan swore, prayed, mastered them with far-reaching lash, then the off leader went down. Dan felt behind him for Hillas and shoved the reins against his arm.

'I'll get him up — or cut leaders — loose! If I don't — come back — drive to light. *Don't — get — out!*'

Dan disappeared in the white fury. There were sounds of a struggle; the sled jerked sharply and stood still. Slowly it strained forward.

Hillas was standing, one foot outside on the runner, as they traveled a team's length ahead. He gave a cry — 'Dan! Dan!' and gripped a furry bulk that lumbered up out of the drift.

'All — right — son.' Dan reached for the reins.

Frantically they fought their slow way toward the blurred light, staggering on in a fight with the odds too savage to last. They stopped abruptly as the winded leaders leaned against a wall interposed between themselves and insatiable fury.

Dan stepped over the dashboard, groped his way along the tongue between the wheel-horses, and reached the leeway of a shadowy square.

'It's the shed, Hillas. Help get the team in.' The exhausted animals crowded into the narrow space without protest.

'Find the guide-rope to the house, Dan.'

'On the other side, toward the shack. Where's — Smith?'

'Here, by the shed.'

Dan turned toward the stranger's voice.

'We're going 'round to the blizzard-line tied from shed to shack.

Take hold of it and don't let go. If you do you'll freeze before we can find you. When the wind comes, turn your back and wait. Go on when it dies down and never let go the rope. Ready? The wind's dropped. Here, Hillas, next to me.'

Three blurs hugged the sod walls around to the northeast corner. The forward shadow reached upward to a swaying rope, lifted the hand of the second who guided the third.

'Hang on to my belt, too, Hillas. Ready — Smith? Got the rope?'

They crawled forward, three barely visible figures, six, eight, ten steps. With a shriek the wind tore at them, beat the breath from their bodies, cut them with stinging needle-points, and threw them aside. Dan reached back to make sure of Hillas who fumbled through the darkness for the stranger.

Slowly they struggled ahead, the cold growing more intense; two steps, four, and the mounting fury of the blizzard reached its zenith. The blurs swayed like battered leaves on a vine that the wind tore in two at last and flung the living beings wide. Dan, clinging to the broken rope, rolled over and found Hillas with the frayed end of the line in his hand, reaching about through the black drifts for the stranger. Dan crept closer, his mouth at Hillas's ear, shouting, 'Quick! Right behind me if we're to live through it!'

The next moment Hillas let go the rope. Dan reached madly. 'Boy, you can't find him — it'll only be two instead of one! Hillas! Hillas!'

The storm screamed louder than the plainsman and began heaping the snow over three obstructions in its path, two that groped slowly and one that lay still. Dan fumbled at his belt, unfastened it, slipped the rope through the buckle, knotted it, and crept its full length back toward the boy. A snow-covered something moved forward guiding another, one arm groping in blind search, reached and touched the man clinging to the belt.

Beaten and buffeted by the ceaseless fury that no longer gave quarter, they slowly fought their way hand-over-hand along the rope, Dan now crawling last. After a frozen eternity they reached the end of the line fastened man-high against a second haven of wall. Hillas pushed open the unlocked door, the three men staggered in and fell panting against the side of the room.

The stage-driver recovered first, pulled off his mittens, examined his fingers, and felt quickly of nose, ears, and chin. He looked sharply at Hillas and nodded. Unceremoniously they stripped off the stranger's gloves; reached for a pan, opened the door, dipped it into the drift, and plunged Smith's fingers down in the snow.

'Your nose is white, too. Thaw it out.'

Abruptly Dan indicated a bench against the wall where the two men seated would take up less space.

'I'm ——' The stranger's voice was unsteady. 'I ——' But Dan had turned his back and his attention to the homesteader.

The eight-by-ten room constituted the entire home. A shed roof slanted from eight feet high on the door and window side to a bit more than five on the other. A bed in one corner took up most of the space, and the remaining necessities were bestowed with the compactness of a ship's cabin. The rough boards of the roof and walls had been hidden by a covering of newspapers, with a row of illustrations pasted picture height. Cushions and curtains of turkey-red calico brightened the homely shack.

The driver had slipped off his buffalo coat and was bending over a baby exhaustedly fighting for breath that whistled shrilly through a closing throat. The mother, scarcely more than a girl, held her in tensely extended arms.

'How long's she been this way?'

'She began to choke up day before yesterday, just after you passed on the down trip.'

The driver laid big finger-tips on the restless wrist.

'She always has the croup when she cuts a tooth, Dan, but this is different. I've used all the medicines I have — nothing relieves the choking.'

The girl lifted heavy eyelids above blue semicircles of fatigue, and the compelling terror back of her eyes forced a question through dry lips.

'Dan, do you know what membranous croup is like? Is this it?'

The stage-driver picked up the lamp and held it close to the child's face, bringing out with distressing clearness the blue-veined pallor, sunken eyes, and effort of impeded breathing. He frowned, putting the lamp back quickly.

'Mebbe it is, Mis' Clark, but don't you be scared. We'll help you a spell.'

Dan lifted the red curtain from the cupboard, found an emptied lard-pail, half filled it with water, and placed it on an oil-stove that stood in the center of the room. He looked questioningly about the four walls, discovered a cleverly contrived tool-box beneath the cupboard shelves, sorted out a pair of pincers and bits of iron, laying the latter in a row over the oil blaze. He took down a can of condensed milk, poured a spoonful of the thick stuff into a cup of water, and made room for it near the bits of heating iron.

He turned to the girl, opened his lips as if to speak with a face full of pity.

Along the four-foot space between the end of the bed and the opposite wall the girl walked, crooning to the sick child she carried. As they watched, the low song died away, her shoulder rubbed heavily against the boarding, her eyelids dropped, and she stood sound asleep. The next hard-drawn breath of the baby roused her and she stumbled on, crooning a lullaby.

Smith clutched the younger man's shoulder. 'God, Hillas, look where she's marked the wall rubbing against it! Do you suppose she's been walking that way for three days and nights? Why, she's only a child — no older than my own daughter.'

Hillas nodded.

'Where are her people? Where's her husband?'

'Down in Yankton, Dan told you, working for the winter. Got to have the money to live.'

'Where's the doctor?'

'Nearest one's in Haney — four days' trip away by stage.'

The traveler stared, frowningly.

Dan was looking about the room again and after prodding the gay seat in the corner, lifted the cover and picked up a folded blanket, shaking out the erstwhile padded cushion. He hung the blanket over the back of a chair.

'Mis' Clark, there's nothing but steam will touch membreenous croup. We saved my baby that way last year. Set here and I'll fix things.'

He put the steaming lard-pail on the floor beside the mother and lifted the blanket over the baby's head. She put up her hand.

'She's so little, Dan, and weak. How am I going to know if she — if she ——'

Dan rearranged the blanket tent. 'Jest get under with her yourself, Mis' Clark, then you'll know all that's happening.'

With the pincers he picked up a bit of hot iron and dropped it hissing into the pail, which he pushed beneath the tent. The room was oppressively quiet, walled in by the thick sod from the storm. The blanket muffled the sound of the child's breathing and the girl no longer stumbled against the wall.

Dan lifted the corner of the blanket and another bit of iron hissed as it struck the water. The older man leaned toward the younger.

'Stove — fire?' with a gesture of protest against the inadequate oil blaze.

Hillas whispered, 'Can't afford it. Coal is nine dollars in Haney, eighteen dollars here.'

They sat with heads thrust forward, listening in the intolerable

silence. Dan lifted the blanket, hearkened a moment, then —
'pst!' another bit of iron fell into the pail. Dan stooped to the
tool chest for a reserve supply when a strangling cough made him
spring to his feet and hurriedly lift the blanket.

The child was beating the air with tiny fists, fighting for breath.
The mother stood rigid, arms out.

'Turn her this way!' Dan shifted the struggling child, face
out. 'Now watch for the ——'

The strangling cough broke and a horrible something —'It's
the membrane! She's too weak — let me have her!'

Dan snatched the child and turned it face downward. The blue-
faced baby fought in a supreme effort — again the horrible something — then Dan laid the child, white and motionless, in her
mother's arms. She held the limp body close, her eyes wide with fear.

'Dan, is — is she —?'

A faint sobbing breath of relief fluttered the pale lips that
moved in the merest ghost of a smile. The heavy eyelids half-
lifted and the child nestled against its mother's breast. The girl
swayed, shaking with sobs, 'Baby — baby!'

She struggled for self-control and stood up straight and pale.
'Dan, I ought to tell you. When it began to get dark with the
storm and time to put up the lantern, I was afraid to leave the
baby. If she strangled when I was gone — with no one to help
her — she would die!'

Her lips quivered as she drew the child closer. 'I didn't go
right away but — I did — at last. I propped her up in bed and
ran. If I hadn't' — her eyes were wide with the shadowy edge of
horror — 'if I hadn't — you'd have been lost in the blizzard
and — my baby would have died!'

She stood before the men as if for judgment, her face wet with
unchecked tears. Dan patted her shoulder dumbly and touched a
fresh, livid bruise that ran from the curling hair on her temple
down across cheek and chin.

'Did you get this then?'

She nodded. 'The storm threw me against the pole when I hoisted the lantern. I thought I'd — never — get back!'

It was Smith who translated Dan's look of appeal for the cup of warm milk and held it to the girl's lips.

She made heroic attempts to swallow, her head drooped lower over the cup and fell against the driver's rough sleeve. 'Poor kid, dead asleep!'

Dan guided her stumbling feet toward the bed that the traveler sprang to open. She guarded the baby in the protecting angle of her arm into safety upon the pillow, then fell like a log beside her. Dan slipped off the felt boots, lifted her feet to the bed, and softly drew covers over mother and child.

'Poor kid; but she's grit, clear through!'

Dan walked to the window, looked out at the lessening storm, then at the tiny alarm-clock on the cupboard. 'Be over pretty soon now!' He seated himself by the table, dropped his head wearily forward on folded arms, and was asleep.

The traveler's face had lost some of its shrewdness. It was as if the white frontier had seized and shaken him into a new conception of life. He moved restlessly along the bench, then stepped softly to the side of the bed and straightened the coverlet into greater nicety while his lips twitched.

With consuming care he folded the blanket and restored the corner seat to its accustomed appearance of luxury. He looked about the room, picked up the gray kitten sleeping contentedly on the floor, and settled it on the red cushion with anxious attention to comfort.

He examined with curiosity the few books carefully covered in a corner shelf, took down an old hand-tooled volume and lifted his eyebrows at the ancient coat of arms on the book plate. He tiptoed across to the bench and pointed to the script beneath the plate. 'Edward Winslow (7) to his dear daughter, Alice (8).'

He motioned toward the bed. 'Her name?'

Hillas nodded. Smith grinned. 'Dan's right. Blood will tell, even to damning the rest of us.'

He sat down on the bench. 'I understand more than I did, Hillas, since — you crawled back after me — out there. But how can you stand it here? I know you and the Clarks are people of education and, oh, all the rest; you could make your way any-where.'

Hillas spoke slowly. 'I think you have to live here to know. It means something to be a pioneer. You can't be one if you've got it in you to be a quitter. The country will be all right some day.' He reached for his greatcoat, bringing out a brown-paper parcel. He smiled at it oddly and went on as if talking to himself.

'When the drought and the hot winds come in the summer and burn the buffalo grass to a tinder and the monotony of the plains weighs on you as it does now, there's a common, low-growing cactus scattered over the prairie that blooms into the gayest red flower you ever saw.

'It wouldn't count for much anywhere else, but the pluck of it, without rain for months, dew even. It's the "colors of courage."'

He turned the torn parcel, showing the bright red within, and looked at the cupboard and window with shining, tired eyes.

'Up and down the frontier in these shacks, homes, you'll find things made of turkey-red calico, cheap, common elsewhere' — he fingered the three-cornered flap — 'It's our "colors."' He put the parcel back in his pocket. 'I bought two yards yesterday after — I got a letter at Haney.'

Smith sat looking at the gay curtains before him. The fury of the storm was dying down into fitful gusts. Dan stirred, looked quickly toward the bed, then the window, and got up quietly.

'I'll hitch up. We'll stop at Peterson's and tell her to come over.' He closed the door noiselessly.

The traveler was frowning intently. Finally he turned toward
the boy who sat with his head leaning back against the wall, eyes
closed.

'Hillas'—his very tones were awkward—'they call me a
shrewd business man. I am; it's a selfish job and I'm not reform-
ing now. But twice tonight you—children have risked your
lives, without thought, for a stranger. I've been thinking about
that railroad. Haven't you raised any grain or cattle that could
be used for freight?'

The low answer was toneless. 'Drought killed the crops, prairie
fires burned the hay, of course the cattle starved.'

'There's no timber, ore, nothing that could be used for east-
bound shipment?'

The plainsman looked searchingly into the face of the older
man. 'There's no timber this side the Missouri. Across the river,
it's reservation—Sioux. We——' He frowned and stopped.

Smith stood up, his hands thrust deep in his pockets. 'I admitted I was shrewd, Hillas, but I'm not yellow clear through,
not enough to betray this part of the frontier, anyhow. I had
a man along here last fall spying for minerals. That's why I'm
out here now. If you know the location, and we both think you
do, I'll put capital in your way to develop the mines and use what
pull I have to get the road in.'

He looked down at the boy and thrust out a masterful jaw.
There was a ring of sincerity no one could mistake when he spoke
again.

'This country's a desert now, but I'd back the Sahara peopled
with your kind. This is on the square, Hillas; don't tell me you
won't believe I'm American enough to trust?'

The boy tried to speak. With stiffened body and clenched
hands he struggled for self-control. Finally in a ragged whisper:
'If I try to tell you what—it means—I can't talk! Dan and
I know of outcropping coal over in the Buttes'—he nodded in

the direction of the Missouri — 'but we haven't had enough money to file mining claims.'

'Know where to dig for samples under this snow?'

The boy nodded. 'Some in my shack too. I ——' His head went down upon the crossed arms. Smith laid an awkward hand on the heaving shoulders, then rose and crossed the room to where the girl had stumbled in her vigil. Gently he touched the darkened streak where her shoulders had rubbed and blurred the newspaper print. He looked from the relentless white desert outside to the gay bravery within and bent his head. 'Turkey-red — calico!'

There was a sound of jingling harness and the crunch of runners. The men bundled into fur coats.

'Hillas, the draw right by the house here.' Smith stopped and looked sharply at the plainsman, then went on with firm careless-ness: 'This draw ought to strike a low grade that would come out near the river level. Does Dan know Clark's address?' Hillas nodded.

They tiptoed out and closed the door behind them softly. The wind had swept every cloud from the sky and the light of the Northern stars etched a dazzling world. Dan was checking up the leaders as Hillas caught him by the shoulder and shook him like a clumsy bear.

'Dan, you blind old mole, can you see the headlight of the Over-land Freight blazing and thundering down that draw over the Great Missouri and Eastern?'

Dan stared.

'I knew you couldn't!' Hillas thumped him with furry fist. 'Dan' — the wind might easily have drowned the unsteady voice — 'I've told Mr. Smith about the coal — for freight. He's going to help us get capital for mining, and after that the road.'

'Smith! Smith! Well I'll be — aren't you a claim-spotter?'

He turned abruptly and crunched toward the stage. His

passengers followed. Dan paused with his foot on the runner and looked steadily at the traveler from under lowered, shaggy brows.

'You're going to get a road out here?'

'I've told Hillas I'll put money in your way to mine the coal. Then the railroad will come.'

Dan's voice rasped with tension. 'We'll get out the coal. Are you going to see that the road's built?'

Unconsciously the traveler held up his right hand. 'I am!'

Dan searched his face sharply. Smith nodded. 'I'm making my bet on the people — friend!'

It was a new Dan who lifted his bronzed face to a white world. His voice was low and very gentle. 'To bring a road here' — he swung his whip-handle from Donovan's light around to Carson's square, sweeping in all that lay behind — 'out here to them' — the pioneer faced the wide desert that reached into a misty space ablaze with stars — 'would be like — playing God!'

The whip thudded softly into the socket and Dan rolled up on the driver's seat. Two men climbed in behind him. The long lash swung out over the leaders as Dan headed the old mail-sled across the drifted right-of-way of the Great Missouri and Eastern.

FANUTZA[1]

KONRAD BERCOVICI

LIGHT and soft, as though the wind were blowing the dust off the silver clouds that floated overhead, the first snow was falling over the barren lands stretching between the Danube and the Black Sea. A lowland wind, which had already hardened and tightened the marshes, was blowing the snow skywards. The fine silvery dust, caught between the two air currents, danced lustily, blown hither and thither until it took hold of folds and rifts in the frozen land and began to form rugged white ridges that stretched in soft silvery curves to meet other growing mountains of snow. The lowland wind, at first a mere breeze playfully teasing the north wind, like a child that kicks the bed-sheets before falling asleep, increased its force and swiftness, and scattered huge mountains of snow, but the steadily rising drone of the north wind soon mastered the situation. Like silver grain strewn by an unseen hand, the snow fell obliquely in steady streams over the land. A great calm followed. The long Dobrudgean winter had started. In the dim steady light, in the wake of the great calm, traveling towards the Danube from the Black Sea, the *Marea Neagra*, four

---

gypsy wagons, each drawn by four small horses, appeared on the frozen plains. The caravan was brought to a standstill within sight of the slowly moving river. The canvas-covered wagons ranged themselves, broadwise, in a straight line with the wind. Between the wagons enough space was allowed to stable the horses. Then, when that part of the business had been done, a dozen men, in furs from head to toe, quickly threw up a canvas that roofed the temporary quarters of the animals and gave an additional overhead protection from the snow and wind to the dwellers of the wheeled homes.

While the unharnessing and quartering of the horses and the stretching of the canvas roof proceeded, a number of youngsters jumped down from the wagons, yelling and screaming with all the power of their lusty lungs. They threw snowballs at one another as they ran, some in search of firewood and others, with wooden pails dangling from ends of curved sticks over the left shoulder, in search of water for the horses and for the cooking pots of their mothers.

Soon afterwards, from little crooked black chimneys that pointed downwards over the roofs of the wagons, thick black smoke told that the fires were already started. The youngsters came back; those with the full water pails marching erectly with legs well apart; the ones with bundles of firewood strapped to their shoulders leaning forward on knotted sticks so as not to fall under the heavy burden.

When everything had been done, Marcu, the tall, gray-bearded chief, inspected the work. A few of the ropes needed tightening. He did it himself, shaking his head in disapproval of the way in which it had been managed. Then he listened carefully to the blowing of the wind and measured its velocity and intensity. He called to his men. When they had surrounded him, he spoke a few words. With shovels and axes they set energetically to work, at his direction packing a wall of snow and wood from the ground up over the axles of the wheels all around the wagons so as to give greater solidity to the whole and to prevent the cold wind from blowing underneath.

By the time the early night settled over the marshes, the camp was quiet and dark. Even the dogs had curled up near the tired horses and had gone to sleep.

Early the following morning the whole thing could not be distinguished from one of the hundreds of mountains of snow that had formed overnight. After the horses had been fed and watered, Marcu, accompanied by his daughter, Fanutza, left the camp and went riverward, in search of the hut of the Tartar whose flat-bottomed boat was moored on the shore. Marcu knew every inch of the ground. He had camped there with his tribe twenty winters in succession. He sometimes arrived before, and at other times after, the first snow of the year. But every time he had gone to Mehmet Ali's hut and asked the Tartar to row him across the Danube, on the old Rumanian side, to buy there fodder for the horses and the men; enough to last until after the river was frozen tight and could be crossed securely with horses and wagon. He had always come alone to Mehmet's hut, therefore the Tartar, after greeting Marcu and offering to do what his friend desired, inquired why the girl was beside the old chief.

'But this is my daughter, Fanutza, Mehmet Ali,' Marcu informed.

'Who, Fanutza? She who was born here fourteen winters ago on the plains here?'

'The same, the same, my friend,' Marcu answered, as he smilingly appraised his daughter.

Mehmet Ali looked at the girl in frank astonishment at her size and full development; then he said, as he took the oars from the corner of the hut: 'And I, who thought that my friend had taken a new wife to himself! Allah, Allah! How fast these youngsters grow! And why do you take her along to the Ghiaour side, to the

heathen side, of the river, friend?' he continued talking as he put
heavy boots on his feet and measured Fanutza with his eyes as he
spoke.

'For everything there is only one right time, say I, Marcu,' the
chief explained in measured, solemn voice. 'And so now is the
time for my daughter to get married. I have chosen her a husband
from amongst the sons of my men, a husband who will become the
Chief when I am no longer here to come to your hut at the beginning of every winter. She shall marry him in the spring. I
now go with her to the bazaars to buy silks and linens which the
women of my tribe will fashion into new clothes for both. And
may Allah be good to them.'

'*Allah il Allah,*' Mehmet assured Marcu. 'And who is he
whom you have chosen from amongst your men?'

'I am old, Mehmet, I would otherwise have chosen a younger
man for my daughter; but because I fear that this or the following
winter will be the last one, I have chosen Stan, whose orphaned
daughter is Fanutza's own age. He is good and true and strong.
Young men never make careful chiefs.'

'That be right and wise,' remarked Mehmet, who was by that
time ready for the trip. During the whole conversation the
young gypsy girl had been looking to her father when he spoke
and sidewise when Mehmet answered.

At fourteen Fanutza was a full-grown woman. Her hair,
braided in tresses, was hanging from underneath a black fur cap
she wore well over her forehead. Her eyes were large and brown,
the long eyebrows were coal black. Her nose was straight and
thin and the mouth full and red. Withal she was of a somewhat
lighter hue than her father or the rest of the gypsy tribe. Yet
there was something of a darker grain that lurked beneath her
skin. And she was light on her feet. Even trudging in the deep
snow she seemed more to float, to skim on top, than to walk.

Unconcerned she had listened to the conversation that had

gone on between her father and the Tartar in the hut of the boatman. She had hardly been interested in the whole affair, yet,
when Mehmet Ali mentioned casually as soon as he was outdoors
that he knew a man who would pay twenty pieces of gold for such
a wife as Fanutza, she became interested in the conversation.

'I sell horses only,' Marcu answered quietly.

'Yet my friend and others from his tribe have bought wives.
Remember that beautiful Circassian girl?' the Tartar continued,
without raising or lowering his voice.

'Yes, Mehmet, we buy wives but we don't sell them.'

'Which is not fair,' Mehmet reflected aloud, still in the same
voice.

By that time they had reached the river shore. Mehmet,
after rolling together the oil cloth that had covered the boat,
helped the gypsy chief and his daughter to the stern. With one
strong push of the oar on the shore rock, the Tartar slid his boat
a hundred feet towards the middle of the stream. Then he seated
himself, face towards his passengers, and rowed steadily without
saying a single word. The gypsy chief lit his short pipe and
looked over his friend's head, trying to distinguish the other
shore from behind the curtain of falling snow. The boat glided
slowly over the thickening waters of the Danube. A heavy snowstorm, the heaviest of the year, lashed the river. When Mehmet
had finally moored his boat to the Rumanian side of the Danube,
he turned around to the gypsy chief and said:

'Be back before sundown. It shall be my last crossing of the
year. For when the sun rises the waters will be frozen still. The
gale blows from the land of the Russians.'

'As you tell me, friend,' answered Marcu, while helping his
daughter out of the boat.

When the two had gone a short distance Fanutza turned her
head. Mehmet Ali was leaning on an oar and looking after them.
A little later, a hundred paces farther, she caught fragments of a

Tartar song that reached her ears in spite of the shrill noises of the wind.

Marcu and his daughter entered the inn that stood a few hundred feet from the shore. The innkeeper, an old, fat, greasy Greek, Chiria Anastasidis, welcomed the gypsy chief. Not knowing the relationship between the old man and the girl, he feared to antagonize his customer by talking to the young woman. He pushed a white pine table near the big stove in the middle of the room and after putting two empty glasses on the table he inquired, 'White or red?'

'Red wine, Chiria. It warms quicker. I am getting old.'

'Old!' exclaimed the Greek, as he brought a small pitcher of wine. 'Old! Why, Marcu, you are as young as you were twenty years ago.'

'This is my daughter, Fanutza, Chiria, and not my wife.'

'A fine daughter you have. Your daughter, eh?'

'Yes, and she is about to marry, too.'

After they had clinked glasses and wished one another health and long years the innkeeper inquired:

'All your men healthy?'

'All. Only One-eyed Jancu died. You remember him. He was well along in years.'

'Bagdaproste. Let not a younger man than he die,' answered Anastasidis, as he crossed himself.

After Marcu felt himself warmed back to life by the fine wine he inquired of Anastasidis the price of oats and straw and hay. The innkeeper's store and his warehouse contained everything from a needle to an oxcart. The shelves were full of dry goods, socks, shirts, silks, belts, fur caps, coats, and trousers. Overhead, hanging from the ceiling, were heavy leather boots, shoes, saddles, harness of all kinds, fishers' nets, and even a red-painted sleigh that swung on heavy chains. In one corner of the store blankets were piled high, while all over the floor were bags of dry beans and peas and corn and oats. At the door were bales of straw and hay, and outside, already half-covered with snow, iron plows hobnobbed with small anchors, harrows, and bundles of scythes that leaned on the wall.

'Oats you wanted? Oats are very high this year, Marcu.'

And the bargaining began. Fanutza sat listlessly on her chair and looked through the window. A few minutes later the two men called one another thief and swindler and a hundred other names. Yet each time the bargain was concluded on a certain article they shook hands and repeated that they were the best friends on earth.

'Now that we have finished with the oats, Chiria, let's hear your price for corn. What? Three francs a hundred kilo? No. I call off the bargain on the oats. You are the biggest thief this side of the Danube.'

'And you, you lowborn *tzigane*, are the cheapest swindler on earth.'

Quarreling and shaking hands alternately and drinking wine, Marcu and the Greek went on for hours. The gypsy chief had already bought all the food for his men and horses and a few extra blankets and had ordered it all carted to the moored boat where Mehmet Ali was waiting, when Fanutza reminded her father of the silks and linens he wanted to buy.

'I have not forgotten, daughter, I have not forgotten.' Fanutza approached the counter behind which the Greek stood ready to serve his customers.

'Show us some silks,' she asked.

He emptied a whole shelf on the counter.

The old gypsy stood aside, watching his daughter as she fingered the different pieces of colored silk, which the shopkeeper praised as he himself touched the goods with thumb and forefinger in keen appreciation of the quality he offered. After she had selected all the colors she wanted and picked out the linen and neckerchiefs and ear-rings and tried on a pair of beautiful patent leather boots that reached over the knees and had stripes of red leather sewed on with yellow silk on the soft vamps, Fanutza declared that she had chosen everything she wanted. The bargaining between the Greek and the Gypsy was about to start anew when Marcu looked outdoors thoughtfully, stroked his beard and said to the innkeeper:

'Put away the things my daughter has selected. I shall come again, alone, to bargain for them.'

'If my friend fears he has not enough money...' suavely intervened Anastasidis, as he placed a friendly hand on the gypsy's arm.

'When Marcu has no money he does not ask his women to select silk,' haughtily interrupted the gypsy. 'It will be as I said it will be. I come alone in a day if the river has frozen. In a day or a week. I come alone.'

'Shall I, then, not take all these beautiful things along with me, now?' asked Fanutza in a plaintive reproachful tone. 'There is Marcia who waits to see them. I have selected the same silk *basma* for her. Have you not promised me, even this morning...'

'A woman must learn to keep her mouth shut,' shouted Marcu, as he angrily stamped his right foot on the floor. He looked at his daughter as he had never looked at her before. Only a few hours ago she was his little girl, a child! He was marrying her off so soon to Stan against his desire, although it was the customary age for gypsies, because of his will to see her in good hands and to give to Stan the succession to the leadership of his tribe.

Only a few hours ago! What had brought about the change? Was it in him or in her? That cursed Tartar, Mehmet Ali, with his silly offer of twenty gold-pieces! He, he had done it. Marcu looked again at his daughter. Her eyelids trembled nervously and there was a little repressed twitch about her mouth. She returned his glance at first, but lowered her eyes under her father's steady gaze. 'Already a shameless creature,' thought the old gypsy. But he could not bear to think that way about his little daughter, about his Fanutza. He also feared that she could read his thoughts. He was ashamed of what passed through his mind. Rapidly enough in self-defense he turned against her the sharp edge of the argument. Why had she given him all those ugly thoughts?

'It will be as I said, Anastasidis. In a day or a week. When the river has frozen, I come alone. And now, Fanutza, we go. Night is coming close behind us. Come, you shall have all your silks.'

The Greek accompanied them to the door. The cart that had brought the merchandise to the boat of the waiting Mehmet was returning.

'The water is thickening,' the driver greeted the gypsy and his daughter.

They found Mehmet Ali seated in the boat expecting his passengers.

'Have you bought everything you intended?' the Tartar inquired, as he slid the oars into the hoops.

'Everything,' Marcu answered, as he watched his daughter from the corner of an eye.

Vigorously Mehmet Ali rowed till well out into the wide river without saying another word. His manner was so detached that the gypsy chief thought the Tartar had already forgotten what had passed between them in the morning. Sure enough. Why! He was an old man, Mehmet Ali. It was possible he had been commissioned by some Dobrudgean Tartar chief to buy him a wife. He had been refused and now he was no longer thinking about her. He would look somewhere else, where his offer might not be scorned. That offer of Mehmet had upset him. He had never thought of Fanutza other than as a child. Of course he was marrying her to Stan ... but it was more like giving her a second father!

Suddenly the old gypsy looked at the Tartar who had lifted his oars from the water and brought the boat to an abrupt standstill. Mehmet Ali laid the paddles across the width of the boat and, looking steadily into the eyes of Marcu, he said:

'As I said this morning, Marcu, it is not fair that you should buy wives from us when you like our women and not sell us yours when we like them.'

'It is as it is,' countered the gypsy savagely.

'But it is not fair,' argued Mehmet, slyly watching every movement of his old friend.

'If Mehmet is tired my arms are strong enough to help if he wishes,' remarked Marcu.

'No, I am not tired, but I should like my friend to know that I think it is not fair.'

There was a long silence during which the boat was carried downstream although it was kept in the middle of the river by skillful little movements of the boatman.

Fanutza looked at the Tartar. He was about the same age as Stan was. Only he was stronger, taller, broader, swifter. When he chanced to look at her his small, bead-like eyes bored through her like gimlets. No man had ever looked at her that way. Stan's eyes were much like her own father's eyes. The Tartar's face was much darker than her own. His nose was flat and his upper lip curled too much noseward and the lower one chinward, and his bulletlike head rose from between the shoulders. There was no neck. No, he was not beautiful to look at. But he was so different from Stan! So different from any of the other men she had seen every day since she was born. Why! Stan ... Stan was like her father. They were all like him in her tribe!

'And, as I said,' Mehmet continued after a while, 'as I said, it is not fair. My friend must see that. It is not fair. So I offer you twenty gold pieces for the girl. Is it a bargain?'

'She is not for sale,' yelled Marcu, understanding too well the meaning of the oars out of the water.

'No?' wondered Mehmet, 'not for twenty pieces of gold? Well, then I shall offer five more. Sure twenty-five is more than any of your people ever paid to us for a wife. It would shame my ancestors were I to offer more for a gypsy girl than they ever received for one of our women.'

'She is not for sale,' roared the gypsy at the top of his voice.

By that time the Tartar knew that Marcu was not armed. He knew the chief too well not to know that a knife or a pistol would have been the answer to his second offer and the implied insult to the race of gypsies.

Twenty-five gold pieces! thought Fanutza. Twenty-five gold pieces offered for her by a Tartar at a second bid. She knew what that meant. She had been raised in the noise of continual bargaining between Tartars and gypsies and Greeks. It meant much less than a quarter of the ultimate sum the Tartar was willing to pay. Would Stan ever have offered that for her? No, surely not. She looked at the Tartar and felt the passion that radiated from him. How lukewarm Stan was! And here was a man. Stopped the boat midstream and bargained for her, fought to possess her. Endangered his life for her. For it was a dangerous thing to do what he did and facing her father. Yet... she would have to marry Stan because her father bade it.

'I don't mean to offend you,' the boatman spoke again, 'but you are very slow in deciding whether you accept my bargain or not. Night is closing upon us.'

Marcu did not answer immediately. The boat was carried downstream very rapidly. They were at least two miles too far down by now. Mehmet looked at Fanutza and found such lively interest in her eyes that he was encouraged to offer another five gold pieces for her.

It was a proud moment for the girl. So men were willing to pay so much for her! But her heart almost sank when her father pulled out his purse from his pocket and said:

'Mehmet Ali, who is my best friend, has been so good to me these twenty years that I have thought to give him twenty gold pieces that he might buy himself a wife to keep his hut warm during the long winter. What says he to my friendship?'

'That is wonderful! Only now, he is not concerned about that, but about the fairness of his friend who does not want to sell wives to the men whose women he buys. I offer five more gold pieces which makes thirty-five in all. And I do that not for Marcu but for his daughter that she may know that I will not harm her and will forever keep her well fed and buy her silks and jewels.'

'Silks!' It occurred to the gypsy chief to look at his daughter at that moment. She turned her head away from him and looked at the Tartar, from under her brows. How had he known?

'A bargain is a bargain only when two men agree on something, says the Koran,' the gypsy chief reminded the Tartar boatman. 'I don't want to sell her.'

'So we will travel downstream for a while,' answered Mehmet Ali and crossed his arms.

After a while the gypsy chief, who had reckoned that they must be fully five miles away from his home across the water, made a new offer.

'A woman, Mehmet Ali, is a woman. They are all alike after you have known them. So I offer you thirty-five pieces of gold with which you can buy for yourself any other woman you please whenever you want.'

Fanutza looked at the Tartar. Though it was getting dark she could see the play of every muscle of his face. Hardly had her father finished making his offer, when Mehmet, after one look at the girl, said:

'I offer fifty gold pieces for the girl. Is it a bargain?'

Fanutza's eyes met the eyes of her father. She looked at him entreatingly, 'Don't give in to the Tartar,' her eyes spoke clearly, and Marcu refused the offer.

'I offer you fifty instead that you buy yourself another woman than my daughter.'

'No,' answered the Tartar, 'but I offer sixty for this one, here.'

Quick as a flash Fanutza changed the encouraging glance she had thrown to the passionate man to a pleading look towards her father. 'Poor, poor girl!' thought Marcu. 'How she fears to lose me! How she fears I might accept the money and sell her to the Tartar!'

'A hundred gold pieces to row us across,' he yelled, for the night was closing in upon them and the boat was being carried swiftly downstream. There was danger ahead of them. Marcu knew it.

'A hundred gold pieces is a great sum,' mused Mehmet, 'a great sum! It has taken twenty years of my life to save such a sum ... yet, instead of accepting your offer, I will give you the same sum for the woman I want.'

'Fool, a woman is only a woman. They are all alike,' roared the gypsy.

'Not to me!' answered Mehmet Ali quietly. 'I shall not say another word.'

'Fool, fool, fool,' roared the gypsy, as he still tried to catch Fanutza's eye. It was already too dark.

'Not to me.' The Tartar's words echoed in the girl's heart. 'Not to me.' Twenty years he had worked to save such a great sum. And now he refused an equal amount and was willing to pay it all for her. Would Stan have done that? Would anybody else have done that? Why should she be compelled to marry whom her father chose when men were willing to pay a hundred gold pieces for her? The old women of the camp had taught her to cook and to mend and to wash and to weave. She must know all that to be worthy of Stan, they had told her. And here was a man who did not know whether she knew any of these things, who staked his life for her and offered a hundred gold pieces in the bargain! Twenty years of savings. Twenty years of work. It was not every day one met such a man. Surely, with one strong push of his arms he could throw her father overboard. He did not do it because he did not want to hurt her feelings. And as the silence continued Fanutza thought her father, too, was a fine man. It was fine of him to offer a hundred gold pieces for her liberty. That was in itself a great thing. But did he do it only for her sake or was it because of Stan, because of himself? And as she thought again of Mehmet's 'Not to me,' she remembered the fierce bitterness in her father's voice when he had yelled, 'All women are alike.' That was not true. If it were true why would Mehmet Ali want her and her only after having seen her only once? Then, too, all men must be alike! It was not so at all! Why! Mehmet Ali was not at all like Stan. And he offered a hundred pieces of gold. No. Stan was of the kind who think all women are alike. That was it. All her people were thinking all women were alike. That was it. Surely all the men in the tribe were alike in that. All her father had ever been to her, his kindness, his love was wiped away when he said those few words. The last few words of Mehmet Ali, 'Not to me,' were the sweetest music she had ever heard.

Marcu waited until it was dark enough for the Tartar not to see, when, pressing significantly his daughter's foot, he said:

'So be it as you said. Row us across.'

'It is not one minute too soon,' Mehmet answered. 'Only a short distance from here, where the river splits in three forks, is a great rock. Shake hands. Here. Now here is one oar. Pull as I count, *Bir, icki, outch, dort.* Again, *Bir, icki, outch, dort.* Lift your oar. Pull again. Two counts only. *Bir, icki.* So, now we row nearer to the shore. See that light there? Row towards it. Good. Marcu, your arm is still strong and steady and you can drive a good bargain.'

Again and again the gypsy pressed the foot of his daughter as he bent over the oar. She should know, of course, that he never intended to keep his end of the bargain. He gave in only when he saw that the Tartar meant to wreck them all on the rocks ahead of them. Why had he, old and experienced as he was, having dealt with those devils of Tartars for so many years, not known better than to return to the boat after he had heard Mehmet say, 'It is not fair!' And after he had reflected on the Tartar's words, why, after he had refused to buy all the silks and linens on that reflection, not a very clear one at first, why had he not told Mehmet to row across alone and deliver the fodder and food. He could have passed the night in Anastasidis's inn and hired another boat the following morning if the river had not frozen meanwhile! He should have known, he who knew these passionate beasts so well. It was all the same with them; whether they set their eyes on a horse that captured their fancy or a woman. They were willing to kill or be killed in the fight for what they wanted. A hundred gold pieces for a woman! Twenty years' work for a woman!

The two men rowed in silence, each one planning how to outwit the other and each one knowing that the other was planning likewise. According to Tartar ethics the bargain was a bargain. When the boat had been pulled out of danger Mehmet hastened to fulfill his end. With one jerk he loosened a heavy belt underneath his coat and pulled out a leather purse which he threw to Marcu. As he did so he met Fanutza's proud eye.

'Here. Count it. Just one hundred.'

'That's good enough,' the gypsy chief answered, as he put the purse in his pocket without even looking at it. 'Row, I am cold. I am anxious to be home.'

'It will not be before daylight, chief,' remarked Mehmet Ali, as he bent again over his oars and counted aloud, '*Bir, icki, Bir, icki.*' An hour later, Fanutza had fallen asleep on the bags of fodder and was covered by the heavy fur coat of the Tartar.

The two men rowed the whole night upstream against the current in the slushy heavy waters of the Danube. A hundred times floating pieces of ice had bent back the flat of the oar Marcu was handling, and every time Mehmet had saved it from breaking by a deft stroke of his own oar or by some other similar movement. He was a waterman and knew the ways of the water as well as Marcu himself knew the murky roads of the marshes. The gypsy could not help but admire the powerful quick movements of the Tartar ... yet ... to be forced into selling his daughter — that was another thing.

At daylight they were within sight of Mehmet's hut on the shore. The storm had abated. Standing up on the bags of fodder Marcu saw the black smoke that rose from his camp. His people must be waiting on the shore. They were a dozen men. Mehmet was one alone. He would unload the goods first; then, when his men would be near enough, he would tell Fanutza to run towards them. Let Mehmet come to take her if he dared!

A violent jerk woke the gypsy girl from her sleep. She looked at the two men but said nothing. When the boat was moored, the whole tribe of gypsies, who had already mourned their chief yet hoped against hope and watched the length of the shore, surrounded the two men and the woman. There was a noisy welcome. While some of the men helped unload the boat a boy came running with a sleigh cart.

When all the bags were loaded on the sleigh Marcu threw the heavy purse Mehmet had given him to the Tartar's feet and grabbed the arm of his Fanutza.

'Here is your money, Mehmet. I take my daughter.'

But before he knew what had happened, Fanutza shook off his grip and picking up the purse she threw it at her father, saying:

'Take it. Give it to Stan so that he can buy with the gold another woman. To him all women are alike. But not to Mehmet

Ali. So I shall stay with him. A bargain is a bargain. He staked his life for me.'

Marcu knew it was the end. 'All women are alike,' he whined to Stan, as he handed him the purse. 'Take it. All women are alike,' he repeated with bitterness, as he made a savage movement towards his daughter.

'All, save those with blood of *Chans* in their veins,' said Mehmet Ali, who had put himself between the girl and the whole of her tribe. And the Tartar's words served as a reminder to Marcu that Fanutza's own mother had been a white woman and the daughter of a Tartar chief.

MY OLD MAN[1]

ERNEST HEMINGWAY

I GUESS looking at it, now, my old man was cut out for a fat guy, one of those regular little roly fat guys you see around, but he sure never got that way, except a little toward the last, and then it wasn't his fault, he was riding over the jumps only and he could afford to carry plenty of weight then. I remember the way he'd pull on a rubber shirt over a couple of jerseys and a big sweat shirt over that, and get me to run with him in the forenoon in the hot sun. He'd have, maybe, taken a trial trip with one of Razzo's skins early in the morning after just getting in from Torino at four o'clock in the morning and beating it out to the stables in a cab and then with the dew all over everything and the sun just starting to get going, I'd help him pull off his boots and he'd get into a pair of sneakers and all these sweaters and we'd start out.

'Come on, kid,' he'd say, stepping up and down on his toes in front of the jock's dressing room, 'let's get moving.'

Then we'd start off jogging around the infield once, maybe, with him ahead, running nice, and then turn out the gate and along one of those roads with all the trees along both sides of them that run out from San Siro. I'd go ahead of him when we hit the road and I could run pretty stout and I'd look around and he'd be jogging easy just behind me and after a little while I'd look around again and he'd begun to sweat. Sweating heavy and he'd just be dogging it along with his eyes on my back, but when he'd catch me looking at him he'd grin and say, 'Sweating plenty?' When my old man grinned, nobody could help but grin too. We'd keep right on running out toward the mountains and then my old man would yell, 'Hey, Joe!' and I'd look back and he'd be sitting under a tree with a towel he'd had around his waist wrapped around his neck.

I'd come back and sit down beside him and he'd pull a rope out of his pocket and start skipping rope out in the sun with the sweat pouring off his face and him skipping rope out in the white dust with the rope going cloppetty, cloppetty, clop, clop, clop, and the sun hotter, and him working harder up and down a patch of the road. Say, it was a treat to see my old man skip rope, too. He could whirr it fast or lop it slow and fancy. Say, you ought to have seen wops look at us sometimes, when they'd come by, going into town walking along with big white steers hauling the cart. They sure looked as though they thought the old man was nuts. He'd start the rope whirring till they'd stop dead still and watch him, then give the steers a cluck and a poke with the goad and get going again.

When I'd sit watching him working out in the hot sun I sure felt fond of him. He sure was fun and he done his work so hard and he'd finish up with a regular whirring that'd drive the sweat out of his face like water and then sling the rope at the tree and come over and sit down with me and lean back against the tree with the towel and a sweater wrapped around his neck.

'Sure is hell keeping it down, Joe,' he'd say and lean back and shut his eyes and breathe long and deep, 'it ain't like when you're a kid.' Then he'd get up before he started to cool and we'd jog along back to the stables. That's the way it was keeping down to weight. He was worried all the time. Most jocks can just about ride off all they want to. A jock loses about a kilo every time he rides, but my old man was sort of dried out and he couldn't keep down his kilos without all that running.

I remember once at San Siro, Regoli, a little wop, that was riding for Buzoni, came out across the paddock going to the bar for something cool; and flicking his boots with his whip, after he'd just weighed in and my old man had just weighed in too, and came out with the saddle under his arm looking red-faced and tired and too big for his silks and he stood there looking at young Regoli standing up to the outdoors bar, cool and kid-looking, and I says, 'What's the matter, Dad?' 'cause I thought maybe Regoli had bumped him or something and he just looked at Regoli and said, 'Oh, to hell with it,' and went on to the dressing room.

Well, it would have been all right, maybe, if we'd stayed in Milan and ridden at Milan and Torino, 'cause if there ever were any easy courses, it's those two. 'Pianola, Joe,' my old man said when he dismounted in the winning stall after what the wops thought was a hell of a steeplechase. I asked him once. 'This course rides itself. It's the pace you're going at, that makes riding the jumps dangerous, Joe. We ain't going any pace here, and they ain't any really bad jumps either. But it's the pace always — not the jumps that makes the trouble.'

San Siro was the swellest course I'd ever seen but the old man said it was a dog's life. Going back and forth between Mirafiore and San Siro and riding just about every day in the week with a train ride every other night.

I was nuts about the horses, too. There's something about it, when they come out and go up the track to the post. Sort of dancy and tight looking with the jock keeping a tight hold on them and maybe easing off a little and letting them run a little going up. Then once they were at the barrier it got me worse than anything. Especially at San Siro with that big green infield and the mountains way off and the fat wop starter with his big whip and the jocks fiddling them around and then the barrier snapping up and that bell going off and them all getting off in a bunch and then commencing to string out. You know the way a bunch of skins gets off. If you're up in the stand with a pair of glasses all you see is them plunging off and then that bell goes off and it seems like it rings for a thousand years and then they come sweeping round the turn. There wasn't ever anything like it for me.

But my old man said one day, in the dressing room, when he was getting into his street clothes, 'None of these things are horses, Joe. They'd kill that bunch of skates for their hides and hoofs up at Paris.' That was the day he'd won the Premio Commercio with Lantorna shooting her out of the field the last hundred meters like pulling a cork out of a bottle.

It was right after the Premio Commercio that we pulled out and left Italy. My old man and Holbrook and a fat wop in a straw hat that kept wiping his face with a handkerchief were having an argument at a table in the Galleria. They were all talking French and the two of them were after my old man about something. Finally he didn't say anything any more but just sat there and looked at Holbrook, and the two of them kept after him, first one talking and then the other, and the fat wop always butting in on Holbrook.

'You go out and buy me a *Sportsman*, will you, Joe?' my old man said, and handed me a couple of soldi without looking away from Holbrook.

So I went out of the Galleria and walked over to in front of the Scala and bought a paper, and came back and stood a little way away because I didn't want to butt in and my old man was sitting back in his chair looking down at his coffee and fooling with a spoon and Holbrook and the big wop were standing and the big wop was wiping his face and shaking his head. And I came up and my old man acted just as though the two of them weren't standing there and said, 'Want an ice, Joe?' Holbrook looked down at my old man and said slow and careful, 'You son of a b——,' and he and the fat wop went out through the tables.

My old man sat there and sort of smiled at me, but his face was white and he looked sick as hell and I was scared and felt sick inside because I knew something had happened and I didn't see how anybody could call my old man a son of a b——, and get away with it. My old man opened up the *Sportsman* and studied the handicaps for a while and then he said, 'You got to take a lot of things in this world, Joe.' And three days later we left Milan for good on the Turin train for Paris, after an auction sale out in front of Turner's stables of everything we couldn't get into a trunk and a suit case.

We got into Paris early in the morning in a long, dirty station the old man told me was the Gare de Lyon. Paris was an awful big town after Milan. Seems like in Milan everybody is going somewhere and all the trams run somewhere and there ain't any sort of a mix-up, but Paris is all balled up and they never do straighten it out. I got to like it, though, part of it, anyway, and say it's got the best race courses in the world. Seems as though that were the thing that keeps it all going and about the only thing you can figure on is that every day the buses will be going out to whatever track they're running at, going right out through everything to the track. I never really got to know Paris well, because I just came in about once or twice a week with the old man from Maisons and he always sat at the Café de la Paix on the Opera side with the rest of the gang from Maisons and I guess that's one of the busiest parts of the town. But, say, it is funny that a big town like Paris wouldn't have a Galleria, isn't it?

Well, we went out to live at Maisons-Lafitte, where just about everybody lives except the gang at Chantilly, with a Mrs. Meyers

that runs a boarding house. Maisons is about the swellest place
to live I've ever seen in all my life. The town ain't so much, but
there's a lake and a swell forest that we used to go off bumming
in all day, a couple of us kids, and my old man made me a sling
shot and we got a lot of things with it but the best one was a
magpie. Young Dick Atkinson shot a rabbit with it one day
and we put it under a tree and were all sitting around and Dick
had some cigarettes and all of a sudden the rabbit jumped up and
beat it into the brush and we chased it but we couldn't find it.
Gee, we had fun at Maisons. Mrs. Meyers used to give me lunch
in the morning and I'd be gone all day. I learned to talk French
quick. It's an easy language.

As soon as we got to Maisons, my old man wrote to Milan for
his license and he was pretty worried till it came. He used to sit
around the Café de Paris in Maisons with the gang, there were
lots of guys he'd known when he rode up at Paris, before the war,
lived at Maisons, and there's a lot of time to sit around because
the work around a racing stable, for the jocks, that is, is all cleaned
up by nine o'clock in the morning. They take the first batch of
skins out to gallop them at 5.30 in the morning and they work the
second lot at 8 o'clock. That means getting up early all right and
going to bed early, too. If a jock's riding for somebody too, he
can't go boozing around because the trainer always has an eye on
him if he's a kid and if he ain't a kid he's always got an eye on
himself. So mostly if a jock ain't working he sits around the Café
de Paris with the gang and they can all sit around about two or
three hours in front of some drink like a vermouth and seltz and
they talk and tell stories and shoot pool and it's sort of like a club
or the Galleria in Milan. Only it ain't really like the Galleria
because there everybody is going by all the time and there's
everybody around at the tables.

Well, my old man got his license all right. They sent it through
to him without a word and he rode a couple of times. Amiens, up

country and that sort of thing, but he didn't seem to get any
engagement. Everybody liked him and whenever I'd come in to
the Café in the forenoon I'd find somebody drinking with him
because my old man wasn't tight like most of these jockeys that
have got the first dollar they made riding at the World's Fair in
St. Louis in nineteen ought four. That's what my old man would
say when he'd kid George Burns. But it seemed like everybody
steered clear of giving my old man any mounts.

We went out to wherever they were running every day with the
car from Maisons and that was the most fun of all. I was glad
when the horses came back from Deauville and the summer.
Even though it meant no more bumming in the woods, 'cause
then we'd ride to Enghien or Tremblay or St. Cloud and watch
them from the trainers' and jockeys' stand. I sure learned about
racing from going out with that gang and the fun of it was going
every day.

I remember once out at St. Cloud. It was a big two hundred
thousand franc race with seven entries and Kzar a big favorite.
I went around to the paddock to see the horses with my old man
and you never saw such horses. This Kzar is a great big yellow
horse that looks like just nothing but run. I never saw such
a horse. He was being led around the paddocks with his head
down and when he went by me I felt all hollow inside he was so
beautiful. There never was such a wonderful, lean, running built
horse. And he went around the paddock putting his feet just so
and quiet and careful and moving easy like he knew just what he
had to do and not jerking and standing up on his legs and getting
wild eyed like you see these selling platers with a shot of dope in
them. The crowd was so thick I couldn't see him again except
just his legs going by and some yellow and my old man started
out through the crowd and I followed him over to the jock's
dressing room back in the trees and there was a big crowd around
there, too, but the man at the door in a derby nodded to my old

man and we got in and everybody was sitting around and getting dressed and pulling shirts over their heads and pulling boots on and it all smelled hot and sweaty and linimenty and outside was the crowd looking in.

The old man went over and sat down beside George Gardner that was getting into his pants and said, 'What's the dope, George?' just in an ordinary tone of voice 'cause there ain't any use him feeling around because George either can tell him or he can't tell him.

'He won't win,' George says very low, leaning over and buttoning the bottoms of his pants.

'Who will?' my old man says, leaning over close so nobody can hear.

'Kircubbin,' George says, 'and if he does, save me a couple of tickets.'

My old man says something in a regular voice to George and George says, 'Don't ever bet on anything, I tell you,' kidding like, and we beat it out and through all the crowd that was looking in over to the 100 franc mutuel machine. But I knew something big was up because George is Kzar's jockey. On the way he gets one of the yellow odds-sheets with the starting prices on and Kzar is only paying 5 for 10, Cefisidote is next at 3 to 1 and fifth down the list this Kircubbin at 8 to 1. My old man bets five thousand on Kircubbin to win and puts on a thousand to place and we went around back of the grandstand to go up the stairs and get a place to watch the race.

We were jammed in tight and first a man in a long coat with a gray tall hat and a whip folded up in his hand came out and then one after another the horses, with the jocks up and a stable boy holding the bridle on each side and walking along, followed the old guy. That big yellow horse Kzar came first. He didn't look so big when you first looked at him until you saw the length of his legs and the whole way he's built and the way he moves. Gosh,

I never saw such a horse. George Gardner was riding him and
they moved along slow, back of the old guy in the gray tall hat
that walked along like he was the ring master in a circus. Back
of Kzar, moving along smooth and yellow in the sun, was a good
looking black with a nice head with Tommy Archibald riding him;
and after the black was a string of five more horses all moving
along slow in a procession past the grandstand and the pesage.
My old man said the black was Kircubbin and I took a good look
at him and he was a nice looking horse, all right, but nothing like
Kzar.

Everybody cheered Kzar when he went by and he sure was one
swell-looking horse. The procession of them went around on the
other side past the pelouse and then back up to the near end of the
course and the circus master had the stable boys turn them loose
one after another so they could gallop by the stands on their way
up to the post and let everybody have a good look at them. They
weren't at the post hardly any time at all when the gong started
and you could see them way off across the infield all in a bunch
starting on the first swing like a lot of little toy horses. I was
watching them through the glasses and Kzar was running well
back, with one of the bays making the pace. They swept down
and around and came pounding past and Kzar was way back
when they passed us and this Kircubbin horse in front and going
smooth. Gee, it's awful when they go by you and then you have
to watch them go farther away and get smaller and smaller and
then all bunched up on the turns and then come around towards
into the stretch and you feel like swearing and goddamming worse
and worse. Finally they made the last turn and came into the
straightaway with this Kircubbin horse way out in front. Everybody was looking funny and saying 'Kzar' in sort of a sick way
and them pounding nearer down the stretch, and then something
came out of the pack right into my glasses like a horse-headed
yellow streak and everybody began to yell 'Kzar' as though they

were crazy. Kzar came on faster than I'd ever seen anything in my life and pulled up on Kircubbin that was going fast as any black horse could go with the jock flogging hell out of him with the gad and they were right dead neck and neck for a second but Kzar seemed going about twice as fast with those great jumps and that head out — but it was while they were neck and neck that they passed the winning post and when the numbers went up in the slots the first one was 2 and that meant Kircubbin had won.

I felt all trembly and funny inside, and then we were all jammed in with the people going downstairs to stand in front of the board where they'd post what Kircubbin paid. Honest, watching the race I'd forgot how much my old man had bet on Kircubbin. I'd wanted Kzar to win so damned bad. But now it was all over it was swell to know we had the winner.

'Wasn't it a swell race, Dad?' I said to him.

He looked at me sort of funny with his derby on the back of his head. 'George Gardner's a swell jockey, all right,' he said. 'It sure took a great jock to keep that Kzar horse from winning.'

Of course I knew it was funny all the time. But my old man saying that right out like that sure took the kick all out of it for me and I didn't get the real kick back again ever, even when they posted the numbers up on the board and the bell rang to pay off and we saw that Kircubbin paid 67.50 for 10. All round people were saying, 'Poor Kzar! Poor Kzar!' And I thought, I wish I were a jockey and could have rode him instead of that son of a b——. And that was funny, thinking of George Gardner as a son of a b—— because I'd always liked him and besides he'd given us the winner, but I guess that's what he is, all right.

My old man had a big lot of money after that race and he took to coming into Paris oftener. If they raced at Tremblay he'd have them drop him in town on their way back to Maisons, and he and I'd sit out in front of the Café de la Paix and watch the people go by. It's funny sitting there. There's streams of people going by and all sorts of guys come up and want to sell you things, and I loved to sit there with my old man. That was when we'd have the most fun. Guys would come by selling funny rabbits that jumped if you squeezed a bulb and they'd come up to us and my old man would kid with them. He could talk French just like English and all those kind of guys knew him 'cause you can always tell a jockey — and then we always sat at the same table and they got used to seeing us there. There were guys selling matrimonial papers and girls selling rubber eggs that when you squeezed them a rooster came out of them and one old wormy-looking guy that went by with post-cards of Paris, showing them to everybody, and, of course, nobody ever bought any, and then he would come back and show the under side of the pack and they would all be smutty post-cards and lots of people would dig down and buy them.

Gee, I remember the funny people that used to go by. Girls around supper time looking for somebody to take them out to eat and they'd speak to my old man and he'd make some joke at them in French and they'd pat me on the head and go on. Once there was an American woman sitting with her kid daughter at the next table to us and they were both eating ices and I kept looking at the girl and she was awfully good looking and I smiled at her and she smiled at me but that was all that ever came of it because I looked for her mother and her every day and I made up ways that I was going to speak to her and I wondered if I got to know her if her mother would let me take her out to Auteuil or Trem- blay but I never saw either of them again. Anyway, I guess it wouldn't have been any good, anyway, because looking back on it I remember the way I thought out would be best to speak to her was to say, 'Pardon me, but perhaps I can give you a winner at Enghien today?' and, after all, maybe she would have thought I was a tout instead of really trying to give her a winner.

We'd sit at the Café de la Paix, my old man and me, and we had
a big drag with the waiter because my old man drank whisky and
it cost five francs, and that meant a good tip when the saucers
were counted up. My old man was drinking more than I'd ever
seen him, but he wasn't riding at all now and besides he said that
whisky kept his weight down. But I noticed he was putting it on,
all right, just the same. He'd busted away from his old gang out
at Maisons and seemed to like just sitting around on the boulevard with me. But he was dropping money every day at the track.
He'd feel sort of doleful after the last race, if he'd lost on the day,
until we'd get to our table and he'd have his first whisky and then
he'd be fine.

He'd be reading the Paris-Sport and he'd look over at me and
say, 'Where's your girl, Joe?' to kid me on account I had told him
about the girl that day at the next table. And I'd get red, but
I liked being kidded about her. It gave me a good feeling. 'Keep
your eye peeled for her, Joe,' he'd say, 'she'll be back.'

He'd ask me questions about things and some of the things I'd
say he'd laugh. And then he'd get started talking about things.
About riding down in Egypt, or at St. Moritz on the ice before
my mother died, and about during the war when they had regular
races down in the south of France without any purses, or betting
or crowd or anything just to keep the breed up. Regular races
with the jocks riding hell out of the horses. Gee, I could listen
to my old man talk by the hour, especially when he'd had a couple
or so of drinks. He'd tell me about when he was a boy in Kentucky and going coon hunting, and the old days in the States
before everything went on the bum there. And he'd say, 'Joe,
when we've got a decent stake, you're going back there to the
States and go to school.'

'What've I got to go back there to go to school for when everything's on the bum there?' I'd ask him.

'That's different,' he'd say and get the waiter over and pay the pile of saucers and we'd get a taxi to the Gare St. Lazare and get on the train out to Maisons.

One day at Auteuil, after a selling steeplechase, my old man bought in the winner for 30,000 francs. He had to bid a little to get him but the stable let the horse go finally and my old man had his permit and his colors in a week. Gee, I felt proud when my old man was an owner. He fixed it up for stable space with Charles Drake and cut out coming in to Paris, and started his running and sweating out again, and him and I were the whole stable gang. Our horse's name was Gilford, he was Irish bred and a nice, sweet jumper. My old man figured that training him and riding him, himself, he was a good investment. I was proud of everything and I thought Gilford was as good a horse as Kzar. He was a good, solid jumper, a bay, with plenty of speed on the flat, if you asked him for it, and he was a nice-looking horse, too.

Gee, I was fond of him. The first time he started with my old man up, he finished third in a 2,500 meter hurdle race and when my old man got off him, all sweating and happy in the place stall, and went in to weigh, I felt as proud of him as though it was the first race he'd ever placed in. You see, when a guy ain't been riding for a long time, you can't make yourself really believe that he has ever rode. The whole thing was different now, 'cause down in Milan, even big races never seemed to make any difference to my old man, if he won he wasn't ever excited or anything, and now it was so I couldn't hardly sleep the night before a race and I knew my old man was excited, too, even if he didn't show it. Riding for yourself makes an awful difference.

Second time Gilford and my old man started, was a rainy Sunday at Auteuil, in the Prix du Marat, a 4,500 meter steeple-chase. As soon as he'd gone out I beat it up in the stand with the new glasses my old man had bought for me to watch them. They started way over at the far end of the course and there was some trouble at the barrier. Something with goggle blinders on was

making a great fuss and rearing around and busted the barrier
once, but I could see my old man in our black jacket, with a white
cross and a black cap, sitting up on Gilford, and patting him with
his hand. Then they were off in a jump and out of sight behind
the trees and the gong going for dear life and the pari-mutuel
wickets rattling down. Gosh, I was so excited, I was afraid to look
at them, but I fixed the glasses on the place where they would
come out back of the trees and then out they came with the old
black jacket going third and they all sailing over the jump like
birds. Then they went out of sight again and then they came
pounding out and down the hill and all going nice and sweet and
easy and taking the fence smooth in a bunch, and moving away
from us all solid. Looked as though you could walk across on their
backs they were all so bunched and going so smooth. Then they
bellied over the big double Bullfinch and something came down.
I couldn't see who it was, but in a minute the horse was up and
galloping free and the field, all bunched still, sweeping around the
long left turn into the straightaway. They jumped the stone wall
and came jammed down the stretch toward the big water-jump
right in front of the stands. I saw them coming and hollered at
my old man as he went by, and he was leading by about a length
and riding way out, and light as a monkey, and they were racing
for the water-jump. They took off over the big hedge of the water-
jump in a pack and then there was a crash, and two horses pulled
sideways out off it, and kept on going and three others were piled
up. I couldn't see my old man anywhere. One horse kneed himself up and the jock had hold of the bridle and mounted and went
slamming on after the place money. The other horse was up and
away by himself, jerking his head and galloping with the bridle
rein hanging and the jock staggered over to one side of the track
against the fence. Then Gilford rolled over to one side off my old
man and got up and started to run on three legs with his off hoof
dangling and there was my old man laying there on the grass flat

out with his face up and blood all over the side of his head. I ran down the stand and bumped into a jam of people and got to the rail and a cop grabbed me and held me and two big stretcher-bearers were going out after my old man and around on the other side of the course I saw three horses, strung way out, coming out of the trees and taking the jump.

My old man was dead when they brought him in and while a doctor was listening to his heart with a thing plugged in his ears, I heard a shot up the track that meant they'd killed Gilford. I lay down beside my old man, when they carried the stretcher into the hospital room, and hung onto the stretcher and cried and cried, and he looked so white and gone and so awfully dead, and I couldn't help feeling that if my old man was dead maybe they didn't need to have shot Gilford. His hoof might have got well. I don't know. I loved my old man so much.

Then a couple of guys came in and one of them patted me on the back and then went over and looked at my old man and then pulled a sheet off the cot and spread it over him; and the other was telephoning in French for them to send the ambulance to take him out to Maisons. And I couldn't stop crying, crying and choking, sort of, and George Gardner came in and sat down beside me on the floor and put his arm around me and says, 'Come on, Joe, old boy. Get up and we'll go out and wait for the ambulance.'

George and I went out to the gate and I was trying to stop bawling and George wiped off my face with his handkerchief and we were standing back a little ways while the crowd was going out of the gate and a couple of guys stopped near us while we were waiting for the crowd to get through the gate and one of them was counting a bunch of mutuel tickets and he said, 'Well, Butler got his, all right.'

The other guy said, 'I don't give a good goddam if he did, the crook. He had it coming to him on the stuff he's pulled.'

'I'll say he had,' said the other guy, and tore the bunch of tickets in two.

And George Gardner looked at me to see if I'd heard and I had all right and he said, 'Don't you listen to what those bums said, Joe. Your old man was one swell guy.'

But I don't know. Seems like when they get started they don't leave a guy nothing.

FOUR GENERATIONS[1]

RUTH SUCKOW

'Move just a little closer together — the little
girl more toward the center — that's good. Now I think we'll
get it.'

The photographer dived once more under the black cloth.

'Stand back, Ma,' a husky voice said. 'You'll be in the picture.'

Aunt Em stepped hastily back with a panicky look. Mercy,
she didn't want to show! She hadn't had time to get her dress
changed yet, had come right out of the kitchen where she was
baking pies to see the photograph taken. She was in her old dark
blue kitchen dress and had her hair just wadded up until she could
get time to comb it. It didn't give her much time for dressing
up, having all this crowd to cook for.

The boys, and Uncle Chris, standing away back on the edges,
grinned appreciatively. Fred whispered to Clarence, 'Laugh
if Ma got in it.' The way she jumped back, and her unconsciousness of the ends sticking up from her little wad of hair,
delighted the boys. When they looked at each other, a little
remembering glint came into their eyes.

[1] From *The American Mercury.* Copyright 1924, by The American Mercury, Inc.
Copyright 1925, by Ruth Suckow.

There was quite a crowd of onlookers. Aunt Em. Uncle Chris
in his good trousers, and his shirt-sleeves, his sunburned face
dark brown above the white collar that Aunt Em had made him
put on because of Charlie's. Uncle Gus and Aunt Sophie Spfierschlage had come over to dinner, and stood back against the
white house wall, Aunt Sophie mountainous in her checked gingham. The boys, of course, and Bernie Schuldt, who was working
for Chris; and another fellow who had come to look at some hogs
and who was standing there, conscious of his old overalls and torn
straw hat, mumbling, 'Well, didn't know I was gona find anything like this goin' on.' . . . Charlie's wife, Ella, had been given a
chair where she could have a good view of the proceedings. She
tried to smile and wave her handkerchief when little Phyllis
looked around at her. Then she put her handkerchief to her
eyes, lifting up her glasses with their narrow light shell rims, still
smiling a little painfully. She had to think from how far Katherine had come.

Aunt Em and Aunt Sophie were whispering: 'Ain't it a shame
Edna couldn't get over! They coulda took one of Chris and her,
and Marine and Merle, with Grandpa, too. . . . That little one
looks awful cute, don't she? . . . Well, what takes him so long?
Grandpa won't sit there much longer. I should think they coulda
had it taken by this time a'ready.'

They all watched the group on the lawn. They had decided
that the snowball bushes would 'make a nice background.' The
blossoms were gone, but the leaves were dark green, and thick.
What a day for taking a picture! It would be so much better out
here than in the house. Katherine had made them take it right
after dinner, so that little Phyllis would not be late for her nap —
nothing must ever interfere with that child's nap. It was the
brightest, hottest time of the day. The tall orange summer lilies
seemed to open and shimmer in the heat. Things were so green —
the country lawn with its thick grass, the heavy foliage of the

maple trees against the blue, summery sky of July. The thin varnished supports of the camera stand glittered yellow and sticky. The black cloth of the lens looked thick, dense, hot. The photographer's shirt was dazzling white in the sun, and when he drew his head out from under the cloth his round face shone pink. His coat made a black splotch tossed on the grass.

'The little girl more toward the center.'

All three of the others tried anxiously to make little Phyllis more conspicuous. 'Here, we've got to have you showing — my, my! — whether the rest of us do or not,' Charlie said jovially. Grandpa's small, aged, frail hand moved a little as if he were going to draw the child in front of him — but, with a kind of delicacy, did not quite touch her little arm.

They had to wait while a little fleecy cloud crossed the sun, putting a brief, strange, cool shadow over the vivid lawn. In that moment the onlookers were aware of the waiting group. Four generations! Great-grandfather, grandfather, mother, daughter. It was all the more impressive when they thought of Katherine and Phyllis having come from so many miles away. The snowball bushes were densely green behind them — almost dusky in the heat. Grandpa's chair had been placed out there — a homemade chair of willow branches. To think that these four belonged together!

Grandpa, sitting in the chair, might have belonged to another world. Small, bent like a little old troll, foreign with his black cambric skullcap, his blue, far-apart peasant eyes with their still gaze, his thin, silvery beard. His hands, gnarled from years of farm work in a new country, clasped the homemade knotted stick that he held between his knees. His feet, in old felt slippers with little tufted wool flowers, were set flat on the ground. He wore the checked shirt of an old farmer. . . . It hardly seemed that Charlie was his son. Plump and soft, dressed in the easy garments, of good quality and yet a trifle careless, of Middle Western small-town prosperity. His shaven face, paler now than it used to be and showing his age in the folds that had come about his chin; his glasses with shell rims and gold bows; the few strands of grayish hair brushed across his pale, luminous skull. A small-town banker. Now he looked both impressed and shamefaced at having the photograph taken.... And then Katherine, taking after no one knew whom. Slender, a little haggard and worn, still young, her pale, delicate face and the cords in her long, soft throat, her little collar bones, her dark, intelligent weak eyes behind her thick black-rimmed glasses. Katherine had always been like that. Refined, 'finicky,' studious, thoughtful. Her hand, slender and a trifle sallow, lay on Phyllis's shoulder.

Phyllis.... Her little yellow frock made her vivid as a canary bird against the dark green of the foliage. Yellow — the relatives did not know whether they liked that, bright yellow. Still, she did look sweet. They hadn't thought Katherine's girl would be so pretty. Of course the care that Katherine took of her — everything had to revolve around that child. There was some-thing faintly exotic about her liquid brown eyes with their jet-black lashes, the shining straight gold-brown hair, the thick bangs that lay, parted a little and damp with the heat, on the pure white of her forehead. Her little precise 'Eastern accent.' ... Grandpa looked wonderingly at the bare arms, round and soft and tiny, white and moist in the heat. Fragile blue veins made a flowerlike tracery of indescribable purity on the white skin. Soft, tender, exquisite ... ach, what a little girl was here, like a princess!

The cloud passed. Katherine's white and Phyllis's yellow shone out again from the green. The others stood back watching, a heavy stolid country group against the white wall of the farm-house that showed bright against the farther green of the grove. Beyond lay the orchard and the rank green spreading cornfields where little silvery clouds of gnats went shimmering over the moist richness of the leaves.

'Watch — he's taking it now!'

In the breathless silence they could hear the long whirr and rush of a car on the brown country road beyond the grove.

Well, the picture was taken. Everyone was glad to be released from the strain.

Grandpa's chair had been placed nearer the house, under some maple trees. Charlie stayed out there with him a while. It was his duty, he felt, to talk to the old man a while when he was here at the farm. He didn't get over very often — well, it was a hundred miles from Rock River, and the roads weren't very good up here in Sac township. His car stood out at the edge of the grove in the shade. The new closed car that he had lately bought, a 'coach,' opulent, shining, with its glass and upholstery and old-blue drapes, there against the background of the evergreen grove with its fallen branches and pieces of discarded farm machinery half visible in the deepest shade.

It wasn't really very hard to get away from Rock River and the bank. He and Ella took plenty of trips. He ought to come and see his father more than he did. But he seemed to have nothing to say to Grandpa. The old man had scarcely been off the place for years.

'Well, Pa, you keep pretty well, do you?'

'Ja, pretty goot . . . ja, for so old as I am ——'

'Oh, now, you mustn't think of yourself as so old.'

Charlie yawned, re-crossed his legs. He lighted a cigar.

'Chris's corn doing pretty well this season?'

'Ach, dot I know nuttings about. Dey don't tell me nuttings.'

'Well, you've had your day at farming, Pa.'

'Ja . . . ja, ja . . .'

He fumbled in the pocket of his coat, drew out an ancient black pipe.

Charlie said cheerfully, 'Have some tobacco?' He held out a can.

The old man peered into it, sniffed. 'Ach, dot stuff? No, no, dot is shust like shavings. I smoke de real old tobacco.'

'Like it strong, hey?'

They both puffed away.

Grandpa sat in the old willow chair. His blue eyes had a look half wistful, half resentful. Charlie was his oldest child. He would have liked to talk with Charlie. He was always wishing that Charlie would come, always planning how he would tell him things — about how the old ways were going and how the farmers did now, how none of them told him things — but when Charlie came, then that car was always standing ready there to take him right back home again, and there seemed nothing to be said. He always remembered Charlie as the young man, the little boy who used to work beside him in the field — and then when Charlie came, he was this stranger. Charlie was a town man now. He owned a bank! He had forgotten all about the country, and the old German ways. To think of Charlie, their son, being a rich banker, smoking cigars, riding round in a fine carriage with glass windows....

'Dot's a fine wagon you got dere.'

Charlie laughed. 'That's a coach, Pa.'

'So? Coach, is dot what you call it? Like de old kings, like de emperors, de kaisers, rode around in. Ja, you can live in dot. Got windows and doors, curtains — is dere a table, too, stove — no? Ja, dot's a little house on wheels.'

He pursed out his lips comically. But ach, such a carriage! He could remember when he was glad enough to get to town in a lumber wagon. Grandma and the children used to sit in the back on the grain sacks. His old hands felt of the smooth knots of his stick. He went back, back, into reverie.... He muttered just above his breath, 'Ach, ja, ja, ja ... dot was all so long ago....'

Charlie was silent, too. He looked at the car, half drew out his watch, put it back again.... Katherine crossed the lawn. His

eyes followed her. Bluish-gray, a little faded behind his modern
glasses — there was resentment, bewilderment, wistfulness in
them at the same time, and loneliness. He was thinking of how he
used to bring Kittie out here to the farm when she was a little
girl, when Chris used to drive to Germantown and get them with a
team and two-seated buggy. They had come oftener than now
when they had the car.... 'Papa, *really* did you live out here —
on this farm?' He had been both proud and a little jealous because she wasn't sunburned and wiry, like Chris's children. A
little, slim, long-legged, soft-skinned, dark-eyed girl. 'Finicky'
about what she ate and what she did — he guessed he and Ella
had encouraged her in that. Well, he hadn't had much when he
was a child, and he'd wanted his little girl to have the things he'd
missed. He wanted her to have more than his brothers' and
sisters' children. He was Charlie, the one who lived in town, the
successful one. Music lessons, drawing lessons, college ... and
here she had grown away from her father and mother. Chris's
children lived close around him, but it sometimes seemed to him
that he and Ella had lost Kittie. Living away off there in the
East. And when she came home, although she was carefully
kind and dutiful and affectionate, there was something aloof.
He thought jealously, maybe it would have been better if they
hadn't given her all those things, had kept her right at home
with them.... It hadn't been as much pleasure as he had anticipated having his little grandchild there. There was her 'schedule'
that Kittie was so pernickety about. He'd been proud to have
people in Rock River see her beauty and perfection, but he
hadn't been able to take her around and show her off as he'd
hoped.

All day he had been seeing a little slim, fastidious girl in a
white dress and white hair ribbons and black patent-leather
slippers, clinging to his hand with little soft fingers when he took
her out to see the cows and pigs.... 'Well, Kittie, do you

wish we lived out here instead of in town?' She shook her head, and her small underlip curled just a little....

He saw Chris and Gus off near the house. They could talk about how crops were coming, and he could tell them, with a banker's authority, about business conditions. He stirred uneasily, got up, yawned, stretched his arms, said with a little touch of shame:

'Well, Pa, I guess I'll go over and talk to Chris a while. I'll see you again before we leave.'

'Ja ——' The old man did not try to keep him. He watched Charlie's plump figure cross the grass. Ja, he had more to say to the young ones.

Aunt Em was through baking. She had gone into the bedroom to 'get cleaned up.' She brought out chairs to the front porch. 'Sit out here. Here's a chair, Ella — here, Katherine. Ach, Sophie, take a better chair than that.' — 'Naw, this un'll do for me, Em.'

'The womenfolks' — Katherine shuddered away from that phrase. She had always, ever since she was a little girl, despised sitting about this way with 'the womenfolks.' Planted squat in their chairs, rocking, yawning, telling over and over about births and deaths and funerals and sicknesses. There was a kind of feminine grossness about it that offended what had always been called her 'finickiness.'

Her mother enjoyed it. She was different from Aunt Em and Aunt Sophie, lived in a different way — a small, plump, elderly woman with waved grayish-silvery hair and a flowered voile dress with little fussy laces, feminine strapped slippers. But still there was something that she liked about sitting here in the drowsy heat and going over and over things with the other women. Sometimes, to Katherine's suffering disgust, she would add items about the birth of Katherine herself — 'Well, I thought

sure Kittie was going to be a boy. She kicked so hard ——'
'Oh, Mother, spare us!' Aunt Em would give a fat, comfortable
laugh — 'Don't look so rambunctious now, does she? Kittie,
ain't you ever gona get a little flesh on your bones? You study
too hard. She oughta get out and ride the horses like Edna
does.'

Aunt Sophie Spfierschlage — that was the way she sat rocking,
her feet flat on the floor, her stomach comfortably billowing,
beads of sweat on her heavy chin and lips and around the roots of
her stiff, dull hair. Well, thank goodness she was only Aunt Em's
sister, she wasn't really related to the Kleins. Aunt Em was bad
enough.

They used to laugh over her fastidious disgust, when she sat
here, a delicate, critical little girl who didn't want to get on one
of the horses or jump from rafters into the hay. 'Kittie thinks
that's terrible. Well, Kittie, that's the way things happen.'
'Ach, she won't be so squeamish when she grows up and has three
or four of her own.' Now she sat beside them, delicate, still too
thin, to Aunt Em's amazement. 'Ain't you got them ribs covered
up yet? What's the matter? Don't that man of yours give you
enough to eat?' — her soft skin pale and her eyes dark from the
heat, dressed with a kind of fastidious precision, an ultra-refine-
ment. A fragile bar pin holding the soft white silk of her blouse,
her fine dark hair drooping about her face. 'Well, you ain't
changed much since you got married!' Aunt Em had said. They
expected to admit her now to their freemasonry, to have *her* add
interesting items about the birth of Phyllis.

Phyllis — her little darling! As if the exquisite miracle of
Phyllis could have anything in common with these things!
Katherine suffered just as she had always suffered from even
small vulgarities. But she sat courteous and ladylike now, a
slight dutiful smile on her lips.

'Where does she get them brown eyes? They ain't the color of yours, are they? Turn around and let's have a look at you — no, I thought yours was kinda darker.'

Aunt Em had come out now, had squatted down into another chair. 'I guess her papa's got the brown eyes.'

'Yes, I think she looks a little like Willis.'

Ella said almost resentfully, 'Well, I don't know whether she takes after Willis's folks or not, but I can't see that she looks one bit like Kittie or any of us.'

'Well,' Aunt Em said, 'but look at Kittie. She don't look like you or Charlie neither. But I guess she's yours just the same, ain't she, Ella? ... Say, you remember that Will Fuchs? Ja, his girl's got one they say don't belong to who it ought to. Her and that young Bender from over South ——'

Katherine did not listen. How long before they could leave? She had thought it right to bring Phyllis over here where her great-grandfather lived, as her father had wished. But it seemed worse to her than ever. She knew that Aunt Em wouldn't let them go without something more to eat, another of her great heavy meals with pie and cake and coffee. Her mother had always said, as if in extenuation of her visible enjoyment of the visit and the food: 'Well, Aunt Em means well. Why don't you try and talk with her? She wants to talk with you.' But Aunt Em and the Spfierschlages and the whole place seemed utterly alien and horrible to Katherine. For a moment, while they had been taking the photograph out on the lawn, she had felt touched with a sense of beauty. But she had never belonged here. She felt at home in Willis's quiet old frame house in New England, with his precise, elderly New England parents — 'refinement,' 'culture,' Willis's father reading 'the classics,' taking the *Atlantic Monthly* ever since their marriage. She had always felt that those were the kind of people she ought to have had, the kind of home. Of course she loved Father and Mother and was loyal to them. They depended upon her as their only child.

This porch! It seemed to express the whole of her visits to the farm. It was old-fashioned now — a long, narrow porch with a fancy railing, the posts trimmed with red. Her ancestral home! It was utterly alien to her.

They were talking to her again.

'Where's the girl — in taking her nap yet?'

'Yes, she's sleeping.'

'Ach, you hadn't ought to make her sleep all the time when she's off visiting. I baked a little piece of piecrust for her. I thought I'd give it to her while it was nice and warm.'

'Oh, better not try to give her piecrust,' Ella said warningly.

'Ach, that ain't gona hurt her — nice homemade pie. Mine always et that.'

'Ja, mine did too.'

Katherine's lips closed firmly. She couldn't hurry and hurt Father and Mother — but oh, to get Phyllis home! Father — he was always trying to give the child something she shouldn't have, he wanted to spoil her as he had tried to spoil Katherine herself.... She shut her lips tight to steel herself against the pitifulness of the sudden vision of Father — getting so much older these last few years — looking like a child bereft of his toy when she had firmly taken away the things with which he had come trotting happily home for his grandchild. He had gradually drawn farther and farther away. Once he had hurt her by saying significantly, when Phyllis had wanted a pink blotter in the bank: 'You'll have to ask your mother. Maybe there's something in it to hurt you. *Grandpa* don't know.' He had wanted to take Phyllis to a little cheap circus that had come to town, to show her off and exhibit her. Mother was more sympathetic, even a little proud of retailing to the other 'ladies' how careful Katherine was in bringing up the child, what a 'nice family' Willis had. But even she was plaintive and didn't understand. Both she and Father thought that Katherine and Willis were 'carrying it too far' when they decided to have Willis teach the child until they could find the proper school for her.

She heard a little sleepy, startled voice from within the house — 'Moth-uh!'

'Uh-huh! There's somebody!' Aunt Em exclaimed delightedly.

Katherine hurried into the darkened bedroom where Phyllis lay on Aunt Em's best bedspread. The shades were down, but there was the feeling of the hot sunlight back of them. Phyllis's bare arms and legs were white and dewy. Her damp golden-brown bangs were pushed aside. Katherine knelt adoring. She began to whisper.

'Is Mother's darling awake? ... Shall we go home soon — see Father? Sleep in her own little room?' ... Her throat tightened with a homesick vision of the little room with the white bed and the yellow curtains.

They had left Grandpa alone again. Charlie and the other men were standing out beside the car, bending down and examining it, feeling of the tires, trying the handles of the doors.

Grandpa had left his chair in the yard and gone to the old wooden rocker that stood just inside the door of his room. His room was part of the old house, the one that he and Grandma had had here on the farm. It opened out upon the back yard, with a little worn, narrow plank out from the door. It looked out upon the mound of the old cyclone cellar, with its wooden door, where now Aunt Em kept her vegetables in sacks on the damp, cool floor, with moist earthen jars of plum and apple butter on the shelf against the cobwebbed wall. The little triangular chicken houses were scattered about in the back yard, and beyond them was the orchard where now small apples were only a little lighter than the vivid summer green of the heavy foliage and where little, dark, shiny bubbles of aromatic sap had oozed out from the rough, crusty bark.

The shadows in the orchard were drawing out long toward the

east, and the aisles of sunlight, too, looked longer. The groups of
people moved about more. Everything had the freshened look of
late afternoon. Grandpa rocked a little. He puffed on his pipe,
took it out and held it between his fingers. It left his lower lip
moist and shining above the fringe of silvery beard. His blue
eyes kept looking toward the orchard, in a still, fathomless gaze.
His lips moved at times.

'Ach, ja, ja, ja. . . .' A kind of mild, sighing groan. It had
pleased him that they had wanted the photograph taken, with the
little great-grandchild. But that was over now. They had left
him alone. And again, with a movement of his head, 'Ja, dot
was all so long ago.'

Beyond the orchard, beyond the dark green cornfields that lay
behind it, beyond the river and the town, beyond all the wide
western country, and the ocean . . . what were his fixed blue eyes,
intent and inward and sad, visioning now?

The rocker was framed in the doorway of his room. Even the
odor of the room was foreign. His bed with a patchwork quilt, a
little dresser, a chest of drawers. The ancient wallpaper had been
torn off and the walls calcimined a sky-blue. Against the inner
one hung his big silver watch, slowly ticking. . . . His eyes, blue,
and his hair under the little black cap, his beard, were silvery. . . .
A German text with gaudy flowers hung on a woolen cord above
the bed. '*Der Herr ist mein Hirte.*'

He started. 'Nun — who is dot?'

He did not know that little Phyllis had been watching him.
Standing outside the door, in her bright canary yellow, her
beautiful liquid brown eyes solemnly studying him. She was half
afraid. She had never seen anything so old as 'Great-grandfather.' The late afternoon sunlight shimmered in the fine
texture of his thin silvery beard. It brought out little frostings
and marks and netted lines on his old face in which the eyes were
so blue. One hand lay upon his knee. She stared wonderingly at

the knots that the knuckles made, the brownish spots, the thick veins, the queer, stretched, shiny look of the skin between the bones. She looked at his black pipe, his funny little cap, his slippers with the tufted flowers. ...

'Ach, so? You t'ink Grandpa is a funny old man, den? You want to look at him? So?'

He spoke softly. A kind of pleased smiling look came upon his face. He stretched out his hand slowly and cautiously, as if it were a butterfly poised just outside his door. A sudden longing to get this small, pretty thing nearer, an ingenuous delight, possessed him now that he was alone with her. He spoke as one speaks to a bird toward which one is carefully edging nearer, afraid that a sudden motion will startle its bright eyes and make it take wing.

'Is dis a little yellow bird? Can it sing a little song?'

A faint smile dawned on the serious parted lips. He nodded at her. She seemed to have come a little closer. He, too, looked in wonderment, as he had done before, at the shining hair, the fragile blue veins on the white temples, the moist, pearly white of the little neck, marveling as he would have marveled at some beautiful strange bird that might have alighted a moment on his doorstep. ...

'Can't sing a little song? No? Den Grandpa will have to sing one to you.'

He had been thinking of songs as he sat here, they had been murmuring somewhere in his mind. Old, old songs that he had known long ago in the old country. ... His little visitor stood quite still as his faint, quavering voice sounded with a kind of dim sweetness in the sunshine. ...

'Du, du liegst mir im Herzen,
Du, du liegst mir im Sinn,
Du, du machst mir viel Schmerzen,
Weist nicht wie gut ich dir bin —
Ja, ja, ja, ja, weist nicht wie gut ich dir bin.'

The gaze of her brown, shining eyes never wavered, and a soft glow of fascinated interest grew in them as the sad wailing simplicity of the old tune quavered on the summer air. For a moment she was quite near, they understood each other.

'You like dot? Like Grandpa's song?'

She nodded. A tiny pleased smile curved her fresh lips.

Then suddenly, with a little delicate scared movement, as if after all she had discovered that the place was strange, she flitted away to her mother.

THE RETURN[1]

SHERWOOD ANDERSON

EIGHTEEN years. Well, he was driving a good car, an expensive roadster, he was well clad, a rather solid, fine-looking man, not too heavy. When he had left the Middle-Western town to go live in New York City he was twenty-two, and now, on his way back there, he was forty. He drove toward the town from the east, stopping for lunch at another town ten miles away.

When he went away from Caxton, after his mother died, he used to write letters to friends at home, but after several months the replies began to come with less and less frequency. On the day when he sat eating his lunch at a small hotel in the town ten miles east of Caxton he suddenly thought of the reason, and was ashamed. 'Am I going back there on this visit for the same reason I wrote the letters?' he asked himself. For a moment he thought he might not go on. There was still time to turn back.

Outside, in the principal business street of the town, people were walking about. The sun shone warmly. Although he had lived for so many years in New York, he had always kept, buried

---

[1] From *The Century Magazine.* Copyright, 1925, by The Century Company. Copyright, 1926, by Sherwood Anderson.

away in him somewhere, a hankering for his own country. All the day before he had been driving through the eastern Ohio country, crossing many small streams, running down through small valleys, seeing the white farmhouses set back from the road, and the big red barns.

The elders were still in bloom along the fences, boys were swimming in a creek, the wheat had been cut, and now the corn was shoulder-high. Everywhere the drone of bees; in patches of woodland along the road a heavy, mysterious silence.

Now, however, he began thinking of something else. Shame crept over him. 'When I first left Caxton, I wrote letters back to my boyhood friends there, but I wrote always of myself. When I had written a letter telling what I was doing in the city, what friends I was making, what my prospects were, I put, at the very end of the letter, perhaps, a little inquiry. "I hope you are well. How are things going with you?" Something of that sort.'

The returning native — his name was John Holden — had grown very uneasy. After eighteen years it seemed to him he could see, lying before him, one of the letters written eighteen years before when he had first come into the strange Eastern city. His mother's brother, a successful architect in the city, had given him such and such an opportunity: he had been at the theater to see Mansfield as *Brutus*, he had taken the night boat upriver to Albany with his aunt; there were two very handsome girls on the boat.

Everything then must have been in the same tone. His uncle had given him a rare opportunity, and he had taken advantage of it. In time he had also become a successful architect. In New York City there were certain great buildings, two or three skyscrapers, several huge industrial plants, any number of handsome and expensive residences, that were the products of his brain.

When it came down to the scratch, John Holden had to admit that his uncle had not been excessively fond of him. It had just

happened that his aunt and uncle had no children of their own.
He did his work in the office well and carefully, had developed a
certain rather striking knack for design. The aunt had liked him
better. She had always tried to think of him as her own son, had
treated him as a son. Sometimes she called him son. Once or
twice, after his uncle died, he had a notion. His aunt was a good
woman, but sometimes he thought she would rather have enjoyed having him, John Holden, go in a bit more for wickedness,
go a little on the loose, now and then. He never did anything she
had to forgive him for. Perhaps she hungered for the opportunity
to forgive.

Odd thoughts, eh? Well, what was a fellow to do? One had
but the one life to live. One had to think of oneself.

Botheration! John Holden had rather counted on the trip
back to Caxton, had really counted on it more than he realized.
It was a bright summer day. He had been driving for days over
the mountains of Pennsylvania, through New York State,
through eastern Ohio. Gertrude, his wife, had died during the
summer before, and his one son, a lad of twelve, had gone away
for the summer to a boys' camp in Vermont.

The idea had just come to him. 'I'll drive the car along slowly
through the country, drinking it in. I need a rest, time to think.
What I really need is to renew old acquaintances. I'll go back to
Caxton and stay several days. I'll see Herman and Frank and
Joe. Then I'll go call on Lillian and Kate. What a lot of fun,
really!' It might just be that when he got to Caxton, the Caxton
ball team would be playing a game, say with a team from Yerington. Lillian might go to the game with him. It was in his mind
faintly that Lillian had never married. How did he know that?
He had heard nothing from Caxton for many years. The ball
game would be in Heffler's field, and he and Lillian would go out
there, walking under the maple trees along Turner Street, past
the old stave factory, then in the dust of the road, past where

the sawmill used to stand, and on into the field itself. He would be carrying a sunshade over Lillian's head, and Bob French would be standing at the gate where you went into the field and charging the people twenty-five cents to see the game.

Well, it would not be Bob; his son, perhaps. There would be something very nice in the notion of Lillian's going off to a ball game that way with an old sweetheart. A crowd of boys, women, and men, going through a cattle gate into Heffler's field, tramping through the dust, young men with their sweethearts, a few gray-haired women, mothers of boys who belonged to the team, Lillian and he sitting in the rickety grandstand in the hot sun.

Once it had been — how they had felt, he and Lillian, sitting there together! It had been rather hard to keep the attention centered on the players in the field. One couldn't ask a neighbor, 'Who's ahead now, Caxton or Yerington?' Lillian's hands lay in her lap. What white, delicate, expressive hands they were! Once — that was just before he went away to live in the city with his uncle and but a month after his mother died — he and Lillian went to the ball field together at night. His father had died when he was a young lad, and he had no relatives left in the town. Going off to the ball field at night was maybe a risky thing for Lillian to do — risky for her reputation if anyone found it out — but she had seemed willing enough. You know how small-town girls of that age are?

Her father owned a retail shoe store in Caxton and was a good, respectable man; but the Holdens — John's father had been a lawyer.

After they got back from the ball field that night — it must have been after midnight — they went to sit on the front porch before her father's house. He must have known. A daughter cavorting about half the night with a young man that way! They had clung to each other with a sort of queer, desperate feeling neither understood. She did not go into the house until

after three o'clock, and went then only because he insisted. He
hadn't wanted to ruin her reputation. Why, he might have ——
She was like a little frightened child at the thought of his going
away. He was twenty-two then, and she must have been about
eighteen.

Eighteen and twenty-two are forty. John Holden was forty
on the day when he sat at lunch at the hotel in the town ten
miles from Caxton.

Now, he thought, he might be able to walk through the streets
of Caxton to the ball park with Lillian with a certain effect. You
know how it is. One has to accept the fact that youth is gone. If
there should turn out to be such a ball game and Lillian would go
with him, he would leave the car in the garage and ask her to
walk. One saw pictures of that sort of thing in the movies — a
man coming back to his native village after twenty years; a new
beauty taking the place of the beauty of youth — something like
that. In the spring the leaves on maple trees are lovely, but they
are even more lovely in the fall — a flame of color; manhood and
womanhood.

After he had finished his lunch John did not feel very comfortable. The road to Caxton — it used to take nearly three
hours to travel the distance with a horse and buggy, but now,
and without any effort, the distance could be made in twenty
minutes.

He lit a cigar and went for a walk not in the streets of Caxton,
but in the streets of the town ten miles away. If he got to Caxton
in the evening, just at dusk, say, now ——

With an inward pang John realized that he wanted darkness,
the kindliness of soft evening lights. Lillian, Joe, Herman, and
the rest. It had been eighteen years for the others as well as for
himself. Now he had succeeded, a little, in twisting his fear of
Caxton into fear for the others, and it made him feel somewhat
better; but at once he realized what he was doing and again felt

uncomfortable. One had to look out for changes, new people, new buildings, middle-aged people grown old, youth grown middle-aged. At any rate, he was thinking of the other now; he wasn't, as when he wrote letters home eighteen years before, thinking only of himself. 'Am I?' It was a question.

An absurd situation, really. He had sailed along so gaily through upper New York State, through western Pennsylvania, through eastern Ohio. Men were at work in the fields and in the towns, farmers drove into towns in their cars, clouds of dust arose on some distant road, seen across a valley. Once he had stopped his car near a bridge and gone for a walk along the banks of a creek where it wound through a wood.

He was liking people. Well, he had never before given much time to people, to thinking of them and their affairs. 'I hadn't time,' he told himself. He had always realized that, while he was a good enough architect, things move fast in America. New men were coming on. He couldn't take chances of going on forever on his uncle's reputation. A man had to be always on the alert. Fortunately, his marriage had been a help. It had made valuable connections for him.

Twice he had picked up people on the road. There was a lad of sixteen from some town of eastern Pennsylvania, working his way westward toward the Pacific coast by picking up rides in cars — a summer's adventure. John had carried him all of one day and had listened to his talk with keen pleasure. And so this was the younger generation. The boy had nice eyes and an eager, friendly manner. He smoked cigarettes, and once, when they had a puncture, he was very quick and eager about changing the tire. 'Now, don't you soil your hands, Mister; I can do it like a flash,' he said, and he did. The boy said he intended working his way overland to the Pacific coast, where he would try to get a job of some kind on an ocean freighter, and that, if he did, he would go on around the world. 'But do you speak any foreign languages?' The boy did not. Across John Holden's mind flashed pictures of hot Eastern deserts, crowded Asiatic towns, wild half-savage mountain countries. As a young architect, and before his uncle died, he had spent two years in foreign travel, studying building in many countries; but he said nothing of this thought to the boy. Vast plans entered into with eager, boyish abandon, a world tour undertaken as he, when a young man, might have undertaken to find his way from his uncle's house in East Eighty-First Street downtown to the Battery. 'How do I know — perhaps he will do it,' John thought. The day in company with the boy had been very pleasant, and he had been on the alert to pick him up again the next morning; but the boy had gone on his way, had caught a ride with some earlier riser. Why hadn't John invited him to his hotel for the night? The notion hadn't come to him until too late.

Youth, rather wild and undisciplined, running wild, eh? I wonder why I never did it, never wanted to do it.

If he had been a bit wilder, more reckless — that night, that time when he and Lillian —— 'It's all right being reckless with yourself, but when someone else is involved, a young girl in a small town, you yourself lighting out' — He remembered sharply that on the night, long before, as he sat with Lillian on the porch before her father's house his hand — It had seemed as though Lillian, on that evening, might not have objected to anything he wanted to do. He had thought — well, he had thought of the consequences. Women must be protected by men, all that sort of thing. Lillian had seemed rather stunned when he walked away, even though it was three o'clock in the morning. She had been rather like a person waiting at a railroad station for the coming of a train. There is a blackboard, and a strange man comes out and writes on it, 'Train Number 287 has been discontinued' — something like that.

Well, it had been all right, everything had been all right.

Later, four years later, he had married a New York woman of good family. Even in a city like New York, where there are so many people, her family had been well known. They had connections.

After marriage, sometimes, it is true, he had wondered. Gertrude used to look at him sometimes with an odd light in her eyes. That boy he picked up in the road — once during the day when he said something to the boy, the same queer look came into his eyes. It would be rather upsetting if one knew that the boy had purposely avoided him next morning. There had been Gertrude's cousin. Once, after his marriage, John heard a rumor that Gertrude had wanted to marry that cousin, but of course he had said nothing to her. Why should he have? She was his wife. There had been, he had heard, a good deal of family objection to the cousin. He was reputed to be wild, a gambler and drinker.

Once the cousin came to the Holden apartment at two in the morning, drunk and demanding that he be allowed to see Gertrude, and she slipped on a dressing-gown and went down to him. That was in the hallway of the apartment, downstairs, where almost anyone might have come in and seen her. As a matter of fact, the elevator boy and the janitor did see her. She had stood in the hallway below talking for nearly an hour. What about? He had never asked Gertrude directly, and she had never told him anything. When she came upstairs again and had got into her bed, he lay in his own bed trembling, but remained silent. He had been afraid that if he spoke he might say something rude; better keep still. The cousin had disappeared. John had a suspicion that Gertrude later supplied him with money. He went out West somewhere.

Now Gertrude was dead. She had always seemed very well, but suddenly she was attacked by a baffling kind of slow fever that lasted nearly a year. Sometimes she seemed about to get better, and then suddenly the fever grew worse. It might be that she did not want to live. What a notion! John had been at the bed-side with the doctor when she died. It was at night, and as the boy was asleep, he was not called. There was something of the same feeling he had had that night of his youth when he went with Lillian to the ball field, an odd sense of futility, of inadequacy. There was no doubt that in some subtle way both women had ac-cused him.

Of what? There had always been, in some vague, indefinable way, a kind of accusation in the attitude toward him of his uncle, the architect, and of his aunt. They had left him their money, but —— It was as though the uncle had said, as though Lillian during that night long ago had said ——

Had they all said the same thing, and was Gertrude his wife saying it as she lay dying? A smile. 'You have always taken such good care of yourself, haven't you, John, dear? You have ob-served the rules. You have taken no chances for yourself or the others.' She had actually said something of that sort to him once in a moment of anger.

II

In the small town ten miles from Caxton there wasn't any park to which a man could go to sit. If one stayed about the hotel, someone from Caxton might come in. 'Hello, what are you doing here?' It would be inconvenient to explain: 'I didn't want to go to Caxton in the daylight. I want the kindliness of evening light for myself and the people I may see there.'

John Holden's boy — he was but twelve — one might say his character had not begun to form yet. One felt in him sometimes a sort of unconscious and casual selfishness, an unawareness of others, a rather unhealthy sharpness about getting the best of others. It was a thing that should be corrected in him and at once. John Holden had got himself into a small panic. 'I must write him a letter at once. Such a habit gets fixed in a boy and then in the man, and it cannot later be shaken off. There are such a lot of people living in the world! Every man and woman has his own point of view. To be civilized, really, is to be aware of the others, their hopes, their gladness, their disillusionments in life.'

John Holden was now walking along a residence street of a small Ohio town composing in fancy a letter to his son in the boys' camp up in Vermont. He was a man who wrote to his son every day. 'I think a man should,' he told himself. 'One should remember that now the boy has no mother.'

He had come to an outlying railroad station. It was neat, with grass and flowers growing in a round bed in the very center of a lawn. Some man, the station agent and telegraph operator, perhaps, passed him and went inside the station. John followed him in. On the wall of the waiting-room there was a framed copy of the timetable, and he stood studying it. A train went to Caxton at five. Another train came from Caxton and passed through the town he was now in at seven-forty-three, the seven-nineteen out of Caxton. The man in the small business section of the station opened a sliding panel and looked at him. The two men just stared at each other without speaking, and then the panel was slid shut again.

John looked at his watch. Two-twenty-eight. At about six he could drive over to Caxton and dine at the hotel there. After he had dined, it would be evening, and people would be coming into the main street.

The seven-nineteen would come in. When John was a lad, sometimes, he, Joe, Herman, and often several other lads climbed on the front of the baggage- or mail-car and stole a ride to the very town he was now in. What a thrill, crouched down in the gathering darkness on the platform as the train ran the ten miles, the car rocking from side to side! When it got a little dark, in the fall or spring, the fields beside the track were lighted up when the fireman opened his firebox to throw in coal. Once John saw a rabbit running along in the glare of light beside the track. He could have reached down and caught it with his hand. In the neighboring town the boys went into saloons and played pool and drank beer. They could depend upon catching a ride back home on the local freight that got to Caxton at about ten-thirty. On one of the adventures John and Herman got drunk, and Joe had to help them into an empty coal car and later get them out at Caxton. Herman got sick, and when they were getting off the freight at Caxton, he stumbled and came very near falling under the wheels of the moving train. John wasn't as drunk as Herman. When the others weren't looking, he had poured several of the glasses of beer into a spittoon. In Caxton he and Joe had to walk about with Herman for several hours, and when John finally got home, his mother was still awake and was worried. He had to lie to her. 'I drove out into the country with Herman, and a wheel broke. We had to walk home.' The reason Joe could carry his beer so well was because he was German. His father owned the town meat market, and the family had beer on the table at home. No wonder it did not knock him out as it did Herman and John.

There was a bench at the side of the railroad station, in the shade, and John sat there for a long time — two hours, three hours. Why hadn't he brought a book? In fancy he composed a letter to his son and in it he spoke of the fields lying beside the road outside the town of Caxton, of his greeting old friends there, of things that had happened when he was a boy. He even spoke of his former sweetheart, of Lillian. If he now thought out just what he was going to say in the letter, he could write it in his room at the hotel over in Caxton in a few minutes without having to stop and think what he was going to say. You can't always be too fussy about what you say to a young boy. Really, sometimes, you should take him into your confidence, into your life, make him a part of your life.

It was six-twenty when John drove into Caxton and went to the hotel, where he registered, and was shown to a room. On the street as he drove into town he saw Billy Baker, who, when he was a young man, had a paralyzed leg that dragged along the sidewalk when he walked. Now he was getting old; his face seemed wrinkled and faded, like a dried lemon, and his clothes had spots down the front. People, even sick people, live a long time in small Ohio towns. It is surprising how they hang on.

John had put his car, of a rather expensive make, into a garage beside the hotel. Formerly, in his day, the building had been used as a livery-barn. There used to be pictures of famous trotting and pacing horses on the walls of the little office at the front. Old Dave Grey, who owned race-horses of his own, ran the livery-barn then, and John occasionally hired a rig there. He hired a rig and took Lillian for a ride into the country, along moonlit roads. By a lonely farmhouse a dog barked. Sometimes they drove along a little dirt road lined with elders and stopped the horse. How still everything was! What a queer feeling they had! They couldn't talk. Sometimes they sat in silence thus, very near each other, for a long, long time. Once they got out of the buggy, having tied the horse to the fence, and walked in a newly cut hayfield. The cut hay lay all about in little cocks. John wanted to lie on one of the haycocks with Lillian, but did not dare suggest it.

At the hotel John ate his dinner in silence. There wasn't even a traveling salesman in the dining-room, and presently the proprietor's wife came and stood by his table to talk with him. They had a good many tourists, but this just happened to be a quiet day. Dull days came that way in the hotel business. The woman's husband was a traveling man and had bought the hotel to give his wife something to keep her interested while he was on the road. He was away from home so much! They had come to Caxton from Pittsburgh.

After he had dined, John went up to his room, and presently

the woman followed. The door leading into the hall had been left open, and she came and stood in the doorway. Really, she was rather handsome. She only wanted to be sure that everything was all right, that he had towels and soap and everything he needed.

For a time she lingered by the door talking of the town.

'It's a good little town. General Hurst is buried here. You should drive out to the cemetery and see the statue.' He wondered who General Hurst was. In what war had he fought? Odd that he hadn't remembered about him. The town had a piano factory, and there was a watch company from Cincinnati talking of putting up a plant. 'They figure there is less chance of labor trouble in a small town like this.'

The woman went, going reluctantly. As she was going along the hallway she stopped once and looked back. There was something a little queer. They were both self-conscious. 'I hope you'll be comfortable,' she said. At forty a man did not come home to his own home town to start —— A traveling man's wife, eh? Well! Well!

At seven-forty-five John went out for a walk on Main Street and almost at once he met Tom Ballard, who at once recognized him, a fact that pleased Tom. He bragged about it. 'Once I see a face, I never forget. Well! Well!' When John was twenty-two Tom must have been about fifteen. His father was the leading doctor of the town. He took John in tow, walked back with him toward the hotel. He kept exclaiming: 'I knew you at once. You haven't changed much, really.'

Tom was in his turn a doctor, and there was about him something —— Right away John guessed what it was. They went up into John's room, and John, having in his bag a bottle of whiskey, poured Tom a drink, which he took somewhat too eagerly, John thought. There was talk. After Tom had taken the drink he sat on the edge of the bed still holding the bottle John had passed to him. Herman was running a dray now. He had married Kit Small and had five kids. Joe was working for the International Harvester Company. 'I don't know whether he's in town now or not. He's a trouble-shooter, a swell mechanic, a good fellow,' Tom said. They drank again.

As for Lillian, mentioned with an air of being casual by John, he, John, knew of course that she had been married and divorced. There was some sort of trouble about another man   Her husband married again later, and now she lived with her mother, her father, the shoe merchant, having died. Tom spoke somewhat guardedly, as though protecting a friend.

'I guess she's all right now, going straight and all. Good thing she never had any kids. She's a little nervous and queer; has lost her looks a good deal.'

The two men went downstairs and, walking along Main Street, got into a car belonging to the doctor.

'I'll take you for a little ride,' Tom said; but as he was about to pull away from the curb where the car had been parked, he turned and smiled at his passenger. 'We ought to celebrate a little, account of your coming back here,' he said. 'What do you say to a quart?'

John handed him a ten-dollar bill, and he disappeared into a near-by drugstore. When he came back he laughed.

'I used your name all right. They didn't recognize it. In the prescription I wrote out I said you had a general breakdown, that you needed to be built up. I recommended that you take a teaspoonful three times a day. Lord! my prescription book is getting almost empty.' The drugstore belonged to a man named Will Bennett. 'You remember him, maybe. He's Ed Bennett's son; married Carrie Wyatt.' The names were but dim things in John's mind. 'This man is going to get drunk. He is going to try to get me drunk, too,' he thought.

When they had turned out of Main Street and into Walnut

Street they stopped midway between two street lights and had
another drink, John holding the bottle to his lips, but putting his
tongue over the opening. He remembered the evenings with Joe
and Herman when he had secretly poured his beer into a spittoon.
He felt cold and lonely. Walnut Street was one along which he
used to walk, coming home late at night from Lillian's house. He
remembered people who then lived along the street, and a list of
names began running through his head. Often the names remained, but did not call up images of people. They were just
names. He hoped the doctor would not turn the car into the
street in which the Holdens had lived. Lillian had lived over in
another part of town, in what was called 'the Red House District.' Just why it had been called that John did not know.

III

They drove silently along, up a small hill, and came to the edge
of town, going south. Stopping before a house that had evidently
been built since John's time, Tom sounded his horn.

'Didn't the fairground use to stand about here?' John asked.
The doctor turned and nodded his head.

'Yes, just here,' he said. He kept on sounding his horn, and a
man and woman came out of the house and stood in the road beside the car.

'Let's get Maud and Alf and all go over to Lylse's Point,'
Tom said. He had indeed taken John into tow. For a time John
wondered if he was to be introduced. 'We got some hooch.
Meet John Holden; used to live here years ago.' At the fairground, when John was a lad, Dave Grey, the livery-man, used
to work out his race-horses in the early morning. Herman, who
was a horse enthusiast, who then dreamed of some day becoming
a horseman, came often to John's house in the early morning, and
the two boys went off to the fairground without breakfast. Herman had got some sandwiches made of slices of bread and cold

meat out of his mother's pantry. They went 'cross-lots, climbing fences and eating the sandwiches. In a meadow they had to cross there was heavy dew on the grass, and the meadow larks flew up before them. Herman had at least come somewhere near expressing in his life his youthful passion: he still lived about horses; he owned a dray. With a little inward qualm John wondered. Perhaps Herman ran a motor truck.

The man and woman got into the car, the woman on the back seat with John, the husband in front with Tom, and they drove away to another house. John could not keep track of the streets they passed through. Occasionally he asked the woman, 'What street are we in now?' They were joined by Maud and Alf, who also crowded into the back seat. Maud was a slender woman of twenty-eight or thirty, with yellow hair and blue eyes, and at once she seemed determined to make up to John. 'I don't take more than an inch of room,' she said, laughing and squeezing herself in between John and the first woman, whose name he could not later remember.

He rather liked Maud. When the car had been driven some eighteen miles along a gravel road, they came to Lylse's farmhouse, which had been converted into a roadhouse, and got out. Maud had been silent most of the way, but she sat very close to John, and as he felt cold and lonely, he was grateful for the warmth of her slender body. Occasionally she spoke to him in a half-whisper. 'Ain't the night swell! Gee! I like it out in the dark this way.'

Lylse's Point was at a bend of the Samson River, a small stream to which John as a lad had occasionally gone on fishing excursions with his father. Later he went out there several times with crowds of young fellows and their girls. They drove out then in Grey's old bus, and the trip out and back took several hours. On the way home at night they had great fun singing at the top of their voices and waking sleeping farmers along the road. Occasionally some of the party got out and walked for a ways. It was a chance for a fellow to kiss his girl when the others could not see. By hurrying a little, they could later easily enough catch up with the bus.

A rather heavy-faced Italian named Francisco owned Lylse's, and it had a dance hall and dining-room. Drinks could be had if you knew the ropes, and it was evident the doctor and his friends were old acquaintances. At once they declared John should not buy anything, the declaration, in fact, being made before he had offered. 'You're our guest, now; don't you forget that. When we come sometime to your town, then it will be all right,' Tom said. He laughed. 'And that makes me think. I forgot your change,' he said, handing John a five-dollar bill. The whiskey got at the drugstore had been consumed on the way out, all except John and Maud drinking heartily. 'I don't like the stuff. Do you, Mr. Holden?' Maud said, and giggled. Twice during the trip out her fingers had crept over and touched lightly his fingers, and each time she had apologized. 'Oh, do excuse me!' she said. John felt a little as he had felt earlier in the evening when the woman of the hotel had come to stand at the door of his room and had seemed reluctant about going away.

After they got out of the car at Lylse's, he felt uncomfortably old and queer. 'What am I doing here with these people?' he kept asking himself. When they had got into the light, he stole a look at his watch. It was not yet nine o'clock. Several other cars, most of them, the doctor explained, from Yerington, stood before the door, and when they had taken several drinks of rather mild Italian red wine, all of the party except Maud and John went into the dance hall to dance. The doctor took John aside and whispered to him. 'Lay off Maud,' he said. He explained hurriedly that Alf and Maud had been having a row and that for several days they had not spoken to each other, although they lived in the same house, ate at the same table, and slept in the same bed.

'He thinks she gets too gay with men,' Tom explained. 'You better look out a little.'

The woman and man sat on a bench under a tree on the lawn before the house, and when the others had danced, they came out, bringing more drinks. Tom had got some more whiskey. 'It's moon, but pretty good stuff,' he declared. In the clear sky overhead stars were shining, and when the others were dancing, John turned his head and saw across the road and between the trees that lined its banks the stars reflected in the water of the Samson. A light from the house fell on Maud's face, a rather strikingly lovely face in that light, but when looked at closely, rather petulant. 'A good deal of the spoiled child in her,' John thought.

She began asking him about life in the city of New York.

'I was there once, but for only three days. It was when I went to school in the East. A girl I knew lived there. She married a lawyer named Trigan, or something like that. You didn't know him, I guess.'

And now there was a hungry, dissatisfied look on her face.

'God! I'd like to live in a place like that, not in this hole! There hadn't no man better tempt me.' When she said that she giggled again. Once during the evening they walked across the dusty road and stood for a time by the river's edge, but got back to the bench before the others had finished their dance. Maud persistently refused to dance.

At ten-thirty, all of the others having got a little drunk, they drove back to town, Maud again sitting beside John. On the drive Alf went to sleep. Maud pressed her slender body against John's, and after two or three futile moves to which he made no special response, she boldly put her hand into his. The second woman and her husband talked with Tom of people they had seen at Lylse's. 'Do you think there's anything up between Fanny and Joe? No; I think she's on the square.'

They got to John's hotel at eleven-thirty, and bidding them all good night, he went upstairs. Alf had awakened. When they were parting, he leaned out of the car and looked closely at John. 'What did you say your name was?' he asked.

John went up a dark stairway and sat on the bed in his room. Lillian had lost her looks. She had married, and her husband had divorced her. Joe was a trouble-shooter. He worked for the International Harvester Company, a swell mechanic. Herman was a drayman. He had five kids.

Three men in a room next John's were playing poker. They laughed and talked, and their voices came clearly to John. 'You think so, do you? Well, I'll prove you're wrong.' A mild quarrel began. As it was summer, the windows of John's room were open, and he went to one to stand, looking out. A moon had come up, and he could see down into an alleyway. Two men came out of a street and stood in the alleyway, whispering. After they left, two cats crept along a roof and began a love-making scene. The game in the next room broke up. John could hear voices in the hallway.

'Now, forget it. I tell you, you're both wrong.' John thought of his son at the camp up in Vermont. 'I haven't written him a letter today.' He felt guilty.

Opening his bag, he took out paper and sat down to write; but after two or three attempts gave it up and put the paper away again. How fine the night had been as he sat on the bench beside the woman at Lylse's! Now the woman was in bed with her husband. They were not speaking to each other.

'Could I do it?' John asked himself, and then, for the first time that evening, a smile came to his lips.

'Why not?' he asked himself.

With his bag in his hand he went down the dark hallway and into the hotel office and began pounding on a desk. A fat old man with thin red hair and sleep-heavy eyes appeared from somewhere. John explained.

'I can't sleep. I think I'll drive on. I want to get to Pittsburgh and as I can't sleep, I might as well be driving.' He paid his bill.

Then he asked the clerk to go and arouse the man in the garage, and gave him an extra dollar. 'If I need gas, is there any place open?' he asked, but evidently the man did not hear. Perhaps he thought the question absurd.

He stood in the moonlight on the sidewalk before the door of the hotel and heard the clerk pounding on a door. Presently voices were heard, and the headlights of his car shone. The car appeared, driven by a boy. He seemed very alive and alert.

'I saw you out to Lylse's,' he said, and, without being asked, went to look at the tank. 'You're all right; you got 'most eight gallons,' he assured John as he climbed into the driver's seat.

How friendly the car, how friendly the night! John was not one who enjoyed fast driving, but he went out of the town at very high speed. 'You go down two blocks, turn to your right, and go three. There you hit the cement. Go right straight to the east. You can't miss it.'

John was taking the turns at racing speed. At the edge of town someone shouted to him from the darkness, but he did not stop. He hungered to get into the road going east.

'I'll let her out,' he thought. 'Lord! It will be fun! I'll let her out.'

AN ARMY WITH BANNERS[1]

KATHARINE FULLERTON GEROULD

Lewis Hunting, like thousands of other young Americans, was a bond salesman. He had a kind of wayward handsomeness that endeared him to women, together with a deep voice and a gravely pleasant manner — both purely physical attributes — which prevented his good looks getting on the nerves of the men he dealt with. He was moderately successful in business, was always well dressed and provided with the comforts of life. A good many of those comforts, naturally, went into his expense account; but when he was not traveling, he lived with his widowed mother, whom he partly supported, in a commonplace but not uncomfortable suburban house. His mother, who adored him, accepted everything he would give her as the reward for her adoration. His father had hoped to send Lewis to a good technical school, but he died at an unlucky moment for Lewis — at the precise time, that is, when Lewis had finished his high-school course and could be considered old enough to earn his living. College would have meant sacrifices on his mother's part which she would have thought unnatural when she

---

[1] From *Harper's Magazine*. Copyright, 1925, by Harper & Brothers. Copyright, 1926, by Katharine Fullerton Gerould.

had a son who was six feet tall. Lewis also would have thought them unnatural — for *his* mother; though he saw the mothers of other young men moving into apartments and doing their own work without thereby disfiguring the noble countenance of Nature.

Lewis Hunting was no moralist. He had to work, and he did work. He was much away from home, and he fell into a few casual adventures that would have shocked his mother hopelessly. These adventures were very few, however; not because Lewis minded doing things that would have shocked his mother, had she known about them, but because even near-dissipation costs money; and he never forgot that his financial margin was hers, not his own. The adventures were fairly sordid, as the limited contacts offered to a young man in strange cities are apt to make them, and his cynicism was deepened by them. In his later twenties Lewis was living about as lonely an existence as a young bond salesman can. When he was at the home office, he spent most of his evenings with his mother (she complained a great deal of loneliness) — reading, talking, or listening to her phonograph. When he was abroad in the land — which was most of the year — he mitigated the solitude of hotel rooms with visits to movie theaters or poolrooms. Mild flirtations he could find anywhere, owing to his good looks and engaging smile; but he was very wary of anything more intimate or dramatic. He knew very little about women, though he considered that he had plumbed female psychology with an unerring lead line. Most women, he decided, were on the make and no good. Girls he had known at school, who had married his more prosperous comrades, seemed — unless they were sunk invisibly into nurseries — as shameless as the others. One or two of them, indeed, made love to him; and that shocked Lewis almost as much as it would have shocked Mrs. Hunting.

You see him, then — young, bewildered, faintly unhappy, and

vaguely aspiring beneath the cynicism that kept its visible smoothness in the face of the smuttiest story or the most shameless of feminine advances. The fact was that Lewis would have expanded most naturally in the society of the nicest people, and he never met them. Mrs. Hunting made it a virtue to be too delicate and too sorrowful for social contacts, and he had no relations that would have knit him up, in this or that city, with the local aristocracy. He was diffident with men who had been through college — probably no one ever knew how he had grieved over the frustration of his and his father's hopes — and his diffidence took the form of refusing, with such, to mix business and pleasure. So even old customers, once rebuffed, did not ask him to their homes. Being, on the whole, irreligious, he eschewed all sociabilities that had a sectarian tinge.

Not a very strong person to stand up against circumstances or events or other people's desires. That cynicism of his, after all, was only skin-deep, and the boy beneath was soft. When Netta Jacobs decided to marry him, he was virtually helpless, for Netta was not only supple and alluring — she was clever. When I say clever, I do not mean to praise her understanding or her wit. She was clever like a very clever animal; she had the instinct of self-preservation so strongly developed that she selected without difficulty the tone, the gesture, the look that would serve her purpose. She was a finished egotist, if you like, though 'egotist' seems too big a word for her. It implies cerebration, and Netta had no cerebration. She had the protective coloring of the white ermine, the adaptability of the giraffe that can lengthen its neck to crop the topmost leaves, of the creature that has developed a lung fit to breathe both air and water. Only, unluckily, she was neither giraffe nor fish; she was human and capable of passion — of that complicated emotion which does not afflict the lower mammals. The lion stalking his prey is far less terrible than the person who wants to possess another human being, not only physically and financially, but socially, mentally, and morally. Netta never put it to herself in that way, but it was so. She fell in love with Lewis Hunting, and her whole organism set itself automatically to the task of acquiring him. It is not often that one person desires another with the totality of his being. Thus Netta desired Lewis. She had no moral sense; but if she had had one, that too would have clung to him. Lewis, of course, had not the faintest chance against her; and between the hour when he first saw her in Jere Wheaton's office, and the hour of the wedding among dusty palms and withering blossoms in the living-room of her married sister's apartment, only four months elapsed.

They lived with Lewis's mother in the not uncomfortable suburban house. Netta intended to change all that; but the best-equipped organism recognizes impossibilities — temporary ones. In order to get his mother to consent to the marriage at all, Lewis had had to make absurd and vast concessions. She made it clear to him that if he chucked her and married without her consent, he would literally end her life. Besides, there was the question of money. Either Netta would have to live with Mrs. Hunting, or Mrs. Hunting would have to go to a cheap boarding-house. Netta, who would not have cared in the least if Mrs. Hunting had had to live in a Salvation Army Home or the State penitentiary, realized that she would have to give in. For the time being, Lewis was not yet completely her creature, and you might as well ask him to break a blood vessel as to turn his mother by force out of her home. Nothing would be easier for her than to make — after marriage — the situation impossible.

That, of course, she proceeded to do, though it took a fairly long time on account of Lewis's protracted absences from home. Given Mrs. Hunting, it was quite easy. Lewis's mother, deprived of her dominance, was acutely uncomfortable. She hated Netta, she thought Lewis deluded and doomed, and she kept herself within bounds only because she knew she was playing a losing game. If Netta had been a gentle soul, Mrs. Hunting would probably have made her supremely unhappy. Netta was not a gentle soul, and she made Mrs. Hunting unhappy instead. When Lewis was at home, both women made him feel them pathetic — suffering untold things for love of him. Netta managed that, too, better than her mother-in-law.

A year, two years wore away, and Lewis began to know despair. Netta was all his, and her kisses made it clear. But she hated his mother, she hated their mode of existence; she was moving slowly but surely to the total elimination of Mrs. Hunting from their lives. So much, for a time, was he Netta's that if she had asked anything less, she might have had it. But what she asked of him, he felt, was to kill his mother. Even for Netta he could not slay. And there came, inevitably, a time when he criticized her for asking him to.

They had it out at last, one evening in their own room, when he was just back from a month's trip in the South. Lewis, who had been listening to mocking-birds and smelling cape jessamine — his sojourns were seldom in such romantic lands — came back with reawakened yearnings, the old hope of beauty revivified in his foolish heart, to find his home uglier than ever. His mother was querulous and plain, and his wife — though she caught him to her breast in greeting and let her bright eyes and hair shimmer above him, he was ravished again — seemed hard, for all the cheaply perfumed softness of her body. He felt that there was no kindness in her, and wondered, for the first time, if Netta would ever develop that tenderness which is the loveliest by-product of passion.

Lewis bent over his suitcase, unpacking things and flinging them about; while Netta, standing between the twin beds, removed and folded counterpanes and pillow covers and wound the clock on the bed-table. Little, intimate, beloved gestures ... but somehow tonight he did not love them. If he closed his tired eyes, he could smell the jessamine. Netta's rustlings forbade him to hear the mocking-bird.

He straightened himself finally and snapped the suitcase shut. Netta came towards him in all the luxury of orchid négligée and cap.

'Tired, honey?' She stretched her arms and yawned a little.

The answer to that was 'No.' If he said 'Yes,' she would be close to him, enfolding him, comforting him, making him forget everything but the physical fact of her. That, he did not wish. 'I've got a beastly headache,' he said quietly.

The barrier was now built between them, and she walked away to her dressing-table. 'Want some aspirin?' she asked over her shoulder.

'No, thanks.' Lewis often made these little mistakes. By his refusal of aspirin he revealed to her that he had no headache.

'Oh — just cross.'

'Isn't it enough to make anybody cross — the kind of thing I come back to?'

'I'm very sorry you have to come back to it, Lewis. But you would have it that way, you know.'

'You certainly don't try to make it any better.'

'You'd better drop that right now,' she warned him. 'It doesn't seem to occur to you that, at least, when you come back to it, I'm here. I live with it, weeks on end, when you aren't here.'

'If you mean, Net, that it's all mother's fault, you're wrong. She wasn't like this until you came and made her so. What makes the house so deadly is that you quarrel with her all the time. I'm always having to apologize to one of you for the other. I'm about fed up with it.'

'Oh, you are, are you? And what about me? I've been pretty patient, I think, but if you're going to crab things, I think I'll have my say. I tell you I live with it all the time. It's a good deal worse when you're not here, because she's afraid of you. And I don't intend to live with it much longer.'

He didn't want to quarrel, he reflected wearily. Why did he have to? But his exacerbated nerves spoke for him. 'I honestly believe it's more your fault than hers, because you're young and strong and she's old and weak. She's a sick woman, half the time — has been for years. It won't be for long, Netta.'

'You can bet it won't be for long,' she murmured intensely. She, too, was irritated; irritated because, as always, his figure there before her set her heart to beating. She did not want to quarrel, either; she wanted him to make love to her. He wouldn't; and therefore they quarreled. But Lewis surprised her. Standing there with folded arms, looking gravely across at her, he went on: 'If you'd have a kid, Netta, I believe everything would come straight. Mother would forget all about both of us if she had a grandchild to fuss over. And you'd be too busy and happy to mind little things.'

She did not recover at once from her astonishment. 'You honestly mean that, Lewis? You'd like me to have a baby?'

'I'd like us to have a baby, of course,' he answered quietly. 'What did you suppose?'

'Well, if you want a child, Lewis' — she too spoke very quietly — 'you'll have to marry somebody else. I'll never have one if I can help it — and I guess I *can* help it.'

'I don't doubt it.' He turned away.

Netta, however, was not through. She had waited long enough for this issue to define itself. As well now as any other time. He had given her the cue with his reproaches.

'And I've got something else to say,' she proceeded. 'I love you, Lewis, and you know it. I've tried out this idea of yours about living with your mother. You can't say I haven't given it a chance — for more than two years. Now, either it gets broken up and you and I take an apartment by ourselves, or I take a job and have a room of my own in town, and you stick with her if you want to. But you can't have us both any longer. And I wouldn't live in this house even if she went away. I don't want a house, anyway, unless I'm a millionaire. It's up to you.'

His face crimsoned. 'You know as well as anything that I can't run an apartment and this house both.'

'I'm willing to take a job, anyhow,' Netta returned triumphantly.

'It would take all you made in any job to dress you. The kind of thing you put on your back costs money.'

'How about your own clothes?'

'I have to be decent to do business. But I don't buy myself fur coats and mesh bags — or the sort of thing you've got on at the present minute. I'm not blaming you for wanting clothes, Net — I guess every woman does — but unless we live right here I can't swing it. Even if you earned money yourself, I couldn't afford to keep mother in this house, with a maid, while we were somewhere else. I'll be making more money next year. We'll see. It would be pretty hard on mother to leave her; but maybe if I can afford to keep her here, the way she is ...'

'All right,' Netta's voice trembled. 'I'll look for that job — *and* that room. It isn't of any importance to me that your mother should live in this house — or any house — or whether she has anybody to work for her or not. I've lived with her for two years, and you can take it from me, she's the limit. You can live with her if you want to. I won't — not another week! This family stuff doesn't go down with me — any of it.' She laughed unpleasantly. 'If you come to your senses any time and want to treat your wife properly, you'll know where to find me. I've never looked at another man and don't expect to. There's nothing gay about me.'

Curiously enough, it was just at the moment when Netta de-

clared herself innocent of intent to wrong him that the idea of
divorce first entered, explicitly, Lewis Hunting's mind. In that
tired, nervous hour he did not care whether she flirted — or more
— with a dozen men. He had come to her that evening after
a journey that had reawakened old desires — for peace, for sweetness, for calm domesticity, for affections normally diffused, for
passion expressed in ways that were not wholly of the flesh.
Netta knew as well as he what he could do and what he could not.
She asked of him to forsake all duties and take her to some perfumed lair where they could lie as beasts at ease. He no longer
cared much for his mother — Netta had finished off that job
very neatly — but her hold on him was immemorial. He had no
desire to live with her, but he would never fling her out of doors to
die. If Netta would only wait another year — but she wouldn't
wait, she said; and after all (he asked himself) what would they
be waiting for? Netta would not have a child, she would not have
a home, she would not have anything — except love-making,
which must some day cease. In that hour he knew that he could
not endure forever the life Netta offered him, and from that moment, really, began his wary plotting for freedom. Standing there
delicately clad, flushed and tempting, she was desirable in his
eyes ... but, inevitably, after two years she had ceased to be
a miracle. She, so prodigal of lures, had neglected every lure she
might have spread for his incorporeal imagination. Even passion
must be bolstered up, quickened, preserved by something besides
itself. Netta, he thought coldly, had counted too much on passion. Oh, yes, he could kiss her and draw her bright head to his
shoulder — and like it; but her perfume would destroy the
memory of jessamine, her voice the echo of the mocking-bird.
Tired, tired he was. . . .

'All right, Netta. Take your job and hire your room. Perhaps
you'll come to feel differently about it.' And already he was
hoping that she wouldn't.

She breathed hard. 'You mean it? You'd rather have your mother than me?'

'No, I wouldn't. I don't like the way we live. But I'm not willing to kill her to please you. So if you can't stand it any longer, you'll have to do as you like. As I say, you may change your mind.'

She wept softly. 'I love you so, Lewis. It isn't fair.'

His lips tightened. 'And I love you, Netta. But it doesn't seem to be enough, does it?' He kept the width of the room between them. He did not wish to be drawn into the quick charm of her proximity. 'I shall have to be away a good deal the next months. They're thinking about a Western branch, and I may have to talk it up out there, more or less. It would be worse than ever for you here, I suppose.'

'And when you come back, Lewis, are you coming to your mother or to me?'

He hadn't thought of that. But of course he couldn't plan anything yet. 'We could both come here, at those times, couldn't we?' he temporized.

Her anger flared up. 'No! When I'm once out of this house, I'll never set foot in it again — except for a funeral.'

That was the end, he thought. Funny that she shouldn't know it was the end — which was not reasonable of Lewis, for cruel things had been said before and ignored if not truly forgotten.

'We'll talk tomorrow. I'm awfully tired now. Good night.' He slipped into his bed, leaving her to put out the lamp and raise the windows. His tone was utterly spent, and beyond 'Good night' she did not speak to him again.

That was the most explicit talk they had. Earlier there had been bickerings, but all the quarrels were intended to be — and were — smoothed out and composed. These particular statements and retorts were never cancelled.

Netta, who really wanted Lewis more than anything else, had made the mistake of permitting herself, temporarily, to want something else more: freedom, frank expression of her hatred and weariness, the luxury of a defiant gesture. Lewis, at the same moment, came to the belief that what he wanted was peace — and love only if it brought peace in its train. Alas! he wanted even more than peace; seemliness in the ordering of his life, beauty in its texture — intimations of immortality, perhaps. But peace was what he called it. 'A man has a right to some peace' — thus he cloaked, or approximated, his yearning.

Destiny then made, in his direction, a few positively affectionate gestures. He wanted to get away, and it became his professional duty to get away. His firm decided to establish a connection on the Coast and kept Lewis for some months traveling between Far-Western cities. Twice, in the interval, he came East for hasty visits to the home office. He worked hard on this job; put his very best into it; for he intended to demand, when arrangements were completed, a Western post. Out there, it seemed to him, he could create life anew. Time enough to make domestic plans when he got his business completed.

Netta had found her job — she made not at all a bad secretary — and had duly given Lewis the address of her office. On his first arrival in the East he telephoned to her. Over the telephone she spoke eagerly — caressed him, as it were; and Lewis exhilarated by Western air, soothed by long absence of domestic fret, found tenderness creeping back into his own voice — almost, indeed, into his heart. He could see her vivid figure across the channeled space between them. He told her he must go to his mother's for the night, asked her to join him. It was good tactics, though at the moment he was not thinking of tactics; he merely wanted everyone to be happy. Perhaps, once out there in another atmosphere, all three of them ... But Netta's voice slid sharply into reproach, and he felt again all the menace that lay in her vividness.

'Indeed I will not, Lewis. You can go and see her, of course, but I'm not going to. I should think you'd want to see me first, but if you don't, you can go and have dinner with her and then come back and meet me. I can't spring you on my landlady very well, since she's never seen you, but we can live at a hotel while you're here.'

His voice changed too. 'We can talk about that later. There's no reason why you shouldn't be decent and go out with me, just for tonight.'

She did not know that it was an ultimatum; she misread his annoyance, taking it for impatience, and laughed harshly. 'Not much, Lewis! When you want me, you'll come to me. I'm a good wife, but I'm a darned poor daughter-in-law ... Where do I meet you tonight?'

'You don't meet me anywhere — tonight.'

He hung up the receiver, and she heard its sharp click. Even then she did not suspect. She was still gloating over the first warmth of his voice and could not know that the warmth had meant very little — that her chance had been very small and that she had thrown that chance away. Lewis did not so much blame Netta for her attitude to his mother as accuse her, in his heart, of being a person who would make no sacrifices to any situation that might arise. Mrs. Hunting was not so much a special case as the sort of thing that, in a hundred forms, might happen to anyone. Netta was hard and always would be. Even suppose his mother were dead: there would always be this or that thing to strike Netta as intolerable. It was the principle of the thing. No; they would never find that peace which, more than ever in an unfamiliar and beautiful landscape, had seemed every man's right. Netta waited in vain for a sign from him. She got none.

Netta, unaware that Hunting was expecting to be definitely settled in the West, thought a waiting game the wisest. If he once came back to living in his mother's house, he wouldn't be able to bear her absence. He'd come running, she believed. But he never did live there without her, and the place never had a chance to stir old memories. He was continuously away and, except in connection with divorce, Netta did not enter his mind. Her clutch was finally off him. He seemed to himself to know her wholly, to be completely aware of her character and to spurn it with reason. He did not know Netta wholly, as he was later to discover; but at this time he felt supremely capable of judging her.

Lewis, whom marriage and discontent had greatly matured, did good work for his firm. When he demanded his promotion and his transfer, he got them both. He had worked overtime for many months, giving to his business not only all his mind, but all his secret stores of energy. He was not working for a woman this time, but to get rid of one. The spur was equally effective. When the 'flu' hit him in San Francisco, it found him ready prey. Later, facing a limp and helpless convalescence, he asked for a long leave of absence, and it was granted. The length of the holiday he asked was the period needed for a divorce under Nevada laws.

In spite of increases and promotions, in spite of the absence of Netta's bills, Lewis had not a large store of money with which to buy his freedom. He would have, he realized, to send less money to his mother, and he wrote her frankly to that effect. He rather dreaded her answer, though he was grim enough about his own intentions. He need not have been afraid. Mrs. Hunting, who could not have lived in an apartment and fended for herself in order to give his youth more scope or his career more chance, could find both strength and money when it came to getting rid of the daughter-in-law she detested. She could even find the old adoration for Lewis, which had been much obscured by jealous resentment. She saw herself once more — with Netta out of the way — playing a winning game with her son; and her heart overflowed with kindness to him. When these troubles were over, she and her darling boy were going to be happy once more as they used to be. There is no doubt that she meant what she said. She really believed that they had been happy before his marriage; she thought of him as her darling boy. When she dismissed her expensive maid, got an ancient cousin in to keep her dismal company, bade Lewis send her no money until he was free and, in addition, sent him a handsome check, she felt these actions right and natural, a duty and a pleasure. Mrs. Hunting had despaired, and now she had hope. Lewis would now be bound forever to his self-sacrificing, generous, devoted mother.

Most people's emotions are even more muddled than their minds; and there can be no question that Mrs. Hunting, playing her unanswerable trumps, loved Lewis more than she had ever loved him. His emotional rejection of Netta she took for an emotional acceptance of herself. She saw herself preferred; and it warmed her confused heart. Lewis was misread by his mother as he had been by his wife. He knew perfectly that they had not been happy before Netta came, and he thought his mother's sacrifices belated. Though he was grateful for her assistance, the past could not be undone, and no new relation could be built up. He was grateful that she helped instead of hindering, as he was grateful for fine weather in place of storm. His loyalty was perhaps increased by gratitude, but the quantity of his affection for her had long since been fixed. He wrote to her regularly and with the utmost kindness; but it was too late for her to push any farther into his heart.

Perhaps he was the happier that no intimate relation needed readjusting. For the first three months of Lewis Hunting's sojourn in the little Nevada town were by all odds the happiest of his life. He saw his future clear, and for once he saw it bright. He had been afraid — though reassured by his lawyer — that Netta would put up a fight; but the fact was that Netta could not. She had no money with which to fight the case; and she discovered very soon that, though New York would have held her a virtuous wife, from the point of view of the more sensitive state of Nevada she had sinned. She had refused to live under what was legally her husband's roof; she had explicitly refused to give him children or a home, even to speak to his aged mother; she had indulged, indeed, in an absolute orgy of mental cruelty. These things were easily proved. It would have taken money to deprive Lewis of his decree, and money she had not. Nor did Lewis have enough to tempt any lawyer to take her case 'on spec.' Netta knew that she was beaten. Yet — had she but known it — she had allies dimly mustering on her side. Netta was all instinct, and Fate looks on instinct with a kindly eye.

Until strength flowed back into him, Lewis was content to lie on the tiny porch of his tiny apartment, staring at the Sierras; and the exertion of going out to his meals and seeing his lawyer, when necessary, was sufficient to his weakened body. After some weeks, however, he tired of watching, in solitude and silence, the dwindling snow patches. Energy returned, subtly heightened by the hope that was his. As the months counted themselves off, he felt Netta a lesser and lesser burden — slipping, slipping from his back. His shoulders ached less with the weight of her. Cheerfulness returned, and he began to welcome the ordinary human contacts. He was not looking for excitement, of which he well knew there was plenty. Neither poker, roulette, bad whiskey, nor rash divorcées appealed to him. Though not overfastidious, he did not care to seize the day. He hoped, instead, to seize the whole of life. Certainly he intended sometime to marry again — some girl opposed at every point to Netta; intended to have a home and kids, and a car, and a radio set, and (so far had he become infected with the West) a view. He didn't know just what she would be like, but he would not find her here.

The doctor whom he felt obliged to consult suggested a car and long drives in the open. He finally bought a small one out of his mother's check, knowing that he could sell it again. But to face the inhuman beauty of that landscape one needs a human companion; someone who is equally dwarfed and conquered by the uncaring peaks and the hostile desert. Rather diffidently — you must remember that Lewis was not vain; he undervalued his charm, indeed, since it had brought him only Netta — he asked Mona Jeffers to drive with him; once, and then again and again.

The girl — a poor relation — was companioning a cousin who soon found that she need not depend on Mona for excitement. Indeed, Mona was a mere hindrance to Mrs. Tilton on most occasions. She needed the girl there on general principles and would not send her home; but she wanted her out of the flat a large part of the time. Mona's insipidity, to Mrs. Tilton's mind, was complete. She used her as she needed her, but she used her less and less — especially after she discovered roulette and acquired a rather shady lover. So the colorless Mona was free to sit beside Lewis while they drove afar. Her quietness, her decency, her very lack of good looks soothed him who was tired alike of Venus and the Furies. Love never entered his head. He expected that shadowy future bride to be handsomer than Mona — for men demand everything and are not satisfied until sex blinds them into thinking they have got it. They were blithe days for Lewis: health recovered, hope enlarging itself on his horizon, the weeks passing swiftly by, the little car for magic carpet, and Mona to exorcise the demons of the hills. Everyone was civil to him, and he rejected far more advances than he accepted. All pointed to his being, through a long life, a happy and useful citizen. Lewis, who was an unimaginative creature, found sanctions all about him for his content. He called them omens or 'hunches.'

Without being superstitious or sentimental one may suspect that Nature lays traps for mortals, and that the trap is no less a trap for being seldom sprung. No doubt, for that matter, a man often comes through unscathed. There is a spot — a sharp turn of the precipitous road, where a man is uplifted for an instant,

defenseless and naked to his stalkers above him on all sides —
which goes (not without reason) by the name of Dead Man's
Point. The term inherits from the days when those who fetched
gold from Virginia City were apt to lose it — and necessarily their
lives — at this place. For a few moments as he toiled past, a man
became, in the nature of things, a target; his best friend would
have taken imaginary sight and aim. When you had finished him
— in the old days — the disposal of the body offered no difficulties. You rolled him over the precipice into the trackless gorge,
and sheriffs were thereby confounded. Booty on that road is now
as rare as bandits. Nature, however, pays little attention to the
infinitesimal changes of human history; her traps remain traps.
Some spots are forever sinister, and this is one of them. The gold
may have gone, but, for a softer generation, the view remains; and
a foolish youth with bad liquor inside him, driving a car too fast,
is as perilous as two guns and a total lack of morals ever were.

There was nothing in Lewis Hunting's heart to cope with that
view, which is desolate and terrifying — and beautiful — beyond
most. He was not in its class; nor was Mona. But the mere size
and scale and arrangement of it impose themselves. You *must*
turn back to look, at Dead Man's Point, before you forsake that
range for others. Lewis and Mona turned to look — and Johnny
Stevens, innocent of everything but that foolish drink, crashed
into them at a curious tangent. Mona was flung free, falling,
with infinite bruising of her tender flesh, upon rock; but the tilt
of the car was such that Lewis was half caught beneath it. It
rocked horridly like a hanging stone — one of those natural
wonders that attract tourists — and then, rolling over, slid down
the path of the corpses. Lewis, whose hands had stretched out
instinctively and caught themselves with desperation in a stiff
clump of sage, was left — though precariously — behind but-
tressed for the moment by a few stones of which the car in its
final plunge had made nothing. They could not deter the ma-

chine, but they sufficed to deter him until Johnny Stevens, sobered by the shock, had dragged him to what is known as safety. Mona came later — half fainting, half crying, but not badly injured. By the time a fresh car came over the pass and picked them up, Lewis was luckily unconscious. They wound slowly home, and Nature — a beast, first, last, and all the time except when she is broken to the service of God — resumed her wise, incomparable smile. A little thing like loose wreckage cannot mar a view like that.

Science, which loves the part more than the whole, took hold of Lewis Hunting and made him one of her choicest fragments. No one could have blamed those able surgeons for being proud of themselves; but, true to type, they were not that: they were proud of Lewis. Half a healthy man is better than a whole man with a trace of sepsis; and Lewis — both legs neatly shorn off between knee and hip — was Exhibit A, a victory, an exultation. His blood was pure, his heart strong, his constitution magnificent, his recovery just what the recovery of the normal man should be. He had not hampered either Nature or Science in any way. The doctors felt affection for him because of his strong heart and untainted blood, and assured him earnestly that there was no reason why he should not live for fifty years. Lewis heard the words, but did not measure their full significance until later.

Numbers of people came to see him in the hospital; flowers and fruits stood about until his eyes wearied of them. He was setting his teeth harder than he had ever done in his life, and he could not unclasp his jaws to breathe the sweetness of roses or taste the pulp of figs. His lawyer had, at his request, written — not telegraphed — to his mother; and in the letter lay a plain request that the news should be kept, by hook or crook, from Netta. The lawyer humored him, writing precisely what Lewis wished; but as that miraculous convalescence progressed, he wondered. No one, of course, would be such a brute as to suggest

to Lewis that he change his plans to match his prospects. But
— well, *but* . . . They moved him to the hotel when he left the
hospital, and guests and employees vied with each other for the
task of pushing his wheel-chair in and out of the elevator and
dining-room. A visiting nurse did the necessary things for a
time. but the wounds healed as by a miracle. Six weeks after the
accident Lewis was tensely calm: adjusting himself; writing to
his firm; trying to apprehend, little by little, what a man with
no legs would be able to do for fifty years. His mental mood had
not yet relaxed to despair, and his body inflicted no fevers, no
relapses, upon him. But as he had not reckoned with Nature, so
he had not reckoned with Netta, who was Nature's protégée.

Mrs. Hunting — distraught, half maddened — had for a
time kept Lewis's command not to let Netta know. But though
Netta never read newspapers and had few intimate friends, the
news eventually came to her. Someone had noticed the identity
of names. The moment Netta heard of it, she asked permission
to absent herself, and rushed to Mrs. Hunting's suburban home.
She made no mistakes this time: her instincts served her well.
Lewis's mother had become, by this stroke, her chief ally, and
from the first moment Netta treated her as such. Within an
hour she had got from Mrs. Hunting precisely what she wanted.
Nor is Mrs. Hunting to be too much blamed for playing into
Netta's hands. She had cried over the maiming of her boy, her
heart had indeed been well-nigh broken. Yet, confusedly, she
saw him as wreckage — beloved wreckage, no doubt; but there
was no triumph in possessing him. She had wanted him all to
herself, and now, inevitably, she had him thus; and her weak old
shoulders trembled under the burden. Being everything to him,
as he had hitherto defined it, was being the chief recipient of his
favors. The poor woman was discouraged to the marrow; she
had no gift for meeting new and shattering situations. Her

grievance against Netta had always been on her own behalf — not really on her son's. She was, of course, leagues away from understanding Lewis, who had indeed never done her the honor of explaining himself to her.

Netta cooed over her, Netta wrapped her in pity and compliments, Netta expressed remorse as inclusive as it was vague. Only the last of their talk need be recorded; and much had been decided between them earlier.

'But Netta, how can I let you go when he told me not to let you know?'

'You can't keep me from him. My boss will lend me the money to go, if I ask him.'

'No, no. I'll give you the money. But do you realize what it means, Netta?'

'Do I realize? What do you take me for? I realize that Lewis is down and out, forever.'

The feeble tears stood in Mrs. Hunting's eyes. 'Yes, that's true. He is. What are you going to do when you get there?'

'Take care of him, of course. He's still my husband.'

'You forgive him for wanting to divorce you?'

Netta's mouth twisted. Forgiveness was something she had never in the least understood. 'It has all been a horrible mistake. And now Lewis will realize it. He'll find that his wife is going to stand by him, no matter what has happened. Bygones are bygones.'

'Netta' — the older woman's voice shook — 'I didn't know you had it in you. I guess I never understood you before.' She had never been further from understanding Netta than she was at that moment, but she spoke in the utmost honesty. To stick to a broken man who could give her nothing, who had cast her off with insult ... why, Netta was wonderful.

'You're going to take him back,' she marveled humbly.

'Sure I am.'

'He ought to worship you, Netta.'

Even Netta was a little at loss to answer that. 'Lewis doesn't worship people, I guess. But we'll be all right.'

'I never did believe in divorce,' sighed Mrs. Hunting. It was quite true, and she felt reminiscently ashamed of having so welcomed her son's.

The two women kissed, and Netta, with Mrs. Hunting's check in her bag, departed to pack and make reservations. Lewis's mother watched her go, and pure admiration filled her heart. She wouldn't have expected it of Netta who could so easily, after a divorce, have married again. If only the dear Lord would help her to carry it through! A little toneless prayer went up that night from Mrs. Hunting's lips that Netta might find her strength and her reward. Netta, meanwhile, alert and flushed, was moving about her room, packing her trunk and humming. Never had she felt less need of pity. *She* was again for Cydnus, to meet Mark Antony.

Her train, she found, would arrive at a hideously inconvenient hour; so she stopped short of her goal, had a night's rest in another town, and motored over in the happy morning light. Her heart was beating hard as she faced the hotel clerk and registered. His quick, excited glance of sympathy and admiration encouraged her. She realized afresh the tremendous handicap in her favor. She was, after all, still a wife.

'I'll telephone up,' stammered the clerk.

Netta bent across the counter and smiled at him gently. The result was to make him feel that some men had all the luck. For a hopeless cripple to get any woman back after trying to get rid of her — and such a good-looking one ...

'No,' she said. 'I've got to see him. And I think it will be easier for both of us if I just walk in. I came as soon as I heard. Does he suffer?' She dropped her voice sympathetically.

'Not now. He's made a wonderful recovery, they say.'

She nodded. 'I'll just go up and knock at his door. What is the number?'

He told her. 'Shall I give you a room?'

Netta flushed a little. 'Suppose you wait until I come down. Here is my trunk check.'

The elevator girl stared at Netta when she revealed her name and her errand. As soon as Netta was well down the corridor, the girl shot the car to the basement where her favorite bellboy would be haunting the poolroom entrance. She crooked a finger at him. 'Say, Ted, who'd you s'pose I just took up to Mr. Hunting's room? His wife! Gosh, she's a wonder — and some looker. Goin' to take him back, I guess. Don't you ever talk to me about women again. There's some of 'em that's worth all the men in creation.' The elevator rose, preventing retort.

Netta already had laid her finger on the pulse of Nevada. She had been a little afraid of this special atmosphere which, she thought, might be like nothing else in our great country. But apparently, even in the stronghold of divorce, fidelity was valued. The mere glances of the clerk and the elevator girl had made that clear. Nevada itself would back her, she now suspected, just as Mrs. Hunting had done. She knocked at Lewis's door and entered.

Lewis sat by the window, a rug spread over him from the waist down. He turned, expecting a bellboy. He saw Netta instead. and so profound was the shock that it seemed instantly inevitable. The fact was too monstrous for doubt. There was hopelessness beneath his hot flush, though his voice was cold and stern.

'Netta! Why are you here?'

Netta took off her gloves, went into the bathroom and washed her hands. She came back, drew up a chair near (but not too near) him and sat down. Only then did she speak.

'I'm here to talk to you, first of all, Lewis. And then to see what I can do for you.'

'How did you hear about this?' He pointed at the rug.

'It must have been in the papers. Someone spoke to me about it, finally. So I went to see Mother Hunting, and she told me everything.'

'Did she know you were coming out here?'

'Why, of course she knew, Lewis. She helped me to come and gave me her blessing.'

More virtue went out of him as he heard these words.

'My mother doesn't understand anything about my position,' he said harshly. 'There's nothing you can do for me. Sorry you had the trip. And now you had better get out as soon as possible. How did they happen to let you up here?'

Netta made no show of temper — which was ominous, Lewis thought. A row, he considered, would be the very best thing that could happen.

'Well, you see, Lewis dear, I am still your wife. And I think' — she spoke gently to veil the brutality of what was to come — 'most people would feel that a man in your position couldn't refuse to see his wife, if she were willing to see him. It isn't as if you ever had any real grounds against me, you know. I suppose you thought you'd marry again. Well, I don't see how you ever can, do you?'

'Of course I shall never marry again,' he said shortly. She had got beneath his skin — Netta always did — and he felt weak tears starting.

'Somebody's got to take care of you, Lewis, you know. And if your mother and I are willing to do it, between us, I guess you can only be thankful to us. I shall keep on working, of course.'

'I'd rather starve,' Lewis answered simply.

'That's foolish,' his wife replied mildly — 'dead silly. Where would you starve? And how? You can be very sure of one thing, Lewis. Your friends aren't going to look after you while your own family stand ready to do it.'

'Why do you come and badger me like this?' It was weak, and he knew it; but he could not tell her in plain words that he hated her. The loss of his physical integrity somehow made it impossible to utter so complete and violent a truth.

Netta rose. 'I suppose if I told you I loved you, Lewis, you wouldn't understand. But I've always loved you. You knew when you left me, when you tried to divorce me, that I loved you. Do you suppose a woman who didn't love you would come back to you, after the way I've been treated, and after what has happened to you? You can put it up to your precious lawyer if you want to. I guess you'll find that even in the State of Nevada people will consider that a wife who's ready to forgive what I'm ready to forgive, and to take care of you the rest of your life, is worth paying some attention to.'

'It's no use talking, Netta. I don't love you — not a damn bit. What do you want me for?'

She bent over him, not touching him. 'Darned if I know, Lewis. But I do want you — and I intend to have you. I don't see how you're going to stop it. No, you needn't worry — I'm not going to kiss you. Some day' — she looked at him strangely, scrutinizingly — 'you'll be asking for it. I'll wait for that, thanks.'

A bellboy knocked and entered just then to take Lewis down to the dining-room. If he was half an hour earlier than usual, he can hardly be blamed. The hotel was buzzing from lobby to kitchen. Word had already gone forth upon the streets of the town concerning the beautiful forgiving wife who had appeared like an angel in the desert. It must be remembered that in Nevada the presumption against the forsaken spouse is not very strong.

'You had better go down alone today, Lewis,' Netta said. 'I'll go out and do an errand or two, and lunch later.'

She left them in the lobby. There were two people she wanted to see before she talked with Lewis again. Thanks to Mrs. Hunting, she knew the names of both, and a telephone book did the rest.

The interview with Lewis's lawyer came first. Netta did not attempt to commit him to anything. She merely announced her presence and her intentions; and she did not fail to refer obliquely to the fact that, however the situation broke, there could be no money in it for anyone.

'Of course I know you'll have to talk with my husband,' she said finally, as she rose. 'But the fact is that he's down and out, and I'm willing to forget everything and work for the rest of my life to support him. I'm afraid I am his only chance.' She shook her tawny head a little pathetically and departed.

Netta permitted herself a sandwich and a cup of coffee before the second encounter. It was possible, she realized, that Lewis had fallen in love; and in spite of Netta's brave sarcasms she knew it also to be possible that another woman had fallen in love with him. If she, Netta, could keep on loving him, another woman might. And if the other woman were rich, she might even allow herself the luxury of a crippled husband. Her hand trembled a little as she rang the bell of Mrs. Tilton's apartment.

She could have shouted for joy, once face to face with Mona Jeffers. If she couldn't cut out that pale creature, she wasn't much good, she opined. She prepared to do battle, rather contemptuously. But Mona surprised her at once.

'We heard that you had come on, Mrs. Hunting. My cousin just came in from shopping. Things get round pretty quickly in this place.' The girl was panting slightly, and Netta watched her, catlike, to see what would come. 'Oh, I do hope it's true, Mrs. Hunting, that you're ready to make it up and take him back!'

So, even if Lewis wanted this chit, she didn't want him. She had only Lewis to fight, after all.

'I certainly am, Miss Jeffers. I only want to stand by him and take care of him, if he'll let me.'

'Oh, how glad I am, Mrs. Hunting! Why' — the girl spoke softly — 'it is almost worth while it should have happened if it brings you together again.'

Precisely what Netta had thought; but she had not expected anyone else to say it. Suspicion attacked her again.

'I wouldn't say that, Miss Jeffers. It's a pretty awful thing that's happened. But he's my husband, and I feel we belong to each other. The real reason I came to see you' — she went on very gravely — 'was that I knew you were together at the time of the accident. I didn't know but you and he had fallen in love with each other — meant to get married when he got his decree.'

The pale girl flushed. 'Oh, no, Mrs. Hunting. There wasn't a thing — ever!' She gave a little involuntary shiver.

Netta noted the shiver and could have laughed aloud. Whatever Lewis might have wanted, this girl didn't want him. Poor old Lewis! His day of charm was over — excepting always for her. Funny: somehow he had 'got' her for all time, but it looked as if he would never 'get' anyone else.

She smiled as she rose to go. 'You must remember, Miss Jeffers, that Mr. Hunting has been trying to divorce me. I don't know yet what he will do.'

'Do?' the girl exclaimed. 'Why, of course he'll worship you. Not many women would do what you are doing.'

Wouldn't they? Netta wondered silently as she went out upon the street. Well, perhaps other people didn't know what they wanted. She had never been troubled that way. But it was clear to her that no one was going to interfere with her taking on the whole burden of Lewis Hunting. Relief was in all their voices. Netta took a room at the hotel, but she did not try to see Lewis again. She dined outside the hotel and filled in the evening at a movie. In the theater she was aware of being covertly pointed out. Before retiring she sent a note to Lewis, saying that she should not see him until he sent for her.

Lewis, however, did not take long to capitulate. After talking with a few people he saw that, in the eyes of public opinion, he had no case. It was cold fact that Netta was behaving with great magnanimity. He was helpless, done for, and she was willing to take him on. The fact that he didn't want to live with her seemed very small in comparison — everybody blew it away, and indeed the mere hint of it seemed to shock. Half a man has no right to the prejudices and preferences of the whole man. How could he fight against the heroine of the hour? He sent for his wife on the second day, and she came at once.

'Well, Lewis?'

'Well, Netta.'

That seemed to be all. Then he said haltingly, 'I am very grateful to you, Netta.'

'You've got reason to be,' she answered briskly. 'I'll move next door tomorrow, and you won't have to hire other people to wait on you. Perhaps I had better begin by taking you down to dinner tonight.' She moved about the room, tidying it. Her presence seemed to flow into the farthest crannies of the chamber, and his nerves began the old gestures of revolt. There was never to be peace.

'Let's go down early,' he said roughly.

'All right.' She wheeled him into the elevator and wheeled him out and into the dining-room. As they moved through the palm room, she heard an unattractive citizen remark aside, 'I've got pretty cynical, living in this place; but, by heck, a woman like that almost gives me back my faith in human nature.' Evidently Lewis had heard it, too, for he flushed.

At the table he ordered, but ate little. Instead, he stared ahead of him — still flushed and curiously, stonily handsome. They talked very little. Netta, too, was flushed and shaken — with victory. She had got Lewis back forever, and food was unimportant. Money was the thing that was going to trouble her next.

Lewis was dealing with the future, as well as she. He was beginning to realize — the overheard words had thrust it on him — that not only must he live with Netta, endure her unmodulated hardness, perhaps even her strong caresses, but must always be humble with gratitude. He would have died rather than kneel to her, three months ago, when he had knees to kneel with; but, symbolically, he must do just that — forever.

'Let's stick round the lobby awhile,' he proposed.

'All right, if you want to.'

But suddenly he clutched the chair-arm. 'No — upstairs!' He had wanted to put off being alone with her, but he had been wrong. It was more terrible to sit there with her, hero and heroine, under those cynical eyes made soft again by the spectacle of them.

'All right,' said Netta again. 'Just wait until I go to the news-stand and get some magazines.' She left him, and he closed his eyes.

A voice in his ear made him open them. 'It's terrible for you — her coming like this. But be brave. Nothing lasts forever. Be brave.' The speaker passed on — a woman he had never known, but whom, like all the other hotel guests, he had noted for her distinction of bearing and garb. She was not in the least of Lewis's — or of the others' — world, and she would never have employed a young woman so aggressive and sharp as Netta.

'Who is your friend?' he heard his wife ask. Strolling back with her magazines, she had noted the clothes, the air, the aspect of the older woman who had paused — though barely — by her husband's chair.

'I never spoke to her before, and I haven't any idea,' he replied. 'There are all sorts of people round this place.'

He spoke very quietly. It was suddenly easier to be patient.

Somehow that woman, with her mere passing murmur of sympathy, had picked his dignity out of the dust and handed it back to him. They had to wait for the elevator, and a cold draft assailed them, blowing directly through the little lobby from the street. Netta took off her scarf and folded it round his shoulders with a solicitous, possessive smile. The world looked on, with moist eyes.... Lewis set his teeth, squared his fine shoulders, and looked straight ahead of him with pride.

HAIRCUT[1]

RING W. LARDNER

I GOT another barber that comes over from Carterville and helps me out Saturdays, but the rest of the time I can get along all right alone. You can see for yourself that this ain't no New York City and besides that, the most of the boys works all day and don't have no leisure to drop in here and get themselves prettied up.

You're a newcomer, ain't you? I thought I hadn't seen you round before. I hope you like it good enough to stay. As I say, we ain't no New York City or Chicago, but we have pretty good times. Not as good, though, since Jim Kendall got killed. When he was alive, him and Hod Meyers used to keep this town in an uproar. I bet they was more laughin' done here than any town its size in America.

Jim was comical, and Hod was pretty near a match for him. Since Jim's gone, Hod tries to hold his end up just the same as ever, but it's tough goin' when you ain't got nobody to kind of work with.

[1] Copyright, 1929, by Charles Scribner's Sons. From *Round Up*, by Ring W. Lardner. Charles Scribner's Sons. 1929.

They used to be plenty fun in here Saturdays. This place is jam-packed Saturdays, from four o'clock on. Jim and Hod would show up right after their supper, round six o'clock. Jim would set himself down in that big chair, nearest the blue spittoon. Whoever had been settin' in that chair, why they'd get up when Jim come in and give it to him.

You'd of thought it was a reserved seat like they have sometimes in a theayter. Hod would generally always stand or walk up and down, or some Saturdays, of course, he'd be settin' in this chair part of the time, gettin' a haircut.

Well, Jim would set there a w'ile without openin' his mouth only to spit, and then finally he'd say to me, 'Whitey,' — my right name, that is, my right first name, is Dick, but everybody round here calls me Whitey — Jim would say, 'Whitey, your nose looks like a rosebud tonight. You must of been drinkin' some of your aw de cologne.'

So I'd say, 'No, Jim, but you look like you'd been drinkin' somethin' of that kind or somethin' worse.'

Jim would have to laugh at that, but then he'd speak up and say, 'No, I ain't had nothin' to drink, but that ain't sayin' I wouldn't like somethin'. I wouldn't even mind if it was wood alcohol.'

Then Hod Meyers would say, 'Neither would your wife.' That would set everybody to laughin' because Jim and his wife wasn't on very good terms. She'd of divorced him only they wasn't no chance to get alimony and she didn't have no way to take care of herself and the kids. She couldn't never understand Jim. He *was* kind of rough, but a good fella at heart.

Him and Hod had all kinds of sport with Milt Sheppard. I don't suppose you've seen Milt. Well, he's got an Adam's apple that looks more like a mushmelon. So I'd be shavin' Milt and when I'd start to shave down here on his neck, Hod would holler, 'Hey, Whitey, wait a minute! Before you cut into it, let's make up a pool and see who can guess closest to the number of seeds.'

And Jim would say, 'If Milt hadn't of been so hoggish, he'd of ordered a half a cantaloupe instead of a whole one and it might not of stuck in his throat.'

All the boys would roar at this and Milt himself would force a smile, though the joke was on him. Jim certainly was a card!

There's his shavin' mug, settin' on the shelf, right next to Charley Vail's. 'Charles M. Vail.' That's the druggist. He comes in regular for his shave, three times a week. And Jim's is the cup next to Charley's. 'James H. Kendall.' Jim won't need no shavin' mug no more, but I'll leave it there just the same for old time's sake. Jim certainly was a character!

Years ago, Jim used to travel for a canned goods concern over in Carterville. They sold canned goods. Jim had the whole northern half of the State and was on the road five days out of every week. He'd drop in here Saturdays and tell his experiences for that week. It was rich.

I guess he paid more attention to playin' jokes than makin' sales. Finally the concern let him out and he come right home here and told everybody he'd been fired instead of sayin' he'd resigned like most fellas would of.

It was a Saturday and the shop was full and Jim got up out of that chair and says, 'Gentlemen, I got an important announcement to make. I been fired from my job.'

Well, they asked him if he was in earnest and he said he was and nobody could think of nothin' to say till Jim finally broke the ice himself. He says, 'I been sellin' canned goods and now I'm canned goods myself.'

You see, the concern he'd been workin' for was a factory that made canned goods. Over in Carterville. And now Jim said he was canned himself. He was certainly a card!

Jim had a great trick that he used to play w'ile he was travelin'.

For instance, he'd be ridin' on a train and they'd come to some little town like, well, like, we'll say, like Benton. Jim would look out the train window and read the signs on the stores.

For instance, they'd be a sign, 'Henry Smith, Dry Goods.' Well, Jim would write down the name and the name of the town and when he got to wherever he was goin' he'd mail back a postal card to Henry Smith at Benton and not sign no name to it, but he'd write on the card, well, somethin' like 'Ask your wife about that book agent that spent the afternoon last week,' or 'Ask your Missus who kept her from gettin' lonesome the last time you was in Carterville.' And he'd sign the card, 'A Friend.'

Of course, he never knew what really come of none of these jokes, but he could picture what *probably* happened and that was enough.

Jim didn't work very steady after he lost his position with the Carterville people. What he did earn, doin' odd jobs round town, why he spent pretty near all of it on gin and his family might of starved if the stores hadn't of carried them along. Jim's wife tried her hand at dressmakin', but they ain't nobody goin' to get rich makin' dresses in this town.

As I say, she'd of divorced Jim, only she seen that she couldn't support herself and the kids and she was always hopin' that some day Jim would cut out his habits and give her more than two or three dollars a week.

They was a time when she would go to whoever he was workin' for and ask them to give her his wages, but after she done this once or twice, he beat her to it by borrowin' most of his pay in advance. He told it all round town, how he had outfoxed his Missus. He certainly was a caution!

But he wasn't satisfied with just outwittin' her. He was sore the way she had acted, tryin' to grab off his pay. And he made up his mind he'd get even. Well, he waited till Evans's Circus was advertised to come to town. Then he told his wife and two kiddies that he was goin' to take them to the circus. The day of the circus, he told them he would get the tickets and meet them outside the entrance to the tent.

Well, he didn't have no intentions of bein' there or buyin' tickets or nothin'. He got full of gin and laid round Wright's poolroom all day. His wife and the kids waited and waited and of course he didn't show up. His wife didn't have a dime with her, or nowhere else, I guess. So she finally had to tell the kids it was all off and they cried like they wasn't never goin' to stop.

Well, it seems, w'ile they was cryin', Doc Stair came along and he asked what was the matter, but Mrs. Kendall was stubborn and wouldn't tell him, but the kids told him and he insisted on takin' them and their mother in the show. Jim found this out afterwards and it was one reason why he had it in for Doc Stair.

Doc Stair come here about a year and a half ago. He's a mighty handsome young fella and his clothes always look like he has them made to order. He goes to Detroit two or three times a year and w'ile he's there he must have a tailor take his measure and then make him a suit to order. They cost pretty near twice as much, but they fit a whole lot better than if you just bought them in a store.

For a w'ile everybody was wonderin' why a young doctor like Doc Stair should come to a town like this where we already got old Doc Gamble and Doc Foote that's both been here for years and all the practice in town was always divided between the two of them.

Then they was a story got round that Doc Stair's gal had throwed him over, a gal up in the Northern Peninsula somewheres, and the reason he come here was to hide himself away and forget it. He said himself that he thought they wasn't nothin' like general practice in a place like ours to fit a man to be a good all round doctor. And that's why he'd came.

Anyways, it wasn't long before he was makin' enough to live on, though they tell me that he never dunned nobody for what they owed him, and the folks here certainly has got the owin' habit, even in my business. If I had all that was comin' to me for just shaves alone, I could go to Carterville and put up at the Mercer for a week and see a different picture every night. For instance, they's old George Purdy — but I guess I shouldn't ought to be gossipin'.

Well, last year, our coroner died, died of the flu. Ken Beatty, that was his name. He was the coroner. So they had to choose another man to be coroner in his place and they picked Doc Stair. He laughed at first and said he didn't want it, but they made him take it. 'It ain't no job that anybody would fight for and what a man makes out of it in a year would just about buy seeds for their garden. Doc's the kind, though, that can't say no to nothin' if you keep at him long enough.

But I was goin' to tell you about a poor boy we got here in town — Paul Dickson. He fell out of a tree when he was about ten years old. Lit on his head and it done somethin' to him and he ain't never been right. No harm in him, but just silly. Jim Kendall used to call him cuckoo; that's a name Jim had for anybody that was off their head, only he called people's head their bean. That was another of his gags, callin' head bean and callin' crazy people cuckoo. Only poor Paul ain't crazy, but just silly.

You can imagine that Jim used to have all kinds of fun with Paul. He'd send him to the White Front Garage for a left-handed monkey wrench. Of course they ain't no such a thing as a left-handed monkey wrench.

And once we had a kind of a fair here and they was a baseball game between the fats and the leans and before the game started Jim called Paul over and sent him way down to Schrader's hardware store to get a key for the pitcher's box.

They wasn't nothin' in the way of gags that Jim couldn't think up, when he put his mind to it.

Poor Paul was always kind of suspicious of people, maybe on account of how Jim had kept foolin' him. Paul wouldn't have much to do with anybody only his own mother and Doc Stair and a girl here in town named Julie Gregg. That is, she ain't a girl no more, but pretty near thirty or over.

When Doc first come to town, Paul seemed to feel like here was a real friend and he hung round Doc's office most of the w'ile; the only time he wasn't there was when he'd go home to eat or sleep or when he seen Julie Gregg doin' her shoppin'.

When he looked out Doc's window and seen her, he'd run downstairs and join her and tag along with her to the different stores. The poor boy was crazy about Julie and she always treated him mighty nice and made him feel like he was welcome, though of course it wasn't nothin' but pity on her side.

Doc done all he could to improve Paul's mind and he told me once that he really thought the boy was gettin' better, that they was times when he was as bright and sensible as anybody else.

But I was goin' to tell you about Julie Gregg. Old Man Gregg was in the lumber business, but got to drinkin' and lost the most of his money and when he died, he didn't leave nothin' but the house and just enough insurance for the girl to skimp along on.

Her mother was a kind of a half invalid and didn't hardly ever leave the house. Julie wanted to sell the place and move somewheres else after the old man died, but the mother said she was born here and would die here. It was tough on Julie, as the young people round this town — well, she's too good for them.

She's been away to school and Chicago and New York and different places and they ain't no subject she can't talk on, where you take the rest of the young folks here and you mention anything to them outside of Gloria Swanson or Tommy Meighan

and they think you're delirious. Did you see Gloria in Wages of
Virtue? You missed somethin'!

Well, Doc Stair hadn't been here more than a week when he
come in one day to get shaved and I recognized who he was as he
had been pointed out to me, so I told him about my old lady.
She's been ailin' for a couple years and either Doc Gamble or
Doc Foote, neither one, seemed to be helpin' her. So he said he
would come out and see her, but if she was able to get out herself,
it would be better to bring her to his office where he could make a
completer examination.

So I took her to his office and w'ile I was waitin' for her in the
reception room, in come Julie Gregg. When somebody comes in
Doc Stair's office, they's a bell that rings in his inside office so as
he can tell they's somebody to see him.

So he left my old lady inside and come out to the front office
and that's the first time him and Julie met and I guess it was what
they call love at first sight. But it wasn't fifty-fifty. This young
fella was the slickest lookin' fella she'd ever seen in this town and
she went wild over him. To him she was just a young lady that
wanted to see the doctor.

She'd came on about the same business I had. Her mother
had been doctorin' for years with Doc Gamble and Doc Foote and
without no results. So she'd heard they was a new doc in town
and decided to give him a try. He promised to call and see her
mother that same day.

I said a minute ago that it was love at first sight on her part.
I'm not only judgin' by how she acted afterwards but how she
looked at him that first day in his office. I ain't no mind reader,
but it was wrote all over her face that she was gone.

Now Jim Kendall, besides bein' a jokesmith and a pretty good
drinker, well, Jim was quite a lady-killer. I guess he run pretty
wild durin' the time he was on the road for them Carterville
people, and besides that, he'd had a couple little affairs of the

heart right here in town. As I say, his wife could of divorced him, only she couldn't.

But Jim was like the majority of men, and women, too, I guess. He wanted what he couldn't get. He wanted Julie Gregg and worked his head off tryin' to land her. Only he'd of said bean instead of head.

Well, Jim's habits and his jokes didn't appeal to Julie and of course he was a married man, so he didn't have no more chance than, well, than a rabbit. That's an expression of Jim's himself. When somebody didn't have no chance to get elected or some-thin', Jim would always say they didn't have no more chance than a rabbit.

He didn't make no bones about how he felt. Right in here, more than once, in front of the whole crowd, he said he was stuck on Julie and anybody that could get her for him was welcome to his house and his wife and kids included. But she wouldn't have nothin' to do with him; wouldn't even speak to him on the street. He finally seen he wasn't gettin' nowheres with his usual line so he decided to try the rough stuff. He went right up to her house one evenin' and when she opened the door he forced his way in and grabbed her. But she broke loose and before he could stop her, she run in the next room and locked the door and phoned to Joe Barnes. Joe's the marshal. Jim could hear who she was phonin' to and he beat it before Joe got there.

Joe was an old friend of Julie's pa. Joe went to Jim the next day and told him what would happen if he ever done it again.

I don't know how the news of this little affair leaked out. Chances is that Joe Barnes told his wife and she told somebody else's wife and they told their husband. Anyways, it did leak out and Hod Meyers had the nerve to kid Jim about it, right here in this shop. Jim didn't deny nothin' and kind of laughed it off and said for us all to wait; that lots of people had tried to make a monkey out of him, but he always got even.

Meanw'ile everybody in town was wise to Julie's bein' wild mad over the Doc. I don't suppose she had any idear how her face changed when him and her was together; of course she couldn't of, or she'd of kept away from him. And she didn't know that we was all noticin' how many times she made excuses to go up to his office or pass it on the other side of the street and look up in his window to see if he was there. I felt sorry for her and so did most other people.

Hod Meyers kept rubbin' it into Jim about how the Doc had cut him out. Jim didn't pay no attention to the kiddin' and you could see he was plannin' one of his jokes.

One trick Jim had was the knack of changin' his voice. He could make you think he was a girl talkin' and he could mimic any man's voice. To show you how good he was along this line, I'll tell you the joke he played on me once.

You know, in most towns of any size, when a man is dead and needs a shave, why the barber that shaves him soaks him five dollars for the job; that is, he don't soak *him*, but whoever ordered the shave. I just charge three dollars because personally I don't mind much shavin' a dead person. They lay a whole lot stiller than live customers. The only thing is that you don't feel like talkin' to them and you get kind of lonesome.

Well, about the coldest day we ever had here, two years ago last winter, the phone rung at the house w'ile I was home to dinner and I answered the phone and it was a woman's voice and she said she was Mrs. John Scott and her husband was dead and would I come out and shave him.

Old John had always been a good customer of mine. But they live seven miles out in the country, on the Streeter road. Still I didn't see how I could say no.

So I said I would be there, but would have to come in a jitney and it might cost three or four dollars besides the price of the shave. So she, or the voice, it said that was all right, so I got

Frank Abbott to drive me out to the place and when I got there, who should open the door but old John himself! He wasn't no more dead than, well, than a rabbit.

It didn't take no private detective to figure out who had played me this little joke. Nobody could of thought it up but Jim Kendall. He certainly was a card!

I tell you this incident just to show you how he could disguise his voice and make you believe it was somebody else talkin'. I'd of swore it was Mrs. Scott had called me. Anyways, some woman.

Well, Jim waited till he had Doc Stair's voice down pat; then he went after revenge.

He called Julie up on a night when he knew Doc was over in Carterville. She never questioned but what it was Doc's voice. Jim said he must see her that night; he couldn't wait no longer to tell her somethin'. She was all excited and told him to come to the house. But he said he was expectin' an important long distance call and wouldn't she please forget her manners for once and come to his office. He said they couldn't nothin' hurt her and nobody would see her and he just *must* talk to her a little w'ile. Well, poor Julie fell for it.

Doc always keeps a night light in his office, so it looked to Julie like they was somebody there.

Meanw'ile Jim Kendall had went to Wright's poolroom, where they was a whole gang amusin' themselves. The most of them had drank plenty of gin, and they was a rough bunch even when sober. They was always strong for Jim's jokes and when he told them to come with him and see some fun they give up their card games and pool games and followed along.

Doc's office is on the second floor. Right outside his door they's a flight of stairs leadin' to the floor above. Jim and his gang hid in the dark behind these stairs.

Well, Julie come up to Doc's door and rung the bell and they was nothin' doin'. She rung it again and she rung it seven or eight times. Then she tried the door and found it locked. Then Jim made some kind of a noise and she heard it and waited a minute, and then she says, 'Is that you, Ralph?' Ralph is Doc's first name.

They was no answer and it must of come to her all of a sudden that she'd been bunked. She pretty near fell downstairs and the whole gang after her. They chased her all the way home, hollerin', 'Is that you, Ralph?' and 'Oh, Ralphie, dear, is that you?' Jim says he couldn't holler it himself, as he was laughin' too hard.

Poor Julie! She didn't show up here on Main Street for a long, long time afterward.

And of course Jim and his gang told everybody in town, everybody but Doc Stair. They was scared to tell him, and he might of never knowed only for Paul Dickson. The poor cuckoo, as Jim called him, he was here in the shop one night when Jim was still gloatin' yet over what he'd done to Julie. And Paul took in as much of it as he could understand and he run to Doc with the story.

It's a cinch Doc went up in the air and swore he'd make Jim suffer. But it was a kind of a delicate thing, because if it got out that he had beat Jim up, Julie was bound to hear of it and then she'd know that Doc knew and of course knowin' that he knew would make it worse for her than ever. He was goin' to do somethin', but it took a lot of figurin'.

Well, it was a couple days later when Jim was here in the shop again, and so was the cuckoo. Jim was goin' duck-shootin' the next day and had came in lookin' for Hod Meyers to go with him. I happened to know that Hod had went over to Carterville and wouldn't be home till the end of the week. So Jim said he hated to go alone and he guessed he would call it off. Then poor Paul spoke up and said if Jim would take him he would go along.

Jim thought a w'ile and then he said, well, he guessed a half-wit
was better than nothin'.

I suppose he was plottin' to get Paul out in the boat and play
some joke on him, like pushin' him in the water. Anyways, he
said Paul could go. He asked him had he ever shot a duck and
Paul said no, he'd never even had a gun in his hands. So Jim
said he could set in the boat and watch him and if he behaved
himself, he might lend him his gun for a couple of shots. They
made a date to meet in the mornin' and that's the last I seen of
Jim alive.

Next mornin', I hadn't been open more than ten minutes when
Doc Stair come in. He looked kind of nervous. He asked me
had I seen Paul Dickson. I said no, but I knew where he was,
out duck-shootin' with Jim Kendall. So Doc says that's what
he had heard, and he couldn't understand it because Paul had
told him he wouldn't never have no more to do with Jim as long
as he lived.

He said Paul had told him about the joke Jim had played on
Julie. He said Paul had asked him what he thought of the joke
and the Doc had told him that anybody that would do a thing
like that ought not to be let live.

I said it had been a kind of a raw thing, but Jim just couldn't
resist no kind of a joke, no matter how raw. I said I thought he
was all right at heart, but just bubblin' over with mischief. Doc
turned and walked out.

At noon he got a phone call from old John Scott. The lake
where Jim and Paul had went shootin' is on John's place. Paul
had came runnin' up to the house a few minutes before and said
they'd been an accident. Jim had shot a few ducks and then give
the gun to Paul and told him to try his luck. Paul hadn't never
handled a gun and he was nervous. He was shakin' so hard that
he couldn't control the gun. He let fire and Jim sunk back in the
boat, dead.

Doc Stair, bein' the coroner, jumped in Frank Abbott's flivver and rushed out to Scott's farm. Paul and old John was down on the shore of the lake. Paul had rowed the boat to shore, but they'd left the body in it, waitin' for Doc to come.

Doc examined the body and said they might as well fetch it back to town. They was no use leavin' it there or callin' a jury, as it was a plain case of accidental shootin'.

Personally I wouldn't never leave a person shoot a gun in the same boat I was in unless I was sure they knew somethin' about guns. Jim was a sucker to leave a new beginner have his gun, let alone a half-wit. It probably served Jim right, what he got. But still we miss him round here. He certainly was a card!

Comb it wet or dry?

THE HALF–PINT FLASK [1]

DuBOSE HEYWARD

I PICKED up the book and regarded it with interest. Even its format suggested the author: the practical linen-covered boards, the compact and exact paragraphing. I opened the volume at random. There he was again: 'There can be no doubt,' 'An undeniable fact,' 'I am prepared to assert.' A statement in the preface leaped from the context and arrested my gaze:

'The primitive American Negro is of a deeply religious nature, demonstrating in his constant attendance at church, his fervent prayers, his hymns, and his frequent mention of the Deity that he has cast aside the last vestiges of his pagan background, and has unreservedly espoused the doctrine of Christianity.'

I spun the pages through my fingers until a paragraph in the last chapter brought me up standing:

'I was hampered in my investigations by a sickness contracted on the island that was accompanied by a distressing insomnia, and, in its final stages, extreme delirium. But I already had sufficient evidence in hand to enable me to prove ——'

Yes, there it was, fact upon fact. I was overwhelmed by the

[1] Copyright, 1929, by Farrar and Rinehart, Inc. From *The Half-Pint Flask*, by DuBose Heyward. Farrar and Rinehart, Inc., 1929.

permanence, the unanswerable last word of the printed page. In the fact of it my own impressions became fantastic, discredited even in my own mind. In an effort at self-justification I commenced to rehearse my *impressions* of that preposterous month as opposed to Barksdale's *facts*; my feeling for effects and highly developed fiction writer's imagination on the one hand; and on the other, his cold record of a tight, three-dimensional world as reported by his five good senses.

Sitting like a crystal gazer, with the book in my hand, I sent my memory back to a late afternoon in August, when, watching from the shore near the landing on Ediwander Island, I saw the 'General Stonewall Jackson' slide past a frieze of palmetto trees, shut off her steam, and nose up to the tenuous little wharf against the ebb.

Two barefooted Negroes removed a section of the rail and prepared to run out the gang plank. Behind them gathered the passengers for Ediwander landing: ten or a dozen Negroes back from town with the proceeds of a month's labor transformed into flaming calico, amazing bonnets, and new, flimsy, yellow luggage; and trailing along behind them, the single white passenger.

I would have recognized my guest under more difficult circumstances and I experienced that inner satisfaction that comes from having a new acquaintance fit neatly into a preconceived pattern. The obstinacy of which I had been warned was evident in the thin immobile line of the mouth over the prognathous jaw. The eyes behind his thick glasses were a bright hard blue and moved methodically from object to object, allowing each its allotted time for classification, then passing unhurriedly on to the next. He was so like the tabloid portrait in the letter of the club member who had sent him down that I drew the paper from my pocket and refreshed my memory with a surreptitious glance.

'He's the museum, or collector type,' Spencer had written; 'spends his time collecting facts — some he sells — some he keeps to play with. Incidentally his hobby is American glass, and he has the finest private collection in the state.'

We stood eyeing each other over the heads of the noisy landing party without enthusiasm. Then when the last Negro had come ashore he picked up his bag with a meticulousness that vaguely exasperated me, and advanced up the gang plank.

Perfunctory introductions followed: 'Mr. Courtney?' from him, with an unnecessarily rising inflection; and a conventional 'Mr. Barksdale, I presume,' from me in reply.

The buckboard had been jogging along for several minutes before he spoke.

'Very good of Mr. Spencer to give me this opportunity,' he said in a close-clipped speech. 'I am doing a series of articles on Negroid Primates, and I fancy the chances for observation are excellent here.'

'Negroid Primates!' The phrase annoyed me. Uttered in that dissecting voice, it seemed to strip the human from the hundred or more Negroes who were my only company except during the duck season when the club members dropped down for the shooting.

'There are lots of Negroes here,' I told him a little stiffly. 'Their ancestors were slaves when the island was the largest rice plantation in South Carolina, and isolation from modern life has kept them primitive enough, I guess.'

'Good!' he exclaimed. 'I will commence my studies at once. Simple souls, I fancy. I should have my data within a month.'

We had been traveling slowly through deep sand ruts that tugged the wheels like an undertow. On either side towered serried ranks of virgin long-leaf pine. Now we topped a gentle rise. Before us was the last outpost of the forest crowning a diminishing ridge. The straight columned trees were bars against a released splendor of sunset sky and sea.

Impulsively I called his attention to it:

'Rather splendid, don't you think?'

He raised his face, and I was immediately cognizant of the keen methodical scrutiny that passed from trees to sea, and from sea back to the last wooded ridge that fell away into the tumble of dunes.

Suddenly I felt his wire-tight grasp about my arm.

'What's that?' he asked, pointing with his free hand. Then with an air of authority, he snapped: 'Stop the cart. I've got to have a look at it.'

'That won't interest you. It's only a Negro burying ground. I'll take you to the quarters tomorrow, where you can study your "live primates."'

But he was over the wheel with surprising alacrity and striding up the slight ascent to the scattered mounds beneath the pines.

The sunset was going quickly, dragging its color from the sky and sea, rolling up leagues of delicately tinted gauze into tight little bales of primary color, then draping these with dark covers for the night. In sharp contrast against the light the burying ground presented its pitiful emblems of the departed. Under the pine needles, in common with all Negro graveyards of the region, the mounds were covered with a strange litter of half-emptied medicine bottles, tin spoons, and other futile weapons that had failed in the final engagement with the last dark enemy.

Barksdale was puttering excitedly about among the graves, peering at the strange assortment of crockery and glass. The sight reminded me of what Spencer had said of the man's hobby and a chill foreboding assailed me. I jumped from the buckboard.

'Here,' I called, 'I wouldn't disturb those things if I were you.'

But my words went unheeded. When I reached Barksdale's side, he was holding a small flat bottle, half filled with a sticky black fluid, and was rubbing the earth from it with his coat sleeve. The man was electric with excitement. He held the flask close to his glasses, then spun around upon me.

'Do you know what this is?' he demanded, then rushed on triumphantly with his answer: 'It's a first issue, half-pint flask of the old South Carolina state dispensary. It gives me the only complete set in existence. Not another one in America. I had hoped that I might get on the trail of one down here. But to fall upon it like this!'

The hand that held the flask was shaking so violently that the little palmetto tree and single X that marked it described small agitated circles. He drew out his handkerchief and wrapped it up tenderly, black contents and all.

'Come,' he announced, 'we'll go now.'

'Not so fast,' I cautioned him. 'You can't carry that away. It simply isn't done down here. We may have our moral lapses, but there are certain things that — well — can't be thought of. The graveyard is one. We let it alone.'

He placed the little linen-covered package tenderly in his inside pocket and buttoned his coat with an air of finality; then he faced me truculently.

'I have been searching for this flask for ten years,' he asserted. 'If you can find the proper person to whom payment should be made I will give a good price. In the meantime I intend to keep it. It certainly is of no use to anyone, and I shan't hesitate for a silly superstition.'

I could not thrash him for it and I saw that nothing short of physical violence would remove it from his person. For a second I was tempted to argue with him; tell him why he should not take the thing. Then I was frustrated by my own lack of a reason. I groped with my instinctive knowledge that it was not to be done, trying to embody the abstract into something sufficiently concrete to impress him. And all the while I felt his gaze upon me, hard, very blue, a little mocking, absolutely determined.

Behind the low crest of the ridge sounded a single burst of laughter, and the ring of a trace chain. A strange panic seized me. Taking him by the arm I rushed him across the short distance to the buckboard and into his seat; then leaped across him and took up the lines.

Night was upon us, crowding forward from the recesses of the forest, pushing out beyond us through the last scattered trees, flowing over the sea and lifting like level smoke into the void of sky. The horse started forward, wrenching the wheels from the clutching sand.

Before us, coming suddenly up in the dusk, a party of field Negroes filled the road. A second burst of laughter sounded, warm now, volatile and disarming. It made me ashamed of my panic. The party passed the vehicle, dividing and flowing by on both sides of the road. The last vestiges of day brought out high lights on their long earth-polished hoes. Teeth were a white accent here and there. Only eyes, and fallen sockets under the brows of the very old, seemed to defy the fading glimmer, bringing the night in them from the woods. Laughter and soft Gullah words were warm in the air about us.

'Howdy, Boss.'

'Ebenin', Boss.'

The women curtsied in their high tucked-up skirts; the men touched hat brims. Several mules followed, grotesque and incredible in the thickening dark, their trace chains dangling and chiming faintly.

The party topped the rise, then dropped behind it.

Silence, immediate and profound, as though a curtain had been run down upon the heels of the last.

'A simple folk,' clipped out my companion. 'I rather envy them starting out at zero, as it were, with everything to learn from our amazing civilization.'

'Zero, hell!' I flung out. 'They had created a Congo art before our ancestors drugged and robbed their first Indian.'

Barksdale consigned me to limbo with his mocking, intolerable smile.

The first few days at the club were spent by my guest in going through the preliminary routine of the systematic writer. Books were unpacked and arranged in the order of study, loose-leaf folders were laid out, and notes made for the background of his thesis. He was working at a table in his bedroom which adjoined my own, and as I also used my sleeping apartment as a study for the fabrication of the fiction which, with my salary as manager of the club, discharged my financial obligations, I could not help seeing something of him.

On the morning of the second day I glanced in as I passed his door, and surprised him gloating over his find. It was placed on the table before him, and he was gazing fixedly at it. Unfortunately, he looked up; our glances met and, with a self-consciousness that smote us simultaneously, remained locked. Each felt that the subject had better remain closed — yet there the flask stood evident and unavoidable.

After a strained space of time I managed to step into the room, pick up a book and say casually:

'I am rather interested in Negroes myself. Do you mind if I see what you have here?'

While I examined the volume he passed behind me and put the flask away, then came and looked at the book with me. 'African Religions and Superstitions,' he said, reading the title aloud; then supplemented:

'An interesting mythology for the American Negro, little more. The African Gullah Negro, from whom these are descended, believed in a God, you know, but he only created, then turned his people adrift to be preyed upon by malign spirits conjured up by their enemies. Really a religion, or rather a superstition, of senseless terror.'

'I am not so sure of the complete obsoleteness of the old rites and superstitions,' I told him, feeling as I proceeded that I was engaged in a useless mission. 'I know these Negroes pretty well.

For them, Plat-eye, for instance, is a very actual presence. If you will notice the cook you will see that she seems to get along without a prayer book, but when she goes home after dark she sticks a sulphur match in her hair. Sulphur is a charm against Plat-eye.'

'Tell me,' he asked with a bantering light in his hard eyes, 'just what is Plat-eye?'

I felt that I was being laughed at and floundered ahead at the subject, anxious to be out of it as soon as possible.

'Plat-eye is a spirit which takes some form which will be particularly apt to lure its victims away. It is said to lead them into danger or lose them in the woods and, stealing their wits away, leave them to die alone.'

He emitted a short acid laugh.

'What amusing rot. And I almost fancy you believe it.'

'Of course I don't,' I retorted, but I experienced the feeling that my voice was over-emphatic and failed to convince.

'Well, well,' he said, 'I am not doing folk lore but religion. So that is out of my province. But it is amusing and I'll make a note of it. Plat-eye, did you say?'

The next day was Thursday. I remember that distinctly because, although nearly a week's wages were due, the last servant failed to arrive for work in the morning. The club employed three of them; two women and a man. Even in the off season this was a justifiable expense, for a servant could be hired on Ediwander for four dollars a week. When I went to order breakfast the kitchen was closed, and the stove cold.

After a makeshift meal I went out to find the yard boy. There were only a few Negroes in the village and these were women hoeing in the small garden patches before the cabins. There were the usual swarms of lean mongrel hounds, and a big sow lay nourishing her young in the warm dust of the road. The women looked up as I passed. Their soft voices, as they raised their

heads one after another to say 'Mornin', Boss,' seemed like
emanations from the very soil, so much a part of the earth did
they appear.

But the curs were truculent that morning: strange, canny,
candid little mongrels. If you want to know how you stand with
a Negro, don't ask him — pat his dog.

I found Thomas, the hired boy, sitting before his cabin watching a buzzard carve half circles in the blue.

'When are you coming to work?' I demanded. 'The day's
half done.'

'I gots de toot-ache, Boss. I can't git ober 'fore ter-morrer.'
The boy knew that I did not believe him. He also knew that
I would not take issue with him on the point. No Negro on the
island will say 'no' to a white man. Call it 'good form' if you
will, but what Thomas had said to me was merely the code for
'I'm through.' I did not expect him and I was not disappointed.

Noon of the following day I took the buckboard, crossed the
ferry to the mainland, and returned at dark with a cheerful,
wholesome Negress, loaned to me by a plantation owner, who
answered for her faithfulness and promised that she would cook
for us during the emergency. She got us a capital supper, retired
to the room adjoining the kitchen that I had prepared for her, as
I did not wish her to meet the Negroes in the village, and in the
morning had vanished utterly. She must have left immediately
after supper, for the bed was undisturbed.

I walked straight from her empty room to Barksdale's sanctum,
entered, crossed to the closet where he had put the flask, and
threw the door wide. The space was empty. I spun around and
met his amused gaze.

'Thought I had better put it away carefully. It is too valuable
to leave about.'

Our glances crossed like the slide of steel on steel. Then
suddenly my own impotence to master the situation arose and

overwhelmed me. I did not admit it even to myself, but that moment saw what amounted to my complete surrender.

We entered upon the haphazard existence inevitable with two preoccupied men unused to caring for their own comfort: impossible makeshift meals, got when we were hungry; beds made when we were ready to get into them; with me, hours put into work that had to be torn up and started over the next day; with Barksdale, regular tours of investigation about the island and two thousand words a day, no more, no less, written out in longhand, and methodically filed. We naturally saw less and less of each other — a fact which was evidently mutually agreeable.

It was therefore a surprise to me one night in the second week to leap from sleep into a condition of lucid consciousness and find myself staring at Barksdale who had opened the door between our rooms. There he stood like a bird of ill omen, tall and slightly stooping, with his ridiculous nightshirt and thin slightly bowed shanks.

'I'll leave this open if you don't mind,' he said with a new note of apology in his voice. 'Haven't been sleeping very well for a week or so, and thought the draft through the house might cool the air.'

Immediately I knew that there was something behind the apparently casual action of the man. He was the type who could lie through conviction; adopt some expedient point of view, convince himself that it was the truth, then assert it as a fact; but he was not an instinctive liar, and that new apologetic note gave him away. For a while after he went back to bed, I lay wondering what was behind his request.

Then for the first time I felt it; but hemmed in by the appalling limitations of human speech, how am I to make the experience plain to others!

Once I was standing behind the organ of a great cathedral when a bass chord was pressed upon the keys; suddenly the air about me was all sound and movement. The demonstration that night was like this a little, except that the place of the sound was taken by an almost audible silence, and the vibrations were so violent as to seem almost a friction against the nerve terminals. The wave of movement lasted for several minutes, then it abated slowly. But this was the strange thing about it: the agitation was not dissipated into the air; rather it seemed to settle slowly, heavily, about my body, and to move upon my skin like the multitudinous crawling of invisible and indescribably loathsome vermin.

I got up and struck a light. The familiar disorder of the room sprang into high relief, reassuring me, telling me coolly not to be a fool. I took the lamp into Barksdale's room. There he lay, his eyes wide and fixed, braced in his bed with every muscle tense. He gave me the impression of wrenching himself out of invisible bonds as he turned and sat up on the edge of his bed.

'Just about to get up and work,' he said in a voice that he could not manage to make casual. 'Been suffering from insomnia for a week, and it's beginning to get on my nerves.'

The strange sensation had passed from my body but the thought of sleep was intolerable. We went to our desks leaving the door ajar, and wrote away the four hours that remained until daylight.

And now a question arises of which due cognizance must be taken even though it may weaken my testimony. Is a man quite sane who has been without sleep for ten days and nights? Is he a competent witness? I do not know. And yet the phenomena that followed my first startled awakening entered into me and became part of my life experience. I live them over shudderingly when my resistance is low and memory has its way with me. I know that they transpired with that instinctive certainty which lies back of human knowledge and is immune from the skepticism of the cynic.

After that first night the house was filled with the vibrations. I closed the door to Barksdale's room, hoping a superstitious hope that I would be immune. After an hour I opened it again, glad for even his companionship. Only while I was wide awake and driving my brain to its capacity did the agitation cease. At the first drowsiness it would commence faintly, then swell up and up, fighting sleep back from the tortured brain, working under leaden eyelids upon the tired eyes.

Ten days and nights of it! Terrible for me: devastating for Barksdale. It wasted him like a jungle fever.

Once when I went near him and his head had dropped forward on his desk in the vain hope of relief, I made a discovery. He was the *center*. The moment I bent over him my nerve terminals seemed to become living antennae held out to a force that frayed and wasted them away. In my own room it was better. I went there and sat where I could still see him for what small solace there was in that.

I entreated him to go away, but with his insane obstinacy he would not hear of it. Then I thought of leaving him, confessing myself a coward — bolting for it. But again, something deeper than logic, some obscure tribal loyalty, held me bound. Two members of the same race; and out there the palmetto jungle, the village with its fires bronze against the midnight trees, the malign beleaguering presence. No, it could not be done.

But I did slip over to the mainland and arrange to send a wire to Spencer telling him to come and get Barksdale, that the man was ill.

During that interminable ten days and nights the fundamental difference between Barksdale and myself became increasingly evident. He would go to great pains to explain the natural causes of our malady.

'Simple enough,' he would say, while his bloodshot eyes, fixed on me, shouted the lie to his words. 'One of those damn swamp fevers. Livingstone complained of them, you will remember, and so did Stanley. Here in this subtropical belt we are evidently subject to the plague. Doubtless there is a serum. I should have inquired before coming down.'

To this I said nothing, but I confess now, at risk of being branded a coward, that I had become the victim of a superstitious terror. Frequently when Barksdale was out I searched for the flask without finding the least trace of it. Finally I capitulated utterly and took to carrying a piece of sulphur next to my skin. Nothing availed.

The strange commotion in the atmosphere became more and more persistent. It crowded over from the nights into the days. It came at noon; any time that drowsiness fell upon our exhausted bodies it was there waging a battle with it behind the closed lids. Only with the muscles tense and the eyes wide could one inhabit a static world. After the first ten days I lost count of time. There was a nightmare quality to its unbreakable continuity.

I remember only the night when I saw *her* in Barksdale's doorway, and I think that it must have been in the third week. There was a full moon, I remember, and there had been unusual excitement in the village. I have always had a passion for moonlight and I stood long on the piazza watching the great disc change from its horizon copper to gold, then cool to silver as it swung up into the immeasurable tranquillity of the southern night. At first I thought that the Negroes must be having a dance, for I could hear the syncopation of sticks on a cabin floor, and the palmettos and moss-draped live oaks that grew about the buildings could be seen the full quarter of a mile away, a ruddy bronze against the sky from a brush fire. But the longer I waited listening the less sure I became about the nature of the celebration. The rhythm became strange, complicated; and the chanting that rose and fell with the drumming rang with a new, compelling quality, and lacked entirely the abandon of dancers.

Finally I went into my room, stretched myself fully dressed on the bed, and almost achieved oblivion. Then suddenly I was up again, my fists clenched, my body taut. The agitation exceeded anything that I had before experienced. Before me, across Barksdale's room, were wide open double doors letting on the piazza. They molded the moonlight into a square shaft that plunged through the darkness of the room, cold, white, and strangely substantial among the half obliterated familiar objects. I had the feeling that it could be touched. That hands could be slid along its bright surface. It possessed itself of the place. It was the one reality in a swimming, nebulous cube. Then it commenced to tremble with the vibrations of the apartment.

And now the· incredible thing happened. Incredible because belief arises in each of us out of the corroboration of our own life experience; and I have met no other white man who has beheld Plat-eye. I have no word, no symbol which can awaken recognition. But who has not seen heat shaking upward from hot asphalt, shaking upward until the things beyond it wavered and quaked? That is the nearest approach in the material world. Only the thing that I witnessed was colored a cold blue, and it was heavy with the perfume of crushed jasmine flowers.

I stood, muscle locked to muscle by terror.

The center of the shaft darkened; the air bore upon me as though some external force exerted a tremendous pressure in an effort to render an abstraction concrete: to mold moving unstable elements into something that could be seen — touched.

Suddenly it was done — accomplished. I looked — I saw *her*.

The shock released me, and I got a flare from several matches struck at once. Yellow light bloomed on familiar objects. I got the fire to a lamp wick, then looked again.

The shaft of moonlight was gone. The open doors showed only a deep blue vacant square. Beyond them something moved. The lamp light steadied, grew. It warmed the room like fire.

It spread over the furniture, making it real again. It fell across Barksdale's bed, dragging my gaze with it. *The bed was empty.*

I got to the piazza just as he disappeared under a wide-armed live oak. The Spanish moss fell behind him like a curtain. The place was a hundred yards away. When I reached it, all trace of him had vanished.

I went back to the house, built a rousing fire, lit all the lamps, and stretched myself in a deep chair to wait until morning.

Then! an automobile horn on Ediwander Island. Imagine that! I could not place it at first. It crashed through my sleep like the trump of judgment. It called me up from the abysses into which I had fallen. It infuriated me. It reduced me to tears. Finally it tore me from unutterable bliss, and held me blinking in the high noon, with my silly lamps still burning palely about me.

'You're a hell of a fellow,' called Spencer. 'Think I've got nothing to do but come to this jungle in summer to nurse you and Barksdale.'

He got out of a big muddy machine and strode forward laughing. 'Oh, well,' he said, 'I won't row you. It gave me a chance to try out the new bus. That's why I'm late. Thought I'd motor down. Had a hell of a time getting over the old ferry; but it was worth it to see the niggers when I started up on Ediwander. Some took to trees — one even jumped overboard.'

He ended on a hearty burst of laughter. Then he looked at me and broke off short. I remember how his face looked then, close to mine, white and frightened.

'My God, man!' he exclaimed, 'what's wrong? You aren't going to die on me, are you?'

'Not today,' I told him. 'We've got to find Barksdale first.'

We could not get a Negro to help us. They greeted Spencer, who had always been popular with them, warmly. They laughed their deep laughter — were just as they had always been with him. Mingo, his old paddler, promised to meet us in half an hour with a gang. They never showed up; and later, when we went to the village to find them, there was not a human being on the premises. Only a pack of curs there that followed us as closely as they dared and hung just out boot reach, snapping at our heels.

We had to go it alone: a stretch of jungle five miles square, a large part of it accessible only with bush hooks and machettes. We dared not take the time to go to the mainland and gather a party of whites. Barksdale had been gone over twelve hours when we started and he would not last long in his emaciated condition.

The chances were desperately against us. Spencer, though physically a giant, was soft from office life. I was hanging on to consciousness only by a tremendous and deliberate effort. We took food with us, which we ate on our feet during breathing spells, and we fell in our tracks for rest when we could go no farther.

At night, when we were eating under the high, white moon, he told me more of the man for whom we were searching.

'I ought to have written you more fully at the start. You'd have been sorry for him then, not angry with him. He does not suggest Lothario now, but he was desperately in love once.

'She was the most fantastically imaginative creature, quick as light, and she played in circles around him. He was never dull in those days. Rather handsome, in the lean Gibson manner; but he was always — well — matter-of-fact. She had all there was of him the first day, and it was hers to do as she pleased with. Then one morning she saw quite plainly that he would bore her. She had to have someone who could *play*. Barksdale could have died for her, but he could not play. Like that,' and Spencer gave a snap of his fingers, 'she jugged him. It was at a house party. I was there and saw it. She was the sort of surgeon who believes

in amputation and she gave it to Barksdale there without an
anesthetic and with the crowd looking on.

'He changed after that. Wouldn't have anything he couldn't
feel, see, smell. He had been wounded by something elusive, in-
tangible. He was still scarred; and he hid behind the defenses of
his five good senses. When I met him five years later he had gone
in for facts and glass.'

He stopped speaking for a moment. The August dark crowded
closer, pressing its low, insistent nocturne against our ears. Then
he resumed in a musing voice: 'Strange the obsession that an
imaginative woman can exercise over an unimaginative man. It
is the sort of thing that can follow a chap to the grave. Celia's
living in Europe now, married — children — but I believe that if
she called him today he'd go. She was very beautiful, you know.'

'Yes,' I replied, 'I know. Very tall, blonde, with hair fluffed
and shining about her head like a madonna's halo. Odd way of
standing, too, with head turned to one side so that she might look
at one over her shoulder. Jasmine perfume, heavy, almost
druggy.'

Spencer was startled: 'You've seen her!'

'Yes, here. She came for Barksdale last night. I saw her as
plainly as I see you.'

'But she's abroad, I tell you.'

I turned to Spencer with a sudden resolve: 'You've heard the
Negroes here talk of Plat-eye?'

He nodded.

'Well, I've got to tell you something whether you believe it or
not. Barksdale got in wrong down here. Stole a flask from the
graveyard. There's been hell turned loose ever since: fires and
singing every night in the village and a lot more. I am sure now
what it all meant — conjuring, and Plat-eye, of course, to lead
Barksdale away and do him in, at the same time emptying the
house so that it could be searched for the flask.'

'But Celia; how could they know about her?'

'They didn't. But Barksdale knew. They had only to break him down and let his old obsession call her up. I probably saw her on the reflex from him, but I'll swear she was there.'

Spencer was leaning toward me, the moon shining full upon his face. I could see that he believed.

'Thank God you see it,' I breathed. 'Now you know why we've got to find him soon.'

In the hour just before dawn we emerged from the forest at the far side of the island. The moon was low and reached long fingers of pale light through the trees. The east was a swinging nebula of half light and vapor. A flight of immense blue heron broke suddenly into the air before us, hurling the mist back into our faces from their beating wings. Spencer, who was ahead of me, gave a cry and darted forward, disappearing behind a palmetto thicket.

I grasped my machette and followed.

Our quest had ended. Barksdale lay face downward in the marsh with his head toward the east. His hands flung out before him were already awash in the rising tide.

We dragged him to high ground. He was breathing faintly in spasmodic gasps, and his pulse was a tiny thread of movement under our finger tips. Two saplings and our coats gave us a make-shift litter, and three hours of stumbling, agonizing labor brought us with our burden to the forest's edge.

I waited with him there, while Spencer went for his car and some wraps. When he returned his face was a study.

'Had a devil of a time finding blankets,' he told me, as we bundled Barksdale up for the race to town. 'House looks as though a tornado had passed through it; everything out on the piazza, and in the front yard.'

With what strength I had left I turned toward home. Behind me lay the forest, dark even in the summer noon; before me, the farthest hill, the sparse pines, and the tumble of mounds in the graveyard.

I entered the clearing and looked at the mound from which Barksdale had taken the flask. There it was again. While it had been gone the cavity had filled with water; now this had flooded out when the bottle had been replaced and still glistened gray on the sand, black on the pine needles.

I regained the road and headed for the club.

Up from the fields came the hands, dinner bound; fifteen or twenty of them; the women taking the direct sun indifferently upon their bare heads. Bright field hoes gleamed on shoulders. The hot noon stirred to deep laughter, soft Gullah accents:

'Mornin', Boss — howdy, Boss.'

They divided and flowed past me, women curtsying, men touching hat brims. On they went; topped the ridge; dropped from view.

Silence, immediate and profound.

NORTH IS BLACK[1]

OLIVER LA FARGE

I<small>T IS</small> true that we say that North is black, and cold, and bad because of the stories of our old men, but those are good stories. They had them from the old men before them, from the time that there were no Americans. The Navajo have been here ever since the land was made, the Americans are new.

It is no use to show me that picture of mountains in the North again. I know it is white because it is all snow. I know those mountains. I have seen them. Yes, why do you suppose they call me North Wanderer? I went there, I came back with many horses. Ask my people about the horses Nahokonss Naga brought with him. Yes, that is why I went, to steal horses. I stood on a high place, praying, and my prayers fell away from me, down into the valleys. My prayers got lost, they would not fly up to the Four Quarters. It is bad there.

Give me more coffee.

I speak with one tongue, I went to steal horses. I was always brave. When I was a boy they took me to San Carlos, where the Apaches are. They taught me to talk American. I ran away, and

---

[1] Copyright, 1935, by Oliver La Farge. From *All the Young Men*, by Oliver La Farge. Houghton Mifflin Company, 1935.

lived all alone until my hair grew. When my hair was long again, I had made myself a bow and arrows, moccasins, a skin blanket. I had stolen two horses. I was always like that.

It is true there are good horses nearer than there. I was three moons going, and three moons coming, but I wanted to see.

Then I will tell you the truth. I am old, it is good someone should know. But you must not tell. I know you, you will not tell; no one would believe.

You see that fire? If you try to shut it up in a box, it will burn the box. I was like that. The soldiers would not let us go on the war-path. There was no work for us. Sometimes we went down to raid the Moqui a little bit, to steal sheep, but not enough. We young men were looking for trouble.

A man with a big red beard came and made a trading post near the railroad, a few miles from my mother's hogahn. I lived there, because I did not think of marriage; all the time I was studying to be a singer, learning about the Gods, and the Medicine. I was like the Black Robed Preachers at Chin Lee, I did not think about women.

Red Beard was not like other traders, he was the other kind of American. They don't have that kind out here, I got to know about them later. They are different. Red Beard was sick, that was why he came out here. He did not care about the trading. He was honest with us and we made money off him. He never understood us. He was a good man.

He had a lot of friends coming to see him, from the East. They, too, were different. They liked to wear little pistols. At this time, Americans only carried pistols when they thought there would be trouble, then they had big pistols, not like the ones most of Red Beard's friends carried. And Red Beard's friends never shot anything. Most of them did not know how to shoot. They had bad manners, like the people at Grand Cañon. We were not used to that then, two or three times we were going to kill them.

Their women came out with them. There was one who was tall, and straight, and had black hair, like an Indian's, and brown eyes. She pulled her hair tight, tying it behind, like a Navajo. I fell in love with her.

I was digging holes to plant corn one day, and I saw She-Rain coming up the valley, with a rainbow behind it. I thought, 'That looks like that American Girl.' Then I was frightened, for I knew I must be in love. How could any man think that the rainbow, which is the Way of the Gods, looked like a woman, unless his eyes were twisted with love?

The next time I was with Mountain Singer, learning Medicine, I sang the Hozoji. When I said, 'I walk with beauty all around me,' my mind wandered to her, I forgot about the Gods and the Holy Things. I said to Mountain Singer, 'My mind is bad.' He told me to fast.

When I had fasted for four days, I returned to my mother's hogahn. When I came in, she said, 'What is the matter with you?' I said, 'Nothing.'

She asked me again, 'What is the matter?' Again I told her, 'Nothing.'

She asked me four times, and the fourth time she said, 'Warrior-with-Gods, tell me what is the matter with you.'

When she called me by that name, I had to answer true. I said, 'I am sick inside, I am bad inside; I must cleanse myself.'

My mother said, 'You will not wash out your sickness, nor pray it out. That is man's talk.'

I had already fasted. Now I let down my hair, praying. I went into a sweat bath. All the time that I was there I sang. When I came out and jumped into the creek, I felt all well again. I ran, singing and leaping.

Then I saw mother-of-pearl dawn in the East, all-colour rain, and the rainbow. I heard the Four Singers on the Four Mountains. But it was midday, and clear, and the desert was silent.

I had seen that American Girl come out of the post to watch me running. So I went back to my hogahn, and sat down, covering my face with my blanket.

My mother said, 'By and by she will go away, then you will get well.'

After that I tried to keep away from the post, but I was like a horse on rope. She used to hire me to guide her to places. When I had been with her and she was friendly to me, I used to feel weak, so that after I went away I sat down and groaned. Sometimes, though, I would want to leap and run, because I had foolish thoughts. When the corn began to sprout, I was like that all the time. She should not have been so friendly to me.

One day she said to me, 'I will give you this bracelet if you will let me ride your pinto horse.'

He was the best horse anybody had around there. I answered, 'You do not need to pay me to ride my horse; but if you will give me the bracelet, I should like it.'

Her face was strange when she gave me the bracelet. I was afraid she would laugh at me, but she did not. My heart sang. I did not understand them, those people.

She wanted to go up to the top of Blue Rock Mesa, where the shrine is, where you can see for many days' ride all around. So I took her up there. She was not like most Americans, the way they act. They talk fast, and shout, and spit over the edge. She was quiet, and looked, and thought about it, like an Indian. Then she made me tell her the names of all the places we could see. I showed her the mountains where the Utes are, you could just see them, like a low line of smoke in the north.

She said, 'Tomorrow I go up there.'

I told her, 'It is far.'

'I am going in the iron-fire-drives. I am going to my brother's house, far beyond there. He lives there because there is good hunting. You can come there.'

When she began, my heart was sick; when she ended, my heart was high with joy, that she should want me to follow her. I thought I would make sure. I said, 'I do not know that trail.'

She told me she would show me on the map when we got back to the post. I did not know about maps, then; I thought it was strong medicine. She told me about the trail, then she told me about one of the mountains you have in that picture. You see it a week before you come to it, and it is marked so that you can tell it. She showed me a picture of it. While she was talking, her expression was strange; again I thought she was going to laugh at me, but she did not, so I read those signs another way, and was glad.

I did not watch her go, there was no use. I went on learning to be a singer, to make myself strong. My heart was happy, and I learned well. I traded close with Red Beard, to get money. I had Mountain Singer make me a fire drill, with turquoise and abalone-shell and mother-of-pearl and black stone on it, because it would be dark in the North, and I knew I would need it. I made more arrows, with fine points to them. A man came to the post who had a rifle, the best I had ever seen, and lots of cartridges for it. It took me three weeks to steal that rifle. Every day, I drew the North Trail in the sand. I gave that girl a name, Nahokonss Atat — that is, in American, Northern Maiden.

A lot of time went by this way. When I was ready, I went and gambled with my money. I knew that I could not lose, my medicine was sure. I gambled with some Americans, with their cards; that was easy. Then I gambled with Indians. I won very much, so that I was rich.

At the moon of tall corn there was a squaw-dance in Blue Cañon. I told my mother I would go there, and see if I could find a girl I liked to marry. She saw me gathering all the jewelry I had won.

'That is well, if you do not lose your way.' She said, 'Have you good medicine, lots of corn pollen?'

My face was ashamed when I heard that, but no one could have stopped me then.

I painted my pinto horse, so that he was an ugly dun colour, and I tied a horsehair around his hock to make him lame. I packed my jewelry and buckskin on him, and my good blankets, and dressed myself in old American clothes, with an old blanket. I had much jewelry for her, and a silver bridle to give her with the pinto horse, I did not want it stolen. I tied turquoise to my gun to make it strong.

It was a long trip. When I was far enough North, I took my hair down and braided it, saying I was a Pah-Ute carrying a message for some Mormons. The Pah-Utes are always poor, and they are friends of the Mormons; they let me pass. I passed beyond the Ute country, through tribes I did not know. I talked signs with them, asking for this mountain. Once I had a fight with some Indians, and two times with Americans. Those Indians scalp everyone they kill, like the Utes.

I was three moons on the trail. Then I came to where snow was. It was the end of harvest moon, too early for snow, I knew I was coming to the North. I hoped to meet some of the Frozen Navajo, who live up there, but I did not. By and by it got to be all snow and colder than it ever is here. That was not like winter snow, but deep like all-year snow that you see on the north side of Dokosli, high up. Then I saw the mountain.

I had not seen Indians for a week, it was all ranches and cattle. There was a railroad, and a big town. I made camp where there were some woods, away from the town. I had stolen a hat from a ranch I passed near, leaving a lot of fine horses, because I was afraid to make trouble. Now I wound my hair up around my head, so that the hat covered it. I took off my headband. With my old American clothes, I looked like a Mexican. I talk a little Mexican. So I went into town.

That town was big. It did not look as though I could ever find

Northern Maiden there. And I could not ask for her, I did not know her name. All I could do was walk around and look. I saw places where they sold bitter-water, and thought I would buy some. I had tasted it before, but never enough. The first place I went into the man said, 'Hey, Injun, get the hell out of here.'

Then I went into another, and I spoke in Mexican before the man noticed me. So he sold me drinks. I bought a lot. They cost ten cents, and I spent a dollar for them. Then I felt so good I began to dance a little bit. One of the men said, 'Hey, that Greaser's drunk, throw him out.'

They threw me out. One of them kicked me hard when I went through the door. I fell down in the snow. My sight was red with anger. I walked away, out of town, to the woods where my things were. There I made ready for the war-path — let down my hair, and took off my American clothes. I thought, none of the people in that town carry guns. Now I shall take my very good gun and shoot them, all those people. I shall burn their houses. While I am doing this, I shall find Northern Maiden; her I shall take away, and go back to my own country, with many horses, and much plunder. That way I thought.

I began making war medicine, praying to the Twin Gods. I held my gun across my knees, that my medicine should be strong for it, too. Praying like that, I fell asleep there in the middle. That is a bad thing.

When I woke up, it was night, and I was cold. I was shivering. The fire was out. My head hurt. When I thought how I had gone to sleep in the middle of my prayer, I was afraid. I put on my clothes, and made a fire with my fire drill. Then I prayed, for a long time I was praying. But my prayer would not go up; it fell down where I said it. All of a sudden I was sick for my own country, for the smell of dust on the trail when the sun is on it, for the sound of my horse's hoofs in the sand. My heart was sick for the blue South, where the rainbow is, and tall corn growing by red rocks. I remembered the smoke of my mother's fire, and the thumping as she pounded the warp down in the loom.

Then I thought how far I had come, and how I was near to Northern Maiden, and how she was waiting for me. My medicine was strong, it was the bitter-water that had made me feel like that. I thought that I would be ashamed to go back now, and I was a brave who did not run away from things. So I rolled up in my blanket and went to sleep again. I was like that, we were warriors in those days.

There was game in the hills behind those woods, so that I had enough to eat. When I was not hunting, I stayed in the town. I stayed eight days, until I began to lose hope. Then I saw her. She was in a wagon with a man. They had two good horses with it; they were not as good as my pinto. I followed them out of town, and saw their tracks in the snow, along a road. Then I ran to my camp.

I threw away my American clothes then. I sang, and while I sang I tied up my hair like a Navajo. My headband was good, my shirt was worked with porcupine quills, my leggings had many silver buttons. My belt was of silver, my necklaces and bow-guard were heavy with silver and turquoise. I put the silver bridle on my horse, to make him look well, and so that when I gave it to her, with the pinto, she should know it was my own. Then I rode out, still singing.

I looked all around me. I said, the North is not black. The ground is white; where the sun strikes it, it is all-colour. The sky is blue as turquoise. Our old men do not know. I galloped along the trail. I sang the song about the wildcat, that keeps time with a horse galloping and makes him go faster. That way I felt.

I started in the morning, I got in just after noon. It was a big ranch, there were many horses in the corral, but no sign of cattle. That is not like an American ranch. They were just getting out of the carriage when I rode in. When they saw me, they cried out.

She was surprised, she did not think I would come. I sat still and rolled a cigarette. Inside I was not still. I looked at her, and my heart kept on saying, 'beautiful, beautiful,' like in a prayer.

She came forward to shake hands with me. Some more men and a woman came out. She told them who I was. One of the men kept on saying, 'George, George!' I thought he was calling someone. Later I found out it was his way of swearing. They were different, those people.

She told me to put my horses in the corral. She went with me while I unsaddled my pony. Her face was flushed, she was glad to see me. I could not speak, I was afraid all those people would see what I was thinking. When we were alone in the corral, I gave her the pinto horse, and the bridle. At first she would not take them. She gave me a room to sleep and keep my things in. Then she took me into the big room where the people were.

There were her brother and his wife. They were good people. There were two other men who were good. One of them knew Indians, he could talk American so that I could understand everything he said. There was another man who was not good. His mouth was not good. He had yellow hair, but there was a dark cloud around his head. I could see that, especially when he was thinking bad things. I did not like him, that one. There were other people who stayed with them and went away again, but these people were there all the time.

They were nice to me. I stayed there a long time. Those men were always going hunting, they took me with them. I was a good hunter, so they thought well of me. They liked a man who could do something better than they could. They thought well of me because I had come so far. They asked me to play cards with them. They did not play cards the way the Americans here taught us, except the man I did not like. I won from them, but never very much. I did not think it was good to win too much from them. They were my friends.

The man I did not like was called Charlie. He, too, wanted Northern Maiden. He was not like those others. Sometimes when they had friends and drank bitter-water, one of the women would tell them they had too much, or one of the other men would. Then they would go out and walk around until they were all right. I did not take anything. Sometimes, when there was another woman staying with them there, one of the men would be making love to her. If she told him to stop, he always stopped. This I saw, different times, when people came to stay with them. But Charlie was the only one who made love to Northern Maiden. He did not stop when she told him to. One day I was coming down the long room they had that ran between the other rooms. He was out there, trying to kiss her, the way Americans do. I walked up. He got red in the face and went away. I made talk to her as if I had not seen anything.

I stayed there a long time. I thought, when it was time for spring in my own country, I should ask Northern Maiden to come with me, and I thought she would say yes.

One day I was walking into the door of the big room, when I heard someone inside say my name. Horse-Tamer they said, that was my name, that people used. The man's voice was angry, so I listened. I could not understand everything that they said, they were talking fast in American. But I understood that Charlie was telling them that I cheated at cards. This made them angry. They said that if they caught me, they would run me out. They called me a damn Indian. I was angry; because I knew that Charlie cheated, too, as I have said. I did not understand this, so I went to Northern Maiden.

I told her that the cowpunchers taught us to cheat at cards, that we thought it was part of that game. An Indian is better at it than an American. I did not say anything about Charlie. She said that her kind of American did not cheat at cards, any more than they told lies. They were always honest. So they trusted

everyone who played in a game, that was why they were so angry.
They would run out anyone who cheated when they trusted him.
Then I understood.

I took my money and went in where they were. I said: 'Here
is your money, that I have won at cards. I did not know you did
not cheat, until I heard you talking. The Americans who played
with us always cheated. Now I will not cheat. That is my word.
It is strong.'

Northern Maiden's brother said, 'The Indian's all right.'

The other one, who knew about Indians, said: 'Yes, what he
says is true. He will not cheat any more. Let him play.'

Charlie was angry, but he was afraid to say anything.

So then I played with them some more, and I watched Charlie.
I knew what I wanted to do, and I took my time, like a good
hunter. Finally my chance came, it was like this — We were
playing poker. Charlie used to hide a good card from the pack.
When he thought he could use it, he put it in the palm of his hand.
Then when he reached down to pick up his draw cards, he mixed
it with them. He discarded one more card than he should. Sometimes he slipped it in with the other discards; sometimes, if it
was a good card, he kept it out. I knew it would be no good to find
the card in his clothes, they would think I had put it there. I had
to catch it in his hand, and he was quick.

This time there were a lot of people there, some men from other
ranches, cowpunchers. There was a lot of money, and Charlie got
excited. I was sitting next him. He did not like to see me next
him. I waited till I saw he was about to use his card. I got my
knife ready. When his hand was sliding along the table, before he
got to the draw, I put my knife through it. He screamed, and
everyone jumped up. I took out my knife. There was the ace of
diamonds, and he held two other aces.

Charlie went out of the room. He was white in the face. The
cowpunchers stood around for a little while, then they went away,

too. I said nothing, waiting for them to thank me. These three men, the ones who lived in the house, went off into a corner and talked. I could not hear what they said. Something was wrong.

The man who understood about Indians came over to me. The rest went out.

'Now,' he said, 'you must go away. It is not your fault. Charlie is one of us. You were right to show that he cheated, but not in front of all those cowpunchers. Now we have lost face with them. We are all made ashamed. You should have told us, and we should have caught him when no one else was here. When we see you, you will make us remember that you, an Indian, showed up our friend in front of those people. When you are here, we shall be ashamed. If a white man caught a friend of yours in front of a lot of Moqui, would you like it?'

I said, 'I see. Now I go.'

He shook hands with me. 'You are a good man,' he said, 'I want to be friends with you. I shall come and see you on your reservation. We shall hunt together.'

I said: 'Your talk is straight. It is good. Now I want meat and coffee and sugar to take on the trail.'

He brought me what I needed while I was saddling my horse. He gave me the money Charlie had won from me. He wanted to give me more.

'He will go to the train tomorrow,' he said, 'he is too weak now, you made him bleed a lot.'

It was in the middle of the afternoon that I rode away. I went up to a high hill behind the ranch-house. There I made camp. When I had a fire lighted, a little one that would not make smoke, I began my medicine. It was not good. My prayers fell away, down into the valley. I saw that a man could not pray there, where there was only one direction, North, the Black One. I wanted to go back to where there was East, and South, and West, Mother-of-Pearl dawn, Blue Turquoise, and Red Shell. I prayed the best I could. I used the last of my corn pollen. When the sun set, I made black paint with ashes. I drew the Bows of the Twin Gods on my chest. I put a black line on my forehead. I stripped to my breechclout, moccasins, and headband. I took off all my jewelry except my bow-guard. I took my bow, because a gun makes too much noise. Long after it was black night I went back to the ranch.

They were all in the big room, except Charlie, sitting round the fire. I came in quietly. I hid in a corner behind a chair. All the time I had my bow ready. They did not say much, but sat, not talking. One by one, they got up to go to bed. I was hoping that Northern Maiden would be the last, but if she was not, I had enough arrows. I could not have come so well to her bedroom, it was upstairs. That house was built like a Moqui house, with two floors.

My medicine was good. She stayed sitting and looking at the fire. I could see that she was sad. That did my heart good. In the firelight she was beautiful. I stood up.

Then Charlie came into the room. I was in the corner. I did not move. He never saw me. I made ready to shoot him. He walked over until he stood in front of Northern Maiden. For a little while they looked at each other. I waited. Then he spoke.

'I'm sorry.'

She said nothing.

'Can't you forgive me?'

Then she spoke to him. She got up and stood very straight. I could not understand all those things that they said. They were talking in American, and using words I did not know. They used words we have not got. But this I understood. She loved him. Now she sent him away, for the thing he had done. She said she was very angry. But I saw that she loved him. She gave him a ring, the ring that Americans give when they are going to marry a woman. Now she gave it back to him. I saw she was that kind, that she sent him away, although she loved him, because his heart was bad. She told him that he was like a snake. She meant he was all bad.

He went away again, holding his face down. His hand was bandaged. He looked like a sick man. I let him go.

Northern Maiden sat down in the chair. She began to cry, like an American, hard, so that it hurts, and does no good. I came, then, and stood in front of her. She looked up. She did not start. She was not afraid of me.

I said: 'I did not know, now I do; I would not have done this. Here is the bracelet you gave me. I should not have it.'

She said, 'I understand.'

Then I went away. I rode all night.

I came home at the time of short corn. I had twelve good horses with me. I met a man prospecting in Chiz-Na-Zolchi. I got a good mule from him. These I showed to the people who asked me why I went away. It was good to see the cañons again, with the washes full of water from the snow. It was good to hear my horse's hoofs in the sand, and smell the dust of the trail.

I sat down by my mother's fire. The smoke was rising up straight. She was weaving a man's blanket. She said: 'This is for you, your blanket is worn out. You must choose yourself a wife, you are too much alone. That is the best medicine for you, to have a house and children. When the corn is green, tell me the one you want. I shall ask for her.'

I saw that she was right. I said, 'It is good. You will ask for one.'

But I did not care if she were old or young, beautiful or ugly.

GOOD MORNING, MAJOR [1]

J. P. MARQUAND

Surely Billy Langwell, in spite of a certain polite indifference toward things which he considered of no importance, had been with brigade headquarters long enough to know that the general was not a funny man. Surely Billy must have known that the general hated all of us, for any one could have read uncomplimentary sentiments in the general's harsh green eyes and in the way his hard lips, straight as a disciplined platoon, moved when he spoke to the young gentlemen. Perhaps, in part, it was the natural dislike and contempt of a disciplined old man who had spent his life in the service for parvenus like us, but any one could tell there was something else.

'Young gentlemen' was what he used to call us. It is easy still to recall his voice those times he came into the mess room late for breakfast, when all the young gentlemen snapped hastily to attention. It was not a pleasant voice, General Swinnerton's — slightly thick, and of a suppressed timbre that made you wonder how it would sound when he was angry. Down in the mess room, one can imagine him walking still, heavy, but straight

---

[1] Copyright, 1926, by The Curtis Publishing Company. By permission of the author.

as a post, and aggressively shaven in that way peculiar to old soldiers risen from the ranks, that way no civilian can imitate; so closely shaven that you would think his epidermis must have been removed by the razor's edge, revealing a pinker, thinner skin beneath. Without a word, he would walk to his place at the table, while the young gentlemen listened to his boot heels hit the floor. Snap — they went, as inevitable as regulations. Snap — and then a pause, a military pause, and it was up to me to say, 'Good morning, general.' It was my part of the drill that he had taught me.

'Good morning, major,' he would answer, and we would shake hands there in the mess room, stiffly, like pugilists posing for the Sunday supplements.

'Good morning, major,' he would say, and sometimes there seemed to be a note in his voice of a lonely man, and sometimes it seemed like the voice of a man slightly puzzled by a changing world.

Then he would pause, and then his heavy neck would move deliberately within the circumference of his stiff white collar — you could almost hear it grate — as he stared down the mess hall. Of course all the overnight lieutenants would be watching him, stiffly trying to look military and knowing that they could not. They were young, so young, without a trace in their faces of any blow from life. They were so fearless, so serenely sure of themselves. Was that what General Swinnerton could not understand, and what he resented most? There was Billy Langwell in his whipcords, much more expensive than the general's; one of those nice New York Langwells, slender and almost delicate, with his yellow hair still moist from his morning bath, and smiling at the general. Billy was always smiling as though he had encountered some amusing private thought. And then there was — what was his name? Sometimes faces are so clear and names so hard to remember — Edwin Bryce, the general's other aide, one of the

Philadelphia Bryces, with a gentle voice, but always with a look that was slightly supercilious. Then there were those other ones, faces new and pleasant voices. Sometimes in our mess hall you might have thought it was a college house party and not a brigade about to sail for France.

As the general looked at those faces before he pulled back his chair, his own face would assume a slightly peculiar expression, almost of bewilderment, you would sometimes think, and then he would speak, precisely still, but somewhat differently.

'Good morning. Sit down, young gentlemen. You won't get any rations like this a month from now.'

Then he would seat himself stiffly and raise his coffee cup with exaggerated ease, and grasp his spoon in his awkward fingers. What was he thinking of as he raised his cup and stared silently above its brim? Was he envious or sad? Was he thinking that he was not and never would be quite like the rest? Was he thinking that we knew it? I wonder — Perhaps he always thought that we were laughing.

What strange intuition or trick of caste made Billy spot the general for what he was? The first time Billy's eyes met the general's eyes he knew, and the general knew he knew.

Of course I can remember — any one can remember those first days when uniforms were new, when Camp Abraham Hicks was just beginning to rise out of its wilderness of yellow pine, a hideous checkerboard of order, when the first men of the draft were herded in, in cheap, baggy clothes which they took off, never to wear again.

Those were the days when brigade headquarters seemed a place of mystery — a veritable religious shrine, in which one could imagine strange rites marching in the night. Headquarters was almost the only wooden house in Camp Abraham Hicks in those days. Typewriters were clicking through the half-open windows; an orderly was standing at the door, one of those jaded Regular

Army orderlies, passive yet sneering, whom the War Department doled out, one to each of our companies.

In front of that wooden shack, the stumps of yellow pine still
obtruded themselves, making you stumble in your new boots.
And a set of awkward men in olive drab were grubbing at those
roots while a young second lieutenant, who had been a lieutenant no longer than they had been soldiers, kept saying, 'Now,
fellows, make it snappy! Make it snappy!'

The orderly at the door had a reason to grin sourly. It was
probably the first time in his life that he had heard enlisted men
addressed as 'fellows.' He was still grinning when I saw him.

'Yes, sir,' he said, 'the general's expecting you. He'll see you
in a minute.' Then he stopped grinning and stared wearily beyond me and wearily saluted, and then I heard a voice behind
me that I knew. It was Billy Langwell, hopping adroitly over
the pine stumps, and only stumbling once over an upthrust
root.

'Oh, now, George,' he said, 'are you here too? How did you
pull it? By writing to your congressman?'

'I don't know,' I answered. The army ways were as strange
to me then as they are today. 'I just got an order and came here
to report.' Billy grinned and flicked at his boot with a swagger
stick that he twirled self-consciously, in nervous knowing
arcs.

'Now don't be so upstagy just because you have those what-
you-may-call-'ems on your shoulders,' he suggested. 'They got
you because you can ride, of course. I bet we're the only people in
this place that can mount without a ladder. It's just as well. I
don't want to be a nurse to those East Side Criminals in my outfit, and anyhow, the family wanted me to be an aide.'

The orderly interrupted us, saluting languidly. 'The general
sends his compliments and says he'll see you now.'

'Both of us?' I asked.

A round solid mass of something moved in the orderly's beefy cheek. 'Yeh,' he said, 'both of you, sir.'

As we entered, from the corner of my eye, I saw the orderly expectorate furtively. It was my first experience with the regular enlisted personnel, and still I do not know how some of them chew tobacco and yet appear not to chew it.

The general was standing in a stuffy little room, with a table, two chairs and a map, showing the squared barrenness of the future Camp Abraham Hicks, pasted on the cardboard-composition wall. He wore the marching shoes of an enlisted man — broad and dusty, like two solid corner stones necessarily large to support his weight. His leather leggings, of an inferior type, were also covered with the camp's red dust, and over his heart was that curious array of ribbons and bits of masonic jewelry that we were even then beginning to stare at with fascination, not to say with envy. They began with the Indian-war ribbon and ran the whole gamut of ribbons — Spanish War, the Philippines and Boxer. Also hanging among them was a silver medal and a pair of crossed rifles. But you needed no service badges to spot him. You could read his service on his face. His jaw and his mouth, without speaking, fairly shouted Regular Army, typical and peculiarly like the eyes of the orderly who sinned in secret by chewing tobacco at the door.

'When you come into my room,' said the general, 'take off your hats. Good morning, major.' And he held out a stubby hand to me and looked me in the eye.

'Good morning, sir,' I answered.

He stood motionless, still looking at me. 'Say, "Good morning, general,"' he replied. 'I consider it better etiquette.'

Then precisely as a machine gun turns on a pivot, his head veered, rising from his white collar, to Billy Langwell.

'Lieutenant,' inquired the general, 'what's that in your hand?'

'A swagger stick, sir,' said Billy.

There was no expression of contempt, no change in the general's face. 'Throw it out the window,' he said.

Without moving from where he was standing, Billy threw it. It made a little whistling arc through the room and was gone.

'Who told you,' asked the general, 'to carry one of those things?'

'Why no one ——' began Billy.

'Sir,' said the general.

'Sir,' said Billy.

The general folded his arms behind his back and rocked backward and forward from his toes to his heels. 'Now listen to me, both of you,' he said. 'Where did you go to school?'

'To Harvard,' I answered. The general's lip contracted.

'Sir,' he said.

'Sir,' I said hastily.

You could tell what the general was thinking. Like a machine gun on a pivot, his eyes again met those of Billy Langwell, who began to smile.

'I am just as effete as he is, sir. I come from Harvard too, sir.'

'Yes?' said the general. 'Well it's no joke, being effete, young man, when there's a war. Now listen to me, both of you.'

He paused and once again rocked from his toes to his heels as though the rocking might give impetus to his thoughts.

'You won't like me,' he said. 'Neither of you will like me, but that makes no difference in the service. In '75 I was a private in Arizona, before either of you was born. There used to be real fighting in '75 and the service used to be a real service. I got my corporal's stripes when I pulled Chief Three Horns off his pony and choked him, back in the Navaho war. I got my majority for going out ahead of my detachment and killing three brown brothers with a bayonet in Mindanao. I'd rather have a bayonet in my hands now than this confounded job. But as long as I'm a general, I'll be a soldier's general' — he scowled slightly and his voice began to sharpen — 'and not one of these bootlicking dancing-party generals with a pull back in the War Department. And the men on my staff will be soldiers, and not like military attachés. I haven't been to Harvard. I haven't been anywhere except to military schools. That's why you won't like me. But you'll be soldiers just the same. That's all. Sit down at that table, major, and go over these reports. And you, Mr. —— I've forgotten your name ——'

'Langwell, sir,' he said — 'William Langwell.'

The general looked at him for a moment in silence. Then for the first time I became aware of that curious, baffled expression in his eyes — half puzzled, almost diffident.

'Langwell? There used to be — where was it? — back in the 65th a shavetail named Langwell. Mr. Langwell, go out and tell that low-lived, no-account orderly that he'll be making little ones out of big ones if I see him chewing tobacco again the way he's chewing it now. If he'd been in the cavalry in '75 he'd know how to stow it in the back of his jaw when he's on duty. Little ones out of big ones — he'll understand if you don't. And then go to the stables, and get my horse and one for yourself. And by the way, major, you'd better go out with him and see that he speaks properly to the enlisted men. There's nothing more important than speaking properly to enlisted men. Salute when you go out. And right-about! One! Two!'

Then we were outdoors again where the men were grubbing at the pine stumps, and Billy was speaking to the orderly.

'My boy,' he said, 'the general has just sent me out to tell you he'll have you making little ones out of big ones if he sees you chewing tobacco. Personally, I can't perceive that you're chewing. But just as a friend — strictly as a friend — I'd advise you to cut it — or shall I say spit it out? — because you didn't serve in the cavalry back in '75.'

I seized Billy by the arm and pulled him out of earshot.

'Don't make an ass of yourself,' I hissed. 'Can't you watch your step?'

Billy smiled at me and blinked. 'Tut-tut, George,' he said. 'Now don't be so continually upstagy because you've got those fig or maple leaves on you! Can't we be boys together once in a while? All right, I'll promise not to do it again. All right, but I somehow couldn't — George' — his smile grew broader and he patted me softly on the arm — 'do you know what I perceived? Really my perception has grown remarkably keen since I embarked on this military business. I perceived, or it seemed to me I perceived' — his voice grew lower, but was very careless, very playful — 'I actually perceived that the general isn't quite a gentleman!'

And there you have it — that stupid inexorable conventionality we all of us have when we are young, incapable of perceiving that a man could be a man and still not quite a gentleman.

Billy was smiling at the tree stumps, but you could see that he was thinking, for his eyes had a curious distant look, and suddenly he tapped my arm again. 'George, my boy,' he said, 'the more I think of it — do you know what I think? Seriously, George, I've got a mission to perform.'

'What sort of a mission?' Somehow you could not help but be amused, for he was never more than half serious even at his worst.

'I feel that it devolves upon me,' said Billy, and tapped my arm again, 'as a representative — I'm hanged if I know of what, but — well, I feel it devolves on me, under the circumstances, to put the general in his place.'

'To what?' I gasped.

'To put the general in his place,' repeated Billy. 'Oh, not crudely; of course, not crudely; but watch me. I'll find a way.'

The egotism of it! It's the sort of thing that always rather shocks you, but Billy Langwell did it. There was that unyielding, curious sense of pride, of decency or position or something of the sort. It took Billy Langwell four months, but just the same he did it — and nicely — oh, so nicely.

It was an afternoon when the thick mud of Camp Abraham Hicks was baking into the clay of spring. You remember those afternoons, dreary as a misspent life, with the weight of a badly cooked dinner resting like a sin upon the conscience. The general was at his table in the orderly room, licking his thumbs the better to turn the papers before him. His blunt thumbs went snap with grim steadiness; his hair was like a gray rat's nest; his coat was unbuttoned at the collar and his eyes were slightly protruding. At the sound of a gentle tap on the door, he muttered something beneath his breath and sighed. It was Billy Langwell in his whipcords, walking delicately in his custom-made riding boots and silver spurs, with his garrison cap pulled smartly over his eyes as he had seen in pictures.

The general cleared his throat, and Billy spoke at once with his inevitable slight smile: 'Excuse me, sir.'

The general looked at him coldly for a moment before he answered. 'Mr. Langwell,' he said at length, 'when you come into the orderly room, take off your cap.'

The slight smile did not leave Billy's lips. His cap was instantly in his hand.

'Certainly, sir. But the general said ——'

Of course the general interrupted him at once, but not unpleasantly — rather with a sort of triumph. 'Don't argue. I can appreciate the way you feel, but don't argue. I won't make pets of second lieutenants because they're aides of mine. Do you remember I told you that?'

'Yes, sir.' Billy had not moved from attention, and his voice was perfectly respectful. 'But the general said ——'

'Well, what did I say?'

'The general told us to keep our hats on when we carried side arms.'

Of course the general had not noticed. There was a moment's pause, and you could almost feel sorry for the general. Of course it was a little thing, but Billy Langwell had the general right on the hip, the way he said he would.

'Side arms?' The general cleared his throat. 'Who told you to put on side arms?'

Yes, he had put the general in his place. Billy's face had the innocent triumph of youth and something more, that indefinable expression that made the general know what Billy thought.

'The general,' he replied, 'told me to report at three with side arms.'

Right on the hip — that was where Billy had him. The general pushed back his chair, but did not rise. The chair creaked and grated beneath his weight, and you could have laughed almost to see his embarrassment. He had made a mistake and he knew he had made one. It might seem little, but not to a Regular Army man.

'Then why' — his voice was thicker — 'then why didn't you tell me in the first place, without all this confounded argument?'

Against the thickness of the general's voice came Billy's answer, pleasant and conventional, devoid of any emotion. He did it nicely, very nicely. 'I tried to, sir,' he said.

'Well,' said the general, 'you didn't try hard enough.'

'No, sir,' said Billy. It was almost sad to watch them. Why could the general not have left it here? Billy was speaking so quietly, leading the general slowly beyond his depth. It was childish, so absurd you could almost laugh, though the pulses were beating in the general's temples.

'Well, you should have,' said the general. 'See here — you put your hand over your holster. You hid it. Did you try to make a fool of me on purpose?'

Billy's answer came at once, perfectly certain, perfectly controlled, and that eternal trace of a smile still flickered on his lips. 'I'm sure I beg the general's pardon,' he replied. 'If the general thinks ——'

General Swinnerton rose slowly from his chair. His voice was chilly, his hand trembling. Something within him, the thing that was always there, burst loose for a moment before he could stop it. 'Can't you speak to me like a man?' he roared.

Why is it that youth is so obtuse and can never understand?

That very evening Billy came into my tent with a stiff parody of a walk and held out his hand.

'Good morning, major,' he said softly, and giggled beneath his breath.

'Stop it!' I whispered. 'Don't be such a fool!'

Billy giggled again. He always had a most engaging way when his friends fell out. 'Don't be such a fool yourself. Just because you've got those fig leaves, or whatever they are, on you — you can't forget we used to go on parties. Oh, I know we're in the Army now, but maybe I didn't have the general dead to rights! What? Didn't I?'

'You ought to be ashamed of yourself ——' I began, but he stopped me with a delicate shrugging gesture.

'Why the deuce should I be ashamed?' he demanded. 'Do you think I'm going to sit still and have the life ragged out of me, my boy? Do you remember what I told you? He isn't a gentleman, George, my boy. I said he wasn't — remember?'

'If you aren't a West Pointer' — I can still hear the general's voice, as he paced about the orderly room one evening when we were there alone — 'if you're not a West Pointer, young man, or if you haven't come from the ranks like me, there isn't any hope for you. You don't know what the Army is, that's all.'

And I suppose in a hundred other barracks, a hundred other

old men with ribbons on their chests were holding forth in the same grim strain. Of course you can't understand; no civilian can fathom the eccentricity of the military mind. That ridiculous affair of the garrison cap and the side arms did something to General Swinnerton.

It has occurred to me sometimes that a monk's life and a soldier's life are really quite the same, for they both have their eternal round of order in which the smallest thing that moves against the methodical current becomes great enough to shatter all existence.

If any one had come to Camp Merritt to see the general off, it might have been a better thing, because I think he would have liked a kindly word; but no one came. No one sent him a box of cigars or candy. No one but the camp commandant said good-by.

He was a short, asthmatic little man, too old to go across, who could only sit and watch others go. He took us down to the Fort Lee Ferry himself, and shook the general's hand. It was what the general had said — you couldn't understand the Army unless you were an army man.

'Good-by, Swinnerton,' he said. 'Give 'em hell.'

Billy Langwell was opening the automobile door.

'So long,' said General Swinnerton. 'Don't drink yourself to death. You needn't help me, Mr. Langwell. I'm still young enough to walk. Run aboard there and give the colonel my compliments and tell him to see his men below and stop their singing. This isn't a Y.M.C.A. social. It's war.'

And that was all the general said as he left his native shores. Yet he seemed to want to talk that night. He called the young gentlemen to his cabin on the boat deck after dinner, where all the portholes were battened tight, and gave them a short lecture.

'Now don't forget,' he ended — and for once that day he seemed to be almost happy — 'don't forget we're through with thés dansants, or however you say it, and pink teas and kissing the girls good-by at those hostess houses, or whatever you call them. Don't forget we're going to war. Don't forget that to-morrow morning or a month from now we may all be dead.' Then he paused, looked a little puzzled at the young gentlemen.

Of course he could not understand the way they took it, and his voice grew louder. 'You don't believe me, do you? You think you've got a return ticket because you're on the staff! What do you find to smile at, Mr. Langwell?'

There was a slight sound of shifting feet above the churning of the engines, and we looked at Billy Langwell. He was standing in the centre of the cabin. He was scarcely smiling; certainly not broadly enough to merit a rebuke. And he answered at once, without embarrassment, as he always did: 'I'm sure I beg the general's pardon. I wasn't smiling at the general.'

'Then what the devil are you smiling at?' General Swinnerton demanded. 'Tell us, Mr. Langwell, if it's funny.'

If Billy Langwell had only blushed or stammered, but he neither blushed nor stammered, and he answered right away:

'It's not exactly funny, sir, but I was only thinking ——'

'Go ahead,' said the general. 'It's obvious that you're thinking.'

'I was only thinking,' said Billy, 'that the general's room used to be the bridal suite, not so many months ago.'

The general looked at the brass bedstead and at the velvet hangings before the portholes, already tawdry from the Army, reeking with stale cigar smoke.

'Major,' he said, 'send my compliments to the gunnery officer and tell him my aides will be on submarine lookout with the other young men from the regiments. Tell him to put them in the bow. Good evening, young gentlemen.'

The general was alone when I returned. He was pacing up and down the bridal suite, and in spite of the slight pitching of the boat, his step was as accurate as ever. His boots went pit-pat on the heavy carpet. In his right cheek was a slight spherical bulge which he caused to disappear when I came in, in the manner of a good cavalryman back in '75.

'I don't understand them,' he said. 'I'm damned if I understand. Young men didn't used to be like that when I was young. Don't they ever think of anything serious?'

I tried to pass it off lightly. Somehow I knew he was oppressed and lonely, and suspected his dinner was not setting right that first night at sea.

'It's their tradition, general,' I said. 'They don't mean anything by it; they're only following the tradition — being *toujours gai.*'

But the general stood stock-still and folded his hands behind him. 'Two joor?' he inquired. 'What does two joor mean? Oh, it means always, does it?' He coughed and moved his jaw hastily, and continued his walk about the bridal suite.

I moved toward the door, was just about to say good night, when he said the most peculiar thing, that made me stop and look at him.

'Just a minute, major.' Was it possible that his voice sounded diffident? 'Would you mind — have you got time — here, I wish you'd read this letter. It's written to my son.'

It was the first time that I knew — the first time that any of us knew — that General Swinnerton had a son. And why he told me of it then I could never understand. Perhaps he was thinking of his farewell from Merritt that morning.

Perhaps he knew that among us all he was a being apart, and for a moment did not want to be.

He handed me a sheet of foolscap paper from a field clerk's box that was set upon a rosewood writing table.

'Dear Earl,' I read. Now you might have known his name would have been Earl! 'Dear Earl: The old man has got off

in a cloud of dust. I am sitting in a bridal suite, surrounded
by a lot of college boys and a Y.M.C.A. secretary, with a bunch
of city boys in the steerage who don't know how to wear their
O.D. breeches. God knows how we can ever fight a war with
a lot of college boys and city boys who think they're soldiers.
I'm glad you're not a college boy. See if you can't be a soldier
even if you are a half-baked shavetail. Do what they tell you
and don't grin about it. So long, Earl. I wish I was going with
you to the front line where there isn't all this damn funny business. Remember what I said — always keep two biscuits and a
clean pair of socks, old army issue if you can get them, in your
back breeches pocket, and be sure to take along a .45 revolver.
Good night, Earl. Your Old Man.'

I handed the letter back. What was there to say? What could
I possibly have said?

The general looked at me curiously, trying to read my comment in my face.

'You think it's a bum letter, don't you?' he inquired. 'But
you see the way I feel.'

'I don't blame you,' I said. I forgot to call him sir.

'Good night, major,' said the general. 'Go round the decks
before you turn in and if you find anybody smoking a cigarette
or showing a light outside, take his name for special court.
That's all. Good night.'

As I turned to close the door I had a glimpse of him standing alone in the bridal suite, staring at the curtains, and I never
told anyone about the letter. Somehow I could never even smile
about it. If it was not a letter from Lord Chesterfield to his
son, at least it was a letter from an army man.

As one thinks of it, it becomes inevitable that Billy Langwell
should have laughed at General Swinnerton. And yet it's so
hidden now that one can scarcely recall all those little things
leading to that end.

Take the history of the Umpty-something Brigade, for instance. You know those stories printed on smooth shiny paper by some local printer and pathetic from their sheer inadequacy. There is only a sentence in it that brings a picture back.

'On the evening of September eighth,' it read, 'the Umpty-something Brigade was carried in trucks to Je Ne Sais Quoi and marched on foot to Ça Ne Fait Rien, where it relieved the Umpty-something-else Brigade of the Fig-Leaf Division at 10:40, occupying a front extending east from and including the town of Quelque Chose along the lines of the Quelque Chose highway, through the farm of Petites Chaussettes and thence to the woods and Je Ne Sais Quoi.' There it is, in black and white, written with all that singular lack of imagination which is characteristic of all things military.

And yet it brings back pictures — a dark, startled obscurity, and noise as constant as silence to the ears, muddy columns of men, sweating startled horses and a grim shape riding on his horse in silence, without a hat.

It was like the general to throw his tin helmet away. 'If they get me they get me,' he said. 'What's the use of all this funny business?'

Those are the sort of things that those pedantic words bring back — even to the shadows of the town of Quelque Chose.

When we took over the brigade P. C. and the front line, of course the enemy specialized on the town of Quelque Chose. You could see its houses two miles off, as it stood there on the hill. They only had to say a number, that was all, and let the guns turn loose.

You should have heard the general swear when those first shells went by. It was enough to have made you laugh, if it had been a time for laughing. You should have seen him scramble in the mud among the wounded horses and have heard his voice, not frightened, only angry, as he shouted to a runner from the

Umpty-something Division. 'Where are we? This is a hell of a place!'

'We're just getting in, sir. It's Quelque Chose,' said the runner. But he was a green man. He had a catch in his voice. 'Damn their hides! Them Jerries know we're moving out tonight. You might 'a' knowed those Blanks 'ud know it.'

Then the general's voice came out of the dark. It really was a funny thing he said, and I felt Billy nudge me in the ribs as the general said it. 'Damn your own hide!' roared General Swinnerton. 'Cut out that swearing!'

We were stumbling over a heap of rubbish that had once been a street. Billy Langwell tripped and grasped instinctively at the general's arm to keep his balance, and I heard him draw a sharp quick breath.

'What is it, Mr. Langwell?' said the general. 'Can't you keep your feet?'

'A man!' said Billy. His voice was a little high. 'General, I stepped on a man!'

You would have known the general was a soldier even in the dark. 'Did you hear Mr. Langwell, young gentlemen?' he inquired. 'Mr. Langwell stepped on a dead man. Don't be surprised. There always are dead men in a war.'

'Here we are, sir,' said the orderly. 'Mind the step, sir. It's in a cellar. Lord! What's that?'

'A heavy gun, you ass,' said the general.

And we were in the headquarters of the town of Quelque Chose. I can still hear the general's voice. It goes with candle-light and the damp and reeking smell of night. 'Give me a map. Where the devil is that map? Are the telephones installed?' And then it is all a nightmare, nothing more.

Quelque Chose I called the town. It isn't its real name, but every town was Quelque Chose in the stretches of those nights. Every town was something that makes you sit up still and stare into the black. As a matter of fact, it was Ouchy, or Coulchy-sur-the-Something-or-Other. The way the old general spluttered and coughed as he pronounced it was enough to make you laugh. It is not so long ago since I saw the place, but though eight years or more have passed, there is a shocked silence, and you can almost think it was the day before yesterday, the time those names meant nothing.

I can remember the general glaring at the French artillery map. The rest is dim, but that part of it seems almost the day before yesterday. There were two candles in that cellar hole where headquarters P. C. were located, shining mellowly upon his face and making the silver stars glitter on his shoulders. And the yellow light gave his face a most peculiar reddish tint which was almost like old copper.

He was in the center of that cellar, quite calm, standing in a welter of equipment that had not been cleared away, between the box where the field telephones were already going and the muddy curtain of blankets by the door. The mud from the road — that strange gray mud of France — came off his stubby fingers on the map he was holding. He was staring at the map with reddish eyes, running his forefinger slowly across it.

'What the devil's the name of this place?' he inquired, looking up for a moment. The young gentlemen were standing around trying to look perfectly calm. 'Oozy-Coozy? What the devil is it? And what the devil are those little gimcracks up ahead?'

It was not peculiar. Maps of all kinds always annoyed the general. He did not have time to get an answer, for the telephone operator interrupted him.

'Call from the division, sir,' he said.

'Confound the division,' said the general. 'Can't they leave a man alone?' And he sat down by the instrument.

His two aides were just behind him, straight and quiet; Billy

Langwell, a little paler than usual, and Edwin Bryce, playing at his belt with his long fingers.

'Stop that noise,' said the general. He seemed to forget that no one could stop that noise until the war was over.

'Hello! Is this what? Is this what? — What? Brewery one? This is General Swinnerton speaking. Headquarters of the Umpty-umph Brigade.'

Billy Langwell looked at me and winked. The color had returned to his cheeks.

'Oh! It's a code word, is it? The Germans will hear me, will they? How many peanuts have I got? What do you mean by peanuts?... Oh! Every man has got a hundred rounds, if the fools know how to fire them.... What's that? The Germans will hear me? Don't make me laugh, sir. You used to talk sense before you got those two stars on you. A hell of a mess? Of course it's a mess. They're turning on everything that they've got. Have I got my front line located? No. How can I be sure when all the wires are out? Well, hold the wire.'

The general tossed the instrument to the telegraph orderly and seized the map again. Of course he knew we were all watching him. Of course we knew he was in a strange position, not knowing where the front line was, not knowing anything — just stumbling in the dark.

'What the devil's the name of this place?' he repeated. 'Oozy? Coozy? Why the devil can't they make sense? and what's that little gimcrack? That's where the Umpty-umph ought to be, isn't it? No, not that. That's a brook. That little square thing, La Ferme. What the devil's a ferme? I came here to fight a war, not to learn French! Confound this light! La Ferme de la Sainte?' The map crumbled beneath the general's fingers. He looked around at the young gentlemen almost stupidly, with his mouth half open. 'That's a deuce of a name to call anything! It isn't a name at all. It's like a piece of underwear. It's like one of those things women put on themselves when they don't wear corsets.'

There was a moment's silence. The word 'corsets' in that place seemed to have a magic sound. The orderly at the telephone looked up. The runners at the door with red bands on their sleeves looked up. And all the rest of us looked at him helplessly, as we listened to the noise outside. Then there came the most incongruous sound. The general's head flew up. Billy Langwell had not meant to laugh. You could see it on his face. It was a reflex of strained nerves, when everyone's nerves were strained. But General Swinnerton heard him. For an instant his face went scarlet and his lips moved without a sound. For an instant even the noise outside seemed to lessen. And then the general spoke — quietly — much more quietly than he had spoken all that night. 'You're laughing, Mr. Langwell?' he inquired.

It was the first time I ever saw Billy startled. In spite of the shadow his helmet cast over his face, his whole face looked drawn and startled.

'I beg the general's pardon,' he said hastily. Even then he did not forget the etiquette he had been taught.

'Well, what were you laughing at?' The general's voice was louder. 'You're laughing at me, Mr. Langwell. You've always been laughing at me! Now tell me what's so funny.'

'I beg the general's pardon,' began Billy again.

General Swinnerton stared at him. He seemed to have forgotten everything — even the noise outside. 'Don't be so damned polite!' he said. 'You're always laughing. Now tell me what's so funny.'

Billy's answer came quickly. He wasn't frightened exactly, but he was embarrassed: 'I'm awfully sorry, sir. I had no business to laugh. I — I don't know why I did, except what you said about the name — the corsets. I ——'

Billy stammered and stopped, and the general nodded. 'I understand,' he said. 'You like to see the old man make a fool of himself.'

You couldn't help but be sorry for Billy Langwell then. Just to see the color in the general's face and the glazed look in his eyes was enough to make you sorry.

For the end of everything was there, or the ultimate result. All that had gone before — the little things, memories of sly glances and half smiles, everything which was hidden beneath courtesy and manners flashed into the general's cheeks and forehead, as though some unseen cauldron had boiled over and had completely spilled its reddish-purple contents even over the general's nose. He blushed and stammered, as though he were fighting against something that had grown too strong at last.

'You second-chop shavetail!' — you would hardly have known it was the general, his face had grown so dark — 'did you think I haven't watched you? Do you flatter yourself I haven't seen you and the lot of you sneering at me because I can't hold a fork? Don't lie to me about it! You think I am a mucker, don't you? — you damned dude! I may be a mucker, but I've got eyes and ears. Don't think I am fit to order you! You don't think I'm a gentleman, do you? I've seen the bunch of you whispering at Hicks and on the boat. You don't think I'm one, do you? Answer me — you! D'you hear?'

The words poured out of him as suddenly as the color had poured into his face, just as ugly and as horrid, and with them came all the pain and resentment he must always have harbored, for he was not under control. No one was under control unless it was Billy Langwell. I saw Edwin Bryce's face flush and his lip curl angrily, but Billy Langwell maintained the most irritating poise — that poise which the general had always hated — and stared at the general placidly.

'The general,' he said, 'has me at a disadvantage. I can't say what I think — what I should have to say — without being misunderstood. Perhaps some other time ——'

The general interrupted him as though the sound of Billy's voice was more than he could bear: 'Say what you mean for once in your life — to my face — like a man — you sniveling coward!'

He was not a sniveling coward. The general ought to have seen that from the way Billy stood and answered.

'You want me to?' he inquired. Every one must have wanted to catch him, to pull him away, but no one did, and his voice continued meticulously distinct. 'You want me to? All right then. I've stood enough. I think you're a bully and a windbag. Stop it! Put down your hand!'

There was no doubt the general was not himself. Edwin Bryce sprang in front of him just in time, and you could almost have been proud of Edwin.

'There, sir,' he said, 'we'll apologize, of course. But let me remind you — The division is on the wire. They want the co-ordinates for the front line.'

'The division is still on the wire, sir.'

The general looked at Edwin Bryce and then back at Billy Langwell. His hand trembled so that the map moved uncertainly in his fingers, and his voice was as unpleasant as I had ever heard it.

'You know everything, don't you?' he remarked — 'you two young men? Orderly, tell headquarters that I'm sending runners up and I'll telephone the co-ordinates when I get them. And now, Mr. Langwell, do you know that word? Can you read it for us?'

Billy leaned over the map. His voice trembled slightly. 'Certainly, sir. It's La Ferme de la St.-Hilaire.'

'De la St.-Hilaire,' mimicked the general, suddenly grotesque and terrible. 'Is it now? And can't you read all these other names, Mr. Langwell?'

Billy looked at the general. Billy no longer looked exactly nonplussed. He took a corner of the map in his thumb and forefinger. 'Certainly — easily,' he answered; 'in fact without any trouble at all.'

The general made no comment. He looked at Edwin Bryce. 'And you, Mr. Bryce?' he inquired with that same unpleasant parody. 'Of course you can read them, Mr. Bryce?'

'Of course,' said Edwin shortly.

And then Billy said something that finished it. Although he was perfectly cool, you could see he was angry — as angry as the general.

'The general must remember,' he said gently, 'that we haven't had — the benefits of an army education.'

The fool! What a fool he was! The coldness and the silence of the general were what made it terrible. He looked at them both with that slightly puzzled expression which changed into something else, and swayed back and forth from his toes to his heels before he finally spoke.

'How fortunate,' said the general, and swayed again from his toes to his heels, 'we've got some one who can locate the front line. Rise and shine, young gentlemen.' They didn't understand him. None of us exactly understood. 'Do you hear me?' The color of the general's face seemed to choke his voice. 'Get out with you both, if you know so much. Go up and find that farm. Go up and see if the line is in front of it, behind it or in it. And come back and let me know.'

And he knew what he was doing. That was what made it worse. He was sending them up to the front line in the dark, under heavy shelling, on the first night that they had ever heard a shell go off — in the dark — without their ever having known the road. Was there any wonder Billy Langwell looked a little sick?

'Of course you'll send us a runner who knows the way?' he said.

'Knows the way?' said the general. 'Can't you see the way — on that road past the little gimcrack and by the thingumajig? What are you standing arguing about? Go up and find that front line and come back and report. Do you think you're any more valuable than any one else because you're on the staff? My aides are expendable. Go out with you! Forward march!'

Even as the general spoke, he must have known how he appeared, from the way that Billy Langwell looked. For Billy Langwell was the better man just then — much the better man.

He gave a slight pull to the gas mask on his chest and nodded to Edwin Bryce. 'Let's get out of this,' he said.

They walked straight to the door, while the general stared at their backs. Once I thought he was going to speak. Once he cleared his throat.

But at the door, Billy Langwell turned and smiled at the general in a most annoying way. 'Will the general excuse me if I don't take off my hat?' he said. 'I may need it on outside.'

Before the general could answer, they were gone. For a moment he stared at the swaying blankets by the door, almost forgetful of where he was.

'Major,' he said at length, 'make a note on Mr. Langwell's record tomorrow morning — that his manner is insolent to his superior officers. Send out two more men from the detail with my compliments to the signal officer and ask him why he cannot mend his wires.'

Then he hesitated, still standing in the center of the room. You see, he was a soldier — too good a soldier to let his anger carry him away for any length of time. He swayed for a moment from his toes to his heels.

'Is there any runner here who knows the way to that farm?' he asked suddenly. And somehow the tension in every one relaxed, soundlessly yet definitely.

'Yes, sir.' It was the single regular orderly from Camp Abraham Hicks who spoke. 'I've been there, sir.'

'Is it hard to find?' The general looked relieved. At last he was speaking to some one he understood.

'No, sir. You gotta go in the fields, though. They're shelling hell out of the roads.'

'Then you better —' began the general. The orderly was moving automatically toward the door, but the general did not have time to finish.

'The regimental wire's in, sir!' cried the telephone orderly.

The general whirled about. 'Which regimental line?' he cried. 'Give me the telephone.... Hello! Who are you? Baggage? How can you get artillery support if you don't send back your co-ordinates? Well, send another man back. Send two more. Now read them before you go out again. Write 'em down, major, as I say 'em — 23 point — I've got that. Two-three point.' There was a silence. The general set down the instrument and swore.

'The damn thing's out again!' he said. 'Orderly, go out and give those lieutenants my compliments and say you'll take one to the farm and send the other back. And the rest of you clean up this mess in here and give me a chair to sit on.'

But when he got the chair the general would not sit down. He began pacing up and down instead, listening to the noise outside. And you could tell what he was thinking. He was wishing he was up there. He understood better than any of us his present uselessness. It was making him restless. It was wearing down his nerves. Once he looked at his wrist watch. It was two o'clock in the morning and you could tell he was wishing it was light.

The suspense — the uncertainty of everything — was enough to get on anybody's nerves. The telephone orderly sat tense, fingering the plugs on his board with tense fingers. The orderlies by the door sat with their shoulders slouched forward, looking at their hands.

But the general's shoulders were the ones that should have sagged. Everything was resting on them, and he knew it. But he still kept walking up and down. He was the first one who heard a noise in the passage — a scraping, hesitating step.

'Pull back those blankets!' he cried. 'Here comes a message.'

We all saw it at the same time.

'What —' began the general. 'What ——'

A private entered — a stupid red-headed farmer's boy, carrying an officer like a bag of meal across the shoulder.

The general was the first person who spoke, for, you see, he was an army man. 'Lay him down,' he said. 'Don't stand there looking at me! Lay him down and put something under his head.' Without surprise, without contrition — quite methodically, the general spoke. And he knew who it was. You could tell by the useless spurs and the whipcords and the exquisite Sam Browne belt, even before you saw his face.

'Break out a first-aid kit, one of you!' he said. 'What are you looking at? Haven't you seen any blood before? One of you orderlies go out and call a stretcher.'

The red-haired private was scrambling to his feet. His shoulder was wet and dripping. 'There was two of 'em,' he said. 'They was walking up the road just like — just like ——'

The general stopped him. His voice was enough to stop anything just then. 'And where's the other one?' he said.

The soldier blinked. He was very stupid and startled — almost dazed. 'Dead,' he answered. And then his voice became querulous and wild. He was seeking relief in words. 'I seen him and he yelled at me,' he said. 'He was coming from here, poor kid, and I was coming here.'

'What's that again?' The general's voice stopped his flow of words.

'You were coming here? Where from?'

The orderly was still dazed. He had difficulty to think. 'From headquarters of the Umpteenth up to that farm with a message.'

'Well, why didn't you say so in the first place?' The general took a step toward him. 'Where is your message?'

That poor red-headed boy was a stupid sight. He blinked, he swallowed, he fumbled at his belt. 'I — I can't remember, sir.'

'Can't remember?' roared the general.

'I — I must have dropped it, sir, when I picked him up.'

General Swinnerton's fingers closed on his palm and opened. Before he even spoke, that red-headed boy cowered away from him. But we never heard what he had to say.

'Don't jump him, sir.' It was Billy Langwell speaking in a curious dreamy way, as he turned his head on his blanket pillow. 'The poor boy did the best he could. We' — he moved slightly and caught his breath — 'we can't all be in the cavalry back in '75.'

The general turned toward him and bent down. Perhaps it was because the candles were flickering that his face looked gray and that he looked older than he had before — much older.

'Don't talk, Mr. Langwell,' he said. 'Are you in pain?'

Some one was applying a rude tourniquet to Billy Langwell's leg. Another was cutting open his whipcord jacket and trying to pull off his Sam Browne belt. But Billy Langwell hardly seemed to notice. He was in that state, you see, where pain has ceased to mean anything or where pain itself brought its own peculiar peace. As he stared at the general, he seemed peculiarly delicate, fragile, as fine as a tenuous thought which a word or a gesture might send away. It was not what he said to the general that made the general's face grow gray and still. It was something in his eyes, rather, and the way he moved his lips.

'Don't bother about me, thank you, sir,' he answered. 'I'm all right — perfectly all right.'

The general turned to the telephone operator. His face had become like a stone — as hard, and quite as gray. 'Get the division,' he said, 'and ask why those casual officers they were sending have not come up.' And then he turned and looked at me.

Except for Billy Langwell, we were the only officers in the cellar then, for the signal officer was out, so was the detachment commander. And of course he saw the way I felt. But he was kind about it — surprisingly kind. He put his hand quite gently on my shoulder.

'Don't look so sick, major,' he said. 'It's the war, that's all; and the next lieutenant that comes in to report will go out the same way if the telephones are not working.'

He was not exactly justifying himself, for he thought it was duty, straight duty. Two stretcher bearers had come in, and the two were working over Billy Langwell, talking in low voices. That constant inflow and outflow of people which is a part of any headquarters was beginning again, like a part of the same vague dream.

Some newcomers had appeared, seemingly from nowhere, as people often did in those vague nights. They stood blinking and looking about them until one of them spoke. 'Beg pardon, sir. Is this brigade headquarters?'

For some reason, I was startled. They were officers — second lieutenants — those casual officers of which the general had spoken. The one in front saluted, holding the salute for exactly the right length of time, almost like a regular officer.

'Sir,' he said, 'Lieutenant Swinnerton reports for duty with the detail.'

The theater — always the theater! Even up there, we had those close-cut banal phrases. Lieutenant Swinnerton! You would have known he was the general's son without any intuition to make you feel it. He had the same heavy shoulders, the same uncompromising head, and he looked from me to the general without showing any recognition. He knew the old man was a soldier. He knew what the old man wanted, and you had to hand it to the general then, for the thing he did was not what he wished to do. I heard him draw a quick breath, but he spoke at once. He could not hesitate, because he was an army man; and if he had not been, how could he have hesitated, with Billy Langwell lying on the floor?

Billy Langwell had not lost consciousness. You could see he was listening and taking a detached interest, as men sometimes do in spite of pain.

'Mr. Swinnerton,' said the general — and once again Billy Langwell had him, though perhaps the general never knew it, or never thought — 'Mr. Swinnerton, do you see that thingu-majig on the map — the ferme-something-er-other? We can't pronounce it now since Mr. Langwell's got laid out. Well, get up there to the Umpteenth Regiment. Give the colonel my compliments and tell him to give you the co-ordinates of the front line, and tell him to send every man he can spare to lay out another wire. That's all.'

The lieutenant saluted. He must have known the old man well enough not to argue, and yet he asked a question: 'Can you let me have a runner, sir, who know's the way?'

There was a slight tremor in the general's voice, but very slight. 'The last one's out, and he hasn't come back yet. But you don't mind a thing like that. You were raised in an army post.'

They were lifting Billy Langwell to the stretcher. They were moving with him to the blankets by the door, when the general noticed. 'Are you comfortable, Mr. Langwell?' he inquired, and Billy opened his eyes.

'Thank you, sir,' he said.

And then there was an embarrassing moment. The stretcher bearers did not know whether to move on or stop; because the general made no sign.

'You don't feel —' The general cleared his throat and seemed to have difficulty with his words. 'I hope you don't feel you've been discriminated against in any way?'

Billy Langwell twisted his lips upward. He was quite himself in that last moment, and careless, but not so careless as we had sometimes seen him.

'Lord, no, sir,' he said. 'It's funny what an idiot I was. I thought you couldn't be real, you know. But now I've seen you working out — ' Without finishing his thought, he waved his hand slightly in a curious, airy way. 'George, give me a cigarette, will you? Now I've seen you working out — Good morning, general! It's just a way I have!' He had ceased waving his hand, and added the truest thing he ever said: 'We're just a different breed of cats — that's all.' What else was there to say — now that he had definitely, completely, put General Swinnerton in his place and himself in his place as well?

When did that regimental wire come in? It might have been an hour or less, although it was impossible to think of time in hours or minutes. The general was seated when they called him, staring at the floor, and no one wished to interrupt him. He might have been asleep, for his chin was sunk on his chest, and his campaign ribbons moved with a regular easy motion. As the telephone orderly spoke, however, General Swinnerton started and seized the instrument.

'Have you heard?' he began. 'Is there —' You could tell what he wanted to say, but he stopped himself. 'Well, it's time you hooked up. This has been a hell of a mess. And those signal officers will get a court for it, or I'll know the reason why. What can I expect? Didn't you get any messages? Didn't?'

The general's shoulder moved forward and he cleared his

throat. 'Didn't a lieutenant report to you with my message? Yes, a new one. His name's Swinnerton. Can't you hear me? Swinnerton. Yes, he's my son, as a matter of fact. But what's that got to do with it? What's that?'

The general's shoulders moved suddenly. He sat up very straight. And suddenly his voice was choked and queer. 'Thanks. Thanks.... But there's no use saying that. There are others who have caught it. Lots of others. Thanks. Now keep the wire.'

There was a noise. The telephone orderly stooped down hastily. The general had dropped the telephone headpiece on the floor and was standing up.

'Major' — his voice was still queer, but perfectly controlled — 'when you get after the morning's report, add on Lieutenant Swinnerton. He — he's dead. I — I think I'll turn in now.'

Now what was there to say? What was there to do? Absolutely nothing, for, you see, he was an army man. No one said a word, and he stood by himself in the light of the guttering candles — alone, as he had always been alone. And why I did it I do not know, but suddenly I found myself holding his hand, trying to say something, anything at all. But still he was an army man, though I felt his fingers closing on mine.

'Don't be a damned fool,' he said. 'What time is it? Three o'clock? Well, I'm turning in till six. Good night — or rather, good morning, major.'

A TELEPHONE CALL [1]

DOROTHY PARKER

Please, God, let him telephone me now. Dear God, let him call me now. I won't ask anything else of You, truly I won't. It isn't very much to ask. It would be so little to You, God, such a little, little thing. Only let him telephone now. Please, God. Please, please, please.

If I didn't think about it, maybe the telephone might ring. Sometimes it does that. If I could think of something else. If I could think of something else. Maybe if I counted five hundred by fives, it might ring by that time. I'll count slowly. I won't cheat. And if it rings when I get to three hundred, I won't stop; I won't answer it until I get to five hundred. Five, ten, fifteen, twenty, twenty-five, thirty, thirty-five, forty, forty-five, fifty. . . . Oh, please ring. Please.

This is the last time I'll look at the clock. I will not look at it again. It's ten minutes past seven. He said he would telephone at five o'clock. 'I'll call you at five, darling.' I think that's where he said 'darling.' I'm almost sure he said it there. I know he called me 'darling' twice, and the other time was when he said good-bye. 'Good-bye, darling.' He was busy, and he can't say much in the office, but he called me 'darling' twice. He couldn't have minded my calling him up. I know you shouldn't keep telephoning them — I know they don't like that. When you do that, they know you are thinking about them and wanting them, and that makes them hate you. But I hadn't talked to him in three days — not in three days. And all I did was ask him how he was; it was just the way anybody might have called him up. He couldn't have minded that. He couldn't have thought I was bothering him. 'No, of course you're not,' he said. And he said he'd telephone me. He didn't have to say that. I didn't ask him to, truly I didn't. I'm sure I didn't. I don't think he would say he'd telephone me, and then just never do it. Please don't let him do that, God. Please don't.

'I'll call you at five, darling.' 'Good-bye, darling.' He was busy, and he was in a hurry, and there were people around him, but he called me 'darling' twice. That's mine, that's mine. I have that, even if I never see him again. Oh, but that's so little. That isn't enough. Nothing's enough, if I never see him again. Please let me see him again, God. Please, I want him so much. I want him so much. I'll be good, God. I will try to be better, I will, if You will let me see him again. If You will let him telephone me. Oh, let him telephone me now.

Ah, don't let my prayer seem too little to You, God. You sit up there, so white and old, with all the angels about You and the stars slipping by. And I come to You with a prayer about a telephone call. Ah, don't laugh, God. You see, You don't know how it feels. You're so safe, there on Your throne, with the blue swirling under You. Nothing can touch You; no one can twist Your heart in his hands. This is suffering, God, this is bad, bad suffering. Won't You help me? For Your Son's sake, help me. You said You would do whatever was asked of You in His name. Oh, God, in the name of Thine only beloved Son, Jesus Christ, our Lord, let him telephone me now.

I must stop this. I mustn't be this way. Look. Suppose a young man says he'll call a girl up, and then something happens, and he doesn't. That isn't so terrible, is it? Why, it's going on all over the world, right this minute. Oh, what do I care what's going on all over the world? Why can't that telephone ring? Why can't it, why can't it? Couldn't you ring? Ah, please, couldn't you? You damned, ugly, shiny thing. It would hurt you to ring, wouldn't it? Oh, that would hurt you. Damn you, I'll pull your filthy roots out of the wall, I'll smash your smug black face in little bits. Damn you to hell.

No, no, no. I must stop. I must think about something else. This is what I'll do. I'll put the clock in the other room. Then I can't look at it. If I do have to look at it, then I'll have to walk into the bedroom, and that will be something to do. Maybe, before I look at it again, he will call me. I'll be so sweet to him, if he calls me. If he says he can't see me tonight, I'll say, 'Why, that's all right, dear. Why, of course it's all right.' I'll be the way I was when I first met him. Then maybe he'll like me again. I was always sweet, at first. Oh, it's so easy to be sweet to people before you love them.

I think he must still like me a little. He couldn't have called me 'darling' twice today, if he didn't still like me a little. It isn't all gone, if he still likes me a little; even if it's only a little, little bit. You see, God, if You would just let him telephone me, I wouldn't have to ask You anything more. I would be sweet to him, I would be gay, I would be just the way I used to be, and then he would love me again. And then I would never have to ask You for anything more. Don't You see, God? So won't You please let him telephone me? Won't You please, please, please?

Are You punishing me, God, because I've been bad? Are You angry with me because I did that? Oh, but, God, there are so many bad people — You could not be hard only to me. And it wasn't very bad; it couldn't have been bad. We didn't hurt anybody, God. Things are only bad when they hurt people. We didn't hurt one single soul; You know that. You know it wasn't bad, don't You, God? So won't You let him telephone me now?

If he doesn't telephone me, I'll know God is angry with me. I'll count five hundred by fives, and if he hasn't called me then, I will know God isn't going to help me, ever again. That will be the sign. Five, ten, fifteen, twenty, twenty-five, thirty, thirty-five, forty, forty-five, fifty, fifty-five. . . . It was bad. I knew it was bad. All right, God, send me to hell. You think You're frightening me with Your hell, don't You? You think Your hell is worse than mine.

I mustn't. I mustn't do this. Suppose he's a little late calling me up — that's nothing to get hysterical about. Maybe he isn't going to call — maybe he's coming straight up here without telephoning. He'll be cross if he sees I have been crying. They don't like you to cry. He doesn't cry. I wish to God I could make him cry. I wish I could make him cry and tread the floor and feel his heart heavy and big and festering in him. I wish I could hurt him like hell.

He doesn't wish that about me. I don't think he even knows how he makes me feel. I wish he could know, without my telling him. They don't like you to tell them they've made you cry. They don't like you to tell them you're unhappy because of them. If you do, they think you're possessive and exacting. And then they hate you. They hate you whenever you say anything you really think. You always have to keep playing little games. Oh, I thought we didn't have to; I thought this was so big I could say whatever I meant. I guess you can't, ever. I guess there isn't ever anything big enough for that. Oh, if he would just telephone, I wouldn't tell him I had been sad about him. They hate sad people. I would be so sweet and so gay, he couldn't help but like me. If he would only telephone. If he would only telephone.

Maybe that's what he is doing. Maybe he is coming up here

without calling me up. Maybe he's on his way now. Something might have happened to him. No, nothing could ever happen to him. I can't picture anything happening to him. I never picture him run over. I never see him lying still and long and dead. I wish he were dead. That's a terrible wish. That's a lovely wish. If he were dead, he would be mine. If he were dead, I would never think of now and the last few weeks. I would remember only the lovely times. It would be all beautiful. I wish he were dead. I wish he were dead, dead, dead.

This is silly. It's silly to go wishing people were dead just because they don't call you up the very minute they said they would. Maybe the clock's fast; I don't know whether it's right. Maybe he's hardly late at all. Anything could have made him a little late. Maybe he had to stay at his office. Maybe he went home, to call me up from there, and somebody came in. He doesn't like to telephone me in front of people. Maybe he's worried, just a little, little bit, about keeping me waiting. He might even hope that I would call him up. I could do that. I could telephone him.

I mustn't. I mustn't, I mustn't. Oh, God, please don't let me telephone him. Please keep me from doing that. I know, God, just as well as You do, that if he were worried about me, he'd telephone no matter where he was or how many people there were around him. Please make me know that, God. I don't ask You to make it easy for me — You can't do that, for all that You could make a world. Only let me know it, God. Don't let me go on hoping. Don't let me say comforting things to myself. Please don't let me hope, dear God. Please don't.

I won't telephone him. I'll never telephone him again as long as I live. He'll rot in hell, before I'll call him up. You don't have to give me strength, God; I have it myself. If he wanted me, he could get me. He knows where I am. He knows I'm waiting here. He's so sure of me, so sure. I wonder why they hate you, as soon as they are sure of you. I should think it would be so sweet to be sure.

It would be so easy to telephone him. Then I'd know. Maybe it wouldn't be a foolish thing to do. Maybe he wouldn't mind. Maybe he'd like it. Maybe he has been trying to get me. Sometimes people try and try to get you on the telephone, and they say the number doesn't answer. I'm not just saying that to help myself; that really happens. You know that really happens, God. Oh, God, keep me away from that telephone. Keep me away. Let me still have just a little bit of pride. I think I'm going to need it, God. I think it will be all I'll have.

Oh, what does pride matter, when I can't stand it if I don't talk to him? Pride like that is such a silly, shabby little thing. The real pride, the big pride, is in having no pride. I'm not saying that just because I want to call him. I am not. That's true, I know that's true. I will be big. I will be beyond little prides.

Please, God, keep me from telephoning him. Please, God.

I don't see what pride has to do with it. This is such a little thing, for me to be bringing in pride, for me to be making such a fuss about. I may have misunderstood him. Maybe he said for me to call him up, at five. 'Call me at five, darling.' He could have said that, perfectly well. It's so possible that I didn't hear him right. 'Call me at five, darling.' I'm almost sure that's what he said. God, don't let me talk this way to myself. Make me know, please make me know.

I'll think about something else. I'll just sit quietly. If I could sit still. If I could sit still. Maybe I could read. Oh, all the books are about people who love each other, truly and sweetly. What do they want to write about that for? Don't they know it isn't true? Don't they know it's a lie, it's a God damned lie? What do they have to tell about that for, when they know how it hurts? Damn them, damn them, damn them.

I won't. I'll be quiet. This is nothing to get excited about.

Look. Suppose he were someone I didn't know very well. Suppose he were another girl. Then I'd just telephone and say, 'Well, for goodness' sake, what happened to you?' That's what I'd do, and I'd never even think about it. Why can't I be casual and natural, just because I love him? I can be. Honestly, I can be. I'll call him up, and be so easy and pleasant. You see if I won't, God. Oh, don't let me call him. Don't, don't, don't.

God, aren't You really going to let him call me? Are You sure, God? Couldn't You please relent? Couldn't You? I don't even ask You to let him telephone me now, God; only let him do it in a little while. I'll count five hundred by fives. I'll do it so slowly and so fairly. If he hasn't telephoned then, I'll call him. I will. Oh, please, dear God, dear kind God, my blessed Father in Heaven, let him call before then. Please, God. Please.

Five, ten, fifteen, twenty, twenty-five, thirty, thirty-five. . . .

DOUBLE BIRTHDAY [1]

WILLA CATHER

Even in American cities, which seem so much alike, where people seem all to be living the same lives, striving for the same things, thinking the same thoughts, there are still individuals a little out of tune with the times — there are still survivals of a past more loosely woven, there are disconcerting beginnings of a future yet unforeseen.

Coming out of the grey stone Court House in Pittsburgh on a dark November afternoon, Judge Hammersley encountered one of these men whom one does not readily place, whom one is, indeed, a little embarrassed to meet, because they have not got on as they should. The Judge saw him mounting the steps outside, leaning against the wind, holding his soft felt hat on with his hand, his head thrust forward — hurrying with a light, quick step, and so intent upon his own purposes that the Judge could have gone out by a side door and avoided the meeting. But that was against his principles.

'Good day, Albert,' he muttered, seeming to feel, himself, all the embarrassment of the encounter, for the other snatched off his hat with a smile of very evident pleasure, and something like pride. His gesture bared an attractive head — small, well-set, definite and smooth — one of those heads that look as if they had been turned out of some hard, rich wood by a workman deft with the lathe. His smooth-shaven face was dark — a warm coffee colour — and his hazel eyes were warm and lively. He was not young, but his features had a kind of quicksilver mobility. His manner toward the stiff, frowning Judge was respectful and admiring — not in the least self-conscious.

The Judge inquired after his health and that of his uncle.

'Uncle Albert is splendidly preserved for his age. Frail, and can't stand any strain, but perfectly all right if he keeps to his routine. He's going to have a birthday soon. He will be eighty on the first day of December, and I shall be fifty-five on the same day. I was named after him because I was born on his twenty-fifth birthday.'

'Umph.' The judge glanced from left to right as if this announcement were in bad taste, but he put a good face on it and said with a kind of testy heartiness, 'That will be an — occasion. I'd like to remember it in some way. Is there anything your uncle would like, any — recognition?' He stammered and coughed.

Young Albert Engelhardt, as he was called, laughed apologetically, but with confidence. 'I think there is, Judge Hammersley. Indeed, I'd thought of coming to you to ask a favour. I am going to have a little supper for him, and you know he likes good wine. In these dirty bootlegging times, it's hard to get.'

'Certainly, certainly.' The Judge spoke up quickly, and for the first time looked Albert squarely in the eye. 'Don't give him any of that bootleg stuff. I can find something in my cellar. Come out to-morrow night after eight, with a gripsack of some sort. Very glad to help you out, Albert. Glad the old fellow holds up so well. Thank'ee, Albert,' as Engelhardt swung the heavy door open and held it for him to pass.

Judge Hammersley's car was waiting for him, and on the ride home to Squirrel Hill he thought with vexation about the Engelhardts. He really was a sympathetic man, and though so stern of manner, he had deep affections; was fiercely loyal to old friends, old families, and old ideals. He didn't think highly of what is called success in the world to-day, but such as it was he wanted his friends to have it, and was vexed with them when they missed it. He was vexed with Albert for unblushingly, almost proudly, declaring that he was fifty-five years old, when he had nothing whatever to show for it. He was the last of the Engelhardt boys, and they had none of them had anything to show. They all died much worse off in the world than they began. They began with a flourishing glass factory up the river, a comfortable fortune, a fine old house on the park in Allegheny, a good standing in the community; and it was all gone, melted away.

Old August Engelhardt was a thrifty, energetic man, though pig-headed — Judge Hammersley's friend and one of his first clients. August's five sons had sold the factory and wasted the money in fantastic individual enterprises, lost the big house, and now they were all dead except Albert. They ought all to be alive, with estates and factories and families. To be sure, they had that queer German streak in them; but so had old August, and it hadn't prevented his amounting to something. Their bringing-up was wrong; August had too free a hand, he was too proud of his five handsome boys, and too conceited. Too much tennis, Rhine wine punch, music, and silliness. They were always running over to New York, like this Albert. Somebody, when asked what in the world young Albert had ever done with his inheritance, had laughingly replied that he had spent it on the Pennsylvania Railroad.

Judge Hammersley didn't see how Albert could hold his head up. He had some small job in the County Clerk's office, was dependent upon it, had nothing else but the poor little house on the

South Side where he lived with his old uncle. The county took care of him for the sake of his father, who had been a gallant officer in the Civil War, and afterwards a public-spirited citizen and a generous employer of labour. But, as Judge Hammersley had bitterly remarked to Judge Merriman when Albert's name happened to come up: 'If it weren't for his father's old friends seeing that he got something, that fellow wouldn't be able to make a living.' Next to a charge of dishonesty, this was the worst that could be said of any man.

Judge Hammersley's house out on Squirrel Hill sat under a grove of very old oak trees. He lived alone, with his daughter, Margaret Parmenter, who was a widow. She had a great many engagements, but she usually managed to dine at home with her father, and that was about as much society as he cared for. His house was comfortable in an old-fashioned way, well appointed — especially the library, the room in which he lived when he was not in bed or at the Court House. To-night, when he came down to dinner, Mrs. Parmenter was already at the table, dressed for an evening party. She was tall, handsome, with a fine, easy carriage, and her face was both hard and sympathetic, like her father's. She had not, however, his stiffness of manner, that contraction of the muscles which was his unconscious protest at any irregularity in the machinery of life. She accepted blunders and accidents smoothly if not indifferently.

As the old coloured man pulled back the Judge's chair for him, he glanced at his daughter from under his eyebrows.

'I saw that son of old Gus Engelhardt's this afternoon,' he said in an angry, challenging tone.

As a young girl his daughter had used to take up the challenge and hotly defend the person who had displeased or disappointed her father. But as she grew older she was conscious of that same feeling in herself when people fell short of what she expected; and she understood now that when her father spoke as if he were savagely attacking someone, it merely meant that he was disappointed or sorry for them; he never spoke thus of persons for whom he had no feeling. So she said calmly:

'Oh, did you really? I haven't seen him for years, not since the war. How was he looking? Shabby?'

'Not so shabby as he ought to. That fellow's likely to be in want one of these days.'

'I'm afraid so,' Mrs. Parmenter sighed. 'But I believe he would be rather plucky about it.'

The Judge shrugged. 'He's coming out here to-morrow night, on some business for his uncle.'

'Then I'll have a chance to see for myself. He must look much older. I can't imagine his ever looking really old and settled, though.'

'See that you don't ask him to stay. I don't want the fellow hanging around. He'll transact his business and get it over. He had the face to admit to me that he'll be fifty-five years old on the first of December. He's giving some sort of birthday party for old Albert, a-hem.' The Judge coughed formally, but was unable to check a smile; his lips sarcastic, but his eyes full of sly humour.

'Can he be as old as that? Yes, I suppose so. When we were both at Mrs. Sterrett's in Rome, I was fifteen, and he must have been about thirty.'

Her father coughed. 'He'd better have been in Homestead!'

Mrs. Parmenter looked up; that was rather commonplace, for her father. 'Oh, I don't know. Albert would never have been much use in Homestead, and he was very useful to Mrs. Sterrett in Rome.'

'What did she want the fellow hanging round for? All the men of her family amounted to something.'

'To too much! There must be some butterflies if one is going to give house parties, and the Sterretts and Dents were all heavyweights. He was in Rome a long while; three years, I think. He had a gorgeous time. Anyway, he learned to speak Italian very well, and that helps him out now, doesn't it? You still send for him at the Court House when you need an interpreter?'

'That's not often. He picks up a few dollars. Nice business for his father's son.'

After dinner the Judge retired to his library, where the gas-fire was lit, and his book at hand, with a paper-knife inserted to mark the place where he had left off reading last night at exactly ten-thirty. On his way he went to the front door, opened it, turned on the porch light, and looked at the thermometer, making an entry in a little note-book. In a few moments his daughter, in an evening cloak, stopped at the library door to wish him good night and went down the hall. He listened for the closing of the front door; it was a reassuring sound to him. He liked the feeling of an orderly house, empty for himself and his books all evening. He was deeply read in divinity, philosophy, and in the early history of North America.

II

While Judge Hammersley was settling down to his book, Albert Engelhardt was sitting at home in a garnet velvet smoking-jacket, at an upright piano, playing Schumann's *Kreisleriana* for his old uncle. They lived, certainly, in a queer part of the city, on one of the dingy streets that run uphill off noisy Carson Street, in a little two-story brick house, a working man's house, that Albert's father had taken over long ago in satisfaction of a bad debt. When his father had acquired this building, it was a mere nothing — the Engelhardts were then living in their big, many-gabled, so-German house on the Park, in Allegheny; and they owned many other buildings, besides the glass factory up the river. After the father's death, when the sons converted houses and lands into cash, this forgotten little house on the South Side had somehow never been sold or mortgaged. A day came when Albert, the last surviving son, found this piece of property the only thing he owned in the world beside his personal effects. His uncle, having had a crushing disappointment, wanted at that time to retire from the practice of medicine, so Albert settled in the South Side house and took his uncle with him.

He had not gone there in any mood of despair. His impoverishment had come about gradually, and before he took possession of these quarters he had been living in a boarding house; the change seemed going up instead of going down in the world. He was delighted to have a home again, to unpack his own furniture and his books and pictures — the most valuable in the world to him, because they were full of his own history and that of his family, were like part of his own personality. All the years and the youth which had slipped away from him still clung to these things.

At his piano, under his Degas drawing in black and red — three ballet girls at the bar — or seated at his beautiful inlaid writing table, he was still the elegant young man who sat there long ago. His rugs were fine ones, his collection of books was large and very personal. It was full of works which, though so recent, were already immensely far away and diminished. The glad, rebellious excitement they had once caused in the world he could recapture only in memory. Their power to seduce and stimulate the young, the living, was utterly gone. There was a complete file of the *Yellow Book*, for instance; who could extract sweet poison from these volumes now? A portfolio of the drawings of Aubrey Beardsley — decadent, had they been called? A slender, padded volume — the complete works of a great new poet, Ernest Dowson. Oscar Wilde, whose wickedness was now so outdone that he looked like the poor old hat of some Victorian belle, wired and feathered and garlanded and faded.

Albert and his uncle occupied only the upper floor of their house. The ground floor was let to an old German glass engraver who had once been a workman in August Engelhardt's factory.

His wife was a good cook, and every night sent their dinner up hot on the dumb waiter. The house opened directly upon the street and to reach Albert's apartment one went down a narrow paved alley at the side of the building and mounted an outside flight of wooden stairs at the back. They had only four rooms — two bedrooms, a snug sitting-room in which they dined, and a small kitchen where Albert got breakfast every morning. After he had gone to work, Mrs. Rudder came up from downstairs to wash the dishes and do the cleaning, and to cheer up old Doctor Engelhardt.

At dinner this evening Albert had told his uncle about meeting Judge Hammersley, and of his particular inquiries after his health. The old man was very proud and received this intelligence as his due, but could not conceal a certain gratification.

'The daughter, she still lives with him? A damned fine-looking woman!' he muttered between his teeth. Uncle Albert, a bachelor, had been a professed connoisseur of ladies in his day.

Immediately after dinner, unless he were going somewhere, Albert always played for his uncle for an hour. He played extremely well. Doctor Albert sat by the fire smoking his cigar. While he listened, the look of wisdom and professional authority faded, and many changes went over his face, as if he were playing a little drama to himself; moods of scorn and contempt, of rakish vanity, sentimental melancholy ... and something remote and lonely. The Doctor had always flattered himself that he resembled a satyr, because the tops of his ears were slightly pointed; and he used to hint to his nephews that his large pendulous nose was the index of an excessively amorous disposition. His mouth was full of long, yellowish teeth, all crowded irregularly, which he snapped and ground together when he uttered denunciations of modern art or the Eighteenth Amendment. He wore his moustache short and twisted up at the corners. His thick grey hair was cut close and upright, in the bristling French fashion. His hands were small and fastidious, high-knuckled, quite elegant in shape.

Across the Doctor's throat ran a long, jagged scar. He used to mutter to his young nephews that it had been justly inflicted by an outraged husband — a pistol shot in the dark. But his brother August always said that he had been cut by glass, when, wandering about in the garden one night after drinking too much punch, he had fallen into the cold-frames.

After playing Schumann for some time, Albert, without stopping, went into Stravinsky.

Doctor Engelhardt by the gas-fire stirred uneasily, turned his important head towards his nephew, and snapped his teeth. 'Br-r-r, that stuff! Poverty of imagination, poverty of musical invention; *fin-de-siècle!*'

Albert laughed. 'I thought you were asleep. Why will you use that phrase? It shows your vintage. Like this any better?' He began the second act of *Pelléas et Mélisande.*

The Doctor nodded. 'Yes, that is better, though I'm not fooled by it.' He wrinkled his nose as if he were smelling out something, and squinted with superior discernment. 'To this *canaille* that is all very new; but to me it goes back to Bach.'

'Yes, if you like.'

Albert, like Judge Hammersley, was jealous of his solitude — liked a few hours with his books. It was time for Uncle Doctor to be turning in. He ended the music by playing half a dozen old German songs which the old fellow always wanted but never asked for. The Doctor's chin sank into his shirt front. His face took on a look of deep, resigned sadness; his features, losing their conscious importance, seemed to shrink a good deal. His nephew knew that this was the mood in which he would most patiently turn to rest and darkness. Doctor Engelhardt had had a heavy loss late in life. Indeed, he had suffered the same loss twice.

As Albert left the piano, the Doctor rose and walked a little stiffly across the room. At the door of his chamber he paused, brought his hand up in a kind of military salute and gravely bowed, so low that one saw only the square upstanding grey brush on the top of his head and the long pear-shaped nose. After this he closed the door behind him. Albert sat down to his book. Very soon he heard the bath water running. Having taken his bath, the Doctor would get into bed immediately to avoid catching cold. Luckily, he usually slept well. Perhaps he dreamed of that unfortunate young singer whom he sometimes called, to his nephew and himself, 'the lost Lenore.'

III

Long years ago, when the Engelhardt boys were still living in the old house in Allegheny with their mother, after their father's death, Doctor Engelhardt was practising medicine, and had an office on the Park, five minutes' walk from his sister-in-law. He usually lunched with the family, after his morning office hours were over. They always had a good cook, and the Allegheny market was one of the best in the world. Mrs. Engelhardt went to market every morning of her life; such vegetables and poultry, such cheeses and sausages and smoked and pickled fish as one could buy there! Soon after she had made her rounds, boys in white aprons would come running across the Park with her purchases. Everyone knew the Engelhardt house, built of many-coloured bricks, with gables and turrets and, on the west a large stained-glass window representing a scene on the Grand Canal in Venice, the Church of Santa Maria della Salute in the background, in the foreground a gondola with a slender gondolier. People said August and Mrs. Engelhardt should be solidly seated in the prow to make the picture complete.

Doctor Engelhardt's especial interest was the throat, preferably the singing throat. He had studied every scrap of manuscript that Manuel Garcia had left behind him, every reported conversation with him. He had doctored many singers, and imagined he had saved many voices. Pittsburgh air is not good for the throat, and travelling artists often had need of medical assistance. Conductors of orchestras and singing societies recommended Doctor Engelhardt because he was very lax about collecting fees from professionals, especially if they sent him a photograph floridly inscribed. He had been a medical student in New York while Patti was still singing; his biography fell into chapters of great voices as a turfman's falls into chapters of fast horses. This passion for the voice had given him the feeling of distinction, of being unique in his profession, which had made him all his life a well-satisfied and happy man, and had left him a poor one.

One morning when the Doctor was taking his customary walk about the Park before office hours, he stopped in front of the Allegheny High School building because he heard singing — a chorus of young voices. It was June, and the chapel windows were open. The Doctor listened for a few moments, then tilted his head on one side and laid his forefinger on his pear-shaped nose with an anxious, inquiring squint. Among the voices he certainly heard one Voice. The final bang of the piano was followed by laughter and buzzing. A boy ran down the steps. The Doctor stopped him and learned that this was a rehearsal for Class Day exercises. Just then the piano began again, and in a moment he heard the same voice alone:

'*Still wie die Nacht, tief wie das Meer.*'

No, he was not mistaken; a full, rich, soprano voice, so easy, so sure; a golden warmth, even in the high notes. Before the second verse was over he went softly into the building, into the chapel, and for the first time laid eyes on Marguerite Thiesinger. He saw a sturdy, blooming German girl standing beside the piano; goodnatured one knew at a glance, glowing with health. She looked like a big peony just burst into bloom and full of sunshine — sunshine in her auburn hair, in her rather small hazel eyes. When she finished the song, she began waltzing on the platform with one of the boys.

Doctor Albert waited by the door, and accosted her as she came out carrying her coat and schoolbooks. He introduced himself and asked her if she would go over to Mrs. Engelhardt's for lunch and sing for him.

Oh, yes! she knew one of the Engelhardt boys, and she'd always wanted to see that beautiful window from the inside.

She went over at noon and sang for them before lunch, and the family took stock of her. She spoke a very ordinary German, and her English was still worse; her people were very ordinary. Her flat, slangy speech was somehow not vulgar because it was so naive — she knew no other way. The boys were delighted with her because she was jolly and interested in everything. She told them about the glorious good times she had going to dances in suburban Turner halls, and to picnics in the damp, smoke-smeared woods up the Allegheny. The boys roared with laughter at the unpromising places she mentioned. But she had the warm bubble in her blood that makes everything fair; even being a junior in the Allegheny High School was 'glorious,' she told them!

She came to lunch with them again and again, because she liked the boys, and she thought the house magnificent. The Doctor observed her narrowly all the while. Clearly she had no ambition, no purpose; she sang to be agreeable. She was not very intelligent, but she had a kind of personal warmth that, to his way of thinking, was much better than brains. He took her over to his office and poked and pounded her. When he had finished his examination, he stood before the foolish, happy young thing and inclined his head in his peculiar fashion.

'Miss Thiesinger, I have the honour to announce to you that you are on the threshold of a brilliant, possibly a great career.'

She laughed her fresh, ringing laugh. 'Aren't you nice, though, to take so much trouble about me!'

The Doctor lifted a forefinger. 'But for that you must turn your back on this childishness, these snivelling sapheads you play marbles with. You must uproot this triviality.' He made a gesture as if he were wringing a chicken's neck, and Marguerite was thankful she was able to keep back a giggle.

Doctor Engelhardt wanted her to go to New York with him at once, and begin her studies. He was quite ready to finance her. He had made up his mind to stake everything upon this voice.

But not at all. She thought it was lovely of him, but she was very fond of her classmates, and she wanted to graduate with her class next year. Moreover, she had just been given a choir position in one of the biggest churches in Pittsburgh, though she was still a schoolgirl; she was going to have money and pretty clothes for the first time in her life and wouldn't miss it all for anything.

All through the next school year Doctor Albert went regularly to the church where she sang, watched and cherished her, expostulated and lectured, trying to awaken fierce ambition in his big peony flower. She was very much interested in other things just then, but she was patient with him; accepted his devotion with good nature, respected his wisdom, and bore with his 'stagey' manners as she called them. She graduated in June, and immediately after Commencement, when she was not quite nineteen, she eloped with an insurance agent and went to Chicago to live. She wrote Doctor Albert: 'I do appreciate all your kindness to me, but I guess I will let my voice rest for the present.'

He took it hard. He burned her photographs and the foolish little scrawls she had written to thank him for presents. His life would have been dull and empty if he hadn't had so many reproaches to heap upon her in his solitude. How often and how bitterly he arraigned her for the betrayal of so beautiful a gift. Where did she keep it hidden now, that jewel, in the sordid life she had chosen?

Three years after her elopement, suddenly, without warning,

Marguerite Thiesinger walked into his office on Arch Street one morning and told him she had come back to study! Her husband's 'affairs were involved'; he was now quite willing that she should make as much as possible of her voice — and out of it.

'My voice is better than it was,' she said, looking at him out of her rather small eyes — greenish-yellow, with a glint of gold in them. He believed her. He suddenly realized how uncommonly truthful she had always been. Rather stupid, unimaginative, but carried joyously along on a flood of warm vitality, and truthful to a degree he had hardly known in any woman or in any man. And now she was a woman.

He took her over to his sister-in-law's. Albert who chanced to be at home, was sent to the piano. She was not mistaken. The Doctor kept averting his head to conceal his delight, to conceal, once or twice, a tear — the moisture that excitement and pleasure brought to his eyes. The voice, after all, he told himself, is a physical thing. She had been growing and ripening like fruit in the sun, and the voice with the body. Doctor Engelhardt stepped softly out of the music-room into the conservatory and addressed a potted palm, his lips curling back from his teeth: 'So we get that out of you, *Monsieur le commis-voyageur*, and now we throw you away like a squeezed lemon.'

When he returned to his singer, she addressed him very earnestly from under her spring hat covered with lilacs: 'Before my marriage, Doctor Engelhardt, you offered to take me to New York to a teacher, and lend me money to start on. If you still feel like doing it, I'm sure I could repay you before very long. I'll follow your instructions. What was it you used to tell me I must have — application and ambition?'

He glared at her: 'Take note, Gretchen, that I change the prescription. There is something vulgar about ambition. Now we will play for higher stakes; for *ambition* read *aspiration*!' His index finger shot upward.

In New York he had no trouble in awakening the interest of his friends and acquaintances. Within a week he had got his protégée to a very fine artist, just then retiring from the Opera, a woman who had been a pupil of Pauline Garcia Viardot. In short, Doctor Engelhardt had realized the dream of a lifetime; he had discovered a glorious voice, backed by a rich vitality. Within a year Marguerite had one of the best church positions in New York; she insisted upon repaying her benefactor before she went abroad to complete her studies. Doctor Engelhardt went often to New York to counsel and advise, to gloat over his treasure. He often shivered as he crossed the Jersey ferry, he was afraid of Fate. He would tell over her assets on his fingers to reassure himself. You might have seen a small, self-important man of about fifty, standing by the rail of the ferry boat, his head impressively inclined as if he were addressing an amphitheatre full of students, gravely counting upon his fingers.

But Fate struck, and from the quarter least under suspicion — through that blooming, rounded, generously moulded young body, from that abundant, glowing health which the Doctor proudly called peasant vigour. Marguerite's success had brought to his office many mothers of singing daughters. He was not insensible to the compliment, but he usually dismissed them by dusting his fingers delicately in the air and growling: 'Yes, she can sing a little, she has a voice; *aber kleine, kleine!*' He exulted in the opulence of his cabbage rose. To his nephews he used to match her possibilities with the singers of that period. Emma Eames he called *die Puritan*, Geraldine Farrar *la voix blanche*, another was *trop raffinée*.

Marguerite had been in New York two years, her path one of uninterrupted progress, when she wrote the Doctor about a swelling of some sort; the surgeons wanted to operate. Doctor Albert took the next train for New York. An operation revealed that things were very bad indeed; a malignant growth, so far advanced that the knife could not check it. Her mother and grandmother had died of the same disease.

Poor Marguerite lived a year in a hospital for incurables. Every week-end when Doctor Albert went over to see her he found great changes — it was rapid and terrible. That winter and spring he lived like a man lost in a dark morass, the Slave in the Dismal Swamp. He suffered more than his Gretchen, for she was singularly calm and hopeful to the very end, never doubting that she would get well.

The last time he saw her she had given up. But she was noble and sweet in mood, and so piteously apologetic for disappointing him — like a child who has broken something precious and is sorry. She was wasted, indeed, until she was scarcely larger than a child, her beautiful hair cut short, her hands like shadows, but still a stain of colour in her cheeks.

'I'm so sorry I didn't do as you wanted instead of running off with Phil,' she said. 'I see now how little he cared about me — and you've just done everything. If I had my twenty-six years to live over, I'd live them very differently.'

Doctor Albert dropped her hand and walked to the window, the tears running down his face. *'Pourquoi, pourquoi?'* he muttered, staring blindly at that brutal square of glass. When he could control himself and come back to the chair at her bedside, she put her poor little sheared head out on his knee and lay smiling and breathing softly.

'I expect you don't believe in the hereafter,' she murmured. 'Scientific people hardly ever do. But if there is one, I'll not forget you. I'll love to remember you.'

When the nurse came to give her her hypodermic, Doctor Albert went out into Central Park and wandered about without knowing where or why, until he smelled something which suddenly stopped his breath, and he sat down under a flowering linden tree. He dropped his face in his hands and cried like a woman.

Youth, art, love, dreams, true-heartedness — why must they go out of the summer world into darkness? *Warum, warum?* He thought he had already suffered all that man could, but never had it come down on him like this. He sat on that bench like a drunken man or like a dying man, muttering Heine's words: 'God is a grimmer humorist than I. Nobody but God could have perpetrated anything so cruel.' She was ashamed, he remembered it afresh and struck his bony head with his clenched fist — ashamed at having been used like this; she was apologetic for the power, whatever it was, that had tricked her. 'Yes, by God, she apologized for God!'

The tortured man looked up through the linden branches at the blue arch that never answers. As he looked, his face relaxed, his breathing grew regular. His eyes were caught by puffy white clouds like the cherub-heads in Raphael's pictures, and something within him seemed to rise and travel with those clouds. The moment had come when he could bear no more. . . . When he went back to the hospital that evening, he learned that she had died very quietly between eleven and twelve, the hour when he was sitting on the bench in the park.

Uncle Doctor now sometimes spoke to Albert out of a long silence: 'Anyway, I died for her; that was given to me. She never knew a death-struggle — she went to sleep. That struggle took place in my body. Her dissolution occurred within me.'

IV

Old Doctor Engelhardt walked abroad very little now. Sometimes on a fine Sunday his nephew would put him aboard a street car that climbs the hills beyond Mount Oliver and take him to visit an old German graveyard and a monastery. Every afternoon, in good weather, he walked along the pavement which ran past the front door, as far as the first corner, where he bought his paper and cigarettes. If Elsa, the pretty little granddaughter of his housekeeper, ran out to join him and see him over the crossings, he would go a little farther. In the morning, while Mrs. Rudder did the sweeping and dusting, the Doctor took the air on an upstairs back porch, overhanging the court.

The court was bricked, and had an old-fashioned cistern and hydrant, and three ailanthus trees — the last growing things left to the Engelhardts, whose flowering shrubs and greenhouses had once been so well known in Allegheny. In these trees, which he called *les Chinoises*, the Doctor took a great interest. The clothes line ran about their trunks in a triangle, and on Monday he looked down upon the washing. He was too nearsighted to be distressed by the sooty flakes descending from neighbouring chimneys upon the white sheets. He enjoyed the dull green leaves of his *Chinoises* in summer, scarcely moving on breathless, sticky nights, when the moon came up red over roofs and smoke-stacks. In autumn he watched the yellow fronds drop down upon the brick pavement like great ferns. Now, when his birthday was approaching, the trees were bare; and he thought he liked them best so, especially when all the knotty, curly twigs were outlined by a scurf of snow.

As he sat there, wrapped up in rugs, a stiff felt hat on his head — he would never hear to a cap — and woollen gloves on his hands, Elsa, the granddaughter, would bring her cross-stitch and chatter to him. Of late she had been sewing on her trousseau, and that amused the Doctor highly — though it meant she would soon go to live in Lower Allegheny, and he would lose her. Her young man, Carl Abberbock, had now a half-interest in a butcher stall in the Allegheny market, and was in a hurry to marry.

When Mrs. Rudder had quite finished her work and made the place neat, she would come and lift the rug from his knees and say: 'Time to go in, Herr Doctor.'

V

The next evening after dinner Albert left the house with a suit-case, the bag that used to make so many trips to New York in the opera season. He stopped downstairs to ask Elsa to carry her sewing up and sit with his uncle for a while; then he took the street car across the Twenty-Second Street Bridge by the blazing steel mills. As he waited on Soho Hill to catch a Fifth Avenue car, the heavy, frosty air suddenly began to descend in snowflakes. He wished he had worn his old overcoat; didn't like to get this one wet. He had to consider such things now. He was hesitating about a taxi when his car came, bound for the East End.

He got off at the foot of one of the streets running up Squirrel Hill, and slowly mounted. Everything was white with the softly falling snow. Albert knew all the places; old school friends lived in many of them. Big, turreted stone houses, set in ample grounds with fine trees and shrubbery and driveways. He stepped aside now and then to avoid a car, rolling from the gravel drives on to the stone-block pavement. If the occupants had recognized Al-bert, they would have felt sorry for him. But he did not feel sorry for himself. He looked up at the lighted windows, the red gleam on the snowy rhododendron bushes, and shrugged. His old schoolfellows went to New York now as often as he had done in his youth; but they went to consult doctors, to put children in school, or to pay the bills of incorrigible sons.

He thought he had had the best of it; he had gone a-Maying while it was May. This solid comfort, this iron-bound security, didn't appeal to him much. These massive houses, after all, held nothing but the heavy domestic routine; all the frictions and jealousies and discontents of family life. Albert felt light and free, going up the hill in his thin overcoat. He believed he had had a more interesting life than most of his friends who owned real es-tate. He could still amuse himself, and he had lived to the full all the revolutions in art and music that his period covered. He

wouldn't at this moment exchange his life and his memories —
his memories of his teacher, Rafael Joseffy, for instance — for
any one of these massive houses and the life of the man who paid
the upkeep. If Mephistopheles were to emerge from the rhodo-
dendrons and stand behind his shoulder with such an offer, he
wouldn't hesitate. Money? Oh, yes, he would like to have some,
but not what went with it.

He turned in under Judge Hammersley's fine oak trees. A car
was waiting in the driveway, near the steps by which he mounted
to the door. The coloured man admitted him, and just as he entered the hall Mrs. Parmenter came down the stairs.

'Ah, it's you, Albert! Father said you were coming in this
evening, and I've kept the car waiting, to have a glimpse of you.'

Albert had dropped his hat and bag, and stood holding her
hand with the special grace and appreciation she remembered in
him.

'What a pleasure to see you!' he exclaimed, and she knew from
his eyes it was. 'It doesn't happen often, but it's always such a
surprise and pleasure.' He held her hand as if he wanted to keep
it there. 'It's a long while since the Villa Scipione, isn't it?'

They stood for a moment in the shrouded hall light. Mrs. Parmenter was looking very handsome, and Albert was thinking
that she had all her father's authority, with much more sweep
and freedom. She was impulsive and careless, where he was
strong and shrinking — a powerful man terribly afraid of little
annoyances. His daughter, Albert believed, was not afraid of anything. She had proved more than once that if you aren't afraid
of gossip, it is harmless. She did as she pleased. People took it.
Even Parmenter had taken it, and he was rather a stiff sort.

Mrs. Parmenter laughed at his allusion to their summer at Mrs.
Sterrett's, in Rome, and gave him her coat to hold.

'You remember, Albert, how you and I used to get up early on
fête days, and go down to the garden gate to see the young king

come riding in from the country at the head of the horse guards? How the sun flashed on his helmet! Heavens, I saw him last summer! So grizzled and battered.'

'And we were always going to run away to Russia together, and now there is no Russia. Everything has changed but you, Mrs. Parmenter.'

'Wish I could think so. But you don't know any Mrs. Parmenter. I'm Marjorie, please. How often I think of those gay afternoons I had with you and your brothers in the garden behind your old Allegheny house. There's such a lot I want to talk to you about. And this birthday — when is it? May I send your uncle some flowers? I always remember his goodness to poor Marguerite Thiesinger. He never got over that, did he? But I'm late, and father is waiting. Good night, you'll have a message from me.'

Albert bent and kissed her hand in the old-fashioned way, keeping it a moment and breathing in softly the fragrance of her clothes, her furs, her person, the fragrance of that other world to which he had once belonged and out of which he had slipped so gradually that he scarcely realized it, unless suddenly brought face to face with something in it that was charming. Releasing her, he caught up his hat and opened the door to follow her, but she pushed him back with her arm and smiled over her shoulder. 'No, no, father is waiting for you in the library. Good night.'

Judge Hammersley stood in the doorway, fingering a bunch of keys and blinking with impatience to render his service and have done with it. The library opened directly into the hall; he couldn't help overhearing his daughter, and he disliked her free and unreproachful tone with this man who was young when he should be old, single when he should be married, and penniless when he should be well fixed.

Later, as Albert came down the hill with two bottles of the Judge's best champagne in his bag, he was thinking that the greatest disadvantage of being poor and dropping out of the world

was that he didn't meet attractive women any more. The men
he could do without, Heaven knew! But the women, the ones
like Marjorie Hammersley, were always grouped where the big
fires burned — money and success and big houses and fast boats
and French cars; it was natural.

Mrs. Parmenter, as she drove off, resolved that she would see
more of Albert and his uncle — wondered why she had let an old
friendship lapse for so long. When she was a little girl, she used
often to spend a week with her aunt in Allegheny. She was fond
of the aunt, but not of her cousins, and she used to escape whenever she could to the Engelhardts' garden only a few doors away.
No grass in that garden — in Allegheny grass was always dirty —
but glittering gravel, and lilac hedges beautiful in spring, and
barberry hedges red in the fall, and flowers and bird cages and
striped awnings, boys lying about in tennis clothes, making mint
juleps before lunch, having coffee under the sycamore trees after
dinner. The Engelhardt boys were different, like people in a book
or a play. All the young men in her set were scornful of girls until
they wanted one; then they grabbed her rather brutally and it was
over. She had felt that the Engelhardt boys admired her without
in the least wanting to grab her, that they enjoyed her aestheti-
cally, so to speak, and it pleased her to be liked in that way.

VI

On the afternoon of the first of December, Albert left his desk
in the County Clerk's office at four o'clock, feeling very much as
he used to when school was dismissed in the middle of the afternoon just before the Christmas holidays. It was his uncle's birthday that was in his mind; his own, of course, gave him no particular pleasure. If one stopped to think of that, there was a shiver
waiting round the corner. He walked over the Smithfield Street
Bridge. A thick brown fog made everything dark, and there was a
feeling of snow in the air. The lights along the sheer cliffs of

Mount Washington, high above the river, were already lighted. When Albert was a boy, those cliffs, with the row of lights far up against the sky, always made him think of some far-away, cloud-set city in Asia; the forbidden city, he used to call it. Well, that was a long time ago; a lot of water had run under this bridge since then, and kingdoms and empires had fallen. Meanwhile, Uncle Doctor was still hanging on, and things were not so bad with them as they might be. Better not reflect too much. He hopped on board a street car, and old women with market baskets shifted to make room for him.

When he reached home, the table was already set in the living-room. Beautiful table linen had been one of his mother's extravagances (he had boxes of it; meant to give some to Elsa on her marriage), and Mrs. Rudder laundered it with pious care. She had put out the best silver. He had forgotten to order flowers, but the old woman had brought up one of her blooming geraniums for a centrepiece. Uncle Albert was dozing by the fire in his old smoking jacket, a volume of Schiller on his knee.

'I'll put the studs in your shirt for you. Time to dress, Uncle Doctor.'

The old man blinked and smiled drolly. 'So? *Die* claw-hammer?'

'Of course *die* claw-hammer! Elsa is going to a masquerade with Carl, and they are coming up to see us before they go. I promised her you would dress.'

'Albert,' the Doctor called him back, beckoned with a mysterious smile; 'where did you get that wine now?'

'Oh, you found it when she put it on ice, did you? That's Judge Hammersley's, the best he had. He insisted on sending it to you, with his compliments and good wishes.'

Uncle Albert rose and drew up his shoulders somewhat pompously. 'From my own kind I still command recognition.' Then dropping into homely vulgarity he added, with a sidelong squint

at his nephew, 'By God, some of that will feel good, running down
the gullet.'

'You'll have all you want for once. It's a great occasion.
Did you shave carefully? I'll take my bath, and then you
must be ready for me.'

In half an hour Albert came out in his dress clothes and found
his uncle still reading his favourite poet. 'The trousers are too
big,' the Doctor complained. 'Why not *die* claw-hammer and my
old trousers? Elsa wouldn't notice.'

'Oh yes, she would! She's seen these every day for five years.
Quick change!'

Doctor Engelhardt submitted, and when he was dressed, surveyed himself in his mirror with satisfaction, though he slyly
slipped a cotton handkerchief into his pocket instead of the linen
one Albert had laid out. When they came back to the sitting-
room, Mrs. Rudder had been up again and had put on the wine
glasses. There was still half an hour before dinner, and Albert
sat down to play for his uncle. He was beginning to feel that it
was all much ado about nothing, after all.

A gentle tap at the door, and Elsa came in with her young man.
She was dressed as a Polish maiden, and Carl Abberbock was in a
Highlander's kilt.

'Congratulations on your birthday, Herr Doctor, and I've
brought you some flowers.' She went to his chair and bent down
to be kissed, putting a bunch of violets in his hand.

The Doctor rose and stood looking down at the violets. 'Hey,
you take me for a Bonapartist? What is Mussolini's flower, Albert? Advise your friends in Rome that a Supreme Dictator
should always have a flower.' He turned the young girl around in
the light and teased her about her thin arms — such an old joke,
but she laughed for him.

'But that's the style now, Herr Doctor. Everybody wants to
be as thin as possible.'

'Bah, there are no styles in such things! A man will always want something to take hold of, till Hell freezes over! Is dat so, Carl?'

Carl, a very broad-faced, smiling young man with outstanding ears was suddenly frightened into silence by the entrance of a fine lady, and made for the door to get his knotty knees into the shadow. Elsa, too, caught her breath and shrank away.

Without knocking, Mrs. Parmenter, her arms full of roses, appeared in the doorway, and just behind her was her chauffeur, carrying a package. 'Put it down there and wait for me,' she said to him, then swept into the room and lightly embraced Doctor Engelhardt without waiting to drop the flowers or take off her furs. 'I wanted to congratulate you in person. They told me below that you were receiving. Please take these flowers, Albert. I want a moment's chat with Doctor Engelhardt.'

The Doctor stood with singular gravity, like someone in a play, the violets still in his hand. 'To what,' he muttered with his best bow, 'to what am I indebted for such distinguished consideration?'

'To your own distinction, my dear sir — always one of the most distinguished men I ever knew.'

The Doctor, to whom flattery was thrice dearer than to ordinary men, flushed deeply. But he was not so exalted that he did not notice his little friend of many lonely hours slipping out of the entry-way — the bare-kneed Highland chief had already got down the wooden stairs. 'Elsa,' he called commandingly, 'come here and kiss me good night.' He pulled her forward. 'This is Elsa Rudder, Mrs. Parmenter, and my very particular friend. You should have seen her beautiful hair before she cut it off.' Elsa reddened and glanced up to see whether the lady understood. Uncle Doctor kissed her on the forehead and ran his hand over her shingled head. 'Nineteen years,' he said softly. 'If the next nineteen are as happy, we won't bother about the rest. *Behüt' dich, Gott!*'

'Thank you, Uncle Doctor. Good night.'

After she fluttered out, he turned to Mrs. Parmenter. 'That little girl,' he said impressively, 'is the rose in winter. She is my heir. Everything I have, I leave to her.'

'Everything but my birthday present, please! You must drink that. I've brought you a bottle of champagne.'

Both Alberts began to laugh. 'But your father has already given us two!'

Mrs. Parmenter looked from one to the other. 'My father? Well, that is a compliment! It's unheard of. Of course he and I have different lockers. We could never agree when to open them. I don't think he's opened his since the Chief Justice dined with him. Now I must leave you. Be as jolly as the night is long; with three bottles you ought to do very well! The good woman downstairs said your dinner would be served in half an hour.'

Both men started towards her. 'Don't go. Please, please, stay and dine with us! It's the one thing we needed.' Albert began to entreat her in Italian, a language his uncle did not understand. He confessed that he had been freezing up for the last hour, couldn't go on with it alone. 'One can't do such things without a woman — a beautiful woman.'

'Thank you, Albert. But I've a dinner engagement; I ought to be at the far end of Ellsworth Avenue this minute.'

'But this is once in a lifetime — for him! Still, if your friends are waiting for you, you can't. Certainly not.' He took up her coat and held it for her. But how the light had gone out of his face; he looked so different, so worn, as he stood holding her coat at just the right height. She slipped her arms into it, then pulled them out. 'I can't, but I just will! Let me write a note, please. I'll send Henry on with it and tell them I'll drop in after dinner.' Albert pressed her hand gratefully and took her to his desk. 'Oh, Albert, your Italian writing-table, and all the lovely things on it, just as it stood in your room at the Villa Scipione! You used to let me write letters at it. You had the nicest way with young girls. If I had a daughter, I'd want you to do it all over again.'

She scratched a note, and Albert put a third place at the table. He noticed Uncle Doctor slip away, and come back with his neck-tie set straight, attended by a wave of eau de Cologne. While he was lighting the candles and bringing in the wine cooler, Mrs. Parmenter sat down beside the Doctor, accepted one of his cigarettes, and began to talk to him simply and naturally about Marguerite Thiesinger. Nothing could have been more tactful, Albert knew; nothing could give the old man more pleasure on his birthday. Albert himself couldn't do it any more; he had worn out his power of going over that sad story. He tried to make up for it by playing the songs she had sung.

'Albert,' said Mrs. Parmenter when they sat down to dinner, 'this is the only spot I know in the world that is before-the-war. You've got a period shut up in here; the last ten years of one century, and the first ten of another. Sitting here, I don't believe in aeroplanes, or jazz, or Cubists. My father is nearly as old as Doctor Engelhardt, and we never buy anything new; yet we haven't kept it out. How do you manage?'

Albert smiled a little ruefully. 'I suppose it's because we never have any young people about. They bring it in.'

'Elsa,' murmured the Doctor. 'But I see; she is only a child.'

'I'm sorry for the young people now,' Mrs. Parmenter went on. 'They seem to me coarse and bitter. There's nothing wonderful left for them, poor things; the war destroyed it all. Where could any girl find such a place to escape to as your mother's house, full of chests of linen like this? All houses now are like hotels; nothing left to cherish. Your house was wonderful! And what music we used to have. Do you remember the time you took me to hear Joseffy play the second Brahms, with Gericke? It was the last time I ever heard him. What did happen to him, Albert? Went to pieces in some way, didn't he?'

Albert sighed and shook his head; wine was apt to plunge him into pleasant, poetic melancholy. 'I don't know if anyone knows. I stayed in Rome too long to know, myself. Before I went abroad, I'd been taking lessons with him right along — I saw no change in him, though he gave fewer and fewer concerts. When I got back, I wrote him the day I landed in New York — he was living up the Hudson then. I got a reply from his housekeeper, saying that he was not giving lessons, was ill and was seeing nobody. I went out to his place at once. I wasn't asked to come into the house. I was told to wait in the garden. I waited a long while. At last he came out, wearing white clothes, as he often did, a panama hat, carrying a little cane. He shook hands with me, asked me about Mrs. Sterrett — but he was another man, that's all. He was gone; he wasn't there. I was talking to his picture.'

'Drugs!' muttered the Doctor out of one corner of his mouth.

'Nonsense!' Albert shrugged in derision. 'Or if he did, that was secondary; a result, not a cause. He'd seen the other side of things; he'd let go. Something had happened in his brain that was not paresis.'

Mrs. Parmenter leaned forward. 'Did he *look* the same? Surely, he had the handsomest head in the world. Remember his forehead? Was he grey? His hair was a reddish chestnut as I remember.'

'A little grey; not much. There was no change in his face, except his eyes. The bright spark had gone out, and his body had a sort of trailing languor when he moved.'

'Would he give you a lesson?'

'No. Said he wasn't giving any. Said he was sorry, but he wasn't seeing people at all any more. I remember he sat making patterns in the gravel with his cane. He frowned and said he simply couldn't see people; said the human face had become hateful to him — and the human voice! "I am sorry," he said, "but that is the truth." I looked at his left hand, lying on his knee. I wonder, Marjorie, that I had the strength to get up and go away. I felt as if everything had been drawn out of me. He got up and took my hand. I understood that I must leave. In desperation I asked him whether music didn't mean anything to him still. "Music," he said slowly, with just a ghost of his old smile, "yes — some music." He went back into the house. Those were the last words I ever heard him speak.'

'Oh, dear! And he had everything that is beautiful — and the name of an angel! But we're making the Doctor melancholy. Open another bottle, Albert — father did very well by you. We've not drunk a single toast. Many returns, we take for granted. Why not each drink a toast of our own, to something we care for.' She glanced at Doctor Engelhardt, who lifted the bunch of violets by his plate and smelled them absently. 'Now, Doctor Engelhardt, a toast!'

The Doctor put down his flowers, delicately took up his glass and held it directly in front of him; everything he did with his hands was deft and sure. A beautiful, a wonderful look came over his face as she watched him.

'I drink,' he said slowly, 'to a memory; to the lost Lenore.'

'And I,' said young Albert softly, 'to my youth, to my beautiful youth!'

Tears flashed into Mrs. Parmenter's eyes. 'Ah,' she thought, 'that's what liking people amounts to; it's liking their silliness and absurdities. That's what it really is.'

'And I,' she said aloud, 'will drink to the future; to our renewed friendship, and many dinners together. I like you two better than anyone I know.'

When Albert came back from seeing Mrs. Parmenter down to her car, he found his uncle standing by the fire, his elbow on the mantel, thoughtfully rolling a cigarette. 'Albert,' he said in a deeply confidential tone, 'good wine, good music, beautiful women; that is all there is worth turning over the hand for.'

Albert began to laugh. The old man wasn't often banal. 'Why, Uncle, you and Martin Luther ...'

The Doctor lifted a hand imperiously to stop him, and flushed darkly. He evidently hadn't been aware that he was quoting — it came from the heart. 'Martin Luther,' he snapped, 'was a vulgarian of the first water; cabbage soup!' He paused a moment to light his cigarette. 'But don't fool yourself; one like her always knows when a man has had success with women!'

Albert poured a last glass from the bottle and sipped it critically. 'Well, you had success to-night, certainly. I could see that Marjorie was impressed. She's coming to take you for a ride to-morrow, after your nap, so you must be ready.'

The Doctor passed his flexible, nervous hand lightly over the thick bristles of his French hair-cut. '*Even in our ashes,*' he muttered haughtily.

DEATH OF RED PERIL[1]

WALTER D. EDMONDS

I

JOHN brought his off eye to bear on me:

What do them old coots down to the store do? Why, one of 'em will think up a horse that's been dead forty year and then they'll set around remembering this and that about that horse until they've made a resurrection of him. You'd think he was a regular Grattan Bars, the way they talk, telling one thing and another, when a man knows if that horse hadn't 've had a breeching to keep his tail end off the ground he could hardly have walked from here to Boonville.

A horse race is a handsome thing to watch if a man has his money on a sure proposition. My pa was always a great hand at a horse race. But when he took to a boat and my mother he didn't have no more time for it. So he got interested in another sport.

Did you ever hear of racing caterpillars? No? Well, it used to be a great thing on the canawl. My pa used to have a lot of them insects on hand every fall, and the way he could get them to run would make a man have his eyes examined.

---

[1] Copyright, 1934, by Walter D. Edmonds. From *Mostly Canallers* by Walter D. Edmonds. Little, Brown, and Company, 1934.

The way we raced caterpillars was to set them in a napkin ring on a table, one facing one way and one the other. Outside the napkin ring was drawed a circle in chalk three feet acrost. Then a man lifted the ring and the handlers was allowed one jab with a darning needle to get their caterpillars started. The one that got outside the chalk circle the first was the one that won the race.

I remember my pa tried out a lot of breeds, and he got hold of some pretty fast steppers. But there wasn't one of them could equal Red Peril. To see him you wouldn't believe he could run. He was all red and kind of stubby, and he had a sort of wart behind that you'd think would get in his way. There wasn't anything fancy in his looks. He'd just set still studying the ground and make you think he was dreaming about last year's oats; but when you set him in the starting ring he'd hitch himself up behind like a man lifting on his galluses, and then he'd light out for glory.

Pa come acrost Red Peril down in Westernville. Ma's relatives resided there, and it being Sunday we'd all gone in to church. We was riding back in a hired rig with a dandy trotter, and Pa was pushing her right along and Ma was talking sermon and clothes, and me and my sister was setting on the back seat playing poke your nose, when all of a sudden Pa hollers, 'Whoa!' and set the horse right down on the breeching. Ma let out a holler and come to rest on the dashboard with her head under the horse. 'My gracious land!' she says. 'What's happened?' Pa was out on the other side of the road right down in the mud in his Sunday pants, a-wropping up something in his yeller hankerchief. Ma begun to get riled. 'What you doing, Pa?' she says. 'What you got there?' Pa was putting his handkerchief back into his inside / pocket. Then he come back over the wheel and got him a chew. 'Leeza,' he says, 'I got the fastest caterpillar in seven counties. It's an act of Providence I seen him, the way he jumped the ruts.' 'It's an act of God I ain't laying dead under the back end of that horse,' says Ma. 'I've gone and spoilt my Sunday hat.' 'Never mind,' says Pa; 'Red Peril will earn you a new one.' Just like that he named him. He was the fastest caterpillar in seven counties.

When we got back onto the boat, while Ma was turning up the supper, Pa set him down to the table under the lamp and pulled out the handkerchief. 'You two devils stand there and there,' he says to me and my sister, 'and if you let him get by I'll leather the soap out of you.'

So we stood there and he undid the handkerchief, and out walked one of them red, long-haired caterpillars. He walked right to the middle of the table, and then he took a short turn and put his nose on his tail and went to sleep.

'Who'd think that insect could make such a break for freedom as I seen him make?' says Pa, and he got out a empty Brandreth box and filled it up with some towel and put the caterpillar inside. 'He needs a rest,' says Pa. 'He needs to get used to his stall. When he limbers up I'll commence training him. Now then,' he says, putting the box on the shelf back of the stove, 'don't none of you say a word about him.'

He got out a pipe and set there smoking and figuring, and we could see he was studying out just how he'd make a world-beater out of that bug. 'What you going to feed him?' asks Ma. 'If I wasn't afraid of constipating him,' Pa says, 'I'd try him out with milkweed.'

Next day we hauled up the Lansing Kill Gorge. Ned Kilbourne, Pa's driver, come abroad in the morning, and he took a look at that caterpillar. He took him out of the box and felt his legs and laid him down on the table and went clean over him. 'Well,' he says, 'he don't look like a great lot, but I've knowed some of that red variety could chug along pretty smart.' Then he touched him with a pin. It was a sudden sight.

It looked like the rear end of that caterpillar was racing the front end, but it couldn't never quite get by. Afore either Ned or Pa could get a move Red Peril had made a turn around the sugar bowl and run solid aground in the butter dish.

Pa let out a loud swear. 'Look out he don't pull a tendon,' he says. 'Butter's a bad thing. A man has to be careful. Jeepers,' he says, picking him up and taking him over to the stove to dry, 'I'll handle him myself. I don't want no rum-soaked bezabors dishing my beans.'

'I didn't mean harm, Will,' says Ned. 'I was just curious.'

There was something extraordinary about that caterpillar. He was intelligent. It seemed he just couldn't abide the feel of sharp iron. It got so that if Pa reached for the lapel of his coat Red Peril would light out. It must have been he was tender. I said he had a sort of wart behind, and I guess he liked to find it a place of safety.

We was all terrible proud of that bird. Pa took to timing him on the track. He beat all known time holler. He got to know that as soon as he crossed the chalk he would get back safe in his quarters. Only when we tried sprinting him across the supper table, if he saw a piece of butter he'd pull up short and bolt back where he come from. He had a mortal fear of butter.

Well, Pa trained him three nights. It was a sight to see him there at the table, a big man with a needle in his hand, moving the lamp around and studying out the identical spot that caterpillar wanted most to get out of the needle's way. Pretty soon he found it, and then he says to Ned, 'I'll race him agin all comers at all odds.' 'Well, Will,' says Ned, 'I guess it's a safe proposition.'

II

We hauled up the feeder to Forestport and got us a load of potatoes. We raced him there against Charley Mack, the bank-walker's, Leopard Pillar, one of them tufted breeds with a row of black buttons down the back. The Leopard was well liked and

had won several races that season, and there was quite a few
boaters around that fancied him. Pa argued for favorable odds,
saying he was racing a maiden caterpillar; and there was a lot of
money laid out, and Pa and Ned managed to cover the most of it.
As for the race, there wasn't anything to it. While we was putting
him in the ring — one of them birchbark and sweet grass ones
Indians make — Red Peril didn't act very good. I guess the smell
and the crowd kind of upset him. He was nervous and kept
fidgeting with his front feet; but they hadn't more'n lifted the
ring than he lit out under the edge as tight as he could make it,
and Pa touched him with the needle just as he lepped the line.
Me and my sister was supposed to be in bed, but Ma had gone
visiting in Forestport and we'd snuck in and was under the table,
which had a red cloth onto it, and I can tell you there was some
shouting. There was some couldn't believe that insect had been
inside the ring at all; and there was some said he must be a cross
with a dragon fly or a side-hill gouger; but old Charley Mack,
that'd worked in the camps, said he guessed Red Peril must be
descended from the caterpillars Paul Bunyan used to race. He
said you could tell by the bump on his tail, which Paul used to put
on all his caterpillars, seeing as how the smallest pointed object
he could hold in his hand was a peavy.

Well, Pa raced him a couple of more times and he won just as
easy, and Pa cleared up close to a hundred dollars in three races.
That caterpillar was a mammoth wonder, and word of him got
going and people commenced talking him up everywhere, so it
was hard to race him around these parts.

But about that time the dock-keeper of Number One on the
feeder come across a pretty swift article that the people round
Rome thought high of. And as our boat was headed down the
gorge, word got ahead about Red Peril, and people began to look
out for the race.

We come into Number One about four o'clock, and Pa tied up

right there and went on shore with his box in his pocket and Red
Peril inside the box. There must have been ten men crowded into
the shanty, and as many more again outside looking in the windows and door. The lock-tender was a skinny bezabor from Stitt-
ville, who thought he knew a lot about racing caterpillars; and,
come to think of it, maybe he did. His name was Henry Buscerck, and he had a bad tooth in front he used to suck at a lot.

Well, him and Pa set their caterpillars on the table for the
crowd to see, and I must say Buscerck's caterpillar was as handsome a brute as you could wish to look at, bright bay with black
points and a short fine coat. He had a way of looking right and
left, too, that made him handsome. But Pa didn't bother to look
at him. Red Peril was a natural marvel, and he knew it.

Buscerck was a sly, twerpish man, and he must've heard about
Red Peril — right from the beginning, as it turned out; for he
laid out the course in yeller chalk. They used Pa's ring, a big
silver one he'd bought secondhand just for Red Peril. They laid
out a lot of money, and Dennison Smith lifted the ring. The way
Red Peril histed himself out from under would raise a man's
blood pressure twenty notches. I swear you could see the hair
lay down on his back. Why, that black-pointed bay was left
nowhere! It didn't seem like he moved. But Red Peril was just
gathering himself for a fast finish over the line when he seen it
was yeller. He reared right up; he must've thought it was butter,
by Jeepers, the way he whirled on his hind legs and went the way
he'd come. Pa begun to get scared, and he shook his needle behind Red Peril, but that caterpillar was more scared of butter
than he ever was of cold steel. He passed the other insect afore
he'd got halfway to the line. By Cripus, you'd ought to've heard
the cheering from the Forestport crews. The Rome men was
green. But when he got to the line, danged if that caterpillar
didn't shy again and run around the circle twicet, and then it
seemed like his heart had gone in on him, and he crept right back

to the middle of the circle and lay there hiding his head. It was the pitifulest sight a man ever looked at. You could almost hear him moaning, and he shook all over.

I've never seen a man so riled as Pa was. The water was running right out of his eyes. He picked up Red Peril and he says, 'This here's no race.' He picked up his money and he says, 'The course was illegal, with that yeller chalk.' Then he squashed the other caterpillar, which was just getting ready to cross the line, and he looks at Buscerck and says, 'What're you going to do about that?'

Buscerck says, 'I'm going to collect my money. My caterpillar would have beat.'

'If you want to call that a finish you can,' says Pa, pointing to the squashed bay one, 'but a baby could see he's still got to reach the line. Red Peril got to wire and come back and got to it again afore your hayseed worm got half his feet on the ground. If it was any other man owned him,' Pa says, 'I'd feel sorry I squashed him.'

He stepped out of the house, but Buscerck laid a-hold of his pants and says, 'You got to pay, Hemstreet. A man can't get away with no such excuses in the city of Rome.'

Pa didn't say nothing. He just hauled off and sunk his fist, and Buscerck come to inside the lock, which was at low level right then. He waded out the lower end and he says, 'I'll have you arrested for this.' Pa says, 'All right; but if I ever catch you around this lock again I'll let you have a feel with your other eye.'

Nobody else wanted to collect money from Pa, on account of his build, mostly, so we went back to the boat. Pa put Red Peril to bed for two days. It took him all of that to get over his fright at the yeller circle. Pa even made us go without butter for a spell, thinking Red Peril might know the smell of it. He was such an intelligent, thinking animal, a man couldn't tell nothing about him.

III

But next morning the sheriff comes aboard and arrests Pa with a warrant and takes him afore a justice of the peace. That was old Oscar Snipe. He'd heard all about the race, and I think he was feeling pleasant with Pa, because right off they commenced talking breeds. It would have gone off good only Pa'd been having a round with the sheriff. They come in arm in arm, singing a Hallelujah meeting song; but Pa was polite, and when Oscar says, 'What's this?' he only says, 'Well, well.'

'I hear you've got a good caterpillar,' says the judge.

'Well, well,' says Pa. It was all he could think of to say.

'What breed is he?' says Oscar, taking a chew.

'Well,' says Pa, 'well, well.'

Ned Kilbourne says he was a red one. '

'That's a good breed,' says Oscar, folding his hands on his stummick and spitting over his thumbs and between his knees and into the sandbox all in one spit. 'I kind of fancy the yeller ones myself. You're a connesewer,' he says to Pa, 'and so'm I and between connesewers I'd like to show you one. He's as neat a stepper as there is in this county.'

'Well, well,' says Pa, kind of cold around the eyes and looking at the lithograph of Mrs. Snipe done in a hair frame over the sink.

Oscar slews around and fetches a box out of his back pocket and shows us a sweet little yeller one.

'There she is,' he says, and waits for praise.

'She was a good woman,' Pa said after a while, looking at the picture, 'if any woman that's four times a widow can be called such.'

'Not her,' says Oscar. 'It's this yeller caterpillar.'

Pa slung his eyes on the insect which Oscar was holding, and it seemed like he'd just got an idee.

'Fast?' he says, deep down. 'That thing run! Why, a snail with the stringhalt could spit in his eye.'

Old Oscar come to a boil quick.

'Evidence. Bring me the evidence.'

He spit, and he was that mad he let his whole chew get away from him without noticing. Buscerck says, 'Here,' and takes his hand off'n his right eye.

Pa never took no notice of nothing after that but the eye. It was the shiniest black onion I ever see on a man. Oscar says, 'Forty dollars!' And Pa pays and says, 'It's worth it.'

But it don't never pay to make an enemy in horse racing or caterpillars, as you will see, after I've got around to telling you.

Well, we raced Red Peril nine times after that, all along the Big Ditch, and you can hear to this day — yes, sir — that there never was a caterpillar alive could run like Red Peril. Pa got rich onto him. He allowed to buy a new team in the spring. If he could only've started a breed from that bug, his fortune would've been made and Henry Ford would've looked like a bent nickel alongside me today. But caterpillars aren't built like Ford cars. We beat all the great caterpillars of the year, and it being a time for a late winter, there was some fast running. We raced the Buffalo Big Blue and Fenwick's Night Mail and Wilson's Joe of Barneveld. There wasn't one could touch Red Peril. It was close into October when a crowd got together and brought up the Black Arrer of Ava to race us, but Red Peril beat him by an inch. And after that there wasn't a caterpillar in the state would race Pa's.

He was mighty chesty them days and had come to be quite a figger down the canawl. People come aboard to talk with him and admire Red Peril; and Pa got the idea of charging five cents a sight, and that made for more money even if there wasn't no more running for the animile. He commenced to get fat.

And then come the time that comes to all caterpillars. And it goes to show that a man ought to be as careful of his enemies as he is lending money to friends.

IV

We was hauling down the Lansing Kill again and we'd just crossed the aqueduct over Stringer Brook when the lock-keeper, that minded it and the lock just below, come out and says there was quite a lot of money being put up on a caterpillar they'd collected down in Rome.

Well, Pa went in and he got out Red Peril and tried him out. He was fat and his stifles acted kind of stiff, but you could see with half an eye he was still fast. His start was a mite slower, but he made great speed once he got going.

'He's not in the best shape in the world,' Pa says, 'and if it was any other bug I wouldn't want to run him. But I'll trust the old brute,' and he commenced brushing him up with a toothbrush he'd bought a-purpose.

'Yeanh,' says Ned. 'It may not be right, but we've got to consider the public.'

By what happened after, we might have known that we'd meet up with that caterpillar at Number One Lock; but there wasn't no sign of Buscerck, and Pa was so excited at racing Red Peril again that I doubt if he noticed where he was at all. He was all rigged out for the occasion. He had on a black hat and a new red boating waistcoat, and when he busted loose with his horn for the lock you'd have thought he wanted to wake up all the deef-and-dumbers in seven counties. We tied by the upper gates and left the team to graze; and there was quite a crowd on hand. About nine morning boats was tied along the towpath, and all the afternoon boats waited. People was hanging around, and when they heard Pa whanging his horn they let out a great cheer. He took off his hat to some of the ladies, and then he took Red Peril out of his pocket and everybody cheered some more.

'Who owns this-here caterpillar I've been hearing about?' Pa asks. 'Where is he? Why don't he bring out his pore contraption?'

A feller says he's in the shanty.

'What's his name?' says Pa.

'Martin Henry's running him. He's called the Horned Demon of Rome.'

'Dinged if I ever thought to see him at my time of life,' says Pa. And he goes in. Inside there was a lot of men talking and smoking and drinking and laying money faster than Leghorns can lay eggs, and when Pa comes in they let out a great howdy, and when Pa put down the Brandreth box on the table they crowded round; and you'd ought to've heard the mammoth shout they give when Red Peril climbed out of his box. And well they might. Yes, sir!

You can tell that caterpillar's a thoroughbred. He's shining right down to the root of each hair. He's round, but he ain't too fat. He don't look as supple as he used to, but the folks can't tell that. He's got the winner's look, and he prances into the centre of the ring with a kind of delicate canter that was as near single-footing as I ever see a caterpillar get to. By Jeepers Cripus! I felt proud to be in the same family as him, and I wasn't only a little lad.

Pa waits for the admiration to die down, and he lays out his money, and he says to Martin Henry, 'Let's see your ring-boned swivel-hocked imitation of a bug.'

Martin answers, 'Well, he ain't much to look at, maybe, but you'll be surprised to see how he can push along.'

And he lays down the dangedest lump of worm you ever set your eyes on. It's the kind of insect a man might expect to see in France or one of them furrin lands. It's about two and a half inches long and stands only half a thumbnail at the shoulder. It's green and as hairless as a newborn egg, and it crouches down squinting around at Red Peril like a man with sweat in his eye. It ain't natural nor refined to look at such a bug, let alone race it.

When Pa seen it, he let out a shout and laughed. He couldn't talk from laughing.

But the crowd didn't say a lot, having more money on the race than ever was before or since on a similar occasion. It was so much that even Pa commenced to be serious. Well, they put 'em in the ring together and Red Peril kept over on his side with a sort of intelligent dislike. He was the brainiest article in the caterpillar line I ever knowed. The other one just hunkered down with a mean look in his eye.

Millard Thompson held the ring. He counted, 'One — two — three — and off.' Some folks said it was the highest he knew how to count, but he always got that far anyhow, even if it took quite a while for him to remember what figger to commence with.

The ring come off and Pa and Martin Henry sunk their needles — at least they almost sunk them, for just then them standing close to the course seen that Horned Demon sink his horns into the back end of Red Peril. He was always a sensitive animal, Red Peril was, and if a needle made him start you can think for yourself what them two horns did for him. He cleared twelve inches in one jump — but then he sot right down on his belly, trembling.

'Foul!' bellers Pa. 'My 'pillar's fouled.'

'It ain't in the rule book,' Millard says.

'It's a foul!' yells Pa; and all the Forestport men yell, 'Foul! Foul!'

But it wasn't allowed. The Horned Demon commenced walking to the circle — he couldn't move much faster than a barrel can roll uphill, but he was getting there. We all seen two things, then. Red Peril was dying, and we was losing the race. Pa stood there kind of foamy in his beard, and the water running right out of both eyes. It's an awful thing to see a big man cry in public. But Ned saved us. He seen Red Peril was dying, the way he wiggled, and he figgered, with the money he had on him, he'd make him win if he could.

He leans over and puts his nose into Red Peril's ear, and he shouts, 'My Cripus, you've gone and dropped the butter!'

Something got into that caterpillar's brain, dying as he was, and he let out the smallest squeak of a hollering fright I ever listened to a caterpillar make. There was a convulsion got into him. He looked like a three-dollar mule with the wind colic, and then he gave a bound. My holy! How that caterpillar did rise up. When he come down again, he was stone dead, but he lay with his chin across the line. He'd won the race. The Horned Demon was blowing bad and only halfway to the line. . . .

Well, we won. But I think Pa's heart was busted by the squeal he heard Red Peril make when he died. He couldn't abide Ned's face after that, though he knowed Ned had saved the day for him. But he put Red Peril's carcase in his pocket with the money and walks out.

And there he seen Buscerck standing at the sluices. Pa stood looking at him. The sheriff was alongside Buscerck and Oscar Snipe on the other side, and Buscerck guessed he had the law behind him.

'Who owns that Horned Demon?' said Pa.

'Me,' says Buscerck with a sneer. 'He may have lost, but he done a good job doing it.'

Pa walks right up to him.

'I've got another forty dollars in my pocket,' he says, and he connected sizably.

Buscerck's boots showed a minute. Pretty soon they let down the water and pulled him out. They had to roll a couple of gallons out of him afore they got a grunt. It served him right. He'd played foul. But the sheriff was worried, and he says to Oscar, 'Had I ought to arrest Will?' (Meaning Pa.)

Oscar was a sporting man. He couldn't abide low dealing. He looks at Buscerck there, shaping his belly over the barrel, and he says, 'Water never hurt a man. It keeps his hide from cracking.' So they let Pa alone. I guess they didn't think it was safe to have a man in jail that would cry about a caterpillar. But then they hadn't lived alongside of Red Peril like us.

THE FAITHFUL WIFE [1]

MORLEY CALLAGHAN

Until a week before Christmas George worked in the station restaurant at the lunch counter. The last week was extraordinarily cold, then the sun shone strongly for a few days, though it was always cold again in the evenings. There were three other men working at the counter. For years they must have had a poor reputation. Women, unless they were careless and easy-going, never started a conversation with them when having a light lunch at noontime. The girls at the station always avoided the red-capped porters and the countermen.

George, who was working there till he got enough money to go back home for a week and then start late in the year at college, was a young fellow with fine hair retreating far back on his forehead and rather bad upper teeth, but he was very polite and generous. Steve the plump Italian, with the waxed black mustaches, who had charge of the restaurant, was very fond of George.

Many people passed the restaurant window on the way to the platform and the trains. The four men, watching them frequently,

[1] Copyright, 1936, by Random House, Inc. From *Now That April's Here*, by Morley Callaghan. Random House, 1936.

got to know some of them. Girls, brightly dressed and highly powdered, loitered in front of the open door, smiling at George, who saw them so often he knew their first names. At noontime, other girls, with a few minutes to spare before going back to work, used to walk up and down the tiled tunnel to the waiting-room, loafing the time away, but they never even glanced in at the countermen. It was cold outside, the streets were slippery, and it was warm in the station, that was all. George got to know most of these girls too, and talked about them with the other fellows.

George watched carefully one girl every day at noon hour. The other men had also noticed her, and two or three times she came in for a cup of coffee, but she was so gentle, and aloofly pleasant, and so unobtrusively beyond them, they were afraid to try and amuse her with easy cheerful talk. George wished earnestly that she had never seen him there in the restaurant behind the counter, even though he knew she had never noticed him at all. Her cheeks were usually rosy from the cold wind outside. When she went out the door to walk up and down for a few minutes, an agreeable expression on her face, she never once looked back at the restaurant. George, following her with his eye while pouring coffee slowly, did not expect her to look back. She was about twenty-eight, pretty, rather shy, and dressed plainly and poorly in a thin blue-cloth coat without any fur on it. Most girls managed to have a piece of fur of some kind on their coats.

With little to do in the middle of the afternoon, George used to think of her because of seeing her every day and looking at her face in profile when she passed the window. Then, on the day she had on the light-fawn felt hat, she smiled politely at him, when having a cup of coffee, and as long as possible, he remained opposite her, cleaning the counter with a damp cloth.

The last night he worked at the station he went out at about half past eight in the evening, for he had an hour to himself, and then worked on till ten o'clock. In the morning he was going home, so he walked out of the station and down the side street to the docks, and was having only pleasant thoughts, passing the warehouses, looking out over the dark cold lake and liking the tang of the wind on his face. Christmas was only a week away. The snow was falling lazily and melting slowly when it hit the sidewalk. He was glad he was through with the job at the restaurant.

An hour later, back at the restaurant, Steve said, 'A dame just phoned you, George, and left her number.'

'Do you know who she was?'

'No, you got too many girls, George. Don't you know the number?'

'I never saw it before.'

He called the number and did not recognize the voice that answered him. A woman was asking him pleasantly enough if he remembered her. He said he did not. She said she had had a cup of coffee that afternoon at noontime, and added that she had worn a blue coat and a tan-colored felt hat, and even though she had not spoken to him, she thought he would remember her.

'Good Lord,' he said.

She wanted to know if he would come and see her at half past ten that evening. Timidly he said he would, and hardly heard her giving the address. Steve and the other boys started to kid him brightly, but he was too astonished, wondering how she had found out his name, to bother with them. The boys, saying goodbye to him later, winked and elbowed him in the ribs, urging him to celebrate on his last night in the city. Steve, who was very fond of him, shook his head sadly and pulled the ends of his mustaches down into his lips.

The address the girl had given him was only eight blocks away, so he walked, holding his hands clenched tightly in his pockets, for he was cold from nervousness. He was watching the automobile headlights shining on slippery spots on the sidewalk. The house, opposite a public-school ground on a side street, was a large old rooming house. A light was in a window on the second story over the door. Ringing the bell he didn't really expect anyone to answer, and was surprised when the girl herself opened the door.

'Good evening,' he said shyly.

'Oh, come upstairs,' she said, smiling and practical.

In the front room he took off his overcoat and hat and sat down slowly, noticing, out of the corner of his eye, that she was even slimmer, and had nice fair hair and lovely eyes. But she was moving very nervously. He had intended to ask at once how she found out his name, but forgot about it as soon as she sat down opposite him on a camp bed and smiled shyly. She had on a red woolen sweater, fitting her tightly at the waist. Twice he shook his head, unable to get used to having her there opposite him, nervous and expectant. The trouble was she had always seemed so aloof.

'You're not very friendly,' she said awkwardly.

'Oh yes I am. Indeed I am.'

'Why don't you come over here and sit beside me?'

Slowly he sat down beside her on the camp bed, smiling stupidly. He was even slow to see that she was waiting for him to put his arms around her. Ashamed of himself, he finally kissed her eagerly and she held on to him tightly. Her heart was thumping underneath the red woolen sweater. She just kept on holding him, almost savagely, closing her eyes slowly and breathing deeply every time he kissed her. She was so delighted and satisfied to hold him in her arms that she did not bother talking at all. Finally he became very eager and she got up suddenly, walking up and down the room, looking occasionally at the cheap alarm clock on a bureau. The room was clean but poorly furnished.

'What's the matter?' he said irritably.

'My girl friend, the one I room with, will be home in twenty minutes.'

'Come here anyway.'

'Please sit down, please do,' she said.

Slowly she sat down beside him. When he kissed her she did not object, but her lips were dry, her shoulders were trembling, and she kept on watching the clock. Though she was holding his wrist so tightly her nails dug into the skin, he knew she would be glad when he had to go. He kissed her again and she drew her left hand slowly over her lips.

'You really must be out of here before Irene comes home,' she said.

'But I've only kissed and hugged you and you're wonderful.' He noticed the red ring mark on her finger. 'Are you sure you're not waiting for your husband to come home?' he said a bit irritably.

Frowning, looking away vaguely, she said, 'Why do you have to say that?'

'There's a ring mark on your finger.'

'I can't help it,' she said, and began to cry quietly. 'Yes, oh yes, I'm waiting for my husband to come home. He'll be here at Christmas.'

'It's too bad. Can't we do something about it?'

'I tell you I love my husband. I do, I really do, and I'm faithful to him too.'

'Maybe I'd better go,' he said uncomfortably, feeling ridiculous.

'Eh, what's that? My husband, he's at a sanitarium. He got his spine hurt in the war, then he got tuberculosis. He's pretty bad. They've got to carry him around. We want to love each other every time we meet, but we can't.'

'That's tough, poor kid, and I suppose you've got to pay for him.'

'Yes.'

'Do you have many fellows?'

'No. I don't want to have any.'

'Do they come here to see you?'

'No. No, I don't know what got into me. I liked you, and felt a little crazy.'

'I'll slide along then. What's your first name?'

'Lola. You'd better go now.'

'Couldn't I see you again?' he said suddenly.

'No, you're going away tomorrow,' she said, smiling confidently.

'So you've got it all figured out. Supposing I don't go?'

'Please, you must.'

Her arms were trembling when she held his overcoat. She wanted him to go before Irene came home. 'You didn't give me much time,' he said flatly.

'No. Irene comes in at this time. You're a lovely boy. Kiss me.'

'You had that figured out too.'

'Just kiss and hold me once more, George.' She held on to him as if she did not expect to be embraced again for a long time, and he said, 'I think I'll stay in the city a while longer.'

'It's too bad, but you've got to go. We can't see each other again.'

In the poorly lighted hall she looked lovely. Her cheeks were flushed, and though still eager, she was quite satisfied with the whole affair. Everything had gone perfectly for her.

As he went out the door and down the walk to the street he remembered that he hadn't asked how she had found out his name. Snow was falling lightly and there were hardly any footprints on the sidewalk. All he could think of was that he ought to go back to the restaurant and ask Steve for his job again. Steve was fond of him. But he knew he could not spoil it for her. 'She had it all figured out,' he muttered, turning up his coat collar.

THE LITTLE WIFE[1]

WILLIAM MARCH

J OE HINCKLEY selected a seat on the shady side of
the train and carefully stowed away his traveling bag and his
heavy, black catalogue case. It was unusually hot for early June.
Outside the heat waves shimmered and danced above the hot
slag roadbed and the muddy river that ran by the station was low
between its red banks. 'If it's as hot as this in June, it sure will be
awful in August,' he thought. He looked at his watch: 2.28 — the
train was five minutes late in getting out. If he had known the
2.23 was going to be late he might have had time to pack his
sample trunk and get it to the station, but he couldn't have
anticipated that, of course. He had had so little time after getting
that telegram from Mrs. Thompkins: barely time to pack his bag
and check out of the hotel. Joe loosened his belt and swabbed his
neck with a limp handkerchief. 'It don't matter so much about
the trunk,' he thought; 'one of the boys at the hotel can express it
to me, or I can pick it up on my way back.'

Joe noticed that one end of his catalogue case protruded
slightly. With his foot he shoved it farther under the seat. It was

a battered, black case, made strongly to withstand constant traveling, and re-enforced at its corners with heavy copper cleats. One of the handles had been broken and mended with newer leather. On the front of the case there had once been stamped in gilt the firm name of Boykin & Rosen, Wholesale Hardware, Chattanooga, Tenn., but time had long since worn away the gold lettering.

The telegram had upset Joe: it had come so suddenly, so unexpectedly. He felt vaguely that somebody was playing a joke on him. He felt confused and helpless. It was difficult to believe that Bessie was so desperately sick. He sat for a time staring at his finger nails. Suddenly he remembered an appointment at four o'clock with the buyer for Snowdoun and Sims and he rose quickly from his seat with some dim idea of telephoning or sending a message to explain his absence. Then he realized that the train was already in motion. 'I'll write him a letter when I get to Mobile,' said Joe to himself; 'he'll understand all right when I explain the circumstances. He won't blame me for breaking that date when I tell him about my wife being so sick.' He sat down heavily in his seat and again looked at his hands.

Ahead of him two young girls were leaning out of the window and waving to their friends. Their eyes were shining and their cheeks were flushed and they were laughing with excitement at the prospect of going away.

Across the aisle sat a gaunt farm-woman. Her red-veined eyes protruded. Her neck was swollen with a goiter. In her arms she held a bouquet of red crêpe-myrtle which was already wilting in the heat. Beside her she had placed her straw suitcase and several bulky, paper-wrapped parcels. She gazed steadily out of the window as if afraid that someone would catch her eye and try to talk to her.

It was very hot in the coach. The small electric fan at the end of the car droned and wheezed sleepily but succeeded only in stirring up the hot air.

Joe took from his pocket the telegram that he had received from his mother-in-law and read it again: 'J. G. Hinckley, American Hotel, Montgomery, Ala. Come home at once. Doctor says Bessie not expected live through day. Will wire again if necessary. It was a boy. Mother.'

Joe's hands clenched suddenly and then relaxed. It had all happened so suddenly; he couldn't quite get it through his head, even yet. He had taken a buyer to lunch that day and they had laughed and talked and told each other stories. Then at two o'clock he had gone back to the hotel to freshen up and the clerk had reached in his box and taken out the key to his room and the telegram. The telegram had been waiting for him for two hours the clerk said. Joe read it through twice and then looked at the address to make sure that the message was really for him. He hadn't understood. Bessie was getting along so nicely — she had had no trouble at all — and the baby wasn't expected for a month. He had arranged his itinerary so that he would be with her when the baby was born. They had gone over all that and had arranged everything. And now everything was upset. He thought: 'I was out talking and laughing with that buyer and the telegram was waiting here all the time.' That thought hurt him. He stood repeating stupidly: 'I was out laughing and telling smutty stories and that telegram was here all the time.'

Joe leaned his head against the red plush of the seat. He felt numb and very tired. At first the signature 'Mother' had puzzled him. He couldn't understand what his mother would be doing in Mobile with Bessie; then he realized that it was Bessie's mother who had sent the telegram. He had never thought of Bessie's mother by any name except Mrs. Thompkins.

When he had married Bessie her mother had come to live with them as a matter of course. He was rather glad of that arrangement; he was really fond of the old lady in an impersonal sort of way. Then, too, it was pleasant for Bessie to have someone with her while he was on the road. His work made it impossible for him to get home oftener than every other week-end, and many times it was difficult for him to get home that often, but he had always managed to make it, one way or another. He couldn't disappoint Bessie, no matter what happened. Their year of married life had been the happiest that he had ever known. And Bessie had been happy too. Suddenly he had a clear picture of her lying on their bed, her face white with suffering, and a quick panic gripped his heart. To reassure himself he whispered: 'Those doctors don't know everything. She'll be all right. Mrs. Thompkins was just excited and frightened. Everything's going to be all right!'

Ahead of him a white-haired old gentleman opened his bag and took out a traveling cap. He had some difficulty in fastening the catch while holding his straw hat in his hand, but his wife, sitting with him, took the bag and fastened it at once. Then she took his hat and held it on her lap. The wife was reading a magazine. She did not look up from the magazine when she fastened the bag.

Down the aisle came the negro porter. He had a telegram in his hand. When he reached the center of the coach he stopped and called out: 'Telegram for Mr. J. G. Hinckley!' Joe let him call the name three times before he claimed the message. The porter explained that the telegram had been delivered to the train by a messenger from the American Hotel just as the train was getting under way. Joe gave the porter twenty-five cents for a tip and went back to his seat.

The country woman looked up for an instant and then turned her eyes away. The young girls giggled and whispered and looked boldly at Joe, and the old gentleman, after settling his cap firmly on his head, took a cigar from his case and went to the smoking-room.

Joe's throat felt tight and he noticed that his hands were

shaking. He wanted to put his head on the window-sill but he was afraid that people would think him sick and try to talk to him. He placed the unopened telegram on the seat beside him and stared at it for a long time. At last he re-read the first telegram very slowly. 'It must be from Mrs. Thompkins, all right,' he thought, 'she said she'd wire again if ——' Then he thought: 'It may not be from Mrs. Thompkins at all; it may be from somebody else; it may be from Boykin & Rosen about that cancellation in Meridian. That's who it's from: it's from the House, it's not from Mrs. Thompkins at all!' He looked up quickly and saw that the two young girls had turned around and were watching him, making laughing remarks to each other behind their hands.

He arose from his seat feeling weak and slightly nauseated, the unopened telegram in his hand. He passed through several coaches until he reached the end of the train and went out on the rear vestibule. He had a sudden wish to jump from the end of the train and run off into the woods, but a brakeman was there tinkering with a red lantern and Joe realized that such an act would look very strange. When the brakeman looked up and saw Joe's face he put down his lantern and asked: 'Are you feeling all right, mister?' Joe said, 'Yes, I'm feeling all right but it's a little hot, though.' Finally the brakeman finished his job and left and Joe was very glad of that. He wanted to be alone. He didn't want anybody around him.

The rails clicked rhythmically and the wilted country-side flew past. A little negro girl . . . in a patched pink dress . . . ran down to the track . . . and waved her hand. A lame old country man . . . ploughing in his stumpy field . . . pulled up his mangy mule . . . to stare at the passing train. The rails clattered and clicked and the train flew over the hot slag roadbed. 'There's no need of going so fast,' thought Joe, 'we've got all the time in the world.' He felt sick. In the polished metal of the car he caught a distorted glimpse of his face. It was white and terrified. He thought: 'No wonder that brakeman asked me how I was feeling.' Then he thought: 'Do I look so bad that people can tell it?' That worried him. He didn't want people to notice him or to talk to him. There was nothing that anybody could say, after all.

He kept turning the telegram over in his hand thinking: 'I've got to open it now; I've got to open it and read it.' Finally he said aloud: 'It's not true! I don't believe it!' He repeated these words a number of times and then he said: 'It's from the House about that cancellation in Meridian — it isn't from Mrs. Thompkins at all.' He tore the unopened telegram into tiny bits and threw the pieces from the end of the train. A wind fluttered and shimmered the yellow fragments before they settled down lightly on the hard, hot roadbed. He thought: 'They look like a cloud of yellow butterflies dancing and settling that way.' Immediately he felt better. He drew back his shoulders and sucked in lungfuls of the country air. 'Everything's all right,' he said. 'I'm going home to see the little wife and everything's all right.' He laughed happily. He felt like a man who has just escaped some terrible calamity. When he could no longer see the scraps of paper on the track he went back to his seat humming a tune. He felt very gay and immensely relieved.

Joe reached his seat just as the conductor came through the train. He nodded pleasantly as he gave up his ticket.

'Don't let anybody talk you out of a free ride,' he said.

'No chance of that, Cap!' said the conductor.

Joe laughed with ringing heartiness and the conductor looked at him in surprise. Then he laughed a little himself. 'You sure are in a good humor, considering how hot it is,' he said.

'And why shouldn't I be in a good humor?' asked Joe. 'I'm going home to see the little wife.' Then he whispered, as if it were a great secret, 'It's a boy!'

'That's fine, that's simply fine!' said the conductor. He put his papers and his tickets on the seat and shook Joe's hand. Joe

blushed and laughed again. As the conductor moved off he
nudged Joe's ribs and said: 'Give my regards to the madam.'

'I sure will,' said Joe happily.

Joe was sorry that the conductor couldn't stay longer. He felt
an imperative need of talking to someone. He felt that he must
talk about Bessie to someone. He looked around the car to see if
he knew anybody on the train. The two young girls smiled at
him. Joe understood perfectly; they were just two nice kids
going on a trip. Either one, alone, would never think of smiling
at a strange man but being together changed things all the way
around. That made it an exciting adventure, something to be
laughed over and discussed later with their friends. Joe decided
that he would go over and talk to them. He walked over casually
and seated himself.

'Well, where are you young ladies going?' he asked.

'Don't you think that you have a great deal of nerve?' asked
the black-eyed girl.

'Sure I have. I wouldn't be the best hardware salesman on the
road if I didn't have a lot of nerve,' said Joe pleasantly.

Both of the girls laughed at that and Joe knew that everything
was all right. He decided that the blue-eyed girl was the prettier
of the two but the black-eyed girl had more snap.

'We're getting off at Flomaton,' said the blue-eyed girl.

'We've been in school in Montgomery,' said the black-eyed
girl.

'We're going home for the summer vacation.'

'And we want the cock-eyed world to know we're glad of it!'

Joe looked at them gravely. 'Don't make a mistake, young
ladies; get all the education you can. You'll regret it later on if
you don't.'

Both the girls started laughing. They put their arms around
each other and laughed until tears came into their eyes. Joe
laughed too although he wondered what the joke was. After

a while the girls stopped laughing, but a sudden giggle from the blue-eyed girl set them off again, worse than before.

'This is awfully silly!' said the black-eyed girl.

'Please don't think us rude,' gasped the blue-eyed girl.

'What's the joke?' asked Joe, who was really laughing as much as either of the girls.

'You sounded so — so —' explained the blue-eyed girl.

'So damned *fatherly!*' finished the black-eyed girl.

They went off into another whirlwind of mirth, laughing and hugging each other. The old lady across the aisle put down her magazine and started laughing too, but the woman with the goiter held her bouquet of crêpe-myrtle rigidly and stared out of the window.

Joe waited until the girls had exhausted themselves. Finally they wiped their eyes and opened their vanity cases to look at themselves in their mirrors and to repowder their faces. He said:

'Well, I guess I ought to sound fatherly: I just got a telegram saying that I was a parent for the first time.'

That interested the young girls and they crowded him with questions: they wanted to know all about it. Joe felt very happy. As he started to talk he noticed that the old lady had been listening and that she had moved over in her seat in order to hear better. Joe felt friendly toward everybody: 'Won't you come over and join us?' he asked.

'Yes, indeed,' said the old lady and Joe moved over and made a place for her.

'Now tell us all about it!' demanded the blue-eyed girl.

'You must be very happy,' said the old lady.

'I sure am happy,' said Joe. Then he added: 'There's not a whole lot to tell except that I got a telegram from Mrs. Thompkins — Mrs. Thompkins is my mother-in-law — saying that Bessie had given birth to a fine boy and that both of them were doing just fine: the doctor said that he'd never seen anybody do so well before, but of course my wife wanted me to be with her and so I just dropped everything and here I am. You see Bessie and I have only been married for a year. We've been very happy. The only bad thing is that I don't get home very often, but it wouldn't do to have everything perfect in the world, would it? She sure is the finest little wife a man ever had. She don't complain at all about my being away so much, but some day we hope to have things different.'

'There isn't anything nicer than a baby,' said the blue-eyed girl.

'What are you going to name him?' asked the old lady.

'Well, Bessie wants to name him for me, but I can't see much sense in that. My first name's Joe and I think that's a little common, don't you? But I'll leave the naming part up to Bessie. She can name him anything she wants to. She sure has been a fine little wife to me.'

Joe started talking rapidly. He told in detail of the first time he had met Bessie. It had been in the home of Jack Barnes, one of the boys he had met on the road, and he had been invited over for dinner and a little stud poker later. Mrs. Barnes didn't play poker so Bessie, who lived across the street, had been invited over to keep Mrs. Barnes company while the men played. He had liked Bessie at once and the boys had kidded him about not keeping his mind on the game. He had never told anybody this before, but when the boys started kidding him he made up his mind not to look at Bessie again as he didn't want her to think that he was fresh, but he couldn't stop looking at her and every time he caught her eye she would smile in a sweet, friendly sort of way. Finally everybody noticed it and they started joking Bessie too, but she hadn't minded at all. He had lost $14.50 that night, but he had met Bessie. You couldn't call Bessie exactly beautiful but she was sweet and nice. Bessie was the sort of girl that any man would want to marry.

He told of their courtship. He quoted whole paragraphs from letters that she had written to prove a particular point which he had brought up. Bessie hadn't liked him especially, not right at first, at any rate; of course she had liked him as a friend from the first but not in any serious way. There were one or two other fellows hanging around, too. Bessie had a great deal of attention; she could have gone out every night with a different man if she had wanted to. Being on the road all the time had been pretty much of a disadvantage. He didn't have an opportunity to see her often. Or maybe that was an advantage — anyway he wrote her every day. Then, finally, they had become engaged. She hadn't even let him kiss her until then. He knew from the first that she would make a wonderful little wife but he was still puzzled why a girl as superior as Bessie would want to marry *him*.

He talked on and on, rapidly — feverishly. He told how he had once determined not to get married at all, but that was before he had met Bessie. She had changed all that. Two hours passed before he knew it. His audience was getting bored, but Joe didn't realize it.

Finally the old gentleman with the cap came back from the smoking-room and his wife, glad of a chance to get away, made her excuses and went over to sit with him. Joe smiled and nodded, but paused only a moment in his story. He was in the midst of a long description of Mrs. Thompkins. Mrs. Thompkins wasn't at all like the comic supplement mother-in-law. Quite the contrary. He didn't see how he and Bessie would get along without her. To show you the sort of woman she really was, she always took his side in any dispute — not that he and Bessie ever quarreled! Oh, no! But occasionally they had little friendly·discussions like all other married couples and Mrs. Thompkins always took his side of the argument. That was unusual, wasn't it? Joe talked and talked and talked, totally unconscious of the passing of time.

Finally the train reached Flomaton and the porter came to help the girls off with their bags. They were very glad to get away. They were getting a little nervous. There was something about Joe that they couldn't understand. At first they had thought him just jolly and high spirited, but after a time they came to the conclusion that he must be a little drunk, or, possibly, slightly demented. For the past hour they had been nudging each other significantly.

Joe helped them off the train and on to the station platform. Just as the train pulled out the black-eyed girl waved her hand and said: 'Give my love to Bessie and the son and heir,' and the blue-eyed girl said: 'Be sure and kiss the baby for me.'

'I sure will,' said Joe.

After the train had passed the girls looked at each other for a moment. Then they started laughing. Finally the black-eyed girl said: 'Well, Bessie certainly has him roped and tied.' The blue-eyed girl said: 'Did you ever see anything like that in your life before?'

Joe came into the coach again. 'Just a couple of nice kids,' he thought to himself. He looked at his watch. It was 5.25. He was surprised. The time had passed very quickly. 'It won't be long now before I'm in Mobile,' he thought.

He went back to his seat, but he was restless. He decided that he would have a cigarette. He found three men in the smoker. One of them was an old man with a tuft of gray whiskers. His face was yellow and sunken and blue veins stood out on his hands. He was chewing tobacco gravely and spitting into the brass cuspidor. The second man was large and flabby. When he laughed his eyes disappeared entirely and his fat belly shook. His finger nails were swollen and his underlip hung down in a petulant droop. The third man was dark and nervous looking. He had on his little finger a ring with a diamond much too large.

They were telling jokes and laughing when Joe came in. Joe

wanted to talk to them about Bessie, but he couldn't bring her name up in such an atmosphere. Suddenly he thought: 'I was laughing and telling smutty stories with that buyer in Montgomery and the telegram was there all the time.' His face contracted with pain. He crushed the thought from his mind. Quickly he threw away his cigarette and went back to his seat.

A bright-skinned waiter came through the train announcing the first call for dinner. At first Joe thought that he would have his dinner on the train as that would break the monotony of the trip and help pass the time, but immediately he remembered that Mrs. Thompkins would have dinner for him at home — a specially prepared dinner with all of the things that he liked. 'I'll wait until I get home,' thought Joe. 'I wouldn't disappoint Mrs. Thompkins and the little wife for the world after they went to all that trouble for me.'

Again he felt that curious, compulsive need of talking about Bessie to someone. He had a feeling that as long as he talked about her she would remain safe. He saw the old lady and her husband in their seat eating a lunch which they had brought and he decided to go over and talk with them. 'Can I come over and talk to you folks?' asked Joe.

'Certainly, sir,' said the old gentleman with the cap. Then, in order to make conversation he said: 'My wife has been telling me that you are going home to see your new son.'

'That's right,' said Joe, 'that's right.' He started talking rapidly, hardly pausing for breath. The old lady looked at her husband reproachfully. 'Now see what you started!' her glance seemed to say.

Joe talked of his wedding. It had been very quiet. Bessie was the sort of a girl who didn't go in for a lot of show. There had been present only a few members of the family and one or two close friends. George Orcutt who traveled a line of rugs out of New York had been his best man. Bessie was afraid that someone would try to play a joke on them: something like tying tin cans to the automobile that was to take them to the station or marking their baggage with chalk. But everything had gone off smoothly. The Barneses had been at the wedding, of course: he had met Bessie in their home and they were such close neighbors that they couldn't overlook them, but almost nobody else outside the family was there.

Then he told of the honeymoon they had spent in New Orleans; all the places they had visited there and just what Bessie had thought and said about each one. He talked on and on and on. He told of the first weeks of their married life and how happy they were. He told what a splendid cook Bessie was and what an excellent housekeeper, how much she had loved the home he had bought for her and her delight when she knew that she was going to have a baby.

The old gentleman was staring at Joe in a puzzled manner. He was wondering if he hadn't better call the conductor as it was his private opinion that Joe had a shot of cocaine in him. The old lady had folded her hands like a martyr. She continued to look at her husband with an 'I-told-you-so!' expression.

Joe had lost all idea of time. He talked on and on, rapidly, excitedly. He had got as far as Bessie's plans for the child's education when the porter touched him on the arm and told him that they were pulling into the station at Mobile. He came to himself with a start and looked at his watch: 7.35! He didn't believe it possible that two hours had passed so quickly.

'It sure has been a pleasure talking to you folks,' said Joe.

'Oh, that's all right,' said the man with the cap.

Joe gave the porter a tip and stepped off the train jauntily. As he turned to pick up his bag he saw that the woman with the goiter was staring at him. He walked over to the window that framed her gaunt face. 'Good-bye, lady; I hope you have a nice trip.' The woman answered: 'The doctors said it wasn't no use operating on me. I waited too long.' 'Well that's fine! — That sure is fine!' said Joe. He laughed gaily and waved his hand. He picked up his bag and his catalogue case and followed the people through the gate. The woman with the goiter stared at him until he was out of sight.

On the other side of the iron fence Joe saw Mrs. Thompkins. She was dressed in black and she wore a black veil. Joe went over to her briskly and Mrs. Thompkins put her arms around him and kissed him twice. 'Poor Joe!' she said. Then she looked at his smiling, excited face with amazement. Joe noticed that her eyes were red and swollen.

'Didn't you get my telegram?' she asked. Joe wrinkled his brow in an effort to remember. Finally he said: 'Oh, sure. I got it at the hotel.'

'Did you get my second telegram?' insisted Mrs. Thompkins. She looked steadily into Joe's eyes. A feeling of terror swept over him. He knew that he could no longer lie to himself. He could no longer keep Bessie alive by talking about her. His face was suddenly twisted with pain and his jaw trembled like a child's. He leaned against the iron fence for support and Mrs. Thompkins held his hand and said: 'You can't give in. You got to be a man. You can't give in like that, Joe!'

Finally he said: 'I didn't read your telegram. I didn't want to know that she was dead. I wanted to keep her alive a little longer.' He sat down on an empty baggage truck and hid his face in his hands. He sat there for a long time while Mrs. Thompkins stood guard over him, her black veil trailing across his shoulder.

'Joe!' she said patiently.... 'Joe!...'

A man in a dirty uniform came up. 'I'm sorry, Mister, but you'll have to move. We got to use that truck.' Joe picked up his catalogue case and his bag and followed Mrs. Thompkins out of the station.

REST CURE[1]

KAY BOYLE

H E SAT in the sun with the blanket about him,
considering, with his hands lying out like emaciated strangers
before him, that today the sun would endure a little longer. Certainly it would survive until the trees below the terrace effaced it,
towards four o'clock, like opened parasols. A crime it had been,
the invalid thought, turning his head this way and that, to have
ever built up one house before another in such a way that one
man's habitation cast a shadow upon another's. The whole sloping coast should have been left a wilderness with no order to it,
stalked and leafed with the great strong trunks and foliage of
these parts. Cactus plants with petals a yard wide and yucca
tongues as thick as elephant trunks were sullenly and viciously
flourishing all about the house. Upon the terrace had a further
attempt at nicety and precision been made: there his wife had
seen to it that geraniums were potted into the wooden boxes that
stood along the wall.

From his lounging chair he could reach out and, with no effort
beyond that of raising the skeleton of his hand, finger the parched

---

stems of the geraniums. The south, and the Mediterranean wind, had blistered them past all belief. They bore their rosy top-knots or their soiled white flowers balanced upon their thick Italian heads. There they were, within his reach, a row of weary washer-women leaning back from the villainous descent of the coast. What parched scions had thrust forth from their stems now served to obliterate in part the vision of the sun. With arms akimbo they surrounded him: thin burned Italian women with their meager bundles of dirty linen on their heads. One after another, with a flicker of irritation for his wife lighting his eye, he fingered them at the waist a moment, and then snapped off each stem. One after another he broke their stalks in two and dropped them away onto the pavings beneath his lounging chair. When he had finished off what plants grew within his reach, he lay back ex-hausted, sank, thin as an archer's bow, into the depths of his cushions.

'They kept the sun off me,' he was thinking in absolution.

In spite of the garden and its vegetation, he would have the last drops of sun. He had closed his eyes, and there he lay look-ing straight ahead of him into the fathomless black pits of his lids. Even here, in the south, in the sun even, the coal-mines remained. His nostrils were sick with the smell of them and on his cheeks he felt lingering the slipping mantle of the English fog. He had not seen the mines since he was a young man, but nothing he had ever done between would alter them. There he sat in the sun with his eyes closed, looking into their depths.

Because his father had been a miner, he was thinking, the black of the pits had put some kind of blasphemy on his own blood. He sat with his eyes closed looking directly into the blank awful mines. Against their obscurity he set the icicles of one winter when the war was on, when he had spent his twilights seeking for pinecones under the tall trees in the woods behind the house. In Cornwall. What a vision! How beautiful that year, and many other years, might have been had it not been for the sour thought of war. Every time his heart had lifted for a hillside or a wave, or for the wind blowing, the thought of the turmoil going on had beset and stricken him. It had lain like a burden on his conscience every morning when he was coming awake. The first light moments of day coming had warned him that despite the blood rising in his body, it was no time to rejoice. The war. Ah, yes, the war. After the mines, it had been the war. Whenever he had believed for half a minute in man, then he had remembered that the war was going on.

For a little while one February, it had seemed that the colors set out in Monte Carlo, facing the Casino, would obliterate forever the angry memories his heart had stored away. The great mauve, white, and deep royal purple bouquets had thrived a week or more, as if rooted in his eyes. Such banks and beds of richly petaled flowers set thick as thieves or thicker on the cultivated lawns conveyed the wish. Their artificial physiognomies masked the earth as well as he would have wished his own features to stand guard before his spirit. The invalid lifted his hand and touched his beard. His mouth and chin, he thought with cunning satisfaction, were marvelously concealed.

The sound of his wife's voice speaking in the room that opened behind him onto the terrace roused him a little as he sat pondering in the sun. She seemed to be moving from one long window to another, arranging flowers in the vases, for her voice would come across the pavings, now strong and close, now distant as if turned away, and she was talking to their guest about some sort of shrub or fern. A special kind, the like of which she could find nowhere on the Riviera. It thrived in the cool brisk fogs of their own land, she was saying. Her voice had turned towards him again and was ringing clearly across the terrace.

'Those are beautiful ones you have there now,' said the voice of the gentleman.

'Ah, take care!' cried out his wife's voice, somewhat dimmed as though she had again turned towards the room. 'I was afraid you had pierced your hand,' she said in a moment.

When the invalid opened his eyes, he saw that the sun was even now beginning to glimmer through the upper branches of the trees, was lolling along the prosperous dark upper boughs as if in preparation for descent. Not yet, he thought, not yet. He raised himself on his elbows and scanned the sky. Scarcely three-thirty, surely, he was thinking. The sun can't be going down at once.

'The sun can't be going down yet awhile, can it?' he called out to the house.

He heard the gravel of the pathway sparkling and spitting out from under the soles of their feet as they crossed it, and then his wife's heels and the boots of the guest struck and advanced across the paving stones.

'Oh, oh, the geraniums ———' said his wife suddenly by his side. The guest had raised his head and stood squinting up at the sun.

'I should say it were going down,' he said after a moment.

He had deliberately stepped before the rays of it and stood leaning back against the terrace-wall. His solid gray head had served to cork the sunlight. Like a wooden stopper, thought the invalid, painted to resemble a man. With the nose of a wooden stopper. And the sightless eyes. And the creases when he speaks or smiles.

'But think what it must be like in Paris now,' said the gentleman. 'I don't know how you feel, but I can't find words to say how grateful I am for being here.' The guest, thought the invalid as he surveyed him, was very conscious of being a guest — of accepting meals, bed, tea, society — and his smile was permanently set beneath his nose.

'Of course you don't know how I feel,' said the invalid. He lay looking sourly up at his guest. 'Would you mind moving out of the sun?' As the visiting gentleman skipped out of the way, the invalid cleared his throat, dissolved the little pellet of phlegm which had leapt to being on his tongue so as not to spit before them, and sank back into his chair.

'The advantage — or rather *one* of the advantages of being a writer,' said the visiting gentleman with a smile, 'is that he can settle down wherever the fancy takes him. Now a publisher ——'

'Why be a publisher?' said the invalid in irritation. He was staring again into the black blank mines.

His wife was squatting and stooping about his chair, gathering up in her dress the butchered geraniums. She said not a word, but crouched there picking them carefully up, one by one. By her side had appeared a little covered basket, and within it rattled a pair of castanets.

'I am sure I can very easily turn these into slips,' she said gently, as if speaking to herself. 'A little snip in the right place and they'll be as good as new.'

'You can make soup out of them,' said the invalid bitterly. 'What's in the basket,' he said, 'making a noise?'

'Oh, a *langouste*!' cried out his wife. She had just remembered. 'We bought you a *langouste*, alive, at the Beausoleil market. It's as lively as a rig!'

The visiting gentleman burst into laughter. The invalid could hear him gasping with enjoyment by his side.

'I can't bear them alive,' said the invalid testily. He lay listening curiously to the animal rattling his jaws and clawing under the basket's lid.

'Oh, but with mayonnaise!' cried his wife. 'Tomorrow!'

'Why doesn't Mr. What-do-you-call-him answer the question I put him?' asked the invalid sourly. His mind was possessed with the thought of the visiting man. 'I asked him why he was a publisher,' said the invalid. What a viper, what a felon, he was thinking, to come and live on me and not give me the satisfaction of a quarrel! He was not a young man, thought the invalid, with his little remains of graying hair, but he had all the endurance and patience of a younger man in the presence of a master. All the smiling and bowing, thought the invalid with contempt, and all the obsequious ways. The man was standing so near to his chair that he could hear his breath whistling through his nostrils. Maybe his eyes were on him, the invalid was thinking. It gave him a turn to think that he was lying there exposed in the sun where the visitor could examine him pore by pore. Hair by hair could the visitor take him in and record him.

'Oh, I beg your pardon,' said the gentleman. 'I'm afraid I owe you an apology. You see, I'm not accustomed to it.'

'To what?' said the invalid sharply. He had flashed his eyes open and looked suspiciously into the publisher's face.

'To seeing you flat on your back,' said the gentleman promptly.

'You covered that over very nicely,' said the invalid. He clasped his hands across his sunken bosom. 'You meant to say something else. You meant to say DEATH,' said the invalid calmly. 'I heard the first letter of it on your tongue.'

He lay back in his chair again with his lids fallen. He could distinctly smell the foul fumes of the pits.

'Elsa,' he said, as he lay twitching in the light, 'I would like some champagne. JUST BECAUSE,' he said sitting up abruptly, 'I've written a few books doesn't mean that you have to keep the truth about me to yourself.'

His wife went off across the terrace, leaving the two men together.

'Don't make a mistake,' said the invalid smiling grimly. 'Don't make any mistake. I'm not quite finished. Not QUITE. I still have a little more to write about,' he said. 'Don't you fool yourself, my dear.'

'Oh, I flatter myself that I don't,' said the gentleman agreeably. 'I'm convinced there's an unlimited amount still to come.

And I hope to have the honor of publishing some of it. I'm counting on that, you know.' He ended on a playful note and looked coyly at the invalid. But every spark of life had suddenly expired in the ill man's face.

'I didn't know the sun would be off the terrace so soon,' he said blankly. His wife had returned and was opening the bottle, carefully and without error, with the end of her pliant thumb. The invalid turned on his side and regarded her: a great strong woman whom he would never forget, never, nor the surprisingly slim crescent of her flexible thumb. All of her fingers, he lay thinking as he watched her, were soft as skeins of silk, and tied in at the joints and knuckles by invisible satin bands of faintest rose. And there was the visiting gentleman hovering about her, with his oh-let-me-please-mrs-oh-do-let-me-now. But her grip on the neck of the bottle was as tenacious as a snake's. She lifted her head, smiled, and shook it at their guest.

'Oh, no,' she said, 'I'm doing beautifully.'

Just as she spoke the cork flew out and hit the gentleman square in the forehead. After it streamed a geyser of purest gold.

'Oh, oh, oh,' cried the invalid. He held out his hands to the golden spray. 'Oh, pour it here!' he cried. 'Oh, buckets of it going! Oh, pour it over me, Elsa!'

The color had flown into Elsa's face and she was laughing. Softly and breathlessly she ran from glass to glass. There in the stems played the clear living liquid, like a fountain springing upward. Ah, that, ah, that, in the inwards of a man, thought the invalid joyfully! Ah, that, springing again and again in the belly and heart! There in the glass it ran, cascaded in needlepoints the length of his throat, went whistling to his pulses.

The invalid set down his empty glass.

'Elsa,' he said gently, 'could I have a little more champagne?'

His wife had risen with the bottle in her hand, but she looked doubtfully at him.

'Do you really think you should?' she asked.

'Yes,' said the invalid. He watched the unbelievably pure stuff flowing out all over his glass. 'Yes,' he said. 'Of course. Of course, I should.'

A sweet shy look of love had begun to arch in his eyes.

'I'd love to see the *langouste*,' he said gently. 'Do you think you could let him out and let me see him run around?'

Elsa set down her glass and stooped to lift the cover of the basket. There was the green armored beast lifting its eyes, as if on hinges, to examine the light. Such an expression he had seen before, thought the invalid immediately. There was a startling likeness in those small audacious eyes. Such a look had there been in his father's eyes: that look, and the long smooth mustaches drooping across the wee clefted chin, gave the *langouste* such a look of his father that he exclaimed aloud.

'Be careful,' said Elsa. 'His claws are tied, but still ——'

'I must have him out,' said the invalid. He gripped the *langouste* firmly about the hips. He looks like my father, he was thinking. I must have him out where I can see.

In spite of its shackles, the animal contrived to wave his wide pinions in the air as the invalid lifted him up and set him on the rug across his knees. There was the same line of sparkling dew-like substance pearling the *langouste's* lip, the same weak disappointed lip, like the eagle's lip, and the bold suspicious eye. Across the sloping shoulders of the beast lay a sprinkling of brilliant dust, as black as coal dust and quite as luminous. Just as his father had looked coming home at night, with the coal dust showered across his shoulders like a deadly mantle. Just such a deadly cloak of quartz and mica and the rotted roots of fern. Even the queer blue toothless look of his father about the jaws. The invalid took another deep swallow of champagne and let it seep quietly through his flesh and blood. Then he lifted his hand and stroked the *langouste* gently. You've never counted, he was thinking mildly. I've led my life very well without you in it. You better go back to the mines where you belong.

When he lifted up the *langouste* to peer into his face, the arms of the beast fell ludicrously open as if he were seeking to embrace the ailing man. He could see his father very well in him, coming home with the coal dirt all over him in the evening, standing by the door that opened in by halves, opening first the upper half and then the lower, swaying a little as he felt for the latch of the lower half of the door. With the beer he had been drinking, or the dew of the Welsh mist shining on his long mustaches. The invalid gave him a gentle shake and set him down again.

I got on very well without you, he was thinking. He sipped at his champagne and regarded the animal upon his knees. As far as I was concerned. As far as I was concerned you need never have been my father at all. Slowly and warily the wondrous eyes and feelers of the beast moved in distrust across the invalid's lap and bosom. A lot of good you ever did me, he was thinking. As he watched the *langouste* groping about as if in darkness, he began to think of the glowing miner's lamp his father had worn strapped upon his brow. Feeling about in the dark and choking to death underground, he was thinking impatiently. I might have been anybody's son. The strong shelly odor of the *langouste* was seasoning the air.

'I've got on very well without you,' he was thinking bitterly. From his wife's face he gathered that he had spoken aloud. The visiting gentleman looked into the depths of his glass of champagne.

'Don't misunderstand me,' said the guest with a forbearing smile. 'I'm quite aware of the fact that, long before you met me, you had one of the greatest publics and following of any living writer ——'

The invalid looked in bewilderment at his wife's face and at the face of the visiting man. If they scold me, he thought, I am going to cry. He felt his underlip quivering. Scold me! he thought suddenly in indignation. A man with a beard! His hand fled to his chin for confirmation. A man with a beard, he thought with a cunning evil gleam narrowing his eye.

'You haven't answered my question,' he said aggressively to the visitor. 'You haven't answered it yet, have you?'

His hand had fallen against the hard brittle armor of the *langouste's* hide. There were the eyes raised to his and the canny feelers lifted. His fingers closed for comfort about the *langouste's* unwieldy paw. Father, he said in his heart, father, help me. Father, father, he said, I don't want to die.

THAT EVENING SUN[1]

WILLIAM FAULKNER

I

Monday is no different from any other week day in Jefferson now. The streets are paved now, and the telephone and electric companies are cutting down more and more of the shade trees — the water oaks, the maples and locusts and elms — to make room for iron poles bearing clusters of bloated and ghostly and bloodless grapes, and we have a city laundry which makes the rounds on Monday morning, gathering the bundles of clothes into bright-colored, specially-made motor cars: the soiled wearing of a whole week now flees apparitionlike behind alert and irritable electric horns, with a long diminishing noise of rubber and asphalt like tearing silk, and even the Negro women who still take in white people's washing after the old custom, fetch and deliver it in automobiles.

But fifteen years ago, on Monday morning the quiet, dusty, shady streets would be full of Negro women with, balanced on their steady, turbaned heads, bundles of clothes tied up in sheets, almost as large as cotton bales, carried so without touch of hand

---

[1] Copyright, 1931, by William Faulkner. From *These Thirteen*, by William Faulkner. Jonathan Cape and Harrison Smith, 1931.

between the kitchen door of the white house and the blackened washpot beside a cabin door in Negro Hollow.

Nancy would set her bundle on the top of her head, then upon the bundle in turn she would set the black straw sailor hat which she wore winter and summer. She was tall, with a high, sad face sunken a little where her teeth were missing. Sometimes we would go a part of the way down the lane and across the pasture with her, to watch the balanced bundle and the hat that never bobbed nor wavered, even when she walked down into the ditch and up the other side and stooped through the fence. She would go down on her hands and knees and crawl through the gap, her head rigid, uptilted, the bundle steady as a rock or a balloon and rise to her feet again and go on.

Sometimes the husbands of the washing women would fetch and deliver the clothes, but Jesus never did that for Nancy, even before father told him to stay away from our house, even when Dilsey was sick and Nancy would come to cook for us.

And then about half the time we'd have to go down the lane to Nancy's cabin and tell her to come on and cook breakfast. We would stop at the ditch, because father told us to not have anything to do with Jesus — he was a short black man, with a razor scar down his face — and we would throw rocks at Nancy's house until she came to the door, leaning her head around it without any clothes on.

'What yawl mean, chunking my house?' Nancy said. 'What you little devils mean?'

'Father says for you to come on and get breakfast,' Caddy said. 'Father says it's over a half an hour now, and you've got to come this minute.'

'I aint studying no breakfast,' Nancy said. 'I going to get my sleep out.'

'I bet you're drunk,' Jason said. 'Father says you're drunk. Are you drunk, Nancy?'

'Who says I is?' Nancy said. 'I got to get my sleep out. I aint studying no breakfast.'

So after a while we quit chunking the cabin and went back home. When she finally came, it was too late for me to go to school. So we thought it was whisky until that day they arrested her again and they were taking her to jail and they passed Mr. Stovall. He was the cashier in the bank and a deacon in the Baptist church, and Nancy began to say:

'When you going to pay me, white man? When you going to pay me, white man? It's been three times now since you paid me a cent ——' Mr. Stovall knocked her down, but she kept on saying, 'When you going to pay me, white man? It's been three times now since ——' until Mr. Stovall kicked her in the mouth with his heel and the marshal caught Mr. Stovall back, and Nancy lying in the street, laughing. She turned her head and spat out some blood and teeth and said, 'It's been three times now since he paid me a cent.'

That was how she lost her teeth, and all that day they told about Nancy and Mr. Stovall, and all that night the ones that passed the jail could hear Nancy singing and yelling. They could see her hands holding to the window bars, and a lot of them stopped along the fence, listening to her and to the jailer trying to make her stop. She didn't shut up until almost daylight, when the jailer began to hear a bumping and scraping upstairs and he went up there and found Nancy hanging from the window bar. He said that it was cocaine and not whisky, because no nigger would try to commit suicide unless he was full of cocaine, because a nigger full of cocaine wasn't a nigger any longer.

The jailer cut her down and revived her; then he beat her, whipped her. She had hung herself with her dress. She had fixed it all right, but when they arrested her she didn't have on anything except a dress and so she didn't have anything to tie her hands with and she couldn't make her hands let go of the window

ledge. So the jailer heard the noise and ran up there and found
Nancy hanging from the window, stark naked, her belly already
swelling out a little, like a little balloon.

When Dilsey was sick in her cabin and Nancy was cooking for
us, we could see her apron swelling out; that was before father
told Jesus to stay away from the house. Jesus was in the kitchen,
sitting behind the stove, with his razor scar on his black face like
a piece of dirty string. He said it was a watermelon that Nancy
had under her dress.

'It never come off of your vine, though,' Nancy said.

'Off of what vine?' Caddy said.

'I can cut down the vine it did come off of,' Jesus said.

'What makes you want to talk like that before these chillen?'
Nancy said. 'Whyn't you go on to work? You done et. You
want Mr. Jason to catch you hanging around his kitchen, talking
that way before these chillen?'

'Talking what way?' Caddy said. 'What vine?'

'I cant hang around white man's kitchen,' Jesus said. 'But
white man can hang around mine. White man can come in my
house, but I cant stop him. When white man want to come in
my house, I aint got no house. I cant stop him, but he cant kick
me outen it. He cant do that.'

Dilsey was still sick in her cabin. Father told Jesus to stay off
our place. Dilsey was still sick. It was a long time. We were in
the library after supper.

'Isn't Nancy through in the kitchen yet?' mother said. 'It
seems to me that she has had plenty of time to have finished the
dishes.'

'Let Quentin go and see,' father said. 'Go and see if Nancy is
through, Quentin. Tell her she can go on home.'

I went to the kitchen. Nancy was through. The dishes were
put away and the fire was out. Nancy was sitting in a chair,
close to the cold stove. She looked at me.

'Mother wants to know if you are through,' I said.

'Yes,' Nancy said. She looked at me. 'I done finished.' She looked at me.

'What is it?' I said. 'What is it?'

'I aint nothing but a nigger,' Nancy said. 'It aint none of my fault.'

She looked at me, sitting in the chair before the cold stove, the sailor hat on her head. I went back to the library. It was the cold stove and all, when you think of a kitchen being warm and busy and cheerful. And with a cold stove and the dishes all put away, and nobody wanting to eat at that hour.

'Is she through?' mother said.

'Yessum,' I said.

'What is she doing?' mother said.

'She's not doing anything. She's through.'

'I'll go and see,' father said.

'Maybe she's waiting for Jesus to come and take her home,' Caddy said.

'Jesus is gone,' I said. Nancy told us how one morning she woke up and Jesus was gone.

'He quit me,' Nancy said. 'Done gone to Memphis, I reckon. Dodging them city *po*-lice for a while, I reckon.'

'And a good riddance,' father said. 'I hope he stays there.'

'Nancy's scaired of the dark,' Jason said.

'So are you,' Caddy said.

'I'm not,' Jason said.

'Scairy cat,' Caddy said.

'I'm not,' Jason said.

'You, Candace!' mother said. Father came back.

'I am going to walk down the lane with Nancy,' he said. 'She says that Jesus is back.'

'Has she seen him?' mother said.

'No. Some Negro sent her word that he was back in town. I wont be long.'

'You'll leave me alone, to take Nancy home?' mother said. 'Is her safety more precious to you than mine?'

'I wont be long,' father said.

'You'll leave these children unprotected with that Negro about?'

'I'm going too,' Caddy said. 'Let me go, Father.'

'What would he do with them, if he were unfortunate enough to have them?' father said.

'I want to go, too,' Jason said.

'Jason!' mother said. She was speaking to father. You could tell that by the way she said the name. Like she believed that all day father had been trying to think of doing the thing she wouldn't like the most, and that she knew all the time that after a while he would think of it. I stayed quiet, because father and I both knew that mother would want him to make me stay with her if she just thought of it in time. So father didn't look at me. I was the oldest. I was nine and Caddy was seven and Jason was five.

'Nonsense,' father said. 'We wont be long.'

Nancy had her hat on. We came to the lane. 'Jesus always been good to me,' Nancy said. 'Whenever he had two dollars, one of them was mine.' We walked in the lane. 'If I can just get through the lane,' Nancy said, 'I be all right then.'

The lane was always dark. 'This is where Jason got scared on Hallowe'en,' Caddy said.

'I didn't,' Jason said.

'Cant Aunt Rachel do anything with him?' father said. Aunt Rachel was old. She lived in a cabin beyond Nancy's, by herself. She had white hair and she smoked a pipe in the door, all day long; she didn't work any more. They said she was Jesus' mother. Sometimes she said she was and sometimes she said she wasn't any kin to Jesus.

'Yes you did,' Caddy said. 'You were scairder than Frony. You were scairder than T. P. even. Scairder than niggers.'

'Cant nobody do nothing with him,' Nancy said. 'He say I done woke up the devil in him and aint but one thing going to lay it down again.'

'Well, he's gone now,' father said. 'There's nothing for you to be afraid of now. And if you'd just let white men alone.'

'Let what white men alone?' Caddy said. 'How let them alone?'

'He aint gone nowhere,' Nancy said. 'I can feel him. I can feel him now, in this lane. He hearing us talk, every word, hid somewhere, waiting. I aint seen him, and I aint going to see him again but once more, with that razor in his mouth. That razor on that string down his back, inside his shirt. And then I aint going to be even surprised.'

'I wasn't scaired,' Jason said.

'If you'd behave yourself, you'd have kept out of this,' father said. 'But it's all right now. He's probably in St. Louis now. Probably got another wife by now and forgot all about you.'

'If he has, I better not find out about it,' Nancy said. 'I'd stand there right over them, and every time he wropped her, I'd cut that arm off. I'd cut his head off and I'd slit her belly and I'd shove ——'

'Hush,' father said.

'Slit whose belly, Nancy?' Caddy said.

'I wasn't scaired,' Jason said. 'I'd walk right down this lane by myself.'

'Yah,' Caddy said. 'You wouldn't dare to put your foot down in it if we were not here too.'

II

Dilsey was still sick, so we took Nancy home every night until mother said, 'How much longer is this going on? I to be left alone in this big house while you take home a frightened Negro?'

We fixed a pallet in the kitchen for Nancy. One night we waked up, hearing the sound. It was not singing and it was not crying, coming up the dark stairs. There was a light in mother's room and we heard father going down the hall, down the back stairs, and Caddy and I went into the hall. The floor was cold. Our toes curled away from it while we listened to the sound. It was like singing and it wasn't like singing, like the sounds that Negroes make.

Then it stopped and we heard father going down the back stairs, and we went to the head of the stairs. Then the sound began again, in the stairway, not loud, and we could see Nancy's eyes halfway up the stairs, against the wall. They looked like cat's eyes do, like a big cat against the wall, watching us. When we came down the steps to where she was, she quit making the sound again, and we stood there until father came back up from the kitchen, with his pistol in his hand. He went back down with Nancy and they came back with Nancy's pallet.

We spread the pallet in our room. After the light in mother's room went off, we could see Nancy's eyes again. 'Nancy,' Caddy whispered, 'are you asleep, Nancy?'

Nancy whispered something. It was oh or no, I dont know which. Like nobody had made it, like it came from nowhere and went nowhere, until it was like Nancy was not there at all; that I had looked so hard at her eyes on the stairs that they had got printed on my eyeballs, like the sun does when you have closed your eyes and there is no sun. 'Jesus,' Nancy whispered. 'Jesus.'

'Was it Jesus?' Caddy said. 'Did he try to come into the kitchen?'

'Jesus,' Nancy said. Like this: Jeeeeeeeeeeeeeeeesus, until the sound went out, like a match or a candle does.

'It's the other Jesus she means,' I said.

'Can you see us, Nancy?' Caddy whispered. 'Can you see our eyes too?'

'I aint nothing but a nigger,' Nancy said. 'God knows. God knows.'

'What did you see down there in the kitchen?' Caddy whispered. 'What tried to get in?'

'God knows,' Nancy said. We could see her eyes. 'God knows.'

Dilsey got well. She cooked dinner. 'You'd better stay in bed a day or two longer,' father said.

'What for?' Dilsey said. 'If I had been a day later, this place would be to rack and ruin. Get on out of here now, and let me get my kitchen straight again.'

Dilsey cooked supper too. And that night, just before dark, Nancy came into the kitchen.

'How do you know he's back?' Dilsey said. 'You aint seen him.'

'Jesus is a nigger,' Jason said.

'I can feel him,' Nancy said. 'I can feel him laying yonder in the ditch.'

'Tonight?' Dilsey said. 'Is he there tonight?'

'Dilsey's a nigger too,' Jason said.

'You try to eat something,' Dilsey said.

'I dont want nothing,' Nancy said.

'I aint a nigger,' Jason said.

'Drink some coffee,' Dilsey said. She poured a cup of coffee for Nancy. 'Do you know he's out there tonight? How come you know it's tonight?'

'I know,' Nancy said. 'He's there, waiting. I know. I done lived with him too long. I know what he is fixing to do fore he know it himself.'

'Drink some coffee,' Dilsey said. Nancy held the cup to her mouth and blew into the cup. Her mouth pursed out like a

spreading adder's, like a rubber mouth, like she had blown all
the color out of her lips with blowing the coffee.

'I aint a nigger,' Jason said. 'Are you a nigger, Nancy?'

'I hellborn, child,' Nancy said. 'I wont be nothing soon. I
going back where I come from soon.'

III

She began to drink the coffee. While she was drinking, holding
the cup in both hands, she began to make the sound again. She
made the sound into the cup and the coffee sploshed out onto her
hands and her dress. Her eyes looked at us and she sat there, her
elbows on her knees, holding the cup in both hands, looking at us
across the wet cup, making the sound.

'Look at Nancy,' Jason said. 'Nancy cant cook for us now.
Dilsey's got well now.'

'You hush up,' Dilsey said. Nancy held the cup in both hands,
looking at us, making the sound, like there were two of them: one
looking at us and the other making the sound. 'Whyn't you let
Mr. Jason telefoam the marshal?' Dilsey said. Nancy stopped
then, holding the cup in her long brown hands. She tried to drink
some coffee again, but it sploshed out of the cup, onto her hands
and her dress, and she put the cup down. Jason watched her.

'I cant swallow it,' Nancy said. 'I swallows but it wont go
down me.'

'You go down to the cabin,' Dilsey said. 'Frony will fix you a
pallet and I'll be there soon.'

'Wont no nigger stop him,' Nancy said.

'I aint a nigger,' Jason said. 'Am I, Dilsey?'

'I reckon not,' Dilsey said. She looked at Nancy. 'I dont
reckon so. What you going to do, then?'

Nancy looked at us. Her eyes went fast, like she was afraid
there wasn't time to look, without hardly moving at all. She
looked at us, at all three of us at one time. 'You member that

night I stayed in yawls' room?' she said. She told about how we waked up early the next morning, and played. We had to play quiet, on her pallet, until father woke up and it was time to get breakfast. 'Go and ask your maw to let me stay here tonight,' Nancy said. 'I wont need no pallet. We can play some more.'

Caddy asked mother. Jason went too. 'I cant have Negroes sleeping in the bedrooms,' mother said. Jason cried. He cried until mother said he couldn't have any dessert for three days if he didn't stop. Then Jason said he would stop if Dilsey would make a chocolate cake. Father was there.

'Why dont you do something about it?' mother said. 'What do we have officers for?'

'Why is Nancy afraid of Jesus?' Caddy said. 'Are you afraid of father, Mother?'

'What could the officers do?' father said. 'If Nancy hasn't seen him, how could the officers find him?'

'Then why is she afraid?' mother said.

'She says he is there. She says she knows he is there tonight.'

'Yet we pay taxes,' mother said. 'I must wait here alone in this big house while you take a Negro woman home.'

'You know that I am not lying outside with a razor,' father said.

'I'll stop if Dilsey will make a chocolate cake,' Jason said. Mother told us to go out and father said he didn't know if Jason would get a chocolate cake or not, but he knew what Jason was going to get in about a minute. We went back to the kitchen and told Nancy.

'Father said for you to go home and lock the door, and you'll be all right,' Caddy said. 'All right from what, Nancy? Is Jesus mad at you?' Nancy was holding the coffee cup in her hands again, her elbows on her knees and her hands holding the cup between her knees. She was looking into the cup. 'What have you done that made Jesus mad?' Caddy said. Nancy let the cup go.

It didn't break on the floor, but the coffee spilled out, and Nancy sat there with her hands still making the shape of the cup. She began to make the sound again, not loud. Not singing and not unsinging. We watched her.

'Here,' Dilsey said. 'You quit that, now. You get aholt of yourself. You wait here. I going to get Versh to walk home with you.' Dilsey went out.

We looked at Nancy. Her shoulders kept shaking, but she quit making the sound. We watched her. 'What's Jesus going to do to you?' Caddy said. 'He went away.'

Nancy looked at us. 'We had fun that night I stayed in yawls' room, didn't we?'

'I didn't,' Jason said. 'I didn't have any fun.'

'You were asleep in mother's room,' Caddy said. 'You were not there.'

'Let's go down to my house and have some more fun,' Nancy said.

'Mother wont let us,' I said. 'It's too late now.'

'Dont bother her,' Nancy said. 'We can tell her in the morning. She wont mind.'

'She wouldn't let us,' I said.

'Dont ask her now,' Nancy said. 'Dont bother her now.'

'She didn't say we couldn't go,' Caddy said.

'We didn't ask,' I said.

'If you go, I'll tell,' Jason said.

'We'll have fun,' Nancy said. 'They wont mind, just to my house. I been working for yawl a long time. They wont mind.'

'I'm not afraid to go,' Caddy said. 'Jason is the one that's afraid. He'll tell.'

'I'm not,' Jason said.

'Yes, you are,' Caddy said. 'You'll tell.'

'I wont tell,' Jason said. 'I'm not afraid.'

'Jason aint afraid to go with me,' Nancy said. 'Is you, Jason?'

'Jason is going to tell,' Caddy said. The lane was dark. We passed the pasture gate. 'I bet if something was to jump out from behind that gate, Jason would holler.'

'I wouldn't,' Jason said. We walked down the lane. Nancy was talking loud.

'What are you talking so loud for, Nancy?' Caddy said.

'Who; me?' Nancy said. 'Listen at Quentin and Caddy and Jason saying I'm talking loud.'

'You talk like there was five of us here,' Caddy said. 'You talk like father was here too.'

'Who; me talking loud, Mr. Jason?' Nancy said.

'Nancy called Jason "Mister,"' Caddy said.

'Listen how Caddy and Quentin and Jason talk,' Nancy said.

'We're not talking loud,' Caddy said. 'You're the one that's talking like father ——'

'Hush,' Nancy said; 'hush, Mr. Jason.'

'Nancy called Jason "Mister" aguh ——'

'Hush,' Nancy said. She was talking loud when we crossed the ditch and stooped through the fence where she used to stoop through with the clothes on her head. Then we came to her house. We were going fast then. She opened the door. The smell of the house was like the lamp and the smell of Nancy was like the wick, like they were waiting for one another to begin to smell. She lit the lamp and closed the door and put the bar up. Then she quit talking loud, looking at us.

'What're we going to do?' Caddy said.

'What do yawl want to do?' Nancy said.

'You said we would have some fun,' Caddy said.

There was something about Nancy's house; something you could smell besides Nancy and the house. Jason smelled it, even. 'I dont want to stay here,' he said. 'I want to go home.'

'Go home, then,' Caddy said.

'I dont want to go by myself,' Jason said.

'We're going to have some fun,' Nancy said.

'How?' Caddy said.

Nancy stood by the door. She was looking at us, only it was like she had emptied her eyes, like she had quit using them. 'What do you want to do?' she said.

'Tell us a story,' Caddy said. 'Can you tell a story?'

'Yes,' Nancy said.

'Tell it,' Caddy said. We looked at Nancy. 'You dont know any stories.'

'Yes,' Nancy said. 'Yes I do.'

She came and sat in a chair before the hearth. There was a little fire there. Nancy built it up, when it was already hot inside. She built a good blaze. She told a story. She talked like her eyes looked, like her eyes watching us and her voice talking to us did not belong to her. Like she was living somewhere else, waiting somewhere else. She was outside the cabin. Her voice was inside and the shape of her, the Nancy that could stoop under a barbed wire fence with a bundle of clothes balanced on her head as though without weight, like a balloon, was there. But that was all. 'And so this here queen come walking up to the ditch, where that bad man was hiding. She was walking up to the ditch, and she say, "If I can just get past this here ditch," was what she say . . .'

'What ditch?' Caddy said. 'A ditch like that one out there? Why did a queen want to go into a ditch?'

'To get to her house,' Nancy said. She looked at us. 'She had to cross the ditch to get into her house quick and bar the door.'

'Why did she want to go home and bar the door?' Caddy said.

IV

Nancy looked at us. She quit talking. She looked at us. Jason's legs stuck straight out of his pants where he sat on Nancy's lap. 'I dont think that's a good story,' he said. 'I want to go home.'

'Maybe we had better,' Caddy said. She got up from the floor. 'I bet they are looking for us right now.' She went toward the door.

'No,' Nancy said. 'Dont open it.' She got up quick and passed Caddy. She didn't touch the door, the wooden bar.

'Why not?' Caddy said.

'Come back to the lamp,' Nancy said. 'We'll have fun. You dont have to go.'

'We ought to go,' Caddy said. 'Unless we have a lot of fun.' She and Nancy came back to the fire, the lamp.

'I want to go home,' Jason said. 'I'm going to tell.'

'I know another story,' Nancy said. She stood close to the lamp. She looked at Caddy, like when your eyes look up at a stick balanced on your nose. She had to look down to see Caddy, but her eyes looked like that, like when you are balancing a stick.

'I wont listen to it,' Jason said. 'I'll bang on the floor.'

'It's a good one,' Nancy said. 'It's better than the other one.'

'What's it about?' Caddy said. Nancy was standing by the lamp. Her hand was on the lamp, against the light, long and brown.

'Your hand is on that hot globe,' Caddy said. 'Dont it feel hot to your hand?'

Nancy looked at her hand on the lamp chimney. She took her hand away, slow. She stood there, looking at Caddy, wringing her long hand as though it were tied to her wrist with a string.

'Let's do something else,' Caddy said.

'I want to go home,' Jason said.

'I got some popcorn,' Nancy said. She looked at Caddy and then at Jason and then at me and then at Caddy again. 'I got some popcorn.'

'I dont like popcorn,' Jason said. 'I'd rather have candy.'

Nancy looked at Jason. 'You can hold the popper.' She was still wringing her hand; it was long and limp and brown.

'All right,' Jason said. 'I'll stay a while if I can do that. Caddy cant hold it. I'll want to go home again if Caddy holds the popper.'

Nancy built up the fire. 'Look at Nancy putting her hands in the fire,' Caddy said. 'What's the matter with you, Nancy?'

'I got popcorn,' Nancy said. 'I got some.' She took the popper from under the bed. It was broken. Jason began to cry.

'Now we cant have any popcorn,' he said.

'We ought to go home, anyway,' Caddy said. 'Come on, Quentin.'

'Wait,' Nancy said; 'wait. I can fix it. Dont you want to help me fix it?'

'I dont think I want any,' Caddy said. 'It's too late now.'

'You help me, Jason,' Nancy said. 'Dont you want to help me?'

'No,' Jason said. 'I want to go home.'

'Hush,' Nancy said; 'hush. Watch. Watch me. I can fix it so Jason can hold it and pop the corn.' She got a piece of wire and fixed the popper.

'It wont hold good,' Caddy said.

'Yes it will,' Nancy said. 'Yawl watch. Yawl help me shell some corn.'

The popcorn was under the bed too. We shelled it into the popper and Nancy helped Jason hold the popper over the fire.

'It's not popping,' Jason said. 'I want to go home.'

'You wait,' Nancy said. 'It'll begin to pop. We'll have fun then.' She was sitting close to the fire. The lamp was turned up so high it was beginning to smoke.

'Why dont you turn it down some?' I said.

'It's all right,' Nancy said. 'I'll clean it. Yawl wait. The popcorn will start in a minute.'

'I dont believe it's going to start,' Caddy said. 'We ought to start home, anyway. They'll be worried.'

'No,' Nancy said. 'It's going to pop. Dilsey will tell um yawl with me. I been working for yawl long time. They wont mind if yawl at my house. You wait, now. It'll start popping any minute now.'

Then Jason got some smoke in his eyes and he began to cry. He dropped the popper into the fire. Nancy got a wet rag and wiped Jason's face, but he didn't stop crying.

'Hush,' she said. 'Hush.' But he didn't hush. Caddy took the popper out of the fire.

'It's burned up,' she said. 'You'll have to get some more popcorn, Nancy.'

'Did you put all of it in?' Nancy said.

'Yes,' Caddy said. Nancy looked at Caddy. Then she took the popper and opened it and poured the cinders into her apron and began to sort the grains, her hands long and brown, and we watching her.

'Haven't you got any more?' Caddy said.

'Yes,' Nancy said; 'yes. Look. This here aint burnt. All we need to do is ——'

'I want to go home,' Jason said. 'I'm going to tell.'

'Hush,' Caddy said. We all listened. Nancy's head was already turned toward the barred door, her eyes filled with red lamplight. 'Somebody is coming,' Caddy said.

Then Nancy began to make that sound again, not loud, sitting there above the fire, her long hands dangling between her knees; all of a sudden water began to come out on her face in big drops, running down her face, carrying in each one a little turning ball of firelight like a spark until it dropped off her chin. 'She's not crying,' I said.

'I aint crying,' Nancy said. Her eyes were closed. 'I aint crying. Who is it?'

'I dont know,' Caddy said. She went to the door and looked out. 'We've got to go now,' she said. 'Here comes father.'

'I'm going to tell,' Jason said. 'Yawl made me come.'

The water still ran down Nancy's face. She turned in her chair. 'Listen. Tell him. Tell him we going to have fun. Tell him I take good care of yawl until in the morning. Tell him to let me come home with yawl and sleep on the floor. Tell him I wont need no pallet. We'll have fun. You member last time how we had so much fun?'

'I didn't have fun,' Jason said. 'You hurt me. You put smoke in my eyes. I'm going to tell.'

V

Father came in. He looked at us. Nancy did not get up.

'Tell him,' she said.

'Caddy made us come down here,' Jason said. 'I didn't want to.'

Father came to the fire. Nancy looked up at him. 'Cant you go to Aunt Rachel's and stay?' he said. Nancy looked up at father, her hands between her knees. 'He's not here,' father said. 'I would have seen him. There's not a soul in sight.'

'He in the ditch,' Nancy said. 'He waiting in the ditch yonder.'

'Nonsense,' father said. He looked at Nancy. 'Do you know he's there?'

'I got the sign,' Nancy said.

'What sign?'

'I got it. It was on the table when I come in. It was a hog-bone, with blood meat still on it, laying by the lamp. He's out there. When yawl walk out that door, I gone.'

'Gone where, Nancy?' Caddy said.

'I'm not a tattletale,' Jason said.

'Nonsense,' father said.

'He out there,' Nancy said. 'He looking through that window this minute, waiting for yawl to go. Then I gone.'

'Nonsense,' father said. 'Lock up your house and we'll take you on to Aunt Rachel's.'

''Twont do no good,' Nancy said. She didn't look at father now, but he looked down at her, at her long, limp, moving hands. 'Putting it off wont do no good.'

'Then what do you want to do?' father said.

'I dont know,' Nancy said. 'I cant do nothing. Just put it off. And that dont do no good. I reckon it belong to me. I reckon what I going to get aint no more than mine.'

'Get what?' Caddy said. 'What's yours?'

'Nothing,' father said. 'You all must get to bed.'

'Caddy made me come,' Jason said.

'Go on to Aunt Rachel's,' father said.

'It wont do no good,' Nancy said. She sat before the fire, her elbows on her knees, her long hands between her knees. 'When even your own kitchen wouldn't do no good. When even if I was sleeping on the floor in the room with your chillen, and the next morning there I am, and blood —'

'Hush,' father said. 'Lock the door and put out the lamp and go to bed.'

'I scared of the dark,' Nancy said. 'I scared for it to happen in the dark.'

'You mean you're going to sit right here with the lamp lighted?' father said. Then Nancy began to make the sound again, sitting before the fire, her long hands between her knees. 'Ah, damnation,' father said. 'Come along, chillen. It's past bedtime.'

'When yawl go home, I gone,' Nancy said. She talked quieter now, and her face looked quiet, like her hands. 'Anyway, I got my coffin money saved up with Mr. Lovelady.' Mr. Lovelady was a short, dirty man who collected the Negro insurance, coming around to the cabins or the kitchens every Saturday morning, to collect fifteen cents. He and his wife lived at the hotel. One morning his wife committed suicide. They had a child, a little girl. He and the child went away. After a week or two he came back alone. We would see him going along the lanes and the back streets on Saturday mornings.

'Nonsense,' father said. 'You'll be the first thing I'll see in the kitchen tomorrow morning.'

'You'll see what you'll see, I reckon,' Nancy said. 'But it will take the Lord to say what that will be.'

VI

We left her sitting before the fire.

'Come and put the bar up,' father said. But she didn't move. She didn't look at us again, sitting quietly there between the lamp and the fire. From some distance down the lane we could look back and see her through the open door.

'What, Father?' Caddy said. 'What's going to happen?'

'Nothing,' father said. Jason was on father's back, so Jason was the tallest of all of us. We went down into the ditch. I looked at it, quiet. I couldn't see much where the moonlight and the shadows tangled.

'If Jesus is hid here, he can see us, cant he?' Caddy said.

'He's not there,' father said. 'He went away a long time ago.'

'You made me come,' Jason said, high; against the sky it looked like father had two heads, a little one and a big one. 'I didn't want to.'

We went up out of the ditch. We could still see Nancy's house and the open door, but we couldn't see Nancy now, sitting before the fire with the door open, because she was tired. 'I just done got tired,' she said. 'I just a nigger. It aint no fault of mine.'

But we could hear her, because she began just after we came up out of the ditch, the sound that was not singing and not unsinging. 'Who will do our washing now, Father?' I said.

'I'm not a nigger,' Jason said, high and close above father's head.

'You're worse,' Caddy said, 'you are a tattletale. If something was to jump out, you'd be scairder than a nigger.'

'I wouldn't,' Jason said.

'You'd cry,' Caddy said.

'Caddy,' father said.

'I wouldn't!' Jason said.

'Scairy cat,' Caddy said.

'Candace!' father said.

BABYLON REVISITED[1]

F. SCOTT FITZGERALD

I

'AND where's Mr. Campbell?' Charlie asked.

'Gone to Switzerland. Mr. Campbell's a pretty sick man, Mr. Wales.'

'I'm sorry to hear that. And George Hardt?' Charlie inquired.

'Back in America, gone to work.'

'And where is the Snow Bird?'

'He was in here last week. Anyway, his friend, Mr. Schaeffer, is in Paris.'

Two familiar names from the long list of a year and a half ago. Charlie scribbled an address in his notebook and tore out the page.

'If you see Mr. Schaeffer, give him this,' he said. 'It's my brother-in-law's address. I haven't settled on a hotel yet.'

He was not really disappointed to find Paris was so empty. But the stillness in the Ritz bar was strange and portentous. It was not an American bar any more — he felt polite in it, and not as if he owned it. It had gone back into France. He felt the stillness from the moment he got out of the taxi and saw the door-man, usually in a frenzy of activity at this hour, gossiping with a *chasseur* by the servants' entrance.

[1] Copyright, 1935, by Charles Scribner's Sons. From *Taps at Reveille*, by F. Scott Fitzgerald. Charles Scribner's Sons, 1935.

Passing through the corridor, he heard only a single, bored voice in the once-clamorous women's room. When he turned into the bar he travelled the twenty feet of green carpet with his eyes fixed straight ahead by old habit; and then, with his foot firmly on the rail, he turned and surveyed the room, encountering only a single pair of eyes that fluttered up from a newspaper in the corner. Charlie asked for the head barman, Paul, who in the latter days of the bull market had come to work in his own custom-built car — disembarking, however, with due nicety at the nearest corner. But Paul was at his country house today and Alix giving him information.

'No, no more,' Charlie said, 'I'm going slow these days.'

Alix congratulated him: 'You were going pretty strong a couple of years ago.'

'I'll stick to it all right,' Charlie assured him. 'I've stuck to it for over a year and a half now.'

'How do you find conditions in America?'

'I haven't been to America for months. I'm in business in Prague, representing a couple of concerns there. They don't know about me down there.'

Alix smiled.

'Remember the night of George Hardt's bachelor dinner here?' said Charlie. 'By the way, what's become of Claude Fessenden?'

Alix lowered his voice confidentially: 'He's in Paris, but he doesn't come here any more. Paul doesn't allow it. He ran up a bill of thirty thousand francs, charging all his drinks and his lunches, and usually his dinner, for more than a year. And when Paul finally told him he had to pay, he gave him a bad check.'

Alix shook his head sadly.

'I don't understand it, such a dandy fellow. Now he's all bloated up ——' He made a plump apple of his hands.

Charlie watched a group of strident queens installing themselves in a corner.

'Nothing affects them,' he thought. 'Stocks rise and fall, people loaf or work, but they go on forever.' The place oppressed him. He called for the dice and shook with Alix for the drink.

'Here for long, Mr. Wales?'

'I'm here for four or five days to see my little girl.'

'Oh-h! You have a little girl?'

Outside, the fire-red, gas-blue, ghost-green signs shone smokily through the tranquil rain. It was late afternoon and the streets were in movement; the *bistros* gleamed. At the corner of the Boulevard des Capucines he took a taxi. The Place de la Concorde moved by in pink majesty; they crossed the logical Seine, and Charlie felt the sudden provincial quality of the left bank.

Charlie directed his taxi to the Avenue de l'Opera, which was out of his way. But he wanted to see the blue hour spread over the magnificent façade, and imagine that the cab horns, playing endlessly the first few bars of *Le Plus que Lent*, were the trumpets of the Second Empire. They were closing the iron grill in front of Brentano's Book-store, and people were already at dinner behind the trim little bourgeois hedge of Duval's. He had never eaten at a really cheap restaurant in Paris. Five-course dinner, four francs fifty, eighteen cents, wine included. For some odd reason he wished that he had.

As they rolled on to the Left Bank and he felt its sudden provincialism, he thought, 'I spoiled this city for myself. I didn't realize it, but the days came along one after another, and then two years were gone, and everything was gone, and I was gone.'

He was thirty-five, and good to look at. The Irish mobility of his face was sobered by a deep wrinkle between his eyes. As he rang his brother-in-law's bell in the Rue Palatine, the wrinkle deepened till it pulled down his brows; he felt a cramping sensation in his belly. From behind the maid who opened the door darted a lovely little girl of nine who shrieked 'Daddy!' and flew up, struggling like a fish, into his arms. She pulled his head around by one ear and set her cheek against his.

'My old pie,' he said.

'Oh, daddy, daddy, daddy, daddy, dads, dads, dads!'

She drew him into the salon, where the family waited, a boy and girl his daughter's age, his sister-in-law and her husband. He greeted Marion with his voice pitched carefully to avoid either feigned enthusiasm or dislike, but her response was more frankly tepid, though she minimized her expression of unalterable distrust by directing her regard toward his child. The two men clasped hands in a friendly way and Lincoln Peters rested his for a moment on Charlie's shoulder.

The room was warm and comfortably American. The three children moved intimately about, playing through the yellow oblongs that led to other rooms; the cheer of six o'clock spoke in the eager smacks of the fire and the sounds of French activity in the kitchen. But Charlie did not relax; his heart sat up rigidly in his body and he drew confidence from his daughter, who from time to time came close to him, holding in her arms the doll he had brought.

'Really extremely well,' he declared in answer to Lincoln's question. 'There's a lot of business there that isn't moving at all, but we're doing even better than ever. In fact, damn well. I'm bringing my sister over from America next month to keep house for me. My income last year was bigger than it was when I had money. You see, the Czechs——'

His boasting was for a specific purpose; but after a moment, seeing a faint restiveness in Lincoln's eye, he changed the subject:

'Those are fine children of yours, well brought up, good manners.'

'We think Honoria's a great little girl too.'

Marion Peters came back from the kitchen. She was a tall woman with worried eyes, who had once possessed a fresh Amer-

ican loveliness. Charlie had never been sensitive to it and was
always surprised when people spoke of how pretty she had been.
From the first there had been an instinctive antipathy between
them.

'Well, how do you find Honoria?' she asked.

'Wonderful. I was astonished how much she's grown in ten
months. All the children are looking well.'

'We haven't had a doctor for a year. How do you like being
back in Paris?'

'It seems very funny to see so few Americans around.'

'I'm delighted,' Marion said vehemently. 'Now at least you
can go into a store without their assuming you're a millionaire.
We've suffered like everybody, but on the whole it's a good deal
pleasanter.'

'But it was nice while it lasted,' Charlie said. 'We were a sort
of royalty, almost infallible, with a sort of magic around us. In
the bar this afternoon' — he stumbled, seeing his mistake —
'there wasn't a man I knew.'

She looked at him keenly. 'I should think you'd have had
enough of bars.'

'I only stayed a minute. I take one drink every afternoon, and
no more.'

'Don't you want a cocktail before dinner?' Lincoln asked.

'I take only one drink every afternoon, and I've had that.'

'I hope you keep to it,' said Marion.

Her dislike was evident in the coldness with which she spoke,
but Charlie only smiled; he had larger plans. Her very aggressive-
ness gave him an advantage, and he knew enough to wait. He
wanted them to initiate the discussion of what they knew had
brought him to Paris.

At dinner he couldn't decide whether Honoria was most like
him or her mother. Fortunate if she didn't combine the traits
of both that had brought them to disaster. A great wave of

protectiveness went over him. He thought he knew what to do for her. He believed in character; he wanted to jump back a whole generation and trust in character again as the eternally valuable element. Everything wore out.

He left soon after dinner, but not to go home. He was curious to see Paris by night with clearer and more judicious eyes than those of other days. He bought a *strapontin* for the Casino and watched Josephine Baker go through her chocolate arabesques.

After an hour he left and strolled toward Montmartre, up the Rue Pigalle into the Place Blanche. The rain had stopped and there were a few people in evening clothes disembarking from taxis in front of cabarets, and *cocottes* prowling singly or in pairs, and many Negroes. He passed a lighted door from which issued music, and stopped with the sense of familiarity; it was Bricktop's, where he had parted with so many hours and so much money. A few doors farther on he found another ancient rendezvous and incautiously put his head inside. Immediately an eager orchestra burst into sound, a pair of professional dancers leaped to their feet and a maître d'hôtel swooped toward him, crying, 'Crowd just arriving, sir!' But he withdrew quickly.

'You have to be damn drunk,' he thought.

Zelli's was closed, the bleak and sinister cheap hotels surrounding it were dark; up in the Rue Blanche there was more light and a local, colloquial French crowd. The Poet's Cave had disappeared, but the two great mouths of the Café of Heaven and the Café of Hell still yawned — even devoured, as he watched, the meagre contents of a tourist bus — a German, a Japanese, and an American couple who glanced at him with frightened eyes.

So much for the effort and ingenuity of Montmartre. All the catering to vice and waste was on an utterly childish scale, and he suddenly realized the meaning of the word 'dissipate' — to dissipate into thin air; to make nothing out of something. In the little hours of the night every move from place to place was an enormous human jump, an increase of paying for the privilege of slower and slower motion.

He remembered thousand-franc notes given to an orchestra for playing a single number, hundred-franc notes tossed to a doorman for calling a cab.

But it hadn't been given for nothing.

It had been given, even the most wildly squandered sum, as an offering to destiny that he might not remember the things most worth remembering, the things that now he would always remember — his child taken from his control, his wife escaped to a grave in Vermont.

In the glare of a *brasserie* a woman spoke to him. He bought her some eggs and coffee, and then, eluding her encouraging stare, gave her a twenty-franc note and took a taxi to his hotel.

II

He woke upon a fine fall day — football weather. The depression of yesterday was gone and he liked the people on the streets. At noon he sat opposite Honoria at Le Grand Vatel, the only restaurant he could think of not reminiscent of champagne dinners and long luncheons that began at two and ended in a blurred and vague twilight.

'Now, how about vegetables? Oughtn't you to have some vegetables?'

'Well, yes.'

'Here's *épinards* and *chou-fleur* and carrots and *haricots*.'

'I'd like *chou-fleur*.'

'Wouldn't you like to have two vegetables?'

'I usually only have one at lunch.'

The waiter was pretending to be inordinately fond of children. *'Qu'elle est mignonne la petite? Elle parle exactement comme une française.'*

'How about dessert? Shall we wait and see?'

The waiter disappeared. Honoria looked at her father expectantly.

'What are we going to do?'

'First, we're going to that toy store in the Rue Saint-Honoré and buy you anything you like. And then we're going to the vaudeville at the Empire.'

She hesitated. 'I like it about the vaudeville, but not the toy store.'

'Why not?'

'Well, you brought me this doll.' She had it with her. 'And I've got lots of things. And we're not rich any more, are we?'

'We never were. But today you are to have anything you want.'

'All right,' she agreed resignedly.

When there had been her mother and a French nurse he had been inclined to be strict; now he extended himself, reached out for a new tolerance; he must be both parents to her and not shut any of her out of communication.

'I want to get to know you,' he said gravely. 'First let me introduce myself. My name is Charles J. Wales, of Prague.'

'Oh, daddy!' her voice cracked with laughter.

'And who are you, please?' he persisted, and she accepted a rôle immediately: 'Honoria Wales, Rue Palatine, Paris.'

'Married or single?'

'No, not married. Single.'

He indicated the doll. 'But I see you have a child, madame.'

Unwilling to disinherit it, she took it to her heart and thought quickly: 'Yes, I've been married, but I'm not married now. My husband is dead.'

He went on quickly, 'And the child's name?'

'Simone. That's after my best friend at school.'

'I'm very pleased that you're doing so well at school.'

'I'm third this month,' she boasted. 'Elsie' — that was her

cousin — 'is only about eighteenth, and Richard is about at the bottom.

'You like Richard and Elsie, don't you?'

'Oh, yes. I like Richard quite well and I like her all right.'

Cautiously and casually he asked: 'And Aunt Marion and Uncle Lincoln — which do you like best?'

'Oh, Uncle Lincoln, I guess.'

He was increasingly aware of her presence. As they came in, a murmur of ' . . . adorable' followed them, and now the people at the next table bent all their silences upon her, staring as if she were something no more conscious than a flower.

'Why don't I live with you?' she asked suddenly. 'Because mamma's dead?'

'You must stay here and learn more French. It would have been hard for daddy to take care of you so well.'

'I don't really need much taking care of any more. I do everything for myself.'

Going out of the restaurant, a man and a woman unexpectedly hailed him!

'Well, the old Wales!'

'Hello there, Lorraine. . . . Dunc.'

Sudden ghosts out of the past: Duncan Schaeffer, a friend from college. Lorraine Quarrles, a lovely, pale blonde of thirty; one of a crowd who had helped them make months into days in the lavish times of three years ago.

'My husband couldn't come this year,' she said, in answer to his question. 'We're poor as hell. So he gave me two hundred a month and told me I could do my worst on that. . . . This your little girl?'

'What about coming back and sitting down?' Duncan asked.

'Can't do it.' He was glad for an excuse. As always he felt Lorraine's passionate, provocative attraction, but his own rhythm was different now.

'Well, how about dinner?' she asked.

'I'm not free. Give me your address and let me call you.'

'Charlie, I believe you're sober,' she said judicially. 'I honestly believe he's sober, Dunc. Pinch him and see if he's sober.'

Charlie indicated Honoria with his head. They both laughed.

'What's your address?' said Duncan sceptically.

He hesitated, unwilling to give the name of his hotel.

'I'm not settled yet. I'd better call you. We're going to see the vaudeville at the Empire.'

'There! That's what I want to do,' Lorraine said. 'I want to see some clowns and acrobats and jugglers. That's just what we'll do, Dunc.'

'We've got to do an errand first,' said Charlie. 'Perhaps we'll see you there.'

'All right, you snob. . . . Good-bye, beautiful little girl.'

'Good-bye.'

Honoria bobbed politely.

Somehow, an unwelcome encounter. They liked him because he was functioning, because he was serious; they wanted to see him, because he was stronger than they were now, because they wanted to draw a certain sustenance from his strength.

At the Empire, Honoria proudly refused to sit upon her father's folded coat. She was already an individual with a code of her own, and Charlie was more and more absorbed by the desire of putting a little of himself into her before she crystallized utterly. It was hopeless to try to know her in so short a time.

Between the acts they came upon Duncan and Lorraine in the lobby where the band was playing.

'Have a drink?'

'All right, but not up at the bar. We'll take a table.'

'The perfect father.'

Listening abstractedly to Lorraine, Charlie watched Honoria's eyes leave their table, and he followed them wistfully about the room, wondering what they saw. He met her glance and she smiled.

'I liked that lemonade,' she said.

What had she said? What had he expected? Going home in a taxi afterward, he pulled her over until her head rested against his chest.

'Darling, do you ever think about your mother?'

'Yes, sometimes,' she answered vaguely.

'I don't want you to forget her. Have you got a picture of her?'

'Yes, I think so. Anyhow, Aunt Marion has. Why don't you want me to forget her?'

'She loved you very much.'

'I loved her to.'

They were silent for a moment.

'Daddy, I want to come and live with you,' she said suddenly.

His heart leaped; he had wanted it to come like this.

'Aren't you perfectly happy?'

'Yes, but I love you better than anybody. And you love me better than anybody, don't you, now that mummy's dead?' .

'Of course I do. But you won't always like me best, honey. You'll grow up and meet somebody your own age and go marry him and forget you ever had a daddy.'

'Yes, that's true,' she agreed tranquilly.

He didn't go in. He was coming back at nine o'clock and he wanted to keep himself fresh and new for the thing he must say then.

'When you're safe inside, just show yourself in that window.'

'All right. Good-bye, dads, dads, dads, dads.'

He waited in the dark street until she appeared, all warm and glowing, in the window above and kissed her fingers out into the night.

III

They were waiting. Marion sat behind the coffee service in a dignified black dinner dress that just faintly suggested mourning. Lincoln was walking up and down with the animation of one who had already been talking. They were as anxious as he was to get into the question. He opened it almost immediately:

'I suppose you know what I want to see you about — why I really came to Paris.'

Marion played with the black stars on her necklace and frowned.

'I'm awfully anxious to have a home,' he continued. 'And I'm awfully anxious to have Honoria in it. I appreciate your taking in Honoria for her mother's sake, but things have changed now' — he hesitated and then continued more forcibly — 'changed radically with me, and I want to ask you to reconsider the matter. It would be silly for me to deny that about three years ago I was acting badly ——'

Marion looked up at him with hard eyes.

'—— but all that's over. As I told you, I haven't had more than a drink a day for over a year, and I take that drink deliberately, so that the idea of alcohol won't get too big in my imagination. You see the idea?'

'No,' said Marion succinctly.

'It's a sort of stunt I set myself. It keeps the matter in proportion.'

'I get you,' said Lincoln. 'You don't want to admit it's got any attraction for you.'

'Something like that. Sometimes I forget and don't take it. But I try to take it. Anyhow, I couldn't afford to drink in my position. The people I represent are more than satisfied with what I've done, and I'm bringing my sister over from Burlington to keep house for me, and I want awfully to have Honoria too. You know that even when her mother and I weren't getting along

well we never let anything that happened touch Honoria. I know
she's fond of me and I know I'm able to take care of her and —
well, there you are. How do you feel about it?'

He knew that now he would have to take a beating. It would
last an hour or two hours, and it would be difficult, but if he
modulated his inevitable resentment to the chastened attitude
of the reformed sinner, he might win his point in the end.

Keep your temper, he told himself. You don't want to be
justified. You want Honoria.

Lincoln spoke first: 'We've been talking it over ever since we
got your letter last month. We're happy to have Honoria here.
She's a dear little thing, and we're glad to be able to help her, but
of course that isn't the question ——'

Marion interrupted suddenly. 'How long are you going to stay
sober, Charlie?' she asked.

'Permanently, I hope.'

'How can anybody count on that?'

'You know I never did drink heavily until I gave up business
and came over here with nothing to do. Then Helen and I began
to run around with ——'

'Please leave Helen out of it. I can't bear to hear you talk
about her like that.'

He stared at her grimly; he had never been certain how fond of
each other the sisters were in life.

'My drinking only lasted about a year and a half — from the
time we came over until I — collapsed.'

'It was time enough.'

'It was time enough,' he agreed.

'My duty is entirely to Helen,' she said. 'I try to think what
she would have wanted me to do. Frankly, from the night you
did that terrible thing you haven't really existed for me. I can't
help that. She was my sister.'

'Yes.'

'When she was dying she asked me to look out for Honoria. If you hadn't been in a sanitarium then, it might have helped matters.'

He had no answer.

'I'll never in my life be able to forget the morning when Helen knocked at my door, soaked to the skin and shivering, and said you'd locked her out.'

Charlie gripped the sides of the chair. This was more difficult than he expected; he wanted to launch out into a long expostulation and explanation, but he only said: 'The night I locked her out ——' and she interrupted, 'I don't feel up to going over that again.'

After a moment's silence Lincoln said: 'We're getting off the subject. You want Marion to set aside her legal guardianship and give you Honoria. I think the main point for her is whether she has confidence in you or not.'

'I don't blame Marion,' Charlie said slowly, 'but I think she can have entire confidence in me. I had a good record up to three years ago. Of course, it's within human possibilities I might go wrong any time. But if we wait much longer I'll lose Honoria's childhood and my chance for a home.' He shook his head, 'I'll simply lose her, don't you see?'

'Yes, I see,' said Lincoln.

'Why didn't you think of all this before?' Marion asked.

'I suppose I did, from time to time, but Helen and I were getting along badly. When I consented to the guardianship, I was flat on my back in a sanitarium and the market had cleaned me out. I knew I'd acted badly, and I thought if it would bring any peace to Helen, I'd agree to anything. But now it's different. I'm functioning, I'm behaving damn well, so far as ——'

'Please don't swear at me,' Marion said.

He looked at her, startled. With each remark the force of her dislike became more and more apparent. She had built up all her fear of life into one wall and faced it toward him. This trivial reproof was possibly the result of some trouble with the cook several hours before. Charlie became increasingly alarmed at leaving Honoria in this atmosphere of hostility against himself; sooner or later it would come out, in a word here, a shake of the head there, and some of that distrust would be irrevocably implanted in Honoria. But he pulled his temper down out of his face and shut it up inside him; he had won a point, for Lincoln realized the absurdity of Marion's remark and asked her lightly since when she had objected to the word 'damn.'

'Another thing,' Charlie said: 'I'm able to give her certain advantages now. I'm going to take a French governess to Prague with me. I've got a lease on a new apartment ——'

He stopped, realizing that he was blundering. They couldn't be expected to accept with equanimity the fact that his income was again twice as large as their own.

'I suppose you can give her more luxuries than we can,' said Marion. 'When you were throwing away money we were living along watching every ten francs.... I suppose you'll start doing it again.'

'Oh, no,' he said. 'I've learned. I worked hard for ten years, you know — until I got lucky in the market, like so many people. Terribly lucky. It didn't seem any use working any more, so I quit. It won't happen again.'

There was a long silence. All of them felt their nerves straining, and for the first time in a year Charlie wanted a drink. He was sure now that Lincoln Peters wanted him to have his child.

Marion shuddered suddenly; part of her saw that Charlie's feet were planted on the earth now, and her own maternal feeling recognized the naturalness of his desire; but she had lived for a long time with a prejudice — a prejudice founded on a curious disbelief in her sister's happiness, and which, in the shock of one terrible night, had turned to hatred for him. It had all happened at a point in her life where the discouragement of ill health and adverse circumstances made it necessary for her to believe in tangible villainy and a tangible villain.

'I can't help what I think!' she cried out suddenly. 'How much you were responsible for Helen's death, I don't know. It's something you'll have to square with your own conscience.'

An electric current of agony surged through him; for a moment he was almost on his feet, an unuttered sound echoing in his throat. He hung on to himself for a moment, another moment.

'Hold on there,' said Lincoln uncomfortably. 'I never thought you were responsible for that.'

'Helen died of heart trouble,' Charlie said dully.

'Yes, heart trouble.' Marion spoke as if the phrase had another meaning for her.

Then, in the flatness that followed her outburst, she saw him plainly and she knew he had somehow arrived at control over the situation. Glancing at her husband, she found no help from him, and as abruptly as if it were a matter of no importance, she threw up the sponge.

'Do what you like!' she cried, springing up from her chair. 'She's your child. I'm not the person to stand in your way. I think if it were my child I'd rather see her ——' She managed to check herself. 'You two decide it. I can't stand this. I'm sick. I'm going to bed.'

She hurried from the room; after a moment Lincoln said:

'This has been a hard day for her. You know how strongly she feels ——' His voice was almost apologetic: 'When a woman gets an idea in her head.'

'Of course.'

'It's going to be all right. I think she sees now that you — can provide for the child, and so we can't very well stand in your way or Honoria's way.'

'Thank you, Lincoln.'

'I'd better go along and see how she is.'

'I'm going.'

He was still trembling when he reached the street, but a walk down the Rue Bonaparte to the quais set him up, and as he crossed the Seine, fresh and new by the quai lamps, he felt exultant. But back in his room he couldn't sleep. The image of Helen haunted him. Helen whom he had loved so until they had senselessly begun to abuse each other's love, tear it into shreds. On that terrible February night that Marion remembered so vividly, a slow quarrel had gone on for hours. There was a scene at the Florida, and then he attempted to take her home, and then she kissed young Webb at a table; after that there was what she had hysterically said. When he arrived home alone he turned the key in the lock in wild anger. How could he know she would arrive an hour later alone, that there would be a snowstorm in which she wandered about in slippers, too confused to find a taxi? Then the aftermath, her escaping pneumonia by a miracle, and all the attendant horror. They were 'reconciled,' but that was the beginning of the end, and Marion, who had seen with her own eyes and who imagined it to be one of many scenes from her sister's martyrdom, never forgot.

Going over it again brought Helen nearer, and in the white, soft light that steals upon half sleep near morning he found himself talking to her again. She said that he was perfectly right about Honoria and that she wanted Honoria to be with him. She said she was glad he was being good and doing better. She said a lot of other things — very friendly things — but she was in a swing in a white dress, and swinging faster and faster all the time, so that at the end he could not hear clearly all that she said.

IV

He woke up feeling happy. The door of the world was open again. He made plans, vistas, futures for Honoria and himself, but suddenly he grew sad, remembering all the plans he and Helen had made. She had not planned to die. The present was the thing — work to do and someone to love. But not to love too much, for he knew the injury that a father can do to a daughter or a mother to a son by attaching them too closely: afterward, out in the world, the child would seek in the marriage partner the same blind tenderness and, failing probably to find it, turn against love and life.

It was another bright, crisp day. He called Lincoln Peters at the bank where he worked and asked if he could count on taking Honoria when he left for Prague. Lincoln agreed that there was no reason for delay. One thing — the legal guardianship. Marion wanted to retain that a while longer. She was upset by the whole matter, and it would oil things if she felt that the situation was still in her control for another year. Charlie agreed, wanting only the tangible, visible child.

Then the question of a governess. Charlie sat in a gloomy agency and talked to cross Bernaise and to a buxom Breton peasant, neither of whom he could have endured. There were others whom he would see tomorrow.

He lunched with Lincoln Peters at Griffons, trying to keep down his exultation.

'There's nothing quite like your own child,' Lincoln said. 'But you understand how Marion feels too.'

'She's forgotten how hard I worked for seven years there,' Charlie said. 'She just remembers one night.'

'There's another thing.' Lincoln hesitated. 'While you and Helen were tearing around Europe throwing money away, we were just getting along. I didn't touch any of the prosperity because I never got ahead enough to carry anything but my insurance. I think Marion felt there was some kind of injustice in it — you not even working toward the end, and getting richer and richer.'

'It went just as quick as it came,' said Charlie.

'Yes, a lot of it stayed in the hands of *chasseurs* and saxophone players and maîtres d'hôtel — well, the big party's over now. I just said that to explain Marion's feeling about those crazy years. If you drop in about six o'clock tonight before Marion's too tired, we'll settle the details on the spot.'

Back at his hotel, Charlie found a *pneumatique* that had been redirected from the Ritz bar where Charlie had left his address for the purpose of finding a certain man.

DEAR CHARLIE: You were so strange when we saw you the other day that I wondered if I did something to offend you. If so, I'm not conscious of it. In fact, I have thought about you too much for the last year, and it's always been in the back of my mind that I might see you if I came over here. We *did* have such good times that crazy spring, like the night you and I stole the butcher's tricycle, and the time we tried to call on the president and you had the old derby rim and the wire cane. Everybody seems so old lately, but I don't feel old a bit. Couldn't we get together some time today for old time's sake? I've got a vile hang-over for the moment, but will be feeling better this afternoon and will look for you about five in the sweet-shop at the Ritz.

Always devotedly

LORRAINE

His first feeling was one of awe that he had actually, in his mature years, stolen a tricycle and pedalled Lorraine all over the Étoile between the small hours and dawn. In retrospect it was a nightmare. Locking out Helen didn't fit in with any other act of his life, but the tricycle incident did — it was one of many. How many weeks or months of dissipation to arrive at that condition of utter irresponsibility?

He tried to picture how Lorraine had appeared to him then —

very attractive; Helen was unhappy about it, though she said nothing. Yesterday, in the restaurant, Lorraine had seemed trite, blurred, worn away. He emphatically did not want to see her, and he was glad Alix had not given away his hotel address. It was a relief to think, instead, of Honoria, to think of Sundays spent with her and of saying good morning to her and of knowing she was there in his house at night, drawing her breath in the darkness.

At five he took a taxi and bought presents for all the Peters — a piquant cloth doll, a box of Roman soldiers, flowers for Marion, big linen handkerchiefs for Lincoln.

He saw, when he arrived in the apartment, that Marion had accepted the inevitable. She greeted him now as though he were a recalcitrant member of the family, rather than a menacing outsider. Honoria had been told she was going; Charlie was glad to see that her tact made her conceal her excessive happiness. Only on his lap did she whisper her delight and the question 'When?' before she slipped away with the other children.

He and Marion were alone for a minute in the room, and on an impulse he spoke out boldly:

'Family quarrels are bitter things. They don't go according to any rules. They're not like aches or wounds; they're more like splits in the skin that won't heal because there's not enough material. I wish you and I could be on better terms.'

'Some things are hard to forget,' she answered. 'It's a question of confidence.' There was no answer to this and presently she asked, 'When do you propose to take her?'

'As soon as I can get a governess. I hoped the day after tomorrow.'

'That's impossible. I've got to get her things in shape. Not before Saturday.'

He yielded. Coming back into the room, Lincoln offered him a drink.

'I'll take my daily whisky,' he said.

It was warm here, it was a home, people together by a fire. The children felt very safe and important; the mother and father were serious, watchful. They had things to do for the children more important than his visit here. A spoonful of medicine was, after all, more important than the strained relations between Marion and himself. They were not dull people, but they were very much in the grip of life and circumstances. He wondered if he couldn't do something to get Lincoln out of his rut at the bank.

A long peal at the door-bell; the *bonne de toute faire* passed through and went down the corridor. The door opened upon another long ring, and then voices, and the three in the salon looked up expectantly; Richard moved to bring the corridor within his range of vision, and Marion rose. Then the maid came back along the corridor, closely followed by the voices, which developed under the light into Duncan Schaeffer and Lorraine Quarrles.

They were gay, they were hilarious, they were roaring with laughter. For a moment Charlie was astounded; unable to understand how they ferreted out the Peters' address.

'Ah-h-h!' Duncan wagged his finger roguishly at Charlie. 'Ah-h-h!'

They both slid down another cascade of laughter. Anxious and at a loss, Charlie shook hands with them quickly and presented them to Lincoln and Marion. Marion nodded, scarcely speaking. She had drawn back a step toward the fire; her little girl stood beside her, and Marion put an arm about her shoulder.

With growing annoyance at the intrusion, Charlie waited for them to explain themselves. After some concentration Duncan said:

'We came to invite you out to dinner. Lorraine and I insist that all this shishi, cagy business 'bout your address got to stop.'

Charlie came closer to them, as if to force them backward down the corridor.

'Sorry, but I can't. Tell me where you'll be and I'll phone you in half an hour.'

This made no impression. Lorraine sat down suddenly on the side of a chair, and focussing her eyes on Richard, cried, 'Oh, what a nice little boy! Come here, little boy.' Richard glanced at his mother, but did not move. With a perceptible shrug of her shoulders, Lorraine turned back to Charlie:

'Come and dine. Sure your cousins won' mine. See you so sel'om. Or solemn.'

'I can't,' said Charlie sharply. 'You two have dinner and I'll phone you.'

Her voice became suddenly unpleasant. 'All right, we'll go. But I remember once when you hammered on my door at four A.M. I was enough of a good sport to give you a drink. Come on, Dunc.'

Still in slow motion, with blurred, angry faces, with uncertain feet, they retired along the corridor.

'Good night,' Charlie said.

'Good night!' responded Lorraine emphatically.

When he went back into the salon Marion had not moved, only now her son was standing in the circle of her other arm. Lincoln was still swinging Honoria back and forth like a pendulum from side to side.

'What an outrage!' Charlie broke out. 'What an absolute outrage!'

Neither of them answered. Charlie dropped into an armchair, picked up his drink, set it down again and said:

'People I haven't seen for two years having the colossal nerve ——'

He broke off. Marion had made the sound 'Oh!' in one swift, furious breath, turned her body from him with a jerk and left the room.

Lincoln set down Honoria carefully.

'You children go in and start your soup,' he said, and when they obeyed, he said to Charlie:

'Marion's not well and she can't stand shocks. That kind of people make her really physically sick.'

'I didn't tell them to come here. They wormed your name out of somebody. They deliberately ——'

'Well, it's too bad. It doesn't help matters. Excuse me a minute.'

Left alone, Charlie sat tense in his chair. In the next room he could hear the children eating, talking in monosyllables, already oblivious to the scene between their elders. He heard a murmur of conversation from a farther room and then the ticking bell of a telephone receiver picked up, and in a panic he moved to the other side of the room and out of earshot.

In a minute Lincoln came back. 'Look here, Charlie. I think we'd better call off dinner for tonight. Marion's in bad shape.'

'Is she angry with me?'

'Sort of,' he said, almost roughly. 'She's not strong and ——'

'You mean she's changed her mind about Honoria?'

'She's pretty bitter right now. I don't know. You phone me at the bank tomorrow.'

'I wish you'd explain to her I never dreamed these people would come here. I'm just as sore as you are.'

'I couldn't explain anything to her now.'

Charlie got up. He took his coat and hat and started down the corridor. Then he opened the door of the dining room and said in a strange voice, 'Good night, children.'

Honoria rose and ran around the table to hug him.

'Good night, sweetheart,' he said vaguely, and then trying to make his voice more tender, trying to conciliate something, 'Good night, dear children.'

v

Charlie went directly to the Ritz bar with the furious idea of finding Lorraine and Duncan, but they were not there, and he realized that in any case there was nothing he could do. He had not touched his drink at the Peters', and now he ordered a whisky-and-soda. Paul came over to say hello.

'It's a great change,' he said sadly. 'We do about half the business we did. So many fellows I hear about back in the States lost everything, maybe not in the first crash, but then in the second. Your friend George Hardt lost every cent, I hear. Are you back in the States?'

'No, I'm in business in Prague.'

'I heard that you lost a lot in the crash.'

'I did,' and he added grimly, 'but I lost everything I wanted in the boom.'

'Selling short.'

'Something like that.'

Again the memory of those days swept over him like a night-mare — the people they had met travelling; then people who couldn't add a row of figures or speak a coherent sentence. The little man Helen had consented to dance with at the ship's party, who had insulted her ten feet from the table; the women and girls carried screaming with drink or drugs out of public places ——

—— The men who locked their wives out in the snow, because the snow of twenty-nine wasn't real snow. If you didn't want it to be snow, you just paid some money.

He went to the phone and called the Peters' apartment; Lincoln answered.

'I called up because this thing is on my mind. Has Marion said anything definite?'

'Marion's sick,' Lincoln answered shortly. 'I know this thing isn't altogether your fault, but I can't have her go to pieces about it. I'm afraid we'll have to let it slide for six months; I can't take the chance of working her up to this state again.'

'I see.'

'I'm sorry, Charlie.'

He went back to his table. His whisky glass was empty, but he shook his head when Alix looked at it questioningly. There wasn't much he could do now except send Honoria some things; he would send her a lot of things tomorrow. He thought rather angrily that this was just money — he had given so many people money....

'No, no more,' he said to another waiter. 'What do I owe you?'

He would come back some day; they couldn't make him pay forever. But he wanted his child, and nothing was much good now, beside that fact. He wasn't young any more, with a lot of nice thoughts and dreams to have by himself. He was absolutely sure Helen wouldn't have wanted him to be so alone.

ONE WITH SHAKESPEARE [1]

MARTHA FOLEY

Yes, Miss Cox was there, sitting at her desk in the almost empty classroom. Elizabeth took in the theme she had written to make up for a class missed because of illness.

A description of people under changing circumstances was the assignment.

Elizabeth had chosen immigrants arriving at a Boston dock. She had got quite excited as she wrote about the black-eyed women and their red and blue dresses, the swarthy men and their ear-rings, and the brightness of a far-away Mediterranean land slipping off a rocking boat to be lost in the greyness of Boston streets.

Elizabeth had liked writing this theme better than anything she had done since the description of a sunset. Amethyst and rose with a silver ribbon of river. Elizabeth shivered. A silver ribbon — that was lovely. And so was 'scarlet kerchief in the night of her hair' in this theme. Words were so beautiful.

Miss Cox read the new theme, a red pencil poised in her authoritative fingers. Miss Cox was so strong. She was strongest

[1] Copyright, 1933, by Whit Burnett and Martha Foley. From *A Story Anthology, 1931–1933*, edited by Whit Burnett and Martha Foley. The Vanguard Press, 1933.

of all the teachers in the school. Stronger even than the two men teachers, Mr. Carpenter of physics and Mr. Cattell of maths. A beautiful strongness. Thought of Miss Cox made Elizabeth feel as she did when two bright shiny words suddenly sprang together to make a beautiful, a perfect phrase.

Elizabeth was glad she had Miss Cox as an English teacher and not Miss Foster any more. Miss Foster had made the class last year count the number of times certain words occurred in *Poor Richard's Almanack* to be sure they read the book right through word for word. And the words were all so ugly. Like the picture of Benjamin Franklin. But Miss Cox made you feel the words. As when she read from *A Tale of Two Cities* in her deep singing voice, 'This is a far, far better thing than I have ever done.' Poor Sydney Carton.

Miss Cox had finished the second page of the theme. She was looking up at Elizabeth, her small dark blue eyes lighting up her glasses.

'Let me give you a pointer, my dear.'

Elizabeth automatically looked toward the blackboard ledge at the chalky pointer until the words 'my dear' bit into her mind. My dear! Miss Cox had called her 'My dear.'

'You have a spark of the divine fire,' Miss Cox said. 'You should make writing your vocation.'

Elizabeth flamed. Miss Cox, 'my dear,' themes about immigrants, blackboards and desks whirled and fused in the divine fire.

Miss Cox marked 'A' in the red pencil at the top of the theme and Elizabeth said 'thank you' and went away.

Elizabeth went back to her desk in the IIIA classroom which was in charge of Miss Perry. Miss Perry was her Greek teacher as well as her room teacher. Somehow Miss Perry made Elizabeth hate Greek. Elizabeth liked to think of Greece. White and gold in a blue Aegean. I, Sappho. Wailing Trojan women. Aristotle

and Plato and Socrates. Grace and brains, said her father, of the
men. But that was outside of Greek class. To Miss Perry Greece
was the aorist of τίθημι and Xenophon's march in the *Anabasis*.
Elizabeth always said to herself as she came into the IIIA room,
'I hate Miss Perry, the aorist and Xenophon. Oh, how I hate
them!'

But this morning Elizabeth only pitied Miss Perry. She had no
spark of the divine fire, poor thing.

Greek was the first class this morning. Elizabeth didn't care.
She should make writing her vocation. That was something Miss
Perry could never do. If she were called on for the list of irregular
verbs this morning she would like to tell Miss Perry that. It
would explain why she hadn't studied her Greek home-lesson.
Why should she be bothered with conjugations when she had to
describe blue and red men arriving on an alien shore?

'Now, Miss Morris, will you please give me the principal parts
of the verb *to give*.'

That was δίδωμι. But what was the perfect tense? Divine
fire, divine fire.

'If you don't know, you may sit down. But I warn you that
unless you do your home-lessons better you are not going to pass
this month.'

Divine fire, divine fire.

The second hour was study class. Under Miss Pratt with the
ugly bulb of a nose, splotchy face and eternal smile. Miss Pratt
taught something or other to the younger girls down in the
sixth class. She always smiled at Elizabeth but Elizabeth seldom
smiled back. Her smile never means anything, thought Elizabeth.

Elizabeth dumped her books down in her desk in Miss Pratt's
room. She opened Virgil at the part she liked — where Aeneas
told Dido the story of his wandering while the stars waned and
drooped in the sky. It was not her lesson. She had had that

months ago. But she liked going back over it, just as she liked
the beginning of the first book. Great bearded Aeneas rang out
in *arma virumque cano*. That was strong. She would write
strong some day. Strong like Virgil, and fine like Swinburne:

> 'I will go back to the great sweet mother,
> Mother and lover of men, the sea.'

Swinburne had divine fire. Keats. Shelley: 'Hail to thee, blithe
spirit.' And Masefield whose autograph she had bought for five
shillings, not to help the British but to have a bit of the man who
wrote *The Widow in the Bye Street*.

Elizabeth looked out into the school courtyard. Fine green
shoots. Yellow on the laburnum. Spring was here. Divine fire,
divine fire.

'Miss Morris, haven't you any work to do?'

Miss Pratt smiling. Nasty, nasty smiling. Didn't she know
whom she was talking to like that? A great writer. A girl who
would be famous. Let her ask Miss Cox. Why, I have a spark
of the divine fire. I am one with Shakespeare and Keats, Thack-
eray and Brontë and all the other great writers.

Elizabeth plumped her head in her hands and stared at the
Latin page. Opposite was an illustration of an old statue, supposed to be Dido. Further on was a pen-and-ink sketch of Dido
mounting the funeral pyre. Further on was a sketch of Aeneas
nearing Rome. Further on was the vocabulary. Then the end
of the book. Elizabeth turned, page by page. She could not
study, and if she looked out the window at spring again Miss
Pratt would be nasty.

'Please, Miss Pratt, may I go to the library?'

'Must you go to the library? What for?'

'I have a reference in my history lesson to look up in the en-
cyclopaedia.'

'Very well.'

The library was large and quiet — a whole floor above Miss Pratt and the study class. It was divided off into alcoves. History in one. Encyclopaedias in another. Languages, sciences. Fiction and poetry were in the farthest end which opened out towards the Fenway. The Fenway with its river and wide sky where Elizabeth liked to walk alone.

Elizabeth had read all the fiction and all the poetry. All of Jane Austen and *The Sorrows of Werther* and lots of other books which had nothing to do with her classes. She was always afraid one of her teachers would come in some day during study class and ask her what she was reading that book for. But that had never happened. And the librarian never paid any attention to her.

Now she went into the fiction and poetry alcove and sat on a small shelf ladder. She looked out the window at the long line of poplars rimming the fens. What would she call them if she were writing about them? Black sentinels against the sky. Oh beautiful, oh beautiful! That was the divine fire.

There was ancient history with Miss Tudor, who had had the smallpox and it showed all over her face; and geometry with Mr. Cattell who had a grey beard and grey eyes and grey clothes and grey manner. Elizabeth liked that — grey manner. That was what the Advanced English Composition called penetrating analysis of character. She would do lots of penetrating analysis when she wrote in earnest.

She would write novels, the greatest, most moving novels ever written, like *Jean-Christophe*, Elizabeth was deciding when the bell rang for the end of the history lesson. And in between the novels she would write fine medallions of short stories like Chekhov's, Elizabeth told herself when the bell rang for the end of the geometry lesson. And she would always write lovely poems in between the novels and the short stories, she was thinking when the bell rang for the end of the school day.

Elizabeth walked past Miss Cox's room on her way out of the building. She slowed down her steps as she came to the door. Miss Cox was putting away her things in the drawer of her desk. Elizabeth would dedicate her first book to Miss Cox. 'To Miss Eleanor G. Cox this book is gratefully dedicated by the author.'

Eileen and Ruth were waiting for Elizabeth at the entrance. Eileen was the cousin of a famous poet and her mother was an Anarchist. Elizabeth liked the thought of anyone being an Anarchist. It sounded so much more beautiful than being a Democrat or a Republican. And Ruth, who was a class ahead, had already had her poems printed in the *Transcript*. Four times. And one of the poems had been reprinted by William Stanley Braithwaite in his anthology. Oh, they were going to be great and famous, all three.

'Let's walk home and save our fares for fudge sundaes,' said Eileen.

'All right, only I am going to have pineapple,' said Ruth.

'I'll go with you but I won't have any sundae,' Elizabeth said. 'I'm going to save my fares this week to buy Miss Cox flowers.'

'You have a crush on Miss Cox.'

'Perhaps I have and perhaps I haven't. Anyway she said something wonderful to me this morning. She said I had a spark of the divine fire and should make writing my vocation.'

'Oh, that is wonderful. She never told me that, not even after Mr. Braithwaite took one of my poems for his anthology.'

'This is the happiest day of my life. Even when I have written many books and proved Miss Cox's faith in me, I shall always look back to this day. I never expected to be so wonderfully happy.'

The three girls, arm in arm, walked through the Fenway.

'I tell you, let's not get sundaes. Since Elizabeth's saving her money, it isn't fair to go in and eat them right before her. Let's you, Ruth, and I buy some of those big frosted doughnuts and

some bananas and eat them on the Charles River esplanade.
Then Elizabeth can have some too.'

'All right, and we can watch the sun set.'

'Oh, but that's what isn't fair. To save my money and then
eat up what you buy.'

'Next time you can give us something.'

Elizabeth loved the Charles River. It always hurt her to think
that it was on a Charles River bridge that Longfellow should
have made up 'I stood on the bridge at midnight.' Perhaps that
wasn't so bad, but so many parodies of the poem had ridiculed
the river. Once Elizabeth had written a 'Letter to a River.'
Elizabeth pretended she was away off somewhere like in New
York, and was writing to the river to tell how much she missed
its beauty. She had put so many lovely phrases in it, she thought,
and she couldn't understand why the editor of the *Atlantic
Monthly* had sent it back to her. But great writers always had
many rejections first. That Scottish writer in whose eyes Ruth
said she saw his soul, had said in his lecture that to write greatly,
one must first suffer greatly.

How she had suffered, thought Elizabeth. Her maths and
Greek teachers were so cruel to her. She who had a spark of
divine fire to be treated as they treated her. Tears came to her
eyes. And now, when she was tired, she was walking home
instead of riding so she could buy Miss Cox flowers. Pink sweetheart roses. Little tight knots of flowers. That was suffering and
sacrifice. But it was for love as well as for literature.

'I felt the rhythm of the universe last night,' Ruth was saying,
'I was sitting on the roof in the dark and I felt the night all
around me.'

'That makes me think of "swiftly walk over the western wave,
spirit of Night." But it always bothers me that the wave is to the
east in Boston,' said Eileen. 'Otherwise I like that poem very
much.'

'The rhythm of the universe? What do you mean?'

'Oh, you know. The way someone said the stars swing round in their courses. And that's why I never, never want to study astronomy. I want only to imagine the stars. That's so much more beautiful than any facts about them can ever be.'

'I don't agree with you at all. Why when you think that the light of the nearest star started coming to you three years ago and what you were doing then and how this minute some star is starting to send you light, that may not get to you until far away and old and ——'

'Stop! Don't give me facts about the stars! You can have those facts about your stars, if you want. But leave me my stars to love as I please.'

'Oh, very well. There, now the sky is colouring. See that lovely clear green high up. Pretty soon the deep colours will come. My, these frosted doughnuts are good! Much better than any near where we live.'

'There's the first light on the other bank. Over near the Tech building.'

That was what it was to have a spark of divine fire. Elizabeth's thoughts flowed on with the darkening river. She could put all this, the river and the sky colours and the lights, into writing. People would feel the loveliness of the world as they had never felt it before. People would no longer walk with their heads bent to the street when there was a sunset to be seen. What have you done to her, masters of men, that her head should be bowed down thus, thus in the deepening twilight and golden angelus? Her father said Noyes wrote maudlin sing-song. It was jingly sometimes but she did like it. And too many heads were bowed down, you masters of men.

'Mother'll scold me if I stay any later,' said Eileen.

'And my mother said she wouldn't get me a new dress for the class party if I came home late again.'

'Yes, we must all be going. But isn't it nice to think when you wake up at home in bed at night that the river is out here, creeping on and on under the stars?'

'No wonder Miss Cox said you had divine fire. Let's put our banana peels in here. This is Spring Clean-Up Week, you know.'

'Good night.'

'Good night.'

'Good night.'

Holding the thought of her own greatness close to her, Elizabeth went home. A sliver of moon curled in the sky. That is the moon Shelley, Shakespeare, Spenser and yes, 'way back, Chaucer looked at. And now I am looking at it.

'Mother, Miss Cox says I have a spark of divine fire. I am to be a great writer some day.'

'Isn't that nice? Did you remember not to wipe your pen-point on your petticoat today?'

'Oh, mother, you know that's not a question of remembering. I never do it when I'm thinking about it. But you didn't half listen to what Miss Cox said about me.'

'Indeed I did. She said you had a divine spark of fire. That means you'll get another A in English this month on your report card.'

'It means more than any old report card. It means my whole life. I'm to be a writer, a great writer.'

'But first you must finish school and college. And that means you have to do your mathematics better. Remember how angry your father was about that E in geometry last month.'

Elizabeth sighed. She went out on the back porch which looked across the city. Lights pricked the blackness. Like a necklace which had spilled over velvet. Oh, words were lovely.

The moon was still there, a more emphatic sliver now. 'Moon of Shelley and Keats and Shakespeare, and my moon,' said Elizabeth, and went in to dinner.

A PRETTY CUTE
LITTLE STUNT[1]

GEORGE MILBURN

I

WELL, R.A., I wish you could of been out to Rotary today. You certainly missed a treat. They pulled off a pretty cute little stunt, and I'm right here to tell you it would of give you something to think about, you old potwalloper, you!

Well, sir, it was a pretty cute little stunt the way they pulled it off. Just as slick as you please. The way it happened, the Chief called me up on the 'phone about 11.30 and says, 'Harry, we've got a bum in jail down here, and he claims that he's an old ex-member of Rotary. He's been aggravating the life out of us, telling us that he's got a message that he's got to get to you boys some way.'

The first thing that occurred to me was that it was some kind of a joke. You know how the Chief is, yourself, R.A., always up to some kind of monkey-business. Sure you do, though, because I remember how the Chief helped pull that fake pinch on you at the station last year, the day you and Alice was starting on your honeymoon. Handcuffed you right there as the train was starting up, and Alice sticking her head out the window, yelling and

---

crying when the train pulled out. I thought I'd 'a' died laughing at the look on your face that day, the way you sputtered when the Chief snapped on those bracelets. And that flabbergasted look of yours all the way on the road when we was making sixty per hour trying to get you to the next station in time to catch up with your missus!

It took you quite a while to catch on to the joke. And, come to think of it, R.A., I don't think Alice ever has acted the same toward we boys since that day she lost her temper. Well, I thought they was carrying the joke a little too far, myself, but I never saw a woman yet that could take a joke in the proper spirit. The way she turned loose on the Chief when we finally caught the train! I mean Alice ought to of seen that the Chief was just helping we boys kid you a little. I mean the Chief was only doing like we asked him to.

But to get back to what I was telling you, I thought to myself, 'This is just some horseplay the Chief's pulling off.' So I says to him, 'Oh, yeah?' You know. Like that. 'Oh, yeah?'

The Chief didn't let on a bit, though. He was just as serious as he could be. He says, 'Yes, he's got the Rotary button and the credentials, but of course he could of stole those some place. But he tells a pretty straight story, and if you've got time, I wish you'd come down to the station and take a look at him.'

Well, just as soon as I saw that the Chief was serious, I quit kidding right away. I says, 'Sure thing, Chief, I'll be right down.' So I hung up and got in my Chivy and drove right on down to the station.

I wish you could of seen this bird the Chief come leading out, R.A. Dirty as rot and looked like he didn't have a shave in a week. He had on an old, worn-out-looking blue-serge suit, all out at the sleeves, and it looked like he didn't have on any shirt, because he had his coat-collar turned up and pinned at the neck with a safety pin.

I was still kind of leery when I walked into the station, but I didn't have no more doubts after I saw this bum the Chief come leading out. He was a little short fellow that looked like he might of seen better days in his time. But it certainly looked like it had been many a day since he had. I mean he had a pretty good-sized stomach on him and he was wearing horn-rim glasses, but I wish you could of seen the way he looked. He just had down-and-outer written all over him.

The Chief introduced us, and I shook hands with him. Then he started in to explaining how he had been setting there in his cell thinking about things, and how good-for-nothing he had got to be. Then he said he just happened to remember that, a little while before the police picked him up, he had seen one of our Rotary-wheel signboards with 'Rotary meets on Mondays — Visitors welcome' on it. Well, the long and the short of it was that he said that he had used to be a Rotarian before he went to the dogs, and he just got to thinking that he would like to meet with the boys again and give them a talk.

He showed me his credentials, they were so dirty and worn I couldn't hardly make out the writing, and his button. He wasn't wearing his button. He was just carrying it in his pocket.

I could see that his feelings were working on him pretty strong. I looked to see him break down and start crying any minute. He was so pitiful I just didn't know what to do about him. But at the same time, I begun to wonder what the boys would think if I was to come walking in with a filthy bum like that to eat with us. You'd have to of seen him to appreciate it. He looked like something somebody had drug up the streets with. Well, I knew that I'd have to decide something quick. It was getting close to noon then. So I says to him, 'You wait here just a minute.' I steps over to the 'phone and calls up Gay Harrison, the secretary.

'Gay,' I says, 'what have we got on the program today?'

'Not a thing that I know of, Harry,' Gay says, 'why?'

'Well,' I says, 'the Chief's got a bum in jail down here that claims he's an old former ex-Rotarian, and this bum wants to come up and eat with us today, and then give us a talk after we eat. What's your reaction?' I says.

Gay fell right in with the notion. He says, 'Harry, that strikes me as being a pretty cute little stunt. Bring him right along!'

And I want to say it *was* a pretty cute little stunt, too.

I went back in to where the bum was standing by the desk, waiting. I hadn't quite caught his name, so I says to him, 'I didn't quite catch what your name was, brother.'

'Just call me Oscar,' he says. 'That's the old Rotary spirit.'

I kind of grinned when he said that, but when I looked at him, just as solemn as a judge when he said it, I didn't lose any time wiping that grin right off my face. I felt kind of ashamed, R.A. I mean the way he looked at me made it seem kind of heathenish to grin at Rotary spirit like that, R.A.

I turned around to the Chief and said, 'Chief, I guess you haven't got any objection, have you, if I took Oscar to Rotary with me today.'

The Chief didn't crack a smile. He said, 'Well, Harry, it's a little irregular, but if I go along to keep him in custody, I guess it'll be all right. I mean we've got him booked on a vag charge here, you see, and we'd be held liable for him.'

Before we started out, though, I looked the bum right straight in the eye and says, 'Before we start, though, Oscar, I want it distinctly understood that there's to be no begging for alms done. The boys wouldn't stand for that. We're glad to have you come eat with us, and to hear your message — but no begging speech, remember that.'

The bum kind of drew himself up and says, 'Why, of course I have no intention of begging for alms. Of course not. That wouldn't be Rotary,' he says. And somehow or another he made me feel pretty cheap again, the way he said that, 'It wouldn't be Rotary.'

II

Well, the upshot of it was, we all piled into my Chivy sedan,
the Chief and the bum and me, and drove right up to the Hotel
Beckman just like we was a delegation of millionaires. I wished
you could of seen that big nigger doorman they got there at the
Beckman, R.A., when we come piling out of my Chivy. That
nigger's eyes just bulged out like stoppers on an organ. I'd give
a pretty to know what he was thinking.

When we walked through the lobby I could see ever'one cran-
ing to get a look at us, and when we come into the dining-room
they had already started eating. But ever'one put down their
knife and fork when we walked up and took our seats at the
speakers' end of the table. They didn't know what to make of it.

And I wished you could of seen that fellow lay away the grub.
He ate like he was half-starved. He just ate up everything in
sight and was ready for more before anybody else had got good
and started. Ever'body was staring down in our direction, and I
was turning about seven different colors. I couldn't hardly eat,
myself, and I was kicking myself for a sucker all through the meal.

After the meal Gay Harrison got up and said, 'I don't believe
there are any visitors today, so we'll proceed with the business.'
Some of the boys began clearing their throat and laughing a
little, and I want to tell you I was about ready to sink right
through that floor. Then Gay says, 'Oh, I beg pardon. Harry
has a guest. Harry, will you introduce your guest.'

I could of kicked Gay around the block for the way he said
that, but I saw then that I was going to have to go on through
with it, so I gets up and kind of grins, and says, 'Well, boys, this
was all about as big a surprise to me as it was to you. And Gay
there is letting on like he didn't know nothing about it, but he
knows just as much as I do. About 11.30 I got a telephone call
from the Chief saying that he had an old ex-Rotarian in jail, and
that this fellow thought he had a message for us. I called up Gay

and he said it would be all right. So I want to introduce Oscar,'
I says, 'and if he'll get up now he can do his own explaining.'

I set down, and this bum, just as ragged and dirty as a Turk,
stood up. The boys clapped for him, but they was all about to
bust laughing. This bum just kind of looked around over the
table, and it got still enough so as you could of heard yourself
think. You talk about magnetism, R.A., well that man had it.
He used psychology on them. Nobody there knew any more
about him than I did, but he stopped that laughing, don't you
forget it.

I wish you could of heard that man talk. He started right in.

'Boys,' he says, 'you don't know me, and I guess none of you
care very much who I am, or what I was once upon a time. And
I'm not going to dwell on that,' he says. 'I came into your fair
city unannounced and I'll be lucky if I can go out the same way,'
he says. 'The way you see me now,' he says, 'I'm on the dog,
just a poor down-and-outer. But,' he says, 'I'm not here to play
on your sympathies. I just want to talk to you a little about
Rotary fellowship, and then I'm through,' he says.

'This morning I was setting in my jail cell meditating,' he says.
'You know that's one thing about being in jail, you get a chance
to do a lot of meditating,' he says. And then he went on to describe about how the early disciples of the Church had all spent
a lot of time in jail, and about how that had give them time to
do a lot of meditating, and that had a lot to do with the purity
and inspiration of their message, and so on and so forth. Well,
R.A., it seems like he was setting there meditating and all of a
sudden he got this inspiration that if he could just give a talk to
Rotary once more, he had a message for them that was worth
hearing.

'I used to be a member of Rotary in good standing,' he
says. 'I'm not going to say where it was, because that don't
make any difference,' he says. And then he talked a little

more and went on and recited that poem, you know that poem
that goes:

> I want to live in the house beside of the road,
>   And see the men go by,
> The men who . . .

Well, I don't remember now just how it goes, something like
that, but anyhow it ends up:

> I want to live in the house beside the road,
>   And be a friend of man.

This bum recited the whole poem from start to finish, and when
he got through, he says, 'Now, that poet had it all wrong,' he
says, 'because that's not Rotary. To be in keeping with Rotary
you have to get out in the middle of the road, and live out in the
middle of the road. You've got to be out in the middle of the road
meeting with men and *mixing* with men, if you're going to be a
friend of man,' he says. 'This old setting down beside of the road
watching men go past won't do at all,' he says.

Well, R.A., his talk was just full of sharp little points like that,
and they hit home, too. A pretty cute little stunt, I want to say.

Another place there he went on and told about how in a town
where he had been a Rotarian one time Rotary had taken all the
kiddies in town, all the poor kiddies, out on an outing out in the
woods. Well, he was a respectable business man back in those
days, and he was getting around among the kiddies, seeing that
they all had a good time, and he come across a little cripple boy
standing over by a tree just crying like his heart would break.

He went up to this little cripple boy and says, 'What's the
matter, sonny?'

And the little cripple boy sobbed out, 'Oh, I can't have any fun.
All the other kids can go around and get red lemonade and ice
cream cones and hot dogs and ever'thing, but I can't. I'm crippled.'

About that time he looks up and he sees a big strapping boy coming up, and he sneaks around on the other side of the refreshment tent to see what this big boy is going to say to this little cripple.

Well, the big boy come up and says, 'What's eatin' yuh, kid?' And the little cripple starts to crying again, and the big boy says, 'Aw, shucks! Come on here and get up on my back.' And he stooped over and got the little cripple up on his back and pretty soon he was loping him all over the picnic ground, handing him up soda pop and hot dogs and ever'thing and the little cripple was having just as good a time as anybody.

R.A., I'm right here to tell you that when that ragged bum finished that story ever'one around that table was a-sniffing and a-snubbing and making dabs at their eyes and trying to grin and make out like they wasn't crying at all. If any speaker ever had magnetism, that man certainly had it. The way he used that psychology on them wasn't even funny.

Well, he finished up by saying that all his message was that if he could just get us to live a little more like the Master Rotarian, and follow in His footsteps, his mission would be fulfilled, and, even if he was a ragged bum, he would 'a' done something worthwhile.

He says, 'Now, boys, you're going to forget me. I'm just a ragged old bum, and I'm going to pass out of your lives. But the idea of fellowship is what I wanted to get across today. The bums and the jailbirds need the grip of a manly hand sometimes. Fellowship, that's all!'

He says, 'Now I know what a lot of you boys been thinking I've been leading up to, but you're wrong. I'm not going to make any plea for money, or for aid of any kind. If you was to offer it to me, I wouldn't take your money. Because that wouldn't be Rotary. But just remember what I told you about fellowship, and try and be a little more like that Master Rotarian of long ago.'

Then he turned around quick and says to the Chief in a kind of tired-out voice, 'Come on, Chief, let's be going.'

The Chief got up and took him by the arm, and they had almost got to the door when old Cliff Oliphant — you know old Cliff, R.A., just as kind-hearted as they make them — jumped up with his eyes streaming tears and began trying to say something.

Well, the whole place was in a hub-bub, and I guess they would of passed the hat, if Gay Harrison hadn't stood up about that time and started to tapping on a glass with his knife. 'Hold on just a minute, boys,' Gay says. 'Hold on there just a minute.'

And then he beckoned to the Chief, and the Chief come leading the bum back to the head of the table.

'Boys,' Gay says, 'I want to introduce you to the Reverend Oscar D. Sneathen, pastor of the First Christian Church over at Garden City.'

The bum reached up and undid the safety pin at his coat collar and threw back his ragged old coat and showed that he had on a collar and tie and a suit just as good as any of us!

III

Well, R.A., we all just set around and goggled and nobody could say a word. It was a regular shock to us to find out that this ragged bum had been a respectable minister of the gospel all along.

And the funny part about it was, none of us suspicioned anything right up to the last. Nobody but Gay and the Chief had been in on the know. It fooled ever'one of us.

I mean, there we was, all ready to show our fellowship to this ragged bum, and shell out some coin if we had to make him take it, and it kind of hit us when we found out he couldn't use our money. But he certainly got his message across. It was a clever little stunt, just as cute as it could be.

Gay made a little talk, telling how Reverend Sneathen had

been going around over the State pulling this stunt at Rotary luncheons, and asked us not to give it away to no one, as that might spoil the effect somewheres else.

It done a lot of good, too, even if it was just a trick. I was talking to Otis Bailey, riding back to the office after it was all over, and he says to me, 'You know, Harry, that bum had it just about right, after all. We've got to get back to fundamentals in this country. After all, a bum is just a human being like us.'

Otis said he wasn't in favor of any new experimenting in this country, like this Dole's System and so on. But he said his point was that we couldn't just let these bums starve.

I told him, 'Sure, Otis, sure. And the way I look at it, that's right where some of this fellowship the speaker was talking about is going to go a long ways toward solving the situation.'

So that just goes to show you, R.A., how a clever little stunt like that can be a big inspiration by getting people to discussing a question.

To get back to what I come to see you about, though, R.A.: Reverend Sneathen is going around over the State putting on this little stunt at Rotary luncheons, and he's out to quite a little expense for traveling expenses and so on. Gay told me to draw $25 out of the entertainment fund for him, but there was only $3.65 left in the treasury after we sent that marble-contest kid to New Jersey to the finals last month. So we're asking the boys all to chip in a dollar or so apiece for the reverend.

It's a pretty cute little stunt he pulls off, all right. I wish you could of been there. I mean it would of give you something to think about, R.A. Well, R.A., give me a ring when it's anything in the insurance line.

SHERREL[1]

WHIT BURNETT

I DO NOT know whether I can do this thing or not. Maybe it is just a thought, maybe I just think it is necessary to do it. I mean about the name. I have thought about it a lot though and it keeps urging at me. It is not easy to understand. But I must try to understand and explain it.

You see, I actually did have a brother. People sometimes asked me, Are you the only boy in the family? And I've said, Yes. This wasn't a lie wholly. I was the first born in my family. But there were others, two others. One died in long clothes. We have his picture at home. The other was named Sherrel.

It is easy to remember him. My mother had us photographed together, for instance. And one especial print was transferred onto little smooth discs the size of a saucer. The discs fit into small twisted wire easels and my brother and I used to sit on the easel like that on my mother's bureau in the bedroom.

He was, as I said, younger than I. This is important. The neighbors used to say, It's the difference in their ages. They tried to explain in that way why I was so mean. And you can see the

---

difference clearly enough on the picture discs. We both stood by the photographer's chair, a plush chair. But I was up to the top of it. My brother's hand rested on the arm. It looks pretty small to me now because I'm twice as old as I was then. We both wore black velvet tam-o'-shanters and dark red velvet coats and pants. My mouth was a little open, too, looking at the photographer. I did not touch my brother. He had one hand, which was very small, on the chair, and the other one had hold of me. His hair was lighter than mine and softer and his eyes wider and bluer. He had a small mouth like a flower and it was smiling. He was a beautiful child. This was the brother I killed.

I am not telling you about a melodrama. I won't be arrested and hanged. I did not kill him yesterday. It was a long time ago, in fact, and I do not remember it all the time, only sometimes when something suggests the way I was then or when someone asks, Have you any other brothers? And I say, No. And here too in this other town at this school except for a girl I know I am quite alone in certain ways and in the winter as now I have seen any number of things to remind me. There is, for example, an epidemic of smallpox here and instead of smooth fast automobile hearses they still have funeral carriages that drag along slowly through the streets. Only once have I ridden in such a carriage. And that was then.

There are some things difficult to remember out of childhood. I do not remember when my brother was born. There was not so much difference then. Only four years before, I had been born. But I remember clearly when I was nine. My brother then was five. And we were two in the family. But I was the first.

Do you know how this is? Nine and five? Well, nine is somebody. Five is still curls. At nine I have seen something of the world. What have you seen at five? Go on, you can't come with us! Go on back to the house! We're going down to the store. You'll get run over. Go on, you can't play with us. You ain't big enough. Go on, grow up some before you come tagging around after us. Who asked you along? Beat it! I know how that is. I said all that, more brutally even. He didn't say anything. He didn't cry or whine or crab. I probably would have. He stopped following simply, and stood there. And then we ran off. He stood alone. Sometimes I found him other places alone, sitting still in a corner thinking quietly about something. I am always a little puzzled now I am older. I have talked it over with others. He would have been important . . . But at nine one is a weed, growing wild. Five is still in the hothouse.

We lived near the sand hills. It wasn't until several years later that I really got into the hills exploring them with a cousin of my own age. Sherrel never did get there. And there was a great liking in both of us for the hills, his maybe different from mine. I often found him sitting dreaming looking at them. But one day late in the spring the hills in a way came down to our house. A cloudburst drenched them, rolling down soft sand, cutting great ditches in the road in front of our place. We weren't long in discovering that, I'll tell you. When Sherrel wandered out of the kitchen the ditch was full of us kids. It was a peach of a ditch as high as our head, gnawed with caves and dangers.

I started the discoveries. There's some hole, I yelled. And down I had gone, doing what the others wanted to do, the first to absorb their wishes. Then they followed, yelling too. Sherrel, I suppose, could hear my voice coming up out of the ground. He came over to the ditch and looked down, standing alone above us. Go on back, I shouted, you'll fall in. He moved away. I paid no more attention then to him and the rest of us ran racing, hiding, searching, together in the wash.

And then, separated from the others for a moment or so, I noticed something odd about my hands. Hey, kids, I cried, lookee! Look at my hands! They looked. They stood back in wonderment. They looked at their own hands. No, they couldn't, they said. It was something funny. Look what Martin can do! Lookee, he can peel off his hands! It was true, something had happened to my hands. I took hold and pulled off long shreds of skin. I amazed them all. They stood astounded.

Let me see, said somebody. It was Sherrel.

Say, I yelled, didn't I say not to come down here? You ain't big enough to be in this here ditch! Let me see your hands, he said. The kids were all looking at me. I'll let you see, all right! I said. He stood his ground and didn't go. That makes me mad, I felt. No, I said. I took him by the shoulder and talked straight in his face, hard. How many times do I have to tell you to get out of this ditch! He turned around and walked up the gorge to a shallower spot and climbed slowly out.

A day or so later Sherrel stayed in bed. There's something the matter with him, my mother said. She didn't know what. Then he took a high fever, they said, and was delirious. I thought it was strange about delirious. Sherrel's eyes were shut and he looked as if he was sleeping but he was talking without any sense. We'll have to have a doctor, my mother said. And that afternoon the doctor came to our house, wiping his feet at the door and entering with a serious look. Let's see the other young fellow, he said. Anything wrong with him? He had a little sore throat, my mother said, but he's all right. He looked down my throat. Look at my hands, I said, ain't they funny?

What I thought, he said.

The same afternoon a man from downtown came and nailed up a yellow flag. It was a cloth sign saying, black on orange, *Scarlet Fever*. I couldn't go out of the yard. That's sure tough, the kids said, peering through the pickets. I even had to keep back from the fence, too. It was catching.

I sat on the steps fronting north from our bare two room brick house and looked at the hills. I had had the Scarlet Fever and hadn't even known it. Why, my mother said, he was playing

around all the time. Why, he was out there playing in the ditch
with all those children. That's bad, said the doctor. But my
brother was worse. He had it good.

I remember the windows in the front room were darkened and
my mother never went to bed. She never took her clothes off.
And my father didn't go to work. My aunt came to the fence with
a bag of oranges and bananas. How is he? she asked. If he isn't
any better Doctor Anderson says he'd better have a consultation,
said my mother. How is Doctor Anderson? asked my aunt. He
is the best doctor in town, my mother said.

I sat in the sun all tired now and weak. But I wasn't sick. I
was big and nine.

I remember the consultation. There were four doctors in the
kitchen standing around and talking low and sitting down and
getting up. I could see in from outside. My mother was nervous
and walking around and my father, who was a big heavy man,
stood around too and sat down and then got up. They were waiting for something definite they spoke of that I could not understand. It was the Crisis. I asked what it was, and my mother had
said, Sherrel will get better then. I didn't know what a Crisis
would be like and I opened the door slowly and got into the house
quietly, past the doctors.

My father and mother were in the front room by the bed where
Sherrel lay. He was still and wasn't talking deliriously. And then
my mother, who was standing by him with my father waiting,
suddenly cried terribly for a minute or so, and she then took hold
of my father and pulled him down by the bed to the floor. I
didn't know what was happening. I was frightened, too. Pray,
she sobbed. Pray, if you never prayed before. O God, she began
... and she was crying more and more. My father was kneeling
heavily and strangely in a big dark bulk. He put his arm around
my mother. There, there, he said. I never saw them like that before. My father is English, my mother is German. I did not think

about that though then. I thought, I am scared; this is all different, and dark. I stood in the doorway, too frightened to move.

Come in, Martin, my mother suddenly cried out to me. Come in to your brother. Come here with us. I came over, and there we were all kneeling down together.

Do you want your brother to die? she asked. No, I said. I was frightened at her, at the strange heavy silence on my father, at my brother even. Go and look at him, she told me.

I got up and looked at my brother's white face. It was like a face of ivory with pale lips. I looked hard. He was different too. What do I do? I thought. I am rough, not like that. My mother is looking at me terribly. Kiss him. I bent over and touched his face. His lips opened with a quiet breath, like a little flower bursting on my cheek.

The crisis came and passed. It came while we were in the room there. My mother could not wait. She went to the bed, trying to wake up my brother. Look, Sherrel, she whispered, we are going to get you the nice pearl-handled pocketknife tomorrow. You won't have to wait till Christmas. Tomorrow. You just get well, now. Sherrel! Do you hear me Sherrel?

Or, he can have mine, I thought.

But he didn't hear us. He didn't hear anybody. Then my mother went to sleep suddenly, it seemed, and drooped down by the bed and they put her in the other room on a couch.

I stood in the dark by a curtain when the doctors came in. Too bad, said Dr. Anderson. He leaned over my brother. Remarkable head, said one of the others. Isn't it! spoke up another one. Artist's head, said the one with the beard. Yes ... Then the doctors walked out together into the room where my mother was and in a little while they all left the house.

A few days later there were the strange preparations for the funeral. I don't want to dwell on the funeral. That is not the point. But we rode in a carriage shut in by ourselves, still quarantined, the others following slowly behind us. I remember we passed the Watsons' place. They were standing at the gate, the family, staring stupidly at the procession as the horse carriages jogged down the hilly street rolling off to the cemetery.

This is all strange, I thought, riding along past the Watsons' house in a carriage like this. My mother and my father and myself. I was taken up with the thought and looked back out of the carriage window now and then at the carriages behind me. My mother pulled me back to sit up straight. My mother's face was drawn and tired and she was crying. My father's eyes had tears in them too. I could not cry. I thought, I ought to cry. How can I cry? I am not hurt any place where I can feel. I squeezed into the corner of the carriage opposite them, pressing up against one hand hard to make it hurt. It turned numb and pained but not in a crying way. You cry easy differently, I thought. Onions, for instance, make you cry. Would it have been a trick, I thought, or right and honest if I had put an onion in my handkerchief, no one seeing me, and then smelt it now and then in the curtained shadows of the carriage? I would have cried then. I wanted to cry. But all I could think was, Sherrel was a queer kid. Were we brothers sure enough? Am I anybody's brother? Why don't I cry? . . .

You see, he would sit in a corner quiet and fraily beautiful. I was nine and active. It's the difference in their ages. Maybe so. There were the Elwell brothers, now. They were twins. They had a carpenter's shop. It was a peach of a shop, down in a cellar, and they worked together great, making book-ends and rabbit hutches and things like that.

I gave him that sickness. I knew that. That killed him. That is why my brother is dead. But I am trying to remember, to clear things up. I am trying to remember if I thought that then. I remember I thought, It's funny just he got it. Why not Leona Eads, Ed or Billy Simons? They touched my hands. I wondered if I hadn't forced my sickness on my brother out of hatred for him, out of my own peculiar older-brother hatred. Did I slap him, maybe strike him in the face with my peeling hand? Perhaps I did. I wondered over this for many weeks now and then.

I'm not even sure now. I might have. It's funny how mean, you see, a person can be. I've thought of that. I've got a girl. I've talked things over with her, not everything, but generally you know. She doesn't like meanness either. I remember when I was about twelve, my sister was just coming along then. She was about two and I had to tend her occasionally. I didn't like it. Once my mother said to me, Do you want your little sister to die too? Well, no, I said. She might even have said, Do you want to kill your little sister too? Maybe this was it, because I asked myself that a lot later, trying to be better. I said, Do you want to kill your sister too? No, I said.

I didn't, either. But I remembered what I'd said when she was born. I said, There's enough in this family already. But I didn't want to kill her. Still I had killed my brother. I had killed Sherrel. Not only by giving him sickness. But by meanness.

This is how I figure it now. I killed my brother by meanness. And it is too bad. I wouldn't do it now. I am not that way. I could have got him a job here in this other town where I am now after he got out of school. I'll be out of school here pretty soon. I'm eighteen next week. Then I'll go on a paper where I've got a stand-in. I'd have said, Now you keep on at school and read a lot of good things, good books you know, poetry and good things and learn how to write. You've got good stuff in you, I can tell. You're going to be an artist. So am I. We'll be two artists, brothers, maybe different, but we can help each other. You've got a poetic style, and I've got a stronger style. I see things more as they are. I'm a little tougher. I can digest more. But that's all right. When I get going, I'll help you. You've got fine things in you. I'll help you bring them out.

That's the kind of a person he would have been. He would have been an artist. There's nothing any bigger than that. Nothing finer. It's the best, in a holy way. It has to be in you first. It hides sometimes and doesn't get a chance to come out where people are.

I've talked that over with people, with that girl I spoke of. I want to be an artist. A writer. I can see back from where I am, though. I've been pretty mean, pretty contemptible. It's funny to look back like that and see yourself in old pictures and things. It's hard to think you had the same name, even.

And that's what I'm puzzling over now. There's nothing wrong with my name, actually. Mark. Mark Stowe. It was first Martin. It was even Martin Tilton Stowe. I didn't like it. All that, I mean. I cut it down to Mark Stowe. It made me feel surer, quicker, stronger.

But even that doesn't quite go. It doesn't all fit. I'm not all blunt, like that. Mark. Mark Stowe. I've got other things. I've written poems, even, and I wouldn't kiss a girl hard. I know how my brother was. He would have been like that too, only a lot more.

And, you know, about the name . . . My folks are getting along now. Sisters don't count, the way I mean, that is. I'm the only boy in the family. And I've been thinking, what if I should write a poem, a long, good one — here I am, alive and everything — and sign it not Mark Stowe but, well Sherrel Stowe? Do you see what I mean? And then by and by there would be another poem, and after a while I would just go ahead and use it right along. Can you understand that? How I would be more him too, then — Sherrel?

NAPOLEON'S HAT UNDER

GLASS[1]

MANUEL KOMROFF

IN THE gorgeous palace of Fontainebleau, just outside of Paris, on an embroidered silk cushion in a glass case, rests Napoleon's hat. This is the very hat he wore when returning from Elba he saluted his gathering army ... the army that he led into the field of Waterloo. But all this was many years ago, over a hundred years ago, guides say when they conduct the large parties of visitors through the palace.

And before this glass case with its showpiece of history now stood a newly married peasant couple from the country. She was a rosy-cheeked farmer's daughter and he was the son of a farmer in southern France. This was their honeymoon.

They stood before the glass case. She fingered her colored ribbons and he stared at the black felt hat in the case. Their red faces and big red hands were reflected in the glass. Their bodies seemed to sway just as they had swayed that very week when the village priest stood before them and recited the marriage vows.

'He was the greatest man in the world,' she said.

[1] Copyright, 1933, by Whit Burnett and Martha Foley. From *A Story Anthology, 1931–1933*, edited by Whit Burnett and Martha Foley. The Vanguard Press, 1933.

'Yes, he was a great man. He was Emperor of almost the whole world.'

'May his soul rest in peace.'

'It must be a hard job to be an Emperor. I don't think I would like it. Too many papers and documents to read, and everything is ... like in the Fall of the year when we have to close ourselves in the house and the leaves become crisp and brittle. It don't seem natural to be an Emperor, does it?'

'Sure not, Emil. It must be very hard. But I think you could do anything you wanted to do. Nobody dreamed you would have the chicken house finished this Summer, especially with all the trouble we had with the old wine barrels that leaked and the bugs on the vegetables. But an Emperor don't have to read many papers. They tell him what it says and all he must do is to sign his name. And you can do that, can't you, Emil?'

'Sure.'

'But it would be harder for me, Emil. This would be a nice place to live. But the servants would be watching you all day long. I would hate to have strange people watching me; but if you were the Emperor I would just have to do it and say nothing.'

'Do what, Marie?'

'Oh, just do everything. Watch the kitchen to see that the rascals did not steal, and do the things that ladies do, like making up the beds and sewing up new dresses. And taking care of the house.'

'It must be a hard job to be an Emperor. I don't think I would like it.'

'If you wanted to be, I am sure you could be anything you like. You are so strong — and I love you so much.'

At length they moved away from the glass case containing Napoleon's hat, and walked out into the gardens. Here they ate their lunch and looked into each other's eyes.

After a long silence she looked up and said: 'You know, Emil, we should go back to the Palace before it closes and see the hat again.'

'Poor Napoleon,' Emil said.

'Yes. It is so sad. He was once Emperor of the whole world, almost, and now he is dead.'

They walked back to have another look at the hat. And in the morning, under the pretext that it was on the way to the station, they went again and had a last gaze at Napoleon's hat under glass.

On the train she sighed: 'It was a wonderful honeymoon, wasn't it, Emil.'

'Sure.'

Then she whispered in his ear, 'I love you, Emil.'

He sat up straight and held her red hand. 'I — thought maybe you loved Napoleon.'

'Oh, yes, but that is different, Emil.'

'How different?'

'Well, he is dead and I feel so sorry for him — it is so sad. He was such a great man and it is such a hard job to be an Emperor. You said yourself it was — you know you did.'

'Yes, I said so, Marie, but I was thinking of myself and not Napoleon. It was easy for him because he always . . . well, he was all the time doing something big . . . he was a general. It is easy for a general to do all kinds of things.'

'He was very brave and that is why . . .'

'That's why you love him.'

'I love you, too, Emil. I want you to be a great man and have people save your hat and . . . but not to be the Emperor.'

Emil was jealous of Napoleon. He kept looking out of the train window watching the green fields and the long rows of tall poplars.

In the evening they were back on the farm. The fragrance of the green shrubbery and the loose damp earth filled their nostrils. In places the grass had grown during their absence. Here was a chance for a second harvest and they lost no time in removing their holiday clothes and getting back into their large comfortable wooden shoes. The shoes that have stamped down the fields of France for centuries. There was only an hour or two before sundown.

At night as they lay in bed breathing heavily, she whispered: 'Oh, Emil, it is so good to be home again.'

He pressed her hand.

'It must be hard to live in a palace,' she added.

Again he pressed her hand.

'And so sad.'

'You are thinking of the dead Emperor's hat!' He let go her hand.

'No, Emil, I was thinking only foolishness. I love you, Emil.'

She put her arms about him and he kissed her eyes and fleshy cheeks and her moist red mouth — moist with the dew of the earth.

And Napoleon never came between them again. Only once did he again appear before them. This happened about a year later when Emil became the proud father of a baby boy.

'He is a prize baby,' said the father.

And she tickled the child under the chin and added: 'We will put him on exhibition ... under glass.'

Then they went through all the names of the ancient kings and Emperors that they could recall, but to their rural ears each sounded foreign and sad.

The grapes were ripe and there was much work to be done around the place, but at odd moments they deliberated and often thought of Napoleon's hat in the show case. But in the end they named their little son John.

THE SHEPHERD OF THE LORD[1]

PETER NEAGOE

THE Lord has many sheep. Through the mouth of his chosen ones he commanded them to go and multiply like the sands of the seas. They are multiplying.

Popa Anghel Boyer is a shepherd of the Lord. A strong man Popa Anghel. The peasants rise when he passes and the women kiss his large hand; the left hand pats the young woman's cheek as she bends her forehead on his right hand. The old he blesses, laying a heavy blessing hand on their bent head. Popa Anghel's boots are shiny and squeak proudly, as the shepherd stamps along the street. When there is a wind his long mustaches are flowing streamers, black and shiny. But his spade-shaped beard, large and thick, flattens like an armor plate against his heavy chest. His long locks fall in curls over a neck, round and strong as a tree-trunk. The wide, muscle-padded shoulders carry easily Popa Anghel's head.

Popa Anghel handles his four oxen with easy grace. The grace of power. Shouting to the heavy, long-horned animals keeps his voice alive. He sings in church and the saints on the windows

---

[1] Copyright, 1935, by Coward-McCann, Inc. From *Winning a Wife*, by Peter Neagoe. Coward-McCann, 1935.

tremble. He booms his sermons upon his congregation, and his words like waves against the breasts of the faithful. The candle flames stretch and shrink, waver and blink, when Popa Anghel booms his sermons in the house of the Lord.

Popa Anghel's wife (priestess Andronica, the peasants call her) is wide-hipped, tall, full-chested. Generous breasts tremble maternally on her full chest when Andronica laughs. Her face and eyes laugh together and the breasts rock in unison. Her skin is smooth as velvet, and her hands white and plump, her voice molten honey. A sweetly fragrant burden in Popa Anghel's powerful arms. 'You crush my bones, you holy bear,' she pants as Popa Anghel holds her, his face against her white throat.

The house is large, the beds are fields of linen and virgin wool. Sweet mint and incense permeate the air of their nest. Popa Anghel's and Andronica's nest.

Popa Anghel has cattle, large-flanked, sleek and strong. Cows, oxen, horses, a bull and a stallion. For in animals the shepherd of the Lord favors the male; in his own species he loves the female.

Popa Anghel has two daughters, Elizabeth and Maria. Priests' wives and daughters are splendid females. The Transylvanian peasant has good eyes. 'She could marry a priest,' he says of a beautiful girl. Elizabeth was seventeen then and Maria fourteen. Elizabeth was not a big girl — but she was plump — feeding on hallowed bread, honey and milk — and her skin was rosy and smooth. Her voice was full and her laughter rippled. The smell of ripe fruit, and her skirt was always snow-white. The colorful aprons she wore had choice designs. The sleeves of her shirt were very full and puffed out from the shoulder to the wrists, where they gathered in an embroidered band, to emerge again in ruffled cuffs. But the wrist-band was loose and when Elizabeth lifted her arms, the sleeves fell back to her very shoulders, a wreath of whiteness from which emerged the pink arms.

But Maria was my friend. She was fourteen and I fifteen. Here my story starts.

Popa Anghel's stone barns are veritable labyrinths. The fragrance of hay and straw seeped into the stone. Even the dust in Popa Anghel's barn is scented. Elizabeth, Maria, myself and two or three village boys played at hide-and-seek there during two of my summer vacations. I hid in the hay, dug myself into the straw and flattened out in some cozy corner. To be found by Maria was the greatest pleasure of my heart. By the time she came upon me Maria was exhausted, had to rest. She would sit down close to me; I would touch her cool arm in the darkness of our hiding-place. At such times we talked in whispers, close to each other, and Maria's breath was sweeter than the fragrance of ripe straw. She often bent so close to my face that the ringlets of her black hair touched my face.

It was the time when I began to feel that girls are very splendid creatures, Maria their queen. The mere sight of Maria, walking across the yard, her apron flaring, released such flow of life in me that I could have jumped over the house or lifted one of the oxen on my back. When we walked side by side, our hands coming together, our fingers timidly embracing, there was a splendor on every object. My eyes were keen as an eagle's. The merest sounds were music. The immense mystery of life gushed from and through everything.

We loved the brook in which we waded. Maria's feet gleaming pink on the shimmering pebbles of its bed — and the water gurgled in its rush. We smiled upon the flowers in the fields and threw ourselves upon the warm ground inhaling the cool scent of the grass we crushed with our bodies. We loved the sparrows who stole kernels from the sheaves stored in the barn. We loved them as we loved the stars and even God, who, we knew, was up in the sky, seeing everything that happened on the earth.

But we knew, Maria and I, that we were the very core of everything, and God looked upon us from above, with grace and love. He was our father.

Maria referred to her own father as Popa Anghel, because the villagers called him so. Maria feared Popa Anghel more than she feared God, because this powerful man lorded over his family with great zest. He was so fond of practical jokes, that in church, he swung the incense-chalice, filled with glowing embers, dangerously near to the mayor's nose. But everybody knew the mayor to be a miser and a tyrant, despite the great piety he showed on Sundays.

In his gold-embroidered priestly garb, Popa Anghel looked very big. He smacked the bundle of sweet mint, soaked in holy water, on the heads of his parishioners with great relish. He kept a serious face but his spade-shaped black beard seemed to laugh as it spread over the shimmering surplice. Often his large mustache pushed out from under his nose as if mocking at someone, just when Popa Anghel raised his hand, with two fingers closed, the other three symbolizing the Holy Trinity.

I noticed that when young women kissed Popa Anghel's hand he would press it against their lips, before they could bow their forehead upon it as the custom is. When he prayed over some young widow whose husband had been taken by the Lord, his hand would caress the woman's cheeks as he adjusted his peplum over her head. But he uttered his prayer in clear words, in a soothing sing-song, so the woman was comforted and left the shelter of the holy peplum refreshed, but with flushed cheeks.

But Popa Anghel did not like the mayor, nor could he bear the mayor's son, a tall square-shouldered young man of twenty, who followed Elizabeth everywhere. This young man, Jacob, was dark and somber of looks, but he smiled so ingratiatingly that mothers of marriageable girls sighed and shook their heads when he did so. But Jacob had no eyes for other girls; only for

Elizabeth. Now I have learned some things — since those days
— so I know that Elizabeth was a great beauty.

Elizabeth was then about seventeen; not tall but of such
grace that even old men turned to look upon her, when she
passed them in the street. And she had a way of changing the
expression of her violet-blue eyes from coldest haughtiness to a
melting warmth which nobody could resist. That is why Jacob
could not live a day without seeing her. For this reason, he
became great friends with me. Passing Popa Anghel's, he would
drop in to call me with every kind of pretext. One time to show
me a thrush he caught that very morning, another time to give
me a new sheath for my belt knife, but more often to ask me into
the fields to help him at some work — which I always loved to do.

I was flattered by Jacob's friendship, because he was stronger
than the other peasants and the best wrestler in the village, not
to mention his dancing. Every girl in the village loved to dance
the reel with him. In the first slow steps of this old dance, the
man barely touches the waist of the two girls — his dancing
partners — while, moving slowly to the right and to the left, he
improvises in rhyme. A satire on someone or some commonly
known event, but more often the man chants out in verse his
heart's yearning. Decided skill is needed to do this, for lacking
that, the poor man will only betray his feelings, to the amusement
of the assembly. Jacob had remarkable skill for this kind of im-
provising. He sang his praises to his adored one, comparing her
to the moon — queen of the stars; to the sun, whose light and
warmth is our life, placing himself, the adorer, in a sad or happy
relation to the symbol of his worship, according to the condition
of his heart at the time.

Everybody listened to Jacob's rhyming, and mothers of lovely
girls attributed his affection to their own daughters. Each one
secretly of course. And many of the girls blushed and blinked to
hide a tear. But I knew to whom Jacob was singing — I did not

even have to look at Elizabeth to know it. And Elizabeth never betrayed her feelings to anybody but myself, and to me only by occasional glances at me. Her big violet-blue eyes remained otherwise screened by their long black lashes.

My admiration for Jacob was especially strong because he could handle a long whip with uncanny skill. He could crack the whip so it sounded like a pistol shot, and by lashing it back and forth, without once striking the ground, he produced with it a succession of reports like that of exploding firecrackers. But what mostly amazed one was the manner in which he would strike down a fruit from the tree. He swung the whip around, then with a quick jerk of the hand would lash the stem of the fruit and bring it to the ground.

In a whip duel he always disarmed his opponent. With frowning eyes he watched for the favoring moment, to lash the whip-handle of his adversary and jerk it out of his hand. The aim of a whip duel is no other than such disarming of the opponent.

Jacob was very generous towards me. He gave me his finest whip, thick as my wrist at the handle, tapering so gently towards the leash that it became twelve feet in length. Jacob had pleated this whip himself, in four strands of white hemp, strong and shining as silk. The handle was hickory, smooth as polished ivory on the upper end but rough, for a better hold, at the lower.

Under Jacob's rigorous tutoring, I succeeded after four weeks in managing the splendid weapon as well as Jacob. So well in fact did I handle the whip, that one day I strangled a crow with it. The poor bird stood perched on a lump of sod in a newly plowed field, its beak in the air and the head tilted to one side. I aimed at the bird's neck. The deadly leash coiled round it, with a snap — and the bird fell over with open beak.

It may have been mere chance, but Jacob praised me for the accuracy of my aim and I felt prouder than Caesar.

Jacob could sing well, in a clear tenor. My voice had broken already and was settling in a deep baritone. Jacob taught me many folk-songs. On evenings we walked up and down the village street, singing in duet.

On a warm night in August, Jacob gathered six or seven young peasants and we went in front of Popa Anghel's house. It was dark but the air was full of the fragrance of the fields. We sat down under the locust tree and began singing. Softly, sadly, an endless tune. Occasionally a breeze would stir the foliage, rendering more sad, even, the melancholy monotone of our song.

I became sadder and sadder under the influence of the night and the never ending song. At length I burst out crying. Jacob, near whom I was seated, put his arm around my shoulders. My crying became a real lament, for with tears in my voice, I kept my place with the singers. Suddenly, Jacob's voice broke also. Then the other fellows' voices caught, and the chorus sounded like a group of mourners.

How long we kept up our wailing, no one could tell, but a rude shock, a terrific donkey-braying, came suddenly, cutting into our lamentation. This unholy braying poured down upon us, from one of the windows in the priest's house. We stopped instantly. We could see nothing, but all guessed that it must be Popa Anghel himself — who indeed it was. For, after his ghastly braying, the priest thundered out in his booming voice:

'Pheu, Satan, may the holy cross kill you! Go back, devil, unto the flaming bowels of hell. Don't disturb the peace of one anointed unto the Lord.'

We crawled off softly on all fours. Once in the street, we took natural positions again and ran away on tiptoes.

Maria told me in the morning that both she and Elizabeth had heard us and cried until their pillows were soaked with tears. Only later she told me that when they heard the braying of their father they got cramps from laughing.

Being at Popa Anghel's, I saw everything that came to pass

there. But the peasants say: 'It is easier to watch a flock of rabbits than a woman in love.' This is gospel truth. I never noticed anything about Elizabeth until one day, going into the barn, I saw something. But what I saw shall never pass my lips. I am honor-bound never to tell a soul. Elizabeth made me swear and then kissed me and pressed me to her heart. For the kiss alone and for her embrace I would keep the secret eternally, not to mention Elizabeth's violet-blue eyes, as they implored me.

In the spring, soon after Easter, Popa Anghel married his daughter Elizabeth to the school teacher. A very handsome young man, with curly black hair, so genuinely patriotic that even now he wears the Roumanian garb on Sundays.

When I arrived in the summer, Elizabeth was marvelously beautiful. She was not as rosy of color as before but a heavenly light shone in her eyes. She was loved, and the peasants said, her husband carried her about on his palms. The school teacher was an ardent lover indeed, for Elizabeth seemed to have forgotten Jacob, who was in the army. When he came for two weeks' leave in August, Jacob only spoke of books. He never mentioned his love. Before we parted he said: 'When I come back from the service, I will go into the mountains to herd our sheep. Don't you see, Peter, the village is so small. It is sad, so small it is.'

I soon forgot my sorrow for Jacob, because to me the village was a gay song; for Maria was there.

We were big enough — Maria and I — to take our amusements otherwise than as children, but we did not. We ran about in bare feet, climbed trees, played in the barn and wandered in the woods. What we both enjoyed most was swinging in the barn. The swing was made of two heavy ropes, attached to the very peak of the barn roof. Usually I sat on the board of the swing while Maria, standing facing me, drove it by bending from the knees and straightening up with a push. We often touched the edge of the roof on both sides. When we swung so fast Maria's skirts flared, catching my head in its folds, and she laughed so much at this that she had to ease her swinging. I was never sorry for that, because then I could tickle her knee, and the smooth spot right in the back of it. All she could do was to wriggle with strident shouts of laughter. When we heard the tramping of Popa Anghel in the yard, we quickly slid off the swing and disappeared in the hay.

But this last summer of my stay at Popa Anghel's, the skies of my happiness began to cloud; Maria grew too fast. She had passed fifteen, and was one inch taller than myself. This was terrible enough in itself, but Maria made it worse. She adopted a protective air towards me — like a big sister managing a frail brother. I had to resort to cunning and the privileges of my sex to offset Maria's patronizing. And often did it at the expense of my feelings.

One of the things I did was — when the horse was needed in the fields — to mount the horse, bareback, and ride proudly through the gate, opened for me by Maria. In the street I set the horse trotting, then goaded him to a clumsy gallop, knowing that Maria was watching and envying me. She could ride the horse as well as I could (she insisted that she did it better, but I never believed her) but the horse was round as a barrel and too much of Maria's bare legs showed from under her skirts for Andronica's approval. Once she had tears in her eyes when she pointed to my trousers saying, 'It is easy for you in those ugly things.' She threw a twig at my head as I trotted out of the yard, haha-ing her. Another time she swished a handful of nettles between the horse's legs and I had to flatten out on him and hold on to his mane. Maria shrieked with joy. Arrived in the fields I worked with the peasants. At noon Maria and two women came with baskets of food. On such occasions Maria never failed to ask me, even coax me, to go back with her and take my luncheon with

the family. Of course I refused, spending a miserable day thinking of her.

But I wanted to show Maria my independence; to show her
how easily I did without her company. In truth, however,
neither the flushed faces of the working girls nor the movements
of their bodies (clad only in a full linen shirt with a belt and two
aprons) consoled me. In fact their laughing and singing increased
my longing for Maria.

At first this stratagem of mine worked very well. Maria told
me that the day was much too long for her without me. But
Maria was much more clever than I thought. Soon she came to
consider my behavior as a childish caprice and told me to my face
that I was not as smart as I imagined. I had to look for other
means, to promote my superiority. An opportunity came.
Being wealthy, Popa Anghel had a bull and a stallion. They were
used for breeding the cows and mares of the villagers. Popa
Anghel called the stallion Nestor. No one but himself was
allowed to exercise Nestor. Daily Popa Anghel would lead the
splendid animal into the yard. A heavy pleated halter on the
stallion's head and a long rope attached to it were the only means
of control used by the priest. Nestor had flaming eyes, a long tail
and a wealth of mane. As soon as he came into the yard he let
out a terrific neighing, arched his neck, whipped his tail and
began prancing. The priest gave him rope, turning on his trunk-
like legs, in the center of a circle formed by the galloping stallion.
Nestor's body was steel-gray. It shone like polished metal. His
black tail and mane flared with his movements. His hoofs,
slender, high, trimmed and carefully filed, were like ivory. He
had a way of picking up his feet as if the ground under them was
red hot. His thin ankles were springs of steel. Popa Anghel, in
his thick, gurgling voice, would talk adoringly to Nestor. 'There,
beauty, there, my brave one, limber up your limbs. Now, now!

Not so rough, my hero; there are no devils here. You can beat the very devil, my boy, so you can, my beauty.'

The spade-shaped beard bobbed up and down on the priest's chest as he spoke.

Popa Anghel loved fecundity. Nestor and the bull were to him symbols of male power and fructifying force. He would caress the bull's flanks, press his face against the shining hide and inhale deeply its odor. The bull would roll his eyes with animal wonderment and stretch his enormous neck. Lifting his massive head, he released, from the depths of his huge body, trombone-like sounds. The priest laughed, answering: 'Yes, my boy, sure — just as you say,' and slapped the bull's belly.

There was a small yard in back of the barns. Wall-enclosed. Nestor and the bull performed their fructifying duties there. Popa Anghel assisted with ritual officiousness, talking admiringly, encouragingly, to Nestor or the bull, as the occasion required, one or the other. But, as soon as a peasant came, with cow or mare, the priest boomed out his order, that all female folk retire into the house. 'Maria — there girl — get in! What are you gaping at, your mouth open as the barn door? Run in to your mother.' Maria had to run into the house at once. But she looked at me enviously and angrily, because I could stay in the yard until the animal was led through the barn gates into the — sanctum; there I was not allowed to enter.

But, reconnoitering in the barn loft, I had found a square ventilator, way up near the roof. It was large enough for me to squeeze through, so that, without being seen from the yard below, I could watch the ceremony. So one day when I saw the mayor come with his mare, I sneaked into the barn. Nobody had seen me. I heard Popa Anghel talking to the mayor. Then he told him to lead the mare — 'In there, you know,' he shouted; adding, 'she's a fine one, your mare.'

I clambered to my post of vantage. Soon I heard Nestor's

tramping on the barn floor. I looked down. The mayor was holding the mare by the bridle.

'Tie her to that post, man! Get away. Want your bones crushed?' shouted the priest. Hurriedly the mayor wound the rope around the post, slipped it through an iron ring and knotted it. Then he ran along the wall into the barn.

Seeing the mare, Nestor let out a piercing neigh and reared on his hind legs. He pushed his tail out straight, then he whipped it so it hissed. The mare flattened her ears, neighing and dancing. Popa Anghel gave rope to the stallion, dodging him: 'Not too rough, my hero; gently, my boy! Now, you devil, don't murder her,' he shouted. Nestor was biting the mare's neck, rearing up and away, when neighing she snapped back at him. Then he pawed the ground, snorting furiously. I heard a noise under his belly as of a club beating on a kettle-drum. Bam, bam, bam, it went, Nestor pawing and snorting. The priest's spade-shaped beard danced on his chest, a thick laugh rumbling out of him.

'Back there!' he shouted to the mayor, who sidled nearer to the scene.

Nestor reared up. His front legs gripped the mare's flanks. The mare danced and neighed — ears flattened — snapping at the stallion's head, as he was mouthing her mane with outstretched lips. Suddenly, resting his whole weight against the mare's body, the stallion set to pummeling her with his front legs. I feared that the savage animal would kill the poor mare, who was being sacrificed to his ferocious passion.

'His little love-play,' grunted the priest over his shoulder to the mayor. Now the 'love-play' stopped. For one instant both animals were still; then I saw Nestor's huge body well up, like a menacing swell, from rump to neck.

'Aha — my hero,' grumbled Popa Anghel.

Leaving my peep-hole, I slid from the straw into the hay, fifteen feet below, where I sank, up to my shoulders. I stood there awaiting my breath, before trying to crawl out, when I heard something stirring in the hay — quite close to me. I listened. Someone was crawling towards me. Then I heard Maria's voice whispering: 'I saw you.'

'Very well, if you did,' I answered as softly.

'Where have you been?' she added, very close to me.

'Up there.'

'Up where?'

'There on top of the straw.' I pointed.

'Just so? What were you doing there?' Maria insisted.

'I? What should I do? Climbed on the straw!'

'To see what?'

'To see? What should I see there? It is dark, on top there.'

'There is a shaft of light; I saw it from ...' She pointed back.

'Yes! Well, there is a bit of light coming in,' I admitted.

'One can look down there.' She pointed towards the back of the barn.

'Maybe.'

'Did you look?' Maria put her mouth close to my ear. This irritated me. She was too insistent and had a manner of questioning which I could not dodge.

'Yes, I did, if you want to know,' I answered brusquely.

'You did — ? Well — if father knew that!'

She certainly was exasperating. I felt my face blushing; my eyes smarted with tears of anger. Whenever we discussed anything Maria had the upper hand of me. Her manner befogged my brain, so that I had to wait too long for the proper answer; she profited by my silence, to cram my head with a lot of words, confusing me still more.

But this time a light had come to me. With cruel relish I snapped at her: 'And why weren't you in the house? Didn't Popa Anghel order you in?'

'No — he did not.' She pulled herself up coldly.

I was not abashed: 'Did he send you in here?' I asked with mock sweetness.

'Oh' — she moaned, 'you are just a bad, vicious, little urchin!' And stretching out on the hay, she cried softly.

I could see her shoulders shake. Something sagged, in the very core of me. I felt limp. With great effort I crawled out. Putting my face close to Maria's head, I began repeating: 'What have I done? What have I done?' She covered her ears, her shoulders shaking the more with stifled sobbing.

I repeated these four words so often, that at length they seemed very stupid to me, in the presence of Maria's grief. I fell silent. I put my hand on her head. Her hair was soft, alive. Her head seemed to beat against my finger-tips, like a heart. That made me terribly sad and compassionate with Maria. Leaning my face softly against her head, I began to cry also. We cried together, like that, for a long time.

At length, a feeling of lightness, a strange happiness invaded me, like the return of health in convalescence. With each passing moment my well-being increased. And not only had my sense of smell become keen and refined, but my entire body was now as sensitive to touch as my finger-tips.

I felt the fragrant air on my face as if it were something alive; my very clothes seemed like living skin, growing from my body. I felt strong. Very strong, I felt as if a living force, a force of growth, were pushing outward, through the wall of my body. Carried away by this power, swung on a wave of warm light, I turned Maria to me — with a quick and agile move, and looked into her astonished eyes. Then, embracing her with all my strength, I bent to her ear, saying: 'Maria — I love you.'

For one short instant Maria looked at me earnestly; then her eyes smiled, her lips and her face smiled. She put up her arms — her sleeves fell back to her armpits — and smoothed my hair.

Her fingers streamed delight into me. Suddenly she encircled my neck and pressed me to herself.

We kissed on the lips, on the eyes, and swore eternal love to each other.

It is known that our greatest weakness lies in the effort to eternalize an emotional state. Only Nirvana can be eternal because it is nothingness. An emotion has an apex. There is to it an ascent and a descent. But this is wisdom, and how could Maria or myself know this, for all we had then was the great urge of life?

I hope, for Maria's sake, that, like her father, she remained on life's side — unwise.

The following summer my uncle took me into the mountains. He made me bathe in warm whey 'to equip you for life,' he said. We fed on corn mush and sweet cream — skimmed from sheep's milk cooling in wooden trays, and on that delicacy of the Carpathian shepherd — frozen mutton stew. The odor of that dish, mixed with the fragrance of rosin and pine-gum, can resurrect the dead.

The whey-bath, the morning baths in spring water, the rolling on the dewy slope, until my body tingled, and my uncle's rations, gave me such vigor and strength that I wrestled with the shepherds the whole day. In the evening I wished for a bear to come along, so we could have a real, rough tussle. And I thought of Maria, wishing she were there. Lying on the carpet of pine-needles, inhaling the heavenly air of the old forest, my thoughts were ever with Maria. That feeling, first experienced in the barn, the feeling of an inner force pushing on the walls of my body, never left me. At times it became painful — for it had no other outlet than shouting, wrestling or running. Because I was aware that this force surged purposefully — towards Maria, my love. Only her presence near me could justify it and, perchance, relieve me from its pain.

I waited endless days, in torturing desire.

Then — Maria came. Elizabeth with her husband, Jacob and Maria. What a day that was.

The presence of a woman in the solitude of the mountains is more welcome than the first day of spring after a hard winter. But who can describe the feeling if the woman happens to be the loved one.

Maria and Elizabeth were the first to appear on the edge of the horizon. The shepherds saw them. With a shout they threw their caps in the air, and began jumping and pushing each other. They baa-ed, moo-ed and neighed—seized with a frantic animal joy.

I stood petrified, scanning the distance. They called to me: 'See there — brave one! Female folks! Mother mine — female folks. Young, too.... Young, sure! Sure as daylight!' — they sang.

'You can see the way they ride. Happy horses! Mother mine — young, plump heifers.'

Even my uncle changed suddenly, when he saw them. His eyes sparkled, his black beard took on a bright sheen. A vibrant ring came into his voice. He moved about quickly, ordering Dan to slaughter a young ram. Before the visitors reached us, the fire roared under the big kettle — started by him. He even peeled the onions, a peck of them, as fast as four womanly hands. He threw the onions in the kettle to simmer and yield up their flavor before the meat was put in. An hour after, we were all seated on blankets, our mouths watering for the fragrant stew.

My uncle lorded it over the shepherds, stroking his beard, his eyes on Elizabeth, who sat pensively, watching the distance, where naked mountain peaks glowed in the setting sun. When we ate, he sat near Elizabeth. With a wooden fork he pointed to the choicest morsels for her to pick.

Aha, good uncle, I must tell this, for you even touched her hand several times. At her faintest smile, you laughed uproariously.

But I was pouting with a fierce joy, watching you jealously, because I did not sit near Maria, as I wished.

When the moon came up, the sheep were safe in the enclosure. The four shepherds played on their fifes. We danced, sang with them, Maria's piercing voice dominating the others like a cry. I never left Maria, but Jacob remained always near her also.

When the hour came for us to go to bed, Maria walked leisurely towards the spring — alone. I followed her, unseen by her or any one else. In front of the little pool into which the water trickled from a wooden pipe stuck in the rock, Maria stopped, stretching like a sleepy cat. I could hear her inhale the air. Then she cupped her hands under the streamlet and drank. With her wetted palms she patted her cheeks. That moment I came up to her.

The moonlight formed a halo around Maria — the water trickled shimmeringly into the basin. A light wind hummed in the fir trees beyond and played with Maria's hair. I felt lighter than the wind. I felt tall, my chest expanded, and I inhaled the scented air in long, deep breaths. A soothing warmth suffused my body, prickled my face.

Quietly, but with all the feeling I could put into my voice, I said to her: 'Maria! Dearest Maria!'

She looked at me steadily, without a smile; without the least move of her lively features. She stood and looked at me, the wind playing with her hair.

'Won't you say a word, Maria?' I asked softly.

Maria moved her arms as if wings. Then she said:

'The air here is — you know — it makes me feel as if I were bathing in very clear water.'

'Oh yes! It is — just exactly — like the purest water. Maria, you know it is one year since we have been together.'

'I know ——' she said, with sudden animation, 'and you have not grown at all. I have been looking at you.'

'I? Oh, yes, Maria, I have grown a lot.'

'It can't be noticed. Not a bit.' There was laughter in her voice.

'But — I can throw you — Maria,' I said courageously. She laughed out loud, slapping her thighs.

'I surely can. Want to try?'

'I'll duck your head in that pool. I'll give you a second baptism,' she laughed.

'All right, then do.' I rushed upon her and the grappling started.

Her legs were like stone pillars. Her arms like cables, around me. I could not budge her feet. Her body bent slightly under my efforts, now one way, now the other, but her spread legs stood planted on the ground. Grinding my teeth, I dug my fists into the middle of her spine. Maria's trunk expanded with a deep breath, her muscles stiffened. Her feet shifted for a better grip on the ground. In a flash I flew up in the air, her arms coiled around my waist. She held me above the ground, pressing my ribs with her arms. Then, with all her force she threw me, as if to plant me in the earth. I struck it with both feet at once, but my knees did not bend: anticipating her move, I spread my legs and stiffened them with all the force in me. Arching my back I feigned pulling her towards me. As she resisted, I quickly pushed her backwards. We fell heavily, but before I could realize it, Maria was on top of me, clutching my shoulders and pressing them to the ground; I could hardly breathe.

She held me like that for a time, then bending to me, so close that her breath struck in my face, she asked pantingly:

'Well, great hero — who won?'

'Didn't I throw you?' I groaned.

'You pushed me all right, but — who is on top? Whose shoulders are pinned to the ground?'

'Who struck ground first?' I asked, trying to laugh.

'What of it? I did! But you — can you move?' With that she put all her weight on her outstretched arms. My shoulders ached under the pressure.

'Yes,' I teased, 'but look where the pool is. You said you'd duck my head.'

Maria turned slightly to look at the spring, unwittingly releasing her hold.

With a swiftness that surprised me even, I turned on my right shoulder and throwing my left arm around her waist, I threw Maria off — to one side. Instantly she grabbed my hair and swung my head backwards. My neck pained from the sudden jerk. I almost cried out in impotent rage.

'God Almighty — give me strength ——' I hissed under my breath. But the coolness of the grass under my cheek felt good. The smell of the ground sweet. The moonlight on Maria's face and shoulders, wonderful to look at. Her forearm rested on my face as she held my hair. She looked at me with smiling eyes. She breathed with parted lips — her strong teeth showing. I made no move for I realized suddenly that it all was wonderful. It was supremely delicious to be lying there, Maria and myself, side by side, on the fragrant grass, in the moonlight, listening to the breathing of the sheep and of the pine-forest.

Maria's warm arm rested on my cheek like a caress. Even the feeling of her fingers clutching my hair was good. Occasionally a wave of pine-drenched air rolled over us and I heard the metallic rustle of some thistles, close to my head. At the spring the water prattled endlessly. The tiny noise as infinite as the sky above.

Maria did not move — thank God — only her eyelids blinked now and then. Silently we looked at each other, then our eyes would turn and dive for an instant into the depth of the sky.

After a time, as if awakened from a reverie, Maria released my hair and pulled her arm away, but remained as she had been.

I was sorry to lose the touch of her arm on my face. I moved my head closer to Maria's, smiling happily. She answered me with her smile, then in a whisper she asked:

'Have I hurt you — Peter?'

'Oh, no, Maria, not at all, not the least, least bit.'

'Truly not?'

'I swear — Maria.'

'Then I am glad.' She reached and stroked my hair. I took her hand, laid it on the ground and rested my face on it. After a while her arm got tired so she moved closer to me, leaving her hand under my face.

For a long time we remained unmoving — looking only at each other. Then — the moon still shining on us, the water still tittering, a common impulse gathered us in each other's arms.

When we returned to the cabin the moon was high. All was silent inside, but Jacob sat leaning against the outside wall of the cabin. The white light of the moon fell on him, spilling from his ruffled hair over his bronzed face and chest — like a shimmering veil of water. Seeing us, Jacob stopped humming, but did not move. He pointed beside him, for us to sit down. Maria sat down close to him; I took my place near her. We sat silently, looking into the distance, an abyss of powdery light.

The forest — close by — hummed softly and breathed upon us its scent.

'This is the queen of all my nights,' Jacob said at length. Leaning forward he turned to me, saying: 'Do you remember — Peter — that song, "Sleepy birds to their nests are flying"?'

I nodded.

'Let us sing it then, all three of us,' he said, touching Maria's hand. We sang. First very softly, then louder, then quietly again, almost whisperingly, repeating many times the words of that melancholy genius — Eminescu. Our song ended, softer than the breath of the forest.

The lamenting song was the swan song of my love, for when we had fallen silent, Jacob turned to Maria, asking:

'Have you told him?'

'No,' answered Maria.

'You have not? Why?'

Maria did not answer. Folding her hands in her lap, she leaned back against the wall and closed her eyes. Jacob bent to look in her face.

'Tell him now, then,' he said.

Maria opened her eyes. Evenly, without a tremor in her voice, without a change on her face, looking straight in front of her, Maria said:

'Peter — I am going to be Jacob's wife; our fathers have agreed.' I jumped up. Looked at them, sitting there, the moonlight full upon them. Then — in a gay but shrill voice — I cried:

'Surely! Of course! Yes, of course! My very best wishes to you — both. My greatest good wishes to you!' And I ran into the cabin.

In the darkness I heard the breathing of Elizabeth and her husband. Cautiously I went to my bed in the chimney corner. Lying in the blanket, I began suddenly to wonder, how it happened that I did not see before the light which, coming from the windows, made two clear, rectangular spots on the floor.

For a long time I tormented my mind with the question: How is it I did not see those pools of light when I entered the cabin?

FAME TAKES THE J CAR[1]

GEORGE ALBEE

Elco Hotel,
3rd & High St.,
Bridgeport, Ohio.

Mr. H. M. Rodney, Esq.,
Personnel Manager,
Riverside St. Ry. Co.,
Riverside, Ohio.

MY DEAR SIR:

Well, Mr. Rodney, I guess you will be sort of surprised to hear from me. I am down here in Bridgeport, fifty miles away from home.

Well, Mr. Rodney, the reason I am writing is, I think the Company is not treating me fair. I think every man has a right to tell their own side of the story, don't you? So I will begin at the beginning, and then maybe you will agree I have a right to say what I'm going to say.

At Polytechnic High, Bertha was the most popular girl, and she was in the Mimerian Society, which has a motto Leadership,

---

Scholarship, and Character. Well, I hate to toot my own horn,
but I was in the Mimerian Society, too. When we told Miss Far-
num we was engaged, she said it was fine, because we would be
civic leaders together all our lives just like we were at Poly High.
Then it was just get out and hustle, for Bertha and me, from the
word Go. But we knew all the biggest men in the country have
started at the bottom of the ladder, and you can not keep a good
man down, just like you say yourself, Mr. Rodney, in your wonderful articles in *Trainmen's Topics* every month. Bertha wanted
to go to clerking at the Five and Dime store. This no-account
brother of hers, Herb, had just gotten married, too, and his wife
was working to support him, and they had a lot of fancy furniture they bought over to the Mercantile. It was no good, because
they got a kind with pink kewpies painted all over it, and then all
the gilt come off right away, but at first I guess Bertha was pretty
jealous. But I always say a woman's place is in the home.

Working my way through Poly, I had one job at Lacey's drug
store, and Mr. Lacey said I was the best soda-jerk he ever had.
Then I had a job delivering the *Clarion-Gazette* on my bicycle.
They give me a bronze button to wear in my button-hole, because
I never had any complaints on my route. Now I was through
school. What was the sense of it all, I figured, if you did not get
a job with a future to it? I knew I was sort of different from most
fellows, with what everyone always said about me and all. We
had a contest at Poly, and I was elected Man Most Likely to
Succeed, and things like that all the time, I mean. So right at
first I didn't know what job to get. But I was in the Hi-Y Club
(that was a club of manly Christian fellows that was the leaders
at school, I guess you remember) and one night at the Y.M.C.A.
you made us a speech, Mr. Rodney! All about what you have
done for Riverside, and about your ideals. And about how the
Riverside Street Railway Company was only hiring men with
high school educations. Gee, I guess you will think I am trying

to softsoap you, but I remember every word you said. I mean, about its being a job for men of ideals, because the Company has such wonderful ideals of service and all. Mr. Rodney, that was the most inspiring moment of my life!

So the next morning bright and early I went down to see you. I went down town on the street-car, and on the way I hung around the back platform and sort of watching the con, you know, and thinking what fine work it was, and how interesting it must be to meet all those folks every day. I guess I am a philosopher, sort of. Most young married couples just go to the movies after supper, but Bert and I will walk up and down Main St. just studying people. I study books on success, too; but Bert does not do that. That is one fault I will have to admit she has. She thinks you get rich by getting lucky breaks. She gets ideas like that from her brother Herb, that is always getting excited over some hairbrained scheme. If it was not for Herb, I would not be in this terrible trouble I am in now, with my heart broken. But what I started to say is, I went down town to our Company building. Gee, I was scared! You know how it is, asking for your first real job. I know you have gone through it, yourself; although some of the fellows say you got your job through pull, because when you got out of college your father owned a lot of stock in our Company. You would be surprised if you knew how much slandering talk like that goes around the car barns every day in the year. I could give you the name of man after man that is always running you and the other executives down, if I was the kind that carries tales. And those men are still working for you right today, and here I am fired! It just don't seem fair, Mr. Rodney. But I will tell you it all, and then you will see for yourself. I was telling you how I came down to the office, that first time, seven years ago. I tell you, it is a mighty big moment when a fellow chooses his life's work. But I was not scared so much, feeling I sort of knew you personally, and what wonderful ideals you had, just like mine. I still wish you had been in your office that morning, Mr. Rodney. If you had talked to me and seen what kind of man I was, and how I felt about service and everything you talked about in your speech at the Y that night, why, last Friday you would have remembered me and you would have not fired me without giving me a chance to finish what I was saying. It is sort of tough, being fired from your job when you have given seven years of the best that is in you. Well, anyhow, that other fellow had me sign the blanks, and see the doctor from the insurance company. And that doctor said I was sound as a dollar all over! And they sent me out on the training-car right off the bat.

I guess maybe you never knew that the guy that took me out on the training-car said he had never seen anyone catch onto things so quick?

Well, now I will have to tell you some of the things about Herb, my wife's brother. Every time Bert and I are happy, he and this wife of his come over and spoil it for us. They try to. To show you, here is what he said that time when I first got my job with the Company. 'This guy Rodney hasn't got any of those ideals he talks about,' he said. 'He made that speech because the company needs some men right now and they sent him out to get them. That is what a personnel manager is for,' Herb says. I mean, that is how he is all the time. Like when I am working on the early shift on the J line and have to get up at 4 A.M. I do not mind it. I know it is the fellows that are willing to put themselves out that get the merit marks and raises and promotions. But then Herb and Hotsy will come over to see us, and he will say: 'Well, Ollie, Bert tells me you are rolling out of bed at 4 A.M. nowadays.'

'That is right,' I will say. 'I do not mind.'

'Why don't you get yourself a real job, like the kind I grab off for myself, where a man can sleep late in the morning?' he will ask.

I am never one to complain, Mr. Rodney. Over the bureau in our bedroom I have a poem that I cut out of the *Clarion-Gazette*, by a poet, that is called 'It's the Man With the Smile That Wins.' And on the wall I have a card, 'The Best Advice is from the Firm of Grin and Barrett.' But that is Herb's attitude. He has no background. He is just ignorant, and does not know anything about loyalty or service or vision. One week he is selling real estate, and the next stock in fake oil wells, and the next washing-machines; one week he is broke and the week after he makes some money and spends every cent of it. He will end up selling lead-pencils on the street, that is what Herb will do! And he and this wop wife of his have the gall to try to tell Bertha and me how to live, that have our little home nearly paid for and not afraid to look any man in the eye! Or like last Xmas, when I was working extra shifts. He and Hotsy came over to see us, and they would say things like, 'Well, Ollie, I guess you will not be taking Bert to the dances down to the Odd Fellows', will you?'

'I don't mind,' Bertha will say. 'Ollie has his future to think of. Ollie has vision.'

Bert is no fool. She knows I am cut out to make a big success. She was a leader, herself, when we was at school. But then, after Herb and Hotsy go, I will hear Bertha crying at night when she thinks I am asleep but when I am really laying awake planning how to give better service to our Company. I am always doing little things extra, like helping old ladies with bundles and things like that; I was trying to tell you about some of the extra things I do last Friday when you told me to get out of your office. But I mean, Bertha is a game little sport, but I know she is thinking about those dances. I mean, all her friends will be there, and they will be saying, 'Oh, Ollie and Bertha are not here. I guess Ollie is ashamed of her and does not want to take her out.' I am not ashamed of my little wife! Sometimes when I am reading the Sunday rotogravure section I look at the pictures and say to myself, 'Gee, I could have gone to New York and made a lot of money on Wall Street and married one of those society girls.' But then I say to myself, 'No sir, you stay right here in Riverside, with this sweet moral little wife of yours, and be thankful.' No, Mr. Rodney, when I am rich I want to have my Bert right alongside with me, that has shared all my early struggles. But when Herb and Hotsy say things like that it makes Bert feel bad. She is crazy about dancing. I am a pretty good dancer if I do say so. We always win the cups down to the Odd Fellows. After all, we are pretty young. I still have my future ahead of me, and, if the Riverside Street Railway Company does not want me, why, maybe some other big corporation will. Maybe you will be sorry you fired me, some day. Ha-Ha. But I tell you, there are times when I would like to take that Herb out in the alley and knock some of the sarcasm and bolshevism out of him. It is enough to make any right-minded man sick to his stomach. Only he is my wife's brother, and I have a weak heart from my mother's side of the family, and anyway fighting is no thing for a gentleman to do. If there is anything my parents brought me up to be, before they passed on to their reward, it is a gentleman. Maybe that is why the passengers on the J line are so crazy about me. I guess some of them will feel pretty sore about my being fired. Maybe some of them will quit using the street-car and start riding on the busses, you can't tell.

You can see what it does, Herb razzing me in front of Bertha all the time. He does it behind my back, too. Why, would you believe it, one time he told Bertha he wanted her to get a divorce, because I did not have brains enough to ever make any big money! I found out about it from a friend of mine that is going with a girl that is one of Hotsy's girl-friends. Of course the things he says do not bother me. I guess no poor excuse for a success like Herb can dominate anyone with my strength of character. All the fortune-tellers I have ever went to have told me I am a

master of men. Of course a man with my education does not believe in fortune-tellers, but it is funny they should all say the
same thing; I wonder why they do? I have developed myself all
along all lines by studying such books like *Power of Will* and *How
to Dominate Others*. So I do not give a darn for Herb and his dirty
anarchistic talk. But you are a married man, Mr. Rodney, and
you know how women are weak. For a long time I did not notice
anything out of the way. Then about two years ago I guess it was,
Bertha began acting kind of different towards me. I tell you, that
no-account brother of hers undermined her morals, that is what
he did! For instance, the night I am thinking of, Herb was over
to the house and I showed him my books.

'Now all you have to do is go out and dominate someone,' he
says. 'Gee, Ollie, the jack you have wasted on those books, you
could have taken Bert down to dance at the Bon Ton every night
for six months.'

Well, after Herb went home, Bertha says to me 'Honey, don't
buy any more books, will you?'

'Well, gee, if I am ever going to be a big executive, Bert, like
you want me to be,' I said, 'I have to educate myself, don't I?'

'But Herb says they are silly.'

'What does he know about things like this?' I ask her. 'He is
nothing but a drifter, living from hand to mouth.'

Bertha stamps her foot. 'He makes twice as much money as
you do, even if he hardly ever does work! That dress Hotsy had
on cost forty dollars.' And then she begins to cry. 'Oh, Ollie,
I know you are going to be a big executive some day, but I want
to have some fun now, like other married couples do.'

Well, Mr. Rodney, I guess that was the worst shock in my life,
Bert saying that. I saw Herb was getting her to be just like him
and Hotsy. Herb is always reading a magazine about how fellows
get lucky breaks and make millions without doing a lick of work;
and he is always shooting craps and playing cards and talking

about his luck. I felt like I didn't have a friend left in the world. I mean, that is why I got married, because my folks had passed on, and when a man has no one in the world he gets sort of shiftless and is not a success. Here I wanted to be a success all for Bert's sake, and she paid me back by falling into ways of wrong thinking, and acting like I was the one that was wrong. I do not want to say anything against my wife, for she is one of the finest; but she is one of the weaker sex.

Once I came right out and said to Herb: 'Herb, I do not like to say this, but I wish you and Hotsy would not come over here any more.'

Well, you would think a man would at least be respected in his own home, but do you know what Herb said? He said: 'Say, listen, you little shrimp, Bert is my sister, and I'll come over here as much as I darn please!' I mean, Herb knows I dominate him, and he is jealous of me. I guess he is afraid that wife of his will fall for me. As if I would have her as a gift! He knows if I did not want to take any of those names he calls me I could just hand him a good sock on the chin and there would be only two blows struck, I would strike him and he would strike the floor, ha-ha. But he knows I have this weak heart from my mother's side, and do not want to start any trouble because he is Bertha's brother, and so he takes advantage of it. Oh, he is clever, all right. A lot it will ever get him! I am not little. I am five foot eight, and some of the greatest captains of industry in this country are that height. I have a nose that looks like Abraham Lincoln, too. It shows how dominating and aggressive I am. A book of mine named *Character Reading at Sight* says so.

Other times, when she is away from Herb's immoral influence, Bertha is just the same sweet little girl I married. She will snuggle up to me, and say, 'Oh, Ollie, I know you will be a big wonderful success some day! You are fifty times more wonderful than Herb. Herb just gets the breaks, that is all.'

'Listen, honey,' I try to teach her, 'don't talk about breaks. It is perseverance, and loyalty, and ideals, and service that gets a man up to the top.'

'Yes, I know,' she will say, 'but a man has to make people notice him. You are better than Herb, but who is going to know it unless you tell them about it yourself? Herb pushes his way into the bosses' offices and tells them all about how wonderful he is. You are too modest, Ollie.'

Well, that is true, Mr. Rodney. I have always been too modest. And the way Bert put it, it began to sound like she might be right about some of it after all. This is just about a year ago, that I am talking about now. I mean, you have read the lives of great business men, and they all say that you have to be aggressive, and sell yourself. Bertha would say, 'Of course you are giving wonderful service to the passengers. But think how many conductors Mr. Rodney has to keep track of. How can he know about you? It's up to you to tell him, Ollie!' Well, you know, I'd never thought about it in just that light before; I sort of figured you knew all about me. For instance, a lot of folks on the J line will wait until I come along, and not ride on any other car but mine. I read your wonderful inspiring articles every month in *Trainmen's Topics*, about giving service, and I guess they just mean more to me than they do to the other fellows. Why, some of the cons and motormen even laugh at those articles of yours! And they are working for you right today, while here I am fired! Herb used to work for an advertising agency once, and he tried to tell me that our *Trainmen's Topics* bought those articles already in print, from a place that writes them in New York; but I out and called him a liar to his face, the bolshevik! No, sir, I knew I was doing work to be proud of, and I figured you knew I was too; only when Bertha began to talk like that, about your being so busy, why, it struck me maybe she was right, and maybe that was why I had not been promoted in seven years like I expected to be.

'Gee, Bert,' I would say, 'nothing will ever happen to make Mr. Rodney notice me. I had just better count on good steady work, and wonderful service, and living up to our Company's ideals, like I am doing.'

'No,' she would say, 'we are going to get a break. We have been waiting for one for seven years, so the Lord only knows we ought to get one soon now.'

Well, that is how she got around me, Mr. Rodney — talking kidding-like, like that, and acting sweet and cute. This is just a couple of months or so ago I am talking about now. Well, I am ashamed to say it, but I guess she talked me into it. I never thought anything like she said would happen, though. The best of us are weak at times, the philosopher says, and pride comes before a fall. Right when I expected nothing would happen, it happened! When I came into your office last Friday, I thought you knew about it, but it seems like you did not, so I will tell you just how it happened. Thursday I came home from work just like always, not knowing anything. At the corner I ran into my next-door neighbor, and he said, 'Well, I guess you won't be speaking to us any more, will you, now you're famous?' I just grinned, thinking he was kidding. But when I got into the house, Bertha ran and kissed me, her eyes just like two stars. 'Oh, Ollie, isn't it wonderful, isn't it wonderful?' she kept saying, over and over. 'Oh, I have phoned Hotsy, and she and Herb are coming over right after supper!' Well, I guess you could have knocked me over with a feather when she showed me the clipping. I just happened to find it when I opened my coin-purse a minute ago, here in Bridgeport, so I will give it to you word for word right out of the *Clarion-Gazette*. Here it is, just like it was in the paper Bert showed me:

Patsy left home that morning on feet as light as sunbeams. Beneath her jaunty little hat her eyes were bright as sunbeams, too. All the flowers along Ridge Street seemed to smile at her, and all the trees to whisper tender secrets into her little pink ears. For had not Hobart Pennington taken her into his strong arms, last night, far out on the Daley Pike in his luxurious coupe, and told her that he loved her with all his heart and soul? Hobart, with the romantic touch of grey at the temples! Hobart, for whom she had been until yesterday just a pretty, efficient secretary! Hobart, the man she had loved in secret these many, many moons! And now — Hobart. Hobart. To her. Hers, to love and cherish. And because she herself was so happy, Patsy noticed the happy face of the handsome young conductor on the street-car she took to work. His number was 432, she read from his cap. He was another happy mortal — Mr. 432 — who had learned the secret of love! Patsy exclaimed to herself, with a little wriggle of ecstasy.

It is a story that is called 'The Sunshine Girl of Riverside,' that is running every day in the *Clarion-Gazette*. When Herb came over that night, he said, 'It is a syndicate story. It is written in New York, but they fix it so whatever town it is printed in it looks like it is written about that town. All that stuff about Ridge Street and the Daley Pike was put in here.' I mean, Herb is jealous of me, and he couldn't see anything as wonderful as being mentioned in the paper happen to me without making at least one nasty crack about it. But a minute later he said, 'Gee, this is a real break for you, Ollie. I sure hope you follow it up.'

Hotsy says: 'You have got about ten thousand dollars' worth of free publicity for yourself and the Riverside Street Railway Company!'

Herb goes on, 'Say, Ollie, when you go down ask Mr. Rodney for a promotion, now, it will be a cinch.'

And Bertha keeps saying, 'Oh, honey, I told you it would happen!'

I can not tell you all the things those three said to me, Mr. Rodney. Herb and Hotsy stayed till after midnight. I thought they were actually being nice to me, for the first time in their

lives. More fool me! Even with all that, I guess I would have had
sense enough not to come down to your office the way I did,
except for all the things that happened the next morning. I
mean, all morning the passengers that got on my car kept looking
at me and whispering to each other. Some of them that knew me
well come right out and said, 'Well, Ollie, I see you got in the
paper!' Others kept smiling at me and whispering to each other,
like I say. I knew they were all talking about me. I guess that
was the last straw, that made me do it. I guess I was just conceited. I am sure sorry, now.

I guess you remember the rest of what happened, all right, Mr.
Rodney, so there is no use in my telling it to you. The girl let me
into your office, and I started talking to you. You looked sort of
different than I remembered you, it being so long since I had seen
you. I guess maybe that is why I got so rattled. I am sorry I
tripped over the edge of the rug and knocked down that big
expensive ash-tray. Oh, Mr. Rodney, I see how crazy it was of
me, now; honest I do! — sitting on your desk and slapping you
on the back, like my wife said her brother did; and telling you I
would not take anything less than an executive position in the
office with you. When you told me to stop pawing you, and stop
shouting, cross my heart and hope to die I did not have any idea I
was pawing you and shouting! Oh, I was a fool. I know it now.
It was all the fault of those three people, working on me the way
they did. I am not like that. If you will ask anyone that knows
me, any of the fellows at the car barns or any passenger that rides
on the J line, they will all tell you I am not conceited. Give me
another chance, Mr. Rodney! Give me a chance to show you I
am not like that. Even the best of us make mistakes.

Well, you told me I was fired. The next thing I knew, I was out
on the street. I have never had such a blow in my life. I walked
up Main Street a ways, and then I saw a Bridgeport bus just
leaving, and I could not go home and face Bertha, and I got on it,

and here I am. I have been here at this Elco Hotel in Bridgeport since Friday afternoon. And so Herb has got me fired, and split up with Bertha, just like he has always wanted. Oh, yes, I see all that now. And so now you know the whole thing, just like it has happened from the very start seven years ago, and I leave it to you if you ought to hire me back. You are a fair-and-square American, and I leave it to you if you think I have been treated unfair and have had hard luck. I will leave it all to you, Mr. Rodney. Whatever you say will be all right with me. It was Sunday I got the idea of writing you this letter, and Monday I went over to the Secretarial School across the street and this young lady here said she would type it for me. I wanted it to be typewritten so it would be easy to read and I will not take any of your valuable time from the affairs of our Company. This young lady here, Miss Dixie Angel, says she will type all this tonight, as a special favor, and bring it to me down here to the hotel on her way to school tomorrow morning. It is mighty nice of her to help me this way.

Well, Mr. Rodney, I guess that is all. I will leave everything to you. I just wanted you to know the whole story, so you can see your way clear to do whatever you think is right. There is a mail train out of here tomorrow morning at ten, so you ought to get this tomorrow afternoon.

Yrs. Respectfully

OLIVER L. SMITH, No. 432

I am writing this on in pencil because there are somethings too sacredd for others to see, Oh Mr. Rodney I never knew till I seen this whole letter together how long it would be, fourteen pages, and I am scairt you will not read all of it, oh Mr. Rodney please read it! Even if you are busy you ougt to read it by Thursday and I have an anser by Friday, I only had my pay check when I come here and it is almost all spent but I will get threw

somehow till Saturday and wait tell then, oh if I don't hear from
you by Friday I will kill myself I swear I will kill myself. Or I
will go away to Cincinnati and get a job there and Riverside the
town where I was born will never see me more, and my own little
wife will never see my face again. Oh Mr. Rodney I can't face
her after this and she thought I would come home with a wonderful position in the office with you, Oh my God I cant face her or
let that Herb and Hotsy have the laugh on me. Oh Mr. Rodney
please give me my job back, please, I will even be a track-walker
and not a con, I do not care, I will tell Bert something or other
and make her believe it, only take me back, Mr. Rodney, give
me another chance! Please read this letter through to the end
and don't just think it is to long and not read it, oh for God's
sake. Oh, in the name of our Saviour, please take me back,
please, please!!!

HELEN, I LOVE YOU[1]

JAMES T. FARRELL

I

'YOU got a goofy look,' Dick Buckford said.

'Yeh,' Dan said.

The two boys stood in front of one of the small gray-stone houses in the 5700 block on Indiana Avenue, glaring at each other.

Dan didn't know what to say. He glanced aside at the hopeless, rainy autumn day. His eyes roved over the damp street, the withered grass and mud by the sidewalk across the street, the three-story apartment buildings, and at the sky which dumped down top-heavily behind the buildings.

'Yeah, you're goofy! You're goofy!' Dick sneered.

'Then so are you,' Dan countered.

'Am I?' Dick challenged.

'Yes!' Dan answered with determination.

'Am I goofy?'

'If you say I am, then you're a goof, too!'

Dan hoped nothing would happen. He knew how, if he lost a fight when he was still new in the neighborhood, everybody would start taking picks on him, bullying him, making a dope out of

---

[1] Copyright, 1937, by The Vanguard Press. From *The Short Stories of James T. Farrell*. The Vanguard Press, 1937.

him, and kidding him all the time because he had been licked. He hoped that he wouldn't be forced into a fight with Dick, who was about ten pounds heavier than he was. But he pretended that he was fighting Dick, beating hell out of him. He pretended that he slugged Dick in the face, and saw the blood spurt from his big nose. He slugged Dick, until Dick was bloody and winded and said quits, and a crowd of guys and girls watching the fight cheered and said that Dan was certainly a fine fighter, and then he pretended that Helen Scanlan came up to him and told him she was so glad.

But he'd already had his chance with her. She had seemed to like him, but he'd been too damn bashful. Once, he could have held her hand and kissed her, and they could have gone over to the park, and kissed some more, if he only hadn't been so bashful. She had even said that she liked him.

They were standing right in front of the parlor window of the Scanlan house. He thought again of himself slamming Dick around, with Helen in the window watching him. Red-haired Helen Scanlan, he loved her. He said to himself:

Helen, I love you!

'Why don't you pull in your ears? Huh?' said Dick.

'Aw, freeze your teeth and give your tongue a sleigh-ride,' Dan said.

He wished Dick would go away, because he wanted to walk around alone, and maybe go over to the park, where it would be all quiet except for the wind, and where the leaves would be wet and yellow, and it would be easy to think of Helen. He could walk around, and think and be a little happy-sad, and think about Helen. And here was Dick before him, and Dick was supposed to be one of the best scrappers in the neighborhood, and he seemed to want to pick a fight, and right here, too, outside of Helen's window. And maybe Dick would win, with Helen there to watch it all.

Dan wanted Dick to go away. He told himself that he loved Helen. He told himself that he was awfully in love with curly, red-haired Helen. He remembered last summer, when he had peddled bills for half a dollar, putting them in mail boxes all over the neighborhood. The day after, they had gone riding on the tail-gate of hump-backed George's grocery wagon, and it had been fun, himself and Helen sitting there on the back of the wagon, holding hands as they bounced through the alleys, and while they waited for George to deliver his orders. And he had spent all his money on her. He told himself that he loved her.

He remembered how, after riding on the wagon, he had gone home, and they had bawled him out because he had worn the soles on his shoes out delivering the bills, and then had gone and spent the money so foolishly, with nothing to show for it. There had been a big scrap, and he had answered them back, and got so sore that he had bawled like a cry-baby. Afterwards, he'd sat in the parlor, crying and cursing, because he was sore. He'd had such a swell time that afternoon, too. And the family just hadn't understood it at all. And then Helen had come around, because all the kids in the neighborhood used to come around to his front steps at night to play and talk. Somebody had called to tell him she was there. He hadn't known what he was doing, and he'd answered that he didn't care if she was there or not.

After that Helen hadn't paid any attention to him.

He told himself:

Helen, I love you!

II

'If I was as goofy as you, I'd do something about it,' Dick said.

'Yeh. Well, I ain't got nothing on you.'

'No? Well, look at it, your stockings are falling down. You can't even keep your stockings up,' said Dick.

'Well, you're sniffin' and don't even know enough to blow your nose.'

'Don't talk to me like that!' Dick said.

'Well, don't talk to me like that, either!'

'I ain't afraid of you!' Dick said.

'And I ain't afraid of you, either!' said Dan.

'Wanna fight?' asked Dick.

'If you do, I do!' said Dan.

'Well, start something,' said Dick.

'You start something,' said Dan.

'But maybe you won't, because you're yellow,' said Dick.

'No, I ain't, neither. I ain't afraid of you.'

Dick smiled sarcastically at Dan.

'I don't know whether to kiss you or kill you,' he said with exaggerated sweetness.

'Yeh, you heard Red Kelly make that crack, and you're just copying it from him. You ain't funny,' Dan said.

'That's all you know about it! Well, I made it up and Red heard me say it. That's where he got it. How you like that?'

'Tie your bull in somebody else's alley,' Dan said.

Dick tried to out-stare Dan. Dan frowned back at him.

'And today in school, when Sister Cyrilla called on you, you didn't even know enough how to divide fractions. You're goofy,' Dick said.

'Well, if I'm goofy, I don't know what you ain't,' Dan said.

Dan again pretended that they were fighting, and that he was kicking the hell out of Dick with Helen watching. And he remembered how last summer when he had gotten those hats advertising Cracker Jack, he had given one to her. He had felt good that day, because she had worn the hat he gave her. And every night they had all played tin-tin, or run-sheep-run, or chase-one-chase-all, or eeny-meeny-miny-mo. He had just moved around then, and he had thought that it was such a good neighborhood, and now, if Dick went picking a fight with him and beat him, well, he just wouldn't be able to show his face any more and would just about have to sneak down alleys and everything.

But if he beat Dick up and Helen saw him, he would be her hero, and he would be one of the leaders of their gang, and then maybe she would like him again, and twice as much, and everything would be all so swell, just like it was at the end of the stories he sometimes read in the *Saturday Evening Post.*

Last summer, too, he had read *Penrod,* and he had thought of Helen because she was like Marjorie Jones in the book, only more so, and prettier, and nicer, and she had nicer hair, because the book said Marjorie Jones's hair was black, and Helen's was red, and red hair was nicer than black hair.

'One thing I wouldn't be called is yellow,' Dick sneered.

'I ain't yellow,' Dan said.

'I wouldn't be yellow,' Dick said.

'And I wouldn't be a sniffer, and not have enough sense to blow my nose,' said Dan.

'Who's a sniffer?' demanded Dick.

'Well, why don't you blow your nose?'

'Why doncha not be so goofy?' demanded Dick.

'I ain't no goofier than you.'

'If I was as goofy as you, I'd quit living,' Dick said.

'Yeh, and if I was like you, I'd drown myself.'

'You better do it then, because you're goofier than anybody I know,' Dick said.

'Yeh?'

'Yeh!'

'Yeh!'

'And let me tell you, I ain't afraid of nobody like you,' Dick said.

'I ain't, neither. Just start something, and see!'

'I would, only I don't wanna get my hands dirty, picking on a goof. If you wasn't afraid of me, you wouldn't stand there, letting me say you're goofy.'

'Well, I'm here saying you're just as goofy.'

'I couldn't be like you.'

'And I couldn't be as dumb as you,' Dan said.

'You're so goofy, I wouldn't be seen with you.'

'Don't, then!' said Dan.

'I ain't! I was here first!'

'I live on this street.'

'I lived in this neighborhood longer than you,' said Dick.

'I live on this street, and you can beat it if you don't like it.'

'You're so goofy you belong in the Kankakee nut house. Your whole family's goofy. My old man says I shouldn't have nothing to do with you because of all the goofiness in your family.'

'Well, my old man and my uncle don't think nothing of your old man,' Dan said.

'Well, don't let my old man hear them sayin' it, because if he does, he's liable to bat their snoots off,' said Dick.

'Let him try! My old man ain't afraid of nothing!'

'Yeh? Don't never think so. My old man could take your old man on blindfolded.'

'Yeh? My old man could trim your old man with his little finger, and it's cut off,' said Dan.

'Say, if my old man's hands were tied behind his back, and he said "Boo," your old man would take to his heels lickety-split down the streets, afraid.'

'Let him start something and see, then!'

'If he ever does, I'd feel sorry for your old man,' said Dick.

'You don't need to be.'

'My old man's strong, and he says I take after him, and when I grow up, I'll be like him, a lineman climbing telephone poles for the telephone company,' said Dick.

'Yeh?' said Dan.

'Yeh!' said Dick.

'Yeh?' said Dan.

'Baloney,' said Dick.

'Bouswah,' said Dan.

'B.S.,' said Dick.

They sneered toughly at one another.

'That for you!' Dick said, snapping his fingers in Dan's face.

'That for you!' Dan said, screwing up his lips and twitching his nose.

'If this is the street you live on, I won't hang around it no more, because it smells just as bad as you do,' said Dick.

'That's because you're on it.'

'I'm going, because I don't want nobody to know that I'm even acquainted with anyone as goofy as you.'

'Good riddance to bad rubbage,' said Dan.

'If you weren't such a clown, I'd break you with my little finger!' said Dick.

'And I'd blow you over with my breath!' said Dan.

III

Dan watched Dick walk away, without looking back. He sat on the iron fence around the grass plot, feeling good because he had proven to himself that he wasn't afraid of Dick. He said to himself:

Helen, I love you!

He sat.

He sat through slow, oblivious minutes. He arose and decided to take a walk. Wishing that he could see Helen, he strolled down to Fifty-eighth Street, and bought five cents' worth of candy. He returned and sat on the iron fence in front of her house, and for about twenty-five minutes he nibbled at his candy, hoping that she would come along, wondering where she was, wishing he could give her some of his candy. He told himself:

Helen, I love you!

He thought of how he had held her hand that day on the grocery wagon. He imagined her watching him while he cleaned the
stuffings out of Dick Buckford.

The day was sad. He wished that it had some sun. The day
wouldn't be sad, though, if she came along and talked to him.

He walked over to Washington Park. It was lonely, and he
didn't see anybody in the park. The wind kept beating against
the trees and bushes, and sometimes, when he listened closely, it
seemed to him like an unhappy person, crying. He walked on and
on, wetting his feet, but he didn't care. He stopped to stand by
the lagoon. There were small waves on it, and it looked dark, and
black, and mean. He said to himself:

Helen, I love you!

He continued gazing at the lagoon. Then, he strolled on.

Yes, if Dick had started something, he would have cleaned the
guts out of him. Dick would have rushed him, and he would have
biffed Dick, giving him a pretty shiner. Dick would have rushed
him again, and he would have biffed Dick a second time, and Dick
would have had a bloody nose. He would have stood back and led
with a left to the solar plexus, and Dick would have doubled up,
and he would have smashed Dick with a right, and Dick would
have fallen down with another black eye. Dick would have yelled
quits, and Helen, who would have been watching it all, would have
yelled for him, and maybe she would have said:

Dan, I want to be your girl!

He walked. He looked all around him at the park stretching
away in wet, darkened, dying grass, with shadows falling down
over it. The light was going out of the sky, and he said good-bye
to Mr. Day. He felt all alone, and thought how nice it would be
if he only had someone to talk to. Maybe Helen. Maybe himself
and Helen walking in the wet grass. Maybe some man would try
to kidnap her. The man would run away with her under his arm

crying for help. And he would pick up a rock and fling at the guy, and it would smack the guy in the skull, and he would drop down unconscious, but Helen wouldn't be hurt. And he would rush up, hit the guy with another rock so that he would be out colder than if he had been hit by Ruby Bob Fitzsimmons in his prime. Police would come, and he would have his picture in the papers, and he would be a real hero, and Helen would say to him:

Dan, I love you, and I'll always love you.

He walked. It was almost dark, and the wind sounds seemed worse than the voices of ghosts. He wished he wasn't so all alone. He had strange feelings. He wondered what he ought to do, and it seemed like there were people behind every tree. The park was too lonely to be in, and he decided that he'd better go home. And it was getting to be supper time.

The wind was awfully sad. There wasn't any moon or stars in the sky yet.

He didn't know what he was afraid of, but he was awfully afraid.

And it would have been so nice, and so different, if he was only with Helen. She would be afraid, too, and he would be protecting her.

He started back toward home, thinking what he would have done to Dick if Dick had really started a fight. Yes, sir, he would have made Dick sorry.

Helen, I love you!

IKE AND US MOONS[1]

NAOMI SHUMWAY

SOMETIME away back in Seventeen and Seventy, on the trek outa Virginia into Kentucky, one of Ike's ancestors saved one of our'ns life at the cost of his own, and ever since then our kin and his'n has sorta stuck together. Only our kin was the kind what prospered and become a power in the community, while Ike's was a fiddling fishing lot what always squatted on a piece of our land and expected us to feed them. I never heared tell of any of us Moons minding either. Reckon they liked having a nest of losels on their homeplace, same as My Dad did. But the Great Rebellion blowed everything to hell. Them of both families what wasn't kilt during the war died fighting the niggers afterwards, till long about Eighteen and Seventy they wasn't anybuddy left sept Ike and My Dad. They woulda stuck it out, even then, but Ike was only eight and My Dad twenty-two, and everything was mortgaged for more than it was worth, so one night they struck a match to their homeplace and climbed in a covered wagon and headed west.

Put near the first I can recollect is Ike telling me of Us Moons.

[1] Copyright, 1933, by Whit Burnett and Martha Foley. From *A Story Anthology: 1931–1933*, edited by Whit Burnett and Martha Foley. The Vanguard Press, 1933.

His memory seemed to stretch clean back to creation. He talked of Jonathan Moon, my first known kin, whats name and farm was all writ up in the Doomsday book like as if they had gone fishing together. 'The Moons always took their living rough handed from the earth,' Ike said. 'No Moon ever lived in any godforsaken city, or any else place but where all the land they could see from their doorsteps belonged to them. They was never a trapsing lot. They clung to their homeplaces as long as they could in honor. None of them was ever knighted, on accounta they never went fighting of any wars. They knowed how it was between a man and his homeplace and they was never the ones to drive any man off'n his. Only Moons what ever took up arms was your grandpa and uncles during the Great Rebellion, and they had to on accounta the Yanks was marching agin their land.'

This would be of a night, and I'd be sitting on Ike's lap, if it was winter, afore the kitchen fireplace, but happen it was summer, we'd sit out on the front porch steps. When I'd get sleepy, Ike would shake my chin and wake me up, for it was fitting I heared what he'd say. The Kids would have snuck away to their beds long afore and Em would be redding up for the night and My Dad would be in his study reading outa a book, it not mattering, for the future of the Moons was in nobuddy's hands but mine.

'No Moons ever worked for other men.' Ike would give my chin an extra hard shake when he'd say this, so's there'd be no danger of my missing it. 'If they planted a tree, or drove a fence post into the ground, it was for themselves and their children's children and not for some other man and his'n. When your Dad and me first come to the Yellowstone over thirty years gone, we slept in a dugout and et nothing but jackrabbits and dough-gods, on accounta we wouldn't join no outfit what wasn't our'n. But look at Moon Manor now! Two thousand acres of the best alfalfa pasturage in the state and racing men from coast to coast coming up to buy our hosses. And here's you, Jonathan Moon, living in a house exactly like what your great-great grandpa built back in Kentucky. Plenty of folks what come to this country same time as your Dad and me are still living in the same soddies they built then, on accounta they was always willing to be working of the railroad, or of somebody better off'n themselves.'

'Leave that baby go to bed,' Em would come with my night things and command. 'Ten o'clock and him wide awake as an owl.'

'Go away, woman!' Ike would start undressing of me then, whether it was on the porch or in the kitchen. It always took him about an hour, so I jest sit still and let him work at me as he talked.

'Everybuddy heared tell of the Sussex Moons. Old Queen Bess herself sent men to learn of them. 'Twas Jeremy Moon what growed the first potatoes in all England and 'twas none less than Sir Francis Drake give him the seed. The Moons ever showed other people the way. 'Twas your great-great grandpa Godfrey Moon what first saw that the Blue Grass was made for hosses. While up here in the Yellowstone where every man turned his hand to cows, your Dad was smart enough to round up the mustangs off'n the range. That's how we got our start, trading ten wild hosses for one thoroughbred.'

Happening we were out on the porch, My Dad woulda been listening at his study window and he'd poke out his head and ask extra serious of Ike, 'Wasn't it Thomas Watt Moon what discovered steam and Eli Whitney Moon what invented the cotton gin?'

Soon as I growed a little more bigger I got on to My Dad's joshing and would try it on Ike myself. I'd tell him stories out of Arabian Nights, and Gulliver's Travels and ask if the Moons had ever heared tell or done such. They wasn't no tale I could tell but what he could tell a taller one about Us Moons. This would generally be at the supper table on accounta I liked an audience.

'Give over, Jonathan,' My Dad would say when he'd see Ike's imagination was near to split from stretching. 'What you mean doubting the abilities of your ancestors?' His voice would be stern like, but there'd be a great twinkle in his eyes. 'Jest you go on Ike and tell this young heathen about Christopher Columbus Moon what discovered America.'

Ike's woman, Em, was so awed by his tales of Us Moons, that she always treated me like as if I was a crown prince or some such. Afore Ike took her she had been the Linden's hired girl. Karl Linden had sent back to the old country for her on accounta he couldn't get enough work outa American girls. She was big and sleepy-eyed, with braids like well ropes wrapped around her head, and she was that strong that when I hid my face agin her big soft breast, I felt that nothing could touch me. Not even death.

Em come to live on Moon Manor after Ike and My Dad built the big white house, and afore she had been there a year the kids come. Folks about were that aggravated, on accounta they couldn't decide who the father was. But Ike didn't keep them long worrit. Soon as ever Doc Sessions said 'Twins,' he got drunk as a lord and jumped on a hoss and rode so far and so fast to tell everybuddy that his mare dropped dead beneath him. When he come home he brought Em a pair of pink satin slippers what was too little for her, but he didn't bring no parson. Even My Dad failed of making him marry her. 'I done made my promises to Em,' Ike said. 'Ain't no skyrider going to hear them. Some things is private.'

The twins was named Jonathan and David, same as My Dad and me. But it was too mixing to call them that, so on accounta one being born a half a head taller than the other and they always staying that way, they was called the Big Kid and the Little Kid. The Big Kid was exactly like Ike, full of reasons and that skinny that My Dad said he ate so much it made him thin to

carry it around. While the Little Kid was more Em's kind,
squat and sturdy and slow thinking. They was always clinging
to some part of each other's anatomy like as if they was Siamese
and couldn't come apart nohow.

After Ike took up with Em, he kept at My Dad's heels like a
barking dog to get him to take a woman. 'If you don't get yourself a son what's to become of the Moons?' He worrit My Dad
with asking: 'Who's my kids going to work for? You want
Moon Manor to fall into strange hands after all we sweat and
dug?'

My Dad would agree with him, but would never do no more
about it than to sit of nights studying the picture in the back of
his watch of the girl he'd left behind him back in the Blue Grass.
So if Big Melody hadn't sent him to Congress I probably would
never of been born, on accounta Washington was where my
mother lived. My Dad wanted a mother for his son and she
wanted a lover. They was never no peace between them and
when My Dad's term of office expired, she was plumb glad to
take the money what he give her and to let him take me off to
my homeplace.

Nobuddy ever tolt me anything about her, but once I overheard My Dad say to Ike, 'I've had another letter from Kathy;
she wants me to let her have the boy for the summer.'

'Tell her you'll see her in hell first,' Ike said awful mad.
'Don't she know Jonathan is the only Moon left 'cept you?'

'You can't have a child by a woman and then jest pick up and
leave,' My Dad said. 'And that's pretty much what I did.
Kathy's a fine girl, it makes me feel like a skunk to say no, but
the life she would give Jonathan would be death to a Moon.'

It didn't bother Ike none that My Dad fetched me home without my mother. He was plumb glad not to have a woman person
interfering with how he should bring me up. Us Kids' education
was a great concern of Ike's. He taught us to read outa Huntly's

'History of the World,' the same outa what My Dad had taught him. We never got very far in books though, on accounta Ike never agreeing with them and spending most of the time showing us they was all wrong. My Dad was always threatening to send back east for a tutor, but Us Kids would beg him not, for how could any strange person know so well as Ike what we'd a need to know? 'More men what's lived been fools than's not,' Ike would say, when we come to an extra disagreeable page. 'So a man's got to be careful, or he'll be believing their nonsense. The Moons never set much store by books anyway, they being mostly writ for folks not smart enough to figure things out for themselves.'

Both Ike and Em put me afore their own kids, but there was one thing Ike wouldn't learn me no matter how I begged. 'Us Wheelers have always fiddled for you Moons,' he said, and would go on learning the Big Kid to fiddle while I sulked in the corner. They was nobody in our parts what could play the fiddle like Ike. Nights when he took a fiddling fit the tall sage brush along the river bank back of our house was all filled up with our Outfit what had snuck up from the Bunkhouse to listen, and happen a stranger passed on the road he said, 'Whoa!' to his team for a spell. His music was awful sad; even when it was happy it was sad, on accounta it made you feel that the happiness had been dearly paid for and might be soon going.

I could never properly decide what I liked best, Ike's fiddling or his singing. He was plumb chuck full of songs. Mostly sad, too. All about homesick cowboys and separated sweethearts and wronged women and such. But the sorrowfullest of all was about a boy what starved to death in the great Irish famine. I recollect that night My Dad had got in late from Sundance and was having a plate of beans at the kitchen table while Ike was singing this'n. When he got to the part, 'Give me three grains of corn, mother, only three grains of corn, 'twill keep the little life I have till the coming of the morn,' Em and Us Kids was all weeping like as if it was a hoss-selling day. 'Will these beans put you outa your misery?' My Dad said, and then threw a spoonful what landed plunk against Ike's bald head.

'You want your son to grow up a hard-hearted losel like your-self?' Ike asked, mad as a wet hen. 'Cause you got no feelings, you got no call to discourage them in your son.'

Them two was always argufying. My Dad wanted Moon Manor to be modern, but Ike hated machinery. He took a ax and chopped up the first mow what My Dad bought on accounta it cut off a jackrabbit's leg and I recollect well the first time he saw a car.

Him and Us Kids had all been berrying and when we come up outa the river bottom we saw that our hitching posts was all filled up with teams and ponies, and that our big corral fence was lined with neighbors. This often happened; folks heard of some-thing and then come to hear what Ike thought about it. As we come up, Big Melody what was sitting long side of My Dad on the corral gate called out, 'Well, Parson, what's the sermon tonight?'

Big Melody always said this and it always made Ike mad, but this night he didn't answer back on accounta we all had saw the thing. We knowed what it was from the papers, but we was all comfluttered to see one standing right there by our corral like as if it had a right. A city man was sitting on the front seat. Ike walked up to him looking so mad that the City Man put up his fists. Ike turned to My Dad. 'You sit there on your goddamned monkey tail and laugh, with a thing like that on your home-place,' Ike said. 'David, you're a disgrace to the Moons.'

'Drive it around the corral a couple of times, Mr. Kalkins,' My Dad said, laughing so he had to put his hands over his heart where the pain always come. 'Let Ike see how it goes.'

It made a noise like thunder in the Firehole Divide when it moved. Ike dropped the berry pails and lifted Us Kids up to

My Dad outa harm's way. The hosses began to scream and kick and one team broke loose and ran with the buggy right out in our potato patch afore the thing stopped.

'It's a magic wonder the earth don't open right up and swallow such a blasphemous thing,' Ike marveled. 'It's worse than a train, 'cause it ain't got no tracks so's you can figure out where it'll go.'

'Twould save a hoss a lot of work,' My Dad said, winking at Big Melody.

'You could go sparking the Merry Widow in Greacewood and be back before Em missed you,' Big Melody said, knowing well that Ike never looked at any woman save Em and was always argufying with men what went outa their own homes for such.

Ike paid them no heed. 'I'd be mortal shamed to be seen in one riding cross-country with all the animals and birds fleeing for their lives.'

'They're a thousand times better than a hoss,' the City Man said, thinking that on accounta all the men was laughing at Ike they was not for him. 'They can do anything.'

'Can they rope a steer?' Ike said quick-like, and reached out and yanked the City Man outa the thing.

My Dad and Big Melody was laughing so they could scarce pull Ike off'n the City Man. 'Best take that thing and get,' Big Melody tolt the City Man, looking kind of sheepish on accounta he didn't want Ike to know he had asked the stranger out.

Folks always laughed at Ike, but they didn't often go against what he said. He sized up new comers and tolt what to expect of them and he'd only to look at a piece of land to know what best would grow there. So our country was pretty slow at buying cars. Long after the happening at the corral, car dealers would meet up with the question, 'Can they rope steers?'

Every Sunday during the summer, Ike would take Us Kids on a walk over the Moon Manor what would last the whole day through. 'You can't know your homeplace too well,' Ike would say as we cut off through the fields. 'For the land can't really be your'n till you've walked over every inch of it.'

'Twas at the end of one of these hikes that our first trouble come, so I recollect it well. We started out afore sunup, the dew wetting us to our knees and Ike bending beneath the grub poke and chewing on a stalk of alfalfa. Ike always chewed alfalfa. He said folks missed a lot by not having a hoss's appetite of it.

We left the fields at Saddle Ridge and from there we could see way off, beyond Big Melody's Ten Sleep, the far purple mountains of the Park. Ike pointed out the divide in the highlands, where he and My Dad first saw Moon Manor. 'We was glad to get outa the mountains,' he said. 'They be no ways fitting for a homeplace, for their canyons yawn like open graves and their heights is a torment to the pride of man.'

The sun was breath warm on the ridge and Ike stretched out on a sandbar to dry his shoes. The Kids gathered sand lilies and got their noses all yellow from the deep smells they took. I walked a spell higher. Below the purple alfalfa moved in the breeze and half choked me with its sweet stinging smell. The big white house and the corrals seemed as growed to the earth as the cottonwoods what shaded them. Frail colored mists hung over the river what was overfull with June meltings. Across it in the pale green stretches of pasture, the young hosses had set themselves agin the mornglome and from the earth I felt the heavy thud of their feet. The ridge showed me my homeplace, and a meadow lark put a tune to what I saw.

'Look good to you, Jonathan?' Ike come up and put his hand on my shoulder. 'Men worshipped the earth afore they growed blasphemous and invented God.' Ike pointed to the highway beyond the Manor what was dotted here and there with buggies. 'Whole Yellowstone is turning out to church, and in strange parts other men are doing the same. They will shut themselves up in a house with windows made of glass what they can't see outa, and they'll read outa a book what's all about some god what was always hurting poor folks just to show them how strong he was. Ain't no need trying to make sense of it.'

The Kids had got so far ahead in their lily hunt that we had to run to catch up with them. At the foot of the ridge we come on a thicket a buffalo berries, and we all broke off branches an' et from them as we walked. Afore noon we was come to Bitter Creek and the old soddy what Ike and My Dad had put up their first year in the Yellowstone. Ike lifted us each up to read the faint printing of 'Moon Manor' above the door, what My Dad had scratched on so long ago with a piece of red sandstone. 'Folks laughed,' Ike said. 'They said as how Moon Manor was a mighty high sounding name for such diggings, but they be laughing outa the other sides of their mouths now.'

There wasn't any windows and only one door, and inside the air was damp like a cave. Hundreds of little lives lived in the walls, and the spiders were that many that between one week and the next we had to break their webs between the table and the chairs. Ike built a smudge in the fireplace to scare out everything, and then we all went down to the creek and stript and went in.

The creek was too shallow for Ike to do much swimming, so he found himself in a clay bed, where the water was only a few inches deep, and laid down. After a spell I left the Kids yelling at magpies what was sitting in the cottonwoods mocking us and waded over and joined him. The clay was as soft and smooth as Em's bosom when she had on her black satin dress. I stretched myself as far as I could in it. The warm live water ebbing up between my armpits and legs and the little threads of moss what drifted agin my skin and clung made me conscious of my body. I was all flesh like a pig in a pasture ditch. I liked it.

Rinsing ourselves off, but not bothering with clothes yet, we went back to the soddy and made us a snack. We had roast apples and potatoes and broiled beef strips, and we et so much Ike said he could see our bellies swelling up like bloated cows. Food always set Ike to recollecting. He tolt us happenings of the Yellowstone what made us mad with jealousy at being born so late.

Our shadows was long like as if we had stilts when we started out. The Kids ran ahead and filled their pockets with isinglass until they come to the collie where the tall sage growed, and then they waited for us. I knowed why they waited. They was scairt.

'I was only a little tad no bigger than you, Jonathan,' Ike said, shouldering the tall sage brush aside so we could pass. 'I was down here hunting our milk cow when I runs on their camp. They was after the corral full of mustangs what your Dad had spent all summer wrangling, and knowing we was all alone felt safe to camp right on our land. In the morning while one of them woulda shot your Dad and me, the others woulda made off with the hosses.

'I knowed they was the famous Rabbit Rustlers as soon as I saw them. Folks called them that on accounta they never give a man they robbed a rabbit's chance afore they kilt him. I ran back and tolt your Dad, but all he could do was to clean his guns and wait for dark, help being so far it was outa the question. So soon as it was good and black we snuck out, leaving the lantern still burning as though we was all unknowing in the soddy. We made a wide circle of their camp and come up on them from behind. All four a them was sitting round their campfire swapping yarns. We was in ten yards of them afore your Dad started to shoot. He shot so fast that only one a them had time to draw his gun afore they was all dead.

'It took us all night to dig their grave, but as soon as we could we took their hosses and outfit into Sundance and turned them over to Big Melody who was sheriff then. Your Dad said he found the rustler's outfit running loose in the hills. Big Melody knowed he was lying and tried to get him to own up, on accounta he thought your Dad should have the five thousand dollar reward what the government offered for them dead or alive, but your Dad went right on saying he didn't know nothing about nothing and he'd jest found the hosses loose in the hills.'

We was all standing around the bare sunken spot where the tall sage wouldn't grow, while Ike talked. He fished in his jumper for his handkerchief and wiped the wet from his eyes, and his voice was all choky when he went on. 'Your Dad was never properly proud of this piece of work. Years after I'd hear him talking in his sleep about it, but he'd no call to let it hurt his happiness. Without the money what the mustangs fetched, he'd not been able to fence Moon Manor, and the squatters woulda took it away from him. A man's got a right to fight for his homeplace, and land what is held at the price of blood grows dearer to the heart. Any Moon woulda done what he done.'

Ike had always a hard time to leave that place and this day Us Kids had to pull him along. He was glum all the way over the hills and cross the river on the highway bridge till we come to the pastures and the hosses started whinnying to him. They come running from all parts, and crowded round him like as if he was one of them. Us Kids couldn't see him at all, but we heared the denim of his pockets rip as they nosed for sugar. Ike tolt us each to get on while they was crowded up agin the fence, and when we did he swung up on Hannibal, the best bid of the year, and we all started off barebacked across the pastures with the unmounted hosses tagging like dogs behind.

The hard pressure of the young mare's back between my legs and the wind whipping down my shirt front and cross my bare body made me feel more than a man. The sky seemed only a step from the earth, and I thought any moment I would rise to it, and I thought that the feel of the red-gold clouds must be even grander than the wind, and I thought that the sun teetering on the tip of Troll Peak was a ripe apple for me to pick as I passed.

The scairt howl of a dog what smelt death come to us 'cross the river from the house. Ike was off'n Hannibal as soon as it reached his ears and running for the bridge and shouting back for Us Kids to follow. We saw Doc Sessions' hoss in the corral and knowed that it meant My Dad. For years the Doc had been telling him to mind his heart, but My Dad always answered, 'To hell with it. If it can't beat strong enough for a man, then the sooner it stops the better.'

Em was at the door to hurry us up the stairs to My Dad's room. Doc Sessions was bending over the bed. 'There's life in him,' he said to Ike, 'but it won't be there long.'

'He was pitching hoss shoes with the Outfit down behind the bunkhouse,' Em said, rolling her apron into a ball. 'And all at onct he jest toppled over and they had to fetch him in.'

I pushed past the grownups so I could see My Dad. His eyes was shut, but his forehead and cheeks peering outa his heavy white hair and beard showed dark red and the quilt scarce moved with his breath.

'Come here, Jonathan.' Ike knelt by the bed and pulled me down with him, Em and the Kids stood behind us. There wasn't any place for the Doc, so he went to the door and turned his back. Snige started howling agin. 'That goddamned dog,' Ike said.

My Dad's eyes opened at Ike's voice and moved back and forth between us till they understood. Then a great twinkle come in them, like as always when he talked to Ike. 'Don't forget to look after the Moons,' he said, his body sort of straightening out.

We looked at My Dad for a long time. Then Ike got up and pulled the sheet over My Dad's face, and it seemed like as if he ought to have pulled something over the purple gray of the sky and over the hills and fields, what was growing more beautiful in the glome. None of us was like I had ever knowed us, but outside the watery roar of the Shoshone hadn't so much as quivered, and the hosses went right on playing in the pastures. It made me mad. Em come up and put her hand on my hair. 'Don't you feel bad, Jonathan,' she said. 'You'll see your Dad some day in a much better world than this'n.'

'Don't lie to him!' Ike grabbed me fiercely from Em. 'He shan't be comforted by lies! Jonathan, your Dad is dead. What's happened to all the people in other years has happened to him, and it will one day happen to you. He's dead and he'll stay that way, and them that says different ain't got the guts to say the truth. But he had a grand life and he'd no kick coming. Don't let me hear none outa you.'

'I ain't kicking,' I said. 'Only I don't want the sky to be so fine, I don't ——'

'The earth can't change on accounta one man has died,' Ike said. 'Not even him,' and he held me close.

That night after they had dressed My Dad up in his Sunday suit, and carried him down to the parlor lounge to wait for the coffin what Big Melody and the Outfit was making out in the back yard, Ike took me in where My Dad was and closed the door. He lifted down the great scythe what hung above the fireplace, what had belonged to Roland Moon the Strong, and handed it to me. Then he went into My Dad's study and fetched the iron chestful of earth, what Peter Moon had brought outa Sussex two hundred and fifty years before. 'A scythe and a bit of earth,' Ike said. 'These be your inheritance from the Moons. They had gold and jewels like other men, but 'twas these they saw fit to hand down to their sons and their sons' sons. They be yours now, Jonathan. Mind you keep faith with them as honorably as your Dad.'

We buried My Dad up on Saddle Ridge, where he'd often said all the Moon Manor was to lie. There was no parson, no nothing, jest us and Big Melody. Ike took a pinch of earth from the iron

chest and flung it into the open grave. 'You and me wouldn't
be worth that,' he said, as he lifted me up in the buggy for going
home.

Them two had always quarreled, My Dad laughing and Ike in
tears, but now that My Dad was up on the Ridge, he belonged to
the Moons; the very best best of the lot and Ike almost forgot the
others in remembering him. Moon Manor ran on, jest like as if
My Dad was still with us. No problem ever come up but what
Ike couldn't recollect something My Dad had said what would
solve it. We was almost getting happy again, the autumn earth
not letting us be sad, and then she come.

Ike was fiddling for us in the kitchen so we never heared her
car on the road, or her knock at the door. We jest looked up and
saw her peering through the screen door at us. She wore a yellow
dress and hat and with the night behind her, she looked like as
if she had jest stepped outa the moon. 'I'm David's wife,' she
said as Ike bid her come in.

She came and stood on our kitchen hearth and shook the dust
from her clothes. Her big black eyes searched me outa behind
Em's chair. 'So you are Jonathan,' she said, and come and pushed
my hair outa my eyes. I felt her studying every inch of me.
'Thank God, you're a Coniston,' she said, meaning her own
people.

'He ain't, he's a Moon!' Ike fair snatched me from her.

His madness didn't scare her a bit, she jest looked at him cool
like and said, 'You are Ike, aren't you? I remember David talking about you. Why wasn't I notified of his death? I learned of
it quite by chance. A friend of mine summered in the Park and
wrote me of it, so I came at once for my son.'

'You ain't got no son what I know of,' Ike said holding me behind him. 'You sold him to David for money! I know, 'cause he
tolt me so.'

'I was a very young girl then,' she said, and the angry red in her cheeks made her look like the lady on the Bank of Cheyenne calendar. 'I had made an unhappy marriage, I wanted to forget it, and I thought that by giving up my son I could live again as though nothing had ever happened. But I couldn't. David knew I couldn't. I wrote him time after time and begged him for my son.'

'What you aim to do now?' Ike said.

'Why, take my son,' she said. 'And give him the life that belongs to him.'

'Jonathan belongs to Moon Manor,' Ike said.

'I've had enough of ranchmen,' she said. 'I shan't have one for my son. Jonathan's education will be expensive. My lawyer will dispose of the ranch for me.'

'I'm pretty much alive,' Ike said, 'and afore you could do that I'd have to be dead. Moon Manor belongs to Jonathan and Jonathan belongs to it. Ain't nothing going to separate them! Never!'

'Now don't be foolish,' she said. 'You have no lawful right to him. David never left a will. I found that out at the bank in Sundance; and we were never divorced. I'm the child's mother and no law court in the world would take him from me.'

'Damn the law,' Ike said. 'A man's got a right to fight for his homeplace. Jonathan ain't big enough, but he's got me.'

'If you were capable of reason,' she said, 'I could talk to you.'

'An' if you was a man I could talk to you.' Ike let go of me and reached for his gun what hanged on the door, handy for hawks and coyotes. He didn't point it at her, but held it down at his side. 'You'd better go,' he said.

She looked at him and laughed and then turned to me like as if she never cared what he had in his hand. She took a handkerchief outa her bag what was softer than anything I ever felt, and wiped my face with it. 'I'm your mother,' she said, 'and God only knows what they've told you about me.' Then she tipped my chin up to kiss me, but I drawed back and went and sat on the milk bench with the Kids. I didn't like nobuddy what Ike didn't.

'You understand who she is, Jonathan? You understand what she wants?' Ike waited for me to nod my head afore he went on. 'Then tell her how it strikes you.'

'I shan't give him a chance to say something to his mother that he will be sorry for afterwards.' She took hold of my hand tight and drew me off'n the bench. 'You're coming with me now. I should never feel safe to leave you here with this man another night.'

'You got the law on your side. I ain't fool enough not to know that. And if I was a man what was feared of it, you could do all you say and I'd stand by and let you. Only I ain't!' Ike pointed the gun square at her now. 'But you ain't got no law with you here tonight. Take your hands off'n that boy and get!'

'You'd never dare,' she said and kept holt my hand. 'You'd hang for it.'

'Not if I turned it on myself afterwards,' Ike said.

'You'd never dare,' she said again, and took a step towards the door pulling me with her. 'If I didn't know how faithfully you'd worked for David all these years, I'd have you arrested as soon as I get to Sundance,' she said, getting braver on accounta he didn't answer her.

She had me almost to the door when the shot come, and when she fell she pulled me down with her. The blood spouted like a little spring from the bosom of her yellow dress. I snatched my hand away and stood up. I looked at Ike and was afraid to go to him, so I ran to where Em and the Kids crouched in the dining room doorway screaming. Ike turned to us and waved the gun like as if it was a whip. 'Go upstairs, you all! Go!' he said.

'Maybe she ain't dead,' Em said. 'Maybe Big Melody can help us.'

'I took you off'n Karl Linden because you was smart,' Ike said. 'Now take the Kids outa here. Quick!'

We was half way up the stairs when the second shot come, and we turned and ran back to the kitchen. Ike lay on the hearth rug, its bright colors growing brighter with his blood. Em sit on the floor and took his head in her lap, and the Kids tugged at his boots.

I walked to the screen door, past her body, and stood studying my homeplace. The northern lights was playing green and red across the pale stubbles of the alfalfa fields, and for half a minute I saw the mound of My Dad's grave up on Saddle Ridge. Then the lights moved on to the river, coloring it like the spreading red on the floor. 'Land what is held at the price of blood grows dearer to the heart,' Ike had once said, and I looked, and knowed he was right.

HORSE THIEF[1]

ERSKINE CALDWELL

I

I DIDN'T steal Lud Moseley's calico horse.

People all over have been trying to make me out a thief, but anybody who knows me at all will tell you that I've never been in trouble like this before in all my life. Mr. John Turner will tell you all about me. I've worked for him, off and on, for I don't know exactly how many years. I reckon I've worked for him just about all my life, since I was a boy. Mr. John knows I wouldn't steal a horse. That's why I say I didn't steal Lud Moseley's, like he swore I did. I didn't grow up just to turn out to be a horse thief.

Night before last, Mr. John told me to ride his mare, Betsy. I said I wanted to go off a little way after something, and he told me to go ahead and ride Betsy, like I have been doing every Sunday night for going on two years now. Mr. John told me to take the Texas saddle, but I told him I didn't care about riding saddle. I like to ride with a bridle and reins, and nothing else. That's the best way to ride, anyway. And where I was going I didn't want to have a squeaking saddle under me. I wasn't up to no mischief.

It was just a little private business of my own that nobody has got a right to call me down about. I nearly always rode saddle Sunday nights, but night before last was Thursday night, and that's why I didn't have a saddle when I went.

Mr. John Turner will tell you I'm not the kind to go off and get into trouble. Ask Mr. John about me. He has known me all my life, and I've never given him or anybody else trouble.

When I took Betsy out of the stable that night after supper, Mr. John came out to the barnyard and asked me over again if I didn't want to take the Texas saddle. That mare, Betsy, is a little rawboned, but I didn't mind that. I told Mr. John I'd just as lief ride bareback. He said it was all right with him if I wanted to get sawn in two, and for me to go ahead and do like I pleased about it. He was standing right there all the time, rubbing Betsy's mane, and trying to find out where I was going, without coming right out and asking me. But he knew all the time where I was going, because he knows all about me. I reckon he just wanted to have a laugh at me, but he couldn't do that if I didn't let on where I was headed. So he told me it was all right to ride his mare without a saddle if I didn't want to be bothered with one, and I opened the gate and rode off down the road towards Bishop's crossroads.

That was night before last — Thursday night. It was a little after dark then, but I could see Mr. John standing at the barnyard gate, leaning on it a little, and watching me ride off. I'd been plowing that day, over in the new ground, and I was dog-tired. That's one reason why I didn't gallop off like I always did on Sunday nights. I rode away slow, letting Betsy take her own good time, because I wasn't in such a big hurry, after all. I had about two hours' time to kill, and only a little over three miles to go. That's why I went off like that.

II

Everybody knows I've been going to see Lud Moseley's young-est daughter, Naomi. I was going to see her again that night. But I couldn't show up there till about nine-thirty. Lud Moseley wouldn't let me come to see her but once a week, on Sunday nights, and night before last was Thursday. I'd been there to see her three or four times before on Thursday nights that Lud Moseley didn't know about. Naomi told me to come to see her on Thursday nights. That's why I had been going there when Lud Moseley said I couldn't come to his house but once a week. Naomi told me to come anyway, and she had been coming out to the swing under the trees in the front yard to meet me.

I haven't got a thing in the world against Lud Moseley. Mr. John Turner will tell you I haven't. I don't especially like him, but that's to be expected, and he knows why. Once a week isn't enough to go to see a girl you like a lot, like I do Naomi. And I reckon she likes me a little, or she wouldn't tell me to come to see her on Thursday nights, when Lud Moseley told me not to come. Lud Moseley thinks if I go to see her more than once a week that maybe we'll take it into our heads to go get married without giving him a chance to catch on. That's why he said I couldn't come to his house but once a week, on Sunday nights.

He's fixing to have me sent to the penitentiary for twenty years for stealing his calico horse, Lightfoot. I reckon he knows good and well I didn't steal the horse, but he figures he's got a good chance to put me out of the way till he can get Naomi married to somebody else. That's the way I figure it all out, be-cause everybody in this part of the country who ever heard tell of me knows I'm not a horse thief. Mr. John Turner will tell you that about me. Mr. John knows me better than that. I've worked for him so long he even tried once to make me out as one of the family, but I wouldn't let him do that.

So, night before last, Thursday night, I rode off from home bare-

back, on Betsy. I killed a little time down at the creek, about a
mile down the road from where we live, and when I looked at my
watch again, it was nine o'clock sharp. I got on Betsy and rode
off towards Lud Moseley's place. Everything was still and quiet
around the house and barn. It was just about Lud's bedtime
then. I rode right up to the barnyard gate, like I always did on
Thursday nights. I could see a light up in Naomi's room, where
she slept with her older sister, Mary Lee. We had always figured
on Mary Lee's being out with somebody else, or maybe being
ready to go to sleep by nine-thirty. When I looked up at their
window, I could see Naomi lying across her bed, and Mary Lee
was standing beside the bed talking to her about something.
That looked bad, because when Mary Lee tried to make Naomi
undress and go to bed before she did, it always meant that it
would take Naomi another hour or more to get out of the room,
because she had to wait for Mary Lee to go to sleep before she
could leave. She had to wait for Mary Lee to go to sleep, and
then she had to get up and dress in the dark before she could
come down to the front yard and meet me in the swing under the
trees.

III

I sat there on Betsy for ten or fifteen minutes, waiting to see
how Naomi was going to come out with her sister. I reckon if
we had let Mary Lee in on the secret she would have behaved all
right about it, but on some account or other Naomi couldn't
make up her mind to run the risk of it. There was a mighty
chance that she would have misbehaved about it and gone
straight and told Lud Moseley, and we didn't want to run that
risk.

After a while I saw Naomi get up and start to undress. I
knew right away that that meant waiting another hour or longer
for her to be able to come and meet me. The moon was starting

to rise, and it was getting to be as bright as day out there in the barnyard. I'd been in the habit of opening the gate and turning Betsy loose in the yard, but I was scared to do it night before last. If Lud Moseley should get up for a drink of water or something, and happen to look out toward the barn and see a horse standing there, he would either think it was one of his and come out and lock it in the stalls, or else he would catch on it was me out there. Anyway, as soon as he saw Betsy, he would have known it wasn't his mare, and there would have been the mischief to pay right there and then. So I opened the barn door and led Betsy inside and put her in the first empty stall I could find in the dark. I was scared to strike a light, because I didn't know but what Lud Moseley would be looking out the window just at that time and see the flare of the match. I put Betsy in the stall, closed the door, and came back outside to wait for Naomi to find a chance to come out and meet me in the swing in the yard.

It was about twelve-thirty or one o'clock when I got ready to leave for home. The moon had been clouded, and it was darker than everything in the barn. I couldn't see my hand in front of me, it was that dark. I was scared to strike a light that time, too, and I felt my way in and opened the stall door and stepped inside to lead Betsy out. I couldn't see a thing, and when I found her neck, I thought she must have slipped her bridle like she was always doing when she had to stand too long to suit her. I was afraid to try to ride her home without a lead of some kind, because I was scared she might shy in the barnyard and start tearing around out there and wake up Lud Moseley. I felt around on the ground for the bridle, but I couldn't find it anywhere. Then I went back to the stall door and felt on it, thinking I might have taken it off myself when I was all excited at the start, and there was a halter hanging up. I slipped it over her head and led her out. It was still so dark I couldn't see a thing, and I had to feel my way outside and through the barnyard gate.

When I got to the road, I threw a leg over her, and started for home without wasting any more time around Lud Moseley's place. I thought she trotted a little funny, because she had a swaying swing that made me slide from side to side, and I didn't have a saddle pommel to hold on to. I was all wrought up about getting away from there without getting caught up with, and I didn't think a thing about it. But I got home all right and slipped the halter off and put her in her stall. It was around one or two o'clock in the morning then.

The next morning after breakfast, when I was getting ready to catch the mules and gear them up to start plowing in the new ground again, Lud Moseley and three or four other men, including the sheriff, came riding lickety-split up the road from town and hitched at the rack. Mr. John came out and slapped the sheriff on the back and told him a funny story. They carried on like that for nearly half an hour, and then the sheriff asked Mr. John where I was. Mr. John told him I was getting ready to go off to the new ground, where we had planted a crop of corn that spring, and then the sheriff said he had a warrant for me. Mr. John asked him what for, a joke or something? And the sheriff told him it was for stealing Lud Moseley's calico horse, Lightfoot. Mr. John laughed at him, because he still thought it just a joke, but the sheriff pulled out the paper and showed it to him. Mr. John still wouldn't believe it, and he told them there was a mix-up somewhere, because, he told them, I wouldn't steal a horse. Mr. John knows I'm not a horse thief. I've never been in any kind of trouble before in all my life.

They brought me to town right away and put me in the cell-room at the sheriff's jail. I knew I hadn't stole Lud Moseley's horse, and I wasn't scared a bit about it. But right after they brought me to town, they all rode back and the sheriff looked in the barn and found Lud Moseley's calico horse, Lightfoot, in Betsy's stall. Mr. John said things were all mixed up, because he knew I didn't steal the horse, and he knew I wouldn't do it. But the horse was there, the calico one, Lightfoot, and his halter was hanging on the stall door. After that they went back to Lud Moseley's and measured my foot tracks in the barnyard, and then they found Betsy's bridle. Lud Moseley said I had rode Mr. John's mare over there, turned her loose, and put the bridle on his Lightfoot and rode him off. They never did say how come the halter to get to Mr. John's stable, then. Lud Moseley's stall door was not locked, and it wasn't broken down. It looks now like I forgot to shut it tight when I put Betsy in, because she got out someway and came home of her own accord sometime that night.

Lud Moseley says he's going to send me away for twenty years where I won't have a chance to worry him over his youngest daughter, Naomi. He wants her to marry a widowed farmer over beyond Bishop's crossroads who runs twenty plows and who's got a big white house with fifteen rooms in it. Mr. John Turner says he'll hire the best lawyer in town to take up my case, but it don't look like it will do much good, because my footprints are all over Lud Moseley's barnyard, and his Lightfoot was in Mr. John's stable.

I reckon I could worm out of it someway, if I made up my mind to do it. But I don't like to do things like that. It would put Naomi in a bad way, because if I said I was there seeing her, and had put Betsy in the stall to keep her quiet, and took Lightfoot out by mistake in the dark when I got ready to leave — well, it would just look bad, that's all. She would have to say she was in the habit of slipping out of the house to see me after everybody had gone to sleep, on Thursday nights, and it would just look bad all around. She might take it into her head some day that she'd rather marry somebody else than me, and by that time she'd have a bad name for having been mixed up with me — and slipping out of the house to meet me after bedtime.

Naomi knows I'm no horse thief. She knows how it all happened — that I rode Lud Moseley's calico horse, Lightfoot, off by mistake in the dark, and left the stall door unfastened, and Betsy got out and came home of her own accord.

Lud Moseley has been telling people all around the courthouse as how he is going to send me away for twenty years so he can get Naomi married to that widowed farmer who runs twenty plows. Lud Moseley is right proud of it, it looks like to me, because he's got me cornered in a trap, and maybe he will get me sent away sure enough before Naomi gets a chance to tell what she knows is true.

But, somehow, I don't know if she'll say it if she does get the chance. Everybody knows I'm nothing but a hired man at Mr. John Turner's, and I've been thinking that maybe Naomi might not come right out and tell what she knows, after all.

I'd come right out and explain to the sheriff how the mix-up happened, but I sort of hate to mention Naomi's name in the mess. If it had been a Sunday night, instead of night before last, a Thursday, I could — well, it would just sound too bad, that's all.

If Naomi comes to town and tells what she knows, I won't say a word to stop her, because that'll mean she's willing to say it and marry me.

But if she stays at home, and lets Lud Moseley and that widowed farmer send me away for twenty years, I'll just have to go, that's all.

I always told Naomi I'd do anything in the world for her, and I reckon this will be the time when I've got to prove whether I'm a man of my word or not.

WINTER[1]

DOROTHY M'CLEARY

Yes, you're kind of thin, and that's a fact.' Hannah ran her finger along his ribs. 'But then I always say that's a good fault — *one* way you look at it, that is.'

They were lying in Hannah's bed. The bed resembled Hannah, in that it was light in colouring, old, time-scarred, yet, in spite of saggings and warped seams, still staunchly durable. It had a bolster, with a wrinkled and spotted cover upon which their heads rested comfortably. Both felt lazily at ease, drowsy and indifferent, satisfied to lie warm in bed, watching the snow sift past the window-pane, listening at intervals to the depressing toll of a church bell.

'It's a Sunday morning,' he muttered, as the bell forced itself into his brain.

'Sunday morning, hell!' said Hannah. 'It's Christmas.'

He half raised himself from the pillow and stared into her face.

'*No!* No, not Christmas,' he pleaded.

'Well, I'm not lyin' to you, am I? There, look for yourself.' She took his head between her long hard hands and turned it in the direction of the wall nearest him. A big calendar hung there, its numbers two inches high, bearing on its upper half a life-size picture of a baby yawning. He studied this for several minutes. 'Yes,' he said, 'that's very nice. That's a very nice calendar.'

'It *is* pretty, ain't it? I got it from Ike's place, that place on the corner — you know it? I like to have something bright to cast my eyes on now and again. You know, I get blue, 'specially in the winter time. God damn it, I get lonesome.' She reached out and put her arm under his head. 'I don't always have congenial company, and that's God's truth.' Under the blankets her feet sought his thin, cold ones and enveloped them in a warm embrace.

'But no joking, now,' he begged. 'Is today the twenty-fifth? For God's sake, girl, tell me the truth. Go on, tell me. I can bear it. But don't *trifle* with me! Don't *jest* ——'

'Say, can't you read a calendar? My God!' cried Hannah.

He looked again at the tremendous chart. But he could not bring his mind to a focus on it. Instead, he began to read the numbers aloud, 'One, two, three, four, five ——'

'Say!' Hannah shouted. 'Lookit where I point. Lookit, see that there 25? That red one. It's *red* — see?'

'Yes,' he said, quickly withdrawing his eyes.

'Well, then, am I lyin' to you?'

He searched her face with painful concentration. His eyes examined every detail, every wrinkle, each hair of her yellow eyelashes, the little ragged white scar at the edge of her lip, the ears, with their soft appetizing lobes, the wild hair. 'Oh, God,' he whispered. He shuddered and turned away from her. 'God, but that hits me hard. That hits me right where I live.' He closed his eyes, and his face contorted itself; he broke into sobbing.

Hannah watched him idly, just as a dog, lying with one eye lolled open, might watch another dog biting at fleas. He had not put up a hand to cover his face, but cried face up, unashamed.

His hair was thin and grey, his neck a criss-cross of wrinkles, and he had little untended tufts of black hair in his ears.

Hannah looked more intently at his face. It began to remind her of something — she couldn't think what it was. She lay, frowning and scratching her head, until all at once it came to her: yes, it was the lion cub she had seen one day at a vaudeville show! It stood on a narrow shelf in the cage and whimpered, and wouldn't go through its tricks. The keeper lashed it in the face with his whip. The cub howled. The keeper lashed it again and again, sometimes across the eyes, until Hannah could stand no more of it. Up she had jumped from her seat, shaking her fist at the keeper. 'Leave that brute be, do you hear me?' she had yelled. 'You lay off that, now — I'm tellin' you — or I'll call a cop!' God, yes, the whole thing came back to her. Maybe she'd had a little extra gin before she left home. Well, anyhow, as she remembered it, she tried to climb up on the stage and kill the man. 'I'll slice you to pieces with your own whip!' she called. 'Aw, she's drunk,' people cried. 'Whyn't you hire a hall, lady?' 'Go on, give 'er the air.' 'Leave me at him!' Hannah yelled savagely. But two men, grabbing hold of her, shoved her along and out through a side-exit. 'And here's your hat, old woman,' somebody had yelled, throwing it after her.

Hannah frowned, and lay staring up at the cracks in the ceiling. Suddenly she gave a hearty guffaw. 'Yes,' she said, laughing until tears came to her eyes, 'Hannah got the bum's rush that time, all right, all right.'

But the face of that poor little cub! With his eyes squeezed shut, and such a pitiful wrinkled look between his eyes. He stood there and just *took* the whip, 'just like a blessed saint,' Hannah said.

'I don't give a God damn on this lousy earth what happens to *people*,' she cried out, 'but I can't stand it to see a dumb beast suffer! Damn if I can. No, it gives me a feeling in the pit of my stomach.'

The man beside her groaned and shook with his sobbing.

'Say, lay off that, will you?' she bawled. She sat up in bed, yawned wide, and clicked her jaws together sharply. 'I'll make a hot cup o' coffee.'

She pushed off the blanket coverings and touched her feet to the cold floor. 'Holy Christmas,' she cried, shivering, 'where's my shoes?' She poked under the bed, but couldn't find them. 'But, my God, what's *this?*' She stretched herself under the bed. 'Lookit here — here's my *umbrella!* Say, it's months since I saw you, babygirl!' She kissed its dusty folds and set it lovingly in a corner of the room. Then she ran to the bureau and pulled a one-burner stove out of the top drawer, attached it to the gas jet, struck a match and warmed her hands over the flame. 'We're pretty comfortable on a day like this, baby, I'll tell the world.'

The man, exhausted and refreshed by his tears, roused himself to watch her. Her great body, with its long yellowish back, its visible ribs, and her tawny haunches and great bare feet, seemed to fill the room with animal warmth. The sight of her was soothing to him, and enlivening, as if a companionable Great Dane were moving about the room on its hind legs.

'What did you say your name was?' he asked.

'Hannah.'

'Hannah? That's funny. I had an old aunt once, named Hannah. Auntie Hannah. She was stone-deaf. You could go up behind her and yell "Fire! Thieves! Bloody murder!"'

He glanced round the room. A bony old trunk stood in one corner, with a piece of goods laid over it. On top of it he saw a bottle, a tumbler, and his own clothes sprawled in a heap. Beside the window was a chair in the last stages of disintegration; a crucifix hung above it. On three hooks beside the bed were Hannah's clothes: a dark skirt or two, hanging limply by their belts; a polka-dot dressing sacque; an old tan coat with a hat stuck into one of the pockets; a flannel petticoat, a man's bath-

robe with several neat patches on it here and there. He looked
again at the dressing sacque, and reached up to touch it; there
came from it a faint reminiscent odour of buckwheat cakes. 'Well,
my girl,' he said, 'you've got a nice, home-like little place here.'

Hannah measured the water and coffee into the coffee pot, then
took up a pair of sharp little scissors and approached the bed.
'Now sit up, baby,' she said, 'I want to trim that hair out of your
ears.'

He sat up, and Hannah wrapped a blanket tenderly round his
shoulders.

'You ought to look after these ears yourself,' she said.

'What for?' he asked impatiently. 'What does it matter?'

Hannah laughed in his face. 'Even a cat keeps herself clean.
Ain't you as good as a cat?'

He shook his head and looked mournfully out at the falling
snow.

'You don't understand me,' he said. 'No, no, you don't understand me, or you wouldn't talk to me that way. Keeping myself
clean — no, that's not the point. No, that signifies nothing at all
to me at the present time.'

'All right. Hold your head *still*, baby!'

'And bringing a *cat* into it . . .' He frowned heavily. 'Yes, a cat
licks itself all over, true! Because it doesn't know any better.
Because a cat's outlook on life is what you might call — shallow
in the extreme!'

'Now, turn the other ear.'

'And furthermore, when a cat's *sick*, it doesn't keep itself clean,
does it?' He looked up at her sharply. 'Indeed no, when it's sick
it has other things to think about. For once in its life it has something to think about besides its own fur. You can mark my words:
a sick cat is a dirty cat! Or, *vice versa*. And rightly so,' he added,
in an oratorical tone, 'for by the outer trappings can we thus
judge of the conditions within. And there, my girl, we have my

situation in a nutshell: I look like a sick man and I *am* a sick man.'

'You don't look very sick to me,' said Hannah.

'It's the *soul* I'm talking of,' he snapped, 'not the body.'

'Oh.' Hannah smiled to herself as she turned the fire out under the coffee. She opened her top bureau drawer, took out a bag of sugar and poured some into a big white cup and some into a tumbler. '*You* can drink out of the cup, baby,' she said, filling it with coffee and handing it to him. Then she unwrapped another bag and took from it part of a loaf of bread; this she tore into two hunks, handing the man one and laying the other on her half of the bolster. Running to the window she jerked it up, letting in a quick sharp blast of snow which made the man's teeth chatter. A bottle half full of frozen milk was buried under the snow on the window-ledge. She scooped some of this into his cup. 'Ice cream, baby,' she murmured; she kissed the top of his head where the hair was sparsest. 'But not for Hannah — gim*me* it as black as hell. God, I can't get it too strong or too black!' She brought her glass of coffee and crawled into the bed beside him.

Leaning against the head of the bed, with the bolster propped up behind their backs, it was cosy and comfortable. The man sipped his coffee gratefully, raising his head like a bird after each sip to stare out of the window.

'Say, I'm cold,' said Hannah. 'Reach me down that jacket, will you, baby?'

He turned and pulled the polka-dot dressing sacque from its hook. As it passed his face he smelled again the faint odour of buckwheat cakes, a familiar and homey smell. As Hannah pulled the sacque round her and slipped her arms into it he watched after it with hungry eyes. 'That's a very pretty dressing sacque,' he said.

'I don't know is it so pretty,' said Hannah, 'but it keeps me warm.'

'Someone I knew once had a dress like that,' he said, 'all polka-dots.' He reached over and took a corner of the goods in his hand, caressing it. 'As a man grows older, you understand, he likes to see things he's seen before. I *love* to see things I've seen before. I'd love to see my old home!' He took a sip of warm coffee and bit off a piece from the nubbin of bread, carefully, fearful of breaking a tooth. 'But — well — I suppose the old home's gone up the spout many a year ago; sold for taxes or what not. But listen to me, my girl: there's not a stone of it, not one square inch of it, not a *nail hole* in it, that's not sacred to me! The old home! Why, it's where I first drew breath. And let me tell you something — it's all in *here!*' He tapped his forehead. 'Yes, I can see it complete.' He looked dreamily at Hannah. 'My mother's dead, too,' he said. 'I know in my heart that she's dead. My poor little mother,' he whimpered, 'behold thy handiwork!'

'My mother was laid away eleven years ago,' said Hannah, 'come Easter.'

He pondered this a while. 'They all come to it,' he said. 'I'll be the next.' He looked at his right hand, stretching the fingers stiff until the bones stood out like a duck's webfoot. 'I live close to the bone these days.'

'Well, for God's sake!' Hannah reached out and boxed his ear. 'You're cheerful company, ain't you? My God, I'd sooner take my cup o' coffee and drink it sittin' on a slab in the morgue.'

'But *Lily's* not dead!' he announced triumphantly. 'No, Lily is as beautiful, as beautiful ——' He paused, and a radiant smile spread over his face. 'She's as beautiful as on the day I took her for my bride. Lily McMasters was her maiden name. And she was sweeter than a flower! We had children, too!' he exclaimed. 'Our first-born was a girl, little Editha; then the boy, later.'

'My married sister has two girls,' said Hannah, 'and that makes it nice for her, what with all the work around the house and all. She had a boy, but she lost him. She had a picture taken of him in his coffin. God, but it was sad! With the eyes closed and everything. My sister said it looked just like he was sleeping. But I said, "Oh, no it don't; it looks like just what it is, a dead baby." And I don't think it's good luck to photograph the dead — do you? You never know, *you* know.'

'I left her,' he moaned. 'I left my dear wife.' He covered his face with one hand. Heavy sobs shook from him.

'Go on, drink your coffee,' said Hannah.

He took a few sips, breathing heavily into the cup. 'Because a young man has hot blood in his veins — he flares up, you understand? A young man's not accountable.... And the babies kept me awake at night. It was summer, and hot as the Old Harry. The flies pestered me. Everything pestered me. Lily was always wanting money, and there *was* no money; none, that is, for fripperies. I had only a clerk's job, for I was new, I was just beginning. I was just a *young* fellow, and —— Well, I'd come home in the evening from the office, tired out, and I'd want nothing but to sit down alone in my comfortable Morris chair — just to sit there, sit there and close my eyes, and think. I'm a dreamer, you know; I'm a philosopher. I must have peace and harmony. But I found no peace there, no, that I did not. Whining babies and filthy diapers, night after night, that's what I found. That's what my life was made up of!'

'Well, say,' asked Hannah, 'what do you expect, with kids?'

'And one night,' he said fiercely, 'I came home with a new book for myself — and I can tell you what the book was!' He glared sternly at Hannah. '*First Principles*, by Herbert Spencer! A gold mine to me! Yes, *better* than finding a gold mine. And I started to sit down in my chair to read the opening chapter. For I hadn't even looked into the preface of it, not even looked over the index! I was saving that great pleasure, mark you, until I should be alone in my own chair. But when I went to sit down, what, think you, did I find in the seat of my chair? I found a puddle! A *puddle* on the cushion of my Morris chair! And Lily just laughed at me!

"Oh, put a cushion on top of it," she called out, laughing, "you'll never feel the difference." Well, that was the last straw. I took up my book and my hat ——'

'God!' said Hannah, bursting into laughter, 'a cushion, she said, eh? "Put a cushion on top!" Say, that's pretty cute, that's ——'

'But oh, what folly,' he cried, 'what bitter, bitter folly! I set my hat on top of my head, and I said to her, *to my Lily*, I said, "Go on and laugh — go right on and live like a pig in a pigpen if you like that way of living, which it seems you do. As for me," I said, "I've had enough of it. I'm *through!*" Lily didn't say one word. She was standing at the little table, looking down at what she was doing, stirring something in a bowl. But something happened to her as she stood there. Something *went out* in her; just as if I'd blown out the light of a candle, do you understand? And she, that was always so sweet, and bright, and —— "Little light of my life" is what I used to call her. But yes, so help me, something went out in Lily. I killed something in Lily, I tell you, with my own voice, my own words ——

'And that made me all the angrier. If she'd flared up at me, or said something, then I might have cooled down. But to see her give way to me, like some meek little rabbit-creature! "Oh, you Patient Griselda, you!" I shouted to her. I looked down to see what she was doing, and I saw that she was putting some kind of custard or other on a pudding, to make a special treat for me — Lily knows I'm dead-set on pudding. Well, she kept stirring it and stirring it and stirring it, until I felt I'd go mad. I up and took hold of the spoon she held, and with a swipe of my hand — like this — I gave it an ugly toss, and a little bit of the custard flew up and hit her on the cheek!'

He groaned, as if from intense pain. Perspiration stood on his face. 'Yes, that's what I did and I won't deny it,' he said. He turned to Hannah. 'Now I've told the worst sin of my life,' he said solemnly, 'and I declare I feel better already for the telling of it. It's been bottling it up, these long years, that's been the ——'

'*Sin!*' said Hannah contemptuously. 'That there's no sin. Lots of couples throw things — plates and things — at each other, and what of it? Say, do you see that crack up there in the ceiling?'

'Couples!' He winced in disgust at the term. 'Ah, no, but not like Lily and me.'

'But, of course, leaving her was a sin,' said Hannah unctuously. 'Say, do you see that big crack up there, the one right over my head?'

'Yes, yes,' he said with impatience.

'Well, that there crack's the Mississippi River!' She looked at him and gave him a sharp nudge with her elbow. 'Or so I call it,' she added. 'That's where my married sister lives, you know. She lives just outside Clarksdale, Mississippi. And she's always been after me and after me, to go down and stay with her — make my home with her, and all, see? She said how nice and quiet it was down there — just her husband and the two girls. I guess she does get kind of lonesome for her own kin, same as anybody else. "Come on down, Sister," she writes me, "I'll send you the cash for your fare if that's what's holdin' you." She's sure a dandy good-hearted woman, and I wouldn't hear a word spoken against her, only.... Well, she kept tellin' me about the peace and quiet I'd have down there in the country, and all, and how grand the Mississippi River was, until I'm damned if I didn't get to thinkin' about it kind of serious.'

She took up the coffee pot from the floor beside her and refilled his cup. 'Drink it up, little baby,' she said.

'Yes, I'd lay here on the bed by the hour, lookin' up at that crack, and turnin' it over in my mind, this way and that. My sister don't know much about me, see? And I studied in my

mind — would we hit it off good, or no? And say,' Hannah
slapped his leg in her amusement, 'I got so's I'd *dream* about that
Mississippi River! And how did it look in my dreams? Wait till
I tell you. Say, do you want to know how it looked in my dreams?
Why, like these here Easter gardens I used to have when we was
kids. Yes, all with green grass, like — and rabbits and lambs, and
baby chicks. Can you beat that? Only there was trees, too, like
some I seen in the movies. They look like these big birds — storks
or ostriches or something. Just a skinny trunk, then a big fat
treepart like a palmleaf fan, and that's all the tree there is to it.
Do you know how I mean?'

'Certainly,' he said. 'You mean the palm of the palmetto.
But you ought to know better than to look for such vegetation in
upper Mississippi! The palm tree requires a moist, semi-tropi-
cal ——'

'Yeah? Well, they don't grow down by my sister's place, and
I'll take oath to that, baby!' Hannah went on. 'But listen
here ——' She tapped him on the arm significantly. 'I dreamed
of it *three nights running!* That's the sign, you know. Yes, that
means Important Changes Are Coming Into Your Life. So I
thought, "Oh, well, all right, anything for a change; I'll go on
down." So I went down.'

'But, on the other hand,' he continued, rousing himself into
animation, 'my supposition would be that down around the delta
of the river the palmetto ——'

'*Baby!*' cried Hannah, 'never again!' She mauled his ear and
kneaded his left cheek, to let him know she meant what she said.
'Never! Inside of seven days by the clock I was back here,
stickin' the key in my own door again. Yes, I'm tellin' you! I
came in and set my old grip down and laid down on the bed and
had a good long laugh at myself. Hannah visitin'! Say, don't
make me laugh. Never again, as long as I'm alive and kickin'.
Lookit, you can take my *corpse* down there, and welcome. I don't

know but that's just what that place's good for. Yes, you can take my dead body down there and throw it in the dirty water. And see if I care!' She looked at him belligerently. He was sighing, and dipping little bits of his bread in the coffee.

'But it wasn't the Mississippi so much,' she said. 'It was my sister's place. "Quiet and peaceful!" Yes, in one way it was so quiet I could've stabbed myself, just for something to do. I couldn't smoke, I didn't know where to get a drink, and there wasn't a living soul I could sit down and have a good long talk with — like you and me now, see? But *peaceful?* Say, I had to listen to Carrie and her husband jawin' at one another all day long and half the night. And Carrie's changed! My God, but that girl has changed! She used to raise the devil, back when we was kids. She rode me a pace, all right — a regular Miss Spitfire. And now I wish't you could see her! God, I cried when I seen her. She's two years younger'n me, and she looks ninety years old! I'm tellin' you. All wrung out like an old rag. No, there's nothin' alive in Carrie now but her tongue. "Say, Carrie," I says, "you don't *live*, girlie. You don't know what life *is!*" And that got her mad. Then her and I had a jawin' match, back and forth and back and forth — My God, I can't live like that. I like things pleasant all round; give and take, like — but in a nice way. I can't stand jawin'!'

'When I shut my eyes like this I can see Lily,' he murmured, nodding his head.

'Do you see this room?' she demanded. 'This room is plenty big enough for me. I get along first-rate here, and nobody's got the right to say to me "Do this," or "Don't do that or I'll kill you!" Understand? No naggin', no jawin'. If people don't like the way I act I can damn quick tell them to get to hell out of here — and I'm not too shy to give 'em a good kick too, so's they'll know who's talkin'. Yes, the way I look at it is, live your own life and live it alone!'

'And so I have done!' he cried. 'I left the bone of my bone and flesh of my flesh. Without a word I walked out of the house and into the street. God knows what I had in mind to do, for I went straight for the docks, down back of the house. I thought to myself, "Life's over for me, now. Now I'm done for." But I was too hot-headed to drown myself. "No, by God," I said, "I'll live my life alone. Free of burdens. I'll live like a flower of the field."' His head sank down on his chest.

'If that ain't you all over!' Hannah roared with laughter. 'Wanted to be free, with nobody to say yes or no to you — like a tomcat, eh? Well, I'd say if you could look after yourself as good as a cat, all right. But look at you, poor baby! Look how scrawny you are. You need a shave, and a good bath, and a hot meal in that little stomach of yours. You need somebody to look after you. Say, my God, if it wasn't that I got my hands full now I'd do it myself!'

'No, no — I need nothing,' he said irritably. 'What I suffer is *here*,' and he pointed to his heart. 'I suffer, and I'm dying, from a dread disease — *remorse!* That's what's killing me. If only I had kissed Lily good-bye — if only I'd gone back and kissed her on the lips. I thought maybe some day I'd go back, with my pockets filled with gold pieces; and I'd bring doll-babies for the girl, and a sled — oh, a sled I fully intended to bring back with me! And a big bag of fruit, all splendid, choice fruit — large pears, big black grapes, plums, et cetera. Why, I can see my little babies so clearly! You'd think I could reach out my hand and touch them, I can see them so clearly. They looked so sweet, so innocent, when they were asleep. The girl had little yellow curls — not like these ninny-pinny clipped heads you see nowadays. No, my girl looked like an angel. Did you ever read a little book called *Editha's Burglar?* There was a picture in it that anyone might take for my Editha. That's why we named her Editha.'

'That's a pretty name, do you know it?' said Hannah.

'It is, isn't it? It's a beautiful name. Editha. Editha. I believe in giving girls pretty names, and boys strong names. It makes men of them.'

'Yes, and my sister did just the other way. She named her boy, the one that died, Archiduke. But the two girls she named Ella and Hannah, the youngest one for me. And I think my name's too plain, don't you? I never was pleased with my name. I wish they'd of called me Phyllis — that's my favourite name for a girl.'

'My name,' he announced impressively, 'is Thomas Quinn O'Hagerty!'

'You're an Irishman, by God!' said Hannah, running her hand affectionately over his hair.

'Scotch-Irish,' he said. 'My people came from County Antrim. Orangemen, all of them. And my boy's the last of the tribe.' He drained his coffee cup and set it on the floor beside the bed.

'I've got some Irish blood in me,' said Hannah. 'But mostly my folks was Swedes.'

She jumped out of bed, ran to the bureau and came back with a small white package. 'Lookit here,' she said. 'My niece sent me this for Christmas. She always sends me something. One year it was a breast-pin, and I got eighty cents for it!' She opened the paper. 'See? Tissue paper and everything. Here's the card that goes with it. You can read it if you want to.'

He took the card from her and held it in the palm of his hand, squinting and frowning to decipher it. '"With dearest love and cheery Xmas greetings to Auntie Hannah from her loving niece, Hannah,"' he read haltingly.

'It's a sachet,' said Hannah. She held a pink satin bag up to his nose. He drew back in anger. 'Don't do so!' he begged. 'I can't bear it.'

'She sent me some peppermint-drops, too. Here.' She put a peppermint in his mouth.

He rolled it on his tongue; his eyes lighted with pleasure. He

smiled, and, reaching out, he linked one of Hannah's hands with
his own and settled himself comfortably against the head of the
bed. 'Merciful God,' he whispered, 'a peppermint!'

'Here, eat another, sweetheart — go ahead, put a whole lot
in your mouth at once.'

'Two things I love in this world,' he said, in a voice faltering
with emotion, 'two things that are *dear* to me are red peppermints
and old-fashioned ginger cookies. But ginger cookies you cannot
get nowadays. You get nothing but leather — flavoured with
glue!'

'You said it, baby.'

'But when I was a boy, by Christ, I knew what good food was!
My mother had a kitchen as big as a sitting-room. And she could
take a piece of meat — *any* piece of meat — and put it in a pan
with a little dab of butter; then she'd pick up an onion and peel it
and slice it and put that in; then she'd open the spice-box and pick
out a snip of sage, about as much as you could hold between your
finger and thumb. Then she'd go and lift the meat up and stir
under it and put it down again. She was a *little* thing, my mother
was, and quick-moving! She wore a long soft white apron; it
always looked too long for her, for she looked like a little girl in it.
And do you know, I never can understand how I could ever have
been born to her! For here I am, a man grown — and she was
just a child, as you might say. Well, she'd lift up the lid of the
pan and peep in, and I declare you'd think she was looking at
a baby in its cradle. Such *love* as she'd get into her face! As if she
were coaxing the meat along. And then, after a time, it would get
done, and she'd set us down to it. Was that *meat?* Oh, Jesus!'

'You can't get good cookin' nowadays,' said Hannah.

He groaned softly to himself, his eyes tight shut. 'My mother's
dead now. I know it without being told. She's gone from me for
ever.'

'Say, I think you need something to eat,' said Hannah.

'No, no, no,' he said irritably.

'I can't cook good here, on account of the damn fire-inspector lookin' in on me any hour of the day or night, till you'd think I was a monkey at the zoo. But I know his step, see? He's got one foot shorter than the other, and he walks like this — da *dum*, da *dum*, da *dum*. God, I nearly die laughin' when I hear him comin' up the stairs! I run and stick my little old hot-plate in the drawer, sizzling hot and all. And whatever's cookin' on top of the stove has to go in the drawer too. Then he knocks at the door, and I call out, "Yoohoo, sweetie, come on in," real lovin' like. And when he opens the door there I stand, makin' like I'm doin' my hair, or takin' a bath or something!' She laughed and tweaked his chin. 'But lookit here, little boy, I'll tell you what you and me'll do. You know Ike's place, up at the corner? Well, Ike's a good friend of mine. There's a damn square fellow, if I ever seen one. Ike's a prince, no mistake. Well, Ike'll let me cook us a little Christmas dinner on his stove, back of the screen, like, from the room where the bar is. I do it any time I please. Ike knows I got to put something hot and solid into my stomach every now and again to keep up my spirits. And the same goes for *you*, or any other friend I want to take there with me, see?'

'My mother could cook pork chops, with a little bit of sage sticking to them, as tender as the day they were born! And hashed brown potatoes — oh, God!' His head rolled distractedly to and fro on the bolster.

'Just the two of us,' said Hannah, 'just you and me. Or maybe Ike'll sit down to the table with us. Ike hasn't got no wife; just a old Chinee woman — she don't come to the table. And I'll get a little chicken! It's dear as hell, but, my God, it won't break me for once. I'll make us up some dumplings, and get a couple of handfuls of rice out of Ike's kitchen; he won't care. And he won't miss it if I just pick up a nice big fat turnip — he keeps them down cellar,' she added in a sly voice. 'Yes, and we'll have something

to celebrate with too. That's where Ike comes in strong. Ike'll
give us something red hot! Oh, *baby!*'

Hannah was so pleased at the prospect that she began to bounce
up and down in bed. 'Whoopee!' she shouted. 'Merry Christmas, baby — same to you and many of 'em!' She caught hold of
him and gave him a terrific kiss that nearly broke his teeth. 'I'll
go out now and get the chicken and leave her sizzle all forenoon.'
She leaped out of bed and began to hunt for her stockings.

'No, no,' he said, lying back in bed and pulling the covers up
to his chin. 'You'll have to count me out of that, my girl.'

'Why?' she asked angrily. 'What's eatin' you now?'

'You don't understand me,' he said. 'You mean me well, and
I thank you for it.' A tear worked its way slowly down his cheek
and fell on his hand. 'But you know.... You don't know what
I feel — in *here.*' He beat his hand against his heart. 'I'm not
just *anybody*, you know; I'm — I'm ——'

'Oh, my God!' Hannah roared with laughter. 'Why, baby,
you're nothin' new to Hannah. I've seen hundreds like you.
Maybe you're some thinner than most, but that's all.'

'I'm Thomas Quinn O'Hagerty,' he said. 'And my grandfather
was an Irish gentleman, with a hickory walking-stick, and lace
cuffs to his coat sleeves. He took snuff!'

'Say, you must think you're some kind of God-damned little
god, eh? Something *special!*'

He shook his head, and looked down with distaste at one of his
bare feet which had worked out from under the covers. 'Oh, no,'
he said. 'No, I guess not. No, I don't set myself up as much. Not
now, I don't. But God knows I did once. When my blood was
young, and I was a youth. For when I was a youth, mark you,
I had the priceless ingredient — the with-out-which-nothing.
I had the eyes to see and the heart to feel. That's the stuff that
makes a philosopher, and a *poet!*'

'God, but you do need a shave, baby,' said Hannah; she
wrapped the blanket more amply round his shoulders.

'I'm fifty-seven years of age!' he declared.

'Well, what of it?' asked Hannah.

'And what am I? I haven't a penny in the world. I haven't a friend. Well, no matter — I'm poor company these days; nobody knows that better than I do. I'm morose, melancholy. It actually *pains* me to laugh! But to think that T. Q. O'Hagerty should live like this — friendless, penniless. Why, I live worse than an animal; for animals, poor things, are not responsible. No blame attaches to a starving dog in the gutter. But when a man, when a *gentleman* — ah, that's what cuts into me; that's the two-edged sword which cuts within and without.'

'Poor baby,' murmured Hannah. 'Say, I've a good mind to give you a shave, myself.'

He squeezed his eyes shut and rubbed his forehead. 'And now lately I feel confused in my head. Things aren't so clear to me as they used to be. When I come to a street-crossing, for instance, I have great difficulty.' He looked up at her piteously. 'I don't know whether it's safe to cross, or not. I can't figure it out, for it all gets into a jumble in my mind. When I see the automobiles stop moving and people going across the street, I'm afraid to start, because I can still see the automobiles going by — in my mind's eye, you understand.'

'Yes, I could tell the minute I laid eyes on you that you didn't know how to take care of yourself,' said Hannah, combing his hair back with her fingers. 'You'll get run down by a heavy truck some day, that's about what'll happen to you — unless you starve to death first.'

'I don't care,' he said, 'what happens to my *body*. Hunger, cold, pain, they mean nothing to me. Reality,' he added proudly, 'means nothing to me — *nothing!*'

'Yeah, but you gotta eat and sleep and keep yourself covered from the cold. And where's your hat, Tom? Answer me that! I found you walkin' around last night in the snow, without a hat to your head, shiverin' and whimperin' like a puppy dog. Haven't you *got* a hat, somewhere?'

'I did have a hat,' he said with dignity, 'but it blew off and got under traffic. I couldn't follow it, could I?'

'Oh, *you!*' cried Hannah, exasperated. 'Well, I'll see what I can do.' She went to the trunk, opened it, and banged the heavy tray out on to the floor. 'Seems like there's always a couple of hats in here — but how they got in here God Himself don't know.' She dug fiercely into the trunk, like a dog in a rabbit's hole, tossing out stray articles: suspenders, torn collars, old dirty corsets, empty bottles, shoes. 'Ah *ha!*' she called, 'here we are — here's a swell little hat! Try her on, baby.'

It was a black derby, frayed along the edges and collapsed at one side of the crown. Hannah punched it out with an experienced fist, rubbed it briskly across her dressing sacque and placed it on his head. 'It might've been *born* on you,' she declared.

He took the hat off and turned it round in his hands. 'That's a very good hat,' he said. 'That's the style I used to wear.' He looked out at the snow, falling now in thin drops almost like rain. He pressed the hat warmly to his breast. 'I wore a hat like this in my courting days,' he said. His face worked. 'But I broke my vows,' he moaned, 'I broke the vows I made to her on bended knee!'

'Now, now, don't blubber again, for God's sake,' said Hannah. 'Get up and get your clothes on, then I'll skip out and buy a nice tender little hen.'

He put on his socks and shoes, and stumbled shivering into his clothes.

'Sit down in this chair,' said Hannah, 'I'm going to give you a shave.' He sat down, and she fastened a flannel petticoat round his neck. She rummaged in the bureau drawer and brought out an old brown-handled razor. 'Yes, I'm gonna give you a shave you won't forget, baby,' she said, feeling his rough cheeks and the

stubble on his chin. 'Just look at you!' She burst out laughing.
'So you're the one that wanted to be free! Wanted to live your
own life. God, that's a good one, all right. Yes, that'll hand me
many a laugh. But say, I'd think you'd had enough of it by this
time. Why don't you go back to your wife, Tom?'

'Go *back?*' He looked up at her, stupefied. 'Back to Lily?
Never! Never while I have a drop of blood in my veins.'

Hannah brushed up a stiff lather in the coffee cup. 'Why not?
She couldn't do nothing to you, could she? If she was gonna have
you up for desertion she'd of done it long ago.'

'You don't understand me,' he said frowning; 'it's not a question of —— Oh, God!' He had caught sight of the top of his
scraggy head in the looking-glass. 'Look at my hair, all grey!
Here I am, all alone in the world, fifty-seven years old. In no
time at all I'll be sixty!'

'Well, ain't that what I'm tellin' you? You're gettin' on in
years, you're not a young man any more — no use in hidin' it
from you. And I say you need someone to look after you. I'd
do it myself and welcome, only I've already got my hands full,
see? You poor babies! God, there's so many of you runnin' loose
in this town, that I —— Say, do you know if your wife's still
alive?'

'That she is!' he cried heartily. '3912 Sycamore Avenue — and
if you don't believe me you can look her up in the telephone
book. There she is, "O'Hagerty, Mrs. Thomas Q." Many's the
time of day I go to the book for no other purpose but to run my
finger over her name. It's written on my heart in letters of
gold!'

'Oh, my God,' said Hannah. She stropped the razor against
a leather panel of the trunk.

'Once,' he said, 'I talked to her over the 'phone. I heard her
dear voice!'

'Say, *did* you?'

'Yes, I did. I'd had a little something to drink, and I couldn't keep from it. I took down the receiver and called her number. Then I'd have run away — but my legs got kind of paralysed. Then *Lily* came to the 'phone; I heard her sweet voice!' He shut his eyes and a beatific smile spread over his face.

'Well, tell me,' said Hannah, 'what did you say to her?'

'She said, "Hello." And at first I couldn't bring myself to speak. My throat, my — I couldn't make sound come. And she said it again, "Hello?" like that, inquiring, as you might say. I said, "Hello, is this Mrs. O'Hagerty?" She said, "Yes, who is this?" And all I could think of to say was, "Well, is *Mr.* O'Hagerty there?"'

'Ain't you the sly one,' said Hannah, laughing.

'Then I heard a voice say, "This is Mr. O'Hagerty"' — he laughed hysterically. 'It was my boy,' he said. 'My second-born. *Mr.* O'Hagerty! And I left him wetting his diaper!' He passed his hand over his face as if to iron his features into repose.

'All right,' said Hannah, 'hold still.' She applied the rich, coffee-coloured lather, and gave the razor a final turn or two across the sole of her shoe. 'Hold still, like my own little baby boy.'

She finished the shaving and gave his hair a good brushing. 'You need a haircut, too; but Hannah's shears ain't sharp enough for it, see? But I tell you what I'll do. I'll give you the price of a haircut — and you see that you get it. Do you hear me?'

'Oh, haircut, haircut!' he cried out in disgust. 'I don't want a haircut. What's all this nonsense — shaving, haircut? It leaves my heart the same, doesn't it? It doesn't change the inside of me. No, no, what I'm after is something to wash me within — *absolution*, that's what I'm after!'

'Sit up, now.'

He sat up, rubbing his stiffened neck, and watched while Hannah combed his hair. 'Now, where do you part it?' she asked. 'In the middle?'

'I don't care,' he said wearily. Hannah made a deep, masterly part, and curved the hair back neatly above each ear.

'You got a cute-shaped little head,' she said.

He looked at himself, then at Hannah, and back again to himself, frowning in bewilderment. 'By God,' he said, 'I've never seen you before in my life, have I? But I've seen that fellow in there. God, if it weren't for my grey hair I'd take oath this had happened before! Tell me, my girl, did you ever stand just like that, and comb my hair, while I sat *here* ——' He stopped and covered his face with his hands. '*No!* Give me the comb!' he commanded sternly. 'I know now what I'm thinking of. I want to part my hair on the *side*.' Laboriously he combed and parted it. 'There,' he said, 'that's the way *Lily* liked me to wear it.'

'Say, that looks good, too,' said Hannah, taking the comb back again to add a little flourish to the forelock. 'You got a handsome little face, do you know it? That is, once you clean it up, so's a body can get a squint at it.'

He looked at himself, his lips trembling and his eyes travelling worshipfully over and over his image. 'Yes,' he said, 'that's T. Q. I'd know that chap anywhere. Now bring me the hat!' he cried. 'Bring it here and put it on me, and let's see.'

Hannah brushed the hat and set it on his head. 'There now,' she said, 'you look like the President of the United States!'

Stiffly he got up out of the chair and drew in a deep breath, swelling out his chest. 'I don't mind telling you,' he said, 'that they had great hopes of me, when I left the university. "Thomas Quinn O'Hagerty, A.B., Maxima cum Laude," that's the way my ticket read! And if you're sceptical about it you can look it up in the records.'

'That's right,' said Hannah, 'that's the way I like to hear you talk. *Loud*, like that, and jolly. You could be damned good company, do you know it? Here, baby,' she brought out a bottle from behind the trunk. 'This is Hannah's best gin. I don't give this out, only to just a few; it's too good, and it's too strong for most.' She took out the paper stopper and handed him the bottle. 'Here's lookin' at you,' she cried. 'Take a good long hot one!'

He closed his eyes and breathed in a long slow draught. 'A-a-ahhh! now could I drink hot blood' — he orated — 'and do such deeds, et cetera.' He looked at himself in the glass. 'I've broken every promise I ever made to a living creature. If I say I'll do a thing, you can lay your bottom dollar on it that I *won't* do it. Never! Not while I've got the breath of life in me to resist!' He beat his breast proudly. Putting his arm around Hannah's waist, he drew her to his side. 'See that fellow in there?' he cried. 'That's the champion breaker-of-promises in the whole *world!*'

'That's nothing,' said Hannah, putting her cheek against his, 'nobody can keep promises — that's why I never make 'em.'

'Yes, but that's just where the difference comes in,' he said loftily. 'You and I, my girl, we're fish of different seas. You don't make promises; well and good. But *I* — I do make them. And I mean to keep them. Deep in my heart I *mean* to keep my promises. Look at that face in there! Look at it and tell me: can't you see, just to look at that face, that my word's as good as my bond?'

'Sure,' said Hannah.

'Yes, *sir*, I'm the genuine article, through and through. When I stood up at the altar beside Lily McMasters, June the twenty-third, eighteen hundred and ninety-five, I looked the minister square in the face. "I will!" I said.' He brought his fist down heavily on the bureau. 'Do you *hear* me?' he thundered.

'Sure I hear you. I been through the marriage service myself.'

'All dressed in white,' he said dreamily. 'With a Lille veil of lace on her head. And white kid gloves. One finger of the glove was split, so that I could put the ring on. And I did put it on. "With this ring I thee wed." Then Lily turned and looked at me. "I, Thomas, take thee, Lily" ——. Afterwards, when she took off her little bridal veil, there was a flower in her hair, caught in her curls — one sweet little orange blossom. I have it to this day!' he shouted. Reaching in his pocket he drew out a few dried particles mixed with tobacco and tinfoil; tenderly he kissed them and put them back again. 'She wears her hair up in the back,' he said, 'with a little yellow back-comb. But below the comb, mark you, are some little golden ringlets. I loved to kiss them. And just behind her ears, ah! that's where I loved best to kiss her. Yes, and on the lips!'

He groaned, and catching hold of Hannah he clung to her, sobbing. 'Fifty-seven years old, today,' he sobbed. 'Just fifty-seven years ago today I was first laid in my mother's arms!'

'What,' Hannah screamed, 'is today your *birthday?* My God, baby doll, why didn't you let Hannah know? Say — wait'll Ike hears about it! Ike's got a special birthday cocktail. It'll half kill you, sweetheart. "Tail of the Rat," Ike calls it. But I call it Rat Poison. But lookit here' — she handed him the bottle again — 'take a birthday gurgle on Hannah, by God, and another, another. *Say,* by God!' She was overcome with solicitude. She pinched him, slapped him on the back and thighs, tickled him in the ribs. 'Baby!' she exclaimed, 'I'm gonna give you a present! God-damned if I'm not.'

She reached inside of her bureau-drawer and brought out her chamois grouch-bag. 'Lemme see, now.' She examined the contents: there were eleven limp and wrinkled one-dollar bills. She counted out five of them. 'Here you are, baby, here's half of all Hannah has in the world. It's for you, baby — with cheery birthday greetings from Hannah. And lookit here' — she held up a sixth bill. 'This here's for you, too; one to grow on, see?' She slapped him affectionately in the face. 'Oh, you little baby doll! He's got just the sweetest, lovin'est little face in the world.'

She put the money in his hand, and his fingers, trembling with emotion, closed around it. 'I'll pay back every cent of this, my

girl,' he said, trying to draw himself erect. 'You can lay your
bottom dollar on *that!*'

'Now give Hannah a nice big birthday kiss,' she said, throwing
her arms around him. He kissed her with gusto. *'Sic semper
tyrannis!'* he shouted. 'Now could I drink hot blood and do such
deeds as hell, et cetera!'

'Well, here's *to* you, Tom,' said Hannah, taking another drink.
She held the bottle to his mouth, tilting it gently as he drank.
'Drink it up, little baby doll.'

'Or to take arms against a sea of troubles!' he thundered out,
gesticulating.

'Now you wait right here,' said Hannah, handing him the
bottle; 'Hannah's gonna run out and get us a nice plump little
hen, and ——'

'Don't leave me!' he cried imperiously. 'Sit down, and lend ear
to my discourse. I'm about to instruct you in regard to a very
important matter ——'

'Oh, *you!* What you need's to lie down on that bed and take
a good sleep till Hannah tells you dinner's ready.'

'Let us be seated, gentlemen,' he said, in a loud rolling voice,
'and engage in friendly discourse.' He took an unsteady step to
the bed and settled down heavily upon it. Hannah drew a blanket
over his legs. 'Go to sleep, Tom,' she said.

'Blood is thicker'n water,' he said.

'Yeah,' said Hannah, sitting down beside him, with the bag of
peppermints in her lap.

'But *love* is thicker than blood! By which I mean to c'nvey to
you, and all of you here assembled, that between Lily and me
there was a bond stronger than the ties of blood, stronger than
—— Why, I love Lily better'n I love *God!* For I've never seen
God.'

'All right, all right,' said Hannah. 'I believe you, baby.'

'No,' he said, 'you don't comprehend. Now let me instruct you

in regard to Lily and me.' He got his hands out from under the
blanket in order to gesticulate freely. 'Now, to bring the matter
to concrete form,' he said, 'suppose that I held in my hand, here
before your eyes, a fine, splendid piece of crockery, let us say a
Limoges tea-cup. Yes, very well and good — a Limoges tea-cup.
Now, then, suppose I held it up like this and *crushed* it, right before your eyes! You'd see the broken pieces, wouldn't you?
You'd comprehend that the cup was broken, gone, done for —?

'Well, then,' he continued, 'now we're getting to the point I
wanted to bring up, specifically and to wit: you saw me break the
cup, didn't you? That is, I told you I broke it!' He paused, bewildered, and shut his eyes sleepily. 'Just so!' he shouted, rousing
himself. 'Just so did I break the bond between Lily and me. I
crushed it, and shattered it, with my own hand. And the broken
pieces,' he added, 'have penetrated into my heart!' An expression of ecstatic joy came over his face. 'Did you hear that?' he
exclaimed. '"Have penetrated into my heart!" Ah, did you
hear that, my girl? That was spoken like a poet!'

He buried his face exultantly against Hannah's dressing
sacque. 'By which I mean to convey,' he murmured dreamily,
'that I want the perfect gem — the cup, do you see? — the *perfect*
gem. Oh, my God, yes, let me have the perfect gem, or nothing
at all! Do you comprehend?' he asked Hannah.

'Sure,' said Hannah. 'I'm right with you, sweetheart.' But
she was not listening. She had suddenly caught sight of her newly
found umbrella, which leaned in the corner by the bureau. 'Say!'
She clutched his arm and pointed to the umbrella. 'That there
means good luck, do you know it? How does that go, now —?
"Find an umbrella, get a new fella!"' she chanted. 'Do you hear
that, baby?'

'She's gone from me forever,' he said, taking a peppermint from
the bag. 'I'll never see her again in this life. But, perhaps, in the
hereafter,' he added. 'What was that?' he asked. '"The here-

after"?' He laughed uproariously. 'The *hereafter!* Look here, my girl,' he said, 'I want to instruct you in regard to that very matter. Listen to me. There's no future life, you know. Let no one deceive you in regard to that most fundamental matter. No, no!' He looked at her with hilarious bloodshot eyes. 'No, you think altogether too much about your conscience, my girl. Forget your conscience! Gather ye rosebuds while ye may, et cetera.'

'Or is it just the other way 'round?' Hannah asked herself in a hushed voice. '"Find an umbrella, *disaster* will follow!" My God, I believe in my heart that's how it goes. Wait'll I find out!'

She lifted up the bolster and pulled her fortune book out from under it. 'Here we are, baby,' she cried, running her finger tempestuously along the index, 'Hold on just a minute, baby, and I'll tell you! Umbrella — umbrella — umbrella ——'

DEATH AND

TRANSFIGURATION[1]

ALAN MARSHALL

THE wind came in cold over the marshes, bending the crisp stubble of salt hay and printing ripples to be frozen upon the pools left at the ebb of tide; charged with the sea and the smell of distant snow, it knotted Grammer Weare's skirt across her knees, and it drove the mist of her breath back into her face and clustered it in hard beads on her blown hair, and snapped the fringes of her thick black shawl as if they had been small woollen whips. And, heavy and sickening with the scent of frost, the wind froze the damp in her nostrils and made them stick together so that she had to breathe through her mouth and let the wind pierce even the soft roots of her teeth, sending chill gimlets into her jaws and making her sick at her stomach with the pain of cold.

The whole of Folly Mill Road was hardened into troughs and crests of earth where the wagon wheels had been, and the hard earth crumbled under Grammer Weare's feet, now and again casting up yellow sparks from the flint. Grammer Weare clutched her green baize bag, spinning on its black cord and thumping against her shanks as she walked. Her tools and pans in the green bag clinked with a dull sound, like coins in a pocket. She hurried on, seeing the pines in Harper's Hollow, thinking of the warmth to be found behind their thick trunks where the wind was baffled and could not reach her and howled instead among the topmost branches. And an early light in a house seaward of the marsh gleamed like a yellow flower in all the desolation of flat, grey land; so Grammer Weare tucked her green bag under an armpit, keeping her eyes off the warm light, and hurried away from it.

When she came to the mouth of the Hollow, dark under the thick boughs of pine that creaked with the frost in their joints, she ran a few steps into its shelter and seated herself upon a stone, laying her bag across her knees and working her fingers inside her mittens to scrape them warm against the rough wool. It was snug and not yet wholly dark, even in the wood; and only two miles were left. When she had been sitting there a moment or two she heard the sound of feet, and looked up, and saw that the man with the lantern was Poll's Matt walking in with a sack from the town.

'It's a foul night to be about, Grammer Weare,' said Poll's Matt.

'It's no worse than need be,' Grammer Weare said.

'There's snow toward,' Poll's Matt then said.

'Never this night,' Grammer Weare said.

Poll's Matt laid his lantern and sack on the ground. A spine of pebble tore a corner of the sack, letting the salt trickle out over the ground. Poll's Matt looked at Grammer's green bag and said:

'It'll be Ting's girl, won't it? Ting Seaver's girl Doll.'

Grammer Weare watched the white salt build a slow mound near the sack.

'Ting Seaver's no friend of yourn,' she said.

Poll's Matt laughed.

'She's been around big three months now,' Poll's Matt cried out. 'Too big to pole up autumn hay. Ting's got along now, too old to rake the marshes. Ting's old woman's too old to rake marshes. Ting's Hipper won't rake the marshes, he won't but trap lobster. It's up to Ting's girl Doll to rake the marshes now, but she was big this autumn hay-time.'

'Ting's girl Doll is frail enough not to rake the marshes,' Grammer Weare said. 'She'll never be a strong woman, that one won't.'

Poll's Matt laughed again; Grammer watched his spilling salt spread in a white pool over the dark ground.

'It's Ting's girl Doll, big and needen you,' Poll's Matt said again, when he had laughed. 'I'll not be fubbed off, Grammer Weare.'

'The wine you drink is made of grapes, Poll's Matt,' she said. Then she laughed; and, warm again, she rose from the stone, dusting the seat of her skirt. She tucked her bag under her armpit and pointed at the sack near the man's feet. 'And the fish you eat is laid up in salt, too,' she said. 'May it not burn your tongue, Poll's Matt.'

Poll's Matt swore and knelt to scrape up the salt, sweeping with his cracked hands over the ground.

'You might have said!' he cried.

'I had naught to say,' Grammer Weare said. 'But now you can munch pebbles in your chowder.'

'Then you can tell Ting's Doll that I've spilled better salt nor this,' Poll's Matt said.

Grammer Weare laughed.

'I would have known that,' she said.

Poll's Matt rose, clutching a stone in his red fist. He stepped across the white stain of salt to Grammer Weare, cursing.

'What you've been told!' he cried. 'You don't know but that!'

Grammer stepped away from him.

'You'll not harm me, Poll's Matt,' she said.

Poll's Matt dropped his stone, and his hand, shaking in the fingers, began to pluck at his lower lip.

'You'll do well to keep an eye on yourself,' Grammer Weare said.

She began to walk away backwards, watching Poll's Matt until he turned and knelt again at his salt, and then she too turned and hurried away at a scuttling gait down the road and past the bend near Turkey Hill. The night had thickened, but was yet clear; for above the pines she could see a few stars blinking in the wind that ran high. But sometimes a gust of wind swept down over the earth and blew what it could find, blowing a pine-cone across the road. The pine-cones, though, were empty in the winter, and their fins were spread open so that they could lay their seeds.

Each man, woman and child of Seabrook village born in the last thirty years had been born into Grammer Weare's hands. Every one of them she had eased out of some woman; every one she had shucked out of some squirming pod of the bleeding flesh, and cut its cord and tied it, had washed the blood from its body and the gum from its eyes. Sometimes the child died, sometimes the mother; sometimes both. When the child died, it was simple; a thing so young — which, indeed, might never have had the breath in its lungs however much the Grammer swung it by its heels and breathed with her own lips into its nostrils — a thing so young and from the start of the woman's time wholly unliving, need only be put in a sack and buried like any thing too rank to keep. It was for Grammer to bury such infants; and if the mother died, to make her ready for burial, too. That also was simple: a matter of straightening the twisted legs, the racked arms, the clawing hands; and if death came later and there had been no one about to ease the dying one, so that there might be a cramp in the legs at death, it was a matter of hamstringing — of cutting the tendons at crotch or knee so that the legs might be brought decently together, side by side, calmly. Then it was a matter of washing the dead thing and changing sheets befouled in death; and, maybe, a matter of getting a pierced lip unclamped from the jaws that gripped it. And the face must be moulded gently, stroked by Grammer Weare's fingers out of anguish and terror, so that when the flesh hardened it would be a calm face, perhaps a face whose lips Grammer's moulding fingers had taught even to smile in peace and resignation.

Underground in the village graveyard there were many such faces, smiling gently; and each smile, until it seeped back into the earth or was chewed away by such things as crawl underground, was the work of Grammer Weare's fingers. Grammer Weare herself smiled, thinking of these things, as she walked out of Harper's Hollow and could see Ting Seaver's shack up the road. Ting Seaver's shack was near the factory which someone had built a year or two back; it was a factory for making shoes, and when the factory had started to make shoes most of the men and women and boys and girls of the village gave up their fishing, their trapping lobsters and digging clams. Before, they had fished through the bright summer, selling their lobsters and clams and salting away their cod and hake and flounders; and in the winter they made lobster-pots and new nets and lines, and ate salt fish. Now they worked in the factory, helping machines to cut and sew shoes, and they lived all year round on what they could buy from the village store. Only a few were left who fished, and husbanded salt hay off the marshes.

And the factory had brought some new blood to the village. There had been little new blood in the village for three hundred years. The Weares and the Seavers and the Morses and the Lowells and all the rest of the village three hundred years ago walked from the ship's landing at Portsmouth; and, finding a river which had fish in it and a harbour at its mouth for fishing-boats, there they had settled and called the place Seabrook, and built cabins and raised children. They had raised governors and lawmakers in the village at first, and sent them to build the state; and they had raised soldiers and sent them to fight the king; and there had been sea-captains too, who had sailed across all the seas in the world; but then the blood of the village grew thin, and the names in the graveyard and in the village registers became fewer and fewer, although there were as many people in the village as ever there had been. For there were twenty or thirty Morses, and twenty or thirty Seavers, and so on; and then the village raised fishermen only — not men who sailed in ships, but who rowed out beyond the breakers in timid dories and who had large heads and drooping mouths and dull eyes.

Now there was the factory, where the men stood at machines all day long, helping the machines; for the machines could not have made shoes without the men, nor the men without the machines. These men of the village lived with their wives and families in small shacks scattered along the roadsides. The shacks were little wooden shells, chinked up with tar-paper and sometimes even with tufts of hay to keep out the winter cold; they rested among sparse trees or in the lee of spurs of New Hampshire granite which glaciers had dragged down from the mountainsides a million years before. Into this village of hovels few people ever came; motorists followed the Lafayette Highway, skirting the village and seeing only a few roadside farms, neat and well-kept. Young men and boys from over the line in Massachusetts used to hire buggies and drive into the village, hoping to entice girls to follow them into the darkly wooded roads; and the men of the village would set upon the invaders with stones and curses. But sometimes these foragers were successful; then the stock of the village was enriched.

Grammer Weare, walking toward Ting Seaver's shack to care for Ting's Doll, listened to the drone and clatter of the cutting and sewing machines, and to the high snarl of the automatic lathes which turned heels out of the beech forests of the village. Being in winter, it was early dark and the factory was all lighted, and Grammer Weare could see the men standing in rows at their machines, their heads bent over hands trained to work as fast as the machines demanded. Ting's shack was lighted, too, and Grammer Weare walked in without knocking.

Ting himself was seated at the table, trimming the wick of the oil lantern which he would carry when it was time for him to go to the factory and watch through the night when the men had stopped work. Ting's old woman, Gathy, stood at the fire stirring a broth of clams and milk which sent fragrant steam through the room, and almost buried the smell of clothes and bodies and kerosene smoke and tarred cord. Ting's Hipper sat weaving cord into the cone-shaped snare of a lobster-pot. And on a bed near the ladder going up to the loft, Ting's girl Doll lay, not looking up, but gazing at her fingers as they fiddled with a button at the waist of her blue gingham dress.

Grammer Weare shut the door behind her and walked to the table and laid her green baize bag upon its white, scarred surface. No one spoke. Grammer took off her thick shawl and folded it and laid it over the back of a chair and sat down. Hipper looked up at Grammer and then bent his head quickly to gnaw the end of a cord free for splicing. Ting lighted his lantern, and sheared a loose strand of wick so that the flame burned even and clear. And at last Ting's old woman, Gathy, dipped out a mouthful of the broth and tasted it, and put the cover back on the pot, and said to Grammer Weare:

'It's an evil night for you to come over with her, Grammer Weare.'

Grammer Weare stretched her thin legs in the warmth of the room, and looked to the window which was frozen thick at the bottom and spangled with water at the top.

'There's been colder,' she said.

'Will you not take off your bonnet?' Ting Seaver said.

Grammer took off her bonnet and knotted the strings again so that she could hang it over a chair. Then she looked at Ting's

Doll, but Ting's Doll would not dare to look at anyone in the room, and lay looking at her own hands.

'She'll be needen you soon,' Ting's Gathy said, 'but we've not had a groan out of her yet.'

'The saucy tart!' Ting's Hipper cried, throwing down the lobster-pot, so that its wooden slats clattered on the floor. 'She'll want you soon, and may she sweat for it!'

'You shut your fat head,' Ting said.

Hipper walked over to the stove and seized up a ladle.

'Give me some broth,' he said.

Ting's Gathy faced him.

'That clam broth's for her,' Gathy said. 'There's none for you here. She'll want all her strength.'

Hipper ladled out a cup of the broth and sat with it in his hands, blowing the steam off the top, and drinking it so hot it burned him, and he swore.

'That's bad talk for now,' Ting said. 'Keep your tongue clean, do you hear?' Then Ting turned to Grammer. 'She'd go foinen at night, night after night,' he said, 'and now she's got what, Grammer Weare.'

'There's been many a girl with child,' Grammer Weare said.

'Ay, Grammer Weare,' Ting's Gathy said. 'But the way she did it!'

Grammer Weare blew on her nails as if to warm her fingers and said:

'There's yet but one way for a girl to get with child, Ting's Gathy.'

'Every mother's son in this village!' Hipper shouted, with his mouth full of clams and potatoes.

'That's not true, you Hipper,' Ting's Doll said from the couch. Her voice was quiet, and there were tears on her cheeks. 'You might have picked your fill of me before.'

Hipper sprang to his feet again and walked to the bedside and stood looking down at the girl.

'You're a fine whoor to talk,' he said. 'I might whip you yet, you and your big belly.'

'And I might thank you for it,' Ting's Doll said.

'So you'll talk back, eh?' Ting's Hipper said. He plucked a hot clam out of his cup of broth and threw it at the girl. It struck her cheek, and stayed there.

'She would have done better to be whipped long since,' Ting said. 'What she's brought down on this roof!'

'We'll not hold up our heads more,' Ting's Hipper said, and walked back to his chair.

Grammer Weare walked over to the girl, who had not moved, and picked the clam off her cheek. Then she held the clam up to Hipper, and said:

'You'll want to eat this yet?'

Ting's Gathy laughed, but Ting said, 'Shut you up!' So Gathy turned to the fire and began rattling with the pots, putting more salt into the broth and saying, 'It's a caution the way we use salt in this house. When I was a girl we laid out sea water in pans and let the sun dry out the salt. Then it was hard to get and we spared it.'

But all this while Doll had been laughing softly, after she dried the clam broth from her cheek, and she turned to Hipper so that she could look at him, and said:

'Have you eat your clam yet?'

Hipper said nothing, but sat chewing in the corner, turning the tough clams over in his mouth. Ting looked at Doll and began to curse her.

'It ain't enough what you've yet done, but you must laugh,' he said. 'Well, you'll not laugh long, young one, when that babe leaps up in you. You'll sing to another tune then, you will.'

Grammer Weare stood up.

'The house will not be for men this night,' she said.

Ting had already closed his lantern and was pulling on his coat.

'It's time for me to go now,' he said. 'There's but a minute yet for the whistle.'

But Ting's Hipper had laid aside his cup of broth and picked up the lobster-pot and was weaving in the snare, having made the cone of mesh so that it would trap lobsters.

'She'll not drive a man from his work,' Hipper said. 'I can work here with such a blowze in labour.'

Doll laughed.

'Go out,' she cried. 'You'll not have sport of me.'

The whistle on the factory then blew, a siren that clamoured in the cold air and echoed on the hills inland. Then all the machines stopped with a falling note, like the sigh of a huge beast.

'Oh, I'll not?' Hipper said to Doll. 'I'll not, eh?'

Grammer Weare opened her bag and took out some sort of instrument, like a plier with ragged jaws.

'You pack your bones out of here,' Grammer Weare said.

Already the men from the factory were walking in the road past the house. Their voices were loud in the dry cold air, and their feet rang on the frozen earth like the shod hooves of animals. They could be heard laughing up the road, but when they came next to Ting's shack there was a hush fell upon them, and then they could be heard laughing down the road. Doll turned on the bed, groaning.

'What now?' Grammer Weare said, bending over Doll.

'It's not the hurt of my body grieves me, Grammer Weare,' Doll said.

'I know, girl,' said Grammer Weare.

Ting coughed. Then he turned to Hipper.

'You lead your damn feet out of here,' he shouted.

Hipper threw down his lobster-pot and rose and put on his coat. Ting said, 'I'll wait and see that you go, too, and if you show your nose in here before daylight I'll break the last bone under your skin.'

Hipper and Ting walked out, and a blast of chill air puffed through the open doorway. The flame in the lamp flickered, and Doll moaned. Grammer pushed the door shut against the wind and drew the bolt.

'We'll need water,' she said to Gathy.

'There's enough and more in the boiler,' Gathy said.

'And clean linens,' Grammer Weare said.

'I've a basket of clouts, fresh washed, Grammer,' Gathy said.

'Then we've naught to do but wait,' Grammer Weare said.

Doll drew up her legs, and, poising her body's weight upon her heels, moved her body, awkward with its size, across the bed a little. Then she swung over, so that she might rest on her side; but in a moment she rolled to her back again.

'There's suthin moves here, Grammer,' she said, drawing her hand across her belly's rise.

'Ay, but does it hurt you, girl?' Grammer Weare said.

Doll's knees collapsed and straightened, and the knees stiffened so that the toes shook. Her eyes closed and her head lay slowly back.

'Fit to mammock out the heart,' she said.

'Ay, girl,' Grammer Weare said.

Ting's Gathy stood at the stove cutting small cubes of salt pork into a pan. The fatty white flesh, striking the smooth iron, writhed and crackled in the heat, and turned crisp and brown and sent up threads of sharp smoke.

'It seems we might take a cup of broth now, Grammer,' Gathy said. She poured the melted fat and the browned meat into the stew of clams and potatoes, so that the fat lay in yellow pools floating upon the white milk. 'She'll want naught until day-break.'

Doll cried out from the bed:

'Ah, Grammer, there's suthin toward here now!'

Grammer spooned up some of her broth and started to blow it cool.

'No,' she said. 'This will be a long night, girl.'

'You'll want to let Grammer Weare get the good of this hot,' Ting's Gathy said to Doll; and then she turned to Grammer, saying: 'A night this cold'll take the very heart out of a body.'

The two old women sat at the table, one opposite the other, eating their broth and savouring it slowly on their lips. Gathy ate cautiously, slicing each clam in two with the edge of her spoon upon the bottom of the dish, and gnawing the clams until her teeth had worried all but the last shred of meat from the tough, black necks. She and Grammer tossed the chewed necks of clams into a dish on the table so that Hipper could use the necks, each with its bright edge of yellow meat, as baits to catch sunfish.

'I do make a fine broth,' Gathy said. 'People have heard tell of my broths in all Seabrook, and in Newbury.'

'Ay,' Grammer Weare said. She sat watching Doll, who lay with her body quiet and her arms straight by her sides, with each fist clenched so that a crest of white bone gleamed through the cracked red flesh of her knuckles.

'We'll want to keep the girl all mobled now,' Grammer said. 'She'll need her gown now.'

Gathy rose and walked to a low chest of fine brown wood, whose slender brass handles had grown dull and green in the sea's air. She took a white woollen gown out of a drawer and held it up, showing it to Grammer.

'It's fresh washed this day,' Gathy said proudly.

Grammer walked over to Doll and stood above her.

'Then lay it by the fire,' Grammer said. She leaned over Doll and opened the buttons on her dress. 'Come, girl, you'll want these off now,' she said.

Doll opened her eyes.

'Is it time now, Grammer Weare?' she said. 'My hands are cold.'

'I'll not need to tell you when it's time,' said Grammer, drawing Doll's arms out of her clothing.

'My hands are cold as paddocks,' Doll said; and Grammer began to take her out of her dress.

Doll's body was not a good body; the sun and the winds off the sea had beaten and blown upon her flesh until it was creased and brown on the arms and neck, and on the legs even to the thighs. And her body had not been made shapely by bending knee-deep in the cold mud-flats seeking clam holes after the run of tide, or by rowing to the buoys of lobster-pots in the calm tides at daybreak, or by stilting up salt hay to dry upon clustered poles driven into the marshes. The food she had eaten had not always been good food, being chiefly fish and shell-fish and potatoes and the other things most easily taken from the sea or the land. Grammer eased Doll upwards on the bed, taking off her underclothing. Her breasts, even heavy as they were with milk, sagged across her armpits, letting the nipples, swollen and cracked and stained purple and dark brown, rest upon the flesh of her arms. Already upon the inner sides of her thighs, below the dark matting at her groins, a fine lacework of blue veins had begun to spread; and the smooth white skin of her belly was now drawn tight, and made ugly by the child within her.

Doll closed her eyes and turned her head aside, and shifted one of her breasts with her hand so that it rested more easily.

'There's been milk?' Grammer Weare said.

'Yes,' Doll said. She laughed briefly. 'I'm like a freshened cow.'

Grammer Weare took one of the nipples of the girl's breast between her fingers and bent over in the lamplight to look at the white globe of milk coming forth, marbled with yellow. Grammer laughed softly, and said: 'You'll feed him well, girl.'

Then the girl laughed again, and Grammer Weare said:

'Gathy, we'll put on her gown now.'

The two old women put Doll's arms and her head into her gown and drew it, still smelling of the fire's warmth, down over her body to her feet. They laid a tarpaulin on the bed under Doll and drew a soft blanket over it, and then another blanket over Doll. Grammer found a length of tarred rope and cut off a stretch of it and made it fast to the foot of the bed, and knotted the other end of it and gave it to Doll, saying: 'When you feel him move within you, heave on this rope. Brace your feet snug on the footboard and heave for what you're worth. It'll ease you.'

Then the women turned the light low and sat by the fire, waiting. There was no sound in the room but the snuffle of the women breathing, and sometimes a coal snapping in the fire and falling through the grate with a crackle of sparks and a soft puff into the grey powder of ashes. And focused on the girl in the bed, the silence and these small sounds turned and settled slowly in the room, like a whorl of blown fog; but outside the house there were the sounds of night and of the cold, the sea-wind falling, the slow beat of a bell in the harbour buoy, and a deep echo of the cold booming across ice on the inland ponds. Then, in a bulky shadow at one corner of the room, there was a sound of fine claws drawn over the rough grain of wood. Doll turned on her bed, laughing.

'It's a mouse there,' she cried. 'It's but a mad mouse, drunk with the heat.'

She laughed again, letting her voice rise like a wind, filling all the room with laughter. She laid her head back on the pillow, making her body rack and twist with laughter until she was weary and sobbing; then her breath came deep and loud and Grammer Weare turned up the light, and Doll said:

'It's now, Grammer. It potches at me now, like a skewer.'

The struggle was then long, through the whole night. Sometimes the two old women could but stand watching the girl on the bed; and then they made themselves busy with the fresh white cloths, casting them into a bucket when they were sodden and heavy. Once when there was a silence the girl lay still on the bed waiting for what was left to her and Gathy sponged the girl's face with cool water, and she raised her head and cried softly:

'Grammer Weare, it was never Poll's Matt. It was never Poll's Matt but once.' She let her head rest back on the pillow and cried out: 'This thing has naught to do with Poll's Matt. It was another,' she said when she had her voice again. 'He was suthin like rain, or the sea on a fresh day.'

The girl put out her hand to Grammer Weare.

'Yes, girl,' the old woman said. 'You be one to know such things.'

Then the girl screamed once only, and the night wore on, being measured by the stretch of sinews in the girl's joints and by the quickening rhythm of pain in her body. And then Grammer Weare's hands were busy with the flesh, coaxing blind tissue, using their skill in all this ritual of agony. Sometimes Grammer Weare bent over the girl's face, trying with words to pierce the layers of ecstasy in which the girl's mind and body were muffled, trying to teach the girl that the world's reaches of time and change, men and women, trees and animals, of hills and waters still endured, and would endure without end. But the girl had been lifted apart and made too remote, she had been borne away from place on earth and away from time of night and day of year, being now sense disjoined of flesh. She was now meaning only and not substance, all the stuff of her body having vapoured away from the thing to the sense only; and anguish swelled in the room until it seemed the walls would burst with it.

So morning came slowly and the child was born. When it had been cut free of her and tied, and touched with cold water to make it breathe, and had been cleansed and swaddled in warm clothing,

Gathy bent over her again and cried, 'It's me now. It's your mother now!' But Doll lay with her eyes open as if she were looking at the ceiling. Gathy bent over the face again and looked into the eyes, saying: 'Grammer, there might be aught you could do now.'

Grammer Weare left the child and walked over to the bed and sat on its edge, and began to strike the girl's face sharply with the hard palms of her hands. This sharp tempo of flesh raised and quickened in the room, and Grammer cried out: 'Bring me a bit of cold glass, Gathy!' Gathy brought a mirror and the two old women held it at Doll's mouth, peering in the lamplight at the smooth glass to see the grey smudge of the girl's breath clinging to the chill surface, and even sparkling in tiny drops in the yellow light of the room.

'She was always frail,' Gathy said. 'She'd never be a strong woman.'

'There's yet life,' Grammer Weare said.

The two old women waved the smoke of burning feathers over Doll's face, and put whiskey in her mouth, and raised her legs to pour the blood back into her brain. Grammer stopped Doll's mouth with her hand and laid her own mouth over the girl's sharpening nostrils and blew her breath into the girl's body; but the girl moved once only after the blue had come into her lips, and Gathy said: 'Ah, well.'

The two old women looked at each other, having nothing to say. At last Gathy walked over to the stove where the child lay, and began to shake down the ashes, gently.

Grammer Weare looked out of the window and said, 'You might turn down the lamp, now.'

Gathy blew down the lamp-chimney, snuffing the light, for the sun had already begun to glow red and blue at the far rim of the sea. For a moment the world seemed to hang between night and morning, like a pendulum at endswing, so still it was; and then

an eddy of gulls whirled over the sea, crying; and the slow chug-
ging of the lobster boats began to sound across the grey marshes.
And Gathy said:

'You'll want to have your breakfast with Ting when he comes
in?'

'I'll want but a cup of broth this morning,' Grammer said.

Then there was a rattling at the door. Grammer drew the bolt
and Hipper walked in, with Poll's Matt following, carrying his
lighted lantern.

'How is the girl, now?' Hipper said, swaggering. 'We've come
to see.'

Grammer closed the door behind them.

'Then look for yourself,' she said.

She pointed to the bed, and Hipper and Poll's Matt looked and
saw the girl under the blanket, and Hipper said, 'Ah, poor girl.'
Then he looked back at the bed, and said, 'You've cut a length
off the painter for my dory. Ah, well, poor thing.'

But Poll's Matt plucked at his lower lip and said, 'I'll see the
babe, then.'

Grammer Weare laughed.

'You'll have naught to do with that infant, you Poll's Matt,'
she said.

Poll's Matt coughed and looked about the room. Then he
picked up his lantern and walked out of the door and looked back
once and began to run up the road. Hipper sprang to the door
after him, crying, 'Was it him, then?'

'No,' Grammer Weare said, pushing him back into the room.
'You sit down to your breakfast now.'

'He ran up the road,' Hipper said sulkily.

'You itch yourself no more of him,' Grammer Weare said.
'There's not only butter in his head, Hipper.'

Hipper blew his nose.

'He's a great fool,' Hipper said, picking up the lobster-pot and beginning to weave in the cone-shaped snare of tarred cord. 'He's not been out by night or day this nine year without he carries his lantern always with him.'

The child in the basket began to wail feebly.

'Corbey Dann's Alice is yet with milk,' Gathy said. 'We might get her to nurse this child now.'

'She'll nurse it sure,' Hipper said.

Then Ting came into the house, stamping his feet for the cold. He did not look at the bed, but cried out, 'I had it just now of Gishy Morse. Poll's Matt told him.' Ting looked at the wailing child and laid his basket down by the fire and sat at the table.

'Well, may it please God, she was a good girl when she was younger.'

He began to eat the breakfast which Gathy had laid out for him. 'I'll sleep up above in the loft this day,' he said, at last looking over at the bed.

'We'll give her tending soon,' Grammer Weare said to Gathy, who was sitting by the fire holding her palms in the warmth of the grate, as if they had been cold.

The child had stopped its crying, and already the men were walking down the road on their way to the factory, casting long shadows before them in the red sun and making their boots ring upon the frozen earth. In a few moments the whistle on the factory howled in a siren note, and then the machines set up their undersong of clatter; but inside the house there was only the sound of breathing and eating, the soft plucking of Hipper's fingers among the woven cords of his snare, the tinkle of Grammer Weare putting her instruments back into the green baize bag, and the creaking of Gathy's chair when she shifted her position at the fire.

OUTSIDE YUMA [1]

BENJAMIN APPEL

THE freight train stopped in blue sky.

The steel tracks nailed down the desert. It smelled like a barn although there was no house to be seen. The steers in the cattle cars mooed.

Four hoboes stared from the caboose to the engine. At both ends heat was helling it down in torrents of bright yellow seeds out of a sun like a gleaming palm. In the hot waves, the shacks came running as if they were going to bump up like two loco-motives. The shacks swung brake-handles, cursing.

'So long, sweethearts,' hollered the Georgian, jumping off. 'Next time I see you lice again, I'll be an oil man.' He was glad to be kicked off. That gave a fellow a chance to speak his mind.

'You lying bum,' yelled a shack. 'You'll be a hobo till you croak.'

The other hoboes grouped around the Georgian, tickled at his smart-aleck toughness. The Georgian sneered at them. 'The shack's right. It don't mean nothing for them to boot us off. And nothing for us to get off.'

The train moved. Steers moaned, the sun ambering their brown eyes as the barn wheeled into cleanliness.

'There's more trains to get on,' said the kid, watching the freight rolling away.

'That's not the point,' said the Georgian. He felt glad to be a man again, free in the emptiness to walk his way with no bulls and shacks to boss him.

From the top of the freight, the desert'd been a sand fake to him, with slanty crooked hills a floor high. The sagebrush, mesquite, chappary cactus and such greenish brownish truck had seemed slopped in here and there as if on old-time stage scenery. That was because the desert had been saying hello and good-bye all at once. And that was how hoboes were built, he thought, hello and good-bye. No use looking at them. None of them had the guts to say boo. They were shaking their heads carefully as if suspecting a fast one. They were hopeless, and he was one of them.

Even as he glanced about him, the desert insinuated itself into his mind. A shiver slashed across his shoulders like a sword. How big the desert, how awful big. He had an idea something in it might have a word to say to him. But nobody'd want to speak to a hobo.

They marched up to the tar road running parallel to the tracks. The tar colour was more friendly than sky and sun and sand. The road shouted to them, in the loneliness, of cities, Houston, St. Louis, Los Angeles. The Georgian led the others who shuffled through the sand, the kid whistling, the Mex and Indian silent. The telegraph posts, tall and arduous as New Englanders, reminded them that men had passed this way. More and more, the Georgian was beginning to look his own strength in the face, the strength that had been cringing in box cars and jungles.

'We'll spread out down the road. No car'd give a lift to the bunch of us.' He pointed to his shadow. 'See that. That's me.

I'm nothing. I'm not a man, nothing but a dirty filthy bum afraid
of his shadow.'

The kid had run away to be a circus man; now whimpering,
bumming them all for a butt. 'What's eating you, Georgia?
Gimme a butt. I got to get to California —— What'll we do?
Where's a freight? You sound like a teacher to be preaching and
all, Georgia.' He gasped after his long bubbling speech, wincing
as the Georgian socked his fist into his thin back. 'Ouch. Lemme
alone.'

'Get a lift, you punk.' He hated the kid's aspect of cleanliness.
How did the punk manage it? Dirt was all over him like another
skin. His neck was rough, scratchy, and only a month ago he'd
been neat, and owner of six ties.

They laid on their bellies in the sands, out of sight of any possible motorists. The kid squatted at the Georgian's heels, who had
separated himself from the caste of the other hoboes by a foot.
The greasy Mex was near the Indian, his felt hat dented like a
cowboy's. What am I highfalutin for? thought the Georgian.
I'm like them, hollow inside, dumb, licked by the world. But they
were worse, never talking, stupid as the cactus.

'It looks like a long wait and it ain't for this I lost my job and
left home.' The highway crawled along loneliness. He stood up,
irritated his strength didn't mean anything, chucking pebbles at
the desert.

'If I had my gun we could bang some lizards. I got a gun. You
bet. I'm a fine shot.' The Indian hadn't forgotten the Reservation school, careful about his words as if he were confronting his
teacher. His black eyes held no further thought of the past than
this. When he was silent he owned neither past nor future.

The Georgian laughed wildly. 'You're a regular Monte Blue.
If you didn't own a gun, you'd never talk. God, I'm glad you got
a gun even if it made the steers so sick they hollered. That's how
the shacks guessed about us.'

'Gila monsters worth plenty dough in town,' said the Indian
gravely. 'That's right, Diego, huh?'

The Mex grinned. 'Si. Si. You betcha.'

'He talks,' exclaimed the Georgian. 'I was thinking I was
alone. That's what we want, Monte; Gilas, dough. I'm sick
panhandling.'

The Mex scratched his brown nose. 'His name — Jacinto.'
His eyes were quick, his hearing like a dog's but he'd heard
nothing but the supposed error. 'Jacinto. Si.'

The Indian declared Monte wasn't his name. The Mex grinned
as if maybe some ancestor was a diplomat. In their company his
heart seemed to fill with sand from the desert and he ached with
a hot self-pity.

They climbed mounds topped by blackish-grey lizards like
reptile feudal barons in armour, and the sun shone. The Georgian
heaved his spangling knife but the lizards were fast as sunlight,
peopling the desert, four inch ones, grand footers. He picked up
his knife, laughing, his knife ahead of his laughter.

The Indian reproved him. What did he want with lizards?
Lizards weren't worth a damn. He was so practical, his red-brown
face so nicely calm it seemed as if he were a shopkeeper behind
a counter. Gila were something else.

More than ever, the Georgian was positive they were dead.
He'd better get to his brother in Texas or he'd be dead, too. The
Mex trudging behind Monte-Jacinto was grinning like a circus, his
sleek cheeks round as if he were blowing a horn. All dead and
playing at life. That was the trouble with hoboes. The sky was
an immense blue wall on the horizon. Between themselves and
the forbidden parapets the desert hilled and wandered and no
joyous things but moonstones. In his misery, hunting for their
cool eyes was fun. Every time he pocketed one he felt he had
stolen from the desert, proved himself a man. And the Mex and
Jacinto duplicated his theft like shadows.

'What'd you wanna leave me?' roared the kid, charging down
a ridge, his voice dynamite. His small peaked face with the scold-
ing mouth was unreal. 'I got sick waiting. Gee whiz. That
wasn't fair leaving me. Who's got a cig? Hey, Georgia, that
was a dirty trick.'

'Any cars pass? Shut up. If you don't stop bellyaching I'll
paste your fishlips to your ears.' He glanced wearily from the
skyblue wall to the land where the kid'd come from. The line of
telegraph posts compassed their haven even if the road was out of
sight. 'You dumb kid, you might've got lost.' He pitied the
dumb goof. Nobody had room for him except maybe the desert.

'Aw, I heard you yelling.' His inquisitive eyes fastened on the
Georgian's closed fist, and when he saw the stones his joy was
deafening to hear. 'Oh, boy! They're nice! Gimme some o'
them stones. What you call them? They worth much?'

He dropped one in the greedy palm. 'Find your own. A man's
got to do things for himself. No one's going to help you, kid.'
He thought of his neckties, the money he'd spent on girls. Again
he turned to the horizon but what it held was only a promise.

'How do you find them? Tell a feller, gee whiz.'

The Indian guided them up and down the rises. How in hell
he'd catch a Gila even if he saw one was beyond anything . . .
But it was fun playing like kids, to curse the flickering lizards.
Jack rabbits were grey disappearances. And always the hope
there'd be something behind the next hill, if only a skull. The
desert. Yes, the desert if that was anything.

The wind whistled up as if the sands were finally getting sick of
the Gila hunters. The sky was yellow-darkish on the edges.

The kid wiped his nose. 'Gee whiz. Let's go. Who's got a
butt?'

The telegraph posts, suddenly, had been hewn behind them.
The hills thronged between the horizons like a herd of buffalo,
the wind ruffling their sand hides. The Mex paled, the kid began

to bawl. The Indian reassured them as if he were Buffalo Bill's right-hand man. He'd lead them out. He went backward from their forward progress but were they going back?

Indians were only fit for the movies, thought the Georgian. The strength that had first greeted him when chased off the train, like another self, a brother long separated, embraced him now. The kid and the two dead hoboes were on his hands. His first responsibility in weeks. Praying, he ran up a tall hill. Christ, they were in luck. There were the telegraph posts or rather their cross-rails lying on top the sand ridges. He hollered directions, cursing the kid for sniffling. They packed together against the desert. Nothing but moonstones, moaned the kid. He wanted to go home.

'Shut up. You ain't got a home. None of you.' He mounted hill after hill to recheck their steering. So that was what the desert had to say to him. The wind was speaking: Death and hard luck and fight for you, Georgia, and never a damn thing else. But with that strength come to him, he wasn't afraid. It wasn't so bad fighting when one was young, the odds weren't so bad.

Finally the telegraph posts were seen from the hollows, taller, getting taller and taller.

They surrounded a post as if it were a fire. The tar road was partly covered by swifter highways of sand. The kid still was crying. The sky was yellow-dark, the sun a dim candle glowing at world's end.

Mica particles got in the Georgian's mouth. 'Shut up.' In the shroudings of sand, the older hoboes were silent but that damn kid'd talk if he were dying. The poor kid. He was right, that kid. What the hell had they roamed into the desert for? Moonstones. His life struck him as useless. Off the train and into the desert, the dry whore, and no one to care or to forbid him. Almighty God, no one to care. He ached to be loved, to have kids, a wife, friends, people to love him. That was how to get even with life.

Not to live unknown, dying like a rat. He had a vision of a stone plunging into water, leaving the ripples of its passing. What had that to do with him? Fool, fool, oh, you fool, Georgia. You came near to dying for nothing at all in the damn desert.

The kid shouted he was going to Texas with him. Georgia's brother'd give him a job. Georgia had to take him. His eyes blinked, furtive and trustful at the same time.

The Georgian growled bitterly. 'You. An oil man. Hell!' But the strength in him like the bottom man of an acrobatic team was glad to be lifting up another.

The highway wanted to steal away from their need, to go wild from its purpose. Cars shot past but there were no lifts. The desert wind sang. They tied handkerchiefs around their nostrils, scraping one foot along the road to feel the smooth tar, the kid hanging on to the Georgian's belt with a drowning man's fist. The Mex tailed Jacinto. The strong hoboes led the weaklings, and behind them all the desert tiptoed after like a huge mocking ghost.

The sun was more yellow than dark. The wind howling against the sun's dying glow but not to blow it out, rather as if trying to fan the day alive. It became lighter. The dirt road into Mexico was an invitation. Two miles down it and they saw houses, trees, more faithful than roads, chanting of settlement. Algodones. They went into the town out of a western movie. Twenty saloons. A river with a gold-dredging barge on it. The Georgian laughed. 'Here we are, boys. The Oasis looks good.'

Americans, Mexicans, and the Oasis women were drinking, having fun. He ordered two whiskies and pushed one to the Indian. 'I'll stand treat to you. You're dead on your feet but a good guy when you're not talking about guns and finding ways out of the desert. You got guts for a dead man.'

The Mex stated Jacinto was not dead man.

The kid fidgeted at the women, whining for him to save a drop.

'I'll save you hell.' He dropped some moonstones on the bar.

'Your pay, cap.' As the bartender growled, he took off his shoe, flipped out a silver dollar. 'Those stones are my pay. Glad to get rid of the cartwheel, it blistered me plenty. Boys, hey Jacinto, kid, Mexico, can you beat it? Moonstones ain't legal tender.'

'If we had a Gila,' said the Indian, looking as if he'd never been near a desert.

The Georgian roared, drunk on one shot. The funny thing was that the yellowbelly Mex, the snotty kid, also appeared as if they'd never been lost. It was all in the day's work. They were dead, sure enough, even if they'd made believe they'd been feared to die. But he was alive. He gritted his teeth tight as if to keep that strength from escaping, thinking of Texas among the drinking phantoms. Texas, I'm bound for Texas.

THE OVERCOAT[1]

SALLY BENSON

It had been noisy and crowded at the Milligans' and Mrs. Bishop had eaten too many little sandwiches and too many iced cakes, so that now, out in the street, the air felt good to her, even if it was damp and cold. At the entrance of the apartment house, she took out her change purse and looked through it and found that by counting the pennies, too, she had just eighty-seven cents, which wasn't enough for a taxi from Tenth Street to Seventy-Third. It was horrid never having enough money in your purse, she thought. Playing bridge, when she lost, she often had to give I.O.U.'s and it was faintly embarrassing, although she always managed to make them good. She resented Lila Hardy who could say, 'Can anyone change a ten?' and who could take ten dollars from her small, smart bag while the other women scurried about for change.

She decided that it was too late to take a bus and she might as well walk over to the subway, although the air down there would probably make her head ache. It was drizzling a little and the sidewalks were wet. And as she stood on the corner waiting for

[1] Copyright, 1936, by Sally Benson. From *People are Fascinating*, by Sally Benson. Covici-Friede, 1936.

the traffic lights to change, she felt horribly sorry for herself. She remembered as a young girl, she had always assumed she would have lots of money when she was older. She had planned what to do with it — what clothes to buy and what upholstery she would have in her car.

Of course, everybody nowadays talked poor and that was some comfort. But it was one thing to have lost your money and quite another never to have had any. It was absurd, though, to go around with less than a dollar in your purse. Suppose something happened? She was a little vague as to what might happen, but the idea fed her resentment.

Everything for the house, like food and things, she charged. Years ago, Robert had worked out some sort of budget for her but it had been impossible to keep their expenses under the right headings, so they had long ago abandoned it. And yet Robert always seemed to have money. That is, when she came to him for five or ten dollars, he managed to give it to her. Men were like that, she thought. They managed to keep money in their pockets but they had no idea you ever needed any. Well, one thing was sure, she would insist on having an allowance. Then she would at least know where she stood. When she decided this, she began to walk more briskly and everything seemed simpler.

The air in the subway was worse than usual and she stood on the local side waiting for a train. People who took the expresses seemed to push so and she felt tired and wanted to sit down. When the train came, she took a seat near the door and, although inwardly she was seething with rebellion, her face took on the vacuous look of other faces in the subway. At Eighteenth Street, a great many people got on and she found her vision blocked by a man who had come in and was hanging to the strap in front of her. He was tall and thin and his overcoat which hung loosely on him and swayed with the motion of the train smelled unpleasantly of damp wool. The buttons of the overcoat were of imitation leather and the button directly in front of Mrs. Bishop's eyes evidently had come off and been sewed back on again with black thread, which didn't match the coat at all.

It was what is known as a swagger coat but there was nothing very swagger about it now. The sleeve that she could see was almost threadbare around the cuff and a small shred from the lining hung down over the man's hand. She found herself looking intently at his hand. It was long and pallid and not too clean. The nails were very short as though they had been bitten and there was a discolored callus on his second finger where he probably held his pencil. Mrs. Bishop, who prided herself on her powers of observation, put him in the white-collar class. He most likely, she thought, was the father of a large family and had a hard time sending them all through school. He undoubtedly never spent money on himself. That would account for the shabbiness of his overcoat. And he was probably horribly afraid of losing his job. His house was always noisy and smelled of cooking. Mrs. Bishop couldn't decide whether to make his wife a fat slattern or to have her an invalid. Either would be quite consistent.

She grew warm with sympathy for the man. Every now and then he gave a slight cough, and that increased her interest and her sadness. It was a soft, pleasant sadness and made her feel resigned to life. She decided that she would smile at him when she got off. It would be the sort of smile that couldn't help but make him feel better, as it would be very obvious that she understood and was sorry.

But by the time the train reached Seventy-Second Street, the smell of wet wool, the closeness of the air and the confusion of her own worries had made her feelings less poignant, so that her smile, when she gave it, lacked something. The man looked away embarrassed.

II

Her apartment was too hot and the smell of broiling chops sickened her after the enormous tea she had eaten. She could see Maude, her maid, setting the table in the dining-room for dinner. Mrs. Bishop had bought smart little uniforms for her, but there was nothing smart about Maude and the uniforms never looked right.

Robert was lying on the living-room couch, the evening newspaper over his face to shield his eyes. He had changed his shoes, and the gray felt slippers he wore were too short for him and showed the imprint of his toes, and looked depressing. Years ago, when they were first married, he used to dress for dinner sometimes. He would shake up a cocktail for her and things were quite gay and almost the way she had imagined they would be. Mrs. Bishop didn't believe in letting yourself go and it seemed to her that Robert let himself go out of sheer perversity. She hated him as he lay there, resignation in every line of his body. She envied Lila Hardy her husband who drank but who, at least, was somebody. And she felt like tearing the newspaper from his face because her anger and disgust were more than she could bear.

For a minute she stood in the doorway trying to control herself and then she walked over to a window and opened it roughly. 'Goodness,' she said. 'Can't we ever have any air in here?'

Robert gave a slight start and sat up. 'Hello, Mollie,' he said. 'You home?'

'Yes, I'm home. I came home in the subway.'

Her voice was reproachful. She sat down in the chair facing him and spoke more quietly so that Maude couldn't hear what she was saying. 'Really, Robert,' she said, 'it was dreadful. I came out from the tea in all that drizzle and couldn't even take a taxi home. I had just exactly eighty-seven cents. Just eighty-seven cents!'

'Say,' he said. 'That's a shame. Here.' He reached in his

pocket and took out a small roll of crumpled bills. 'Here,' he repeated. And handed her one. She saw that it was five dollars. Mrs. Bishop shook her head. 'No, Robert,' she told him. 'That isn't the point. The point is that I've really got to have some sort of allowance. It isn't fair to me. I never have any money! Never! It's got so it's positively embarrassing!'

Mr. Bishop fingered the five-dollar bill thoughtfully. 'I see,' he said. 'You want an allowance. What's the matter? Don't I give you money every time you ask for it?'

'Well, yes,' Mrs. Bishop admitted. 'But it isn't like my own. An allowance would be more like my own.'

'Now, Mollie,' he reasoned. 'If you had an allowance, it would probably be gone by the tenth of the month.'

'Don't treat me like a child,' she said. 'I just won't be humiliated any more.'

Mr. Bishop sat turning the five-dollar bill over and over in his hand. 'About how much do you think you should have?' he asked.

'Fifty dollars a month,' she told him. And her voice was harsh and strained. 'That's the very least I can get along on. Why, Lila Hardy would laugh at fifty dollars a month.'

'Fifty dollars a month,' Mr. Bishop repeated. He coughed a little, nervously, and ran his fingers through his hair. 'I've had a lot of things to attend to this month. But, well, maybe if you would be willing to wait until the first of next month, I might manage.'

'Oh, next month will be perfectly all right,' she said, feeling it wiser not to press her victory. 'But don't forget all about it. Because I shan't.'

As she walked toward the closet to put away her wraps, she caught sight of Robert's overcoat on the chair near the door. He had tossed it carelessly across the back of the chair as he came in. One sleeve was hanging down and the vibration of her feet on the floor had made it swing gently back and forth. She saw that the cuff was badly worn and a bit of the lining showed. It looked dreadfully like the sleeve of the overcoat she had seen in the subway. And, suddenly, looking at it, she had a horrible sinking feeling, like falling in a dream.

RESURRECTION OF A

LIFE[1]

WILLIAM SAROYAN

EVERYTHING begins with inhale and exhale, and
never ends, moment after moment, yourself inhaling, and exhaling, seeing, hearing, smelling, touching, tasting, moving,
sleeping, waking, day after day and year after year, until it is
now, this moment, the moment of *your* being, the last moment,
which is saddest and most glorious. It is because we remember,
and I remember having lived among dead moments, now deathless because of my remembrance, among people now dead, having
been a part of the flux which is now only a remembrance, of myself and this earth, a street I was crossing and the people I saw
walking in the opposite direction, automobiles going away from
me. Saxons, Dorts, Maxwells, and the streetcars and trains, the
horses and wagons, and myself, a small boy, crossing a street,
alive somehow, going somewhere.

First he sold newspapers. It was because he wanted to do something, standing in the city, shouting about what was happening
in the world. He used to shout so loud, and he used to need to
shout so much, that he would forget he was supposed to be selling

---

papers; he would get the idea that he was only supposed to shout, to make people understand what was going on. He used to go through the city like an alley cat, prowling all over the place, into saloons, upstairs into whore houses, into gambling joints, to see: their faces, the faces of those who were alive with him on the earth, and the expressions of their faces, and their forms, the faces of old whores, and the way they talked, and the smell of all the ugly places, and the drabness of all the old and rotting buildings, all of it, of his time and his life, a part of him. He prowled through the city, seeing and smelling, talking, shouting about the big news, inhaling and exhaling, blood moving to the rhythm of the sea, coming and going, to the shore of self and back again to selflessness, inhale and newness, exhale and new death, and the boy in the city, walking through it like an alley cat, shouting headlines.

The city was ugly, but his being there was splendid and not an ugliness. His hands would be black with the filth of the city and his face would be black with it, but it was splendid to be alive and walking, of the events of the earth, from day to day, new headlines every day, new things happening.

In the summer it would be very hot and his body would thirst for the sweet fluids of melons, and he would long for the shade of thick leaves and the coolness of a quiet stream, but always he would be in the city, shouting. It was his place and he was the guy, and he wanted the city to be the way it was, if that was the way. He would figure it out somehow. He used to stare at rich people sitting at tables in hightone restaurants eating dishes of ice cream, electric fans making breezes for them, and he used to watch them ignoring the city, not going out to it and being of it, and it used to make him mad. Pigs, he used to say, having everything you want, having everything. What do you know of this place? What do you know of me, seeing this place with a clean eye, any of you? And he used to go, in the summer, to the Crystal

Bar, and there he would study the fat man who slept in a chair all summer, a mountain of somebody, a man with a face and substance that lived, who slept all day every summer day, dreaming what? This fat man, three hundred pounds? What did he dream, sitting in the saloon, in the corner, not playing poker or pinochle like the other men, only sleeping and sometimes brushing the flies from his fat face? What was there for him to dream, anyway, with a body like that, and what was there hidden beneath the fat of that body, what grace or gracelessness? He used to go into the saloon and spit on the floor as the men did and watch the fat man sleeping, trying to figure it out. Him alive, too? he used to ask. That great big sleeping thing alive? Like myself?

In the winter he wouldn't see the fat man. It would be only in the summer. The fat man was like the hot sun, very near everything, of everything, sleeping, flies on his big nose. In the winter it would be cold and there would be much rain. The rain would fall over him and his clothes would be wet, but he would never get out of the rain, and he would go on prowling around in the city, looking for whatever it was that was there and that nobody else was trying to see, and he would go in and out of all the ugly places to see how it was with the faces of the people when it rained, how the rain changed the expressions of their faces. His body would be wet with the rain, but he would go from one place to another, shouting headlines, telling the city about the things that were going on in the world.

I was this boy and he is dead now, but he will be prowling through the city when my body no longer makes a shadow upon the pavement, and if it is not this boy it will be another, myself again, another boy alive on earth, seeking the essential truth of the scene, seeking the static and precise beneath that which is in motion and which is imprecise.

The theatre stood in the city like another universe, and he entered its darkness, seeking there in the falsity of pictures of man in motion the truth of his own city, and of himself, and the truth of all living. He saw their eyes: *While London Sleeps*. He saw the thin emaciated hand of theft twitching toward crime: *Jean Valjean*. And he saw the lecherous eyes of lust violating virginity. In the darkness the false universe unfolded itself before him and he saw the phantoms of man going and coming, making quiet horrifying shadows: *The Cabinet of Doctor Caligari*. He saw the endless sea, smashing against rocks, birds flying, the great prairie and herds of horses, New York and greater mobs of men, monstrous trains, rolling ships, men marching to war, and a line of infantry charging another line of infantry: *The Birth of a Nation*. And sitting in the secrecy of the theatre he entered the houses of the rich, saw them, the male and the female, the high ceilings, the huge marble pillars, the fancy furniture, great bathrooms, tables loaded with food, rich people laughing and eating and drinking, and then secrecy again and a male seeking a female, and himself watching carefully to understand, one pursuing and the other fleeing, and he felt the lust of man mounting in him, desire for the loveliest of them, the universal lady of the firm white shoulders and the thick round thighs, desire for her, he himself, ten years old, in the darkness.

He is dead and deathless, staring at the magnification of the kiss, straining at the mad embrace of male and female, walking alone from the theatre, insane with the passion to live. And at school their shallowness was too much. Don't try to teach me, he said. Teach the idiots. Don't try to tell me anything. I am getting it direct, straight from the pit, the ugliness with the loveliness. Two times two is many millions all over the earth, lonely and shivering, groaning one at a time, trying to figure it out. Don't try to teach me. I'll figure it out for myself.

Daniel Boone? he said. Don't tell me. I knew him. Walking through Kentucky. He killed a bear. Lincoln? A big fellow walking alone, looking at things as if he pitied them, a face like the

face of man. The whole countryside full of dead men, men he
loved, and he himself alive. Don't ask me to memorize his speech.
I know all about it, the way he stood, the way the words came
from his being.

He used to get up before daybreak and walk to the San Joaquin
Baking Company. It was good, the smell of freshly baked bread,
and it was good to see the machine wrapping the loaves in wax
paper. *Chicken bread*, he used to say, and the important man in
the fine suit of clothes used to smile at him. The important man
used to say. What kind of chickens you got at your house, kid?
And the man would smile nicely so that there would be no insult, and he would never have to tell the man that he himself
and his brother and sisters were eating the chicken bread. He
would just stand by the bin, not saying anything, not asking for
the best loaves, and the important man would understand, and
he would pick out the best of the loaves and drop them into the
sack the boy held open. If the man happened to drop a bad loaf
into the sack the boy would say nothing, and a moment later the
man would pick out the bad loaf and throw it back into the bin.
Those chickens, he would say, they might not like that loaf. And
the boy would say nothing. He would just smile. It was good
bread, not too stale and sometimes very fresh, sometimes still
warm, only it was bread that had fallen from the wrapping machine and couldn't be sold to rich people. It was made of the same
dough, in the same ovens, only after the loaves fell they were
called chicken bread and a whole sackful cost only a quarter.
The important man never insulted. Maybe he himself had known
hunger once; maybe as a boy he had known how it felt to be hungry for bread. He was very funny, always asking about the chickens. He knew there were no chickens, and he always picked out
the best loaves.

Bread to eat, so that he could move through the city and shout.
Bread to make him solid, to nourish his anger, to fill his substance

with vigor that shouted at the earth. Bread to carry him to death and back again to life, inhaling, exhaling, keeping the flame within him alive. Chicken bread, he used to say, not feeling ashamed. We eat it. Sure, sure. It isn't good enough for the rich. There are many at our house. We eat every bit of it, all the crumbs. We do not mind a little dirt on the crust. We put all of it inside. A sack of chicken bread. We know we're poor. When the wind comes up our house shakes, but we don't tremble. We can eat the bread that isn't good enough for the rich. Throw in the loaves. It is too good for chickens. It is our life. Sure we eat it. We're not ashamed. We're living on the money we earn selling newspapers. The roof of our house leaks and we catch the water in pans, but we are all there, all of us alive, and the floor of our house sags when we walk over it, and it is full of crickets and spiders and mice, but we are in the house, living there. We eat this bread that isn't quite good enough for the rich, this bread that you call chicken bread.

Walking, this boy vanished, and now it is myself, another, no longer the boy, and the moment is now this moment, of my remembrance. The fig tree he loved: of all graceful things it was the most graceful, and in the winter it stood leafless, dancing, sculptural whiteness dancing. In the spring the new leaves appeared on the fig tree and the hard green figs. The sun came closer and closer and the heat grew, and he climbed the tree, eating the soft fat figs, the flowering of the lovely white woman, his lips kissing.

But always he returned to the city, back again to the place of man, the street, the structure, the door and window, the hall, the roof and floor, back again to the corners of dark secrecy, where they were dribbling out their lives, back again to the movement of mobs, to beds and chairs and stoves, away from the tree, away from the meadow and the brook. The tree was of the other earth, the older and lovelier earth, solid and quiet and of godly grace, of earth and water and of sky and of the time that was before, ancient places, quietly in the sun, Rome and Athens, Cairo, the white fig tree dancing. He talked to the tree, his mouth clenched, pulling himself over its smooth limbs, to be of you, he said, to be of your time, to be there, in the old world, and to be here as well, to eat your fruit, to feel your strength, to move with you as you dance, myself, alone in the world, with you only, my tree, that in myself which is of thee.

Dead, dead, the tree and the boy, yet everlastingly alive, the white tree moving slowly in dance, and the boy talking to it in unspoken, unspeakable language; you, loveliness of the earth, the street waits for me, the moment of my time calls me back, and there he was suddenly, running through the streets, shouting that ten thousand Huns had been destroyed. Huns? he asked. What do you mean, Huns? They are men, aren't they? Call me, then, a Hun. Call me a name, if they are to have a name dying. And he saw the people of the city smiling and talking with pleasure about the good news. He himself appreciated the goodness of the news because it helped him sell his papers, but after the shouting was over and he was himself again, he used to think of ten thousand men smashed from life to violent death, one man at a time, each man himself as he, the boy, was himself, bleeding, praying, screaming, weeping, remembering life as dying men remember it, wanting it, gasping for breath, to go on inhaling and exhaling, living and dying, but always living somehow, stunned, horrified, ten thousand faces suddenly amazed at the monstrousness of the war, the beastliness of man, who could be so godly.

There were no words with which to articulate his rage. All that he could do was shout, but even now I cannot see the war as the historians see it. Succeeding moments have carried the germ of myself to this face and form, the one of this moment, now, my being in this small room, alone, as always, remembering the boy, resurrecting him, and I cannot see the war as the historians see it.

Those clever fellows study all the facts and they see the war as a large thing, one of the biggest events in the legend of man, something general, involving multitudes. I see it as a large thing too, only I break it into small units of one man at a time, and I see it as a large and monstrous thing for each man involved. I see the war as death in one form or another for men dressed as soldiers, and all the men who survived the war, including myself, I see as men who died with their brothers, dressed as soldiers.

There is no such thing as a soldier. I see death as a private event, the destruction of the universe in the brain and in the senses of one man, and I cannot see any man's death as a contributing factor in the success or failure of a military campaign. The boy had to shout what had happened. Whatever happened, he had to shout it, making the city know. *Ten thousand Huns killed, ten thousand,* one at a time, one, two, three, four, inestimably many, ten thousand, alive, and then dead, killed, shot, mangled, ten thousand Huns, ten thousand men. I blame the historians for the distortion. I remember the coming of the gas mask to the face of man, the proper grimace of the horror of the nightmare we were performing, artfully expressing the monstrousness of the inward face of man. To the boy who is dead the war was the international epilepsy which brought about the systematic destruction of one man at a time until millions of men were destroyed.

There he is suddenly in the street, running, and it is 1917, shouting the most recent crime of man, extra, extra, ten thousand Huns killed, himself alive, inhaling, exhaling, *ten thousand, ten thousand,* all the ugly buildings solid, all the streets solid, the city unmoved by the crime, *ten thousand,* windows opening, doors opening, and the people of the city smiling about it, good, ten thousand of them killed, good. *Johnny, get your gun, get your gun, Johnny get your gun: we'll be over, we're coming over, and we won't come back till it's over, over there,* and another trainload of boys in uniforms, going to the war. And the fat man, sleeping in a corner of the Crystal

Bar, what of him? Sleeping there, somehow alive in spite of the lewd death in him, but never budging. Pig, he said, ten thousand Huns killed, ten thousand men with solid bodies mangled to death. Does it mean nothing to you? Does it not disturb your fat dream? Boys with loves, men with wives and children. What have you, sleeping? They are all dead, all of them dead. Do you think you are alive? Do you dream you are alive? The fly on your nose is more alive than you.

Sunday would come, *O day of rest and gladness, O day of joy and light, O balm of care and sadness, Most beautiful, most bright*, and he would put on his best shirt and his best trousers, and he would try to comb his hair down, to be neat and clean, meeting God, and he would go to the small church and sit in the shadow of religion: in the beginning, the boy David felling the giant Goliath, beautiful Rebecca, mad Saul, Daniel among lions, Jesus talking quietly to the men, and in the boat shouting at them because they feared, angry at them because they had fear, calm yourselves, boys, calm yourselves, let the storm rage, let the boat sink, do you fear going to God? Ah, that was lovely, that love of death was lovely, Jesus loving it: calm yourselves, boys, God damn you, calm yourselves, why are you afraid? *Still, still with thee, when purple morning breaketh, abide, abide, with me, fast falls the eventide*, ah, lovely. He sat in the basement of the church, among his fellows, singing at the top of his voice. I do not believe, he said. I cannot believe. There cannot be a God. But it is lovely, lovely, these songs we sing, *Saviour, breathe an evening blessing, sun of my soul, begin, my tongue, some heavenly theme, begin, my tongue, begin, begin.* Lovely, lovely, but I cannot believe. The poor and the rich, those who deserve life and those who deserve death, and the ugliness everywhere. Where is God? Big ships sinking at sea, submarines, men in the water, cannon booming, machine guns, men dying, ten thousand, where? But our singing, *Joy to the world, the Lord is come. Let earth receive her King. Silent night, holy night. What grace, O Lord, my dear redeemer. Ride on, ride on, in majesty. Angels, roll the rock away; death, yield up thy mighty prey.* No, he could not believe. He had seen for himself. It was there, in the city, all the godlessness, the eyes of the whores, the men at cards, the sleeping fat man, and the mad headlines, it was all there, unbelief, ungodliness, everywhere, all the world forgetting. How could he believe? But the music, so good and clean, so much of the best in man: *lift up, lift up your voices now. Lo, he comes with clouds descending once for favored sinners slain. Arise, my soul, arise, shake off thy guilty fears, O for a thousand tongues to sing. Like a river glorious, holy Bible, book divine, precious treasure, thou art mine.* And spat, right on the floor of the Crystal Bar. And into Madam Juliet's Rooms, over the Rex Drug Store, the men buttoning their clothes, ten thousand Huns killed, madam. *Break thou the bread of life, dear Lord, to me, as thou didst break the loaves, beside the sea.* And spat, on the floor, hearing the fat man snoring. Another ship sunk. The Marne. Ypres. Russia. Poland. Spat. *Art thou weary, art thou languid, art thou sore distressed?* Zeppelin over Paris. The fat man sleeping. *Haste, traveler, haste, the night comes on.* Spat. *The storm is gathering in the west.* Cannon. Hutt! two three, four! Hutt! two three, four, how many men marching, how many? Onward, onward, unChristian soldiers. *I was a wandering sheep.* Spat. *I did not love my home.* Your deal, Jim. Spat. *Take me, O my father, take me.* Spat. *This holy bread, this holy wine. My God, is any hour so sweet?* Submarine plunging. Spat. *Take my life and let it be consecrated, Lord, to thee.* Spat.

He sat in the basement of the little church, deep in the shadow of faith, and of no faith: I cannot believe: where is the God of whom they speak, where? *Your harps, ye trembling saints, down from the willows take.* Where? Cannon. *Lead, oh lead, lead kindly light, amid the encircling gloom.* Spat. *Jesus, Saviour, pilot me.* Airplane: spat: smash. *Guide me, O thou great Jehovah. Bread of heaven, feed me till I want no more.* The universal lady of the dark theatre: thy lips, beloved, thy shoulders and thighs, thy sea-surging blood. The tree, black figs in sunlight. Spat. *Rock of ages, cleft for me, let me hide myself in thee.* Spat. *Let the water and the blood, from thy riven side which flowed, be of sin the double cure.* Lady, your arm, your arm: spat. The mountain of flesh sleeping through the summer. Ten thousand Huns killed.

Sunday would come, turning him from the outward world to the inward, to the secrecy of the past, endless as the future, back to Jesus, to God; *when the weary, seeking rest, to thy goodness flee;* back to the earliest quiet: *He leadeth me, O blessed thought.* But he did not believe. He could not believe. Jesus was a remarkable fellow: you couldn't figure him out. He had a pious love of death. An heroic fellow. And as for God. Well, he could not believe.

But the songs he loved and he sang them with all his might: *hold thou my hand, O blessed nothingness, I walk with thee. Awake, my soul, stretch every nerve, and press with vigor on. Work, for the night is coming, work, for the day is done.* Spat. Right on the floor of the Crystal Bar. It is Sunday again: O blessed nothingness, we worship thee. Spat. And suddenly the sleeping fat man sneezes. Hallelujah. Amen. Spat. Sleep on, beloved, sleep, and take thy rest. *Lay down thy head upon thy Saviour's breast.* We love thee well, but Jesus loves thee best. Jesus loves thee. For the Bible tells you so. Amen. The fat man sneezes. He could not believe and he could not disbelieve. Sense? There was none. But glory? There was an abundance of it. Everywhere. Madly everywhere. Those crazy birds vomiting song. Those vast trees, solid and quiet. And clouds. And sun. And night. And day. *It is not death to die,* he sang: *to leave this weary road, to be at home with God.* God? The same. Nothingness. Nowhere. Everywhere. The crazy glory, everywhere: Madam Juliet's Rooms, all modern conveniences, including beds. Spat. *I know not, O I know not, what joys await us there.* Where? Heaven? No. Madam Juliet's.

In the church, the house of God, the boy singing, remembering the city's lust.

Boom: Sunday morning: and the war still booming: after the singing he would go to the newspaper office and get his Special Sunday Extras and run through the city with them, his hair combed for God, and he would shout the news: amen, *I gave my life for Jesus.* Oh, yeah? Ten thousand Huns killed, and I am the guy, inhaling, exhaling, running through the town, I, myself, seeing, hearing, touching, shouting, smelling, singing, wanting, I, the guy, the latest of the whole lot, alive by the grace of God: ten thousand, two times ten million, by the grace of God dead, by His grace smashed, amen, extra, extra: five cents a copy, extra, ten thousand killed.

I was this boy who is now lost and buried in the succeeding forms of myself, and I am now of this last moment, of this small room, and the night hush, time going, time coming, breathing, this last moment, inhale, exhale, the boy dead and alive. All that I have learned is that we breathe, and remember, and we see the boy moving through a city that has become lost, among people who have become dead, alive among dead moments, crossing a street, the scene thus, or standing by the bread bin in the bakery, a sack of chicken bread please so that we can live and shout about it, and it begins nowhere and it ends nowhere, and all that I know is that we are somehow alive, all of us in the light, making shadows, the sun overhead, space all around us, inhaling, exhaling, the face and form of man everywhere, pleasure and pain, sanity and madness, war and no war, and peace and no peace, the earth solid and unaware of us, unaware of our cities, our dreams, the earth everlastingly itself, and the sea sullen with movement like my breathing, waves coming and going, and all that I know is that I am alive and glad to be, glad to be of this ugliness and this glory, somehow glad that I can remember the boy climbing the fig tree, unpraying but religious with joy, somehow of the earth, of the time of earth, somehow everlastingly of life, nothingness, blessed or unblessed, somehow deathless, insanely glad to be here, and so it is true, there is no death, somehow there is no death, and can never be.

THIS TOWN AND

SALAMANCA[1]

ALLAN SEAGER

I

So WHEN he returned, we asked him why had he gone to live there and he said he'd just heard of it and thought it might be a nice place to live in for a while. He had lived in an old house built around a court. The walls were four feet thick and the windows were larger on the inside than they were on the outside; the sills slanted. They kept goats' milk there on the window-sills because the stone made the air cool. You could see the sticks of a hawk's nest hanging over one corner of the roof, and Jesus the landlady's son — he looked up here to see if we thought it was funny that a man should be named Jesus, but none of us said anything. We read a great deal — he often whistled to it evenings. Yes, the food was good. They had a sausage with tomatoes in it that was very good and the wine was not like French wine, it was heavier and sweeter. And there were no fireplaces for heating but things they called braseros. They were big pans like that with his arms stretched and on cold mornings they set it alight and covered the flame with ashes. They would put the brasero under a big table. The table had a sort of plush cover to it that hung down to

the floor with slits in it. You put your feet through the slits and
wrapped the cover around your waist. Then although your feet
roasted, you could still see your breath and you couldn't stay in
the room long because of the fumes, and sitting by the brasero
gave you chilblains but they were a common thing and no one
minded. Klug asked him about the women. Were they — you
know? The women were all right he said. The peasant girls were
very pretty but they faded early and got fat. Yes, but, Klug said
impatiently, but he was talking then about the riots, how they
used beer bottles full of black powder for bombs and when they
bombed the convent, the nuns all ran out crying and waving their
arms after the explosion and some fell on their knees and prayed
in the midst of the rioters but the bomb had not even chipped the
wall, it was four feet thick. All the houses were like that with big
thick walls and the streets were narrow and the town was quiet.
They could not hang the washing in the courtyards because it was
too cool for it to dry, so they spread it on rocks beside the river
when they finished. It was a very old town and they lived in the
same way year after year. Gordon asked him about the spiritual
remnants of medievalism. He answered that the people were very
pious and went to the cathedral to pray for everything, even lost
articles. The cathedral had small windows and the light was
yellow inside not like the grey light inside the cathedrals in Ile de
France.

Well, I thought, as they talked on into the evening, it is not
anything like that here. You see I remember this particular evening very clearly and all that we said, because it was the last time
John had anything new to tell us, and from that time on, he has
lived here with us in this town. We never thought he would settle
here. It is a good enough town but nothing to the places he has
seen, not even the kind of place you would close your book to
watch if you went through on the train. First there are the ball-
bearing factory and the electric bell factory, with the other fac-

tories hidden behind them; then there are trees hiding the houses with their backs turned toward you and vegetable gardens beside the tracks; and then you would see the spire, not of a cathedral, but of the Methodist church, and the town would soon dwindle away into the cornfields and just after that you could look at your watch to see how long before Chicago. It is not like Salamanca, but the four of us were born and grew up here and only John had gone away. And when he came home to see his mother, he would tell us these things that made us seem fools to ourselves for having stayed but we were busy with our work and could not follow him. There are maple trees on both sides of the streets and in summer it is like driving through a tunnel of green leaves.

You see he never answered Gordon's intelligent questions and he always disappointed Klug who thinks that all the women in foreign countries wait on street corners after dark winking and motioning yonder with their heads. John seldom was an actor in his own play — he merely looked, it seemed, and told us what he saw. It was the best way, keeping himself out, but they would not admit it, so they kept on with the questions. They admitted it to themselves though. Klug said he thought of the peasant girls with their ankles shining under their tucked-up skirts doing the washing by the river bank when he was scrubbing his hands after taking the cancer out of Mrs. Gira, the Polish washwoman, and the nurse was counting the used wet sponges and the hospital smell made his stomach turn. And when the aldermen brought the plans of the new railroad station to Gordon and sat down to talk and object for hours, he saw the smoke drifting from where the bomb exploded and the nuns praying in the confusion and one of the aldermen had spots on his waistcoat that he kept picking at. Though we had nothing but questions when he came, we all knew that the questions were merely little signs to show that we too might very well have been there and seen these things, and that it was nothing more important than chance that we had stayed here. He talked late and I remember there was a bat lurching to and fro under a light down the street.

Mrs. Gira got well though and it is a fine new railroad station.

II

He was in an old boat-house whistling. We heard him when we came down the path. The boat-house was so old the shingles curled and weeds grew on the roof, and we used to tell him that some day the whole thing would give way with him in it and he would have to swim out with the rafters round his neck. He had borrowed the use of it from Old Man Suggs who hadn't kept a boat in years. When we were kids I remember seeing it when we went to the river-flats to look for dog-tooth violets. It was a motor launch and he sold it when the tomato cannery started up. Every summer the river is full of blobs of red tomato pulp and no one wants to go out in a boat then. But John was building a sail boat. It was May then and he had worked all his spare time on it since the August before; every Saturday afternoon, and nights after supper he would go down and work by the light of three oil lamps he got from his mother. That was the winter we played so much poker and sometimes we would go to the boat-house at midnight and ask John to take a hand. He was always pleasant about it, without any scruples against gambling, but he never stopped working and we would shout above the hammer blows, 'Where do you think you're going in this boat when it's finished? Going to haul tomatoes for the cannery?' He would laugh and say that a good many waters would wet this hull before she was much older. We would laugh because we knew he had got the phrase out of some book, and we would start up the path. The ripples on the water always shone in the lamplight and we could hear his hammer as far as the dirt road where we turned to Klug's house. Often we played till midnight. I won a lot of money that winter.

When we entered the boat-house we could see it was nearly
finished. It looked very big and white and seemed not too much
to have put a winter's work into. He was planing some teak for
the deck, and when we came near there was the acrid leathery
odour of the fresh shavings. We had seen pictures of yachts, and
once or twice the ore boats on the big lakes, but the things we saw
every day, the houses, trees and grain elevators, went straight up
from the ground. They had roots. If they had not, as they
seemed, been always in one place, they always would be. John's
boat was a strange shape, curved for the water. Even in the dim
boat-house, propped up with blocks, she seemed ready for movement. I looked at John with the handle of the plane easy in his
hand, a carpenter's tool, and we were going to be 'professional'
men, and I knew he would go away. The boat had sprung from
some matrix within him that we would never understand, just as
he was puzzled when Gordon asked him how long she was and
how many tons weight as if she were a heifer fattened for market.
When we went out of the boat-house, Klug said, 'So long,
skipper.'

He went away in the boat as I had thought he would and after
this he never came back for long at a time. God knows how he
got the blocks from under her without any help, but one afternoon
he launched her all by himself, and in ten days he had her rigged
and the galley full of stores. He sailed away without saying anything to anyone, down our little river into the Ohio and then into
the Mississippi and out into the Gulf below New Orleans. He was
gone all summer into October. I saw him on the street when he
returned. He was tanned almost black. We shook hands and I
said:

'Where did you go? Did you have a good trip?'

He looked at me a moment before answering. 'Trip' means
a journey you take in a car during your two-weeks' vacation in
the summer, maybe to Yellowstone or the Grand Canyon or

Niagara. It is a relaxation from your work. I could see as I said it that 'trip' was the wrong word, but just how far wrong, it took me years to find out and then I never was certain. I thought of his boat, a strange and unfamiliar shape, and how he, whom we had seen unsuspectingly every day through his boyhood, had made it.

'Yes, I had a good time.'

'Where did you go?'

'Well, down into the Gulf and around.'

'Cuba?'

'Yes, I put in at Havana,' and then as if he had at last found something he could tell me, 'you know, Klug would like that place — they've got a park there where you can get free beer. It's owned by a brewing company and you can go there and drink all you want, free.'

'Where else did you go?'

'Oh, the Tortugas, Hayti, Vera Cruz.'

He showed me a gold piece he had got off a pawnbroker in Port-au-Prince. He said it was a moidore. He was nineteen then.

III

When he returned next time, he was less reticent. It was not because he was proud of being a traveller but more, I think, that he saw we really wanted to hear about the distant places he had been. When his boat was coming into the harbour of Singapore, he said you could see the junks waiting with their crinkled sails. And when the ship came near, they sailed right in front of the bow as close as they could. Sometimes they didn't make it and they all smashed up and drowned. He said they did it to cut off the devils following behind. The day after he told us that Gordon asked Tom Sing, who runs the chop suey joint, if he believed in devils but Tom only grinned. Gordon said it was the oriental inscrutability. Gordon is quite serious.

During the next ten years John did all the things we said we'd do that time in the apple orchard. He joined the army to fly and left the army after a time and went to Italy. I went to his house from the office the day he got home. He was dressed in white, lunging at himself in a long mirror with a foil in his hand. The French held their foils this way with the thumb so, but the Italians that way. After that he was a sailor on one of the crack clippers that still bring the wheat up from Australia, and from Liverpool I had a postcard with a picture of Aintree racecourse on the back. It said, 'Give Gordon my congratulations.' Gordon had been elected mayor and we were very proud of him. How John heard of it we couldn't figure out.

One time there was a card from Aden and another from Helsingfors. You can see he travelled. No one in the town had ever gone so far and people used to stop his mother on the street to ask where he was then, not that they really cared but because the thread that tied them to him as a local boy tied them also to the strange name his mother answered when they asked.

When he was a sailor in the Pacific, spinal meningitis broke out on board. Eighteen people died and they put the bodies down in the hold. The ship's doctor examined all the crew and said John was the healthiest and the captain ordered him to go below and sew up the bodies in shrouds and heave them overboard.

John got a roll of canvas, a reel of pack-thread, a leather palm-guard and a needle and went down into the hold. He rigged up an electric light in a wire cage and swung it from a hook over his head. The eighteen lay there in a row. They were quite stiff, and when the ship rolled, sometimes an arm would come up and pause until the ship rolled back. But they were in the shadow and he did not watch them much because the sewing was hard work about an hour to each one. He jabbed his finger with the needle three or four times and that made it harder. When he got one ready, he would put it over his shoulder and stagger up the companionway to the deck.

High up above him beside the funnel, to escape the risk of infection, stood an Anglican parson, one of the passengers. He had an open prayer book and said the service very quickly the leaves fluttering in the wind. Then John would pick up the corpse again and heave it over the side. Sometimes a shark ripped the shroud almost as it hit the water; others he could see jerked from the ring of foam of their impact and carried quickly below. There were at least a dozen sharks and John said he knew his work was useless and he took bigger and bigger stitches in the canvas. There was quite a wind and John could never hear the whole service because the wind blew the words away but a few snatches would come down to him. He and the parson were all alone, the other people having hidden from fear; and they did not speak to each other. When John brought up the last corpse, it had been a Portuguese merchant from Manila on his way to Goa to see his daughter, the wind stopped suddenly and there was a moment of calm. ' ... to the deep to be turned into corruption,' the parson said. John picked up the merchant, balanced him on the rail and shoved him over and the sharks came.

IV

'And Eloise said it was when she was getting the coffee after dinner. Mr. and Mrs. Booth were setting in the parlour and Mr. Booth was drinking brandy like he always does and both of them quiet as mutes at a funeral when all at once the door bell rang and Eloise answered it and there stood John Baldwin. My, I think he's handsome. Oh, he's much better looking than him. And he asked could he see Mr. Booth and Eloise said he could; he was right in the parlour. So Mr. Baldwin come in but he wouldn't give Eloise his hat. He kept it and said he was only staying a minute. Well Eloise said she went to the kitchen to get another cup naturally expecting Mr. Baldwin would have some coffee and when she come back through the dining-room she was so surprised she nearly dropped it.

'She said Mr. Baldwin was standing right in front of Mr. Booth and he says, "Dennis, I've come for your wife." Just like that. And Mr. Booth says, "What do you mean — you've come for my wife?" Eloise said she got behind the window drapes so they wouldn't see her and Mr. Baldwin says, "Frances loves me. I want you to divorce her." Mr. Booth was drunk on all that brandy and he jumped up and began to shout that it was damned cool and a lot of things about throwing Mr. Baldwin out of the house only Eloise don't think for a minute he could have even if he was sober. Why, John Baldwin's way over six feet and a sailor and always fighting with them little swords and all, but Mr. Booth got white, he was so mad, and Mrs. Booth she didn't say anything. She just sat there and looked at them and Eloise said it was like Mr. Baldwin didn't hear a word Mr. Booth said because he was looking at Mrs. Booth all the time and when Mr. Booth stopped talking Mr. Baldwin looked up at him quick like you do when a clock stops. Then he just says, "Well, Dennis," and Mr. Booth began to swear something terrible but he didn't try to throw him out, he didn't even come close to him. Then Mr. Baldwin looked at Mrs. Booth and smiled and says, "Come along, Frances," and Mrs. Booth smiled back and they walked right out of the house without her even packing any clothes. And that's all there was to it. Eloise says Mrs. Booth walked right out of her house into a new life, never to return. And Mrs. Booth they say has gone to Paris to get a divorce from Mr. Booth. Well, all I got to say is, it serves him right — he was always running around after them dirty little factory girls. Certainly he was. Everybody knows it. Why you know that little Muller girl, the one with the fox fur. Why Eloise says that....'

I stopped listening then. I always liked to look even at the

Italian flags on bottles of olive oil when I was a kid. I had the
same feeling then: no one does things like that here, walking into
a man's house and taking his wife. If you want a man's wife, you
meet her by chance in Chicago and she goes on being his wife
afterwards. Or maybe it was like the boat. We hadn't lived with
him. He was only the things he had done and those at a distance.
Now that he had begun his marriage this way I did not think he
would change the pattern, but that was before I knew he intended to settle here.

He was, I thought then, rootless and invincible. He didn't seem
to want what we had, what we had remained here and worked for.
Which comes down to this, I suppose, and little more: the same
trees every day when you go to work, in summer hanging over the
lawns beside the walks, and bare with snow at the forks of the
limbs and the sound of snow shovels scraping the walks; and
when you look up, the line of the roof of the house next door
against the sky. You could call it peace. It is just peace with no
brilliance. I remembered how bright the gold piece was in his
hand.

But he didn't go away again. He settled here very quietly and
took a nice little house. He and Frances were very happy, and we
all used to say how glad we were that they were so happy. We
used to say it very loudly to ourselves and sometimes to him, and
we put ourselves out to help him meet people. He had been away
so long that he had forgot or never had known them. We got him
into the golf club the first week he was in the bank. Everything
we could show him about the town we did gladly.

After he had been married a year, we all came to Gordon's one
night to drink beer. Most of the evening we taught John poker,
and after that we just sat around and talked. John said,

'You know Roy Curtis from out Fruit Ridge way? Well, he
came in today and wanted to borrow ten thousand dollars to buy
another hundred acres. That piece there by the bridge. Belongs
to Dick Sheppard.'

'He'll raise wheat. There's no money in wheat now,' we said.

'That's what I told him, but he wants to have a shot at it just the same. He offered a second mortgage. I don't know though. What do you think?'

We told him that Roy Curtis was a fool if he thought he could make money in wheat at fifty-six cents a bushel.

'He's got a combine you know. He says he'll have five hundred acres in wheat, and he and his boy can work it all by themselves.'

We remembered when he'd bought the combine. Five hundred acres is too small for a combine. This isn't Dakota.

'You wouldn't lend him the money, then? He's coming in Thursday. It's good security, a second mortgage on his place.'

We told him that we wouldn't lend the money, but John had drunk a lot of beer. He kept on talking about it.

'He's a smart farmer, Roy. Look at that house he's got there. It's a fine place, as good as any of these here in town. Got a Packard and a big radio. Why, he said he got Rome on that radio the other night. He didn't make his money doing foolish things. I don't know about the loan.'

Roy's aunt had left him money, but that was while John was away. We didn't tell him. I said:

'Do you fence any now, John?'

He got up laughing and went out into the hall and got a mashie out of Gordon's golf bag and came in with it. He began standing with a bent leg and one hand flung up behind him. He went through the lunges and parries laughing.

'Getting fat,' he said, 'I can't do 'em any more.'

I had to leave then because I had to be at the office early next day. John was still talking about the loan when I left. It had been raining and the wind had blown down leaves from the maples. The evening had been unsatisfactory and I thought about it as I walked along. I was in sight of my house before I thought why, and I stopped to pick off the red leaves stuck to my shoes.

I remembered him in white with his face grave. 'You see, the French hold a foil this way. It's not like the Italians. I learned in Marseilles.' That was the way he used to talk. We knew all about loans; we knew all about him now. Of course I could never do more than just remind him of these things because he was so happy. But I did not think he would ever go away again to return and tell us these things, because of his happiness. Suddenly I felt old. It was as if we had trusted him to keep our youth for us and he had let it go. But our youth only.

MAN ON A ROAD[1].

ALBERT MALTZ

A<small>T ABOUT</small> four in the afternoon I crossed the bridge at Gauley, West Virginia, and turned the sharp curve leading into the tunnel under the railroad bridge. I had been over this road once before and knew what to expect — by the time I entered the tunnel I had my car down to about ten miles an hour. But even at that speed I came closer to running a man down than I ever have before. This is how it happened.

The patched, macadam road had been soaked through by an all-day rain and now it was as slick as ice. In addition, it was quite dark — a black sky and a steady, swishing rain made driving impossible without headlights. As I entered the tunnel a big cream colored truck swung fast around the curve on the other side. The curve was so sharp that his headlights had given me no warning. The tunnel was short and narrow, just about passing space for two cars, and before I knew it he was in front of me with his big, front wheels over on my side of the road.

I jammed on my brakes. Even at ten miles an hour my car skidded, first toward the truck and then, as I wrenched on the wheel, in toward the wall. There it stalled. The truck swung around hard, scraped my fender, and passed through the tunnel about an inch away from me. I could see the tense face of the young driver with the tight bulge of tobacco in his cheek and his eyes glued on the road. I remember saying to myself that I hoped he'd swallow that tobacco and go choke himself.

I started my car and shifted into first. It was then I saw for the first time that a man was standing in front of my car about a foot away from the inside wheel. It was a shock to see him there. 'For Chrissakes,' I said.

My first thought was that he had walked into the tunnel after my car had stalled. I was certain he hadn't been in there before. Then I noticed that he was standing profile to me with his hand held up in the hitch-hiker's gesture. If he had walked into that tunnel, he'd be facing me — he wouldn't be standing sideways looking at the opposite wall. Obviously I had just missed knocking him down and obviously he didn't know it. He didn't even know I was there.

It made me run weak inside. I had a picture of a man lying crushed under a wheel with me standing over him knowing it was my car.

I called out to him 'Hey!' He didn't answer me. I called louder. He didn't even turn his head. He stood there, fixed, his hand up in the air, his thumb jutting out. It scared me. It was like a story by Bierce where the ghost of a man pops out of the air to take up his lonely post on a dark country road.

My horn is a good, loud, raucous one and I knew that the tunnel would re-double the sound. I slapped my hand down on that little black button and pressed as hard as I could. The man was either going to jump or else prove that he was a ghost.

Well, he wasn't a ghost — but he didn't jump either. And it wasn't because he was deaf. He heard that horn all right.

He was like a man in a deep sleep. The horn seemed to awake

him only by degrees, as though his whole consciousness had been sunk in some deep recess within himself. He turned his head slowly and looked at me. He was a big man, about thirty-five with a heavy-featured face — an ordinary face with a big, fleshy nose and a large mouth. The face didn't say much. I wouldn't have called it kind or brutal or intelligent or stupid. It was just the face of a big man, wet with rain, looking at me with eyes that seemed to have a glaze over them. Except for the eyes you see faces like that going into the pit at six in the morning, or coming out of a steel mill or foundry where heavy work is done. I couldn't understand that glazed quality in his eyes. It wasn't the glassy stare of a drunken man, or the wild, mad glare I saw once in the eyes of a woman in a fit of violence. I could only think of a man I once knew who had died of cancer. Over his eyes, in the last days, there was the same dull glaze, a far away, absent look as though behind the blank, outward film there was a secret flow of past events on which his mind was focussed. It was this same look that I saw in the man on the road.

When at last he heard my horn, the man stepped very deliberately around the front of my car and came toward the inside door. The least I expected was that he would show surprise at an auto so dangerously close to him. But there was no emotion to him whatsoever. He walked slowly, deliberately, as though he had been expecting me and then bent his head down to see under the top of my car. 'Kin yuh give me a lift, friend?' he asked me.

I saw his big, horse teeth chipped at the ends and stained brown by tobacco. His voice was high-pitched and nasal with the slurred, lilting drawl of the deep South. In West Virginia few of the town folk seem to speak that way. I judged he had been raised in the mountains.

I looked at his clothes — an old cap, a new blue work shirt, and dark trousers, all soaked through with rain. They didn't tell me much.

I must have been occupied with my thoughts about him for some time, because he asked me again. 'Ahm goin' to Weston,' he said. 'Are you a'goin' thataway?'

As he said this, I looked into his eyes. The glaze had disappeared and now they were just ordinary eyes, brown and moist.

I didn't know what to reply. I didn't really want to take him in — the episode had unnerved me and I wanted to get away from the tunnel and from him too. But I saw him looking at me with a patient, almost humble glance. The rain was streaked on his face and he stood there asking for a ride and waiting in simple concentration for my answer. I was ashamed to tell him 'no.' Besides, I was curious. 'Climb in,' I said.

He sat down beside me, placing a brown paper package on his lap. We started out of the tunnel.

From Gauley to Weston is about a hundred miles of as difficult mountain driving as I know — a five mile climb to the top of a hill, then five miles down, and then up another. The road twists like a snake on the run and for a good deal of it there is a jagged cliff on one side and a drop of a thousand feet or more on the other. The rain, and the small rocks crumbling from the mountain sides and littering up the road, made it very slow going. But in the four hours or so that it took for the trip I don't think my companion spoke to me half a dozen times.

I tried often to get him to talk. It was not that he wouldn't talk, it was rather that he didn't seem to hear me — as though as soon as he had spoken, he would slip down into that deep, secret recess within himself. He sat like a man dulled by morphine. My conversation, the rattle of the old car, the steady pour of rain were all a distant buzz — the meaningless, outside world that could not quite pierce the shell in which he seemed to be living.

As soon as we had started, I asked him how long he had been in the tunnel.

'Ah don' know,' he replied. 'A good tahm, ah reckon.'

'What were you standing there for — to keep out of the rain?'

He didn't answer. I asked him again, speaking very loudly. He turned his head to me. 'Excuse me, friend,' he said, 'did you say somethin'?'

'Yes,' I answered. 'Do you know I almost ran you over back in that tunnel?'

'No-o,' he said. He spoke the word in that breathy way that is typical of mountain speech.

'Didn't you hear me yell to you?'

'No-o.' He paused. 'Ah reckon ah was thinkin'.'

'Ah reckon you were,' I thought to myself. 'What's the matter, are you hard of hearing?' I asked him.

'No-o,' he said, and turned his head away looking out front at the road.

I kept right after him. I didn't want him to go off again. I wanted somehow to get him to talk.

'Looking for work?'

'Yessuh.'

He seemed to speak with an effort. It was not a difficulty of speech, it was something behind, in his mind, in his will to speak. It was as though he couldn't keep touch between his world and mine. Yet when he did answer me, he spoke directly and co-herently. I didn't know what to make of it. When he first came into the car I had been a little frightened. Now I only felt terribly curious and a little sorry.

'Do you have a trade?' I was glad to come to that question. You know a good deal about a man when you know what line of work he follows and it always leads to further conversation.

'Ah ginerally follows the mines,' he said.

'Now,' I thought, 'we're getting somewhere.'

But just then we hit a stretch of unpaved road where the mud was thick and the ruts were hard to follow. I had to stop talking and watch what I was doing. And when we came to paved road again, I had lost him.

I tried again to make him talk. It was no use. He didn't even hear me. Then, finally, his silence shamed me. He was a man lost somewhere within his own soul, only asking to be left alone. I felt wrong to keep thrusting at his privacy.

So for about four hours we drove in silence. For me those hours were almost unendurable. I have never seen such rigidity in a human being. He sat straight up in the car, his outward eye fixed on the road in front, his inward eye seeing nothing. He didn't know I was in the car, he didn't know he was in the car at all, he didn't feel the rain that kept sloshing in on him through the rent in the side curtains. He sat like a slab of molded rock and only from his breathing could I be sure that he was alive. His breathing was heavy.

Only once in that long trip did he change his posture. That was when he was seized with a fit of coughing. It was a fierce, hacking cough that shook his big body from side to side and doubled him over like a child with the whooping cough. He was trying to cough something up — I could hear the phlegm in his chest — but he couldn't succeed. Inside him there was an ugly scraping sound as though cold metal were being rubbed on the bone of his ribs, and he kept spitting and shaking his head.

It took almost three minutes for the fit to subside. Then he turned around to me and said, 'Excuse me, friend.' That was all. He was quiet again.

I felt awful. There were times when I wanted to stop the car and tell him to get out. I made up a dozen good excuses for cutting the trip short. But I couldn't do it. I was consumed by a curiosity to know what was wrong with the man. I hoped that before we parted, perhaps even as he got out of the car, he would tell me what it was or say something that would give me a clew.

I thought of the cough and wondered if it were T.B. I thought of cases of sleeping sickness I had seen and of a boxer who was punch drunk. But none of these things seemed to fit. Nothing physical seemed to explain this dark, terrible silence, this intense, all-exclusive absorption within himself.

Hour after hour of rain and darkness!

Once we passed the slate dump of a mine. The rain had made the surface burst into flame and the blue and red patches flickering in a kind of witch glow on a hill of black seemed to attract my companion. He turned his head to look at it, but he didn't speak, and I said nothing.

And again the silence and rain! Occasionally a mine tipple with the cold, drear, smoke smell of the dump and the oil lamps in the broken down shacks where the miners live. Then the black road again and the shapeless bulk of the mountains.

We reached Weston at about eight o'clock. I was tired and chilled and hungry. I stopped in front of a café and turned to the man.

'Ah reckon this is hit,' he said.

'Yes,' I answered. I was surprised. I had not expected him to know that we had arrived. Then I tried a final plunge. 'Will you have a cup of coffee with me?'

'Yes,' he replied, 'thank you, friend.'

The 'thank you' told me a lot. I knew from the way he said it that he wanted the coffee but couldn't pay for it; that he had taken my offer to be one of hospitality and was grateful. I was happy I had asked him.

We went inside. For the first time since I had come upon him in the tunnel he seemed human. He didn't talk, but he didn't slip inside himself either. He just sat down at the counter and waited for his coffee. When it came, he drank it slowly, holding the cup in both hands as though to warm them.

When he had finished, I asked him if he wouldn't like a sandwich. He turned around to me and smiled. It was a very gentle, a very patient smile. His big, lumpy face seemed to light up with it and become understanding and sweet and gentle.

The smile shook me all through. It didn't warm me — it made me feel sick inside. It was like watching a corpse begin to stir. I wanted to cry out, 'My God, you poor man!'

Then he spoke to me. His face retained that smile and I could see the big, horse teeth stained by tobacco.

'You've bin right nice to me, friend, an' ah do appreciate it.'

'That's all right,' I mumbled.

He kept looking at me. I knew he was going to say something else and I was afraid of it.

'Would yuh do me a faveh?'

'Yes,' I said.

He spoke softly. 'Ah've got a letter here that ah done writ to mah woman, but ah can't write very good. Would you all be kind enough to write it ovah for me so it'd be proper like?'

'Yes,' I said, 'I'd be glad to.'

'Ah kin tell you all know how to write real well,' he said, and smiled.

'Yes.'

He opened his blue shirt. Under his thick woolen underwear there was a paper fastened by a safety pin. He handed it to me. It was moist and warm and the damp odor of wet cloth and the slightly sour odor of his flesh clung to it.

I asked the counterman for a sheet of paper. He brought me one. This is the letter I copied. I put it down here in his own script.

My dere wife —

i am awritin this yere leta to tell you somethin i did not tell you afore i lef frum home. There is a cause to wy i am not able to get me any job at the mines. i told you hit was frum work abein slack. But this haint so.

Hit comes frum the time the mine was shut down an i worked in the tunel nere Gauley Bridge where the company is turnin the river inside the mounten. The mine supers say they wont hire any men war worked in thet tunel.

Hit all comes frum thet rock thet we all had to dril. Thet rock was silica and hit was most all of hit glass. The powder frum this glass has got into the lungs of all the men war worked in thet tunel thru their breathin. And this has given to all of us a sickness. The doctors writ it down for me. Hit is silicosis. Hit makes the lungs to git all scab like and then it stops the breathin.

Bein as our hom is a good peece frum town you aint heerd about Tom Prescott and Hansy McCulloh having died two days back. But wen i heerd this i went to see the doctor.

The doctor says i hev got me thet sickness like Tom Prescott and thet is the reeson wy i am coughin sometime. My lungs is agittin scab like. There is in all ova a hondred men war have this death sickness frum the tunel. It is a turible plague becus the doctor says this wud not be so if the company had gave us masks to ware an put a right fan sistem in the tunel.

So i am agoin away becus the doctor says i will be dead in about fore months.

I figger on gettin some work maybe in other parts. i will send you all my money till i caint work no mohr.

i did not want i should be a burdin upon you all at hum. So thet is wy i hev gone away.

i think wen you doan here frum me no mohr you orter go to your grandmaws up in the mountens at Kilney Run. You kin live there and she will take keer of you an the young one.

i hope you will be well an keep the young one out of the mines. Doan let him work there.

Doan think hard on me for agoin away and doan feel bad. But wen the young one is agrowed up you tell him wat the company has done to me.

i reckon after a bit you shud try to git you anotha man. You are a young woman yit.

Your loving husband,

Jack Pitckett.

When I handed him the copy of his letter, he read it over. It took him a long time. Finally he folded it up and pinned it to his undershirt. His big, lumpy face was sweet and gentle. 'Thank you, friend,' he said. Then, very softly, with his head hanging a little — 'Ahm feelin' bad about this a-happenin' t'me. Mah wife was a good woman.' He paused. And then, as though talking to himself, so low I could hardly hear it, 'Ah'm feelin' right bad.'

As he said this, I looked into his face. Slowly the life was going out of his eyes. It seemed to recede and go deep into the sockets like the flame of a candle going into the night. Over the eyeballs came that dull glaze. I had lost him. He sat deep within himself in his sorrowful, dark absorption.

That was all. We sat together. In me there was only mute emotion — pity and love for him, and a cold, deep hatred for what had killed him.

Presently he arose. He did not speak. Nor did I. I saw his thick, broad back in the blue work shirt as he stood by the door. Then he moved out into the darkness and rain.

A LIFE IN THE DAY OF A

WRITER[1]

TESS SLESINGER

O SHINING stupor, O glowing idiocy, O crowded vacuum, O privileged pregnancy, he prayed, morosely pounding x's on his typewriter, I am a writer if I never write another line, I am alive if I never step out of this room again; Christ, oh, Christ, the problem is not to stretch a feeling, it is to reduce a feeling, *all* feeling, all thought, all ecstasy, tangled and tumbled in the empty crowded head of a writer, to one clear sentence, one clear form, and still preserve the hugeness, the hurtfulness, the enormity, the unbearable all-at-once-ness, of being alive and knowing it too . . .

He had been at it for three hours, an elbow planted on either side of his deaf-mute typewriter, staring like a passionate moron round the walls that framed his life — for a whole night had passed, he had nothing or everything to say, and he awoke each morning in terror of his typewriter until he had roused it and used it and mastered it, he was always afraid it might be dead forever — when the *telephone* screamed like an angry siren across his nerves. It was like being startled out of sleep; like being caught making faces at yourself in the mirror — by an editor or a book-

---

critic; like being called to account again by your wife. His hand on the telephone, a million short miles in time and space from his writing-desk, he discovered that he was shaking. He had spoken to no one all the morning since Louise — shouting that she could put up with being the wife of a non-best-seller, or even the wife of a chronic drunk with a fetich for carrying away coat-hangers for souvenirs, but not, by God, the duenna of a conceited, adolescent flirt — had slammed the door and gone off cursing to her office. Voices are a proof of life, he explained gently to the angry telephone, and I have not for three hours heard my own; supposing I have lost it? Courage, my self! he said, as he stupidly lifted the receiver and started when nothing jumped out at him. All at once he heard his own voice, unnaturally loud, a little hoarse. *I wish to report a fire*, he wanted to say, but he said instead, roaring it: *Hello*. The answering *Hello, sunshine*, came from an immeasurable distance, from America, perhaps, or the twentieth century — a rescue party! but he had grown, in three long hours, so used to his solitary island! And though he was a writer and said to be gifted with a fine imagination, it was beyond his uttermost power to imagine that this voice addressing him was really a voice, that since it was a voice it must belong to a person, especially to the person identifying herself as Louise.

Ho, Louise! he said, going through with it for the purpose of establishing his sanity, at least in her ears if not actually in his own: he spoke courteously as though her voice were a voice, as though it did belong to her, as though she really were his wife; *now, darling, don't go on with* —— But then he discovered that she was not going on with anything but being a wife, a voice, an instrument of irrelevant torture. *How goes the work*, she said kindly. What in hell did she think he was, a half-witted baby playing with paper-dolls? *Oh, fine, just fine*, he answered deprecatingly. (I'm a writer if I never write another line, he said fiercely to his typewriter, which burst out laughing.) *Well, look*, she was saying,

Freddie called up (who in hell was Freddie?), and then her voice
went on, making explanations, and it seemed that he was to put
away his paper-dolls and meet her at five at Freddie's, because
Freddie was giving a cocktail party. *Cocktail party,* he said obediently; *wife; five.* Cocktail party, eh — and a dim bell sounded in
his brain, for he remembered cocktail parties from some other
world, the world of yesterday; a cocktail party meant reprieve
from typewriters, rescue from desert islands; and it might also
mean Betsey — he cocked a debonair eye at his typewriter to see
if it was jealous — Betsey, who, along with half a dozen coat-
hangers, had been the cause of this morning's quarrel! *Yes, your*
wife for a change, came the off-stage tinkle over the telephone again;
and you might try taking her home for a change too, instead of some-
one else's — and by the way, my treasure, don't bring those coat-
hangers with you, Freddie has plenty of his own. — Right you are,
my pet, he said, feeling smart and cheap and ordinary again, *right*
you are, my lamb-pie, my song of songs, ace of spades, queen of
hearts, capital of Wisconsin, darling of the Vienna press — But
she had got off somewhere about Wisconsin.

He looked, a little self-conscious, about his now twice-empty
room; aha, my prison, my lonely four-walled island, someone has
seen the smoke from my fire at last, someone has spied the waving
of my shirt-tails; at five o'clock today, he said, thumbing his nose
at his typewriter, the rescue plane will swoop down to pick me up,
see, and for all you know, my black-faced Underwood, my noise-
less, portable, publisher's stooge, my conscience, my slave, my
master, my mistress — for all you know it may lead to that elegant creature Betsey, whom my rather plump Louise considers a
bit too much on the thin side ... ah, but my good wife is a bit
short-sighted there, she doesn't look on the *other* side, the bright
side, the sunny side, the side that boasts the little, hidden ripples
that it takes imagination, courage, to express; the little hiding
ripples that the male eye can't stop looking for ...

He seated himself again before his typewriter, like an embarrassed schoolboy.

Black anger descended upon him. It was easy enough for her, for Louise, to put out a hand to her telephone where it sat waiting on her office desk, and ring him up and order him to report at a cocktail party — Louise, who sat in a room all day surrounded matter-of-factly by people and their voices and her own voice. But for him it was gravely another matter. Her ring summoned him out of his own world — what if he hadn't written a line all morning except a complicated series of coat-hanger designs in the shape of X's? — and because he couldn't really make the crossing, it left him feeling a little ashamed, a little found-out, caught with his pants down, so to speak — and a little terrified, too, to be reminded again that he was not 'like other people.' He was still shaking. She had no right, damn it, no damn right, to disturb him with that sharp malicious ringing, to present him with the bugbear, the insult, the indignity, of a cocktail party — she, who was proud enough of him in public (Bertram Kyle, author of *Fifty Thousand Lives*, that rather brilliant book), although at home she was inclined to regard him, as his family had when he refused to study banking, as something of a sissy.

Still, when you have accepted an invitation to a party for the afternoon, you have that to think about, to hold over your typewriter's head, you can think of how you will lock it up at half-past four and shave and shower and go out with a collar and a tie around your neck to show people that you can look, talk, drink, like any of them, like the worst of them. But a party! Christ, the faces, the crowds of white faces (like the white keys of the typewriter I had before you, my fine Underwood), and worst of all, the voices. . . . The party became abnormally enlarged in his mind, as though it would take every ounce of ingenious conniving — not to speak of courage! — to get to it at all; and as he fell face downward on his typewriter, he gave more thought to the party than

even the party's host was likely to do, Freddie, whoever the devil
'Freddie' was . . .

O degrading torture, lying on the smug reproachful keys with
nothing to convey to them. He remembered how he had once been
afraid of every woman he met until he kissed her, beat her, held
her captive in his arms; but this typewriter was a thing to master
every day, it was a virgin every morning. If I were Thomas Wolfe,
he thought, I should start right off: O country of my birth and
land I have left behind me, what can I, a youth with insatiable appetite, do to express what there is in me of everlasting hunger,
loneliness, nakedness, a hunger that feeds upon hunger and a loneliness that grows in proportion to the hours I lend to strangers . . .
If I were Saroyan I should not hesitate either: But I am young,
young and hungry (thank God), and why must I listen to the rules
the old men make or the rich ones, this is not a story, it is a life, a
simple setting down in words of what I see of men upon this earth.
No, no, I am not Saroyan (thank God), I am not Thomas Wolfe
either, and I am also not Louise's boss (ah, *there's* a man!). And I
cannot write an essay; I am a natural liar, I prefer a jumbled order
to chronology, and poetry to logic; I don't like facts, I like to
imagine their implications. O to get back, get back, to the pre-
telephone stupor, the happy mingled pregnancy, the clear confusion of myself only with myself . . .

And so Bertram Kyle opened up his notebooks. He felt again
that the story he had outlined so clearly there, of the 'lousy guy'
whom everyone thought was lousy including himself, but who was
so only because of a simple happening in his childhood, might be
a fine story; but it was one he could not do today. Nor could he do
the story (which had occurred to him on a train to Washington)
of the old lady, prospective grandmother, who went mad thinking
it was her own child to be born. Nor could he do the story —
partly because he did not know it yet — which would begin:
'He lived alone with a wife who had died and two children who

had left him.' Perhaps, he thought bitterly, he could never do those stories, for in the eagerness of begetting them he had told them to Louise; too often when he told her a story it was finished then, it was dead, like killing his lust by confiding an infidelity.

And so, desperately, he turned to those thoughtful little flaps in the backs of his notebooks, into which he poured the findings in his pockets each night; out came old menus, the torn-off backs of matchbooks, hotel stationery that he had begged of waiters, ticket-stubs, a time-table, a theatre program, and odd unrecognizable scraps of paper he had picked up anywhere. The writing on these was born of drinking sometimes; of loneliness in the midst of laughing people; of a need to assert himself, perhaps, a desire to remind himself — that he was a writer; but more than anything, he thought, for the sheer love of grasping a pencil and scratching with it on a scrap of paper. 'If I were a blind man I should carry a typewriter before me on a tray suspended from my neck by two blue ribbons; I think I *am* blind' — he had written that on a tablecloth once, and Louise was very bored.

'It is always later than you think, said the sundial finding itself in the shade' — from the back of an old match-box, and undoubtedly the relic of an evening on which he had strained to be smart. A night-club menu: 'Dear Saroyan: But take a day off from your writing, *mon vieux* or your writing will get to be a habit ...' Another menu — and he remembered the evening well, he could still recall the look of tolerance growing into anger on Louise's face as he wrote and wrote and went on writing: 'Nostalgia, a nostalgia for all the other nostalgic nights on which nothing would suffice ... a thing of boredom, of content, of restlessness, *velleities*, in which the sweetness of another person is irrelevant and intolerable, and indifference or even cruelty hurt in the same way ... linking up with gray days in childhood when among bewilderingly many things to do one wanted to do none of them, and gray evenings with Louise when everything of the adult

gamut of things to do would be the same thing...' (At that point
Louise had reached down to her anger and said, 'All right,
sunshine, we come to a place I loathe because you like to see
naked women and then, when they come on, you don't even
watch them; I wouldn't complain if you were Harold Bell Wright
or something...') 'In order to make friends,' he discovered
from another match-box, 'one need not talk seriously, any more
than one needs to make love in French' — and that, he recalled
tenderly, was plagiarized from a letter he had written to a very
young girl, Betsey's predecessor in his fringe flirtations. 'A
man's underlying motives are made up of his thwarted, or unreal-
ized, ambitions.' 'The war between men and women consists of
left-overs from their unsatisfactory mating.' 'But the blinking
of the eye' — this on a concert program — 'must go on; perhaps
one catches the half-face of the player and sees, despite the fren-
zied waving of his head, a thing smaller than his playing, but
perhaps the important, the vital thing: like the heart-beat, at
once greater and smaller than the thing it accompanies...'
'We are not so honest as the best of our writing, for to be wholly
honest is to be brave, braver than any of us dares to be with
another human being, especially with a woman.' *'At bottom one is
really grave.'*

He was pulled up short by that last sentence, which was the
only one of the lot that made sense. 'At bottom one is really
grave.'

Suddenly he raised his head and stared wildly round the room.
He was terrified, he was elated. Here was his whole life, in these
four walls. This year he had a large room with a very high ceiling;
he works better in a big room, Louise told people who came in.
Last year he had worked in a very small room with a low ceiling;
he works better, Louise used to tell people, in a small place. He
worked better at night, he worked better in the daytime, he
worked better in the country, better in the city, in the winter, in

the summer... But he was frightened. Here he was all alone with his life until five o'clock in the afternoon. Other people (Louise) went out in the morning, left their life behind them somewhere, or else filed it away in offices and desks; he imagined that Louise only remembered her life and took it up again in the late afternoon when she said good night to her boss and started off for home — or a cocktail party. But he had to live with his life, and work with it; he couldn't leave it alone and it couldn't leave him alone, not for a minute — except when he was drunk, and that, he said, smugly surveying the scattered coat-hangers, relic of last night's debauch, that is why a writer drinks so much. Hell, he thought, proud, I'm living a life, my own whole life, right here in this room each day; I can still feel the pain I felt last night when I was living part of it and Louise said... and I can still feel the joy I felt last week when Betsey said... and I can feel the numbness and the excitement of too many Scotch-and-sodas, of too perfect dancing, of too many smooth-faced, slick-haired women; I can remember saying *Listen — listen* to anyone who would or would not, and the truth of it is I had nothing to say anyway because I had too much to say... Hell, he thought, my coat-hangers lie on the floor where I flung them at three this morning when Louise persuaded me that it was better not to sleep in my clothes again, I have not hung up my black suit, I have not emptied yesterday's waste-basket nor last week's ashtrays (nor my head of its thirty years' fine accumulation)... everything in my room and in my head is testimony to the one important fact, that I am alive, alive as hell, and all I have to do is wait till the whole reeling sum of things adds itself up or boils itself down, to a story...

There seemed now to be hunger in his belly, and it was a fact that he had not eaten since breakfast and then only of Louise's anger. But the turmoil in his insides was not, he felt, pure hunger. It came from sitting plunged in symbols of his life, it came because he did not merely have to live with his life each day, but he had to give birth to it over again every morning. Of course, he thought with a fierce joy, I am hungry. I am ravenously hungry, and I have no appetite, I am parched but I am not thirsty, I am dead tired and wide awake and passionately, violently alive.

But he lifted his elbows now from his typewriter, he looked straight before him, and he could feel between his eyes a curious knot, not pain exactly, but tension, as though all of him were focused on the forefront of his brain, as though his head were a packed box wanting to burst. It was for this moment that, thirty years before, he had been born; for this moment that he had tossed peanuts to an elephant when he was a child; that he had by a miracle escaped pneumonia, dropping from an airplane, death by drowning, concussion from football accidents; that he had fallen desperately and permanently in love with a woman in a yellow hat whose car had been held up by traffic, and whom he never saw again; that he had paused at sight of the blue in Chartres Cathedral and wept, and a moment later slapped angrily at a mosquito; that he had met and married Louise, met and coveted Kitty Braithwaite, Margery, Connie, Sylvia, Elinor, Betsey; for this moment that he had been born and lived, for this moment that he was being born again.

His fingers grew light. The room was changing. Everything in it was integrating; pieces of his life came together like the odd-shaped bits of a puzzle-map, forming a pattern as one assembles fruits and flowers for a still-life. Listen, there is a name. Bettina Gregory. Bettina is a thin girl, wiry, her curves so slight as to be ripples, so hidden that the male eye cannot stop searching for them; she drinks too much; she is nicer when she is sober, a little shy, but less approachable. Bettina Gregory. She is the kind of girl who almost cares about changing the social order, almost cares about people, almost is *at bottom really grave*. She is the kind of girl who would be at a cocktail party when someone named

Fr — named Gerry — would call up and say he couldn't come because he was prosecuting a taxi-driver who had robbed him of four dollars. She is the kind of girl who would then toss off another drink and think it funny to take old Carl along up to the night-court to watch old Gerry prosecute a taxi-man. She is the kind of girl who will somehow collect coat-hangers (I give you my coat-hangers, Betsey-Bettina, Bertram Kyle almost shouted in his joy) — and who will then go lilting and looping into the night-court armed to the teeth with coat-hangers and defense mechanisms, who will mock at the whores that have been rounded up, leer at the taxi-driver, ogle the red-faced detective, mimic the rather sheepish Gerry — all the time mocking, leering, ogling, mimicking — nothing but herself. Frankly we are just three people, she explains to the detective, with an arm about Gerry and Carl, who love each other veddy veddy much. She must pretend to be drunker than she is, because she is bitterly and deeply ashamed; she must wave with her coat-hangers and put on a show because she knows it is a rotten show and she cannot stop it. It is not merely the liquor she has drunk; it is the wrong books she has read, the Noel Coward plays she has gone to, the fact that there is a drought in the Middle West, that there was a war when she was a child, that there will be another when she has a child, that she and Carl have something between them but it is not enough, that she is sorry for the taxi-driver and ashamed of being sorry, that *at bottom she is almost grave.* In the end, Bertram Kyle said to anybody or nobody, in the end I think ...

But there was no reason any more to think. His fingers were clicking, clicking, somehow it developed that Gerry had muddled things because he was drunk so that the taxi-man must go to jail pending special sessions, and then Bettina and Gerry and Carl take the detective out to a bar some place; explaining frankly to waiters that they are just four people who love each other veddy veddy much ... and, perhaps because they all hate themselves so veddy veddy much, Carl and Gerry let Bettina carry them all off in her car for a three-day spree which means that Gerry misses the subpoena and the taxi-driver spends a week in jail, earning himself a fine prison record because he stole four dollars to which Carl and Gerry and Bettina think him wholly and earnestly entitled, and perhaps in the end they give the four dollars to the Communist Party, or perhaps they just buy another round of drinks, or perhaps they throw it in the river, or perhaps they frankly throw themselves...

And is this all, Bertram Kyle, all that will come out today of your living a life by yourself, of your having been born thirty years ago and tossed peanuts to elephants, wept at the Chartres window, slapped at mosquitoes, survived the hells and heavens of adolescence to be born again, today — is this all, this one short story which leaves out so much of life? But neither can a painter crowd all the world's rivers and mountains and railroad tracks onto one canvas, yet if his picture is any good at all it is good because he has seen those rivers and mountains and puts down all that he knows and all that he has felt about them, even if his painting is of a bowl of flowers and a curtain... And here, thought that thin layer of consciousness which went on as an undercurrent to his fingers' steady tapping, here is my lust for Betsey, my repentance for Louise, my endless gratitude to the woman who wore a yellow hat, my defeatism, my optimism, the fact that I was born when I was, all of my last night's living and much that has gone before...

The room grew clouded with the late afternoon and the cigarettes that he forgot to smoke. His fingers went faster, they ached like the limbs of a tired lover and they wove with delicacy and precision because the story had grown so real to him that it was physical. He knew that his shoulders were hunched, that his feet were cramped, that if he turned his desk about he would have a better light — but all the time he was tearing out sheet after sheet and with an odd accuracy that was not his own at any other time, inserting the next ones with rapidity and ease, he typed almost perfectly, he made few mistakes in spelling, punctuation, or the choice of words, and he swung into a rhythm that was at once uniquely his and yet quite new to him.

Now each idea as he pounded it out on his flying machine gave birth to three others, and he had to lean over and make little notes with a pencil on little pieces of paper that later on he would figure out and add together and stick in all the gaping stretches of his story. He rediscovered the miracle of something on page twelve tying up with something on page seven which he had not understood when he wrote it, the miracle of watching a shapeless thing come out and in the very act of coming take its own inevitable shape. He could feel his story growing out of the front of his head, under his moving fingers, beneath his searching eye . . . his heart was beating as fast as the keys of his typewriter, he wished that his typewriter were also an easel, a violin, a sculptor's tools, a boat he could sail, a plane he could fly, a woman he could love, he wished it were something he could not only bend over in his passion but lift in his exultation, he wished it could sing for him and paint for him and breathe for him.

And all at once his head swims, he is in a fog, sitting is no longer endurable to him, and he must get up, blind, not looking at his words, and walk about the room, the big room, the small room, whether it is night or day or summer or winter, he must get up and walk it off . . . *Listen, non-writers, I am not boasting when I tell you that writing is not a sublimation of living, but living is a pretty feeble substitute for art. Listen, non-writers, this is passion. I am trembling, I am weak, I am strong, pardon me a moment while I go and make love to the world, it may be indecent, it may be mad — but as I stalk about the room now I am not a man and I am not a woman, I am Bettina Gregory and Gerry and the taxi-driver and all the whores and cops and stooges in the night-court, I am every one of*

the keys of my typewriter, I am the clean white pages and the word-
sprawled used ones, I am the sunlight on my own walls — rip off
your dress, life, tear off your clothes, world, let me come closer; for
listen: I am a sated, tired, happy writer, and I have to make love to
the world.

Sometimes it was night when this happened and then he must
go to bed because even a writer needs sleep, but at those times he
went to bed and then lay there stark and wide awake with plots
weaving like tunes in his head and characters leaping like mad
chess-men, and words, words and their miraculous combinations,
floating about on the ceiling above him and burying themselves
in the pillow beneath him till he thought that he would never
sleep and knew that he was mad ... till Louise sometimes cried
out that she could not sleep beside him, knowing him to be lying
there only on sufferance, twitching with his limbs like a madman
in the dark ...

Louise! For it was not night, it was late afternoon, with the
dark of coming night stealing in to remind him, to remind him
that if he were ever again to make the break from his life's world
back to sanity, back to normalcy and Louise, he must make it
now, while he remembered to; he must leave this room, stale with
his much-lived life, his weary typewriter, he must shake off his
ecstasy and his bewilderment, his passion, his love, his hate, his
glorious rebirth and his sated daily death — and go to meet
Louise; go to a cocktail party ...

He was shocked and terrified when he met his own face in the
mirror because it was not a face, it was a pair of haggard, gleaming
eyes, and because like Rip Van Winkle he seemed to have grown
heavy with age and yet light with a terrible youth. He managed
somehow to get by without letting the elevator man know that
he was crazy, that he was afraid of him because he was a face and
a voice, because he seemed to be looking at him queerly. On the
street Bettina appeared and walked beside him, waving her

drunken coat-hangers and announcing, 'Frankly there is nothing
like a coat-hanger,' while Gerry leaned across him rather bitterly
to say, 'If I hear you say frankly again, Bettina, frankly I shall
kill you.' But they walked along, all of them, very gay and
friendly, despite the taxi-driver's slight hostility, and then at the
corner they were joined by Carl with the detective's arm about
him, and Carl was saying to anybody and nobody that they passed
— 'Frankly we are veddy veddy mad.' And they came at last
to Freddie's house, and there Bertram Kyle stood for a moment,
deserted by Bettina and Carl and Gerry — even the detective
was gone — hiding behind a collar and a tie and frankly panic-
stricken. The door opens, he enters mechanically — good God,
is it a massacre, a revolution, is it the night-court, a nightmare? . . .

But he pushed in very bravely and began to reel toward all his
friends. 'Hello, I'm cockeyed!' he roared at random. 'Hell, I've
been floating for forty days, where's a coat-hanger, Freddie,
frankly, if there's anything I'm nuts about it's coat-hangers, and
frankly have you seen my friends, some people I asked along,
Bettina Gregory, Gerry, and a detective?' He saw Louise,
ominous and tolerant, placing her hands in disgust on her soft hips
at sight of him. Frankly, he shouted at her, frankly, Louise, I am
just three or four people who love you veddy veddy much, and
where's a drink, my pearl, my pet, my bird, my cage, my night-
court, my nightmare — for frankly I need a little drink to sober
down . . .

AMERICAN NOCTURNE [1]

ROBERT WHITEHAND

IT WAS their last night.

Neither Carl nor Irene had mentioned it, yet all afternoon the thought had lain between them with sweet, muted sadness. As they were eating their picnic lunch, she had almost alluded to it. Although she caught herself in time and began spreading a film of butter over her sandwich, Carl looked up intently, and she knew that he had read the thought in her eyes. Then, after rolling up blanket and tablecloth, they burned the paper plates and wandered through the park, oblivious to a few September stragglers who strolled gratefully in the languid warmth of these last days of summer.

It wasn't until sunset, when Irene coaxed Carl down to the dock, that the thought again bubbled in their minds. This time it was Carl. He balanced the canoe while she stepped into it to lie back against some cushions packed into the prow. Watching her, he suddenly leaned forward and said, 'Irene...'

'What?'

But when her eyes met his, he straightened up on his knees and began paddling. 'Shall we go to a dance?' he asked.

'Do you feel like dancing?'

'Not if you don't,' he answered eagerly.

'Let's not.'

They cruised about the lake, watching shadows grow out of the sunset to stretch across the water and become silhouettes of jagged, undulating shade on the ruffled water. After a while Irene saw that Carl was steering up 'Lovers' Lane' where low-hanging trees dangled mossy hair in the lake and clasped their branches above the narrow headwaters in a long arch of matted leaves.

Sitting upright, she breathed deeply of air that was fragrant with the promise of autumn. 'Carl! It's all so pretty!'

'Isn't it!'

She lay back on the pillows again, careful to set her head at the angle Carl liked. Her hands dropped over the sides to let her fingers comb the soft, warm water. She knew that Carl was watching. 'Maybe he's thinking how much he likes me.' The thought lingered in her mind, pleasantly, as a kind of solace, and through occasional openings in the interlaced branches she saw a cauldron of burning clouds in the west.

Finally her eyes turned back toward him, met his gaze, and turned hastily away again. But after a moment she was looking at him once more. Twilight had softened the angles of his face into dim lines, and she liked them that way. It seemed as if all the sadness of her life were gathered into this moment. 'He's my own,' she thought. 'He may go away tomorrow, but he'll always be my sweetheart — my first love!'

But she mustn't make this farewell hard on him; she must be brave. She smiled a bit. Sadly. Then she spoke:

'Carl, this is our last night.'

'Yes.' He laid the paddle across his thighs.

'Tomorrow you'll be gone to the university, and I'll be getting ready for that silly finishing school.'

'I wish we were going to the same place.'

'Dad wouldn't change his mind, though, once he gets it set.'

'And I can't go to a finishing school.'

'Will you miss me, darling?' While she was speaking, she kept singing over and over to herself: 'He's good-looking! He's the best-looking boy at school!'

'You know I will,' he answered.

'We've just known each other six months.'

'It seems like longer.'

She laughed. 'You'll never know how jealous the other girls were when you began taking me to dances and parties.'

'I don't want to know. What do I care about them?'

Her hands floated upward and lay quivering against her breast. 'I could write a sonnet like Rossetti now,' she thought. Her heart began to swell.

'Will you study hard?' Carl asked after a moment.

'Yes.' Her hands unclasped and settled in her lap. 'Will you?'

'I guess so.'

'And lots of pretty girls will flirt with you.'

'I won't like any of them.'

'We'll both have to learn fast so that we can make enough money to get married on right after we graduate.'

Still drifting slowly, the canoe bumped against the grassy shore. Irene raised her head to peer over the gunwale.

'Carl, let's get out and go for a walk!'

He jumped to the bank to help her step ashore. They went up the hillside to a spot where a circular opening, scalloped with a fringe of leaves, revealed a disk of evening sky. Carl spread the blanket and they sat down.

'Do you want to put your head on my lap?' she asked. He crept to her and lay back, looking up into her face. With her fingers she felt the smoothness of his cheeks and laid her palms against them.

'Your hands are cool and nice,' he said.

She tickled the corners of his mouth with her fingertips, smiling down at him. Then she traced the line of his cheek. 'I hate to see you leave.'

'We'll be home again Thanksgiving.'

'But that's so long.' Reaching up to take the hairpins from a pliant knot on the nape of her neck, she tried to laugh. 'Now we're getting sad on our last night.' As her head shook backward, the fine, yellow hair streamed over her shoulders.

Fascinated, Carl watched it. 'Your hair's prettier and longer than any girl's at school.'

'What if I should get it cut?' she teased.

'You do, and I'll shave my head.'

She flipped his nose with a finger. 'Did you think I really would?'

Twisting around, he poked his fingers lightly between her ribs. 'You devil!' They wrestled for a moment, tickling, pulling hair and trying to blow into each other's ears. After a while Irene sat up, laughing. 'You'll get me all grass-stained and mussed up,' she said. 'Then what'll mother think?'

Subsiding for the while, she wriggled her dress back into place.

Everything was going fine. Carl wasn't being gloomy and she had kept from crying. Now if only something momentous would happen, something which she could recall each night as she lay in the solitude of her room at school. When she had finished smoothing herself, Carl asked, 'Did you ever sleep "hobo"?'

'Hobo?'

'Sure. Lie on your back and put your head on my shoulder, and I lie on my back and put my head on your shoulder. Like this...' She listened carefully. Then both lay on their backs, legs stretching out in opposite directions and their heads, cheek to cheek, resting on each other's shoulder.

'I'm not going to sleep, though,' Irene said.

'Do you like it?'

'It's fun. I can hear your heart beating.'

Her hair was spread over Carl's shoulder, and she knew that some of it was caressing his cheek as softly as a breeze so light that you feel only its coolness and never its passage. 'You've got the prettiest hair in the whole world,' she heard him say. Her heart floundered with the sudden thrill. Rolling over quickly, she rose to her elbows, leaned over him and showered his face with its softness.

'That tickles,' he said.

'I meant for it to.'

As she lay down again, one of her slender arms pointed toward an opening in the leaves. 'There's the moon coming up.'

'It's pretty.'

'Let's go up the hill and watch it.'

'It'll come to us in a little while.'

'Well, lazy, we *could* go up and meet it.'

'All right.'

She lay still until Carl arose, grinning, lifted her up to her feet and helped her over the rough places in their path. From the hilltop they watched the moon float up into the blue darkness, turning whiter and whiter and growing smaller and smaller, until it was like a plate of glowing chinaware tossed among the stars. Irene's hand slipped up against Carl's breast. 'He's mine,' she thought. 'He'll always be mine.' She looked out across the mist which lay in the small valley. The distant city was a glittering jewel, and shadowy trees about her became huge vases of spreading ferns.

Her head bent to his shoulder and her eyes closed. 'I wish we could get married before you go.'

'So do I.'

'Then we'd always belong to each other.'

'It would be swell.'

'And we'd be sure of our love.'

'Aren't we now?'

'Of course, silly. But I mean *more sure.*'

While they strolled back to the blanket, arm in arm, she kept thinking over and over to herself: 'He's mine and nobody else's. He's all mine.' She wondered if any other woman had ever felt this way — as if something kept growing inside you until you were about to burst. But you didn't want to because the thing growing was so nice you wanted to feel that way always.

Arriving at the blanket, they lay down again, stretched out full length, with their hands folded behind them, pillowing their heads. The sound of waves slapping the sides of the canoe came up the hillside. 'I'm in love,' Irene kept repeating to the rhythm of an artery pulsing in her breast. 'I'm in love ... I'm in love ...'

'What's that star?' she asked after a while, pointing toward a bright planet, hanging motionless and unblinking, where the western sky gleamed with its myriad flecks of light.

'Which one?'

'The one over that tall tree there.'

Carl looked for a moment. 'I don't know. Evening Star, I guess.'

Then they were quiet for a long time. Irene listened to the lisping of the grass as it undulated with each breeze. Finally she said, 'I tell you what let's do.'

'What?'

'If you wouldn't be afraid,' she went on, and added hastily, 'Wouldn't be ashamed, I mean.'

'Ashamed of what?'

She turned her head away from the cone of moonlight shining through the opening in the branches and kept her eyes in the shadow of her forehead. Her hands unfolded and she followed a seam of her dress with a finger. Then her answer came, almost a whisper: ' ... of taking off our clothes.'

His startled 'What!' made her smile.

'If we saw each other that way, neither of us could ever love anyone else; could we?'

His answer was lost somewhere in a sudden rustling of wind among the leaves.

'And we'd really be married then — just as if we had gone to a minister.'

'Do you think we ought to?' he asked.

'We love each other; don't we?'

'Sure. But...'

'Then it's all right.' Standing up, she unsnapped her dress. It slipped back over her shoulders and fell around her feet. Glancing down at Carl who still sat, rigid, staring up at her, she asked, 'Aren't you going to?'

He stood up then and began undressing.

After a moment their bodies glistened white. The moonlight streamed like milk over Irene's young breasts and poured down her long, slender legs into the shadows about her feet. She stood, motionless, looking at Carl's browner body and trying to hide the wonder in her eyes. The tip of his tongue slipped between his lips before he spoke.

'You're beautiful!'

A rapturous, tingling wave flowed through her heart and away from her body filling the whole world with its ecstasy. 'He thinks I'm beautiful.... He thinks I'm beautiful....' The thought hummed in her mind like the purl of water in slow rapids above a roaring falls. But it seemed to her that of all the people who had mated since the beginning of time, only her love for Carl was real.

Everything around them was etched by the moon and the moment into brilliant clarity — at the foot of the hill a scimitar of water glistened between the curved shores, two leaves coasted downward from the trees, a bird twinkled somewhere overhead. ... And directly in front of her stood Carl. Above the tumult of her thoughts she heard him whisper:

'Irene! You're wonderful!'

She crossed the space between them. 'And you're like a Greek god.' She leaned forward and kissed him lightly. Her body warmed at the touch of his dry lips. 'Now we'll always love each other; won't we?'

'Yes!'

'Forever and ever.'

He nodded.

'We'd better dress now.'

They turned their backs to each other as they lifted their clothing from the ground, but after a few minutes she called to him: 'Help me with this. I can't get it fastened.' She stood with her back still toward him, holding the ends of her unclasped brassiere against her shoulder blades. His steps sounded loud on the brittle grass, then she felt him fumble with the snaps and heard his breathy words:

'You're beautiful! I love you!'

She laughed quietly.

When they were dressed, Carl picked up the blanket, and Irene slipped a hand through his arm. She looked around once more before they left, memorizing every detail of the spot. 'This is where I gave my heart away,' she said to herself. 'My heart that's his for always. This is our shrine.' After a final glance at the well of moonlight, she followed Carl down the hill, without speaking, without wanting to speak, and it wasn't until they arrived at the canoe that either spoke. Lying back once more in the prow, Irene said, 'I'll always remember it just like this.'

'It was wonderful.' Carl knelt in the stern.

'You'll write to me often; won't you?'

'Every day,' he promised.

She watched the paddle slip into the water, then glanced back toward the hill. 'Love is beautiful.' Turning around, she asked aloud, 'Isn't love beautiful, Carl?'

His quiet nod was her only answer.

The canoe swerved about, pointed toward the dock across the water, then glided out onto the lake which was an upturned sky with a galaxy of pin-point stars and the reflection of Venus, clearer than all the others, shifting back and forth among the small waves like a bright light swinging in the wind.

ONLY THE DEAD KNOW

BROOKLYN[1]

THOMAS WOLFE

Dere's no guy livin' dat knows Brooklyn t'roo an' t'roo, because it'd take a guy a lifetime just to find his way aroun' duh f—— town.

So like I say, I'm waitin' for my train t' come when I sees dis big guy standin' deh — dis is duh foist I eveh see of him. Well, he's lookin' wild, y'know, an' I can see dat he's had plenty, but still he's holdin' it; he talks good an' is walkin' straight enough. So den, dis big guy steps up to a little guy dat's standin' deh, an' says, 'How d'yuh get t' Eighteent' Avenoo an' Sixty-sevent' Street?' he says.

'Jesus! Yuh got me, chief,' duh little guy says to him. 'I ain't been heah long myself. Where is duh place?' he says. 'Out in duh Flatbush section somewhere?'

'Nah,' duh big guy says. 'It's out in Bensonhoist. But I was neveh deh befoeh. How d'yuh get deh?'

'Jesus,' duh little guy says, scratchin' his head, y'know — yuh could see duh little guy didn't know his way about — 'yuh got me, chief. I neveh hoid of it. Do any of youse guys know where it is?' he says to me.

'Sure,' I says. 'It's out in Bensonhoist. Yuh take duh Fourt' Avenoo express, get off at Fifty-nint' Street, change to a Sea Beach local deh, get off at Eighteent' Avenoo an' Sixty-toid, an' den walk down foeh blocks. Dat's all yuh got to do,' I says.

'G'wan!' some wise guy dat I neveh seen befoeh pipes up. 'Whatcha talkin' about?' he says — oh, he was wise, y'know. 'Duh guy is crazy! I tell yuh what yuh do,' he says to duh big guy. 'Yuh change to duh West End line at Toity-sixt',' he tells him. 'Get off at Noo Utrecht an' Sixteent' Avenoo,' he says. 'Walk two blocks oveh, foeh blocks up,' he says, 'an' you'll be right deh.' Oh, a *wise* guy, y'know.

'Oh, yeah?' I says. 'Who told *you* so much?' He got me sore because he was so wise about it. 'How long you been livin' heah?' I says.

'All my life,' he says. 'I was bawn in Williamsboig,' he says. 'An' I can tell you t'ings about dis town you neveh hoid of,' he says.

'Yeah?' I says.

'Yeah,' he says.

'Well, den, you can tell me t'ings about dis town dat nobody else has eveh hoid of, either. Maybe you make it all up yoehself at night,' I says, 'befoeh you go to sleep — like cuttin' out papeh dolls, or somp'n.'

'Oh, yeah?' he says. 'You're pretty wise, ain't yuh?'

'Oh, I don't know,' I says. 'Duh boids ain't usin' my head for Lincoln's statue yet,' I says. 'But I'm wise enough to know a phony when I see one.'

'Yeah?' he says. 'A wise guy, huh? Well, you're so wise dat someone's goin' t'bust yuh one right on duh snoot some day,' he says. 'Dat's how wise *you* are.'

Well, my train was comin', or I'da smacked him den and dere, but when I seen duh train was comin', all I said was, 'All right, mugg! I'm sorry I can't stay to take keh of you, but I'll be seein' yuh sometime, I hope, out in duh cemetery.' So den I says to duh big guy, who'd been standin' deh all duh time, 'You come wit me,' I says. So when we gets onto duh train I says to him, 'Where yuh goin' out in Bensonhoist?' I says. 'What numbeh are yuh lookin' for?' I says. *You* know — I t'ought if he told me duh address I might be able to help him out.

'Oh,' he says. 'I'm not lookin' for no one. I don't know no one out deh.'

'Then whatcha goin' out deh for?' I says.

'Oh,' duh guy says, 'I'm just goin' out to see duh place,' he says. 'I like duh sound of duh name — Bensonhoist, y'know — so I t'ought I'd go out an' have a look at it.'

'Whatcha tryin' t'hand me?' I says. 'Whatcha tryin' t'do — kid me?' *You* know, I t'ought duh guy was bein' wise wit me.

'No,' he says, 'I'm tellin' yuh duh troot. I like to go out an' take a look at places wit nice names like dat. I like to go out an' look at all kinds of places,' he says.

'How'd yuh know deh was such a place,' I says, 'if yuh neveh been deh befoeh?'

'Oh,' he says, 'I got a map.'

'A *map?*' I says.

'Sure,' he says, 'I got a map dat tells me about all dese places. I take it wit me every time I come out heah,' he says.

And Jesus! Wit dat, he pulls it out of his pocket, an' so help me, but he's *got* it — he's tellin' duh troot — a big map of duh whole f—— place with all duh different pahts mahked out. You know — Canarsie an' East Noo Yawk an' Flatbush, Bensonhoist, Sout' Brooklyn, duh Heights, Bay Ridge, Greenpernt — duh whole goddam layout, he's got it right deh on duh map.

'You been to any of dose places?' I says.

'Sure,' he says, 'I been to most of 'em. I was down in Red Hook just last night,' he says.

'Jesus! Red Hook!' I says. 'Whatcha do down deh?'

'Oh,' he says, 'nuttin' much. I just walked aroun'. I went into a coupla places an' had a drink,' he says, 'but most of the time I just walked aroun'.'

'Just walked aroun'?' I says.

'Sure,' he says, 'just lookin' at t'ings, y'know.'

'Where'd yuh go?' I asts him.

'Oh,' he says, 'I don't know duh name of duh place, but I could find it on my map,' he says. 'One time I was walkin' across some big fields where deh ain't no houses,' he says, 'but I could see ships oveh deh all lighted up. Dey was loadin'. So I walks across duh fields,' he says, 'to where duh ships are.'

'Sure,' I says, 'I know where you was. You was down to duh Erie Basin.'

'Yeah,' he says, 'I gues dat was it. Dey had some of dose big elevators an' cranes an' dey was loadin' ships, an' I could see some ships in drydock all lighted up, so I walks across duh fields to where dey are,' he says.

'Den what did yuh do?' I says.

'Oh,' he says, 'nuttin' much. I came on back across duh fields after a while an' went into a coupla places an' had a drink.'

'Didn't nuttin' happen while yuh was in dere?' I says.

'No,' he says. 'Nuttin' much. A coupla guys was drunk in one of duh places an' started a fight, but dey bounced 'em out,' he says, 'an' den one of duh guys stahted to come back again, but duh bartender gets his baseball bat out from under duh counteh, so duh guy goes on.'

'Jesus!' I said. 'Red Hook!'

'Sure,' he says. 'Dat's where it was, all right.'

'Well, you keep outa deh,' I says. 'You stay away from deh.'

'Why?' he says. 'What's wrong wit it?'

'Oh,' I says, 'It's a good place to stay away from, dat's all.
It's a good place to keep out of.'

'Why?' he says. 'Why is it?'

Jesus! Whatcha gonna do wit a guy as dumb as dat? I saw it
wasn't no use to try to tell him nuttin', he wouldn't know what
I was talkin' about, so I just says to him, 'Oh, nuttin'. Yuh
might get lost down deh, dat's all.'

'Lost?' he says. 'No, I wouldn't get lost. I got a map,' he says.
A map! Red Hook! Jesus!

So den duh guy begins to ast me all kinds of nutty questions:
how big was Brooklyn an' could I find my way aroun' in it, an'
how long would it take a guy to know duh place.

'Listen!' I says. 'You get dat idea outa yoeh head right now,'
I says. 'You ain't neveh gonna get to know Brooklyn,' I says.
'Not in a hunderd yeahs. I been livin' heah all my life,' I says,
'an' I don't even know all deh is to know about it, so how do you
expect to know duh town,' I says, 'when you don't even live
heah?'

'Yes,' he says, 'but I got a map to help me find my way about.'

'Map or no map,' I says, 'yuh ain't gonna get to know Brooklyn
wit no map,' I says.

'Can you swim?' he says, just like dat. Jesus! By dat time,
y'know, I begun to see dat duh guy was some kind of nut. He'd
had plenty to drink, of course, but he had dat crazy look in his
eye I didn't like. 'Can you swim?' he says.

'Sure,' I says. 'Can't you?'

'No,' he says. 'Not more'n a stroke or two. I neveh loined
good.'

'Well, it's easy,' I says. 'All yuh need is a little confidence.
Duh way I loined, me older bruddeh pitched me off duh dock one
day when I was eight yeahs old, cloes an' all. "You'll swim," he
says. "You'll swim all right — or drown." An' believe me, I

swam! When yuh know yuh got to, you'll do it. Duh only t'ing yuh need is confidence. An' once you've loined,' I says, 'you've got nuttin' else to worry about. You'll neveh forget it. It's somp'n dat stays wit yuh as long as yuh live.'

'Can yuh swim good?' he says.

'Like a fish,' I tells him. 'I'm a regulah fish in duh wateh,' I says. 'I loined to swim right off duh docks wit all duh oddeh kids,' I says.

'What would you do if yuh saw a man drownin'?' duh guy says.

'Do? Why, I'd jump in an' pull him out,' I says. 'Dat's what I'd do.'

'Did yuh eveh see a man drown?' he says.

'Sure,' I says. 'I see two guys — bot' times at Coney Island. Dey got out too far, an' neider one could swim. Dey drowned befoeh anyone could get to 'em.'

'What becomes of people after dey've drowned out heah?' he says.

'Drowned out where?' I says.

'Out heah in Brooklyn.'

'I don't know whatcha mean,' I says. 'Neveh hoid of no one drownin' heah in Brooklyn, unless you mean a swimmin' pool. Yuh can't drown in Brooklyn,' I says. 'Yuh gotta drown some-where else — in duh ocean, where dere's wateh.'

'Drownin',' duh guy says, lookin' at his map. 'Drownin'.' Jeus! I could see by den he was some kind of nut, he had dat crazy expression in his eyes when he looked at you, an' I didn't know what he might do. So we was comin' to a station, an' it wasn't my stop, but I got off anyway, an' waited for duh next train.

'Well, so long, chief,' I says. 'Take it easy, now.'

'Drownin',' duh guy says, lookin' at his map. 'Drownin'.'

Jesus! I've t'ought about dat guy a t'ousand times since den an' wondered what eveh happened to 'm goin' out to look at

Bensonhoist because he liked duh name! Walkin' aroun' t'roo
Red Hook by himself at night an' lookin' at his map! How many
people did I see get drowned out heah in Brooklyn! How long
would it take a guy wit a good map to know all deh was to know
about Brooklyn!

Jesus! What a nut *he* was! I wondeh what eveh happened to
'im, anyway! I wondeh if someone knocked him on duh head,
or if he's still wanderin' aroun' in duh subway in duh middle of
duh night wit his little map! Duh poor guy! Say, I've got to
laugh, at dat, when I t'ink about him! Maybe he's found out by
now dat he'll neveh live long enough to know duh whole of
Brooklyn. It'd take a guy a lifetime to know Brooklyn t'roo an'
t'roo. An' even den, yuh wouldn't know it all.

MARCHING ORDERS[1]

I. V. MORRIS

NICOLAS ZAPHIRO, *né* Zaphiropoulos, pushed away
the plate of fried potatoes with which he usually finished off his
breakfast, and sank back in his armchair. He had no appetite
this morning, and he had had no appetite yesterday either, nor
the whole week before. It was a bad sign for a man to have no
appetite for breakfast. Not that he was ill — he had never felt
healthier in his life — but he simply had lost his taste for food —
and for other things.

For instance, his wife and he had visited some friends last night,
Greeks like themselves, and they had had Greek wine. Now, as
a rule there was nothing Zaphiro so relished as a glass, or even
several glasses, of good Greek wine, but on this occasion he had
raised it to his lips and put it down untasted; when they urged
him to drink, he had complied with their wishes so as not to hurt
their feelings, and the liquid had tasted bitter and unfermented
as it ran down his throat. It was the same with his other pleasures,
too — with the pleasures of carnal love, and even of making a
good trade, which he had once thought the greatest joy of all. As

[1] From *New Stories*, 1936.

Nicolas Zaphiro sat there, puffing a cigarette and staring at his overladen breakfast table, it came to him with a shock that it was a long time since he had really enjoyed life.

He was a tailor by profession, and a very good one; he was said to be one of the best in Paris. Thirty years before, this Nicolas Zaphiro had had a dream. In that dream there had been many people: there had been men, keen and eager as himself, moving about with rolls of fine materials in their hands, while others, seated at low tables, cut the cloth; there had been still others perched high on stools, adding up in black ledgers rows of figures which represented money. There had also been a woman in his dream: a plump, appetizing woman, replete with curves and bangles; there had been a great foreign city; an apartment with soft beds, soft sofas; an endless row of dishes, sizzling in luscious oils.

And now that dream was realized. He, once an illiterate urchin in the back streets of Salonika, employed more than a dozen workmen in his expensive Paris shop, while the gold bracelets on his wife's arms had accumulated till she had to wear them above the elbows; he had gained security, wealth, and a high measure of recognition in his chosen trade. Indeed, he had achieved more than he set out to do, and the trouble was that there was nothing left to achieve. Of course he might have increased his business — might eventually have doubled or tripled his capital — but this lay outside the scope of his dream; he was not interested in it. If he still worked ten hours daily in the shop, it was through force of habit, and with the knowledge that his assistants could have managed almost as well without him. Perhaps, had Zaphiro been asked, he would have found it as difficult to say why he worked as to say what he still expected out of life.

So there he was on the morning in question, sitting by his breakfast table, when there came the soft sound of the morning post falling through the letter slot. Crushing out his cigarette, he rose and made his way into the corridor, where a number of envelopes lay scattered near the outer door of his apartment. He stooped to pick them up, grunting as he did so, for with all his other possessions, he had come into a paunch. Just then the bedroom door opened, and he caught sight of his wife in her flannel nightgown, standing in the entrance; probably the thud of the letters on the carpet had awakened her.

'Anything of interest?' she asked, yawning. Even with each other they spoke French, which had become far more their language than their native Greek.

'No, all business things,' he answered.

But then he saw one which was not business — a personal letter, though in an unknown handwriting. He was about to mention it, and for some reason decided not to.

His wife asked: 'Were you going to say something?'

'No, nothing. What made you think so?'

Later, as he was going downstairs in the lift, he took out the letter and looked at it again. No, he certainly did not know the writing. Then he split it open, read 'Dear Zaphiro,' and looked down at the foot of the page for the signature. 'A. Lopez.'

This Lopez was a client of Zaphiro's, an Argentine who had spent most of his life in Paris. He had begun coming to the Greek tailor for his clothes three years before, and since then had ordered a great many suits — at least two dozen — though as yet he had never paid a penny on account. About a year before, Zaphiro, grown worried, began to hint that a small payment would be welcome, but Lopez had put him off, both through his airy promises to discharge the bill, and because of the intimate, almost affectionate manner he had adopted towards Zaphiro from the start. It flattered the little Greek's vanity to be treated as an equal by a gentleman of the world; though it was true that he had never seen Lopez outside his shop, he could, when he spoke to him, feel himself part of the gay, luxurious life at which the other was always hinting in his conversation.

By the time Zaphiro unlocked the door of his tailor shop, which occupied the ground floor of the same premises, he had read through Lopez' letter and digested its contents. In a few lines, the Argentine told his creditor that he was about to leave the country, returning to South America, and that if Zaphiro dropped in to see him at his hotel, he was sure they could come to a 'friendly understanding' about the bill. Zaphiro, as he stuffed the letter into his pocket, wondered why he did not feel more upset. He knew just how much was to be expected from these 'friendly understandings,' and a year before he would have cursed himself for a fool for allowing anyone such large credit. As it was, he simply wasn't interested — but surely it was another bad sign for a man not to be interested in his own business!

He even would have put off the visit to another day had an errand not taken him near the hotel that same morning; finding himself unexpectedly in a nearby street, he remembered Lopez' letter and on the spur of the moment decided to call. It was then a little after eleven.

Zaphiro had to wait some moments in the hotel lobby while the operator rang the Argentine's apartment. Just when he was despairing of getting a reply, was about to tell the girl not to trouble, he heard the other receiver being lifted off the hook, and a sleepy voice asked what he wanted.

'I came about your letter.'

'Letter? Ah, yes!' There was a pause; then Lopez asked him to come up. 'I'll see you in a moment.'

Zaphiro followed a uniformed boy into the lift, and later through the upstairs corridors of the hotel; they walked a long way, the thick carpet on which they trod drowning the sound of their footsteps. They passed a maid, who squeezed against the wall to make room for them, bowing respectfully to Zaphiro, looking at him with servile eyes.

At length the boy stopped before a glass-partitioned door.

'This is the suite, sir,' he said, and knocked. Zaphiro gave him a small tip.

He had to wait about a minute before Lopez came to let him in. The South American was dressed in a pair of pale-blue pyjamas with a large monogram on one breast pocket; over these hung loosely an orange dressing-gown of heavy silk. He was not yet shaved, but he had pomaded his hair, which was brushed back from his thin, pale forehead.

'Please forgive me,' said the tailor. 'I didn't know — you said ——'

'It's quite all right.' The other cut short his apologies. 'Come in.'

He opened the door to a large sitting-room, with many pieces of furniture about, etchings on the wall, and a large table at one end, on which were arrayed a number of China figures; it looked much more like a room in a private house than a hotel parlour.

'Ah, you have it very nice here,' said Zaphiro, glancing about.

'Not bad. Sit down. Do you smoke?'

'Thank you.' He accepted from an alabaster box a cigarette on which Lopez had had printed his initials. 'That's nice,' he said. 'I've never seen that before.'

Lopez did not answer him, but began at once to talk about the object of the visit; he seemed in a hurry to get the conversation over with.

'Yes, as I wrote you, it's impossible for me to pay just now. I've explained to you already that we can't get money out of our country, at least not very much. Still, you needn't worry; it's a temporary state — I mean to pay you.'

'I haven't said anything,' said Zaphiro. 'It's you who wrote.'

'I know, I know. Well, what's to be done? I don't want you to suffer, and at the same time I can't do the impossible. Now, what I want to suggest is this: I'll give you something I own and which

I can't take away. When I come back, I'll give you the money; it will be a sort of security.'

'I see. And what did you think of giving me?'

'I don't know — we'll find something suitable. I was thinking perhaps my car. I have a Citröen — last year's model.'

'And I, too,' said Zaphiro.

'Oh! That's unfortunate. Well, what else can I suggest? Perhaps my aeroplane.'

'An aeroplane! What should I be doing with an aeroplane?'

'You could learn to fly — as I did. It's most amusing; I go up almost every afternoon.'

Zaphiro began to laugh at the absurdity of the suggestion.

'But I'm afraid I was born to be a tailor — not an aviator.'

Suddenly he had the queerest sensation: he felt without the shadow of a doubt that all this had happened to him somewhere before — that he had once already pronounced that last phrase, in reply to somebody's statement that he went up in the air each afternoon. Was it recently or long ago? He was not sure. It was as if he were at that moment dreaming, but this time *consciously* dreaming, an old dream which always eluded his memory in daytime hours. And the most uncanny thing of all, but a thing of which he was absolutely sure, was that his dream had a direct bearing on his lethargy, on his boredom, in fact on his whole changed state of being. It came like a flash of intuition, but next moment all was dark again.

Lopez was talking.

'You're old-fashioned, my dear Zaphiro! What would have happened to aviation if we'd all of us thought like that? Do you think I believe that I was "born to be an aviator"? But you catch on to it — it's like learning a new language. Soon you feel that you've known it always.'

He stood there with his bright dressing-gown falling from his slender shoulders, his hair glistening in the morning sunlight. He was a representative of another world, apart from the world of tailors, of Greek immigrants, of *petits bourgeois*. Zaphiro, from his limitless distance, smiled self-consciously.

'I'm a busy man, Mr. Lopez. I haven't the leisure to fly about in aeroplanes all day.'

'Oh, it isn't a question of all day. An hour in the evening is all you need, and it's April — remember that the evenings are getting longer. I assure you that it's fascinating — but don't think that I'm trying to argue you into it.'

'It's a fantastic idea,' said Zaphiro — 'quite fantastic.'

He wanted to say something else, to drop this subject of the aeroplane, which had come to its logical conclusion, and to his surprise, he found himself continuing it instead.

'But what was your suggestion — that I actually buy the aeroplane? Or keep it as a security? To do that would be very complicated, I think.'

'Yes, you'd better buy it; then if you decide that you don't want it, you can sell it later. Of course the amount of your bill would be considered already paid.'

Zaphiro was astonished at the way the other, all without pressing the matter, seemed to consider the deal as good as finished; he spoke as if only the details were still to be arranged, and despite himself, Zaphiro was swept along.

'Then there wouldn't be much more to pay,' he observed, his old bargaining instinct coming to the fore.

'No, not much. We'll fix on a fair price for the aeroplane — there's a regular tariff, as for second-hand cars — and the difference you can pay me when you please.'

'I quite understand. Now if I oblige you, I think that you should let me have it cheap — considering the circumstances.'

'We won't argue about the price.'

Just then a door leading to a bedroom flew open, and to Zaphiro's embarrassment a young woman in a light green dressing-

gown came into the room; he noticed immediately two things
about her: her beauty and the abnormal pallor of her face.

'What do you want?' asked Lopez irritably. 'I'm very busy.'

'Can't you choose some other moment for your business? You
may be an Argentine, Lopez, but I beg of you, behave as if you
had some manners!'

'We are having a most important conversation. We are reaching a deal about my aeroplane.'

'Oh, is that it? If you're trying to get rid of that old kite, no
wonder that you have to do a lot of arguing. The machine's not
fit to taxi across the field in! I presume you are a flyer?' she asked,
turning to Zaphiro and smiling at him in a way to which he was
not accustomed in his clients.

'No,' he answered, 'but Mr. Lopez is trying to turn me into
one.'

'Zaphiro makes my clothes,' explained Lopez. 'He's the best
tailor in the city. Don't you think he'd make a splendid aviator?'

'Why, yes, of course,' said the South American's mistress,
glancing at Zaphiro again, and laughing. 'The only trouble is his
weight; he'd better try to reduce, or he'll never manage a decent
take-off.'

It struck Zaphiro that her manner towards him changed the
moment that she learned that he was not an aviator; previously,
no doubt, she had taken him to be a gentleman.

'Does Madame fly also?' asked the Greek, when she had left
the room.

'Yes, she is an excellent aviatrix. In fact, I met her at the airport.'

'Which airport do you use?'

'Orly. It's the most convenient — only fifteen kilometres'
drive from the Concorde. You ought to do it in your Citröen in
twenty minutes. By the way, how about going up with me for
a trial spin this afternoon? You will see how you like it.'

'Oh — well, thank you very much. You mean that you would take me up?'

'Why, yes. You needn't be frightened — I'm an authorized pilot; I take friends up all the time.'

'No, no — I'm not frightened, though I've never been up before. I was just figuring out if I could manage it today. If you'd really be so kind, I should like it very much.'

'All right.'

As soon as Zaphiro left Lopez' apartment, he began to blame himself for the outcome of the interview. Looking at matters logically, he had to admit that he'd acted like a woefully bad business man; once he had consented to so much as discuss Lopez' proposition, he had said good-bye to all hope of recovering the cash. Not that he meant to buy that aeroplane! Certainly not! Still, he did not obligate himself in any way by allowing the Argentine to take him up; it would be rather amusing, and without doubt an experience.

It was past noon when he returned to the tailor shop, and the clerks and the cutters had all gone out for lunch. Zaphiro went upstairs, and on opening the door of his flat, his nostrils were assailed by the rich smell of goulash; the maid came hurrying by, a huge platter of stuffed egg plants on her arm.

'You're ten minutes late. They've begun to eat.'

Zaphiro went at once into the dining-room, to find his wife, his mother-in-law, and the three children seated before high-stacked plates. His wife greeted him with a raised fork.

'We couldn't wait. We were hungry.'

He seated himself in his usual chair and waited for the maid to serve him; but when, having handed about the vegetables, she brought him in his meat, he found that all desire for food had fled. His wife watched him angrily as he picked out a few small morsels.

'Why don't you eat anything? Isn't it what you like?'

'Yes — I'm just not hungry.'

He wondered how he should break the news that he was to go flying that afternoon. He thought of saying it quite casually, or else of asking them to guess what he meant to do, and then surprising them, but decided against both alternatives. He was sure that his wife would forbid him, and he feared a scene, for suddenly he knew definitely that he was going up; nothing would prevent him. He did not know why, but he had begun to think of it as intensely important that he make the trial flight that afternoon with Lopez. After consideration he decided to say nothing; it was the safest plan.

The meal dragged to its end, Zaphiro sitting moodily at his end of the table without once talking. The memory of his brief encounter with Lopez served as a barrier behind which he hid himself from his family; he felt himself strangely foreign to these greasy, dark-skinned children, to this squat wife of his with her negroid hair and mountainous bosoms which welled up over her loose corsets. Catching sight of himself in the oval wall mirror, he noted with satisfaction his pale skin, his thick-set but handsome face, his square shoulders, over which the pepper-and-salt suit, cut with his own hands, lay creaselessly; and for almost the first time there stirred within him a feeling of irritation at this family of Greeks which had sprung up around him, claiming him as their own. If it weren't for them — and for his name — not a soul would have taken him for anything but a Frenchman.

He escaped from the flat as soon as possible and went downstairs, taking with him a thick sweater and a motoring cap, which he deemed suitable garments for his flight. It was ten minutes past two by the clock in the tailor shop, and one of the clerks was just coming in through the street door, returning tardily from lunch; he jumped with terror on catching sight of the boss, for as a rule Zaphiro did not return to the shop till three, taking a nap, Oriental fashion, after lunch. To the man's surprise, he escaped without a reprimand or a glance of enquiry. Zaphiro had absentmindedly lit a cigarette and was striding up and down the little room. Soon afterwards he went into the office where the books were kept, presumably to study Lopez' account, but actually to be alone. He sat at the table for some minutes with the unopened ledger before him.

He was not in the least frightened, or even excited, at the thought of the approaching adventure, but he had the most peculiar feeling about it, the like of which he had had only two or three times in his life before. He remembered distinctly the first of these occasions. He had been a small boy of twelve, in Greece. It was Christmas. Someone, he forgot whom, had sent his mother a roll of cloth to make a dress for herself, and perhaps other garments for the children. He could still see it lying in a corner of the crowded living-room, could to this day feel the satiny texture of the cloth. By what strange coincidence had he that very Christmas received a large pair of 'cutting-out' scissors? Suddenly he is walking towards the roll of cloth, the scissors in his outstretched hand. Nearer and nearer he comes, and at each step he feels strong within him that same curious, inexplicable sensation which is to overwhelm him again almost forty years later on. How is he to describe it? An awareness of fatality — of the inevitable about to be realized — of the future rolled into the present? He knows that he must cut the cloth — that therein lies his destiny, lies self-realization, lies beauty. And today in the same way, or almost the same way, he knows that he must fly through the clouds with Lopez. Consciously, he is going towards his fate. The present and the past are made one by the recurrence of an emotion long since forgotten; he is a child; life like a pattern, woven and unchangeable, lies before him, and he must *live* that pattern.

Returning to the other room, he was surprised to see Lopez' Citröen parked outside; the Argentine was waiting for him, smoking a cigar.

'I thought you said three o'clock,' Zaphiro apologized. 'I didn't want to keep you waiting.'

'It is three, Zaphiro — ten past, to be exact. But don't worry; I've only this moment arrived.'

So that meant that he had been sitting in the little alcove almost an hour!

He went to get his sweater and motoring cap, and to tell the clerks that he would not be back that day. Lopez eyed the checked headgear askance on his return.

'That won't do you any good,' he said. 'I'll lend you a regular aviator's helmet when we get to the flying field.'

They drove through the southern suburbs of Paris and out along the Fontainebleau road. Neither of them spoke more than a few words till they were almost at the aerodrome.

'Is that it?' asked Zaphiro, sitting up in his seat, as he caught sight of a row of hangars to the left; at the same time he noticed two aeroplanes circling in the sky.

'Yes, that's Orly,' said Lopez, swinging his car in through the open gates. A uniformed attendant took off his cap and bowed.

Having alighted from the car, Zaphiro accompanied the Argentine down a cinder path into a newly constructed white stone building, above the portico of which he read the words: 'Cercle Roland Garros.'

'This is a club,' explained Lopez. 'You have to be elected a member, though of course you may fly at Orly even if you do not belong. But I'll arrange it for you. You'll find it useful to join.'

If — if I decide to fly! thought Zaphiro, protesting inwardly at the other's presumption. To hear him talk, one would suppose that the whole matter had been settled!

In the large reading-room, which still smelt of paint and varnish, several members, both men and women, sat about conversing or perusing magazines. They nearly all nodded to Lopez, and two men came up to speak to him. Zaphiro was introduced, and just as that morning, when Lopez' mistress had addressed him, before she knew he was a tailor, he was impressed and delighted by their respectful manner towards him. Lopez left him to get into his flying togs, so for several moments he stood speaking with these gentlemen, who owned their own aeroplanes and flew, like Lopez, as a hobby.

When Lopez came back, they left the building, following the cinder path towards one of the hangars. It was raining a thin drizzle and the visibility was bad, but Lopez replied with a laugh to Zaphiro's question as to whether it was not a poorish flying day.

'You're not backing out now, are you?'

'No, of course not. What an idea!'

In front of the hangar, two mechanics were engaged in turning over the propeller of an open two-seater monoplane.

'It's still cold,' explained Lopez. 'It takes some moments to get the engine started.'

Just as they came up to the plane, the propeller started with a whirr, blowing a strong current of air in their direction, which tore off Zaphiro's cap and sent it scurrying across the field. Lopez laughed loudly at the other's discomfiture.

'Here, put this on,' he said, tossing him a helmet with goggles attached, which he drew from the pocket of his leather jacket.

A moment later they had stepped into the aeroplane, and the mechanic was showing Zaphiro how to fasten the safety straps which attach one to the seat. Lopez accelerated the motor; they began slowly, then more rapidly, to taxi across the field; imperceptibly they left the ground, which moved away from them, to leave them suspended fearsomely in space.

It was a novel experience for Zaphiro. Yet it was not so very novel either. Had he read so extensively about flying and the accompanying sensations that he seemed to have felt them all before, or was it possible that he had dreamed about this also, so that when Lopez in the forward cockpit turned about to shout something at him, at the same time pointing downwards to the toy palaces of Versailles, the gesture merely repeated that of some dream figure in the past? But if this was reality and the other experience a dream, it was strange that the dream, tenuous and broken though it remained in his memory, had a vividness that the present moment lacked. Everything now was as hazy and unreal as if the flight were being made upon a magic carpet. They passed through a heavy bank of mist, and for some moments not even the tips of the wings or the back of his companion's neck were visible to Zaphiro from where he sat; it seemed to him that he was flying into a new world, that he had left upon the old all consciousness of his former life; he could feel the damp air against his cheeks, stinging his eyes so that he had to close the lids, and he relished these sensations, as a man who never in his life has suffered might hold out his arms to pain. When they came out of the mist, he felt that he had been bathed clean, and his skin, when he touched it, seemed to him soft and strange. After an experience like this, flashed through his mind, a man can never be the same again. They passed over Versailles and over St. Germain, just perceptible through the shreds of mist which they had left below them, and then Lopez doubled the plane about and bore towards Orly. Arrived above the flying field, he began to circle downwards, the plane tipping sideways, so that the bodies of the two men lay almost horizontal to the ground. Zaphiro could feel the air rushing at his head, while the ground below revolved rapidly, as on a pivot, at the same time rising up to meet him.

He was not scared, not for a moment, although he did not realize that this was quite the safest method of losing altitude. Seeing Lopez turn about, he waved his hand at him and smiled. He wanted to go on forever, and it was with a disappointed feeling that he perceived they were about to land. When the aeroplane skimmed low across the field, and finally, a land vehicle again, bumped its way awkwardly towards the hangars, Zaphiro relaxed with a sigh of utter satisfaction. So that was it! Yes, he had known that it would be like that — he had known it always. He was going to buy Lopez' aeroplane and learn to fly.

Every afternoon at five Zaphiro had a lesson at the aerodome. He did not use his own machine to make these flights, but sat in the instruction plane, equipped with dual control. The Farman stood under canvas in a corner of one of the hangars, and often Zaphiro would have the cover stripped off to have a good look at his possession. He had only been up in it that once, but already he had a real affection for this plane, believing without reason that it was handsomer and more graceful than its sisters. He now took it quite for granted that he was to be an aviator, and he deemed it a bit of extraordinary luck that he had fallen on such a splendid little plane. He, who had never been possessive by nature, found himself quite blown up with pride when it came to the Farman monoplane. He did not like to think of its having belonged to someone else, and on one occasion when the mechanics moved it to the other end of the hangar without his authorization, he was furious, and to their surprise, quite lost his temper.

But in many other ways his character had changed, at least it seemed so to his wife and family. It was not so much that he treated them casually of late, or rather ignored their existence, as the fact that his attitude towards everything, small and large, had become practically reversed. If it was months since he had seemed entirely himself, the change in him lately was both more general and more pronounced. His ennui and occasional disgust with his family, which he took no pains to hide, extended gradually to the whole circle of his former acquaintances, so that in the end he insulted his childhood friend, Diamantopoulos, by not showing up at his birthday party. And he did not care. When Diamantopoulos came to see him next day, Zaphiro received him in such an offhand manner that it only made matters worse; as his old friend said to Zaphiro's wife afterwards, 'He seemed so absent-minded — as if the whole matter didn't concern him at all.'

Zaphiro's wife thought that he had a mistress, and believed that she even knew the name of the lady in question. Naturally she did not like the thought that the sharer of her bed for twenty years had been unfaithful to her, but she was a clever woman and would have put up with that, if only he had not grown so strange and callous. What made matters worse was that while he never denied her accusation, he refused to discuss the matter with her, simply relapsing into a dogged silence. As he no longer made any advances to her, she never for a moment doubted his unfaithfulness, and she would have been greatly surprised if told that her rival had wings instead of legs, and a smooth aluminum body with the tricolour painted on it in concentric circles. His daily relations with his new love were as yet of a platonic nature, but soon the day would come when physical intimacy could commence. He would rather have died than introduce this mistress to his wife, or indeed tell her of the illicit world to which she belonged, and where he visited her surreptitiously after office hours.

About four Zaphiro used to leave his shop, call for his Citröen at the garage, and take the road for Orly. He was always overcome by an intense, almost painful excitement, as the hour approached, but once he was in the car and on the way it vanished completely; he was already then in the new world, and as oblivious of the old as if it did not exist. He never thought of his family, of his business, of anything to do with his ordinary existence; he did not deny these things, nor was he ashamed of them, but they seemed so far away that he could hardly remember, for instance, the names of his three children, or the colour of a suit which a customer had ordered that same morning.

He would arrive at the aerodrome half an hour before his lesson.

This was at first accidental, for he was terrified of annoying his instructor by coming late; afterwards it became purposeful, when he found that the spare moments could be passed delightfully in the lounge of the Cercle Roland Garros. He had not made any friends, but possessed innumerable acquaintances who greeted him, and sometimes asked him to have a drink. It was known that Zaphiro was a tailor, but flying people are not snobbish, and his occupation did not alter the cordiality of their feelings towards him; only Zaphiro himself was shocked on seeing the word 'tailor' printed after his name on the posted list of new candidates for election to the club.

At five promptly, Zaphiro stepped into the cockpit of the instruction plane, though he often had to wait some moments for the arrival of his mentor, who used to have a drink at the bar between flights. At length the man could be seen coming down the cinder path, perhaps still fastening the buckle of his helmet, and taking his good time about it; Zaphiro could hardly wait to get started, nor control his annoyance at this daily delay, which cut ten minutes off his half-hour. The instructor climbed languidly into his seat, threw away his cigarette, and with hardly a word to his passenger, started off the plane. Zaphiro disliked this man who, of all the people he had met at the aerodrome, seemed alone to look down on him. Yet on the instructor's own statement his pupil had made astonishingly rapid progress. Did he realize that Zaphiro was a tailor and a Greek, and was that the reason for his attitude? Be that as it may, he succeeded in thoroughly riling Zaphiro, who sought the opportunity to snub him in turn when he met him later in the clubhouse.

After the flight, it was pleasant to come back into the heated room, which at that hour of the day was usually well filled with people. There would be a game or two of bridge going on, and sometimes a table of poker, at which Zaphiro used to take a hand. Every now and then the door would open to admit new people who had just descended from their planes; Zaphiro, seated at the card table or standing at the bar, would call out to one or the other to ask how the flight had gone. He had even met the stunt flyers, Detroyat and Doret, both of whom flew frequently at Orly, and he used to nod to them quite intimately; he could hardly believe that a month before he had not known a single one of all these people.

He always stayed until quite late and, as they served a light supper in the club, it happened frequently that he telephoned his wife that he could not be home for dinner. Standing in the dimly lit telephone booth, while the receiver at his ear gave forth a rhythmic drone, it seemed to Zaphiro, as he waited for the familiar voice to answer, that the lien which still bound him to his family and his former life was slenderer, oh, far slenderer, than the thin wire stretching from this instrument to his flat in Passy. How little it would take now to snap that bond, so that normal living as he used to know it would cease entirely! And then what? His future was as dark, as unhomely as this leather-padded cell, yet he knew that he must live in it. There was no going back to security, to order and to rest.

After he had conveyed his message, he would linger in the booth a moment longer, straightening his tie or using his pocket comb upon his hair — finding some excuse to prolong this little interlude between his two so different lives. When he pushed open the door and wandered back into the smoky lounge, he felt like a high diver, hurling himself from land into a foreign element.

One day when he came into the club lounge after flying there was a woman, whom he seemed to know, seated with a group of people in a corner. He had to go closer before he noticed her extreme pallor and recognized her as Lopez' mistress whom he had met when he called at the hotel that morning. Lopez by this time was well out on the high seas, but the people with whom she was conversing were known to Zaphiro.

'Have you met Madame ——?' said one of them, when he came up to the table.

'Why, yes, I think I have.'

She looked up at Zaphiro curiously but without recognition.

'Madame once told me that I was too fat to fly. I'm afraid that she was wrong.'

She remembered then and laughed.

'But you haven't reduced as I told you to. You're fatter still today.'

'So sorry not to have taken your advice,' said Zaphiro, piqued. 'I get on quite well as it is.'

Everyone laughed.

'Oh, yes,' agreed one of the men enthusiastically. 'Zaphiro gets on all right. He's made terribly rapid progress — the instructor says that he simply can't teach him fast enough. When do you make your first solo flight, Zaphiro?'

'I have — today.'

'Really? That's splendid. You'll be taking your licence, soon.'

'I won't lose any time.'

'I'm sure you won't,' said Lopez' mistress. 'You don't look like a fellow who'd waste much time. And I suppose you've learned how to hustle in your calling.'

'Why, yes,' said Zaphiro, flushing deeply but trying to smile.

'No dilly-dallying when a customer's suit is to be got ready, eh?'

Zaphiro became intensely embarrassed and walked off to the bar. The others in the group smiled sheepishly, as people do when they feel that one of their number has made a tactless joke.

A few moments later, as he was finishing a drink and pretending to himself that he did not mind her remarks, he noticed that she was standing close beside him; her pale face smiled into his.

'Why, Mr. Zaphiro, don't you speak to me any more?'

'Why shouldn't I?'

'No reason. But I don't know what on earth you meant by walking off like that.'

'I'm sorry,' said Zaphiro, at once apologetic. 'Forgive me if I was rude.'

They talked for a while and she accepted his offer of a drink. Zaphiro found her very charming, easy to talk to, amusing in her repartees. He was delighted now that he had met her and the insult was quite forgotten; but just as they were saying good-bye another gentleman came up and asked her what the two of them had been discussing so earnestly.

'Nothing of great importance,' she said. 'Our friend here has just been telling me the best way to sew on buttons.'

This time Zaphiro was clever enough not to let on that he had been hit, though the insult rankled all the same.

'What does she mean by making fun of me — the little whore?' he thought. 'I could tell them a thing or two about her, too, if I felt like it.'

But he soon discovered that he really had nothing to tell — that is, nothing which she did not tell herself. She was quite brazen in discussing her relationship with Lopez and with various other men, in fact went out of the way to relate all the juicy details, and one day stated calmly that there was not a single ace in France who had not at some time been her lover. Zaphiro discovered that she was a woman of independent wealth, the widow of a famous stunt aviator who had been killed two years before, and that she kept three aeroplanes of her own at Orly. Nevertheless she flew only infrequently nowadays and usually in other people's planes. The reason, she told Zaphiro, was not that she did not enjoy piloting, but simply that she could not be bothered; she preferred having someone else do the work. Since her husband's death, she had gradually lost her energy and power of initiative till the smallest effort now seemed too great for her to make; she merely existed and allowed circumstance to control her movements, but as to living in an active sense that was a thing of the past. Hence the disordered manner of her life, the three idle aeroplanes, the love affairs with every ace in France.

The better Zaphiro knew this woman, the more interested in her he became. At first he explained his attachment by the fact that she was so unlike anyone he had ever met before; she was a strange species of being who did and said exactly what came into her head with no regard to conventionality, decency, or sense. If she felt like being rude to him she could be ruder than anybody else; and whereas the instructor's rudeness was concealed under a semblance of deference, hers was outspoken and purposefully cruel; the next moment she was talking to him with absorption and evident pleasure, signalling him out for her undivided attention. Then Zaphiro felt recompensed for the slights she had inflicted and even felt that, if he had the courage and bided his opportunity, it was on him that the mantle of Lopez and the hundred aces eventually would fall.

That something lay between them subtler than a developing flirtation Zaphiro was to realize late one rainy evening at the club. They had had dinner together — for the first time — and later swallowed any number of brandies, seated on a sofa by a window facing the flying field. In the half dark outside, the drizzle could be seen spattering down on the muddy tract, crisscrossing which the double tracks of aeroplane wheels were faintly visible; a row of sentinel lights picked out the boundaries of the field, while the sudden stab of the searchlight swept it periodically from end to end. The lounge where they sat was dimly lit; they were the only people.

Suddenly she leaned forward, not looking at Zaphiro, but out of the window at the flying ground, and in a voice curiously lacking in the usual ironical undertone, she said:

'Yes, you see, that's how it is; one day one's life comes to a full stop — and then what? How shall one go on?'

Zaphiro's heart gave a thud; he looked at her intently, waiting for her to continue, feeling that her next words would throw light on the great darkness which he felt about him. But she smiled.

'Shrug your shoulders, my friend, shrug your shoulders. We lost people have no right to ask such questions.'

'What are you saying? I don't understand.'

'I said nothing. But you understand all too well. Don't let's try and fool each other, whatever else we do. It's too cheap a game to play.'

Zaphiro was silent; he felt that he had grown pale and that if he reached for the bottle to pour out brandy, he would spill some on the table.

'So it's all up with us?' he said after a moment.

'Oh, it's very pleasant to go on living.'

After that evening neither he nor she ever mentioned that conversation again. But it was not forgotten; it trembled in the air between them, and at times he was forcibly reminded of it, as of an undigested dinner.

Zaphiro planned to take his pilot's licence at the end of May and to begin flying his own aeroplane. His progress had really been remarkably rapid, for he had started learning less than six weeks before. All his acquaintances were astonished at his perseverance, his eagerness to get through the period of tuition in as brief a time as possible; many days he would fly twice, both mornings and afternoons, so as to have more flying hours to his credit; even when the weather hardly warranted a flight, he insisted on going up as usual. It was as if he were pressing towards a goal, the attainment of which was of supreme importance, though the reason for his undue haste he himself could not have stated.

He had not yet taken up the Farman, preferring to rent a plane for these trial flights. He did not want to risk crashing his darling, not having mastered the fine points of taking off and landing, and besides, his insurance policy forbade him to use the plane without a licence. But he loved looking at it all the same. Once he had the covers stripped off, filled the tank with petrol, and taxied back and forth across the field, just to get the feel of the controls; he almost changed his mind and took it up on that occasion, actually accelerated the motor till it only needed a jerk at the joy stick for the monoplane to leave the ground; but at the last moment prudence prevailed, and he steered it back home to its hangar. No, the time had not yet come; he would have to wait a little longer.

As he was walking back to the clubhouse, he caught sight of Lopez' ex-mistress sitting on the stairs, watching him.

'What have you been doing, crawling around the field like that?' she called out, as he came up. 'Did you get cold feet, Zaphiro?'

He explained to her that it was Lopez' former aeroplane, and gave her the reason for his not wishing to take it up.

'Oh, so you bought the old rattletrap after all, did you?'

'Rattletrap? It's a beautiful machine!'

She looked at him curiously, as if she meant to say something, then changed her mind.

'All right — it's a beautiful machine. Seeing that you bought it, I suppose you ought to know.'

'You've been up in it?'

'Oh, several times. Lopez was a brilliant pilot — and a daring one.'

'Perhaps you'll come up with me some day?' said Zaphiro.

'Yes, perhaps I will — if I feel like it.'

'I'll tell you what,' pursued the Greek, struck by an idea. 'Why don't you come with me the first time I try it out? I ought to have my licence in a fortnight. It will be a sort of inauguration trip, and we'll go and drink some champagne afterwards.'

'Do you think that would be nice?'

'Yes, very nice. Will you do it?'

'I don't know. Perhaps. And after the champagne, what will happen then?'

'Anything you wish,' he answered.

'Shall we spend that night together?' she asked him suddenly.

Zaphiro felt a rush of blood into his face; his throat contracted with excitement, so that he could hardly speak.

'Are you joking with me?' he asked.

'No, I am not joking. I promise that if I go up in your plane I will spend the night with you afterwards — if I do decide to go up, that is.'

'Perhaps I'll hold you to your promise.'

'I'm sure you will, Zaphiro. You wouldn't be a Greek otherwise, would you?'

She began to laugh, rocking back and forth on the steps where she sat; she laughed loudly but without mirth, keeping her eyes wide open and fixed on Zaphiro the whole time. He did not know if she was laughing at him or at herself — probably at both of them, he decided in the end. He went indoors.

There was a spell of fine summer weather now, and Zaphiro spent most of his days up in the air. He neglected his business utterly, leaving matters in the hands of the two clerks, who hardly knew what to do with their new authority. His family saw him rarely, some days not at all, as he used to leave early in the morning and only come back late at night. Rapidly he was flying through the dwindling hours which separated him from his licence; the desired goal was almost within his reach.

Ten days later he called her up at her apartment, for she had not shown up at the clubhouse since their conversation.

'I hope you haven't forgotten,' he began.

'I don't forget.'

'I received my licence half an hour ago; it looks very beautiful. When are we going flying in my aeroplane?'

'When are you?'

'Tomorrow, perhaps. Are you coming with me?'

'I don't know.'

'If not tomorrow, any day you like.'

'Oh, tomorrow is as good as any other day. I haven't quite decided. What hour are you going up?'

'Four o'clock, if it suits you — or earlier.'

'No, four is perfect. If I'm not there, you must go up without me.'

'I'll postpone the flight.'

'No, no, it won't do you any good, my friend. If I'm not there by four tomorrow, I shan't go up with you at all.'

'Very well.' He knew better than to argue. 'I hope very sincerely that you'll join me; for such an occasion one doesn't want to be alone. I desire it passionately for other reasons too.'

'Naturally — we know all about that. Don't try and telephone me again; I'll either come, or else I won't.'

Zaphiro woke up very early the next morning. He lay for some time in bed, excited and fully awake, staring at the ceiling with his hands behind his head. The room lay in near darkness, but in the dawn which filtered in through the tightly shuttered windows he could make out a couple of flies chasing each other around the hanging lamps suspended from the ceiling, buzzing as they made contact and attempted to accomplish the fornicating act in air, then chasing each other again. How strange, he reflected, that at every moment there are billions of lives around us, completing their small cycle, living, loving, dying — lives of which we are aware at best only for a second! Why, even within each person there are several hundred million separate organisms, each for all we know with his own consciousness, his sense of self-importance, if one may use the expression! Yes, they must all have consciousness, to a greater or a less degree, for otherwise they would cease to be alive, becoming part of the inanimate world, like a rock or bit of sediment.

And suddenly the thought occurred to him: yes, that is what has happened to me — just that. I have lost my sense of consciousness, the realization that I am myself, Nicolas Zaphiro, a tailor, a Greek. I have been looking at myself abstractly, from without, as I look at a man passing in the street or at those flies, and my sense of being alive has grown so weak that practically it does not exist. I have become a mere organism, moving instinctively, controlled by forces outside myself; I am just a man existing in the world; I have lost contact with myself.

He lay there quietly for a while, digesting this thought, not finding it unpleasant or disturbing, but merely extraordinary, as any self-evident truth which has so far escaped one seems extraordinary. He had lost his identity like those poor shell-shocked fellows one read about who could not for the life of them remember their real names; but with him no catastrophe, no sudden blighting of the senses, was to blame — he had drifted into the condition slowly and inevitably. And he asked himself if many people at some period come to a state resembling suspended animation and if it is possible to pass beyond it into another life.

In her sleep his wife stirred uneasily, throwing her arm above her head. He turned his eyes towards her and for some moments lay looking at that face which had once been dear to him, at the plump arm and the ineffective little hand that clenched the pillow. She sighed in an unhappy dream and he felt pity for her, not because he knew that he was the cause of her sigh but because he thought of her now as one of those hundred billion living creatures feeling and conscious as he once had been.

All at once and for no reason in particular he remembered a promise he had made her to change his will. The change concerned some Greek government bonds he owned and which he had stipulated should go to his younger brother, but he had quarrelled with this same brother a good time ago and had determined to transfer the bonds to his capital estate whence they would pass to his wife upon his death. Months had gone by but he had as yet done nothing. He made up his mind that he would put it off no longer; he would pay a visit to his lawyer that very morning.

. As he was dressing a half-hour later, it struck him that there was something else he ought to do: look up Diamantopoulos. It was curious that he should have remembered his old friend just on that day which was already so well occupied, for he had neither seen him nor thought of him since the unfortunate episode following the birthday party. Looking back at his behaviour now, it seemed to him almost inconceivable that he could have acted so unkindly; without a doubt he must take steps to patch up their quarrel, and that with the least possible delay.

He had a busy morning. First he went to the lawyer and arranged about his will — actually insisted on signing the new codicil then and there, though the lawyer suggested that he post him on the document; next he called up Diamantopoulos and made an engagement with him for lunch. In the meanwhile he had thought of several other things to see to — matters which had been hanging over for long, and which ought finally to be settled. He could not understand why he had put off doing all these things till now.

He did not get to the aerodrome till half-past three, though he had meant to arrive much earlier to attend to the fuelling of the plane, and also to test the engine and the body struts, seeing that it was almost two months since it had been flown. His lunch with Diamantopoulos had been a great success; not only had they entirely made up their misunderstanding but they had agreed to see each other in the future as often as they always used to in the past. Zaphiro kept asking himself how he could have allowed the two of them to drift apart; he was pleased that he had had the idea of calling up his friend, and that he had not put off their reconciliation another day. Now it was almost four o'clock and he was standing by the aeroplane, the propellers of which were turning

slowly as the mechanic completed his brief tuning up of the machine.

Zaphiro kept glancing down the cinder path towards the entrance of the aerodrome through which his passenger would be
bound to arrive. She was not late yet, but he became more nervous with every passing minute, for she had said that she would
come promptly if she came at all. He had practically given up
hope when he caught sight of the yellow and black cabriolet turning in through the gates and, with the now familiar sensation of
the inevitable fulfilling itself, realized that he had known in his
heart that she would come; despite his superficial surprise at seeing her, he was aware that this was right — that everything was
working out according to schedule. A few moments later she was
standing beside him in her green flying kit; her manner was aloof
and vaguely bored, as if a hundred times already she had lived
through the experiences that lay ahead of her and they had lost
their poignancy and zest.

'Well, you've come!' said Zaphiro, trying to control the excitement which he felt rising in his throat.

'So you see. Is everything ready?'

'All ready. I was terribly afraid that you would not show up.
I can't tell you how glad ——'

'Don't, Zaphiro, don't. What's the use? Do let's get started if
we're going.'

He helped her into the rear cockpit and stood fastening his helmet strap underneath his chin.

'Zaphiro!' she called, as he was about to climb into his seat.

'Yes, what is it?'

'Let's see what you can do in the way of tricks — try a few
spins and loops. It's a beautiful little aeroplane for stunt flying.'

'And you've kept on telling me that it's a rattletrap!'

'Oh, I was joking — I assure you that I was joking. You
mustn't believe everything I say.'

He put his foot on the grooved aluminum step and swung himself into his seat. Twice he accelerated the motor, each time allowing it to die down again; it was running beautifully. Then he raised his arm as a signal for the mechanic to kick away the wooden props beneath the wheels. Slowly the aeroplane left the concrete foundation, taxied the full length of the field tilting slightly from side to side — then with a roar of its engine shot forward and eventually upwards into the blue.

Of all the planes Zaphiro had used since he began to fly, first the instruction planes, then those he rented for his trial flights, he never had been in one which suited him so perfectly as this. It responded to his wishes almost before he touched the controls; he had the 'feel' of the plane after he had flown a hundred yards. He knew that this plane had been made for him, or perhaps it was he who had been born to fly the plane.

After they had been in the air ten minutes he let the motor full out and he thrilled to see the red arrow on his dashboard mount up to the two hundred kilometre mark and stay there quivering as long as his foot pressed down on the accelerator; then he let it swerve back to a hundred and eighty — a hundred and sixty — a hundred and forty, and kept it there with the lightest pressure upon the pedal; this was the normal cruising speed of the monoplane.

Adjusting his goggles, he turned around to see if his passenger were enjoying it. She sat quite still with her eyes closed, breathing deeply; he might have thought she was asleep except that as he watched her she carried her hand to her high forehead and passed her palm gently across its surface. She was even paler than usual, her thin face was as white as if she had powdered to excess, and the thin line of the lips was barely visible.

'What a woman!' he thought. 'She seems hardly human. Perhaps she was right when she told me that she had died two years ago.'

But he was not frightened of her, nevertheless; he was beyond feeling fear.

The aeroplane rushed along faster than any bird has flown and presently Zaphiro saw beneath him the blue ribbon of the Marne. He followed the river up as far as the hills of Chennevières, then left it near its junction with the Seine to speed back towards Orly with the wind behind him and the aeroplane riding on its lap as smoothly as a galleon before a steady breeze.

Espying the familiar landing field below, Zaphiro remembered his passenger's request to perform some stunts, and he headed the aeroplane downwards for a nose spin. The plane responded perfectly as ever to his touch; it tilted forward till it had reached an angle almost perpendicular to the ground, then shot downwards at a terrific speed while Zaphiro, fingering the joy stick with loving and sensitive fingers, waited for the exact moment when he should break the fall and allow the plane to right itself. The wind whistled in his ears; the hangar at which he drove grew larger, larger. Zaphiro's fingers closed about the lever and he drew it towards him.

And then he realized that there was something wrong — so wrong that it would never be set right. The aeroplane lurched sideways in its fall and, casting a glance in that direction, he saw the wing even as he looked detaching itself from the body, the struts split in twain; he saw the hangar and the field and beyond them the white thread of the road, but they were all swinging rapidly upwards and around, making him as it were the axis of an enormous circle.

This all he saw clearly and he realized that he would die, but he realized also that he had known this before — known it a very long time, it seemed to him. Now he understood much that had been troubling him of late. Viewing these last months as a preparatory period to death, he saw that he had long since come to a point when he had no further reason to go on living, when his life

logically speaking had reached its end. He had received his
marching orders at that time and, all without knowing it, had
gone off to seek the instrument of destruction. No wonder that
he had snatched so eagerly at Lopez' aeroplane! Then he must
have realized all along that it would end like this. How clear and
simple it seemed now! Everything fitted in down to the smallest
details — even to his desire that morning to transfer the stock.
So death is always suicide, flashed through his mind. He understood, and he wondered why he was the only man to grasp the
truth.

The aeroplane with ever greater speed was hurtling to the
ground. The wing detached itself completely and, writhing in mid-
air, fell slower than the body; for a brief moment it lived its independent life, then crashed and crumbled some distance from the
plane.

HAIR[1]

JESSE STUART

I

IF YOU'VE never been to Plum Grove then you wouldn't know about that road. It's an awful road, with big ruts and mudholes where the coal wagons with them nar-rimmed wheels cut down. There is a lot of haw bushes along this road. It goes up and down two yaller banks. From Lima Whitehall's house in the gap it's every bit of a mile and a half to Plum Grove. We live just across the hill from Lima's house. I used to go up to her house and get with her folks and we would walk over to Plum Grove to church.

Lima Whitehall just went with one boy. I tried to court her a little, but she wouldn't look at me. One night I goes up to her and I takes off my hat and says: 'Lima, how about seeing you home?' And Lima says: 'Not long as Rister is livin'.' Lord, but she loved Rister James. You ought to see Rister James — tall with a warty face and ferret eyes, but he had the prettiest head of black curly hair you ever saw on a boy's head. I've heard the girls say: 'Wish I had Rister's hair. Shame such an ugly boy has to have that pretty head of hair and a girl ain't got it. Have to

---

[1] From *The American Mercury.* Copyright, 1936, by the American Mercury Publishing Company.

curl my hair with a hot poker. Burnt it up about, already. Shame a girl don't have that head of hair.'

Well, they don't say that about my hair. My hair is just so curly I don't know which end of it grows in my head until I comb it. I've prayed for straight hair — or hair of a different color. But it don't do no good to pray. My hair ain't that pretty gold hair, or light gold hair. It's just about the color of a weaned Jersey calf's hair. I'll swear it is. People even call me Jersey.

There was a widder down in the Hollow and she loved Rister. Was a time, though, when she wouldn't look at him. She was from one of those proud families. You've seen them. Think they're better'n everybody else in the whole wide world — have to watch about getting rain in their noses. That's the kind of people they were in that family. And when a poor boy marries one of them girls he's got to step. They are somebody around here and they boss their men. So Rister James went with the woman I loved, Lima Whitehall, when he could have gone with Widder Ollie Spriggs. Widder Ollie wasn't but seventeen years old and just had one baby. Rister was nineteen and I was eighteen. Lima was seventeen. If Rister would have gone with Widder Ollie it would have made things come out right for me. God knows I didn't want Widder Ollie and she didn't want me. I wanted Lima. I told her I did. She wanted Rister. She told me she did.

Widder Ollie was a pretty girl — one of them women that just makes a good armful — small, slim as a rail, with hair pretty as the sunlight and teeth like peeled cabbage stalks. She'd have made a man a pretty wife. She might not have made a good wife — that's what Effie Spriggs told me. Effie is John Spriggs' mother and Ollie married John when she was fifteen. Effie said Ollie broke a whole set of plates, twelve of 'em, on John's head over nothing in God Almighty's world. And he just had too much honor in his bones to hit a woman with his fist. He just stood there and let her break them. And when she got through, John was kind of addled but he got out of the house and came home to his mother Effie, who is Widder Effie here in the Hollow. (She tried to pizen her man, but he found the pizen in his coffee and left her.) Widder Ollie went to live with Widder Effie later. They had a-plenty — a big pretty farm down in the Hollow, fat barns, and plenty of milk cows. They were kindly rich people with heads so high you couldn't reach them with a ten-foot pole.

Widder Ollie, as I said, wouldn't look at Rister at first. She laughed at him when he used to hoe corn for her pappie for twenty-five cents a day. She made fun of poor old Rister's snaggled-toothed mother and said she looked like a witch. She laughed at Rister's pappie and said he looked like old Lonesy Fannin. That was an old bald-headed horse-doctor who used to go from place to place pulling the eyeteeth out of blind horses, saying they would get their sight back. And she said all the children in the James family looked like varmints. She'd laugh and laugh at 'em and just hold her head high. Then suddenly she was after Rister to marry him. But that's the way — pride leads a woman to a fall. And after she gets up, with a little of the pride knocked out of her, she's a different woman.

But I didn't blame Rister for not wanting her when he could get Lima. Lima was the sweetest little black-headed armload you ever put your two eyes on. I was in the market for Lima the first time I ever saw her. And I guess that was when we were babies. But I didn't know how to get her. I think I was a durn sight better-looking boy than Rister. It's funny how a woman will take to an uglier feller that way and just hold on to his coat-tails whether or not. Hang on just as long as she can. I always thought the reason Lima did that was because she knew Widder Ollie wanted Rister. And if there'd a been another girl around in the market for a man *she* would have wanted Rister because Lima wanted him and Widder Ollie wanted him.

But nobody was after me. I was left out in the cold — just

because of my hair, Mom always told me. Mom said I was a good-looking boy all but the color of my hair, and women wouldn't take to that kind of hair. Of course, it don't matter how ugly a man is, his Mom always thinks he's the best-looking boy in the district.

II

I used to go down past Lima's house last June when the roses were in bloom, and the flags. Them blue and yaller flags just sets a yard off and makes it a pretty thing. Now Rister never saw anything pretty in flowers. He never saw anything pretty in a woman's voice or the things she said, or the shape of her hands. He would watch a woman's legs — and go with them far as he could. He was that kind of a feller. I knew it all the time. I'd pass Whitehall's house. It would be on a Wednesday when Mom would run out of sugar or salt and I'd have to get on the mule and go to the store and get it. Rister would be down to see Lima on a weekday. Now God knows, when a man is farming he don't have no time to play around with a woman like a lovesick kitten. He's got to strike while the iron is hot. If he don't he won't get much farming done. When I saw Rister and Lima I reined my mule up to the palings. And I started talking to them as if I didn't care what they were doing. But I did care. I says: 'How you getting along with your crop, Rister?'

'Oh, pretty well,' he says. 'Nothing extra. Terbacker's getting a little weedy on me. Too wet to hoe in it today. Ground will ball up in your hand. Too wet to stir the ground when it is like that.'

Well, I knew he was a-lying. But I never said anything. I know when ground is wet and when ground ain't wet. I'd been out working in it all morning. It was in good shape to work. Rister used to be a good worker. But you know how a man is when he gets lovesick after a woman. Take the best man in the world to work and let him get his mind on a woman and he goes hog-wild. That was the way with Rister.

While I was there looking over the palings, Lima went right up into his arms. He kissed her right there before me. Mom always says a woman that would kiss around in front of people was a little loose with herself. Well, I would have told Mom she lied about Lima if she'd said that about her to my face. I just didn't want to believe anything bad about Lima. I wanted her for my wife. But, men, how would you like to look over the palings from a mule's back and see your dream-wife in the arms of a man bad after women — right out among the pretty roses and flags — and her right up in his arms, her arms around his neck, and his arms around her waist pulling her up to him tight enough to break her in two. And he would say to her: 'Oo love me, oo bitsy baby boopy-poopy oo?' And she would say: 'I love U, U bitsy 'itsy boopy-poopy oo. I love my 'ittle 'itsy 'itsy bitsy turly-headed boopy-poopy oo.' God, it made me sick as a horse. It's all right when *you're* loving a woman. It don't look bad to *you*. But when you see somebody else gumsuck around, then you want to get the hell out of the way and in a hurry. It's a sickening thing.

I reined my mule away and I never let him stop till I was a mile beyond the house. I went on to the store and got the sugar. That was Wednesday night and Prayer-Meeting night at Plum Grove, so I had to hurry back and do up the work and go to Prayer Meeting.

I'm a Methodist — I go to church — but God knows they won't have my name on the Lamb's Book of Life because I saw the fiddle, play set-back, and dance at the square dances. Some of them even say terbacker is a filthy weed and none of it will be seen in heaven. Some won't even raise it on their farms. But I go to church even if they won't have me until I quit these things. I just up and go to see and to be seen — that's what we all go for. It is a place to go and about the only place we got to go.

I hurried and got my work done. I put the mule up and fed him. I helped milk the cows. I slopped the hogs, got in stove-wood and kindling. I drew up water from the well — got every-thing done around the house and I set out to church. Well, when I got down to Whitehall's place, there was Lima and Rister. They were getting ready to go. I gave them a head start and followed after. But I hadn't more than walked out in the big road until here come Widder Ollie and that baby of hers. He was just big enough to walk a little and talk a lot. We started down the road. I said to Ollie: 'Rister and Lima's just on ahead of us.'

And Ollie says: 'They're on ahead? C'mon, let's catch up with them. Take my baby boy, you carry him awhile.'

So I took her baby and started in a run with her to catch up with Lima and Rister. You know, a woman will do anything when she loves a man. I could tell Widder Ollie loved Rister. She was all nervous and excited. She had her mind set on getting Rister. And when a woman has her mind set on getting a man she can about get him. That made me think if she could get Rister I'd have a chance to get Lima. That was the only reason I'd be carrying a widder's baby around. I had heard that baby was the meanest young'n in the world. Now I believed it. It had been spiled by them two women — its mother and its grandmother. He would kick me in the ribs and say: 'Get up hossy! Get up there! Whoa back, Barnie.' And when he would say 'Whoa back' he would glomb me in the eyes with his fingers like he was trying to stop a horse. Then he would say: 'Get up, hossy, or I'll bust you one in the snoot.' And then he started kicking me in the ribs again. I was sweating, carrying that load of a young'n and keep-ing up with Widder Ollie. I felt like pulling him off my back and burning up the seat of his pants with my hand.

We saw them — Rister had his left arm around Lima's back and she had her right arm around his back. They were climbing up the first hill, that little yaller hill on this side of the haw bushes.

It was light as day. The moon had come up and it lit the fields
like a big lamp. Pon my word and honor I couldn't remember in
all my life a prettier night than that one. You ought to have seen
my corn in the moonlight. We had to pass it. I was glad for the
girls to go by it and see what a clean farmer I was and what
a weedy farmer Rister was. Not a weed in any of my corn. Pretty
and clean in the moonlight and waving free as the wind. Lord,
I felt like a man with religion to see my corn all out of the weeds
and my terbacker clean as a hound dog's tooth — my land all
paid for — not a debt in the world — didn't owe a man a penny.
Raised what I et and et what I raised. All I needed was a wife
like Lima. She'd never want for anything. And I thought: 'What
if this baby on my back was mine and Lima's? I'd carry him the
rest of my days. I'd let him grow to be a man a-straddle of my
back. But if I had my way now, I'd bust his little tail with my
hand.'

We got right up behind Rister and Lima. And they looked
around. Widder Ollie had me by the arm. I had her baby on my
back yet. God, it hurt me. But I held the baby while Lima won
the battle. You know women are dangerous soldiers. They fight
with funny weapons. The tongue is a dangerous cannon when
a woman aims it right. We just laughed and talked. We just
giggled before Rister and Lima got to giggling at us. I was afraid
they'd laugh at me for carrying the baby. They went on up the
next hill — us right behind them. We went past the haw bushes
and on to church. We just laughed and laughed and went on
crazy. That baby on my back, a-making a lot of noise. We went
up the hill at the church and the boys said: 'Look at that pack
mule, won't you?'

Well, to tell the truth I'd ruther be called a pack mule as to
be called Jersey. So I just let them whoop and holler to see me
with Widder Ollie and carrying her baby. Everybody out on the
ground laughed and hollered enough to disturb the Methodist

Church. Church was going on inside. But there was more people
out in the yard than there was inside. They could see more on the
outside than they could hear going on inside. I just wagged the
baby right in the church house. Everybody looked around and
craned their necks.

Rister and Lima acted like they were ashamed of us. Tried to
sidle out of the way and get us in front so they could dodge us.
But we stayed right with them. They set down on a seat. We set
right beside them as if we were all together. People looked around.
I had Widder Ollie's boy in my lap. He tried to hit the end of my
nose. I had a time with him. I could see the girls whisper to one
another. They watched us more than they did the preacher. He
was telling them about widders and orphans. He was preaching
a sermon on that. Rister would flinch every now and then. He
wanted to be on another seat. But he couldn't very well move.
So he just set there and took it. And I took it from that young'n.
But I thought: 'There'll be the time when I come back to this
church house with a different woman. I'll come right here and
marry her. It will be different from what they see tonight.'

III

We set right there and listened through that sermon. Boys
would come to the winder and point to me from the outside —
being with a widder woman who hadn't been divorced from her
man very long. Boys around home thinks it's kindly strange to
go with a widder woman — but I don't think so. They say a body
is in adultery. But when two can't go on loving each other and
start breaking plates — twelve at a crack — it's time they were
getting apart. Especially when two has to go through life tied
together when the mother-in-law tied the knot. I just felt sorry
for Widder Ollie. She had always loved Rister and would have
married him to begin with if it hadn't been for that mother of hers
telling her so many times that she got to believing it that she was
better than any man in the Hollow.

Well, they got us in front coming out of the church house. I thought we'd better take advantage of getting out first. So we took the lead going back. Boys just giggled and hollered at me when I came out of the house with the baby on my back. I didn't care. I was seeing ahead. So we just went out the road. The moon was pretty on the fields. A thousand thoughts came into my mind. I didn't want Rister to have Lima. I loved Lima. God, I loved her. Widder Ollie said to me going home: 'Don't think it has done much good for both of us tonight. We'll have to think of something different. I love that boy till it hurts. I could love him forever. I can't get him; Lima don't love him. She holds him because I want him. That is the way of women. You want what you can't get. When you get what you want you don't want it. I have always loved Rister. But my people wanted me to marry John. I married him. My mother married him. Life is not worth while without Rister. And here you've been out carrying my baby around and letting people talk about you so you could help me get Rister and you could get Lima.'

That was right. Life was not fair. The night so pretty. The moon above my clean corn. My house on the hill where I would take Lima. I needed a wife. I wanted the woman I loved. I loved Lima Whitehall. And when we passed her home I wouldn't look across the palings at the roses. I remembered the weekday I passed and saw Rister out there with her. I just took Widder Ollie on home. And when we got to the gate I said: 'Widder Ollie, I am Rister kissing you. You are Lima kissing me. You are Lima for one time in your life. I am Rister one time in my life. Shut your eyes and let's kiss. Let's just pretend.' So we did.

Then I started on the long walk home up the branch. I had to pass Lima's house. Moonlight fell on the corn. Wind blew through the ragweeds along the path. Whip-poor-wills hollered so lonely that they must have been in love with somebody they couldn't get. I went in Lima's yard to draw me a drink of water.

And right by the well-gum stood Rister and Lima. They weren't
a-saying a word. They didn't see me; I didn't let myself be
known; I just stepped back into the moonshade of one of the yard
trees. I just stood there and watched. Lima went into the house
after kissing and kissing Rister. When Lima left, Rister stood at
the well-gum. He looked down at the ground. He kicked the toe
of his shoe against the ground. There was something funny about
the way he was acting. He kept his eye on the upstairs winder in
that house. I had one of them pole ladders — we call them
chicken ladders — just one straight pole with little tiny steps
nailed across it. It was setting up back of the house — from the
ground to the winder.

Then, suddenly, Rister let out one of the funniest catcalls you
ever heard. It would make the hair stand up on your head, it
wasn't a blue yodel, but it was something like a part of that yodel
Jimmie Ridgers used to give. He done it someway down in his
throat. It started out like the nip-nip-nipping of scissor-blades,
then it clanked like tin cans, then like a fox horn, way up there
high, then it went like a bumblebee, then it rattled like a rattlesnake, and ended up like that little hissing noise a black snake
makes when it warns you. I never heard anything like it. If it
hadn't been for me knowing where it had come from I'd set sail
off of that hill and swore it was a speret that made the noise.
Rister gave the catcall once — held his head high in the air — no
answer. So he gave it again. And from upstairs came the answer
— a soft catcall like from a she-cat. So he takes right out in front
of me and runs up that ladder like a tom and pops in at the winder.

I thought I'd go home and get the gun and come back and when
he came down that ladder I'd fill his behind so full of shot it would
look like a strainer. Then again I thought I'd go over and pull the
ladder down and make him go down the front way. God, I was
mad! But I didn't do neither one. The whole thing made me so
sick I just crawled out of the moonshade and sneaked over the

hill home. I didn't know what to do. It just made me sick — sick at life. I just couldn't stand it. I couldn't bear to think of Lima in the dark upstairs with Rister.

I thought about taking the gun and going back and blowing Rister's brains out when he came back through that upstairs winder. I could have done it — God knows I could have done it. But they'd have got out the bloodhounds and trailed me home. Lima would have known who did it. I thought there must be a way for me to get Lima yet, and for her to come to her senses. But then I thought they are up in that dark room together. Lord, it hurt me. Pains shot through and through me. Life wasn't worth the pain one got out of it. I had something for her — a farm, a little money, clean crops, and plenty of food for cold days when the crows fly over the empty fields hunting last year's corn-grains. Rister didn't have nothing to take a woman to but his father's house, and den her with his own father's young'ns.

I went upstairs and got the gun from the rack. I put a shell into its bright blue barrel. Just one shell for Rister. I would kill him. Then I put the gun down. I would not kill Rister. I could see blood and brains all over the wall. Old Sol Whitehall would run out in his nightshirt. He would kill Lima if he knew. And I wouldn't get Lima. It is better not to let a man know everything — it is better to live in silence and hold a few things than to lose your head and get a lot of people killed. I put the gun back, took the shell out of it, and set it back on the rack. I went to bed. But I couldn't sleep. I could see Lima and Rister in a settee in the front yard, kissing. I could hear that catcall. I memorized it. I said it over and over in bed. It came to me — every funny noise in it. I called it out, several times. It made the hair stand up on my head. It waked Pa up and he said: 'I've been hearing something funny in this house or my ears are fooling me. Funniest thing I ever heard. Like a pheasant drumming on a brushpile. Goes something like a rattlesnake, too. I can't go to sleep.' But

Pa went back to sleep. I kept my mouth shet. I just laid there the rest of the night and thought about Rister and Lima.

I didn't eat much breakfast the next morning. I went out and got the Barnie mule and I started plowing my terbacker. I couldn't get Lima off my mind. I prayed to God. I did everything I knew to do. And it all came to me like a flash. It just worked out like that.

So I waited. I just waited about ten hours. I plowed all day, worked hard in the fields. After I'd fed the mule, et my supper, done up the rest of the work, I slipped back up the path that I had come over the night before.

All the lights in the Whitehall house were out. The ladder was up at the winder at the back of the house. Everything was quiet. The old house slept in the moonlight. The hollyhocks shone in the moonlight. Old Buck came around and growled once or twice. But he knew me when I patted his head. He walked away contented. Brown, he was, in the moonlight — like a wadded-up brown carpet thrown among the flowers.

I held my head in the air, threw my chin to the stars, and gave that catcall — just as good as Rister gave it. Lima answered me from upstairs. The dog started barking at the strange sounds. My cap pulled low over my funny-colored hair I climbed the ladder and went in through the winder. The dog barked below. I was afraid. If Sol Whitehall found me there he would kill me. But I had to do this thing. I just had to.

Lima said: 'Oo bitsy 'itsy boopy-poopy oo. My turly-headed baby boy.'

I kept away from the streak of moonlight in the room. . . . Well, no use to tell you all. A man's past belongs to himself. His future belongs to the woman he marries. That's the way I look at it. That's the way I feel about it. This is a world where you have to go after what you get or you don't get it. Lima would not stand and say: 'Here I am. Come and get me.' No. She couldn't say it long as she was free — free without a care in the world. If she was like Widder Ollie, she'd be glad to find a nice young man like me even if I did have hair the color of a Jersey calf and so curly you couldn't tell which end grew in my head. I know that much about women.

When my hat come off in the moonlight upstairs Lima just screamed to the top of her voice. Screamed like she had been stabbed. I made for the winder. She hollered: 'That hair! That hair!' She knew who I was. I went out of that winder like a bird. I heard Sol getting out the bed. I landed on soft ground right in the hollyhock bed, as God would have it. I took down over the bank — circled up in the orchard through the grass so they couldn't track me. I hadn't got two hundred feet when I heard Sol's gun and felt the shot sprinkling all around me in the sassafras like a thin rain falls on the green summer leaves.

I went on to bed that night. I dreamed of Lima. I loved her. I didn't care about Rister and his past with Lima. The way I looked at it, that belonged to them. A girl has the same right to her past that a boy has to his. And when a man loves, nothing matters. You just love them and you can't help it. You'll go to them in spite of the world — no matter what a man has done or a woman has done. That's the way I look at it. Be good to one another in a world where there's a lot of talking about one another, a lot of tears, laughter, work, and love — where you are a part of the world and all that is in it and the world is a part of you. I dreamed about Lima that night. She was in my arms. I kissed her. She was in the trees I'd seen in the moonlight. She was in the wild flowers I saw — the flowers on the yaller bank. She was in my corn and my terbacker. She was in the wind that blows. She was my wife. She wasn't Rister's. She was mine. I loved her.

IV

Well, August ended, and September came along with the changing leaves. Then October when all the world turned brown and
dead leaves flew through the air. The wind whistled lonesome
over the brown fields. The crows flew high through the crisp
autumn air.

The months dragged by. We went to church, but I barely ever
spoke to Lima or to Rister. I went with Widder Ollie sometimes.
People were talking about Lima. People understood. A woman,
with her crooked finger over the paling fence, said: 'That poor
Lima Whitehall was raised under a decent roof, and in the House
of the Lord, a church-going girl with as good a father and mother
as ever God put breath in. And look how she's turned out. You
just can't tell about girls nowadays. They'll fool you — especially
when they run around with a low-down boy like Rister James.
Curly-headed thing — everybody's crazy about his hair. Look
at that bumpy face and them ferret eyes and you'll get a stomach-
ful, won't you?'

And the woman driving home from town with an express and
buggy said: 'You are right, Miss Fairchild. It's them low-down
James people. That boy. He ought to be tarred and feathered,
bringing a poor girl to her ruint. She's a ruint girl. Never can
stand in the church choir any more with the other girls and play
the organ and sing at church. Her good times are over. That
James boy won't marry her now. They say he's got to dodging
her. Poor thing.'

So I went to Widder Ollie and I said: 'Everybody's down on old
Rister now. You ought to go talk to him. He's down and out.
Now is when he needs help. You know what they are accusing
him of. I guess it's the truth. Wait till after I see the baby and
I might take Lima and the baby. Be glad to get them. If I do,
you can grab Rister.'

'I'll do it,' said Widder Ollie. 'I'll spin my net for him like

a spider. I'll get the fly. I love that boy. I love him. He's got
the prettiest hair you nigh ever see on any boy's head.'

The land was blanketed in snow. The cold winds blew. Winter
was here. We heard the people talk: 'W'y, old Sol Whitehall's
going to march that young man Rister right down there at the
pint of his gun and make him marry Lima. It's going to be a shot-
gun wedding. Something is going to happen.'

The talk was all over the neighborhood. Everybody in the
district knew about Lima. It is too bad when a girl gets in trouble
and everybody knows about it. Around home she can never get
a man. She's never respected again. For the man it don't matter
much. He can go right back to the church choir and sing when
they play the organ. Nothing is ever said about the man.

'I won't marry her,' said Rister, 'and old Sol can't gun me into
it. I'll die first. I'll go away to the coal mines and dig coal till it is
all over. I'll go where Widder Ollie's pappie is — up in West
Virginia.'

So Widder Ollie goes to West Virginia after Rister has been
there awhile. She leaves her boy with her mother and she goes to
stay awhile with her pappie. I thought that was the right move.
It just looked like everything was coming nicely to my hands.
I had worked hard. I had prayed hard. I had waited. It was
time to get something. But what a mess. What a risk to run over
a woman. How she had suffered. How I had suffered. The
lonely nights I'd gone out to the woods — nights in winter when
the snow dusted the earth — when the trees shook their bare tops
in the wind and the song of the wind in the trees was long and
lonesome and made a body want to cry — lonely nights when
a body wondered if life was worth living — white hills in the
moonlight — the barns with shaggy cows standing around them
and sparrows mating in the eaves. Life is strange. Lima there,
and the Lord knew what she'd do the way people were talking in
the district. I was just waiting to see. It would soon be time.

The winter left. Birds were coming back from the South —
robins had come back. And Rister was gone. Rister was at the
mines — had a job — making more money than he'd ever made
in his life. He wasn't working for twenty-five cents a day no
more. He was working on the mine's tipple for three dollars a day.
He was wearing good clothes. He was courting Widder Ollie right
up a tree. And he had her up the tree a-barking at 'er like a
hound-dog trees a possum.

The days went swiftly. April was here — green in the hills and
the plow again in the furrows. Mom was there that ninth of
April. She was with Lima. Doctor so far away and hard for poor
people to get. Lima came through all right. She had the baby.
Mom came home the next morning — I was waiting to see. She
said: 'It's got that funny-colored hair — that Jersey hair with
two crowns on its head. But it ain't no Harkreader. It's the first
time I ever saw any other person but a Harkreader have hair like
that.'

I never said a word. I was so happy I couldn't say a word. I
had the almanac marked and it had come out just right. So I up
and went down to Whitehall's to see the baby. I went in by the
bed. I reached over and picked up that baby. It was my baby.
I knew it. It was like lifting forty farms in my hands. I kissed it.
It was a boy. I never lifted a little baby before or never saw a
pretty one in my life. But this baby was pretty as a doll. I loved
it. I said: 'I'll go to the store and get its dresses right now, Lima.'

And she said: 'W'y, what are you talking about?'

'Look at its hair,' I said. 'Only a Harkreader has that kind of
hair, you know that.'

Fire popped in her eyes — then tears to quench the fire. They
flowed like water. 'When you get out of bed,' I said, 'we'll go to
church and get married. We'll go right out there where we went
to school and where we played together. We'll forget about
Rister.'

She started out of the bed. I put her back. When a girl is down and out — a girl you love — a girl who is good and who lives as life lets a woman and a man love — I could shed tears. I could cuss. I could cry. But what I did was to run out and chop up that settee. I dug up the green sprouts of the flags and the roses. My daddy-in-law, old Sol Whitehall, ran around the house on me and yelled: 'What the devil are you doing? Am I crazy to see you in my yard digging up my flowers?'

And I said: 'You are crazy, for I am not here, and you are not Sol Whitehall. You are somebody else.'

I dumped the flower roots over the palings. I left Sol standing there, looking at the wind.

I ran toward the store. I said to myself: 'I got her! I'll plow more furrows. Clear more ground. Plant more corn. I'll do twice as much work. I got her! And I am going to get my boy some dresses. Hell's fire! He's greater to look at than my farm!'

I got him the dresses. I ran back and told the preacher to be ready soon. She must be mine. And when I got back with the dresses my pappie-in-law said: 'And that scoundrel — married. Rister married to Widder Ollie Spriggs. Damn him to hell! God damn his soul to hell and let it burn with the chaff!'

But let them talk. Let them talk. They'll never know.

We went to the church. We were married there. Made Lima feel better to be married there. I could have been married in a barn. Would have suited me.

You ought to see my boy now. Takes after me — long Jersey-colored hair. He's my image. He don't look like his ma — not the least. He's up and going about.

Rister's back home now. He works for Widder Ollie and her mother. They all live in the house together. Everything came out just fine. We went to church together the other night, all of us. Rister and Widder Ollie walked behind. We went into the church house carrying our babies. I know people thought I was carrying

Rister's baby, and that he was carrying the one I ought to carry. The Widder Ollie's brat was digging Rister in the ribs and saying: 'Get up, hossy. Get up, hossy, or I'll hit you on the snoot.'

And he'd have done it too, if Rister hadn't stepped up a little faster. That kid is twice as big as he was the night I carried him. Ollie says he won't walk a step when she takes him any place. Makes Rister carry him everywhere. People look at us and grin. They crane their necks back over the seats to look at us all together again. Ollie understands. Lima understands. Rister don't understand so well.

And we go back across the hills shining in moonlight. Summer is here again. Corn is tall on the hills. Then I hold my head in the air, throw my chin to the stars, and I give that strange catcall once more. Rister looks a little funny. He understands now better than he did.

THE IRON CITY[1]

LOVELL THOMPSON

THERE is a rawness in the city of Liverpool that permeates the flesh and grips the vitals of a man who, like Gideon Grimes, is not vigorous. The city, as it stood in his mind, appeared coated with cold, cohesive dust. When he thought of the city he felt sticky particles rasping upon his fingertips and saw heavy dust-hardened raindrops, and fog stiffened by the filth of Liverpool. The odor of Liverpool was to him that of stale grease; even after he had crossed the Mersey Bar a taste of Liverpool clung in the back of his throat. Was it the queer name of the city that stamped this impression on him, or was it that it was the place where he had met Shank?

Gideon Grimes hated the city — and yet it was this city, phlegmatic and depraved, that beyond all others lay closest to the varied and beautiful ocean. The graceful ships of a hundred nations rested here close to the stinking rawboned docks. In the harbor the water was smooth, sluggish, and crusted with a gelatinous scum. Yet here, in spite of ugliness and crudity, the thousand-fingered hand of the ocean gently soothed the land. The

---

[1] From *Story.* Copyright, 1936, by Story Magazine, Inc.

mighty rhythm of the ocean's breath is sensitively felt in Liverpool. The scum upon the surface of the water assiduously charts upon the piles of the docks the record of each breath. Twice a year the ocean heaves a few vast equinoctial signs, the tide rises high and in Liverpool the highest tide is more permanently recorded than the rest, by the scum mark on the piles, by the bits of débris shoved far up to a damp and rotting security beneath the bellies of the docks. Here on the harbor's edge human scum is also deposited and left till the next high tide reaches up for it once more. Thus the hand of the ocean reached for the man Shank, on the same September night that Gideon Grimes also embarked for America.

Under the shelter of the dock a few electric light bulbs shone listlessly. They were on the ends of long rods which stretched down out of darkness. They lit up the sordid dirt and scraps of paper upon the dock floor. Gideon Grimes tightened his muscles to try to stop shivering. The anguished clatter of a winch banged at the back of his head. He was weak. He was depressed. He gazed down the dockway into the murk as if in search of a reason.

And out of the murk came the man Shank whose name he did not then know. He, too, bore a duffle bag upon his shoulder. He leaned forward with it and thus was able to support it partly on his back and partly also upon his elbow, cocked up for the purpose with a hand upon his hip. His other arm, the left, with the fingers of the hand hooked into the fastening of the sea bag upon his right shoulder, concealed his face. So Grimes observed the rest of him. He was shabby, neither dirty nor clean, neither tidy nor unkempt — he was utterly ordinary and he bent beneath his load like a tallow taper before a hot blaze.

When he had come quite close to the gangplank before which Grimes stood, he threw down his duffle bag. He was small, about the size of Gideon, and astonishingly thin, and his pinched face except for his eyes was no more unusual than the rest of him. His eyes looked as if their owner's line of vision traveled about twenty feet and then turned a right angle. The man looked as if he were trying to see around a corner; looked as if he did see around one; looked as if he saw nowhere else. He looked at Gideon Grimes, seeming to have to look away to get him in his line of vision, and he spoke.

'Say, Brother, ain't there extra quarters on these ships, fellars like you going back — extra bunks I mean? Think I could stow away with you fellars — no one would notice? Won't show up for boat drill. Slip ashore in Boston. What do you think, eh?'

'I guess so,' said Gideon.

'I'll stick close to you,' said Shank, and close he remained.

They labored into the black belly of the ship.

On a ship of this type what is often called the first deck is beneath the actual outside deck of the ship. By outside deck is meant what the ordinary man considers the deck of a ship — the outermost uppermost side which roofs in the hold and upon which the officers' quarters, funnels, and what not appears to be a superstructure. Beneath this outside deck then is the first deck — a subterranean deck, as it were, and on it, forward in the bow, are quarters for the crew, rooms lined with bunks.

They walked this deck, Shank and Grimes, between rows of iron supports. The deck was dark and for the most part empty.

On this freighter, as on other ships of the same line, there were the extra quarters which Shank had asked about. These had been put in after the building of the ship, to accommodate extra hands required for the shipping of certain cargoes — a deckload of livestock, for instance. Thereafter these quarters were used as a sort of unofficial sub-steerage, where men whom the line desired to transport across the ocean were quartered.

The *Iron City* had a cabin for four next these quarters. It was designed for those who were in charge of the men who worked on the cargo. Grimes made for this cabin, in the hope that the other

free passengers might be sufficiently few for him to occupy it
alone. Shank, however, followed him into the room, so Grimes
directed him to throw his bag into a lower bunk and to crawl into
an upper himself. Gideon did the same and the cabin was occupied. Other men following looked in but were directed to the
larger bunk-room further along.

Shank's scheme of stowing away was extraordinarily feasible.
The captain of a freighter pays no attention to this idle element
of his crew. There are say ten men in the extra quarters — most
of them probably have been employed in bringing livestock from
America to England; no one ever sees them all together. The
face of the stowaway becomes familiar. No one realizes that he is
an extra. The officers are searching for a name on their lists which
has no corresponding face, not for a face which has no name.

With blankets given out later by the purser, and with a dry
straw mattress beneath him, Gideon felt warm and slept. As he
dropped off, he noticed that a rod of light from one of the bulbs
on the dock came through a doorway and through a port and at
last rested upon the recumbent figure of Shank — this leech who
clung to him — it lit Shank's face, his strange eyes now closed and
his mouth now gently ajar.

During the next day, the *Iron City* steamed through choppy
water along the coast of Ireland. Hour after hour the high green
coast passed by — the long miles marked by bulging headlands.
Each, when first seen, appeared to come no nearer; ship and head-
land moved together, carried on the same subaqueous belt. But
when attention was turned from the progress of the boat the headlands leapt up upon it and stopped again when the eye was turned
upon them as if they played a game.

As the day dwindled, the long, blinking beam of Fastnet Light
rose in the west. The beam of this revolving star, like a gigantic
compass describing an arc, traversed every few seconds a three-

hundred-mile circle and yet found time in its passing to pierce the eyeball of Grimes, who looked at it, with a fierce, curious stare.

Summoned by this wonder, and still smelling of stale daylight sleep, up the forward hatchway, rose the fate-sent Shank to ask, 'What light is that?'

'Fastnet,' said Grimes.

Shank looked while the night wind, sharp upon the forecastle-head, hewed his heavy frowsy hair into a sculptured grace. Then he turned away to walk a stretch down the deck and return. Thus he came at intervals, bringing his pale face to meet the swinging light, then turned again to vanish as if into another world. And each time he came Gideon asked a question and Shank replied, gradually drawing the picture of a life.

With an artificial tension produced by his periodic walks down the deck, from which he would return still more stirred by the contemplation of his past, Shank held his listener, there on the deck of the *Iron City*. A constantly freshening wind gave to the man's talk an ominous crescendo and the scene was unified by one powerful trait of the man which emerged slowly from his story.

This was a genius for taking care of himself in perilous situations — a genius for always attaching himself to the person who was best fitted to look after him — a genius which had thus far never forsaken him.

In Egypt during the war he had found a six-foot-five Australian. He had followed this man as a jackal does a lion; he had watched with furtive curiosity the unending process of satisfying the lion's appetites, and he had picked up the mouthfuls which were thrown aside as too small to fill the throat of his patron.

Into Arab villages where voluminous Arab women with tattooed faces beckoned, Shank followed Australia; he wet his feet where the big man wallowed; drank a glass where his companion drank a gallon; used the Australian's size and boldness to aid him in gleaning a small harvest of dissipation which Shank alone would never have had the courage or impressiveness to find, and in the end he would take Australia home.

'Women listen,' said Shank, 'when six-foot-five speaks to them.'

On the bow of the battleship that the English were to beach as part of their desperate plan to land at Gallipoli, stood the big Australian. After the vessel had gently forced its keel into the smooth sand, he was one of the first over the gangplank toward shore, and one of the many to be killed on that gangplank — his superhuman appetites quenched by human death. Perhaps the last tremor of departing life woke the big man to consciousness once more, told him that, in his loneliness, many feet were stepping over him; then left him only time to curse the day that man was born to die. Perhaps, however, he never knew that Shank was not to take him home from this night of adventure as from the others.

Shank saw, and the bile of his belly was sour in his throat. Turkish lights and Turkish guns were trained upon the landing point. Shank knew that the other end of that plank did not lie on the beach but in unending unconsciousness.

Then he saw a few men running to the unnoticed and slightly more seaward side of the bow, from there they dropped into the water and swam ashore. This was the thin road out that fate always sent to Shank. He hurled himself over the side and fell feet first into the bloody water with a thick splash like a June-bug in a mug of beer. But he was soon gathering his feet under him in the shallow water, safely landed beyond the feline stare of the search-lights.

Fastnet Light was barely discernible now and as the *Iron City* left the sheltering coast of Ireland, the wind grew stronger. The ship took the waves on her quarter. She wallowed deeply while each wave rolled upward along her side toward the scuppers amidships. Then as the lifting power of the wave passed forward beneath the center of the boat, the stern fell back and the bow rose dripping and stars and shreds of cloud appeared beneath the ship's rail. The last step in the cycle was a shuffling, falling movement as the ship fell backward and crabwise down the long back of the wave, while the wave cantered easily forward into the darkness like some unwieldy prehistoric animal wearing a small white nightcap of phosphorescent foam. The light upon the mast indicated upon the sky, as if with an extended little finger, an ellipse; and drew it neatly to a close as each wave passed. Shank's talk ceased; he felt sick and went below.

Often during the next thirty-six hours Grimes watched Shank stick his head out of the port hole above his bunk. He looked at these moments like a mouse with its head in a trap, hind quarters protruding, passionately limp. He was very sick.

The fourth morning, however, was sunny with a light steadying headwind, and Shank with a two days' beard upon his face peered over the edge of his bunk with the light of life in his eye. After breakfast Shank followed Gideon up to the wheelhouse where it was sheltered — where the sun was tropical and where they lay half naked upon the deck. Here, stimulated by his sudden freedom from nausea and by his heavy drinking of tea, and hypnotized by the droning of the ship's propeller beneath them — Shank grew confidential.

'I've got a girl,' said Shank. 'And I've got money.'

He reached for his coat, stiffly, as one from death revivified, and pulled out of it a worn imitation-leather wallet. From the wallet he drew a photograph and holding it in his wan yellow palm, he studied it for a long time. Grimes leaned over the man's shoulder to look at the picture and noticed that he smelt like an old man, and that the high sun made the hairs on his chest cast long shadows on his belly.

Gideon was looking down at the picture of a woman — Shank's

'girl.' Momentarily the bright day and all it showed to his eyes became a frame to the picture. The tarry pleasant smell of a bit of marlin he was twisting in his hands perfumed the moment.

There was a long silence, for the face before Grimes was beautiful. The face of that woman had the seductive patience of a fair-weather sea. It was a smooth-skinned face, deeply shadowed beneath the eyes, which were lighter than the surrounding skin. The hair was heavy, like the flow of oil, and was drawn back from the round cheeks to leave the pale ears showing. The woman wore a round-necked dress with a collar that lay smooth upon it and a sort of coif above her smooth crown. The points of her shoulders were thrown forward slightly so that there was an area above a full, deep bosom which was slightly concave.

'There's the girl,' said Shank, and added abruptly, 'She's a trained nurse.'

'Now,' said Shank, 'I'll tell ye how I got the money.' So he began, blinking at the wide ocean with his eyes that made only the knight's move.

The new regiment to which, after Gallipoli and toward the end of the war, Shank was shifted was in a camp, close behind the lines in France. In this regiment there was a man who owned a roulette wheel. Daily this man spread out the marked cloth that was the board and amid an attendant circle he spun the wheel and was the banker — but Shank was the croupier.

And Shank was glad to be croupier, for he felt that he won, himself, and yet at no risk; the banker in turn permitted Shank's offices good-humoredly at first, and then as his game grew larger depended on them. The banker was Sergeant Cooper — a man with a squat frame and a huge U-shaped smile and a nose that plunged down between the upright arms of the U. His smile parted his lips from one corner of his mouth to the other; it looked like a horseshoe turned upright for luck.

One night a soldier came hurrying to the grinning sergeant's group to say that the regiment was ordered forward.

On the following night Shank got himself settled comfortably in a front-line trench. After settling himself he took a walk down the trench to pay a call and to ask a question. He called on a second lieutenant whom he had known before and who had been given a command which included Sergeant Cooper. His question was, 'How's Sergeant Cooper?' 'Oh, he's fine,' replied the lieutenant, and Shank retired.

Regularly once a day for four days Shank made this inquiry, and at last on the fourth day the answer he sought was given him.

'I sent Cooper out this morning with a couple of men, to look around, and he didn't come back. They all got separated and Cooper's two men don't know what became of him.' Shank thanked the lieutenant and returned to his place.

He shed no tears for the good sergeant whose wheel had given so much pleasure to so many and so much profit to its owner and who somewhere in No Man's Land had encountered a run on the bank.

'I got back then quick to my post.' Shank went on, and he waited at his post until full darkness, then crawled over the parapet and began, on hands and knees, a search for Sergeant Cooper.

Now and then a star shell went up and caught the thin little man turning over a corpse with his hand for a better look at the face. Instantly he would crouch and be like the dead man himself, using the light, however, for a glance at the dead face, looking eagerly for that horseshoe smile.

Shank told Grimes that it was safer to be in No Man's Land than in a trench, if you knew the shell holes, for there was less shelling there and less sniping.

Sometimes Shank could tell by the smell of a body that it was not that of Sergeant Cooper, for Cooper had not been dead long. Sometimes Shank must have turned over one that still retained life enough to roll a comprehending eye; but he never said this. Perhaps he crept quickly away when this happened, disliking the suspicious glance of these men whose problem was suddenly so far removed from his and who were already cooling in the final chill. He would then have had to come back when such a man had died to make sure that none of them was Cooper. He continued with perseverance his squirming inspection of that dark rat-ridden graveyard for the unburied, returning in the gray of morning.

Thus the man worked to rob the dead. And when Gideon said this Shank turned upon him and said, dropping his 'H' as he seldom did: 'Well, 'oo are the dead?'

'It was the third night,' said Shank, 'I found him, and in the pocket of his tunic the money, mostly coins.'

Shank took the grinning sergeant's identification disk, his money, and his wrist watch and warily returned to the home trench. He was not one to believe fortune a friend because fortune had done him a favor. . . .

Shank's voice had stopped and the regular beat of the propeller upon the water now became noticeable. It rose, this sound, to take the place of Shank's voice, to fill in the interval as water runs into a depression, leveling it off. The small waves ran out from the wake, upon the surface of the ocean, as upon a hard surface; and the sound of them came regularly as upon a beach. The long, straight wake appeared to have been once a flowing substance, long since congealed, though retaining still the pattern of its boiling. It lay now behind the ship like a fault in the surface of a vast blue earth. Shank pulled a layer of skin-like red paint off the deck and made no further move to speak. The slow strong pulse of calm weather beat everywhere about them.

While Grimes fidgeted, Shank slept, and between the blue concentric spheres of sky and ocean, three white birds appeared, painted when they flew high a yellowed amber by the late afternoon light and reflecting the blue light from the ocean on their bellies when they flew low. The birds looked like tubby cigars with a stiff unjointed wing, shaped like a razor blade attached to each side of the center of the cigar. With wings as unmoving as if transfixed by the taxidermist's wire, these birds apparently freed from the laws of gravity rose and fell in the air. Going nowhere, seeking no food, they were only superficially appropriate, the touch of a landlubber's brush upon the afternoon marine.

The birds passed on ahead of the ship, outdistancing it as did the sun and the lazy waves. One bird before it disappeared, swept toward the boat and passed over it, casting thus a momentary shadow, like a mask, across Shank's eyes. With the passing of the shadow and the resuming of the glare of the sun upon his face, Shank opened his eyes and looked at once at Gideon. He started, feeling guilty at having been caught thus staring at Shank while he slept.

'I've been thinking the face of that girl was familiar, Shank. Just let me have another glance at the photo, will you?' Gideon repeated these words to himself trying to find the casual emphasis.

When at last he spoke the question aloud, Shank said, 'What girl?'

'I mean the photo of the trained nurse you showed me.'

'You don't know her,' said Shank, as if to close the conversation.

But Grimes persisted, 'Let me see it at any rate.'

'What the Jesus for?' mumbled Shank; but he unfolded his coat and reached into the inner pocket. Then at last he placed that beautiful victim in Gideon's hand.

Gideon looked but did not dare to gaze too long. Passing the photo back he said, 'What's her name?'

'She's Mary Slade,' said Shank.

Before Grimes slept that night he dared to ask Shank another question. 'Shank,' he said, 'where is she now, your friend Mary Slade?'

And at this Shank rose out of his bunk, and Grimes saw his head silhouetted against the portal which showed, a round gray hole in the surrounding darkness. 'Say,' said Shank, 'you're struck on that picture, ain't you?'

Grimes saw as he examined the silhouette from the shelter of his dark bunk that Shank was right; Gideon was struck on Mary Slade.

At last the silhouette vanished and Grimes saw the round port unbroken once more; the straw of Shank's mattress hissed dryly with the movement of his body and Shank's voice said: 'She's in Blackwell. A town in the east of England.' No more was said that night.

What had taken seed on the fourth day, on the fifth grew rankly, so that the position of Shank as tyrant keeper of the well was a thing established by night. This was natural since Shank and Grimes were day and night together, and had no occupation to keep them from continual consciousness of one another's thoughts; and since there could come no other woman's face to divert these two from the voluptuous contemplation of the face of Mary Slade.

Furthermore it was necessary for Shank not to displease Grimes too much, for at disembarkation comes another time when the stowaway must have a man to assist him. Someone must carry his duffle ashore, leaving him in hiding aboard until nightfall, when he can walk off unquestioned by the authorities on shore. Once ashore, he can look up his accomplice, get his baggage, and depart about his business. For this task Grimes was the ideal man. And the desire of Grimes's fingers to know exactly the temperature of the gray opalescent fine-textured skin on Mary Slade's throat was Shank's assurance.

On the sixth day of the voyage the *Iron City* passed in the late afternoon a ship headed back to England. The smokestack of this vessel was a rich weathered pink that shone out even at a great distance. The smoke from the vessel's funnel rose gently upward — for the wind was on her quarter — and then lay in a huge flimsy cloud above the ship. Thoughtful and brooding, as if with a distracted eye upon the ship, the cloud appeared like a mother who patiently slows her pace for the child that bustles by her hand. Other shreds of cloud, fatigued by their defeat at the hands of the sunny day, struggled down the sky and made a white background for the dark brooding smoke.

On one of the *Iron City's* tarpaulin-covered hatches a stoker sat; his face was pasty, his eyes were darkened about the lashes by coal dust imperfectly removed. He looked like a great actor wearied and resting after the playing of a tragic rôle. He crooned upon a harmonica softly to the receding day, and noiselessly dusk gathered in the zenith.

And Gideon, too, sat there on the hatch and watched the ship go slowly back to England. Shank sat beside him.

'That ship,' said Shank, 'will be steaming up the Mersey in a week, and if ye were aboard her ye'd be in Blackwell the same day.'

'I'll go back there, as soon as I get to America,' said Grimes. It was a threat, but Shank laughed. He laughed first silently with his lower jaw agape, like the swinging jaw of a steam shovel; then he laughed through his nose, noisily and with his mouth wide open and his stinking breath pouring out between his rotten teeth. Then he banged the tragic actor on the back and asked him did he hear that. The harmonica sputtered, uttered a discord, and then resumed exactly where it left off ... 'save the king.'

Then in the full early night, while Shank beside him dreamed not of the deadly thrust he made at him, Grimes swore to himself to visit Blackwell as soon as he could get back to England. Shank in silence enjoyed Grimes's despondent air. He did not know that

Gideon's oath made him like a man pushed from a cliff-top; as yet unharmed, he fell through space.

Shank felt a need to play upon Grimes's admiration for Mary and thus to assure himself of Gideon's protection. Every time that Grimes was permitted to see the picture of Mary, and this was really often though never without preliminary resistance, Shank accompanied the revelation of the beautiful face with a new tale of the woman's extraordinary humbleness. These relations, coming with the sight of the picture as they did, filled Grimes with envy and passion. This made Shank exaggerate. None the less, the succession of anecdotes as the days passed built a picture detailed and essentially truthful.

Mary's strength drew her to Shank's weakness. The more she battled for him and against him, the more she had at stake and the further she was from leaving him. She was like a mother persisting in her love for a vicious child.

During the war the poor women of Blackwell had been organized to do a share in the war work. They knitted and rolled bandages; and Mary, whose hands were quick, soon began to be noticed. A hospital was started in the neighborhood, and Mary's capabilities soon drew her out of her natural sphere and into another. Mary became a trained nurse.

As a nurse Mary was distinguished by her calm strength. She tended her patients placidly, disregarding their complaints, her mind fixed only on the signs of their recovery.

The war ended. Mary Slade returned to Blackwell; and when Shank returned also, all her natural affection and all her newly acquired gift for watching over the unreasonable flowed out upon him. In this nerve-racking atmosphere of endless patience Shank soon grew restless again.

There was still one other chapter in the six-day epic of Shank's leechdom. It was apparently almost a final scene in that part of

Shank's life which preceded his brief acquaintance with Grimes. The effect of its telling upon Gideon's mind was subtle and final. It grew into his mind during the next day of the voyage like roots into soft earth, laying a fine fatal tendril on every particle. For it showed to Grimes how the fear of dying hung over Shank, excluding consideration for the world. It made Grimes feel strong — he seemed to hold a weapon built and weighted to his hand. . . .

During the summer following the peace Shank was finally mustered out of France and crossed the Channel on his way to Blackwell. He found among the troops that accompanied him another man who was also going to Blackwell. With this man Shank made friends. They had drunk many drinks together by the time, Blackwell was reached, and Shank had shown his friend the picture of Mary. Meanwhile Shank had thought of a joke with which to celebrate his homecoming.

'Go to her house and tell her I'm dead,' said Shank.

Shank's friend, a handsome man, impressed by Mary's beauty and feeling that the embrace of a handsome man is often a quick road away from grief for the death of a runt, consented — already feeling the soft skin of Mary on his lips.

The handsome man went to the house where Mary lived and spoke his piece, and Mary wept at the news and screamed under his kisses and he fled.

Such was Shank's joke — and Shank waited at a near-by saloon to hear the outcome. His friend, of course, never bothered to report, and Shank after waiting and drinking set out for Mary's house himself. The woman who came to the door in answer to Shank's ring said that Mary had left the house. Shank knew Blackwell and knew where she would have gone. Shank was pretty drunk but he kept walking. Just outside of the town the road crossed a brook, and at its crossing there was a break in the hedge that bordered the road and a footway ran through it along the side of the brook. The path ended where the brook crossed another road a mile further along its course. Here Shank and Mary had walked in the early days of Shank's courting.

Unsteadily then Shank walked down this path in search of his beautiful Mary. He found her remembering in torture the kisses of the handsome man, and wondering in yet greater pain if the terrible story he had told her was true.

Shank's snuffling laugh announced to Mary his return from death, for the sight of Mary's grief was funny to him. Shaken with laughter he half fell, half willingly sat down in the coarse strong-growing grass at the brook's edge. Mary seeing him ran to him, crouched beside him pressing her wet face upon his in joy. Shank laughed on, and between drunken giggles explained his joke. Mary was not a woman to spank a long-lost child because he had run away. She was glad of Shank's return and went on kissing him. Under her kisses his gloating suddenly turned from mirth to heat.

The soft upper edge of Mary's breast might just have showed at the pointed neck of her dress — so Grimes thought where its smooth arch sprang from her chest. It might have looked in the half light of the long twilight a gray cream color — soft and giving way elusively under the touch as if the skin actually floated upon a smooth rich liquid.

Shank's breath smelling of stale beer warmed Mary's neck; perhaps she saw in his face more human emotion than she had seen for many years. Thus the picture was before Grimes's eyes when Shank paused to grab the shoulder of the intent listener, startling him so that he shivered. 'Wot 'appened then? 'ere's wot 'appened — a goddam rabbit, his guts a-swim with fear, scrambled clean over the two of us' — as intent upon its separate terror as Shank upon the soft throat of Mary. But here something had laid hold of Mary. Suddenly the smell of decaying vegetation in the brook bed, the reasonless cancerous profusion of growth all about her, smothered for a moment the intentness of her love of Shank. She stopped him in mid-caress.

While he paused, the rabbit, still near, began to scream; the enemy that had invisibly pursued had now caught up. The rabbit gave forth a series of cries each less strong, a significant diminuendo, without emotion, a purely mechanical announcement that that which was alive understood that it was losing in agony all the world of created things. The mad desire to go on living, the great condition of all life, was in the presence of Mary and Shank undergoing the final chastening which it was born to meet, the ultimate agony which dwarfs all joy. Shank felt Mary's body stiffen and relax as if the outcry were her own, and Shank's hand, like a scaled lizard, withdrew cringing from that dim and oddly cool chamber between Mary's breasts where it had crept.

Between that time and the time of his seeking out the *Iron City*, Shank did not again make love to Mary Slade. Death had waggled a finger at him. He was impressed by his bad luck. Perhaps he had hoped the *Iron City* would wall it out, but it had walled it in. Grimes, too, feared it and felt himself shaken by a strange anticipatory tremble, like a bride before her lover, but the embrace that now encircled him was sinister and invisible.

'Does Mary know why you have gone or where?' asked Grimes.

'I'll write,' said Shank, 'when I'm well ready.'

There were two things only which served to make one day different from the next aboard the *Iron City*. The weather and the photograph of Mary Slade. The rotation of stew and hash was as monotonous and as inevitable as the turn of the ship's propeller. The rotation of distant officers upon the bridge was the same. One had a beard, one had a mustache, one was clean-shaven. These faces appeared against the sky in a succession as imperturbable as the alternation of sun and moon against the same sky, and the faces seemed, if anything, more distant. Sun and moon and officers and hash all moved like figures on an elaborate clock to the rhythmic, melodious, distant sound of the ship's bells.

But the weather and the photograph were full of change. They maintained an interrelationship of mood, an irrelevant coquettishness. They smiled, then sneered; they played tricks with time, they spun the moon in its orbit at will; they rang the ship's bells and toyed with the succession of beards and mustaches. Gideon was bound by their spell day and night. He was alone with the *Iron City* surrounded by hallucinations; he sailed in an empty sea.

By the eighth day Mary was flesh and blood for Grimes and he had set up about her picture all those fetishes of love that men set up about the moods of real women.

It was a cruel tyranny. He tried to think of a way by which he might break it. In the first place he might steal the photograph. When Shank discovered its absence, he would become infuriated — for he would thus lose a hostage for his security, and the implement with which, in this dull interval, he tortured Grimes. He would realize just where his picture had gone and Grimes would not dare sleep in a room with a man thus enraged who was moreover in possession of a bag of murderous tackler's tools — mechanic's hammers nicely weighted, punches, and the like. If he dared not sleep with Shank after the theft, so Grimes reasoned, he should have to get rid of him, and this he might do by hastily informing the ship's officers of the presence of a stowaway aboard the ship. This scheme would leave Grimes quit of Shank and in possession of the photograph.

In the darkness of the eighth night — stimulated by the wheezing of the unconscious Shank — Grimes plotted on. A stowaway is put in the brig and he goes back with the ship to his native port. Shank would go back to England and very likely, after a short jail term, back to Mary. Grimes, without money, having to work his passage back, could hardly get there before Shank. It would not do to expose Shank.

Here the sleeping Shank paused in his wheezing to moisten his lips, and for Gideon from this thought there arose another anxiety. Suppose Shank were to lose the photograph? He would be quite as sure that Grimes had taken it, as if he really had, and Grimes would be in the same danger of violence.

On the ninth day of the voyage a new piece of information was thrust at Gideon. The finger of God appeared and pointed to it.

Early in the ninth night Shank and Grimes stood on the fo'c'sle-head. The wind was behind the ship so that it was comfortable to be in the bow. Two figures moved silently on the bridge. A third man was tinkering with the searchlight on the bridge; it went on and off at rare intervals; a lantern was near him to light his work.

There were only two topics of conversation between Grimes and Shank now. There was the problem of getting Shank ashore, and there was Mary Slade.

'Mary's a fine big woman,' said Shank. He drew out his wallet. 'If the searchlight comes on again ye might have a look.' Grimes tried in the half darkness to prepare his eyes to take advantage of every moment of light by filling them in advance with the image of the photograph so that no time should be wasted in recognition of details already sufficiently impressed on his mental eye. Thus his eye was fixed upon Shank's hands that held his wallet and the photograph. Many moments passed but the light was not turned on. After a while it went on and shone out over the water, throwing only a reflected grayness upon the photograph.

Shank and Grimes waited, but at last Shank grew tired and began to put it back in its place. As he was doing this and while Gideon's eyes still stared at his hands, a rod of light leapt into the air. It did not progress from the searchlight and illuminate Shank's hands. It was dropped into place whole; one end rested in the socket of the searchlight on the bridge, the other rested on the wallet in Shank's hands and slipped a tributary beam into every crevice and pocket in it. The finger of light pointed into the long pocket at the back of the wallet. There, deep in the bowels of the greasy wallet, ephemeral, perishable, Grimes perceived two notes of the Bank of England. The bar of light vanished, not sucked in like a lizard's tongue, but lifted out of place whole and instantaneously, and put down somewhere else out of sight. Grimes had not fixed his anxious gaze upon Mary's face, but what had he seen?

In the darkness that follows blinding light and that slowly returns again to the normal gray like blood returning to a frightened face, Grimes saw that Shank's eyes were fixed upon his and that they asked him that same question.

Grimes had not envisaged the winnings of Sergeant Cooper in the form of two bank notes in Shank's pocket. He had supposed the money hidden or in a bank. Now it appeared to be within reach of his hand. That money, could he procure it, would see him back to England at once.

After an interval Shank went below but Grimes remained where he was. Smoke, black and angry, was pushed out of the funnel and blown forward above him, darkening the night. The many sounds of the traveling ship made in his ear a monotonous whisper, a woven harlequin pattern of sound unheard. An ocean of jet a-sparkle with gray highlights stood before his eyes unseen. Eyes and ears turned inwards and fixed themselves upon one thought. When Grimes took the photograph from Shank, he must also take the money.

He saw himself upon the bridge telling the two men about the stowaway. He saw an officer asking him why he had not reported this sooner; he heard Shank's voice saying that he had only done it now because he had taken Shank's money; Grimes saw himself locked with Shank below decks. While Shank had a voice, a memory, while Shank was on the ship, Grimes would not be safe.

Then, upon that instant, Shank must have no voice, no memory; he must leave the ship.

From every angle both in space and in time, Gideon saw a long line of circumstances converging with a fitness born of fatality upon the deed of murder. No one knew that Shank was aboard the *Iron City*. A day or so before the vessel's arrival in harbor it was necessary that Shank disappear so that when the final roundup came he would be well hidden, waiting for evening to enable him to slip off the ship unseen. When Shank was no longer on the ship, Grimes would only have to say to his companions, who knew Shank was a stowaway, that Shank had begun his term of hiding. Grimes then would walk off the vessel when it made port with Shank's duffle as already arranged, and who was to know that Shank, who had been last seen in Blackwell, had met death upon the Grand Banks of Newfoundland?

The heavy bag of tools, the mechanic's hammer, now seemed to Gideon as providential as the revelation of the money and the chance of having come to know the photograph.

With this thought of violence tightening its unfamiliar grip upon him, Gideon waited upon the bow beneath the heavy train of smoke that went into the west. Its mass concealed him, its hot breath warmed him. He wanted to go beneath it, toward the shore. He felt that the smoke would guide him, and conceal him from the stars. He saw himself upon a bicycle outdistancing the ship, riding upon the sea with Shank already done to death in stealth.

He climbed down the iron stairway to the castle deck. At the foot of it was the doorway to that four-bunk cabin which Shank and he had so successfully held against their companions. The round brass ring that was a doorknob stared at him as soon as he had stepped off the last step; he laid hand upon it; he stepped over the high sill and closed the door behind him. Into the deeper blackness of the cabin the grayer light of the open night flowed from the portal over Shank's bunk and lit with a faint austere light the head that Gideon hoped to crush, forty-eight hours hence; the eyes, their uneven flicker of deceit now vanished, moved idly beneath their lids. The faithful, forward motion of the ship gave peace. Shank's face wore the composed yet faintly drawn expression of a death mask. Below the gray, calm sharpened face Gideon saw, as his eyes became accustomed to yet deeper shades of night, protruding from the bunk beneath Shank's, the handle of his mechanic's hammer.

Grimes undressed silently so as not to wake Shank. He climbed into his bunk. He did not sleep. Hour upon hour his muscles twitched with the effort of wielding that hammer. He caught it with both hands and swung it above his head, but found he had swung it too freely and the metal girder above Shank's bunk rang where the blow fell. He realized that he could not strike as he would drive a spike with a sledge. He struck again, with a more circumspect swing; the blow fell strong upon the face of Shank, but the high side of the bunk was struck by the handle of his weapon at the same time that its head struck the sleeping face, the force of the blow was broken, it was not fatal, it did not even stun. Gideon wiped the slate clean again, and the next time he stood upon the lower bunk giving himself thus height from which to strike. His stroke this time was very cramped but the hammer was heavy, it shattered the skull like cardboard. It caught inside the hole it had made and could not easily be withdrawn. Gideon did not have the remotest idea how much force a skull would resist nor did he know how it would resist. Was it like a hen's egg, he wondered, or like a turtle's egg? A last time he rehearsed the blow, and this time he used the flat of the hammer and was successful. Would there be blood, he wondered? Was it a sure way to kill a man?

The ship traveled methodically on. It carried Shank and Gideon; and it carried all about Gideon a thousand other Shanks all variously mutilated and resisting his hammer. The room was crowded with their forms, they overlapped. There was one form with many heads; not one was whole. Gideon suffered the tortures of one who repents a crime. Yet he had not as yet committed any crime and certainly did not regret it. In the light of morning he resolved against the business and then slept.

Grimes opened his eyes, puffed with short hours of stuffy sleep. He knew at once that his life had become an unpleasant business. He looked forward to the day with dread and to all days. He sought in his mind for the reason and found at once the feeling of the murder of Shank, hastily following down the thoughts of the passed day, to overtake the present, he found his mind too slow for his anxiety. He rose out of his bed and hastily and fearfully looked into Shank's bunk. Shank lay there asleep. Grimes was at once overjoyed and disappointed: the situation was unchanged. He had nothing to fear today that he did not have to fear yesterday; he had no new hope today. Then in the same moment he remembered the outcome of the night's deliberations — he had decided not to kill Shank. He was free.

From the breakfast of sluggish gruel, stiffened bread, dusty butter, brightened only by the sunny light of marmalade, the untouchables on the tenth day arose and went on deck. The sun drew them up as it drew the light mists that lay here and there upon the ocean, like clouds dozing.

Grimes chose the forward end of the ship. He paced back and forth on the windward side of the deck and slowly he felt purged of the night. For this tenth day was lively. In its light all things moved lightly, briskly — waves, clouds, sun, and ship. The officer on the bridge moved quickly. He minced as if he walked a treadmill which supplied the power for the sprightly motion of the world around him. There in the ship's bow, Shank found Grimes, and crept away again frightened by his fierce silence.

Grimes stood staring at the flat sea as it came toward the ship.

The boat was stationary, only the sea moved. Someone behind drew the huge flat sheet of water toward the vessel. The sheet was torn asunder in its exact center by the bow of the stationary boat. The material parted with a faint hiss. The dark scar of those parted edges showed behind the ship as far as the eye could see. Grimes watched the roll come toward him from the west. The lunch hour came and passed, he did not go below. The sea grew flatter. The cloth ran from the bolt smoothly and still more smoothly. The sun leapt with one exuberant bound into the zenith and through the bright morning. There it stood as still as if Grimes were a Joshua, and while it stood there and while the sea grew calm it waned, it paled. It was like a last ember in the grate at which you warm your hands. It died in mid-leap, and before the day had reached maturity it had dwindled into a premature and waxen twilight.

Then at last as the day fainted and night stood close — Grimes perceived the end of the bolt on which the smooth ocean was wound, the loom from which it came. For all about there now appeared wisps of mist, string-like shreds of vapor rising from the taut silken surface. And while Grimes watched, the ship was swallowed in the machinery of the loom. It plunged into a wall of fog.

Grimes now found himself in a new, cramped world, a world hardly bigger than the ship itself, and far from other worlds. Heralding this accomplished passage out of the world that Grimes knew, came an enormous sound. It filled the fog-bound sphere in which the ship was cased. This sound flowed alike between the particles of air and the particles of Gideon's body. It was as loud in his stomach as in the air above his head. It drew his knees toward his chin in a convulsion of fear. Upon the bridge the officer with a mustache had drawn down the wire that ran up the fog horn upon the funnel. Summoned by that trumpet of doom, Gideon went to his cabin scarce knowing whether he was judge or judged and fearing to be either.

He was too late for supper. He could only crawl shivering between his blankets; and his belly made savage with hunger paced within him like a caged cat, and at two-minute intervals throughout the night his whole body was dissolved in sound.

At every blast throughout the unrelenting night, Gideon's eyes leapt open. Morning came again, the eleventh morning, and as the sun rose higher the fog withdrew, not altogether but to a good distance — a besieging army which takes counsel after an unexpected rebuff. The fog horn ceased its braying — the wind had not risen since it had dropped twenty hours before. There was no sound of waves rebounding from iron flanks, no grunting of strained bolts; the ship moved stealthily. Relieved from the tension produced by the blasts of the horn which seemed to demand an accounting of him, Gideon fell asleep.

The morning passed. After lunch, feeling more cheerful, Grimes returned on deck with Shank. The sun was losing its strength, the boat still skated upon a stricken sea. Then the sun vanished altogether and the world, bounded by fog, shrank. With this new contraction of the cage surrounding Grimes and Shank, announcing their approach to a fog-bound Newfoundland, announcing the beginning of the end of the voyage, the separation of Grimes from Shank and consequently the separation of Grimes from the picture of Mary, came a scream from the fog horn, and Grimes jumped the more because this time he saw the sound was coming, but could not tune his ears to its loudness. He winced before it as if it were a cry for help that called him into danger. In two minutes the scream came again and yet again, the fog came closer and the afternoon crept on, two minutes at a time.

A half hour later there came out of the fog another sign of the approaching end of the voyage. Four gulls signifying anew the nearness of land appeared in the ship's wake. Two of the birds cackled malevolently, one wailed melodiously and pityingly, and one made a sound that was like the voice of a woman. This voice,

low, smooth and rich, was raised in speech, but before it had time
to articulate it halted as if embarrassed by emotion. Unmoved,
however, by threat or tears the ship slid slowly forward and the
afternoon drew to a close.

After supper with the world about the *Iron City* even more
constricted by darkness, that arrived to re-enforce the fog,
Grimes went to the wheelhouse. Here also came Shank. They
leaned upon the ship's rail together. The voices of the gulls spoke
to them of the end of the strange voyage watched over by the
beauty of Mary Slade. 'Shank,' said Grimes, finally, 'let's have
a look at Mary before it's too dark.'

Shank reached into his inner pocket and brought out his wallet.
He held it in his hand. Grimes waited and under the pressure of
Shank's delay he added another plea. 'Give me the picture,' he
said. 'You'll never give happiness more easily.'

'I can give it easier to Mary,' said Shank, but he drew from the
wallet the picture — he was about to do as Grimes asked.

Holding the small white square between his hands, his elbows
on the rail, and hands above the wake of the ship, his deliberations produced the effect of a pause. During this pause, while
Grimes was putting forth a hand to receive from Shank the photograph, Shank let slip the picture of Mary just before Gideon's
fingers could close upon it. While the face of Mary was still
visible to Gideon, the falling photograph was far beyond his
reach, as irrevocably removed as are the living from the dead.
Mary was gone.

With her went Grimes's tolerance of Shank. He began to get
angry. Shank laughed at the accident. He, in that moment,
reached the peak of his power over Grimes. Had some breath of
wind played the final trick that Shank dared not play, yet now
he could laugh and appear as if he had permitted the accident.

Grimes was helpless. 'God damn you, Shank,' he said. 'You

bastard.' He sought for some supreme blasphemy, there was none; only the daily oaths came to his tongue.

Shank savored the impotent insults, they rolled down his scraggy throat as easily as they shot up from Grimes's. Grimes rattled the loose ship's rail in his hand. He stamped his foot. Then suddenly a great feeling of freedom rolled over him; there was now no reason to preserve the forms of friendship with Shank. He had tolerated Shank's nauseous personality in order that he might be permitted to look at the picture of Mary. What reason was there for Grimes to control his dislike now? And Shank's laughs were echoed by Grimes's own. Shank stopped in surprise. Grimes, watching, grew cold and deliberate.

'You think you've got Mary, Shank,' he said. 'Why do you think I've asked questions about her? Why do I know her address and where she works: because I'm going back to Blackwell and get her. I'm going to have her now, not you. What's more, you're going to be damn polite the rest of this voyage or I'll tell an officer you're a stowaway and you'll be starved below decks handcuffed so you can't brush off the rats. Damn you, Shank.'

Shank might have tried to hit Gideon then; but Grimes turned and left him.

The fog horn split the silence. Its two-minute interval had just bracketed the scene. It hurried Gideon on his way.

The fog about the ship shut out sound and sight and air and held in the demon who yelled in the cabin. Grimes slept; awoke and perceived that not yet had Shank come to bed. Why in hell was he up so late? Was he out behind the wheelhouse, terrified by threats and wondering how he could escape exposure?

One more night and the *Iron City* would raise Highland Light; the fog horn bellowed, there might be fishing schooners near.

What was Shank thinking? Gideon asked himself. Then he saw. 'Where's my Buddy, did ye ask?' Shank would say to the fo'c'sle cook; "e's going to hide out this last day. Let me get his landing card. The officers don't know one of us for another. I'll get ashore, then he'll have his passport, says he can manage all right.' It wasn't a very good idea, but who would think about it, and where would Gideon be? Gideon asked in the dark cabin and Gideon answered. He would be overboard with the hammer thrown after, gone the way he had thought of sending Shank. Shank would have his papers, passport and all. It was simple; that was what Shank was thinking. He, who had crawled about in the cold blood of dead men, would not fumble the doing. He simply waited for Gideon to go to sleep. 'I must not sleep,' thought Gideon.

He turned on the light to help him stay awake. He lay and blinked at the dull light. Now the blaring fog horn became a lullaby. When it blew, its loudness suspended the action of Gideon's senses and held his eyes closed. They flew open again as soon as the sound ceased to tell him if Shank had come into the room. There was a perceptible time between the moment at which Gideon's eyes flew open and the succeeding temporary allaying of his fears. During this moment he could visualize the form of Shank, head and shoulders leaning over his bunk, hammer poised flat side toward his head. Feverishly Gideon's brain would hasten to compare this anticipated image with what his eyes actually saw. When he found that they did not coincide, his terror was allayed for two minutes more, but when his eyes closed again the hammer rose as before and his scalp crawled upon his skull, awaiting the shock. He rubbed the place.

Then he dozed and dreamed.

He dreamed that he opened his eyes, that he hastened to compare as always the two images, the one that he feared with the one that he actually beheld, and that he found to his utter terror that they exactly coincided. This time with certainty and in spite of the fact that his eyes were surely open he still beheld the thin wrist, the bony hand with fingers whitened by the strength of the grip upon the handle of the heavy hammer. He tried to grab the wrist, to shout. He writhed in his bunk in a death agony and then he overcame the force that held shut his eyes. The deafening horn which held him asleep suddenly ceased, his eyelids flew up; and waking he beheld neither the familiar sight of the iron girder above his bunk or the anticipated grim face and upraised hammer. He beheld nothing. The room was dark. The light had been turned out.

Was Shank there above him? He did not know. He rose up. He could see only the round port, dimly gray. He got out of his bunk and he reached into the bunk below Shank's to see if the hammer were there. He felt the handle; why had he not thought to possess himself of it before? Next, he stood upon the edge of the lower bunk and looked into Shank's bunk to see if he were there. He was there, and in the faint light from the port his eyes showed dark in the lighter tone of his face. They were open. He must be seeing Gideon leaning over him with the hammer in his hand. He would kill Gideon. Gideon must strike while sleep still stifled his mind, if not his sight. Gideon brought down the hammer flat side foremost, swinging short from his elbow to avoid the girder: Shank tried to shout; sleep still held him for one split instant more. The flat side of the hammer struck the head. It was not like a hen's egg; it was not like a turtle's egg; it was like an apple inside a sock.

The fog horn blew again. It was two minutes since Gideon had got out of his bunk.

Gideon shuddered and — rolled in his blankets. Shank too shuddered, as if the idea of death were repugnant to him. Gideon did not dare to touch Shank's heart to see if he were dead; instead he put his heavy blanket over Shank's head so that if he should not be dead and should groan the sound would be muffled. Then Gideon dressed, and went to the galley.

This part was simple and Gideon was quick, for he had thought it out before. In the galley was a sackful of potato peelings and the galley was empty. Gideon took the sack to his cabin quickly lest Shank should be alive. Shank had not moved. He emptied the sack on the floor of the cabin.

Then he climbed laboriously into the top bunk and straddling the warm form of Shank which, for all he knew, might still be alive, he shudderingly pulled the blanket from Shank's head and all in one motion hurled it to the floor among the potato peelings. The head was still and Gideon saw that it was queerly shaped. He pulled the bag hastily over it, then down to the waist of the limp little man.

In the end, after lifting the whole unwieldy burden to the floor, he was able to shake the whole of the man, Shank, in an inverted squat down into the bag. He tried not to jounce the crushed head too hard upon the floor in doing this. Once he waited for the blare of the fog horn to conceal the sound of his operation. When the little man was in the bag, Gideon shoved his tool kit in after him, tying it to one ankle. He got the burden onto his shoulder by resting it on an upper bunk, paused, adjusting the weight, and it seemed to him that the pulse of the ship's engine went slower. The world became still more quiet; between the blasts of the fog horn there was no sound in the world but the expiring distant beat of the ship's engine.

Gideon opened the door of the cabin and peered out as well as he could with that awkward hundred-odd pounds upon his shoulder. He saw no one, once out of his room he was all right or almost. He might have been working late for the cook and now be carrying the week's collection of potato peels to the door in the ship's side to throw it out. He staggered out upon the darkened underdeck.

The concrete floor was slippery with dampness of the fog. Bent as Shank had been bent that first day in Liverpool when he came down the dock with his duffle bag, Gideon walked uncertainly aft.

Before he had taken two steps the dying rhythm of the ship's engine ceased altogether. Silence fell upon the world. Gideon, too, felt forced to stop, his bundle settled upon his shoulder as if making itself comfortable. Now creeping up behind Gideon came that deadly brazen shout. The bridge again! Gideon started aft in the dead ship with a dead burden nestling to him and there came to him now a faint answering bellow, as if spectators were assembling for the burial of Shank at sea.

Gideon came to the door in the side of the ship. The whole un-rippling ocean waited to hear the sound of Shank's plunge. He lowered the bag to the deck and waited for the salute from the bridge which would conceal the sound of the splash. In the slug-gish sea the ship was losing way. Across the water came the answering bleat. He knew that the call of the *Iron City* would follow soon. He got ready. 'Get set,' it said to him and GO cried the signal from the bridge.

Forward and outward fell the bag. Gideon leaned over and grasped the two lower corners and whipped back his body. That shrivelled parasite, Grimes's strange companion, Shank, fell free of the bag, unsheltered by any shroud, into the ocean which quiv-ered now beneath the *Iron City's* brazen blast. As Shank struck the water it seemed to Gideon to fall away beneath, forming momentarily a smooth bowl-like cradle for the huddled form, a cradle festooned about its edges with a pale fire of phosphores-cence. Then the water grew calm above the spot where Shank had fallen. He sank slowly, dragged down by the feet to which Gideon had tied the kit of tools. The face looked up and Gideon could see it; for phosphorescent bubbles issued from the nose and mouth and escaped from the hair and drew in livid light the out-line of a bodiless, eyeless face.

While Gideon looked down thus and Shank looked up there came, winding like a garter snake through tall grass, a gigantic serpent of light, a curious fish which left behind it a trail of phosphorescence and was drawn by this sudden commotion in the sea. For one final instant the upturned face seemed like the head of this serpentine body, like the fabulous serpent of the garden of Eden human-headed; then all was lost in a knot of fiery coils which fell shining into a hell of velvet in the shadow of the ship.

Gideon straightened his aching back and turned about. Little Shank was gone like big Australia, a cockroach in a mug of beer.

In the end it was light. Grimes got himself on deck. He rose, still stupid with the shock of murder, out of the darkness and stench of the ship, out of the cabin where the smell of Shank's living body still hung, into the opalescent misty morning. The fog had retreated somewhat and the fog horn no longer blew. He went to the rail and looked upon the sea. No wind stirred it; yet everywhere there was life. As far as he could see, spread out at geometrically even intervals like fleur-de-lis on a wallpaper, there were small black and white birds. They could not rise off the water because the day was still. They rested each in its appointed place upon the endless pewter plane and waited for the wind. As the ship moved upon this strange sea, the birds became frightened by its approach and flapped their short strong wings vainly. Around each bird then ripples arose widening evenly, slowly, until the graceful circles became tangent to one another. The *Iron City* lay upon a sheet of ancient silver chased with an inscrutable design.

CHRIST IN CONCRETE[1]

PIETRO DI DONATO

$\mathbf{M}$ARCH whistled stinging snow against the brick walls and up the gaunt girders. Geremio, the foreman, swung his arms about, and gaffed the men on.

Old Nick, the 'Lean,' stood up from over a dust-flying brick pile, and tapped the side of his nose.

'Master Geremio, the devil himself could not break his tail any harder than we here.'

Burly Vincenzo of the walrus moustache, and known as the 'Snoutnose,' let fall the chute door of the concrete hopper and sang over in the Lean's direction: 'Mari-Annina's belly and the burning night will make of me once more a milk-mouthed strippling lad . . .'

The Lean loaded his wheelbarrow and spat furiously. 'Sons of two-legged dogs . . . despised of even the devil himself! Work! Sure! For America beautiful will eat you and spit your bones into the earth's hole! Work!' And with that his wiry frame pitched the barrow violently over the rough floor.

Snoutnose waved his head to and fro and with mock pathos wailed, 'Sing on, oh guitar of mine . . .'

Short, cherry-faced Joe Chiappa, the scaffoldman, paused with hatchet in hand and tenpenny spike sticking out from small dice-like teeth to tell the Lean as he went by, in a voice that all could hear, 'Ah, father of countless chicks, the old age is a carrion!'

Geremio chuckled and called to him: 'Hey, little Joe, who are you to talk? You and big-titted Cola can't even hatch an egg, whereas the Lean has just to turn the doorknob of his bedroom and old Philomena becomes a balloon!'

Coarse throats tickled and mouths opened wide in laughter.

Mike, the 'Barrel-mouth,' pretended he was talking to himself and yelled out in his best English ... he was always speaking English while the rest carried on in their native Italian: 'I don't know myself, but somebodys whose gotta bigga buncha keeds and he alla times talka from somebodys elsa!'

Geremio knew it was meant for him and he laughed. 'On the tomb of Saint Pimplelegs, this little boy my wife is giving me next week shall be the last! Eight hungry little Christians to feed is enough for any man.'

Joe Chiappa nodded to the rest. 'Sure, Master Geremio had a telephone call from the next bambino. Yes, it told him it had a little bell there instead of a rosebush ... It even told him its name!'

'Laugh, laugh all of you,' returned Geremio, 'but I tell you that all my kids must be boys so that they some day will be big American builders. And then I'll help them to put the gold away in the basements for safe keeping!'

A great din of riveting shattered the talk among the fast-moving men. Geremio added a handful of 'Honest' tobacco to his corncob, puffed strongly, and cupped his hands around the bowl for a bit of warmth. The chill day caused him to shiver, and he thought to himself, 'Yes, the day is cold, cold ... but who am I to complain when the good Christ himself was crucified?

'Pushing the job is all right (when has it been otherwise in my life?) but this job frightens me. I feel the building wants to tell me something; just as one Christian to another. I don't like this. Mr. Murdin tells me, "Push it up!" That's all he knows. I keep telling him that the underpinning should be doubled and the old material removed from the floors, but he keeps the inspector drunk and... "Hey, Ashes-ass! Get away from under that pilaster! Don't pull the old work. Push it away from you or you'll have a nice present for Easter if the wall falls on you!" ... Well, with the help of God I'll see this job through. It's not my first, nor the... "Hey, Patsy number two! Put more cement in that concrete; we're putting up a building, not an Easter cake!"'

Patsy hurled his shovel to the floor and gesticulated madly. 'The padrone Murdin-sa tells me, "Too much, too much! Lil' bit is plenty!" And you tell me I'm stingy! The rotten building can fall after I leave!'

Six floors below, the contractor called: 'Hey Geremio! Is your gang of dagos dead?'

Geremio cautioned to the men: 'On your toes, boys. If he writes out slips, someone won't have big eels on the Easter table.'

The Lean cursed that 'the padrone could take the job and shove it...!'

Curly-headed Sandino, the roguish, pigeon-toed scaffoldman, spat a clod of tobacco-juice and hummed to his own music.

'Yes, certainly yes to your face, master padrone... and behind, this to you and all your kind!'

The day, like all days, came to an end. Calloused and bruised bodies sighed, and numb legs shuffled towards shabby railroad flats....

'Ah, *bella casa mio*. Where my little freshets of blood, and my good woman await me. Home where my broken back will not ache so. Home where midst the monkey chatter of my piccolinos I will float off to blessed slumber with my feet on the chair and the head on the wife's soft full breast.'

These great child-hearted ones leave each other without words or ceremony, and as they ride and walk home, a great pride swells the breast....

'Blessings to Thee, oh Jesus. I have fought winds and cold. Hand to hand I have locked dumb stones in place and the great building rises. I have earned a bit of bread for me and mine.'

The mad day's brutal conflict is forgiven, and strained limbs prostrate themselves so that swollen veins can send the yearning blood coursing and pulsating deliciously as though the body mountained leaping streams.

The job alone remained behind... and yet, they too, having left the bigger part of their lives with it. The cold ghastly beast, the Job, stood stark, the eerie March wind wrapping it in sharp shadows of falling dusk.

That night was a crowning point in the life of Geremio. He bought a house! Twenty years he had helped to mould the New World. And now he was to have a house of his own! What mattered that it was no more than a wooden shack? It was his own!

He had proudly signed his name and helped Annunziata to make her **X** on the wonderful contract that proved them owners. And she was happy to think that her next child, soon to come, would be born under their own rooftree. She heard the church chimes, and cried to the children: 'Children, to bed! It is near midnight. And remember, shut-mouth to the *paesanos*! Or they will send the evil eye to our new home even before we put foot.'

The children scampered off to the icy yellow bedroom where three slept in one bed and three in the other. Coltishly and friskily they kicked about under the covers; their black iron-cotton stockings not removed... what! and freeze the peanut-little toes?

Said Annunziata, 'The children are so happy, Geremio; let them be, for even I would a Tarantella dance.' And with that she turned blushing. He wanted to take her on her word. She patted his hands, kissed them, and whispered, 'Our children will dance for us ... in the American style some day.'

Geremio cleared his throat and wanted to sing. 'Yes, with joy I could sing in a richer feeling than the great Caruso.' He babbled little old country couplets and circled the room until the tenant below tapped the ceiling.

Annunziata whispered: 'Geremio, to bed and rest. Tomorrow is a day for great things ... and the day on which our Lord died for us.'

The children were now hard asleep. Heads under the cover, over ... moist noses whistling, and little damp legs entwined.

In bed Geremio and Annunziata clung closely to each other. They mumbled figures and dates until fatigue stilled their thoughts. And with chubby Johnnie clutching fast his bottle and warmed between them ... life breathed heavily, and dreams entertained in far, far worlds, the nation-builder's brood.

But Geremio and Annunziata remained for a while staring into darkness, silently.

'Geremio?'

'Yes?'

'This job you are now working. . . .'

'So?'

'You used always to tell me about what happened on the jobs ... who was jealous, and who praised. . . .'

'You should know by now that all work is the same. . . .'

'Geremio. The month you have been on this job, you have not spoken a word about the work ... And I have felt that I am walking in a dream. Is the work dangerous? Why don't you answer . . . ?'

Job loomed up damp, shivery grey. Its giant members waiting. Builders quietly donned their coarse robes, and waited.

Geremio's whistle rolled back into his pocket and the symphony of struggle began.

Trowel rang through brick and slashed mortar rivets were machine-gunned fast with angry grind Patsy number one check Patsy number two check the Lean three check Vincenzo four steel bellowed back at hammer donkey engines coughed purple Ashesass Pietro fifteen chisel point intoned stone thin steel whirred and wailed through wood liquid stone flowed with dull rasp through iron veins and hoist screamed through space Carmine the Fat twenty-four and Giacomo Sangini check ... The multitudinous voices of a civilization rose from the surroundings and welded with the efforts of the Job.

To the intent ear, Nation was voicing her growing pains, but, hands that create are attached to warm hearts and not to calculating minds. The Lean as he fought his burden on looked forward to only one goal, the end. The barrow he pushed, he did not love. The stones that brutalized his palms, he did not love. The great God Job, he did not love. He felt a searing bitterness and a fathomless consternation at the queer consciousness that inflicted the ever mounting weight of structure that he HAD TO! HAD TO! raise above his shoulders! When, when and where would the last stone be? Never ... did he bear his toil with the rhythm of song! Never ... did his gasping heart knead the heavy mortar with lilting melody! A voice within him spoke in wordless language.

The language of worn oppression and the despair of realizing that his life had been left on brick piles. And always, there had been hunger and her bastard, the fear of hunger.

Murdin bore down upon Geremio from behind and shouted:

'Goddamnit, Geremio, if you're givin' the men two hours off today with pay, why the hell are they draggin' their tails? And why don't you turn that skinny old Nick loose, and put a young wop in his place?'

'Now, listen-a to me, Mister Murdin ——'

'Don't give me that! And bear in mind that there are plenty of good barefoot men in the streets who'll jump for a day's pay!'

'Padrone — padrone, the underpinning gotta be make safe and ——'

'Lissenyawopbastard! If you don't like it, you know what you can do!'

And with that he swung swaggering away.

The men had heard, and those who hadn't knew instinctively.

The new home, the coming baby, and his whole background, kept the fire from Geremio's mouth and bowed his head. 'Annunziata speaks of scouring the ashcans for the children's bread in case I didn't want to work on a job where ... But am I not a man, to feed my own with these hands? Ah, but day will end and no boss in the world can then rob me of the joy of my home!'

Murdin paused for a moment before descending the ladder.

Geremio caught his meaning and jumped to, nervously directing the rush of work... No longer Geremio, but a machine-like entity.

The men were transformed into single, silent, beasts. Snout-nose steamed through ragged moustache whip-lashing sand into mixer Ashes-ass dragged under four by twelve beam Lean clawed wall knots jumping in jaws masonry crumbled dust billowed thundered choked....

At noon, Geremio drank his wine from an old-fashioned magnesia bottle and munched a great pepper sandwich ... no meat on Good Friday. Said one, 'Are some of us to be laid off? Easter is upon us and communion dresses are needed and ...'

That, while Geremio was dreaming of the new house and the joys he could almost taste. Said he: 'Worry not. You should know Geremio.' It then all came out. He regaled them with

his wonderful joy of the new house. He praised his wife and children one by one. They listened respectfully and returned him
well wishes and blessings. He went on and on.... 'Paul made a
radio — all by himself, mind you! One can hear Barney Google
and many American songs! How proud he.'

The ascent to labour was made, and as they trod the ladder,
heads turned and eyes communed with the mute flames of the
brazier whose warmth they were leaving, not with willing heart,
and in that fleeting moment, the breast wanted so, so much to
speak of hungers that never reached the tongue.

About an hour later, Geremio called over to Pietro: 'Pietro,
see if Mister Murdin is in the shanty and tell him I must see him!
I will convince him that the work must not go on like this ... just
for the sake of a little more profit!'

Pietro came up soon. 'The padrone is not coming up. He was
drinking from a large bottle of whisky and cursed in American
words that if you did not carry out his orders ——'

Geremio turned away disconcerted, stared dumbly at the structure and mechanically listed in his mind's eye the various viola-
tions of construction safety. An uneasy sensation hollowed him.
The Lean brought down an old piece of wall and the structure
palsied. Geremio's heart broke loose and out-thumped the floor's
vibrations, a rapid wave of heat swept him and left a chill touch
in its wake. He looked about to the men, a bit frightened. They
seemed usual, life-size, and moved about with the methodical
deftness that made the moment then appear no different than the
task of toil had ever been.

Snoutnose's voice boomed into him. 'Master Geremio, the
concrete is rea—dy!'

'Oh, yes, yes, Vincenz.' And he walked gingerly towards the
chute, but, not without leaving behind some part of his strength,
sending out his soul to wrestle with the limbs of Job, who threatened in stiff silence. He talked and joked with Snoutnose. No-

thing said anything, nor seemed wrong. Yet a vague uneasiness was to him as certain as the foggy murk that floated about Job's stone and steel.

'Shall I let the concrete down now, Master Geremio?'

'Well, let me see — no, hold it a minute. Hey, Sandino! Tighten the chute cables!'

Snoutnose straightened, looked about, and instinctively rubbed the sore small of his spine. 'Ah,' sighed he, 'all the men feel as I — yes, I can tell. They are tired but happy that today is Good Friday and we quit at three o'clock . . .' And he swelled in human ecstasy at the anticipation of food, drink, and the hairy flesh-tingling warmth of wife, and then, extravagant rest. In truth, they all felt as Snoutnose, although perhaps with variations on the theme.

It was the Lean only who had lived, and felt otherwise. His soul, accompanied with time, had shredded itself in the physical war to keep the physical alive. Perhaps he no longer had a soul, and the corpse continued from momentum. May he not be the Slave, working on from the birth of Man — He of whom it was said, 'It was not for Him to reason?' And probably He who, never asking, taking, nor vaunting, created God and the creatable? Nevertheless, there existed in the Lean a sense of oppression suffered, so vast that the seas of time could never wash it away.

Geremio gazed about and was conscious of seeming to understand many things. He marvelled at the strange feeling which permitted him to sense the familiarity of life. And yet — all appeared unreal, a dream pungent and nostalgic. Life, dream, reality, unreality, spiralling ever about each other. 'Ha,' he chuckled, 'how and from where do these thoughts come?'

Snoutnose had his hand on the hopper latch and was awaiting the word from Geremio. 'Did you say something, Master Geremio?'

'Why, yes, Vincenz, I was thinking — funny! A — yes, what is the time — yes, that is what I was thinking.'

'My American can of tomatoes says ten minutes from two o'clock. It won't be long now, Master Geremio.'

Geremio smiled. 'No, about an hour... and then, home.'

'Oh, but first we stop at Mulberry Street, to buy their biggest eels, and the other finger-licking stuffs.'

Geremio was looking far off, and for a moment happiness came to his heart without words, a warm hand stealing over. Snoutnose's words sang to him pleasantly, and he nodded.

'And Master Geremio, we ought really to buy the seafruits with the shells — you know, for the much needed steam they put into the ——'

He flushed despite himself and continued. 'It is true, I know it — especially the juicy clams... uhmn, my mouth waters like a pump.'

Geremio drew on his unlit pipe and smiled acquiescence. The men around him were moving to their tasks silently, feeling of their fatigue, but absorbed in contemplations the very same as Snoutnose's. The noise of labour seemed not to be noise, and as Geremio looked about, life settled over him a grey concert — grey forms, atmosphere, and grey notes... Yet his off-tone world felt so near, and familiar.

'Five minutes from two,' swished through Snoutnose's moustache.

Geremio automatically took out his watch, rewound, and set it. Sandino had done with the cables. The tone and movement of the scene seemed to Geremio strange, differently strange, and yet, a dream familiar from a timeless date. His hand went up in motion to Vincenzo. The molten stone gurgled low, and then with heightening rasp. His eyes followed the stone-cementy pudding, and to his ears there was no other sound than its flow. From over the roofs somewhere, the tinny voice of *Barney Google* whined its way, hooked into his consciousness and kept itself a revolving record beneath his skull-plate.

'Ah, yes, Barney Google, my son's wonderful radio machine . . . wonderful Paul.' His train of thought quickly took in his family, home and hopes. And with hope came fear. Something within asked, 'Is it not possible to breathe God's air without fear dominating with the pall of unemployment? And the terror of production for Boss, Boss and Job? To rebel is to lose all of the very little. To be obedient is to choke. Oh, dear Lord, guide my path.'

Just then, the floor lurched and swayed under his feet. The slipping of the underpinning below rumbled up through the undetermined floors.

Was he faint or dizzy? Was it part of the dreamy afternoon? He put his hands in front of him and stepped back, and looked up wildly. 'No! No!'

The men poised stricken. Their throats wanted to cry out and scream but didn't dare. For a moment they were a petrified and straining pageant. Then the bottom of their world gave way. The building shuddered violently, her supports burst with the crackling slap of wooden gunfire. The floor vomited upward. Geremio clutched at the air and shrieked agonizingly. 'Brothers, what have we done? Ahhhh-h, children of ours!' With the speed of light, balance went sickeningly awry and frozen men went flying explosively. Job tore down upon them madly. Walls, floors, beams became whirling, solid, splintering waves crashing with detonations that ground man and material in bonds of death.

The strongly shaped body that slept with Annunziata nights and was perfect in all the limitless physical quantities, thudded as a worthless sack amongst the giant debris that crushed fragile flesh and bone with centrifugal intensity.

Darkness blotted out his terror and the resistless form twisted, catapulted insanely in its directionless flight, and shot down neatly and deliberately between the empty wooden forms of a foundation wall pilaster in upright position, his blue swollen face pressed against the form and his arms outstretched, caught securely through the meat by the thin round bars of reinforcing steel.

The huge concrete hopper that was sustained by an independent structure of thick timber, wavered a breath or so, its heavy concrete rolling uneasily until a great sixteen-inch wall caught it squarely with all the terrific verdict of its dead weight and impelled it downward through joists, beams and masonry, until it stopped short, arrested by two girders, an arm's length above Geremio's head; the grey concrete gushing from the hopper mouth, and sealing up the mute figure.

Giacomo had been thrown clear of the building and dropped six floors to the street gutter, where he lay writhing.

The Lean had evinced no emotion. When the walls descended, he did not move. He lowered his head. One minute later he was hanging in mid-air, his chin on his chest, his eyes tearing loose from their sockets, a green foam bubbling from his mouth and his body spasming, suspended by the shreds left of his mashed arms pinned between a wall and a girder.

A two-by-four hooked little Joe Chiappa up under the back of his jumper and swung him around in a circle to meet a careening I-beam. In the flash that he lifted his frozen cherubic face, its shearing edge sliced through the top of his skull.

When Snoutnose cried beseechingly, 'Saint Michael!' blackness enveloped him. He came to in a world of horror. A steady stream, warm, thick, and sickening as hot wine bathed his face and clogged his nose, mouth, and eyes. The nauseous syrup that pumped over his face, clotted his moustache red and drained into his mouth. He gulped for air, and swallowed the rich liquid scarlet. As he breathed, the pain shocked him to oppressive semi-consciousness. The air was wormingly alive with cries, screams, moans and dust, and his crushed chest seared him with a thousand fires. He couldn't see, nor breathe enough to cry. His right hand moved to his face and wiped at the gelatinizing substance, but it kept coming on, and a heart-breaking moan wavered about him, not far. He wiped his eyes in subconscious despair. Where was he? What kind of a dream was he having? Perhaps he wouldn't wake up in time for work, and then what? But how queer; his stomach beating him, his chest on fire, he sees nothing but dull red, only one hand moving about, and a moaning in his face!

The sound and clamour of the rescue squads called to him from far off.

Ah, yes, he's dreaming in bed, and far out in the streets, engines are going to a fire. Oh poor devils! Suppose his house were on fire? With the children scattered about in the rooms he could not remember! He must do his utmost to break out of this dream! He's swimming under water, not able to raise his head and get to the air. He must get back to consciousness to save his children!

He swam frantically with his one right hand, and then felt a face beneath its touch. A face! It's Angelina alongside of him! Thank God, he's awake! He tapped her face. It moved. It felt cold, bristly, and wet. 'It moves so. What is this?' His fingers slithered about grisly sharp bones and in a gluey, stringy, hollow mass, yielding as wet macaroni. Grey light brought sight, and hysteria punctured his heart. A girder lay across his chest his right hand clutched a grotesque human mask, and suspended almost on top of him was the twitching, faceless body of Joe Chiappa. Vincenzo fainted with an inarticulate sigh. His fingers loosed and the bodyless-headless face dropped and fitted to the side of his face while the drippings above came slower and slower.

The rescue men cleaved grimly with pick and axe.

Geremio came to with a start ... far from their efforts. His brain told him instantly what had happened and where he was. He shouted wildly. 'Save me! Save me! I'm being buried alive!'

He paused exhausted. His genitals convulsed. The cold steel

rod upon which they were impaled froze his spine. He shouted louder and louder. 'Save me! I am hurt badly! I can be saved, I can — save me before it's too late!' But the cries went no farther than his own ears. The icy wet concrete reached his chin. His heart was appalled. 'In a few seconds I shall be entombed. If I can only breathe, they will reach me. Surely they will!' His face was quickly covered, its flesh yielding to the solid, sharp-cut stones. 'Air! Air!' screamed his lungs as he was completely sealed. Savagely, he bit into the wooden form pressing upon his mouth. An eighth of an inch of its surface splintered off. Oh, if he could only hold out long enough to bite even the smallest hole through to air! He must! There can be no other way! He is responsible for his family! He cannot leave them like this! He didn't want to die! This could not be the answer to life! He had bitten half way through when his teeth snapped off to the gums in the uneven conflict. The pressure of the concrete was such, and its effectiveness so thorough, that the wooden splinters, stumps of teeth, and blood never left the choking mouth.

Why couldn't he go any farther?

Air! Quick! He dug his lower jaw into the little hollowed space and gnashed in choking agonized fury. 'Why doesn't it go through? Mother of Christ, why doesn't it give? Can there be a notch, or two-by-four stud behind it? Sweet Jesu! No! No! Make it give. . . . Air! Air!'

He pushed the bone-bare jaw maniacally; it splintered, cracked, and a jagged fleshless edge cut through the form, opening a small hole to air. With a desperate burst the lung-prisoned air blew an opening through the shredded mouth and whistled back greedily a gasp of fresh air. He tried to breathe, but it was impossible. The heavy concrete was settling immutably, and its rich cement-laden grout ran into his pierced face. His lungs would not expand, and were crushing in tighter and tighter under the settling concrete.

'Mother mine — mother of Jesu-Annunziata — children of mine — dear, dear, for mercy, Jesu-Guiseppe e 'Maria,' his blue-foamed tongue called. It then distorted in a shuddering coil and mad blood vomited forth. Chills and fire played through him and his tortured tongue stuttered, 'Mercy, blessed Father — salvation, most kind Father — Saviour — Saviour of His children help me — adored Saviour — I kiss your feet eternally — you are my Lord — there is but one God — you are my God of infinite mercy — Hail Mary divine Virgin — our Father who art in heaven hallowed be thy — name — our Father — my Father,' and the agony excruciated with never-ending mount, 'our Father — Jesu, Jesu, soon Jesu, hurry dear Jesu Jesu! Je-sssu....!' His mangled voice trebled hideously, and hung in jerky whimperings.

The unfeeling concrete was drying fast, and shrinking into monolithic density. The pressure temporarily de-sensitized sensation; leaving him petrified, numb, and substanceless. Only the brain remained miraculously alive.

'Can this be death? It is all too strangely clear. I see nothing nor feel nothing, my body and senses are no more, my mind speaks as it never did before. Am I or am I not Geremio? But I am Geremio! Can I be in the other world? I never was in any other world except the one I knew of; that of toil, hardship, prayer . . . of my wife who awaits with child for me, of my children and the first home I was to own. Where do I begin in this world? Where do I leave off? Why? I recall only a baffled life of cruelty from every direction. And hope was always as painful as fear, the fear of displeasing, displeasing the people and ideas whom I could never understand; laws, policemen, priests, bosses, and a rag with colours waving on a stick. I never did anything to these things. But what have I done with my life? Yes, my life! No one else's! Mine — mine — MINE — Geremio! It is clear. I was born hungry, and have always been hungry for freedom — life! I married and ran away to America so as not to kill and be killed in Tripoli for things they call "God and Country." I've never known the freedom I wanted in my heart. There was always an arm upraised to hit at me. What have I done to them? I did not want to make them toil for me. I did not raise my arm to them. In my life I could never breathe, and now without air, my mind breathes clearly for me. Wait! There has been a terrible mistake! A cruel crime! The world is not right! Murderers! Thieves! You have hurt me and my kind, and have taken my life from me! I have long felt it — yes, yes, yes, they have cheated me with flags, signs and fear ... I say you can't take my life! I want to live! My life! To tell the cheated to rise and fight! Vincenz! Chiappa! Nick! Men! Do you hear me? We must follow the desires within us for the world has been taken from us; we, who made the world! Life!'

Feeling returned to the destroyed form.

'Ahhh-h, I am not dead yet. I knew it — you have not done with me. Torture away! I cannot believe you, God and Country, no longer!' His body was fast breaking under the concrete's closing wrack. Blood vessels burst like mashed flower stems. He screamed. 'Show yourself now, Jesu! Now is the time! Save me! Why don't you come! Are you there! I cannot stand it — ohhh, why do you let it happen — it is bestial — where are you! Hurry, hurry, hurry! You do not come! You make me suffer, and what have I done! Come, come — come now — now save me, save me now! Now, now, now! If you are God, save me!'

The stricken blood surged through a weltering maze of useless pipes and exploded forth from his squelched eyes and formless nose, ears and mouth, seeking life in the indifferent stone.

'Aie — aie, aie — devils and Saints — beasts! Where are you — quick, quick, it is death and I am cheated — cheat — ed! Do you hear, you whoring bastards who own the world? Ohhh-ohhhh aie-aie — hahahaha!' His bones cracked mutely and his sanity went sailing distorted in the limbo of the subconscious.

With the throbbing tones of an organ in the hollow background, the fighting brain disintegrated and the memories of a baffled lifetime sought outlet.

He moaned the simple songs of barefoot childhood, scenes flashed desperately on and off in disassociated reflex, and words and parts of words came pitifully high and low from his inaudible lips, the hysterical mind sang cringingly and breathlessly, 'Jesu my Lord my God my all Jesu my Lord my God my all Jesu my Lord my God my all Jesu my Lord my God my all,' and on as the whirling tempo screamed now far, now near, and came in soul-sickening waves as the concrete slowly contracted and squeezed his skull out of shape.

THE CHRYSANTHEMUMS [1]

JOHN STEINBECK

THE high grey-flannel fog of winter closed off the Salinas Valley from the sky and from all the rest of the world. On every side it sat like a lid on the mountains and made of the great valley a closed pot. On the broad, level land floor the gang ploughs bit deep and left the black earth shining like metal where the shares had cut. On the foot-hill ranches across the Salinas River, the yellow stubble fields seemed to be bathed in pale cold sunshine, but there was no sunshine in the valley now in December. The thick willow scrub along the river flamed with sharp and positive yellow leaves.

It was a time of quiet and of waiting. The air was cold and tender. A light wind blew up from the southwest so that the farmers were mildly hopeful of a good rain before long; but fog and rain do not go together.

Across the river, on Henry Allen's foothill ranch there was little work to be done, for the hay was cut and stored and the orchards were ploughed up to receive the rain deeply when it should come. The cattle on the higher slopes were becoming shaggy and rough-coated.

[1] Copyright, 1938, by The Viking Press. From *The Long Valley* by John Steinbeck. The Viking Press, 1938.

Elisa Allen, working in her flower garden, looked down across the yard and saw Henry, her husband, talking to two men in business suits. The three of them stood by the tractor shed, each man with one foot on the side of the little Fordson. They smoked cigarettes and studied the machine as they talked.

Elisa watched them for a moment and then went back to her work. She was thirty-five. Her face was lean and strong and her eyes were as clear as water. Her figure looked blocked and heavy in her gardening costume, a man's black hat pulled low down over her eyes, clod-hopper shoes, a figured print dress almost completely covered by a big corduroy apron with four big pockets to hold the snips, the trowel and scratcher, the seeds and the knife she worked with. She wore heavy leather gloves to protect her hands while she worked.

She was cutting down the old year's chrysanthemum stalks with a pair of short and powerful scissors. She looked down toward the men by the tractor-shed now and then. Her face was eager and mature and handsome; even her work with the scissors was over-eager, over-powerful. The chrysanthemum stems seemed too small and easy for her energy.

She brushed a cloud of hair out of her eyes with the back of her glove, and left a smudge of earth on her cheek in doing it. Behind her stood the neat white farm house with red geraniums close-banked around it as high as the windows. It was a hard-swept-looking little house, with hard-polished windows, and a clean mud-mat on the front steps.

Elisa cast another glance toward the tractor shed. The strangers were getting into their Ford coupé. She took off a glove and put her strong fingers down into the forest of new green chrysanthemum sprouts that were growing around the old roots. She spread the leaves and looked down among the close-growing stems. No aphids were there, no sow bugs or snails or cutworms. Her terrier fingers destroyed such pests before they could get started.

Elisa started at the sound of her husband's voice. He had come near quietly, and he leaned over the wire fence that protected her flower garden from cattle and dogs and chickens.

'At it again,' he said. 'You've got a strong new crop coming.'

Elisa straightened her back and pulled on the gardening glove again. 'Yes. They'll be strong this coming year.' In her tone and on her face there was a little smugness.

'You've got a gift with things,' Henry observed. 'Some of those yellow chrysanthemums you had this year were ten inches across. I wish you'd work out in the orchard and raise some apples that big.'

Her eyes sharpened. 'Maybe I could do it, too. I've a gift with things, all right. My mother had it. She could stick anything in the ground and make it grow. She said it was having planters' hands that knew how to do it.'

'Well, it sure works with flowers,' he said.

'Henry, who were those men you were talking to?'

'Why, sure, that's what I came to tell you. They were from the Western Meat Company. I sold those thirty head of three-year-old steers. Got nearly my own price, too.'

'Good,' she said. 'Good for you.'

'And I thought,' he continued, 'I thought how it's Saturday afternoon, and we might go into Salinas for dinner at a restaurant; and then to a picture show — to celebrate, you see.'

'Good,' she repeated. 'Oh, yes. That will be good.'

Henry put on his joking tone. 'There's fights tonight. How'd you like to go to the fights?'

'Oh, no,' she said breathlessly. 'No, I wouldn't like fights.'

'Just fooling, Elisa. We'll go to a movie. Let's see. It's two now. I'm going to take Scotty and bring down those steers from the hill. It'll take us maybe two hours. We'll go in town about five and have dinner at the Cominos Hotel. Like that?'

'Of course I'll like it. It's good to eat away from home.'

'All right, then. I'll go get up a couple of horses.'

She said: 'I'll have plenty of time to transplant some of these sets, I guess.'

She heard her husband calling Scotty down by the barn. And a little later she saw the two men ride up the pale yellow hillside in search of the steers.

There was a little square sandy bed kept for rooting the chrysanthemums. With her trowel she turned the soil over and over, and smoothed it and patted it firm. Then she dug ten parallel trenches to receive the sets. Back at the chrysanthemum bed she pulled out the little crisp shoots, trimmed off the leaves of each one with her scissors and laid it on a small orderly pile.

A squeak of wheels and plod of hoofs came from the road. Elisa looked up. The country road ran along the dense bank of willows and cottonwoods that bordered the river, and up this road came a curious vehicle, curiously drawn. It was an old spring-wagon, with a round canvas top on it like the cover of a prairie schooner. It was drawn by an old bay horse and a little grey-and-white burro. A big stubble-bearded man sat between the cover flaps and drove the crawling team. Underneath the wagon, between the hind wheels, a lean and rangy mongrel dog walked sedately. Words were painted on the canvas, in clumsy, crooked letters. 'Pots, pans, knives, sisors, lawn mores, Fixed.' Two rows of articles, and the triumphantly definitive 'Fixed' below. The black paint had run down in little sharp points beneath each letter.

Elisa, squatting on the ground, watched to see the crazy, loose-jointed wagon pass by. But it didn't pass. It turned into the farm road in front of her house, crooked old wheels skirling and squeaking. The rangy dog darted from between the wheels and ran ahead. Instantly the two ranch shepherds flew out at him. Then all three stopped, and with stiff and quivering tails, with taut straight legs, with ambassadorial dignity, they slowly

circled, sniffing daintily. The caravan pulled up to Elisa's wire
fence and stopped. Now the newcomer dog, feeling out-num-
bered, lowered his tail and retired under the wagon with raised
hackles and bared teeth.

The man on the wagon seat called out: 'That's a bad dog in a
fight when he gets started.'

Elisa laughed. 'I see he is. How soon does he generally
get started?'

The man caught up her laughter and echoed it heartily.
'Sometimes not for weeks and weeks,' he said. He climbed
stiffly down, over the wheel. The horse and the donkey drooped
like unwatered flowers.

Elisa saw that he was a very big man. Although his hair
and beard were greying, he did not look old. His worn black
suit was wrinkled and spotted with grease. The laughter had disappeared from his face and eyes the moment his laughing voice
ceased. His eyes were dark, and they were full of the brooding
that gets in the eyes of teamsters and of sailors. The calloused
hands he rested on the wire fence were cracked, and every crack
was a black line. He took off his battered hat.

'I'm off my general road, ma'am,' he said. 'Does this dirt road
cut over across the river to the Los Angeles highway?'

Elisa stood up and shoved the thick scissors in her apron
pocket. 'Well, yes, it does, but it winds around and then fords
the river. I don't think your team could pull through the sand.'

He replied with some asperity: 'It might surprise you what
them beasts can pull through.'

'When they get started?' she asked.

He smiled for a second. 'Yes. When they get started.'

'Well,' said Elisa, 'I think you'll save time if you go back to
the Salinas road and pick up the highway there.'

He drew a big finger down the chicken wire and made it sing.
'I ain't in any hurry, ma'am. I go from Seattle to San Diego and

back every year. Takes all my time. About six months each way. I aim to follow nice weather.'

Elisa took off her gloves and stuffed them in the apron pocket with the scissors. She touched the under edge of her man's hat, searching for fugitive hairs. 'That sounds like a nice kind of a way to live,' she said.

He leaned confidentially over the fence. 'Maybe you noticed the writing on my wagon. I mend pots and sharpen knives and scissors. You got any of them things to do?'

'Oh, no,' she said quickly. 'Nothing like that.' Her eyes hardened with resistance.

'Scissors is the worst thing,' he explained. 'Most people just ruin scissors trying to sharpen 'em, but I know how. I got a special tool. It's a little bobbit kind of thing, and patented. But it sure does the trick.'

'No. My scissors are all sharp.'

'All right, then. Take a pot,' he continued earnestly, 'a bent pot, or a pot with a hole. I can make it like new so you don't have to buy no new ones. That's a saving for you.'

'No,' she said shortly. 'I tell you I have nothing like that for you to do.'

His face fell to an exaggerated sadness. His voice took on a whining undertone. 'I ain't had a thing to do today. Maybe I won't have no supper tonight. You see I'm off my regular road. I know folks on the highway clear from Seattle to San Diego. They save their things for me to sharpen up because they know I do it so good and save them money.'

'I'm sorry,' Elisa said irritably. 'I haven't anything for you to do.'

His eyes left her face and fell to searching the ground. They roamed about until they came to the chrysanthemum bed where she had been working. 'What's them plants, ma'am?'

The irritation and resistance melted from Elisa's face. 'Oh, those are chrysanthemums, giant whites and yellows. I raise them every year, bigger than anybody around here.'

'Kind of a long-stemmed flower? Looks like a quick puff of coloured smoke?' he asked.

'That's it. What a nice way to describe them.'

'They smell kind of nasty till you get used to them,' he said.

'It's a good bitter smell,' she retorted, 'not nasty at all.'

He changed his tone quickly. 'I like the smell myself.'

'I had ten-inch blooms this year,' she said.

The man leaned farther over the fence. 'Look. I know a lady down the road a piece, has got the nicest garden you ever seen. Got nearly every kind of flower but no chrysantheums. Last time I was mending a copper-bottom washtub for her (that's a hard job but I do it good), she said to me: "If you ever run acrost some nice chrysantheums I wish you'd try to get me a few seeds." That's what she told me.'

Elisa's eyes grew alert and eager. 'She couldn't have known much about chrysanthemums. You *can* raise them from seed, but it's much easier to root the little sprouts you see there.'

'Oh,' he said. 'I s'pose I can't take none to her, then.'

'Why yes you can,' Elisa cried. 'I can put some in damp sand, and you can carry them right along with you. They'll take root in the pot if you keep them damp. And then she can transplant them.'

'She'd sure like to have some, ma'am. You say they're nice ones?'

'Beautiful,' she said. 'Oh, beautiful.' Her eyes shone. She tore off the battered hat and shook out her dark pretty hair. 'I'll put them in a flower pot, and you can take them right with you. Come into the yard.'

While the man came through the picket gate Elisa ran excitedly along the geranium-bordered path to the back of the house. And she returned carrying a big red flower-pot. The gloves were forgotten now. She kneeled on the ground by the starting bed and dug up the sandy soil with her fingers and scooped it into the bright new flower-pot. Then she picked up the little pile of shoots she had prepared. With her strong fingers she pressed them into the sand and tamped around them with her knuckles. The man stood over her. 'I'll tell you what to do,' she said. 'You remember so you can tell the lady.'

'Yes, I'll try to remember.'

'Well, look. These will take root in about a month. Then she must set them out, about a foot apart in good rich earth like this, see?' She lifted a handful of dark soil for him to look at. 'They'll grow fast and tall. Now remember this: In July tell her to cut them down, about eight inches from the ground.'

'Before they bloom?' he asked.

'Yes, before they bloom.' Her face was tight with eagerness. 'They'll grow right up again. About the last of September the buds will start.'

She stopped and seemed perplexed. 'It's the budding that takes the most care,' she said hesitantly. 'I don't know how to tell you.' She looked deep into his eyes, searchingly. Her mouth opened a little, and she seemed to be listening. 'I'll try to tell you,' she said. 'Did you ever hear of planting hands?'

'Can't say I have, ma'am.'

'Well, I can only tell you what it feels like. It's when you're picking off the buds you don't want. Everything goes right down into your fingertips. You watch your fingers work. They do it themselves. You can feel how it is. They pick and pick the buds. They never make a mistake. They're with the plant. Do you see? Your fingers and the plant. You can feel that, right up your arm. They know. They never make a mistake. You can feel it. When you're like that you can't do anything wrong. Do you see that? Can you understand that?'

She was kneeling on the ground looking up at him. Her breast swelled passionately.

The man's eyes narrowed. He looked away self-consciously. 'Maybe I know,' he said. 'Sometimes in the night in the wagon there——'

Elisa's voice grew husky. She broke in on him: 'I've never lived as you do, but I know what you mean. When the night is dark — why, the stars are sharp-pointed, and there's quiet. Why, you rise up and up! Every pointed star gets driven into your body. It's like that. Hot and sharp and — lovely.'

Kneeling there, her hand went out toward his legs in the greasy black trousers. Her hesitant fingers almost touched the cloth. Then her hand dropped to the ground. She crouched low like a fawning dog.

He said: 'It's nice, just like you say. Only when you don't have no dinner, it ain't.'

She stood up then, very straight, and her face was ashamed. She held the flower-pot out to him and placed it gently in his arms. 'Here. Put it in your wagon, on the seat, where you can watch it. Maybe I can find something for you to do.'

At the back of the house she dug in the can pile and found two old and battered aluminum saucepans. She carried them back and gave them to him. 'Here, maybe you can fix these.'

His manner changed. He became professional. 'Good as new I can fix them.' At the back of his wagon he set a little anvil, and out of an oily tool-box dug a small machine hammer. Elisa came through the gate to watch him while he pounded out the dents in the kettles. His mouth grew sure and knowing. At a difficult part of the work he sucked his under-lip.

'You sleep right in the wagon?' Elisa asked.

'Right in the wagon, ma'am. Rain or shine I'm dry as a cow in there.'

'It must be nice,' she said. 'It must be very nice. I wish women could do such things.'

'It ain't the right kind of a life for a woman.'

Her upper lip raised a little, showing her teeth. 'How do you know? How can you tell?' she said.

'I don't know, ma'am,' he protested. 'Of course I don't know. Now here's your kettles, done. You don't have to buy no new ones.'

'How much?'

'Oh, fifty cents'll do. I keep my prices down and my work good. That's why I have all them satisfied customers up and down the highway.'

Elisa brought him a fifty-cent piece from the house and dropped it in his hand. 'You might be surprised to have a rival some time. I can sharpen scissors, too. And I can beat the dents out of little pots. I could show you what a woman might do.'

He put his hammer back in the oily box and shoved the little anvil out of sight. 'It would be a lonely life for a woman, ma'am, and a scarey life, too, with animals creeping under the wagon all night.' He climbed over the single-tree, steadying himself with a hand on the burro's white rump. He settled himself in the seat, picked up the lines. 'Thank you kindly, ma'am,' he said. 'I'll do like you told me; I'll go back and catch the Salinas road.'

'Mind,' she called, 'if you're long in getting there, keep the sand damp.'

'Sand, ma'am? . . . Sand? Oh, sure. You mean around the chrysanthemums. Sure I will.' He clucked his tongue. The beasts leaned luxuriously into their collars. The mongrel dog took his place between the back wheels. The wagon turned and crawled out the entrance road and back the way it had come, along the river.

Elisa stood in front of her wire fence watching the slow progress of the caravan. Her shoulders were straight, her head thrown back, her eyes half-closed, so that the scene came vaguely into them. Her lips moved silently, forming the words 'Good-bye — good-bye.' Then she whispered: 'That's a bright direction.

There's a glowing there.' The sound of her whisper startled her. She shook herself free and looked about to see whether anyone had been listening. Only the dogs had heard. They lifted their heads toward her from their sleeping in the dust, and then stretched out their chins and settled asleep again. Elisa turned and ran hurriedly into the house.

In the kitchen she reached behind the stove and felt the water tank. It was full of hot water from the noonday cooking. In the bathroom she tore off her soiled clothes and flung them into the corner. And then she scrubbed herself with a little block of pumice, legs and thighs, loins and chest and arms, until her skin was scratched and red. When she had dried herself she stood in front of a mirror in her bedroom and looked at her body. She tightened her stomach and threw out her chest. She turned and looked over her shoulder at her back.

After a while she began to dress, slowly. She put on her newest underclothing and her nicest stockings and the dress which was the symbol of her prettiness. She worked carefully on her hair, pencilled her eyebrows and rouged her lips.

Before she was finished she heard the little thunder of hoofs and the shouts of Henry and his helper as they drove the red steers into the corral. She heard the gate bang shut and set herself for Henry's arrival.

His step sounded on the porch. He entered the house calling: 'Elisa, where are you?'

'In my room, dressing. I'm not ready. There's hot water for your bath. Hurry up. It's getting late.'

When she heard him splashing in the tub, Elisa laid his dark suit on the bed, and shirt and socks and tie beside it. She stood his polished shoes on the floor beside the bed. Then she went to the porch and sat primly and stiffly down. She looked toward the river road where the willow-line was still yellow with frosted leaves so that under the high grey fog they seemed a thin band of

sunshine. This was the only colour in the grey afternoon. She
sat unmoving for a long time. Her eyes blinked rarely.

Henry came banging out of the door, shoving his tie inside his
vest as he came. Elisa stiffened and her face grew tight. Henry
stopped short and looked at her. 'Why — why, Elisa. You look
so nice!'

'Nice? You think I look nice? What do you mean by
"nice"?'

Henry blundered on. 'I don't know. I mean you look different,
strong and happy.'

'I am strong? Yes, strong. What do you mean "strong"?'

He looked bewildered. 'You're playing some kind of a game,'
he said helplessly. 'It's a kind of a play. You look strong enough
to break a calf over your knee, happy enough to eat it like a watermelon.'

For a second she lost her rigidity. 'Henry! Don't talk like that.
You didn't know what you said.' She grew complete again. 'I'm
strong,' she boasted. 'I never knew before how strong.'

Henry looked down toward the tractor shed, and when he
brought his eyes back to her, they were his own again. 'I'll get
out the car. You can put on your coat while I'm starting.'

Elisa went into the house. She heard him drive to the gate and
idle down his motor, and then she took a long time to put on her
hat. She pulled it here and pressed it there. When Henry turned
the motor off she slipped into her coat and went out.

The little roadster bounced along on the dirt road by the river,
raising the birds and driving the rabbits into the brush. Two
cranes flapped heavily over the willow-line and dropped into the
river-bed.

Far ahead on the road Elisa saw a dark speck. She knew.

She tried not to look as they passed it, but her eyes would not
obey. She whispered to herself sadly: 'He might have thrown
them off the road. That wouldn't have been much trouble, not

very much. But he kept the pot,' she explained. 'He had to keep the pot. That's why he couldn't get them off the road.'

The roadster turned a bend and she saw the caravan ahead. She swung full around toward her husband so she could not see the little covered wagon and the mis-matched team as the car passed them.

In a moment it was over. The thing was done. She did not look back.

She said loudly, to be heard above the motor: 'It will be good, tonight, a good dinner.'

'Now you're changed again,' Henry complained. He took one hand from the wheel and patted her knee. 'I ought to take you in to dinner oftener. It would be good for both of us. We get so heavy out on the ranch.'

'Henry,' she asked, 'could we have wine at dinner?'

'Sure we could. Say! That will be fine.'

She was silent for a while; then she said: 'Henry, at those prize-fights, do the men hurt each other very much?'

'Sometimes a little, not often. Why?'

'Well, I've read how they break noses, and blood runs down their chests. I've read how the fighting gloves get heavy and soggy with blood.'

He looked around at her. 'What's the matter, Elisa? I didn't know you read things like that.' He brought the car to a stop, then turned to the right over the Salinas River bridge.

'Do any women ever go to the fights?' she asked.

'Oh, sure, some. What's the matter, Elisa? Do you want to go? I don't think you'd like it, but I'll take you if you really want to go.'

She relaxed limply in the seat. 'Oh, no. No. I don't want to go. I'm sure I don't.' Her face was turned away from him. 'It will be enough if we can have wine. It will be plenty.' She turned up her coat collar so he could not see that she was crying weakly — like an old woman.

CORPORAL HARDY[1]

RICHARD ELY DANIELSON

I

IN THOSE days, during the haying season, it was my duty to keep the men in the fields supplied with sufficient cooling drink to enable them to support the heat and burden of the day. According to our established custom, this cooling drink consisted of cold water from the spring, flavored, for some obscure New England reason, with molasses, and it had to be freshly renewed every hour. We had plenty of ice in the icehouse, but there was a stubborn tradition that ice water was 'bad' for men working in hayfields under the hot sun.

So every hour I carried down a brown jug containing the innocent mixture of 'molasses 'n' water' to the hands, each one of whom would pause in his work, throw the jug over his upper arm, drink deeply thereof, wipe the sweat off his forehead, say 'Thanks, Bub,' and go on making hay. I was only ten years old, but it was no hardship to carry the jug, and it was fun to see their Adam's apples working as they drank.

This was routine practice on our Connecticut farm. Mostly the farm hands — 'hired men,' we called them — came back to the house at noon and ate in the kitchen, after washing up at the

[1] From *The Atlantic Monthly*. Copyright, 1938, by The Atlantic Monthly Company.

pump outside. But in haymaking season each man sought a patch of shade, and his meal was carried to him there, to be eaten in the fields. I suppose the men's overheated bodies cooled off in the wisps of breeze drifting across the scorching 'mowings' more effectively and comfortably than would have been possible in a hot summer kitchen. I am sure that my father did everything he could to make their lot as comfortable and healthy as possible. He worked with them, under the same conditions, setting them an example of careful, efficient labor. He differed from his men only in the fact that he was always cleanly shaved, that he gave orders and directions, and that he wore a silk shirt even in the hayfields. Nobody objected in the least to this token, for he was 'the owner,' and he had been to college, and everyone admitted that he was fair and square.

On such occasions, when the men were given their 'dinners' out of doors, I always carried his victuals to Mr. Hardy, because I liked to sit with him while he ate and listen to his stories. I think he enjoyed talking, in his racy Connecticut vernacular, to such a fascinated audience of one. He was a Civil War veteran, like my father, who, however, had been too young to enlist until the last year of the war and had seen almost no active service. But Mr. Hardy was a soldier. Congress had given him a medal — of honor — and all men regarded him with respect.

As I look back and remember his stories, I think he must have been the most modest man I have ever known. Certainly he never thought of himself as a hero. He would accept no pension. 'I'm able-bodied. I can work, can't I?' But, alas, he was not really able-bodied. He had been grievously wounded several times, and in 1895, when I fetched and carried for him and sat at his feet, it was pitiful to see his valiant efforts to fork hay on the wagon or do the other farming tasks which require muscular strength. He was thin and bent, but his face was brown and clean and his blue eyes bright and indomitable.

My father employed Mr. Hardy whenever there was work to give him, and treated him — I did not, at that time, know why — differently from the other hired men. He was poor, he lived alone, he was unsuccessful, and in New England then we rated people by their comparative 'success.' But he worked stoutly and asked no favors of anyone. It was generally conceded that Mr. Hardy, if a failure, was nevertheless a good man.

I remember the last day I served him. I brought him his dinner in a basket — cold meat 'n' potatoes, 'n' bread 'n' butter, 'n' cold coffee, 'n' pie. He was seated in the shade of an oak tree, leaning against a stack of hay. I put the food down beside him and sat down, hugging my knees and rocking back and forth. It was pleasant there, with the smell of the hay and the drone of the bees, and the good, warm feeling of the earth.

Mr. Hardy lay back against the haymow. 'Thanks, Jackie,' he said. 'I don't seem to be hungry today. It's hot and this tree don't give much shade. Why, dammit, it's like that mean little oak tree down to Chancellorsville.'

I said, 'Oh, Mr. Hardy, you've told me about Antietam and the Wilderness, but you've never told me about Chancellorsville. What was it like?'

He said slowly, 'I ain't never told nobody about Chancellorsville, and I don't aim to tell nobody — grown-up, that is. But I'd kind of like to tell somebody that don't know nothing — like you — about it, for the first and last time. You'll forget it, and it would kind of ease my mind.'

II

Mr. Hardy hoisted himself a little higher on the haymow and made a pretense of eating some bread and meat.

'Chancellorsville,' he said, 'was a bad battle, an awful bad battle. We didn't fight good and they was too many of them and I lost my captain.'

'Who was he?' I asked.

'Why,' he said, incredulously, 'you oughta know that! He was Captain William Armstrong, commandin' Company B, 39th Connecticut. 'N' his twin brother, Ezra, was lootenant. He was younger by an hour or so, and they was twins. They never was two men as much alike — in looks, that is, for they was quite unlike inside. The lootenant was always stompin' around an' shoutin' an' wavin' his arms, an' the captain, he was always quiet an' soft spoken an' brave an' gentle. He was a good man — he was an awful good man. I guess he was the best man I ever knowed.'

He paused and took a sip of his cold coffee. Then he said, 'Why, when we come to leave town to go in the cars to Hartford and then to Washington, their father — he was old Judge Armstrong, who lived in that big place up on Armstrong Hill — the Judge come up to me and says, "Nathan, you look after my boys," he said. "They're younger than you be. You kind of keep an eye on them, for my sake," he says. "They is good boys," he says. "I will, Judge," I says. "I'll do my best." An' he says to me, "I know you will, Nathan Hardy."'

'But tell me, Mr. Hardy,' I broke in, for I was not interested in the Armstrong twins, 'what happened at Chancellorsville?'

'It was a bad battle, as I said. Them Rebs come charging out of the woods, hollerin' and yellin' and helligolarrupin', and they was too many of them. The lootenant, he kept stomping up and down, shouting, "Never give ground, boys! Stay where you are! Take careful aim! Never retreat!" Those was his words. I will never forget them, because he meant them. But my captain — I was next to him — says, "They're too many; we can't stop 'em. Tell the men to retreat slowly, firing as often as they can reload." Just then it hit him right in the chest. *Thunk!* was the noise it made; just like thet — *thunk!* I caught him as he fell, and the blood began to come out of his mouth. He tried to speak, but he was vomiting blood dreadful, so all he could do was to make faces, and his lips said, "Tell Elizabeth . . . ." and then he died. I put him down and noticed we was under a mean little oak tree on the edge of our trenches.

'Then they was around us, hairy men with bayonets, stabbin' and shootin' and yellin', and we soldiers had kind of drifted together in groups and the lootenant was shouting, "Don't retreat, men!" and he got hit right in the knee and fell down; and so I picked him up and put him across my shoulder and started for the rear. He kep' hittin' me in the face and swearing. "You damn coward! You left my brother there and you're making me retreat!" I says to him, "Ezra, be reasonable; I'm takin' you to an ambulance. You ain't fit to fight, and as soon as I can I'm goin' back to bury William. They ain't goin' to shovel him into no trench," I said. So he stopped hitting at me.

'I was strong then, and I must a carried him what seemed a mile or a mile and a few rods when we come to some stretcher men near a house, and I said, "You take this officer to the nearest surgeon. They got to saw his leg off." And they said, "We ain't carryin' no wounded. We're a burial detail." I said, pulling my pistol out, "You will be if you don't carry this man. I'm kind of tuckered, but I ain't too tuckered to shoot." So two of them carried him, and I went along with my pistol till we come to a place where surgeons was carving men up and I handed over the lootenant. He come to as I did so, and said, "You scoundrel, you made me retreat. I'll never forgive you!" I said, "Ezra, they're going to saw your leg off and you'll never fight again, but I'll bury William if it's the last thing I do." He says, "Is that a promise?" And I says, "That's a promise. But it ain't a promise to you — it's one I made to your pa."

'So I stayed with him and helped hold him while they sawed his leg off. They havin' run out of chloroform, it took four of us to hold him. And when it was over he was unconscious, and they

put him in a cart with some others and took him away. So I went
back to the house where the burial men were loafing. It was
pretty ruined, but I found a shingle that was almos' clean and
I wrote on it, in the light of a fire, 'cause it was dark then:

CAPT. WILLIAM ARMSTRONG
COMMANDING CO. B., 39 CONNECTICUT
He was an awful good man

'Then I borrowed a spade from this burial party. We had an
argument about it, but I persuaded them with my pistol and I
started off toward the Rebel lines. I hadn't gone very far when
I come to a place which was thick with men moanin' and screamin'
and lots that wasn't sayin' nothing at all. I didn't want to walk
on them an' I couldn't help them, having nothing on me but a
shingle and a spade and a pistol, an' I decided I couldn't find the
captain in the dark anyhow, so I set down and tried to sleep, for
I was tuckered. ... But they was one man bothered me. He kep'
callin' out, "Won't someone for Jesus Christ's sake kill me?
Won't someone kill me?" And he kep' it up so long I knew he
couldn't die and was in pain. So I crept around till I located him
and I says, "Is it bad, brother?" And he says, "For Christ's
sake kill me. I can't die." So I felt around in my pockets and
found a sulphur match and looked at him and he was all torn to
pieces. And I said, "I don't blame you. I'll do it." And he says,
"God bless you." So I took out my pistol and put it right between his eyes and shot him. Then I threw away my pistol.
I set there the rest of the night waitin' for the dawn. It was a
long time comin'.

III

'When it come gray, I started out with my shingle and my
spade and I went along till I was challenged by the Rebel pickets
and sentries. I answered, "Union burial detail. I'm comin' for

to bury my captain." They begun shootin' at me and I don't know as I blame them. I was comin' out of the mist and they couldn't see that I was alone an' wasn't armed. So they shot real hard, and one bullet struck me in the left thigh and I fell down. Fortu*nate*ly I had a belt, and I sat up and took it off and strapped it real tight over my wound, and my britches was tight at the waist so they didn't come down, and I got up and went on.

'They stopped shootin' and a man with a bayonet got up and said, "Yank, you're my pris'ner." And I said, "I know I be, but I ain't your pris'ner till I bury my captain." And I held up my shingle and spade. He said, "Where's he lie?" And I said, "About quarter mile from here and maybe a few rods, under a mean little oak tree; and," I says, "you take me there and I'll bury him and then I'm your pris'ner. They ain't goin' to stuff my captain into no ditch," I says. He says, "You may be crazy, Yank, or you may be a spy. You come with me an' I'll turn you over to the captain."

'"Your captain alive?" I asks.

'"I reckon so," he says.

'"Mine's dead," I says, "and I aim for to bury him."

'So he tuk me away with his bayonet in my back and the blood was squilchin' in my boot, but I got along to where his captain was and the captain asked questions, and the Rebel soldier, he tol' all he knew, an' the captain says, "Where's he lie?" An' I says, "By a mean little oak, where our lines was yesterday mornin'."

'An' the captain says, "That ain't far away. I'll send a detail to bury him." I says, "Ain't nobody goin' to bury the captain but me," I says. "After that, I'll be your pris'ner."

'They was a young man dressed up all pretty with gold braid on his uniform, and he laughed kind of loud and he says, "Saves us the trouble of buryin' him!" an' the captain turns on him, real stern, and says, "Lootenant, this is a brave soldier," he says, "who come back under fire and was wounded to bury his company commander and give himself up as pris'ner. I will not have him insulted or laughed at," he says. Then he turns to me an' says, "What is your name an' rank?"

'"Corporal Nathan Hardy, Co. B, 39th Connecticut," I says.

'An' he says, "Corporal, you and I an' these men," turnin' around to the five or six Rebs who was listenin', "will go together to find your captain."

'So we went and I found him, underneath that mean little oak tree, and he looked dreadful. His eyes was open and they was an awful lot of blood on his shirt where his coat was torn open, and he was lyin' all sprangled out an' undignified. An' the first thing I done was to straighten him out. I spit on my sleeve and wiped the blood off his mouth the best I could. An' I closed his eyes an' buttoned his coat an' crossed his arms. They was kind of stiff, but I done it, an' I brushed him off and layed him out regular.

'Then I started diggin', an' it would have been easy if it hadn't been for my leg and all the blood was in my boot. Six foot four or thereabouts it was, and three foot deep — not as deep as I wanted, but I couldn't dig no deeper, I was so tuckered. But it was an honest grave, for I was real handy with a spade in them days. Then I stood up and said, "Will two o' you Rebs hand the captain to me?" Which they done, and I laid him in the grave. An' as I stood lookin' down at him lyin' there, I says to myself, "Ain't nobody goin' to shovel no dirt on the captain's face — nobody, nobody, nobody at all, not even me!" So I took my coat off and laid it over him, coverin' up his face best I could. I didn't want to go to no Rebel prison in my shirt, but I wouldn't have no one shovel dirt on the captain.

'Then the two Rebs pulled me out of the grave, real gentle and considerate. An' then I noticed they was a Rebel general there settin' on a blood horse. How long he bin there I don't know. He looked at me and see I was wounded and peaked, and he says, stern an' hard, "Captain, what's the meanin' of this? This man's wounded and weak," he says. "Do you force wounded men to bury the dead?"

'The captain went over to him and began talkin' to him low and earnest, seemed like, all the time I was fillin' in the grave. An' when I had patted the mound even, so it looked good, and had stuck the shingle in the new earth at the head of the grave, I come over to where the general was, limpin' and leanin' on my spade, an' I saluted — couldn't help it; I kind of forgot he was a Rebel — an' I says, "General, I'm your pris'ner. I buried my captain. I ain't a great hand at askin' favors, an' your captain and these Rebs has been real good to me. But I wanta ask one more. I was raised Episcopal, which was unusual in our town, and so was the captain. I'd kind of like to say a prayer before I surrender . . ."'

IV

Here Mr. Hardy seemed to doze for a little. 'Where was I?' he asked, rousing after a few minutes.

'You had just gone up to the general and asked if you could say a prayer before you surrendered.'

'Yes, yes, so it was. The general said, "Corporal Hardy, I am an Episcopalian too, and you shall say your prayer."

'So he dismounted and took off his hat, and he and I kneeled down by the grave, and it was awful hard for me to kneel. And when we was there kneelin' I looked up for a minute and all them Rebs was standin' with their caps off and their heads bowed, nice and decent, just like Northern people. An' then I had a dreadful time, for to save my life I couldn't remember a prayer, not a line, not a word. I had heard the burial service often enough and too often, what with Pa and Ma an' all kinds of relations, but my brains was all watery an' thin, seemed like, an' I couldn't remember nothin' at all. I don't know how long 't was till some-

thin' come driftin' into my mind. It wa'n't from the burial
service; 't was somethin' we used to chant in Evenin' Prayer.
So I says it, loud as I could, for I was gettin' awful feeble.

'"Lord," I says, "now lettest Thou Thy servant depart in
peace, according to Thy Word..." An' I couldn't remember or
say any more. The general, he helped me to my feet, spade an'
all, an' I looked him in the face and, by creepers, they was tears
in his beard. Soon as I could speak I says, "General, you've
been real good to me and I thank you. An' now I'm your pris'ner,
wherever you want to send me."

'An' he says, "Corporal Hardy, you will never be a pris'ner of
our people as long as I live and command this corps."

'An' I broke in, awful scared he had misunderstood, and I says,
"General, you don't think I was prayin' for *me* to go in peace!
I'm your pris'ner; I'm not askin' for no favors. I was thinkin'
of the captain — and me too, perhaps, but not that way. I can
go anywhere now. I ——"

'He cut me short. "Corporal Hardy," he says, "I know to
Whom you was prayin' and why, an' I haven't misunderstood
you at all. Captain," he says, "I want a detail of six men an' a
stretcher and a flag of truce to take this brave soldier an' — an'
Christian gentleman back to the Union lines; an' I want this
message, which I have dictated and signed, delivered to the commanding officer to be forwarded through channels to the Secretary of War or the President. Those people can hardly decline
this courtesy, under the circumstances.... Wait, Carter, I wish
to add a few lines." So he put the paper against his saddle and
he wrote for some time.

'Then, kind of in a dream, I heard the Rebel captain say,
"Sir, if the General permits, I would like to lead this detail to
the Union lines and ask to be blindfolded and deliver your message to the Division Commander."

'An' the General says, "Captain, I am very glad you made

that request, and I commend your behavior. It is only fittin' that the officer escortin' Corporal Hardy with my message should be of field rank, and I shall put in my order for your promotion. You are a pretty good soldier, yourself," he says — only he didn't say it that way.

'All this time I was kind of waverin' around, but I heard most all they said; and because I was feeble from losing blood an' the battle an' buryin' the captain an' a kind of feverish feelin', things begun to spin around, and I started walkin' this way and that way with my spade, tryin' to stand up, knowin' I couldn't much longer. I heard someone yell, "Catch him!" An' the next thing I knowed I was in a bed of straw and they was probin' for the bullet in my leg. Then I don't remember nothin' till I woke up in a bed, a clean bed, with a nice-lookin' woman leanin' over me, wipin' my head with a cold, wet towel. I says, "Where am I?"

'An' she says, "You're in the hospital of the Sanitary Commission in Washington. An' oh, Corporal Hardy," she says, "I'm so glad you're conscious, for today the President is comin' to give you the Medal of Honor." An' I says, "Listen, Sister, I gotta get out of here. I don't care for no President or no medal — I gotta bury the captain. He's lyin' down there under a mean little oak. Gimme my clothes," I says; "I want a spade and a shingle." An' she says, "Corporal, you buried your captain an' buried him fine. That's why the President is comin' to see you. Now you just drink this and go to sleep for a while, and I'll wake you when the President comes."

'So I drank it and kind of slept, and when I woke up there was the ugliest man I ever see, leanin' over and pinnin' something to my nightshirt, an' he says, "Corporal Hardy, even the enemy call you a brave soldier and a good man. Congress has voted you this medal. God bless you," he says.'

V

Mr. Hardy yawned and closed his eyes, and leaned against the haymow. He had told the tale he had to tell — once, to one person.

'But, Mr. Hardy,' I said, 'what happened to the lieutenant, and who was Elizabeth?' I wanted the story all tied up in ribbons.

'Who?' he said. 'The lootenant? Oh, Ezra come back and married Elizabeth and they went to live in Massachusetts. Seems he went aroun' sayin' he couldn't live in no town where people pointed at him and thought he had run away leavin' his dead brother. Naturally no one done so or thought so. But, for all his stompin' and shoutin', he was sensitive, an' he bore me a grudge for takin' him away. I don't see as how I could-a done different. I'd promised the old Judge I'd look after his boys an' I've allus aimed to keep my promises.'

Just then my father came up to us. It was unlike Mr. Hardy to sit in the shade while other men had started to work again, and Father looked worried. 'How are you feeling, Nathan?' he asked.

'Why, John, I'm plumb tuckered out, and that's a fact. I don' know as I can do much more work today. Seems like I never did fare good under these mean little oak trees,' and he glanced sharply at me with an expression that was almost a wink. We shared a secret.

Father looked startled, as if he thought Mr. Hardy's wits were wandering.

'I tell you what, Nathan,' he said, 'you've had all the sun you need. I'll send the wagon and they'll take you up to the house, where you can be cool and rest for a while.' And, for once in his life, Mr. Hardy made no protest over having 'favors' done for him. Father took me aside. 'Jackie,' he said, 'you run up to the house and tell your mother to make the bed in the spare room ready, and then you go to the village and tell Dr. Fordyce he's wanted. I don't like Nathan's looks.'

Before I started running I glanced at Mr. Hardy, and I saw what Father meant. He was pale and flushed in the wrong places, though I hadn't noticed it at all when he was telling me about Chancellorsville.

So Mr. Hardy was put to bed in the spare room, and given such care and aid as we knew how to give. For several days he lay quietly enough, and, as I look back on it after all these years, I think that the weight and burden of his long, valiant struggle must suddenly have proved too great. He couldn't go on forever. Mr. Hardy was tuckered out.

Then for some time he alternated between unconsciousness and a mild delirium. He kept mumbling phrases: 'Take that quid out o' your mouth. 'T ain't soldierly!' ... 'Ain't nobody goin' to bury the captain but me.' I knew what lots of his bewildered sayings meant, but there were many which were obscure. I sat with him every day for an hour or so when the rest of the household were busy, and I had instructions to call my elders if Mr. Hardy needed help or became conscious.

One day he opened his eyes and said, 'Here I am and I'm real easy in my mind — but I can't just remember what I said.' I went out and called my parents, who told me to stay outside. But I listened and I heard Mr. Hardy say, 'Call the boy in. He knows what I want said and I can't remember. He's young and 't won't hurt him and he'll forget.' So Mother beckoned me to come in and I said, 'What can I do, Mr. Hardy?'

'You can say what I said for the captain when I knelt down with the general.'

So I knelt down, and, having the parrot-like memory of childhood, I said, 'You knelt down and so did the general, and then you couldn't remember any of the words of the burial service, but you did remember something that was sung in the evening, and you said, "Lord, now lettest Thou Thy servant depart in peace, according to Thy Word..."' And I began to cry.

'That's right,' he said very faintly, 'that's right; that's it. Yes, Captain...'

My mother gathered me up and took me out and held me very close, rocking back and forth with me while I wept out how I loved Mr. Hardy and what a good man he was.

And that was why I was sent to my aunt and cousins at New London, where I could swim and fish and forget about battles and wounds and Mr. Hardy. But I didn't forget.

NOTE. The characters and situations, the incidents, even the military units mentioned in this story are entirely imaginary, and do not portray and are not intended to portray persons or events which may have existed in reality.

BRIGHT AND MORNING

STAR [1]

RICHARD WRIGHT

SHE stood with her black face some six inches from the moist window-pane and wondered when on earth would it ever stop raining. It might keep up like this all week, she thought. She heard rain droning upon the roof, and high up in the wet sky her eyes followed the silent rush of a bright shaft of yellow that swung from the airplane beacon in far-off Memphis. Momently she could see it cutting through the rainy dark; it would hover a second like a gleaming sword above her head, then vanish. She sighed, troubling, Johnny-Boys been trampin in this slop all day wid no decent shoes on his feet.... Through the window she could see the rich black earth sprawling outside in the night. There was more rain than the clay could soak up; pools stood everywhere. She yawned and mumbled: 'Rains good n bad. It kin make seeds bus up thu the groun, er it kin bog things down lika watah-soaked coffin.' Her hands were folded loosely over her stomach and the hot air of the kitchen traced a filmy veil of sweat on her forehead. From the cookstove came the soft singing

[1] From *New Masses*. Copyright, 1938, by Weekly Masses Co., Inc.

of burning wood and now and then a throaty bubble rose from a
pot of simmering greens.

'Shucks, Johnny-Boy coulda let somebody else do all tha
runnin in the rain. Theres others bettah fixed fer it than he is.
But, naw! Johnny-Boy ain the one t trust nobody t do nothin.
Hes gotta do it *all* hissef. . . .'

She glanced at a pile of damp clothes in a zinc tub. Waal, Ah
bettah git to work. She turned, lifted a smoothing iron with a
thick pad of cloth, touched a spit-wet finger to it with a quick,
jerking motion: *smiiitz!* Yeah; its hot! Stooping, she took a blue
work-shirt from the tub and shook it out. With a deft twist of
her shoulder she caught the iron in her right hand; the fingers of
her left hand took a piece of wax from a tin box and a frying sizzle
came as she smeared the bottom. She was thinking of nothing
now; her hands followed a life-long ritual of toil. Spreading a
sleeve, she ran the hot iron to and fro until the wet cloth became
stiff. She was deep in the midst of her work when a song rose out
of the far off days of her childhood and broke through half-parted
lips:

> Hes the Lily of the Valley, the Bright n Mawnin Star
> Hes the Fairest of Ten Thousan t mah soul . . .

A gust of wind dashed rain against the window. Johnny-Boy
oughta c mon home n eat his suppah. Aw Lawd! Itd be fine ef
Sug could eat wid us tonight! Itd be like ol times! Mabbe aftah
all it wont be long fo he'll be back. Tha lettah Ah got from im
las week said *Don give up hope.* . . . Yeah; we gotta live in hope.
Then both of her sons, Sug and Johnny-Boy, would be back with
her.

With an involuntary nervous gesture, she stopped and stood
still, listening. But the only sound was the lulling fall of rain.
Shucks, ain no usa me ackin this way, she thought. Ever time
they gits ready to hol them meetings Ah gits jumpity. Ah been a
lil scared ever since Sug went t jail. She heard the clock ticking

and looked. Johnny-Boys a *hour* late! He sho mus be havin a time doin all tha trampin, trampin thu tha mud. . . . But her fear was a quiet one; it was more like an intense brooding than a fear; it was a sort of hugging of hated facts so closely that she could feel their grain, like letting cold water run over her hand from a faucet on a winter morning.

She ironed again, faster now, as if the more she engaged her body in work the less she would think. But how could she forget Johnny-Boy out there on those wet fields rounding up white and black Communists for a meeting tomorrow? And that was just what Sug had been doing when the sheriff had caught him, beat him, and tried to make him tell who and where his comrades were. Po Sug! They sho musta beat tha boy something awful! But, thank Gawd, he didnt talk! He ain no weaklin' Sug ain! Hes been lion-hearted all his life long.

That had happened a year ago. And now each time those meetings came around the old terror surged back. While shoving the iron a cluster of toiling days returned; days of washing and ironing to feed Johnny-Boy and Sug so they could do party work; days of carrying a hundred pounds of white folks' clothes upon her head across fields sometimes wet and sometimes dry. But in those days a hundred pounds was nothing to carry carefully balanced upon her head while stepping by instinct over the corn and cotton rows. The only time it had seemed heavy was when she had heard of Sug's arrest. She had been coming home one morning with a bundle upon her head, her hands swinging idly by her sides, walking slowly with her eyes in front of her, when Bob, Johnny-Boy's pal, had called from across the fields and had come and told her that the sheriff had got Sug. That morning the bundle had become heavier than she could ever remember.

And with each passing week now, though she spoke of it to no one, things were becoming heavier. The tubs of water and the smoothing iron and the bundle of clothes were becoming harder to lift, her with her back aching so, and her work was taking longer, all because Sug was gone and she didn't know just when Johnny-Boy would be taken too. To ease the ache of anxiety that was swelling her heart, she hummed, then sang softly:

> He walks wid me, He talks wid me
> He tells me Ahm His own. . . .

Guiltily, she stopped and smiled. Looks like Ah jus cant seem t fergit them ol songs, no mattah how hard Ah tries. . . . She had learned them when she was a little girl living and working on a farm. Every Monday morning from the corn and cotton fields the slow strains had floated from her mother's lips, lonely and haunting; and later, as the years had filled with gall, she had learned their deep meaning. Long hours of scrubbing floors for a few cents a day had taught her who Jesus was, what a great boon it was to cling to Him, to be like Him and suffer without a mumbling word. She had poured the yearning of her life into the songs, feeling buoyed with a faith beyond this world. The figure of the Man nailed in agony to the Cross, His burial in a cold grave, His transfigured Resurrection, His being breath and clay, God and Man — all had focused her feelings upon an imagery which had swept her life into a wondrous vision.

But as she had grown older, a cold white mountain, the white folks and their laws, had swum into her vision and shattered her songs and their spell of peace. To her that white mountain was temptation, something to lure her from her Lord, a part of the world God had made in order that she might endure it and come through all the stronger, just as Christ had risen with greater glory from the tomb. The days crowded with trouble had enhanced her faith and she had grown to love hardship with a bitter pride; she had obeyed the laws of the white folks with a soft smile of secret knowing.

After her mother had been snatched up to heaven in a chariot of fire, the years had brought her a rough workingman and two black babies, Sug and Johnny-Boy, all three of whom she had wrapped in the charm and magic of her vision. Then she was tested by no less than God; her man died, a trial which she bore with the strength shed by the grace of her vision; finally even the memory of her man faded into the vision itself, leaving her with two black boys growing tall, slowly into manhood.

Then one day grief had come to her heart when Johnny-Boy and Sug had walked forth demanding their lives. She had sought to fill their eyes with her vision, but they would have none of it. And she had wept when they began to boast of the strength shed by a new and terrible vision.

But she had loved them, even as she loved them now; bleeding, her heart had followed them. She could have done no less, being an old woman in a strange world. And day by day her sons had ripped from her startled eyes her old vision; and image by image had given her a new one, different, but great and strong enough to fling her into the light of another grace. The wrongs and sufferings of black men had taken the place of Him nailed to the Cross; the meager beginnings of the party had become another Resurrection; and the hate of those who would destroy her new faith had quickened in her a hunger to feel how deeply her strength went.

'Lawd, Johnny-Boy,' she would sometimes say, 'Ah jus wan them white folks t try t make me tell *who* is *in* the party n who *ain!* Ah jus wan em t try, n Ahll show em something they never thought a black woman could have!'

But sometimes like tonight, while lost in the forgetfulness of work, the past and the present would become mixed in her; while toiling under a strange star for a new freedom the old songs would slip from her lips with their beguiling sweetness.

The iron was getting cold. She put more wood into the fire, stood again at the window and watched the yellow blade of light

cut through the wet darkness. Johnny-Boy ain here yit. . . . Then,
before she was aware of it, she was still, listening for sounds.
Under the drone of rain she heard the slosh of feet in mud. Tha
ain Johnny-Boy. She knew his long, heavy footsteps in a million. She heard feet come on the porch. Some woman. . . . She
heard bare knuckles knock three times, then once. Thas some
of them comrades! She unbarred the door, cracked it a few inches,
and flinched from the cold rush of damp wind.

'Whos tha?'

'Its me!'

'Who?'

'Me, Reva!'

She flung the door open.

'Lawd, chile, c mon in!'

She stepped to one side and a thin, blonde-haired white girl
ran through the door; as she slid the bolt she heard the girl gasping
and shaking her wet clothes. Somethings wrong! Riva wouldna
walked a mile t mah mouse in all this slop fer nothin! Tha gals
stuck onto Johnny-Boy; Ah wondah ef anything happened t im?

'Git on inter the kitchen, Reva, where its warm.'

'Lawd, Ah sho is wet!'

'How yuh reckon yuhd be, in all tha rain?'

'Johnny-Boy ain here *yit?*' asked Reva.

'Naw! N ain no usa yuh worryin bout im. Jus yuh git them
shoes off! Yuh wanna ketch yo deatha col?' She stood looking
absently. Yeah; its something bout the party er Johnny-Boy
thas gone wrong. Lawd, Ah wondah ef her pa knows how she feels
bout Johnny-Boy? 'Honey, yuh hadnt oughta come out in sloppy
weather like this.'

'Ah had t come, An Sue.'

She led Reva to the kitchen.

'Git them shoes off an git close t the stove so yuhll git dry!'

'An Sue, Ah got something to tell yuh . . .'

The words made her hold her breath. Ah bet its something
bout Johnny-Boy!

'Whut, honey?'

'The sheriff wuz by our house tonight. He come see pa.'

'Yeah?'

'He done got word from somewheres bout tha meetin tomorrow.'

'Is it Johnny-Boy, Reva?'

'Aw, naw, An Sue! Ah ain hearda word bout im. Ain yuh
seen im tonight?'

'He ain come home t eat yit.'

'Where kin he be?'

'Lawd knows, chile.'

'Somebodys gotta tell them comrades tha meetings off,' said
Reva. 'The sheriffs got men watchin our house. Ah had t slip
out t git here widout em followin me.'

'Reva?'

'Hunh?'

'Ahma ol woman n Ah wans yuh t tell me the truth.'

'Whut, An Sue?'

'Yuh ain tryin t fool me, is yuh?'

'*Fool* yuh?'

'Bout Johnny-Boy?'

'Lawd, naw, An Sue!'

'Ef theres anything wrong jus tell me, chile. Ah kin stan it.'

She stood by the ironing board, her hands as usual folded
loosely over her stomach, watching Reva pull off her waterclogged
shoes. She was feeling that Johnny-Boy was already lost to her;
she was feeling the pain that would come when she knew it for
certain; and she was feeling that she would have to be brave and
bear it. She was like a person caught in a swift current of water
and knew where the water was sweeping her and did not want to
go on but had to go on to the end.

'It ain nothin bout Johnny-Boy, An Sue,' said Reva. 'But we gotta do something er we'll all git inter trouble.'

'How the sheriff know bout tha meetin?'

'Thas whut pa wans t know.'

'Somebody done turned Judas.'

'Sho looks like it.'

'Ah bet it wuz some of them new ones,' she said.

'Its hard t tell,' said Reva.

'Lissen, Reva, yuh oughta stay here n git dry, but yuh bettah git back n tell yo pa Johnny-Boy ain here n Ah don know when hes gonna show up. *Some*bodys gotta tell them comrades t stay erway from yo pas house.'

She stood with her back to the window, looking at Reva's wide, blue eyes. Po critter! Gotta go back thu all tha slop! Though she felt sorry for Reva, not once did she think that it would not have to be done. Being a woman, Reva was not suspect; she would have to go. It was just as natural for Reva to go back through the cold rain as it was for her to iron night and day or for Sug to be in jail. Right now, Johnny-Boy was out there on those dark fields trying to get home. Lawd, don let em git im tonight! In spite of herself her feelings became torn. She loved her son and, loving him, she loved what he was trying to do. Johnny-Boy was happiest when he was working for the party, and her love for him was for his happiness. She frowned, trying hard to fit something together in her feelings: for her to try to stop Johnny-Boy was to admit that all the toil of years meant nothing; and to let him go meant that sometime or other he would be caught, like Sug. In facing it this way she felt a little stunned, as though she had come suddenly upon a blank wall in the dark. But outside in the rain were people, white and black, whom she had known all her life. Those people depended upon Johnny-Boy, loved him and looked to him as a man and leader. Yeah; hes gotta keep on; he cant stop now. . . . She looked at Reva; she was crying and pulling her shoes back on with reluctant fingers.

'Whut yuh carryin on tha way fer, chile?'

'Yuh done los Sug, now yuh sendin Johnny-Boy ...'

'Ah got t, honey.'

She was glad she could say that. Reva believed in black folks and not for anything in the world would she falter before her. In Reva's trust and acceptance of her she had found her first feelings of humanity; Reva's love was her refuge from shame and degradation. If in the early days of her life the white mountain had driven her back from the earth, then in her last days Reva's love was drawing her toward it, like the beacon that swung through the night outside. She heard Reva sobbing.

'Hush, honey!'

'Mah brothers in jail too! Ma cries ever day ...'

'Ah know, honey.'

She helped Reva with her coat; her fingers felt the scant flesh of the girl's shoulders. She don git ernuff t eat, she thought. She slipped her arms around Reva's waist and held her close for a moment.

'Now, yuh stop tha cryin.'

'A-a-ah c-c-cant hep it. ...'

'Everythingll be awright; Johnny-Boyll be back.'

'Yuh think so?'

'Sho, chile. Cos he will.'

Neither of them spoke again until they stood in the doorway. Outside they could hear water washing through the ruts of the street.

'Be sho n send Johnny-Boy t tell the folks t stay erway from pas house,' said Reva.

'Ahll tell im. Don yuh worry.'

'Good-bye!'

'Good-bye!'

Leaning against the door jamb, she shook her head slowly and watched Reva vanish through the falling rain.

II

She was back at her board, ironing, when she heard feet sucking in the mud of the back yard; feet she knew from long years of listening were Johnny-Boy's. But tonight with all the rain and fear his coming was like a leaving, was almost more than she could bear. Tears welled to her eyes and she blinked them away. She felt that he was coming so that she could give him up; to see him now was to say good-bye. But it was a good-bye she knew she could never say; they were not that way toward each other. All day long they could sit in the same room and not speak; she was his mother and he was her son; most of the time a nod or a grunt would carry all the meaning that she wanted to say to him, or he to her.

She did not even turn her head when she heard him come stomping into the kitchen. She heard him pull up a chair, sit, sigh, and draw off his muddy shoes; they fell to the floor with heavy thuds. Soon the kitchen was full of the scent of his drying socks and his burning pipe. Tha boys hongry! She paused and looked at him over her shoulder; he was puffing at his pipe with his head tilted back and his feet propped up on the edge of the stove; his eyelids drooped and his wet clothes steamed from the heat of the fire. Lawd, tha boy gits mo like his pa ever day he lives, she mused, her lips breaking in a faint smile. Hols tha pipe in his mouth jus like his pa usta hol his. Wondah how they woulda got erlong ef his pa hada lived? They oughta liked each other, they so mucha like. She wished there could have been other children besides Sug, so Johnny-Boy would not have to be so much alone. A man needs a woman by his side. . . . She thought of Reva; she liked Reva; the brightest glow her heart had ever known was when she had learned that Reva loved Johnny-Boy. But beyond Reva were cold white faces. Ef theys caught it means *death*. . . . She jerked around when she heard Johnny-Boy's pipe clatter to the floor. She saw him pick it up, smile sheepishly at her, and wag his head.

'Gawd, Ahm sleepy,' he mumbled.

She got a pillow from her room and gave it to him.

'Here,' she said.

'Hunh,' he said, putting the pillow between his head and the back of the chair.

They were silent again. Yes, she would have to tell him to go back out into the cold rain and slop; maybe to get caught; maybe for the last time; she didn't know. But she would let him eat and get dry before telling him that the sheriff knew of the meeting to be held at Lem's tomorrow. And she would make him take a big dose of soda before he went out; soda always helped to stave off a cold. She looked at the clock. It was eleven. Theres time yit. Spreading a newspaper on the apron of the stove, she placed a heaping plate of greens upon it, a knife, a fork, a cup of coffee, a slab of cornbread, and a dish of peach cobbler.

'Yo suppahs ready,' she said.

'Yeah,' he said.

He did not move. She ironed again. Presently, she heard him eating. When she could no longer hear his knife tinkling against the edge of the plate, she knew he was through. It was almost twelve now. She would let him rest a little while longer before she told him. Till one er'clock, mabbe. Hes so tired. . . . She finished her ironing, put away the board, and stacked the clothes in her dresser drawer. She poured herself a cup of coffee, drew up a chair, sat, and drank.

'Yuh almos dry,' she said, not looking around

'Yeah,' he said, turning sharply to her.

The tone of voice in which she had spoken let him know that more was coming. She drained her cup and waited a moment longer.

'Reva wuz here.'

'Yeah?'

'She lef bout a hour ergo.'

'Whut she say?'

'She said ol man Lem hada visit from the sheriff today.'

'Bout the meetin?'

'Yeah.'

She saw him stare at the coals glowing red through the crevices of the stove and run his fingers nervously through his hair. She knew he was wondering how the sheriff had found out. In the silence he would ask a wordless question and in the silence she would answer wordlessly. Johnny-Boys too trustin, she thought. Hes tryin t make the party big n hes takin in folks fastern he kin git t know em. You cant trust ever white man yuh meet....

'Yuh know, Johnny-Boy, yuh been takin in a lotta them white folks lately ...'

'Aw, ma!'

'But, Johnny-Boy ...'

'Please, don talk t me bout tha now, ma.'

'Yuh ain t ol t lissen n learn, son,' she said.

'Ah know whut yuh gonna say, ma. N yuh wrong. Yuh cant judge folks jus by how yuh feel bout em n by how long yuh done knowed em. Ef we start tha we wouldnt have *no*body in the party. When folks pledge they word t be with us, then we gotta take em in. Wes too weak t be choosy.'

He rose abruptly, rammed his hands into his pockets, and stood facing the window; she looked at his back in a long silence. She knew his faith; it was deep. He had always said that black men could not fight the rich bosses alone; a man could not fight with every hand against him. But he believes so hard hes blind, she thought. At odd times they had had these arguments before; always she would be pitting her feelings against the hard necessity of his thinking, and always she would lose. She shook her head. Po Johnny-Boy; he don know ...

'But ain nona our folks tol, Johnny-Boy,' she said.

'How yuh know?' he asked. His voice came low and with a

tinge of anger. He still faced the window and now and then the
yellow blade of light flicked across the sharp outline of his black
face.

'Cause Ah know em,' she said.

'*Any*body mighta tol,' he said.

'It wuzgnt nona *our* folks,' she said again.

She saw his hand sweep in a swift arc of disgust.

'*Our* folks! Ma, who in Gawds name is *our* folks?'

'The folks we wuz born n raised wid, son. The folks we *know!*'

'We cant make the party grow tha way, ma.'

'It mighta been Booker,' she said.

'Yuh don know.'

' ... er Blattberg ...'

'Fer Chrissakes!'

' ... er any of the fo-five others whut joined las week.'

'Ma, yuh jus don wan me t go out tonight,' he said.

'Yo ol ma wans yuh t be careful, son.'

'Ma, when yuh start doubtin folks in the party, then there ain
no end.'

'Son, Ah knows ever black man n woman in this parta the
county,' she said, standing too. 'Ah watched em grow up; Ah
even heped birth n nurse some of em; Ah knows em *all* from way
back. There ain none of em tha *coulda* tol! The folks Ah know
jus don open they dos n ast death t walk in! Son, it wuz some of
them white folks! Yuh jus mark mah word!'

'Why is it gotta be *white* folks?' he asked. 'Ef they tol, then
theys jus Judases, thas all.'

'Son, look at whuts befo yuh.'

He shook his head and sighed.

'Ma, Ah done tol yuh a hundred times Ah cant see white an Ah
cant see black,' he said. 'Ah sees rich men an Ah sees po men.'

She picked up his dirty dishes and piled them in a pan. Out of
the corners of her eyes she saw him sit and pull on his wet shoes.

Hes goin! When she put the last dish away he was standing fully dressed, warming his hands over the stove. Just a few mo minutes now n he'll be gone, like Sug, mabbe. Her throat swelled. This black mans fight takes *ever*thing! Looks like Gawd puts us in this worl jus t beat us down!

'Keep this, ma,' he said.

She saw a crumpled wad of money in his outstretched fingers.

'Naw; yuh keep it. Yuh might need it.'

'It ain mine, ma. It berlongs t the party.'

'But, Johnny-Boy, yuh might hafta go erway!'

'Ah kin make out.'

'Don fergit yosef too much, son.'

'Ef Ah don come back theyll need it.'

He was looking at her face and she was looking at the money.

'Yuh keep tha,' she said slowly. 'Ahll give em the money.'

'From where?'

'Ah got some.'

'Where yuh git it from?'

She sighed.

'Ah been savin a dollah a week fer Sug ever since hes been in jail.'

'Lawd, ma!'

She saw the look of puzzled love and wonder in his eyes. Clumsily, he put the money back into his pocket.

'Ahm gone,' he said.

'Here; drink this glass of soda watah.'

She watched him drink, then put the glass away.

'Waal,' he said.

'Take the stuff outta yo pockets!'

She lifted the lid of the stove and he dumped all the papers from his pocket into the hole. She followed him to the door and made . him turn round.

'Lawd, yuh tryin to maka revolution n yuh cant even keep yo

coat buttoned.' Her nimble fingers fastened his collar high around his throat. 'There!'

He pulled the brim of his hat low over his eyes. She opened the door and with the suddenness of the cold gust of wind that struck her face, he was gone. She watched the black fields and the rain take him, her eyes burning. When the last faint footstep could no longer be heard, she closed the door, went to her bed, lay down, and pulled the cover over her while fully dressed. Her feelings coursed with the rhythm of the rain: Hes gone! Lawd, Ah *know* hes gone! Her blood felt cold.

III

She was floating in a gray void somewhere between sleeping and dreaming and then suddenly she was wide awake, hearing and feeling in the same instant the thunder of the door crashing in and a cold wind filling the room. It was pitch black and she stared, resting on her elbows, her mouth open, not breathing, her ears full of the sound of tramping feet and booming voices. She knew at once: They lookin fer im! Then, filled with her will, she was on her feet, rigid, waiting, listening.

'The lamps burnin!'

'Yuh see her?'

'Naw!'

'Look in the kitchen!'

'Gee, this place smells like niggers!'

'Say, somebodys here er been here!'

'Yeah; theres fire in the stove!'

'Mabbe hes been here n gone?'

'Boy, look at these jars of jam!'

'Niggers make good jam!'

'Git some bread!'

'Heres some cornbread!'

'Say, lemme git some!'

'Take it easy! Theres plenty here!'

'Ahma take some of this stuff home!'

'Look, heres a pota greens!'

'N some hot cawffee!'

'Say, yuh guys! C mon! Cut it out! We didnt come here fer a feas!'

She walked slowly down the hall. They lookin fer im, but they ain got im yit! She stopped in the doorway, her gnarled, black hands as always folded over her stomach, but tight now, so tightly the veins bulged. The kitchen was crowded with white men in glistening raincoats. Though the lamp burned, their flashlights still glowed in red fists. Across her floor she saw the muddy tracks of their boots.

'Yuh white folks git outta mah house!'

There was quick silence; every face turned toward her. She saw a sudden movement, but did not know what it meant until something hot and wet slammed her squarely in the face. She gasped, but did not move. Calmly, she wiped the warm, greasy liquor of greens from her eyes with her left hand. One of the white men had thrown a handful of greens out of the pot at her.

'How they taste, ol bitch?'

'Ah ast yuh t git outta mah house!'

She saw the sheriff detach himself from the crowd and walk toward her.

'Now Anty ...'

'White man, don yuh *Anty* me!'

'Yuh ain got the right sperit!'

'Sperit hell! Yuh git these men outta mah house!'

'Yuh ack like yuh don like it!'

'Naw, Ah don like it, n yuh knows dam waal Ah don!'

'What yuh gonna do about it?'

'Ahm tellin yuh t git outta mah house!'

'Gittin sassy?'

'Ef tellin yuh t git outta mah house is sass, then Ahm sassy!'

Her words came in a tense whisper; but beyond, back of them, she was watching, thinking, and judging the men.

'Listen, Anty,' the sheriff's voice came soft and low. 'Ahm here t hep yuh. How come yuh wanna ack this way?'

'Yuh ain never heped yo *own* sef since yuh been born,' she flared. 'How kin the likes of yuh hep me?'

One of the white men came forward and stood directly in front of her.

'Lissen, nigger woman, yuh talkin t *white* men!'

'Ah don care who Ahm talkin t!'

'Yuhll wish some day yuh did!'

'Not t the likes of yuh!'

'Yuh need somebody t teach yuh how t be a good nigger!'

'*Yuh* cant teach it t me!'

'Yuh gonna change yo tune.'

'Not longs mah bloods warm!'

'Don git smart now!'

'Yuh git outta mah house!'

'Spose we don go?' the sheriff asked.

They were crowded around her. She had not moved since she had taken her place in the doorway. She was thinking only of Johnny-Boy as she stood there giving and taking words; and she knew that they, too, were thinking of Johnny-Boy. She knew they wanted him, and her heart was daring them to take him from her.

'Spose we don go?' the sheriff asked again.

'Twenty of yuh runnin over one ol woman! Now, ain yuh white men glad yuh so brave?'

The sheriff grabbed her arm.

'C mon, now! Yuh done did ernuff sass fer one night. Wheres tha nigger son of yos?'

'Don yuh wished yuh knowed?'

'Yuh wanna git slapped?'

'Ah ain never seen one of yo kind tha wuznt too low fer . . .'

The sheriff slapped her straight across her face with his open palm. She fell back against a wall and sank to her knees.

'Is tha whut white men do t nigger women?'

She rose slowly and stood again, not even touching the place that ached from his blow, her hands folded over her stomach.

'Ah ain never seen one of yo kind tha wuznt too low fer . . .'

He slapped her again; she reeled backward several feet and fell on her side.

'Is tha whut we too low t do?'

She stood before him again, dry-eyed, as though she had not been struck. Her lips were numb and her chin was wet with blood.

'Aw, let her go! Its the nigger we wan!' said one.

'Wheres that nigger son of yos?' the sheriff asked.

'Find im,' she said.

'By Gawd, ef we hafta find im we'll kill im!'

'He wont be the only nigger yuh ever killed,' she said.

She was consumed with a bitter pride. There was nothing on this earth, she felt then, that they could not do to her but that she could take. She stood on a narrow plot of ground from which she would die before she was pushed. And then it was, while standing there feeling warm blood seeping down her throat, that she gave up Johnny-Boy, gave him up to the white folks. She gave him up because they had come tramping into her heart demanding him, thinking they could get him by beating her, thinking they could scare her into making her tell where he was. She gave him up because she wanted them to know that they could not get what they wanted by bluffing and killing.

'Wheres this meetin gonna be?' the sheriff asked.

'Don yuh wish yuh knowed?'

'Ain there gonna be a meetin?'

'How come yuh astin me?'

'There *is* gonna be a meetin,' said the sheriff.

'Is it?'

'Ah gotta great mind t choke it outta yuh!'

'Yuh so smart,' she said.

'We ain playin wid yuh!'

'Did Ah say yuh wuz?'

'Tha nigger son of yos is erroun here somewheres an we aim t find im,' said the sheriff. 'Ef yuh tell us where he is n ef he talks, mabbe he'll git off easy. But ef we hafta find im, we'll kill im! Ef we hafta find im, then yuh git a sheet t put over im in the mawnin, see? Git yuh a sheet, cause hes gonna be dead!'

'He wont be the only nigger yuh ever killed,' she said again.

The sheriff walked past her. The others followed. Yuh didnt git whut yuh wanted! she thought exultingly. N yuh ain gonna *never* git it! Hotly something ached in her to make them feel the intensity of her pride and freedom; her heart groped to turn the bitter hours of her life into words of a kind that would make them feel that she had taken all they had done to her in her stride and could still take more. Her faith surged so strongly in her she was all but blinded. She walked behind them to the door, knotting and twisting her fingers. She saw them step to the muddy ground. Each whirl of the yellow beacon revealed glimpses of slanting rain. Her lips moved, then she shouted:

'Yuh didn't git whut yuh wanted! N yuh ain gonna nevah git it!'

The sheriff stopped and turned; his voice came low and hard.

'Now, by Gawd, thas ernuff outta yuh!'

'Ah know when Ah done said ernuff!'

'Aw, naw, yuh don!' he said. 'Yuh don know when yuh done said ernuff, but Ahma teach yuh ternight!'

He was up the steps and across the porch with one bound. She backed into the hall, her eyes full on his face.

'Tell me when yuh gonna stop talkin!' he said, swinging his fist.

The blow caught her high on the cheek; her eyes went blank; she fell flat on her face. She felt the hard heel of his wet shoes coming into her temple and stomach.

'Lemme hear yuh talk some mo!'

She wanted to, but could not; pain numbed and choked her. She lay still and somewhere out of the gray void of unconsciousness she heard someone say: *Aw fer chrissakes leave her erlone its the nigger we wan.* . . .

IV

She never knew how long she had lain huddled in the dark hallway. Her first returning feeling was of a nameless fear crowding the inside of her, then a deep pain spreading from her temple downward over her body. Her ears were filled with the drone of rain and she shuddered from the cold wind blowing through the door. She opened her eyes and at first saw nothing. As if she were imagining it, she knew she was half-lying and half-sitting in a corner against a wall. With difficulty she twisted her neck, and what she saw made her hold her breath — a vast white blur was suspended directly above her. For a moment she could not tell if her fear was from the blur or if the blur was from her fear. Gradually the blur resolved itself into a huge white face that slowly filled her vision. She was stone still, conscious really of the effort to breathe, feeling somehow that she existed only by the mercy of that white face. She had seen it before; its fear had gripped her many times; it had for her the fear of all the white faces she had ever seen in her life. *Sue* . . . As from a great distance, she heard her name being called. She was regaining consciousness now, but the fear was coming with her. She looked into the face of a white man, wanting to scream out for him to go; yet accepting his presence because she felt she had to. Though some remote part of her mind was active, her limbs were powerless. It was as if an invisible knife had split her in two, leaving one half of her lying there helpless, while the other half shrank in dread from a forgotten but familiar enemy. *Sue its me Sue its me* ... Then all at once the voice came clearly.

'Sue, its me! Its Booker!'

And she heard an answering voice speaking inside of her, Yeah, its Booker ... The one whut jus joined ... She roused herself, struggling for full consciousness; and as she did so she transferred to the person of Booker the nameless fear she felt. It seemed that Booker towered above her as a challenge to her right to exist upon the earth.

'Yuh awright?'

She did not answer; she started violently to her feet and fell.

'Sue, yuh hurt!'

'Yeah,' she breathed.

'Where they hit yuh?'

'Its mah head,' she whispered.

She was speaking even though she did not want to; the fear that had hold of her compelled her.

'They beat yuh?'

'Yeah.'

'Them bastards! Them Gawddam bastards!'

She heard him saying it over and over; then she felt herself being lifted.

'Naw!' she gasped.

'Ahma take yuh t the kitchen!'

'Put me down!'

'But yuh cant stay here like this!'

She shrank in his arms and pushed her hands against his body; when she was in the kitchen she freed herself, sank into a chair, and held tightly to its back. She looked wonderingly at Booker; there was nothing about him that should frighten her so; but even that did not ease her tension. She saw him go to the water bucket, wet his handkerchief, wring it, and offer it to her. Distrustfully, she stared at the damp cloth.

'Here; put this on yo fohead ...'

'Naw!'

'C mon; itll make yuh feel bettah!'

She hesitated in confusion; what right had she to be afraid when someone was acting as kindly as this toward her? Reluctantly, she leaned forward and pressed the damp cloth to her head. It helped. With each passing minute she was catching hold of herself, yet wondering why she felt as she did.

'Whut happened?'

'Ah don know.'

'Yuh feel bettah?'

'Yeah.'

'Who all wuz here?'

'Ah don know,' she said again.

'Yo head still hurt?'

'Yeah.'

'Gee, Ahm sorry.'

'Ahm awright,' she sighed and buried her face in her hands. She felt him touch her shoulder.

'Sue, Ah got some bad news fer yuh ...'

She knew; she stiffened and grew cold. It had happened; she stared dry-eyed with compressed lips.

'Its mah Johnny-Boy,' she said.

'Yeah; Ahm awful sorry t hafta tell yuh this way. But Ah thought yuh oughta know ...'

Her tension eased and a vacant place opened up inside of her. A voice whispered, Jesus, hep me!

'W-w-where is he?'

'They got im out t Foleys Woods tryin t make im tell who the others is.'

'He ain gonna tell,' she said. 'They just as waal kill im, cause he ain gonna nevah tell.'

'Ah hope he don,' said Booker. 'But he didnt hava chance t tell the others. They grabbed im just as he got t the woods.'

Then all the horror of it flashed upon her; she saw flung out over the rainy countryside an array of shacks where white and black comrades were sleeping; in the morning they would be rising and going to Lem's; then they would be caught. And that meant terror, prison, and death. The comrades would have to be told; she would have to tell them; she could not entrust Johnny-Boy's work to another, and especially not to Booker as long as she felt toward him as she did. Gripping the bottom of the chair with both hands, she tried to rise; the room blurred and she swayed. She found herself resting in Booker's arms.

'Lemme go!'

'Sue, yuh too weak t walk!'

'Ah gotta tell em!' she said.

'Set down, Sue! Yuh hurt; yuh sick!'

When seated she looked at him helplessly.

'Sue, lissen! Johnny-Boys caught. Ahm here. Yuh tell me who they is n Ahll tell em.'

She stared at the floor and did not answer. Yes; she was too weak to go. There was no way for her to tramp all those miles through the rain tonight. But should she tell Booker? If only she had somebody like Reva to talk to. She did not want to decide alone; she must make no mistake about this. She felt Booker's fingers pressing on her arm and it was as though the white mountain was pushing her to the edge of a sheer height; she again exclaimed inwardly, Jesus, hep me! Booker's white face was at her side, waiting. Would she be doing right to tell him? Suppose she did not tell and then the comrades were caught? She could not ever forgive herself for doing a thing like that. But maybe she was wrong; maybe her fear was what Johnny-Boy had always called 'jus foolishness.' She remembered his saying, Ma we cant make the party ef we start doubtin everybody. . . .

'Tell me who they is, Sue, n Ahll tell em. Ah just joined n Ah don know who they is.'

'Ah don know who they is,' she said.

'Yuh *gotta* tell me who they is, Sue!'

'Ah tol yuh Ah don know!'

'Yuh *do* know! C mon! Set up n talk!'

'Naw!'

'Yuh wan em all t git *killed?*'

She shook her head and swallowed. Lawd, Ah don blieve in this man!

'Lissen, Ahll call the names n yuh tell me which ones is in the party n which ones ain, see?'

'Naw!'

'Please, Sue!'

'Ah don know,' she said.

'Sue, yuh ain doin right by em. Johnny-Boy wouldnt wan yuh t be this way. Hes out there holdin up his end. Les hol up ours. . . .'

'Lawd, Ah don know. . . .'

'Is yuh scareda me cause Ahm *white?* Johnny-Boy ain like tha. Don let all the work we done go fer nothin.'

She gave up and bowed her head in her hands.

'Is it Johnson? Tell me, Sue?'

'Yeah,' she whispered in horror; a mounting horror of feeling herself being undone.

'Is it Green?'

'Yeah.'

'Murphy?'

'Lawd, Ah don know!'

'Yuh gotta tell me, Sue!'

'Mistah Booker, please leave me erlone. . . .'

'Is it Murphy?'

She answered yes to the names of Johnny-Boy's comrades; she

answered until he asked her no more. Then she thought, How he know the sheriffs men is watchin Lems house? She stood up and held onto her chair, feeling something sure and firm within her.

'How yuh know bout Lem?'

'Why ... How Ah know?'

'Whut yuh doin here this tima night? How yuh know the sheriff got Johnny-Boy?'

'Sue, don yuh blieve in me?'

She did not, but she could not answer. She stared at him until her lips hung open; she was searching deep within herself for certainty.

'You meet Reva?' she asked.

'Reva?'

'Yeah; Lems gal?'

'Oh, yeah. Sho, Ah met Reva.'

'She tell yuh?'

She asked the question more of herself than of him; she longed to believe.

'Yeah,' he said softly. 'Ah reckon Ah oughta be goin t tell em now.'

'Who?' she asked. 'Tell *who?*'

The muscles of her body were stiff as she waited for his answer; she felt as though life depended upon it.

'The comrades,' he said.

'Yeah,' she sighed.

She did not know when he left; she was not looking or listening. She just suddenly saw the room empty, and from her the thing that had made her fearful was gone.

V

For a space of time that seemed to her as long as she had been upon the earth, she sat huddled over the cold stove. One minute

she would say to herself, They both gone now; Johnny-Boy n Sug
. . . Mabbe Ahll never see em ergin.   Then a surge of guilt would
blot out her longing. 'Lawd, Ah shouldna tol!' she mumbled.
'But no man kin be so lowdown as t do a thing like tha . . .'
Several times she had an impulse to try to tell the comrades herself; she was feeling a little better now. But what good would
that do? She had told Booker the names. He just couldnt be
a Judas t po folks like us . . . He *couldnt!*

'An Sue!'

Thas Reva! Her heart leaped with an anxious gladness. She
rose without answering and limped down the dark hallway.
Through the open door, against the background of rain, she saw
Reva's face lit now and then to whiteness by the whirling beams
of the beacon. She was about to call, but a thought checked her.
Jesus, hep me! Ah gotta tell her bout Johnny-Boy . . . Lawd, Ah
cant!

An Sue, yuh there?'

'C mon in, chile!'

She caught Reva and held her close for a moment without
speaking.

'Lawd, Ahm sho glad yuh here,' she said at last.

'Ah thought something had happened t yuh,' said Reva,
pulling away. 'Ah saw the do open . . . Pa tol me to come back
n stay wid yuh tonight . . .' Reva paused and stared. 'W-w-
whuts the mattah?'

She was so full of having Reva with her that she did not understand what the question meant.

'Hunh?'

'Yo neck . . .'

'Aw, it ain nothin, chile. C mon in the kitchen.'

'But theres blood on yo neck!'

'The sheriff wuz here . . .'

'Them fools! Whut they wanna bother yuh fer? Ah could kill
em! So hep me Gawd, Ah could!'

'It ain nothin,' she said.

She was wondering how to tell Reva about Johnny-Boy and Booker. Ahll wait a lil while longer, she thought. Now that Reva was here, her fear did not seem as awful as before.

'C mon, lemme fix yo head, An Sue. Yuh hurt.'

They went to the kitchen. She sat silent while Reva dressed her scalp. She was feeling better now; in just a little while she would tell Reva. She felt the girl's finger pressing gently upon her head.

'Tha hurt?'

'A lil, chile.'

'Yuh po thing.'

'It ain nothin.'

'Did Johnny-Boy come?'

She hesitated.

'Yeah.'

'He done gone t tell the others?'

Reva's voice sounded so clear and confident that it mocked her. Lawd, Ah cant tell this chile...

'Yuh tol im, didnt yuh, An Sue?'

'Y-y-yeah...'

'Gee! Thas good! Ah tol pa he didn't hafta worry ef Johnny-Boy got the news. Mabbe thingsll come out awright.'

'Ah hope...'

She could not go on; she had gone as far as she could; for the first time that night she began to cry.

'Hush, An Sue! Yuh awways been brave. Itll be awright!'

'Ain nothin awright, chile. The worls just too much fer us, Ah reckon.'

'Ef yuh cry that way itll make me cry.'

She forced herself to stop. Naw; Ah cant carry on this way in fronta Reva... Right now she had a deep need for Reva to believe in her. She watched the girl get pine-knots from behind the stove, rekindle the fire, and put on the coffee pot.

'Yuh wan some cawffee?' Reva asked.

'Naw, honey.'

'Aw, c mon, An Sue.'

'Jusa lil, honey.'

'Thas the way t be. Oh, say, Ah fergot,' said Reva, measuring out spoonfuls of coffee. 'Pa tol me t tell yuh t watch out fer tha Booker man. Hes a stool.'

She showed not one sign of outward movement or expression, but as the words fell from Reva's lips she went limp inside.

'Pa tol me soon as Ah got back home. He got word from town . . .'

She stopped listening. She felt as though she had been slapped to the extreme outer edge of life, into a cold darkness. She knew now what she had felt when she had looked up out of her fog of pain and had seen Booker. It was the image of all the white folks, and the fear that went with them, that she had seen and felt during her lifetime. And again, for the second time that night, something she had felt had come true. All she could say to herself was, Ah didnt like im! Gawd knows, Ah didnt! Ah tol Johnny-Boy it wuz some of them white folks . . .

'Here; drink yo cawffee . . .'

She took the cup; her fingers trembled, and the steaming liquid spilt onto her dress and leg.

'Ahm sorry, An Sue!'

Her leg was scalded, but the pain did not bother her.

'Its awright,' she said.

'Wait; lemme put something on tha burn!'

'It don hurt.'

'Yuh worried bout something.'

'Naw, honey.'

'Lemme fix yuh so mo cawffee.'

'Ah don wan nothin now, Reva.'

'Waal, buck up. Don be tha way . . .'

They were silent. She heard Reva drinking. No; she would not tell Reva; Reva was all she had left. But she had to do something, some way, somehow. She was undone too much as it was; and to tell Reva about Booker or Johnny-Boy was more than she was equal to; it would be too coldly shameful. She wanted to be alone and fight this thing out with herself.

'Go t bed, honey. Yuh tired.'

'Naw; Ahm awright, An Sue.'

She heard the bottom of Reva's empty cup clank against the top of the stove. Ah *got* t make her go t bed! Yes; Booker would tell the names of the comrades to the sheriff. If she could only stop him some way! That was the answer, the point, the star that grew bright in the morning of new hope. Soon, maybe half an hour from now, Booker would reach Foley's Woods. Hes boun t go the long way, cause he don know no short cut, she thought. Ah could wade the creek n beat im there.... But what would she do after that?

'Reva, honey, go t bed. Ahm awright. Yuh need res.'

'Ah ain sleepy, An Sue.'

'Ah knows whuts bes fer yuh, chile. Yuh tired n wet.'

'Ah wanna stay up wid yuh.'

She forced a smile and said:

'Ah don think they gonna hurt Johnny-Boy...'

'Fer *real*, An Sue?'

'Sho, honey.'

'But Ah wanna wait up wid yuh.'

'Thas mah job, honey. Thas whut a mas fer, t wait up fer her chullun.'

'Good night, An Sue.'

'Good night, honey.'

She watched Reva pull up and leave the kitchen; presently she heard the shucks in the mattress whispering, and she knew that Reva had gone to bed. She was alone. Through the cracks of the stove she saw the fire dying to grey ashes; the room was growing cold again. The yellow beacon continued to flit past the window and the rain still drummed. Yes; she was alone; she had done this awful thing alone; she must find some way out, alone. Like touching a festering sore, she put her finger upon that moment when she had shouted her defiance to the sheriff, when she had shouted to feel her strength. She had lost Sug to save others; she had let Johnny-Boy go to save others; and then in a moment of weakness that came from too much strength she had lost all. If she had not shouted to the sheriff, she would have been strong enough to have resisted Booker; she would have been able to tell the comrades herself. Something tightened in her as she remembered and understood the fit of fear she had felt on coming to herself in the dark hallway. A part of her life she thought she had done away with forever had had hold of her then. She had thought the soft, warm past was over; she had thought that it did not mean much when now she sang: 'Hes the Lily of the Valley, the Bright n Mawnin Star.' ... The days when she had sung that song were the days when she had not hoped for anything on this earth, the days when the cold mountain had driven her into the arms of Jesus. She had thought that Sug and Johnny-Boy had taught her to forget Him, to fix her hope upon the fight of black men for freedom. Through the gradual years she had believed and worked with them, had felt strength shed from the grace of their terrible vision. That grace had been upon her when she had let the sheriff slap her down; it had been upon her when she had risen time and again from the floor and faced him. But she had trapped herself with her own hunger; to water the long dry thirst of her faith her pride had made a bargain which her flesh could not keep. Her having told the names of Johnny-Boy's comrades was but an incident in a deeper horror. She stood up and looked at the floor while call and counter-call, loyalty and counter-loyalty struggled in her soul. Mired she was between two abandoned worlds, living, dying without the strength of the grace that either gave. The clearer she felt it the fuller did something well up from the depths of her for release; the more urgent did she feel the need to fling into her black sky another star, another hope, one more terrible vision to give her the strength to live and act. Softly and restlessly she walked about the kitchen, feeling herself naked against night, the rain, the world; and shamed whenever the thought of Reva's love crossed her mind. She lifted her empty hands and looked at her writhing fingers. Lawd, whut kin Ah do now? She could still wade the creek and get to Foley's Woods before Booker. And then what? How could she manage to see Johnny-Boy or Booker? Again she heard the sheriff's threatening voice: Git yuh a sheet, cause hes gonna be dead! The sheet! Thas it, the sheet! Her whole being leaped with will; the long years of her life bent toward a moment of focus, a point. Ah kin go wid mah sheet! Ahll be doin whut he said! Lawd Gawd in Heaven, Ahma go lika nigger woman wid mah windin sheet t git mah dead son! But then what? She stood straight and smiled grimly; she had in her heart the whole meaning of her life; her entire personality was poised on the brink of a total act. Ah know! Ah know! She thought of Johnny-Boy's gun in the dresser drawer. Ahll hide the gun in the sheet n go aftah Johnny-Boys body.... She tiptoed to her room, eased out the dresser drawer, and got a sheet. Reva was sleeping; the darkness was filled with her quiet breathing. She groped in the drawer and found the gun. She wound the gun in the sheet and held them both under her apron. Then she stole to the bedside and watched Reva. Lawd, hep her! But mabbe shes bettah off. This had t happen sometimes... She n Johnny-Boy couldna been together in this here South... N Ah couldnt tell her bout Booker. Itll come out awright n she wont nevah know. Reva's trust would never be shaken. She caught her breath as the shucks in the mattress rustled dryly; then all was quiet and she breathed easily again. She tiptoed to the door, down the hall, and stood on the porch. Above her the yellow beacon whirled through the rain. She went over muddy ground, mounted a slope, stopped and looked back at her house. The lamp glowed in her window, and the yellow beacon that swung every few seconds seemed to feed it with light. She turned and started across the fields, holding the gun and sheet tightly, thinking, Po Reva... Po critter... Shes fas ersleep...

VI

For the most part she walked with her eyes half shut, her lips tightly compressed, leaning her body against the wind and the slanting rain, feeling the pistol in the sheet sagging cold and heavy in her fingers. Already she was getting wet; it seemed that her feet found every puddle of water that stood between the corn rows.

She came to the edge of the creek and paused, wondering at what point was it low. Taking the sheet from under her apron, she wrapped the gun in it so that her finger could be upon the trigger. Ahll cross here, she thought. At first she did not feel the water; her feet were already wet. But the water grew cold as it came up to her knees; she gasped when it reached her waist. Lawd, this creeks high! When she had passed the middle, she knew that she was out of danger. She came out of the water, climbed a grassy hill, walked on, turned a bend and saw the lights of autos gleaming ahead. Yeah; theys still there! She hurried with her head down. Wondah did Ah beat im here? Lawd, Ah hope so! A vivid image of Booker's white face hovered a moment before her eyes and a driving will surged up in her so hard and strong that it vanished. She was among the autos now. From nearby came the hoarse voices of the men.

'Hey, yuh!'

She stopped, nervously clutching the sheet. Two white men with shotguns came toward her.

'Whut in hell yuh doin out here?'

She did not answer.

'Didnt yuh hear somebody speak t yuh?'

'Ahm comin aftah mah son,' she said humbly.

'Yo *son?*'

'Yessuh.'

'Whut yo son doin out here?'

'The sheriffs got im.'

'Holy Scott! Jim, its the niggers ma!'

'Whut yuh got there?' asked one.

'A sheet.'

'A *sheet?*'

'Yessuh.'

'Fer whut?'

'The sheriff tol me t bring a sheet t git his body.'

'Waal, waal...'

'Now, ain tha something?'

The white men looked at each other.

'These niggers sho love one ernother,' said one.

'N tha ain no lie,' said the other.

'Take me t the sheriff,' she begged.

'Yuh ain givin us *orders*, is yuh?'

'Nawsuh.'

'We'll take yuh when wes good n ready.'

'Yessuh.'

'So yuh wan his body?'

'Yessuh.'

'Waal, he ain dead yit.'

'They gonna kill im,' she said.

'Ef he talks they wont.'

'He ain gonna talk,' she said.

'How yuh know?'

'Cause he ain.'

'We got ways of makin niggers talk.'

'Yuh ain got no way fer im.'

'Yuh thinka lot of tha black Red, don yuh?'

'Hes mah son.'

'Why don yuh teach im some sense?'

'Hes mah son,' she said again.

'Lissen, old nigger woman, yuh stan there wid yo hair white. Yuh got bettah sense than t blieve tha niggers kin make a revolution . . .'

'A black republic,' said the other one, laughing.

'Take me t the sheriff,' she begged.

'Yuh his ma,' said one. 'Yuh kin make im talk n tell whos in this thing wid im.'

'He ain gonna talk,' she said.

'Don yuh wan im t live?'

She did not answer.

'C mon, les take her t Bradley.'

They grabbed her arms and she clutched hard at the sheet and gun; they led her toward the crowd in the woods. Her feelings were simple; Booker would not tell; she was there with the gun to see to that. The louder became the voices of the men the deeper became her feeling of wanting to right the mistake she had made; of wanting to fight her way back to solid ground. She would stall for time until Booker showed up. Oh, ef theyll only lemme git close t Johnny-Boy! As they led her near the crowd she saw white faces turning and looking at her and heard a rising clamor of voices.

'Whos tha?'

'A nigger woman!'

'Whut she doin out here?'

'This is his ma!' called one of the men.

'Whut she wans?'

'She brought a sheet t cover his body!'

'He ain dead yit!'

'They tryin t make im talk!'

'But he will be dead soon ef he don open up!'

'Say, look! The niggers ma brought a sheet t cover up his body!'

'Now, ain tha sweet?'

'Mabbe she wans hol a prayer meetin!'

'Did she git a preacher?'

'Say, go git Bradley!'

'O.K.!'

The crowd grew quiet. They looked at her curiously; she felt their cold eyes trying to detect some weakness in her. Humbly, she stood with the sheet covering the gun. She had already accepted all that they could do to her.

The sheriff came.

'So yuh brought yo sheet, hunh?'

'Yessuh,' she whispered.

'Looks like them slaps we gave yuh learned yuh some sense, didnt they?'

She did not answer.

'Yuh don need tha sheet. Yo son ain dead yit,' he said, reaching.

She backed away, her eyes wide.

'Naw!'

'Now, lissen, Anty!' he said. 'There ain no use in yuh ackin a fool! Go in there n tell tha nigger son of yos t tell us whos in this wid im, see? Ah promise we wont kill im ef he talks. We'll let im git outta town.'

'There ain nothin Ah kin tell im,' she said.

'Yuh wan us t kill im?'

She did not answer. She saw someone lean toward the sheriff and whisper.

'Bring her erlong,' the sheriff said.

They led her to a muddy clearing. The rain streamed down through the ghostly glare of the flashlights. As the men formed a semi-circle she saw Johnny-Boy lying in a trough of mud. He was tied with rope; he lay hunched, one side of his face resting in a pool of black water. His eyes were staring questioningly at her.

'Speak t im,' said the sheriff.

If she could only tell him why she was there! But that was impossible; she was close to what she wanted and she stared straight before her with compressed lips.

'Say, nigger!' called the sheriff, kicking Johnny-Boy. 'Here's yo ma!'

Johnny-Boy did not move or speak. The sheriff faced her again.

'Lissen, Anty,' he said. 'Yuh got mo say wid im than anybody. Tell im t talk n hava chance. Whut he wanna pertect the other niggers n white folks fer?'

She slid her finger about the trigger of the gun and looked stonily at the mud.

'Go t him,' said the sheriff.

She did not move. Her heart was crying out to answer the amazed question in Johnny-Boy's eyes. But there was no way now.

'Waal, yuhre astin fer it. By Gawd, we gotta way to *make* yuh talk t im,' he said, turning away. 'Say, Tim, git one of them logs n turn tha nigger upsidedown n put his legs on it!'

A murmur of assent ran through the crowd. She bit her lips; she knew what that meant.

'Yuh wan yo nigger son crippled?' she heard the sheriff ask.

She did not answer. She saw them roll the log up; they lifted Johnny-Boy and laid him on his face and stomach, then they pulled his legs over the log. His knee-caps rested on the sheer top of the log's back, the toes of his shoes pointing groundward. So absorbed was she in watching that she felt that it was she that was being lifted and made ready for torture.

'Git a crowbar!' said the sheriff.

A tall, lank man got a crowbar from a near-by auto and stood over the log. His jaws worked slowly on a wad of tobacco.

'Now, its up t yuh, Anty,' the sheriff said. 'Tell the man whut t do!'

She looked into the rain. The sheriff turned.

'Mabbe she think wes playin. Ef she don say nothin, then break em at the knee-caps!'

'O.K., Sheriff!'

She stood waiting for Booker. Her legs felt weak; she wondered if she would be able to wait much longer. Over and over she said to herself, Ef he came now Ahd kill em both!

'She ain sayin nothin, Sheriff!'

'Waal, Gawddammit, let im have it!'

The crowbar came down and Johnny-Boy's body lunged in the mud and water. There was a scream. She swayed, holding tight to the gun and sheet.

'Hol im! Git the other leg!'

The crowbar fell again. There was another scream.

'Yuh break em?' asked the sheriff.

The tall man lifted Johnny-Boy's legs and let them drop limply again, dropping rearward from the knee-caps. Johnny-Boy's body lay still. His head had rolled to one side and she could not see his face.

'Jus lika broke sparrow wing,' said the man, laughing softly.

Then Johnny-Boy's face turned to her; he screamed.

'Go way, ma! Go way!'

It was the first time she had heard his voice since she had come out to the woods; she all but lost control of herself. She started violently forward, but the sheriff's arm checked her.

'Aw, naw! Yuh had yo chance!' He turned to Johnny-Boy. 'She kin go ef yuh talk.'

'Mistah, he ain gonna talk,' she said.

'Go way, ma!' said Johnny-Boy.

'Shoot im! Don make im suffah so,' she begged.

'He'll either talk or he'll never hear yuh ergin,' the sheriff said. 'Theres other things we kin do t im.'

She said nothing.

'Whut yuh come here fer, ma?' Johnny-Boy sobbed.

'Ahm gonna split his eardrums,' the sheriff said. 'Ef yuh got anything t say t im yuh bettah say it *now!*'

She closed her eyes. She heard the sheriff's feet sucking in mud. Ah could save im! She opened her eyes; there were shouts of eagerness from the crowd as it pushed in closer.

'Bus em, Sheriff!'

'Fix im so he cant hear!'

'He knows how t do it, too!'

'He busted a Jew boy tha way once!'

She saw the sheriff stoop over Johnny-Boy, place his flat palm over one ear and strike his fist against it with all his might. He placed his palm over the other ear and struck again. Johnny-Boy moaned, his head rolling from side to side, his eyes showing white amazement in a world without sound.

'Yuh wouldn't talk t im when yuh had the chance,' said the sheriff. 'Try n talk now.'

She felt warm tears on her cheeks. She longed to shoot Johnny-Boy and let him go. But if she did that they would take the gun from her, and Booker would tell who the others were. Lawd, hep me! The men were talking loudly now, as though the main business was over. It seemed ages that she stood there watching Johnny-Boy roll and whimper in his world of silence.

'Say, Sheriff, heres somebody lookin fer yuh!'

'Who is it?'

'Ah don know!'

'Bring em in!'

She stiffened and looked around wildly, holding the gun tight. Is tha Booker? Then she held still, feeling that her excitement might betray her. Mabbe Ah kin shoot em both! Mabbe Ah kin shoot twice! The sheriff stood in front of her, waiting. The crowd parted and she saw Booker hurrying forward.

'Ah know em all, Sheriff!' he called.

He came full into the muddy clearing where Johnny-Boy lay.

'Yuh mean yuh got the names?'

'Sho! The ol nigger...'

She saw his lips hang open and silent when he saw her. She stepped forward and raised the sheet.

'Whut...'

She fired, once; then, without pausing, she turned, hearing them yell. She aimed at Johnny-Boy, but they had their arms around her, bearing her to the ground, clawing at the sheet in her hand. She glimpsed Booker lying sprawled in the mud, on his face, his hands stretched out before him; then a cluster of yelling men blotted him out. She lay without struggling, looking upward through the rain at the white faces above her. And she was suddenly at peace; they were not a white mountain now; they were not pushing her any longer to the edge of life. Its awright...

'She shot Booker!'

'She hada gun in the sheet!'

'She shot im right thu the head!'

'Whut she shoot im fer?'

'Kill the bitch!'

'Ah *thought* something wuz wrong bout her!'

'Ah wuz fer givin it t her from the firs!'

'Thas whut yuh git fer treatin a nigger nice!'

'Say, Bookers dead!'

She stopped looking into the white faces, stopped listening. She waited, giving up her life before they took it from her; she had done what she wanted. Ef only Johnny-Boy... She looked at him; he lay looking at her with tired eyes. Ef she could only tell im!

'Whut yuh kill im fer, hunh?'

It was the sheriff's voice; she did not answer.

'Mabbe she wuz shootin at yuh, Sheriff?'

'Whut yuh kill im fer?'

She felt the sheriff's foot come into her side; she closed her eyes.

'Yuh black bitch!'

'Let her have it!'

'Yuh reckon she foun out bout Booker?'

'She mighta.'

'Jesus Christ, whut yuh dummies *waitin* on!'

'Yeah; kill her!'

'Kill em *both!*'

'Let her know her nigger sons dead firs!'

She turned her head toward Johnny-Boy; he lay looking puzzled in a world beyond the reach of voices. At leas he cant hear, she thought.

'C mon, let im have it!'

She listened to hear what Johnny-Boy could not. They came, two of them, one right behind the other; so close together that they sounded like one shot. She did not look at Johnny-Boy now; she looked at the white faces of the men, hard and wet in the glare of the flashlights.

'Yuh hear tha, nigger woman?'

'Did tha surprise im? Hes in hell now wonderin whut hit im!'

'C mon! Give it t her, Sheriff!'

'Lemme shoot her, Sheriff! It wuz mah pal she shot!'

'Awright, Pete! Thas fair ernuff!'

She gave up as much of her life as she could before they took it from her. But the sound of the shot and the streak of fire that tore its way through her chest forced her to live again, intensely. She had not moved, save for the slight jarring impact of the bullet,

She felt the heat of her own blood warming her cold, wet back.
She yearned suddenly to talk. 'Yuh didnt git whut yuh wanted!
N yuh ain gonna nevah git it! Yuh didnt kill me; Ah come here
by mahsef . . .' She felt rain falling into her wide-open, dimming
eyes and heard faint voices. Her lips moved soundlessly. *Yuh
didnt git yuh didnt yuh didnt . . .* Focused and pointed she was,
buried in the depths of her star, swallowed in its peace and
strength; and not feeling her flesh growing cold, cold as the rain
that fell from the invisible sky upon the doomed living and the
dead that never dies.

BIOGRAPHICAL NOTES

BIOGRAPHICAL NOTES

WILBUR DANIEL STEELE

Wilbur Daniel Steele was born in Greensboro, North Carolina, in 1886. He is a graduate of the University of Denver and has studied art in Paris, New York, and Boston. He is the author of several novels, several collections of short stories, and several plays. His most distinguished short stories are *The Yellow Cat, Down on Their Knees, Ching, Ching, Chinaman, The Dark Hour, Out of Exile, The Shame Dance, From the Other Side of the South,* and *How Beautiful With Shoes.* His best short stories were written between 1914 and 1922. Essentially a romantic, he has always sought novel settings and atmospheric effects for his stories. He is probably the best short-story writer at the beginning of our period, but hardly foreshadows the future course of the American short story. His narrative power at its best is outstanding.

THEODORE DREISER

Theodore Dreiser was born in Terre Haute, Indiana, in 1871. He was educated at Indiana University and had wide experience as a newspaper man and as a magazine editor. His novel *Sister Carrie,* when it appeared in 1900, foreshadowed prophetically the course which American writing was to take from then till now. It took over twenty years for the American public to catch up with this and the other distinguished novels which came from his pen. Anderson and Hemingway owe much to him. He has published several volumes of short stories, of which the most distinguished is *Free. The Lost Phoebe* seems to me his most important story, and it stands quite apart from the natural course of his realistic writing. It has taken root already as one of the great American legends.

BENJAMIN ROSENBLATT

Benjamin Rosenblatt was born in a small Russian village in 1880 and brought to New York by his parents when he was ten. After leaving the normal training school he taught English to foreigners and opened a preparatory school. He has not collected his stories in book form. His best stories are *Zelig, The Menorah,* and *The Madonna.* When these stories appeared for the first time in magazines, they were at once recognized as notable contributions to American writing because of the intense Rembrandt-like quality of the pictures which he presented of Russian Jewish life at home and in America.

THOMAS BEER

Thomas Beer was born in Council Bluffs, Iowa, in 1889. He was educated at Yale and Columbia Universities. He was in the American army during the war. He has written several distinguished novels, a brilliant life of Stephen Crane, and many short stories. Of these last, *Onnie* is probably the most important. Reminiscent of Flaubert's masterpiece *A Simple Heart,* it is a moving portrait of a faithful family servant with deep and exact characterization and much dramatic power. Thomas Beer's work as a social critic in his other stories is of considerable distinction.

IRVIN S. COBB

Irvin S. Cobb was born in Paducah, Kentucky, in 1876. He was educated in public and private schools and had a long career as a newspaper man. He has published a great many humorous books, mostly collections of short stories, but others reflect his philosophy of life in other ways. He has acted in motion pictures and has written numerous screen stories. He has inherited to some degree and worn modestly the mantle of Mark Twain. He has added to American literature one character of distinction, Judge Priest, and it is in his Judge Priest stories that he is most successful. His most outstanding stories are *The Belled Buzzard, Boys Will Be Boys, The Great Auk,* and *Darkness.* His stories would gain greatly by compression, but we must grant him the privilege of a certain verbosity for the sake of his rich delineation of character when he is writing at his best.

JOSEPH   HERGESHEIMER

Joseph Hergesheimer was born in Philadelphia in 1880. He was educated at the Pennsylvania Academy of Fine Art. A long series of fine novels have come from his pen since he published *The Lay Anthony* in 1914. His output of short stories has been large, but he has not seen fit to collect all of them. As a writer he marks the turning-point between the American writing of romantic escape and the new interest in the American scene for its own immediate human value. In general, we may say that his short stories are less important than his novels, but *The Meeker Ritual* stands by itself as a vividly realized fantasy with its roots in reality. Published twenty years ago, it anticipates remarkably the later impulse of contemporary writers to use the discoveries of Freud to illuminate their probing of reality.

FRANCES   GILCHRIST   WOOD

Frances Gilchrist Wood was born about seventy years ago near the small prairie town of Carthage, Illinois. She was educated at Carthage College and at Columbia University. She began to write short stories in later life, after working as a reporter and editor on western newspapers. She has also been engaged in railway administration with her father. Her best stories are *The White Battalion, Shoes,* and *Turkey Red. Turkey Red* is one of the best pioneer stories ever written by an American. As a feat of construction, it has seldom been surpassed. There was a danger in the very elaborateness of the construction, but the vitality of the characterization and the sheer human interest of the story itself overcome the structural difficulty.

KONRAD   BERCOVICI

Konrad Bercovici was born in Rumania in 1882 and came to the United States in 1916. He had published other books before his reputation was finally consolidated by the collection of short stories entitled *Ghitza,* which appeared in 1919. Since then he has published numerous other books including several collections of short stories. His chief contribution to American short stories are his Rumanian gypsy tales of which *Fanutza* is an excellent example. Based on first-

hand knowledge and experience, these warm-blooded gypsy tales all
have fine characterization, fresh, crisp narrative value, and fine
atmospheric backgrounds. Konrad Bercovici's best short stories
appeared between 1920 and 1925. One of his most distinguished stories
is entitled *Ghitza*.

ERNEST HEMINGWAY

Ernest Hemingway was born in Oak Park, Illinois, in 1898. He
was educated in private schools and joined the Italian army during
the World War. He has been a newspaper man and an amateur bull-
fighter. He is equally distinguished as a novelist and as a short-story
writer, and the publication of the little pamphlet in Paris in 1923
entitled *Three Stories and Ten Poems* may almost be said to mark the
complete coming of age of the American short story. I recognized the
fact at the time by breaking a rule and reprinting from this pamphlet
My Old Man, although it had not previously appeared in a magazine.
It is Ernest Hemingway's distinction that he has been able to render
for the first time with the utmost economy of means the inarticulate
thoughts and emotions of the little man in America. While Ernest
Hemingway's stories are superficially colorless, they are actually
charged most subtly with emotional and intellectual perception.
Nowhere is the emphasis of understatement carried further more successfully than in these stories. His best work which is to be found in
the volumes entitled *In Our Time, Men Without Women, Winner Take
Nothing*, and *To Have and Have Not*, rank with the greatest short
stories of any country and any time.

RUTH SUCKOW

Ruth Suckow was born in Hawarden, Iowa, in 1892. She was
educated at Grinnell College and at the University of Denver. She
has published several novels and collections of short stories. Her
best short stories are to be found in *Iowa Interiors*, and in *Children and
Older People*. Her two most distinguished stories are probably *Renters*
and *Four Generations*. She excels in the deft and quiet portrayal of
middle-western country people. Her pictures are intimate, affectionate, and a little ironic. Her very unpretentiousness achieves a certain
heightened effect.

SHERWOOD ANDERSON

Sherwood Anderson was born in Camden, Ohio, in 1876, and had a public school education. He had already won critical esteem by two novels and a collection of poems before the publication of *Winesburg, Ohio*, in 1919 made us realize that a great new American short-story writer had appeared on the horizon. This book, which anticipated the work of Ernest Hemingway by several years, shares with Hemingway's first book the distinction of being one of the two chief landmarks in the American short-story writing of our time. Taken in conjunction with two other collections by Sherwood Anderson entitled *The Triumph of the Egg* and *Horses and Men*, this collection ranks in literature with the best work of Chekhov and Maupassant. The body of Sherwood Anderson's short stories is the most important portrait gallery that exists of the America of our time.

KATHARINE FULLERTON GEROULD

Katharine Fullerton Gerould was born in Brockton, Massachusetts, in 1879. She was educated at Radcliffe College and has taught English at Bryn Mawr College. She has published several collections of short stories, notably *Vain Oblations*, *The Great Tradition*, and *Valiant Dust*. Influenced strongly by Henry James and Edith Wharton, she has evolved a manner of her own of considerable dramatic power. Her most distinctive stories are *The Knight's Move*, *Habakkuk*, *French Eva*, *Belshazzar's Letter*, *An Army With Banners*, and *The Nature of an Oath*. She has also written novels of some distinction.

RING W. LARDNER

Ring W. Lardner was born in Niles, Michigan, in 1885. He was educated at the Armour Institute of Technology, and spent most of his life as a sporting writer and editor for American newspapers. Before his untimely death he published several collections of short stories, the best of which have been reprinted in *Round Up*. Mistaken by the general public for many years for an idle entertainer, he was actually a devastating portrayer of the American jungle. With a contained fury that reminds us of Swift, his portraits of his contemporaries are deeply bitten with acid perception of reality. Among his outstanding stories, special attention must be called to *Haircut, The Love Nest, The Golden Honeymoon, Horseshoes, Anniversary, Reunion,* and *Some Like Them Cold.*

DuBOSE HEYWARD

DuBose Heyward was born in Charleston, South Carolina, in 1885. He had a public school education. As a novelist and playwright he has mirrored southern life with considerable distinction. As a short-story writer, his reputation rests on *The Half-Pint Flask* which is memorable because of the inevitable quality of the drama which it portrays. Told with great compression, it is beautifully focused and its impartiality is arresting.

OLIVER LA FARGE

Oliver La Farge was born in New York City in 1901. He was educated at Harvard University and has been assistant in ethnology at Tulane University and research associate in anthropology in Columbia University. He has made numerous archaeological and ethnological expeditions to Arizona, Mexico, and Guatemala. He is an expert on Indian affairs. He has written several novels and one of them, *Laughing Boy,* has been awarded the Pulitzer Prize. His short stories have been collected in *All the Young Men. North is Black* is perhaps the best of his Indian stories. It shows extraordinary penetration into the reticence of the Indian mind.

J. P. MARQUAND

J. P. Marquand was born in Wilmington, Delaware, in 1893. He was educated at Harvard University. He has published numerous successful novels, the best of which is probably *The Late George Apley,* and many short stories which he has not seen fit to collect. *Good Morning, Major,* is his most effective short story. It is developed with considerable subtlety and dramatic force.

DOROTHY PARKER

Dorothy Parker was born in West End, New Jersey, in 1893. She was educated at private schools. She has been an editor and dramatic critic, has published several volumes of verse, and is the author of two fine collections of short stories, *Laments for the Living* and *After Such Pleasures*. She excels as a witty social critic with much subtle penetration and a sense of pity which is a little cruel. She has an unusual ear for spoken speech, and especially for monologue. Her stories are unusually neat, crisp, and conclusive.

WILLA CATHER

Willa Cather was born in Winchester, Virginia, in 1876. She was educated at the University of Nebraska. In early life she was engaged in newspaper work and as a magazine editor. She is one of the most distinguished novelists of our time and a fine poet. She has written few short stories. With the exception of *Double Birthday*, the best of these are reprinted in *Youth and the Bright Medusa* and *Obscure Destinies*. Most of these stories deal with the contrast between the outward appearance and the inner life of individuals, and some of them are preoccupied with the problems of the American artist. In *Double Birthday* it is interesting to observe how the story is observed from several angles and how the author builds up a unity of impression out of several converging strands.

WALTER D. EDMONDS

Walter D. Edmonds was born in Boonville, New York, in 1903. He was educated at Harvard University and at Union College. He has published several excellent novels and numerous short stories dealing with life on the old Erie Canal and along the Mohawk Trail. He has a fine sense of historical background, good characterization, and a fine ear for humorous speech. *Death of Red Peril* is one of his best stories and shows his humor in its richest form.

MORLEY CALLAGHAN

Morley Callaghan was born in Toronto, Ontario, in 1903. He was educated at the University of Toronto. He has studied law and has done newspaper work. As a short-story writer he was much influenced at first by Ernest Hemingway, but eventually won through to a manner of his own. He is now the most distinguished living Canadian writer by reason of his novels as well as his short stories. The latter have been collected in *A Living Argosy* and *Now That April's Here*. *The Faithful Wife* illustrates Morley Callaghan's work at its best. He usually prefers to take a single static situation and to invite us to look on while he presents it as it is without resolution or comment.

WILLIAM MARCH

William March was born in Mobile, Alabama, and has lived in many parts of the United States. He was educated at the University of Valparaiso and the University of Alabama. He was in the Marine Corps during the World War, and has been an officer of a large shipping corporation. He has written several novels, and three collections of short stories, *The Little Wife*, *Company K*, and *Some Like Them Short*. *The Little Wife* is probably his best story. It is masterly in the terseness of its construction and the reticence with which the situation is portrayed.

KAY BOYLE

Kay Boyle was born in St. Paul, Minnesota, in 1903. She has spent a large part of her life abroad. She has written several distinguished novels and three collections of short stories, *Wedding Day*, *The First Lover*, and *The White Horses of Vienna*. Her most important stories are probably *Rest Cure* and *The First Lover*. She has often been compared to Katherine Mansfield, and the stories of these two writers have a similar incisiveness. Kay Boyle is more impersonal than Katherine Mansfield. *Rest Cure* was obviously suggested by the last years in the life of D. H. Lawrence.

WILLIAM FAULKNER

William Faulkner was born in New Albany, Mississippi, in 1897. He was educated at the University of Mississippi. He served with the British Air Force in 1918. He has published many distinguished novels, and among his collections of short stories may be mentioned *These Thirteen* and *Doctor Martino*. His best short story is undoubtedly *That Evening Sun Go Down*. Among other outstanding stories may be mentioned *Smoke*, *Beyond*, *Lo!*, *Bear Hunt*, *That Will Be Fine*, *Fool About a Horse* and *Skirmish at Sartoris*. William Faulkner excels at creating his effects by indirect implication, and *That Evening Sun Go Down* conveys to us the truth about a family through the half-unrealized perceptions of the children who witness the events which transpire.

F. SCOTT FITZGERALD

F. Scott Fitzgerald was born in St. Paul, Minnesota, in 1896. He was educated at Princeton University. He served in the American army during the World War. He has published several novels, notably *The Great Gatsby*, and four collections of short stories, *Flappers and Philosophers*, *Tales of the Jazz Age*, *All the Sad Young Men*, and *Taps at Reveille*. His best short story is probably *Babylon Revisited*. The reader will not soon forget the protagonist of this story who lost all he wanted in the boom. F. Scott Fitzgerald was the typical writer of the jazz age immediately after the war and one of its best social critics.

MARTHA FOLEY

Martha Foley was born in Boston, Massachusetts. She was educated at Boston University. With her husband Whit Burnett, she founded *Story* in Vienna in 1931. She has had a varied and colorful newspaper career. Her short stories are as yet uncollected. The most important are *One With Shakespeare*, *She Walks in Beauty*, and *Her Own Sweet Simplicity*. No American writer has penetrated more deeply and with more wistful humor into the mind of a little girl.

GEORGE MILBURN

George Milburn was born in Coweta, Indian Territory, in 1906. He was educated at the University of Tulsa, Oklahoma Agricultural and Mechanical College, Commonwealth College, and the University of Oklahoma. He has engaged in newspaper work. He has published a novel and two collections of short stories, *Oklahoma Town* and *No More Trumpets*. As a chronicler of the American scene in brief Rabelaisian anecdote, he is unsurpassed. *A Pretty Cute Little Stunt* is his most distinctive story.

WHIT BURNETT

Whit Burnett was born in Salt Lake City, Utah, in 1899. He was educated at the University of Southern California, the University of Utah, and the University of California. He is married to Martha Foley. His short stories are collected in *The Maker of Signs*. He has also published a volume of essays entitled *The Literary Life and the Hell With It*. With Martha Foley he founded and has since edited *Story*, the best short-story magazine in the world. A file of *Story* since 1931 will reveal the names of most of the significant American short-story writers of our time. Whit Burnett and Martha Foley discovered nearly all of them. Whit Burnett's chief stories are *Sherrel*, *A Day in the Country*, *The Cats Which Cried*, *Herr Qualla*, and *Two Men Free*. *Sherrel* is probably his most important story.

MANUEL KOMROFF

Manuel Komroff was born in New York City in 1890. He was privately educated. He has published a number of successful novels. The best of his earlier short stories are reprinted in *The Grace of Lambs*. His later short stories await collection. All his work is noteworthy for his light and fantastic treatment of themes which deeply move him and for his poetic approach to reality. He has been strongly influenced by Maupassant. *Napoleon's Hat Under Glass* is characteristic of his economy and understatement and of the manner in which he touches reality with fantasy.

PETER NEAGOE

Peter Neagoe was born in Transylvania of Rumanian parents about 1890. He spent his vacations in childhood living the life of a rugged mountaineer among the Carpathian shepherds. He was educated at the University of Bucharest. He came to America at the age of twenty-one. He has written several novels and a collection of short stories entitled *Storm. Shepherd of the Lord* is his best story. His Rumanian peasant tales are warm-blooded, richly human, and full of a riotous pagan zest.

GEORGE ALBEE

George Albee was born in Wisconsin in 1905. He has since lived in the Middle West and Southwest. He began writing in 1924 and has published two or three novels of distinction. His short stories are infrequent and uncollected, and of these the best is *Fame Takes the J Car*. This story in the form of a letter shows brilliant talents for characterization and a fine ear for folk speech.

JAMES T. FARRELL

James T. Farrell was born in Chicago, Illinois, in 1904. He was educated at the University of Chicago. He has produced several long novels dealing with the life of the poor in Chicago streets and three collections of short stories which have been reprinted in the single volume entitled *The Short Stories of James T. Farrell. Helen, I Love You!* seems to me to be the best of his short stories. James T. Farrell has little selective power and in consequence his writing is of unequal quality, but no one surpasses him in photographic realism and in quick ear for speech, and his passion for social justice imposes a roughly effective form on much of his best work.

NAOMI SHUMWAY

Naomi Shumway was born on a ranch in northwestern Wyoming about 1909. She had a public school education which she abandoned at seventeen to go on a mission for the Mormon Church. She lost her faith and came to New York to do housework. She is now a librarian in New York. She has only written occasional short stories of which *Ike and Us Moons* is the best. I regard this story as one of the most outstanding American stories which have appeared in the last ten years.

ERSKINE CALDWELL

Erskine Caldwell was born in White Oak, Georgia, in 1902. He was educated at Erskine College, the University of Virginia, and the University of Pennsylvania. He has been a newspaper writer, a cotton-picker, a stage-hand, a professional football player, an editor, and a screen writer. He has written a number of distinguished novels and three collections of short stories, *American Earth*, *We Are the Living*, and *Kneel to the Rising Sun*. His novel *Tobacco Road* has been successfully dramatized. Erskine Caldwell's short stories are noteworthy for their impartial presentation of poor-white life in the South. Their philosophy is implicit and their psychological attitude behaviorist. Among his best stories may be mentioned *Dorothy*, *Warm River*, *The First Autumn*, *Horse Thief*, *The Cold Winter*, and *Picking Cotton*.

DOROTHY M'CLEARY

Dorothy M'Cleary was born in Washington, D.C., in 1894. She was educated at George Washington University. She has engaged in newspaper work and is the author of three novels. Her short stories have been infrequent and are uncollected. Her most important stories are *Winter*, *Sunday Morning*, and *The Shroud*. She has a gift for pathetically humorous dialogue and her characterization is excellent.

ALAN MARSHALL

Alan Marshall was born in Rutherglen, Scotland, in 1905. His parents brought him to America in 1912. He was educated at the Carnegie Institute of Technology and at Columbia University. He has taught at the College of the City of New York. He has published few short stories. *Death and Transfiguration* is his most important story. In this story he has succeeded in cloaking simple realism with a poetic treatment that is not unlike the best of Hawthorne.

BENJAMIN APPEL

Benjamin Appel was born in New York City in 1907. He was educated at Lafayette College. He is the author of several novels and numerous uncollected short stories. He is at his best when describing the gangster life of the American cities and the life of roaming, un-attached workers who have nothing to lose.

SALLY BENSON

Sally Benson was born in St. Louis. She is the author of two col-lections of short stories, *People are Fascinating* and *Emily*. She is also a frequent contributor to the *New Yorker*. *The Overcoat* is her best story. The quietness of her narration gives special force to the flashing revelation at the end of the story.

WILLIAM SAROYAN

William Saroyan is a young Armenian born in the San Joaquin Valley, California, about thirty years ago. He has published several collections of short stories of which the most noteworthy are *The Daring Young Man on the Flying Trapeze, Inhale and Exhale, Little Children, The Trouble With Tigers,* and *Love, Here Is My Hat!* His literary fecundity is extreme and in consequence the quality of his work is unequal. At its best, however, it is a free fantasia in which he pours forth his thoughts and feelings about himself and America with extraordinary brilliance and perceptive power. *Resurrection of a Life* is one of his best stories. He has invented a new form successfully for the short story.

ALLAN SEAGER

Allan Seager was born in Adrian, Michigan, in 1906. He was edu-cated at the University of Michigan and at Oxford University. He has been assistant editor of *Vanity Fair* and has taught English at the University of Michigan. His short stories are so far uncollected. *This Town and Salamanca* was at once recognized on its appearance as one of the most important short stories of our time, entitling the author to rank with Sherwood Anderson and Ernest Hemingway. Other important stories by Allan Seager are *Pommery 1921, Fugue for Har-monica,* and *Berkshire Comedy.*

ALBERT MALTZ

Albert Maltz was born in Brooklyn, New York, in 1908. He was educated at Columbia University and Yale University. He is a member of the Executive Board of the Theatre Union. He has written several plays and a collection of short stories entitled *The Way Things Are*. *Man on a Road* is his best story. Few American writers have embodied the growing social consciousness of our time in better stories.

TESS SLESINGER

Tess Slesinger was born in New York City in 1905. She was educated at Swarthmore College and Columbia University. She has been engaged in newspaper work. She is the author of a novel entitled *The Unpossessed* and a collection of short stories entitled *Time: The Present*. Her best stories are *Missis Flinders*, *The Old Lady Counts Her Injuries*, *Jobs in the Sky*, and *A Life in the Day of a Writer*. Tess Slesinger is the most successful American short-story writer using the stream-of-consciousness technique.

ROBERT WHITEHAND

Robert Whitehand was born in San Francisco, California, in 1910. He has lived in many parts of the United States. He was educated at the University of Oklahoma and the University of Iowa. He has written several plays and a few short stories of which *American Nocturne* is the best. This delicate idyl might easily have failed through excess of sentiment, but as it stands it is nearly faultless.

THOMAS WOLFE

Thomas Wolfe was born in Asheville, North Carolina, in 1900, and died in 1939. He was educated at the University of North Carolina and Harvard University. He taught English at New York University. He is best known for his important novels *Look Homeward, Angel!* and *Of Time and the River*. He published one collection of short stories, *From Death to Morning*. *Only the Dead Know Brooklyn* is his most important short story. It is quite unlike the rest of his work and is a *tour de force*.

I. V. MORRIS

I. V. Morris was born in Chicago, Illinois, in 1903. He was educated at Harvard University and at Heidelberg University. He is married to Edita Morris, who is also a distinguished short-story writer. He has spent most of his life in Europe and now lives in France. He is the author of two novels, *Covering Two Years* and *Marching Orders*. The latter is an expansion of the short story reprinted in this volume. His short stories are still uncollected. Among them may be mentioned *A Tale From the Grave*, *The Kimono*, and *The Sampler*.

JESSE STUART

Jesse Stuart was born in 1907 near Riverton, Kentucky. He was educated at Lincoln Memorial College and at Vanderbilt University. He has published an autobiography and a distinguished volume of poems and many of his stories have been collected in a volume entitled *Head o' W-Hollow*. All his short stories deal with the life of the Kentucky mountaineers who are his own people. They are rich in drama and comedy and full of a native poetry which is unusual among American short-story writers. Among his best stories may be mentioned *Battle Keaton Dies*, *Three Hundred Acres of Elbow Room*, *Woman in the House*, *Fern*, *Hair*, *Toes*, and *Eustacia*.

LOVELL THOMPSON

Lovell Thompson was born in Nahant, Massachusetts, in 1902. He was educated at Harvard University. Since then he has been associated with publishing houses in Boston. He is best known by his short story *The Iron City* which attracted wide attention when it was published in *Story* in 1937. This sustained effort in the vein of Joseph Conrad is an unforgettable story.

PIETRO DI DONATO

Pietro di Donato was born in West Hoboken, New Jersey, in 1911. He left grammar school at thirteen to support his widowed mother and seven brothers and sisters. When his father was killed on the job, he picked up his tools and went to work on the scaffold as a bricklayer. He has been tied to the job ever since. *Christ in Concrete* is his first short story and now forms the opening chapter of a novel with the same title. In its relentless inevitability it is an unforgettable story.

JOHN STEINBECK

John Steinbeck was born in Salinas, California, in 1902. He was educated at Stanford University. He is the author of many notable novels and his most important short stories have been collected in a volume entitled *The Long Valley*. Stories worthy of special mention are *The Chrysanthemums, Harness,* and *A Snake of One's Own.*

RICHARD ELY DANIELSON

Richard Ely Danielson was born in Brooklyn, Connecticut, in 1885. He was educated at Yale University. He was a captain in the American army during the World War. He has edited the *Independent* and the *Sportsman. Corporal Hardy* is his best short story and one of the best stories of the American Civil War ever written.

RICHARD WRIGHT

Richard Wright was born in Natchez, Mississippi, in 1908. He is a Negro and the most distinguished writer his own people have so far produced. He is the author of *Uncle Tom's Children*, a collection of short stories of permanent merit. *Bright and Morning Star* is his best short story.